Dhoombak Goobgoowana

Dhoombak Goobgoowana

A History of Indigenous Australia and the University of Melbourne

Volume 1: Truth

Edited by
Ross L Jones,
James Waghorne
and Marcia Langton

MELBOURNE
UNIVERSITY
PRESS

Melbourne University Publishing acknowledge the traditional owners of the unceded land on which we work, learn and live: the Wurundjeri Woiwurrung peoples of the Kulin Nation. We pay respect to elders past, present and future, and acknowledge the importance of Indigenous knowledge.

MELBOURNE UNIVERSITY PRESS
An imprint of Melbourne University Publishing Limited
Level 1, 715 Swanston Street, Carlton, Victoria 3053, Australia
mup-contact@unimelb.edu.au
www.mup.com.au

First published 2024
This edition published 2024
Reprinted 2024

Cover design by Pfisterer + Freeman
Cover image: Purunda (Warwick), Chance, Erlikilyika (Jim Kite), Frank Gillen, and Baldwin Spencer, members of the 1901–1902 Expedition, Alice Springs, Central Australia, 18 May 1901. Spencer and Gillen Collection. Museums Victoria.
Typeset in 10¾pt Minion 3 by Cannon Typesetting
Printed in Malaysia by Papercraft

A catalogue record for this book is available from the National Library of Australia

9780522880434 (hardback)
9780522881059 (paperback)
9780522880441 (ebook)

Contents

II Human Remains

III Settler-Colonial Knowledge

IV Indigenous Knowledge

Editors' Note

Dhoombak Goobgoowana can be translated as 'truth-telling' in the Woi Wurrung language of the Wurundjeri Woi Wurrung people on whose unceded lands several University of Melbourne campuses are located.

The cover photograph shows the members of a 1901 expedition through central Australia led by Frank Gillen (seated, left) and Baldwin Spencer (seated, right). To the rear stands mounted constable Harry Chance. Beside these white men are two Arrernte men, Erlikilyika (to the left) and Purunda (to the right). We have used this image to represent the unacknowledged participation of Indigenous people in the activities of academics in the University's history. The uncredited work of Erlikilyika as interpreter of both language and culture informed many of the conclusions of the white ethnographers and the anthropologists who followed. The expedition would have been impossible without the knowledge of these Indigenous men, and the scholarship it produced exists only because of them. Today at the University of Melbourne we pay respect to Elders past, present and future, and acknowledge the importance of Indigenous knowledge in the Academy. As a community of researchers, teachers, professional staff and students, we are privileged to work and learn every day with Indigenous colleagues and partners.

Aboriginal and Torres Strait Islander readers are advised that this book contains images and names of people who have died. Readers are also advised that they may be disturbed by the content of this book, which includes distressing images and descriptions, and derogatory terms for Indigenous people used in their historical context.

In writing this history, we sought to use culturally appropriate and respectful terminology. The following terms are used interchangeably throughout the book: Aboriginal and Torres Strait Islander, First Nations, First Peoples, Indigenous Australians (inclusive of Aboriginal and Torres Strait Islander peoples), Aboriginal peoples and Indigenous peoples (commonly used for First Nations peoples internationally). We also use the term non-Indigenous to refer to those who do not identify as Aboriginal or Torres Strait Islander or First Nations people.

When referencing Traditional Owner groups in Victoria, we have followed the Victorian Aboriginal Heritage Council determinations of the Registered Aboriginal Party in place as at November 2023. For Traditional Owner groups in other states, we have consulted with Elders and community leaders to ensure that we are using the most accurate names. The name of the Indigenous leader Trukanini is one that has changed in recent years from 'Truganini' or other variations. We have adopted the current preferred spelling.

Foreword

DUNCAN MASKELL

IT IS WITH recognition of the vital role of Indigenous people in our institution that I welcome the publication of the first volume of this long-awaited work of truth-telling. We live in a period when public recognition of the brutal treatment of Indigenous people in Australia—and indeed in many countries around the world that are grappling with their settler-colonial pasts—seems ever more important. More voices are raised now than in the past, in speaking to the need for truth-telling about this history. At the same time, more people in Australia and in other postcolonial countries are becoming aware of the strength and power of Indigenous cultures and Indigenous knowledge, and of the unique contribution that Indigenous citizens and communities are making to the future of their wider nations.

Dhoombak Goobgoowana, which means 'truth-telling' in the language spoken by the Indigenous people of the central and eastern Melbourne area—the Wurundjeri Woi Wurrung people—plays an important part in this growing national and international dialogue. The University of Melbourne, one of Australia's founding knowledge institutions and the first university established in the colony (later state) of Victoria, prides itself on both its historic foundational role and its present responsibility for shaping future leaders. As part of its mission, the University has initiated its *Murmuk Djerring* strategy, which, among other priorities, has pledged to engage in full and honest truth-telling about its history. This scholarly work is the first outcome of this truth-telling commitment.

I am confident that this book will challenge, even shock, many people who have previously held too rosy a view of the University's past engagements with Indigenous people. Some of these engagements are cause for shame. Yet serious attempts have also been made in recent years by the University and its people to play a more positive role for the future. This has involved not only acknowledging the errors of the past but also empowering Indigenous people to participate in the life of the University and the nation: as students, academics, graduates and leaders, and as Indigenous community leaders. *Dhoombak Goobgoowana* addresses both the positive and negative aspects of the historical record.

Led by Indigenous and non-Indigenous academics, and bringing together the voices of a wide range of scholars, participants and leaders, this book is a thorough and unique social document. It not only puts the facts on record but also critically interrogates these facts and begins new conversations. It is the kind of work that a leading contemporary research university is obliged to undertake. By supporting it, we seek to make a positive difference for the future.

I commend the work done by the editors and contributors in bringing the first volume of *Dhoombak Goobgoowana* into existence.

Professor Duncan Maskell
Vice-Chancellor, University of Melbourne

Introduction

ROSS L JONES, JAMES WAGHORNE and MARCIA LANGTON

'We had a trouble here in this country ...'

Address by William Barak and fifteen Coranderrk residents to Graham Berry, 22 March 1886[1]

IN 1853, TWO years after the colony of Victoria was declared, the University of Melbourne was founded in Carlton on the edges of Narrm, then grasslands and woodlands, watered by seasonal creeks and wetlands rich in biodiversity. There were still a few Wurundjeri Woi Wurrung, Bunurong and Wadawurrung people and others living in the area in their traditional living places, harvesting foods, hunting birds and trapping eels. These Traditional Owners must have watched in horror when, from the mid-1830s, the invaders set up their tent encampments along the Yarra River and foully polluted the water, resulting in outbreaks of typhoid fever and other diseases. Wonga Wonga or Simon Wonga, born before colonisation, in 1824, was the *ngurungaeta* or leader of the Woi Wurrung and Taungurung Ngurai-illum Wurrung clans of the Kulin confederacy, and son of Billibellary. At the age of thirteen he had witnessed the signing of Batman's 'Treaty', and he was living in the Melbourne area when the University was established. The ugly behaviour towards the Traditional Owners, disastrous first contact with diseases, hunger and dispossession had reduced their numbers radically.

The impact on the peoples of the Kulin confederacy was profound, but the worst was just beginning. As the Indigenous population fell, the settler population surged. In 1852 alone the population of Melbourne ballooned from 24 000 to over 100 000 with the arrival of gold-hungry immigrants headed for the goldfields around Ballarat and Bendigo. The gold boom gripped the colony for the next forty years, while the land boom never ended.

Wonga had learnt some English and passages from the Bible and was valiant in his political efforts to ensure his people survived the disaster of the invasion, claiming land for them to live on, but without success.[2] In 1863 Wonga, with his cousin William Barak and inspector John Green, led the forty or so survivors in a trek over the Dandenong Ranges to Coranderrk Station, where the colony granted them 'permissive occupancy'. After his death, Wonga was succeeded as *ngurungaeta* by Barak.[3]

The failed treaty negotiated by John Batman and overruled by the governor of the Colony of New South Wales was long forgotten. The establishment of the University of Melbourne was a foundational settler-colonial act designed to secure the place of the invaders and displace the Traditional Owners in several ways: physically, materially and, as will be explained below, intellectually and epistemically.

To the Honble Graham Berry.

Melbourne, March 22nd/86.

We have come to see you because you have done a great deal of work for the Aborigines.

I feel very sorrowful and first time I hear you was going home I was crying. you do all that thing for the Station when we were in trouble. when the Board would not give us much food and clothes and wanted to drive us off the land we come to you and told you our trouble and you gave us the land for our own as long as we live and gave us more food and clothes and blankets and better houses and the people all very thankful.

And now you leave this country. Victoria to go to England where we may never see you no more. we give you small present with our love, when you go away keep remembering the Natives for the Natives will remember you for your doing good to Coranderrk.

We had a trouble here in this Country but we can all meet up along "Our Father" we hope that God will lead you right through the water and take you safe to England and keep you in the straight way and give you eternal life through Jesus Christ Our Saviour.

Signed Barak ×
Chief of the Yarra Yarra tribe of Aborigines, Victoria Australia.

Bertdrak ×	Mooney ×	Patterson ×
Katawarmin ×	Manton ×	Cogle ×
Wort se ilum ×	Hamilton ×	Stewart ×
Ngiaqueon ×	Rowan ×	Logan ×
Berrinel ×	Were ×	Gable ×

Illuminated address presented by William Barak and fifteen Coranderrk residents to Graham Berry, 1886.

This first volume is an attempt to acknowledge and publicly address the long, complex and troubled relationship between the Indigenous people of what we now call Australia and the University of Melbourne. It is a book about race and how it has been constructed by academics in the University. It is also about power and how academics have wielded it and justified its use against Indigenous populations, and about knowledge, especially the Indigenous knowledge that silently contributed to many early research projects and collection endeavours. Only recently has this knowledge been recognised and brought forward to contribute new approaches and methodologies. It is not just about individuals: the University as an institution has encouraged these ideas and benefited from them. It has enabled the transference of racist ideas from one academic discipline to another. In 2019, the University convened the Research Colloquium on Place and Indigenous Cultural Recognition to address the complexity of this history. These books are one of the outcomes of that meeting.

The University of Melbourne is not alone in this. Universities worldwide have grappled with their histories of racism. The connection between the dispossession of Indigenous land and universities presents moral challenges, notably in the case of US land-grant universities, but also, as this history will show, the universities in Australia.[4] Universities' role in justifying the settler-colonial project of imperial powers has also been revealed, undermining claims to neutrality and objectivity. The dark legacy of slavery has also only recently been acknowledged, with university endowments funded from its proceeds, academics and administrators owning and even trading slaves on university campuses, and racist academic theory upholding its virtues.[5]

This book documents some of the worst failings of our intellectual leaders, both in empathy and listening, but also against their own standards and knowledge systems. By appropriating Wurundjeri land for its buildings, and accepting donations drawn from the proceeds of colonisation of Indigenous Country, the University advertised its superiority as a whole institution to Indigenous people. Within these buildings, academics and students explored a worldview that effectively banished Indigenous knowledge and culture. As a scholarly community the University has fostered the application of racist ideas across disciplines, repeating common themes. Architects adopted racist hierarchies as ways of interpreting buildings; leaders from across the University joined organisations that promoted eugenics. These examples are discussed in the chapters that follow. The University has supported injustices called progress, half-truths presented as facts, and prejudices pretending at objectivity. It follows the failings of many biographies and institutional histories that excluded race from their stories of achievement, overlooking how racist ideas complicated and shaped their narratives. Although many things have changed, the stain of the past remains. The land has not been returned; racism persists in the institution. But the University no longer wishes to look away.

Exposing these histories should prompt academics today to reflect on their own practices, and how they might enable the kinds of intolerance that this project has uncovered. The chapters that follow ask why individuals acted in the ways that they did, how academic practices informed their actions, and how ideas that have since been discredited can re-emerge at times. This is intended to be unsettling, but conversely recognition of Indigenous expertise and knowledge and adopting decolonising methodologies can also reveal new approaches to academic work that can be stimulating and challenging.[6] It is striking that in 2023 four major new university strategies have incorporated Indigenous knowledge, in recognition of the vitality of this field. Along with the establishment of the Indigenous Knowledge Institute in 2020, the University's new *Indigenous Strategy 2023–2027* (*Murmuk Djerring*) has Indigenous knowledge as a strategic priority.[7] It is also exemplified in the overarching *Advancing Melbourne* strategy, with its objectives to incorporate Indigenous knowledge research and education into the academy, improve the quality of Indigenous research and increase the number of Indigenous researchers.[8] The University's *Sustainability Plan 2030* draws on Indigenous perspectives to increase understanding of sustainability.[9] The *Advancing Students and Education* strategy aims to ensure that all students leave the University with an appreciation of Indigenous knowledge.[10]

Settler-Colonial University

From its foundation the University of Melbourne was an institution created by a settler-colonial society to inform and support settler-colonial endeavours. Until 1958 it was Victoria's only university, and it has remained an eminent national and international institution since. It has contributed significantly to the intellectual and moral justification of settler-colonial society, doing so for over a century and a half. At the opening of the University in 1855, the first chancellor, Redmond Barry, defined the University as supplanting Indigenous knowledge with what he deemed

Sir Redmond Barry.

superior Western knowledge.[11] In his inaugural address, he explained that the University of Melbourne would rise above the 'first rude efforts of constructive efficiency ... such as we behold amongst the remnant of aboriginal inhabitants of the soil still lingering around their former haunts'. These the University would replace with 'progressive improvement of architectural, mechanical, and scientific invention and intellectual art'.[12] Barry's speech established the overriding principle of all the various manifestations of settler-colonial intellectual work, which presumed the inferiority of Indigenous Australians. 'Civilisation' involved the imposition of a hierarchy of knowledge. 'Colonisation' was the process by which Western peoples claimed the Australian continent, and their 'rightful' dominance of Indigenous people.

Indigenous people became the subjects of university research, helping to justify the settler-colonial hierarchy, and develop ways of managing its impact on Indigenous society. Barry himself studied the culture and language of the local tribes and created the first dictionary—a Western technology that categorised and captured knowledge. In Barry's legal work he explored the morality of the imposition of European ideas and legal institutions and their effect on Indigenous society. He became the unofficial standing counsel for the Wurundjeri Woi Wurrung people without claiming any fees. When defending two Tasmanian men, Tunnerminnerwait and Maulboyheenner, on murder charges, he argued that, since they were not naturalised subjects, they should be tried by a jury that included Indigenous members.[13] This work took place in the midst of the violent destruction of Indigenous society and dispossession of Indigenous lands. Barry's worldview tended towards amelioration. He was influenced by Rousseau's concept of the 'noble savage', which upheld the moral qualities of people uncontaminated by the evils of Western society.[14]

Increasingly, however, as civilising projects became more insistent, amelioration came to be viewed as ineffective. By the second half of the nineteenth century, Darwinian evolution provided new intellectual justifications for Indigenous disadvantage and informed policies that preserved inequality. These ideas inspired reformers across the University, as they did in universities across the Western world, who saw in them ways of solving public problems. The modernity that these ideas expressed was swept up in the national fervour in the years leading up to Federation. Students such as Alfred Deakin, later prime minister of Australia and a champion of White Australia—after whom Deakin Court at the University was named in 1975—espoused such views. The writer Nettie Palmer described him holding a group of students spellbound in the University quadrangle while he was a student in the 1870s, explaining to them that all traditional subjects such as classics and mathematics had been superseded by the social Darwinism of Herbert Spencer. He told them that the 'world was entering on a new epoch in history: everyone should start anew from Spencer's theories'.[15]

There was no stronger champion of evolutionary thought than Walter Baldwin Spencer, who arrived to take up the chair in biology in 1887.[16] Melbourne's intellectuals began regularly to parrot Darwinian ideas of competitive evolution, which divided races into the 'fit' and 'unfit'.[17] The 'unfit' races would always lag, thus 'the survival of the fittest' trope justified inaction in the face of destruction. The influence of social Darwinism is apparent in Spencer's anthropology. When Spencer was protector of the Aborigines in the Northern Territory in 1912–13, he mobilised the separation of 'half-caste' Indigenous children from their families on a racial argument that these children would be inherently superior to their 'full blood' community. He diminished Indigenous people in his publications, albeit acknowledging the extraordinary feats of memory or firm attachment to honourable causes exhibited by those few he took the time to befriend. Ultimately, however, he concluded that Indigenous people were 'mentally, about the level of a child who has little control over his feelings and is liable to give way to violent fits of temper ... He has no sense of responsibility and ... no initiative.'[18] These assumptions influenced Spencer's work in the Northern Territory, leading him to justify the malpractices of settler colonisers.[19] Yet Spencer's earlier anthropological work with Francis Gillen, studying and documenting the social and cultural life of Indigenous tribes in central and northern Australia, has provided an incalculably rich and important legacy upon which many land rights claims are based today, as well as establishing a body of knowledge and set of interpretative frameworks that became central to twentieth-century anthropological understanding of Indigenous Australians worldwide.[20]

Sir Walter Baldwin Spencer.

Spencer was invited to be the founding president of the Victorian Eugenics Society in 1914, an offer he declined because of other commitments.[21] Social Darwinism and eugenics, though often classed together, are in fact conflicting expressions of race science. While social Darwinism allowed the free expression of racial and social dominance, eugenics involved selective social engineering for national efficiency—although in practice they were often indiscriminately applied either alone or together to support the accepted 'superiority' of whites.[22] These were international movements, championed by modern, progressive thinkers. The Victorian Eugenics Society included a sweep of prominent citizens, including Deakin.[23] The University of Melbourne claimed status in this international sphere through its great interest in this science.

Spencer's interest in eugenics also sat comfortably within the University of Melbourne. He was joined by colleagues such as Richard Berry, who arrived in 1906 as the first professor of anatomy, and Melbourne became a centre for eugenic thought.[24] The chapters that follow on eugenics trace the breadth of membership across the University, drawing in a range from

Richard Berry.

medical and biological scientists to educationists and anthropologists. Berry was a leader of the eugenic movement in Australia. He saw his purpose not only to teach his students but also to apply his knowledge and lead reforms in what he saw as the public interest. As Berry was aware, during this period professors could have outsized public influence.[25] He found many like-minded, powerful backers for his eugenic project to mould a new society, and he was supported over decades by the University, the Victorian Government, the major newspapers and international philanthropic organisations such as the Rockefeller Foundation.[26] Berry's project resulted in the active disparagement, exclusion and punishment of the Indigenous population.

Throughout its history the University had many members who, like Berry, expressed grim confidence in the inevitable extinction of Indigenous people. Many of them populate this book. Others, troubled by a Christian or humanitarian conscience, allowed themselves to be convinced by the 'science' of settler-colonial superiority and acquiesced with unease. Only a few individuals up until the 1950s rejected the dominant racial paradigm that justified the superiority of whiteness and spoke out about the appalling treatment of Indigenous people. Berry's successor, Frederic Wood Jones, for example, was a prominent public activist who attacked the theories of Indigenous inferiority and advocated for policies to improve the life of Indigenous Australians—although he feared for their future. He is discussed in greater detail in other chapters.

This seemingly confused and often contradictory story of the University's history was rooted in the ideologies that fuelled colonial expansion. Liberal progressivism, national efficiency and limited notions of democracy resulted in individuals taking positions that seem to be mutually antagonistic. Historians have documented this among leading intellectuals of the period.[27] For instance, University of Melbourne graduate Frank Tate, the first director of education in Victoria and longstanding University councillor, was one of Australia's greatest educational reformers.[28] Among his many notable accomplishments were the development of post-primary education in Victoria in the first decades of the twentieth century, and the transformation of teaching from an apprentice-trained, under-educated and poorly paid occupation into a profession. Yet these reforms were attained by creating a two-tiered public secondary-education system. Street 'roughs' from the slums might have access to technical education leading to industrial or agricultural work, while limited pathways through selective schools

Frank Tate.

would support only the 'strongest' students. Such an arrangement helped to improve 'national efficiency', Tate argued repeatedly.[29] This presented an illiberal progressivism as enlightened policy.[30] Despite the ambiguity of his record, Tate received the honour of having a building named after him in the former Teachers' College, which merged with the University in 1989, although his name was removed in 2022.

There are many more such examples, but in Barry, Spencer, Berry, Tate and Wood Jones we can find the various contrasting ways in which the early University thought of Indigenous Australia: the willingness to dismiss and disparage and only study Indigenous Australians to place them in a racial hierarchy; the belief that Indigenous Australians were to be pitied but protected from 'progress'; and the minority view that valued Indigenous accomplishments but feared they were doomed.

Telling the Whole Truth

One of the reasons this book is so urgently needed is to correct the longstanding failure to engage with this troubling history. Frequent misrepresentation has generated a complacency that denies justice to those who have been wronged and understates the significance of the problem faced by the University. In the decades after World War II, social Darwinism and eugenics receded from public discourse. The sequencing of the human genome has undermined the validity of attempts to categorise populations by race, as lay at the heart of eugenic thinking before World War II, both at the University of Melbourne and internationally. The ongoing debates over eugenics after the war are discussed in 'Eugenics, the 1950s and Beyond' in this volume. However, the prewar eugenic movement attracted little by way of sustained criticism at the University. Rather than highlighting the break with the past and censuring past academic leaders, new language was substituted that more closely represented contemporary scientific canons. Issues such as slum clearance and immigration were discussed in medicalised terms, or reframed in terms of personal choice, rather than as state intervention. Wrong thinking from the past came to be seen as 'unscientific' and was thus excised from the narrative.[31] New generations of students were not exposed to racial elements formerly part of university curriculum. The University's racist history went unacknowledged and came to be largely forgotten, except among a small group of academics and critical thinkers.

Many histories and biographies of the prewar University omitted references to the racist, eugenicist or social Darwinist views so ubiquitous in the research and public pronouncements of leading academics. A series of biographies and biographical essays of prominent eugenicists, published in the twenty years from the 1970s, celebrated their lives. Biographies such as Mulvaney and Calaby's monumental work on Spencer, *So Much That Is New*, catalogued their subjects' achievements and public contributions.[32] Departmental histories of this period are bereft of any consideration of these matters.[33] Kenneth Russell's history of the Medical School, as well as his publications on Richard Berry, described at length Berry's work in anatomy, and university and hospital administration and reform, yet failed to discuss his preferred subject of study—eugenics.[34] The *Australian Dictionary of Biography* is currently offering new and more complete biographies alongside the partial biographies from its past.

Perhaps this mischaracterisation was motivated to protect these eminent intellectuals; perhaps it saw racist activities as inconsequential in the greater picture of their lives. However, this overlooks the profound influence of racist thinking on their intellectual outlook and public contributions. As Gabriela Soto Laveaga has observed, these 'historical silences are not confined to archival gaps, contestations of memory or methodology. The strongest silence is sustained by academic networks and their gatekeepers'. This form of 'privilege ... is not extended to the colonized'.[35]

The need to recover this history is only now beginning. Richard Selleck's 2003 history of the University began the process of uncovering historical racism. His work identified the University's role in justifying Aboriginal dispossession and overriding Indigenous knowledge with Western science. He traced Australian analogues of international debates over social Darwinism. Yet he did not pursue its structural implications for the University's academic work and he offered less insight into the emergence of eugenic ideas that revealed ambivalent aspects of progressivism or its influence on the emerging welfare state.[36] It is perhaps not surprising that two of the most important scholars of settler-colonialism and the fetishising of whiteness, Patrick Wolfe and Warwick Anderson, both come from this University.[37] Both were very involved in Indigenous matters at the University—Wolfe taught some of the earliest courses on Indigenous history, and Anderson was instrumental in setting up the Onemda VicHealth Koori Health Unit in his Centre for the Study of Health and Society in the Medical Faculty, discussed in the second volume. Anderson contributes yet another perspective on the University's attraction to whiteness in a chapter in this book.[38]

And Nothing but the Truth

The need for a detailed history of the relationship between Indigenous peoples and the University was urged by Uncle Jim Berg at the 2019 colloquium. A key theme was the vexed issue of the naming of buildings after past professors whose work denigrating Indigenous peoples had been challenged over decades by Indigenous student leaders and others. The COVID-19 pandemic delayed the project's beginning until the end of 2020, when it was decided to prepare a collective history. Ross Jones began in 2021 with co-editors Marcia Langton (Associate Provost) and James Waghorne (University Historian). Margot Eden (Director, Indigenous Strategy) has managed the project, and offered leadership, information and essential support throughout. The whole project has been overseen by a steering committee with majority Indigenous membership. It was chaired during 2021 by pro vice-chancellor (place and Indigenous) Shaun Ewen and then, after Ewen left the University in 2022, by Deputy Vice-Chancellor (Indigenous) Barry Judd.

From initial discussions, it immediately became apparent that the University's Indigenous history was far more multifaceted and complex than was possible to cover in a narrowly focused history written by a few specialists. Indeed, the desire to engage in a truth-telling process led to extensive consultation across the University to find topics worthy of inclusion and to present multiple perspectives. The response to this call was overwhelming. Soon the contributors' list reached thirty and, with more possibilities appearing every week, it was decided to limit the contributors to members of staff and honoraries of the University. By the time of publication, the number of contributors had grown to over seventy.

More than a third of the contributors are Indigenous. This was a monumental ask on already overburdened members of the University community. Some felt unable to contribute but many have. While we prioritised Indigenous voices, this history should not only be their responsibility. It is also the responsibility of non-Indigenous members of the University to confront this past, to understand it and appreciate its significance. As the story moves closer to the present, more Indigenous scholars take it up, as is reflected in the title of the second volume, *Voice*. These volumes do not consider people's lives beyond their connection to Indigenous Australia—we have pointed to other materials that provide that context. We show in part how the University of Melbourne compares with other Australian and international universities, but we do not offer a systematic analysis. These books are a beginning, an attempt to present a basis of common understanding, and we look forward to Indigenous scholars taking the lead in future endeavours arising from this project.

This volume begins with a section on the idea of 'Place', which discusses the University's connection with stolen land, the Indigenous landscape on which the University has been constructed, and attempts to reconnect with the past to shape the future identity of the University's campuses. The next section, titled 'Human Remains', traces the historical initiatives of the University to collect the human remains of Indigenous people, and the moves to return them to communities. This volume closes with two sections grappling with the clashes between Western and Indigenous knowledge systems. 'Settler-Colonial Knowledge' and 'Indigenous Knowledge' explore the University's role in developing and promoting scientific forms of racism, and the mostly unacknowledged reliance of the University's scientists on Indigenous knowledge, and follow the growing understanding of Indigenous knowledge and its significance for showing new approaches to

University work. This book concludes with an essay on the contested issue of naming, particularly concerning buildings and lecture theatres named after individuals who form the subject of this book.

If we acknowledge, as we so often do, the Traditional Owners whose entire worlds were taken from them by the greedy colonists, then we must also acknowledge this history and our own parts in it as members of the University community. Our University has precipitated a wholesale ecological and epistemic transformation of Country. We cannot regain what was destroyed but we can play a role in reviving the cultural and knowledge systems that predated colonisation. We can ensure that our research and education are respectful of those traditions and those who continue to maintain them. We can recognise them and incorporate them into the academy in myriad ways. We can pay homage to the ancestors of these places. A just vision of our University in the future would draw inspiration from the chapters that follow. Our academics would be inspired to tell the truth to their students and offer a more just and inclusive account of our histories, cultures and knowledges. With knowledges both Indigenous and Western now available, we can transform the institution into a respectful place of learning, uniquely drawing on ancient Australian and global knowledges as tributaries of a great river.

Notes

1 'Mr Berry and the Aborigines', *Argus*, 25 March 1886, p. 7, https://trove.nla.gov.au/newspaper/article/6089151 (accessed 13 October 2023).

2 Cheryl Glowrey, 'Tarra Bobby (1834–1874)', *Australian Dictionary of Biography*, National Centre of Biography, Australian National University, Canberra, 2020, https://adb.anu.edu.au/biography/tarra-bobby-29711/text36783 (accessed 13 October 2023).

3 Patricia Marcard, 'William Barak (1824–1903)', *Australian Dictionary of Biography*, National Centre of Biography, Australian National University, Canberra, 2006, https://adb.anu.edu.au/biography/barak-william-2930/text4239 (accessed 13 October 2023).

4 Sharon Stein, 'A Colonial History of the Higher Education Present: Rethinking Land-Grant Institutions through Processes of Accumulation and Relations of Conquest', *Critical Studies in Education*, vol. 61, no. 2, 2020, pp. 212–28; Theresa Rocha Beardall, 'Settler Simultaneity and Anti-Indigenous Racism at Land-Grant Universities', *Sociology of Race and Ethnicity*, vol. 8, no. 1, 2022, pp. 197–212.

5 Craig Steven Wilder, *Ebony & Ivy: Race, Slavery, and the Troubled History of America's Universities*, Bloomsbury, New York, 2013; Leslie M Harris, James T Campbell and Alfred L Brophy (eds), *Slavery and the University: Histories and Legacies*, University of Georgia Press, Athens, 2019; Stephen Mullen, 'British Universities and Transatlantic Slavery: The University of Glasgow Case', *History Workshop Journal*, vol. 91, no. 1, 2021, pp. 210–33; Joel Barnes,

'Australian Universities and Atlantic Slavery', *History Australia*, vol. 20, no. 1, 2023, pp. 41–63.

6 Sharon Stein, *Unsettling the University*, Johns Hopkins University Press, Baltimore, 2022.

7 The University of Melbourne, *Murmuk Djerring: The University of Melbourne Indigenous Strategy 2023–2027*, 2023.

8 The University of Melbourne, *Advancing Melbourne 2030*, 2020.

9 The University of Melbourne, *Sustainability Plan, 2030*, 2022.

10 The University of Melbourne, *Advancing Students and Education Strategy: 2023–2030*, 2023.

11 Ann Galbally, *Redmond Barry: An Anglo-Irish Australian*, Melbourne University Press, Carlton, 1995; Peter Ryan, 'Sir Redmond Barry (1813–1880)', *Australian Dictionary of Biography*, National Centre of Biography, Australian National University, Canberra, 2006, https://adb.anu.edu.au/biography/barry-sir-redmond-2946/text4271 (accessed 13 October 2023).

12 *Proceedings on the Occasion of the Inauguration of the University of Melbourne, on Friday, the 13th of April 1855*, John Ferres, Government Printer, Melbourne, 1855, pp. 18–19.

13 Susanne Davies, 'Aborigines, Murder and the Criminal Law in Early Port Phillip, 1841–1851', *Historical Studies*, vol. 22, no. 88, April 1987, p. 316.

14 David McVilly, '"Something to Blow about?": The State Library of Victoria, 1856–1880', *The La Trobe Journal*, no 8, October 1971, p. 81; Barry W Butcher, 'Gorilla Warfare in Melbourne: Halford, Huxley and "Man's Place in Nature"', in RW Home (ed.), *Australian Science in the Making*, Cambridge University Press, Cambridge, 1988.

15 Nettie Palmer, *Henry Bournes Higgins: A Memoir*, George Harrap, London, 1931, p. 74; JA La Nauze, *Alfred Deakin: A Biography*, Melbourne University Press, Carlton, 1965; Barry W Butcher, 'Darwinism, Social Darwinism, and the Australian Aborigines: A Reevaluation', in Roy MacLeod and Philip Rehbock (eds), *Evolutionary Theory and Natural History in the Pacific: Darwin's Laboratory*, University of Hawaii Press, Honolulu, 1994.

16 DJ Mulvaney and JH Calaby, *So Much That Is New: Baldwin Spencer, 1860–1929, a Biography*, Melbourne University Press, Carlton, 1985; DJ Mulvaney, 'Sir Walter Baldwin Spencer (1860–1929)', *Australian Dictionary of Biography*, National Centre of Biography, Australian National University, Canberra, 2006, https://adb.anu.edu.au/biography/spencer-sir-walter-baldwin-8606 (accessed 13 October 2023).

17 Butcher, 'Gorilla Warfare in Melbourne'; Mark Francis, 'Social Darwinism and the Construction of Institutionalised Racism in Australia', *Journal of Australian Studies*, vol. 20, nos 50–51, 1996, pp. 90–105.

18 W Baldwin Spencer, 'Preliminary Report on the Aboriginals of the Northern Territory', *Bulletin of the Northern Territory*, Department of External Affairs, Melbourne, 7 July 1913, pp. 14–15.

19 Tim Calabria, 'The Origins of Segregated Education in Central Australia: A Tale of Two Families', *History Australia*, vol. 19, nos 2–3, April 2022, pp. 210–29.

20 Patrick Wolfe, 'On Being Woken Up: The Dreamtime in Anthropology and in Australian Settler Culture', *Comparative Studies in Society and History*, vol. 33, no. 2, 1991, pp. 197–224; Alison Petch, 'Spencer and Gillen's Work in Australia: The Interpretation of Power and Collecting in the Past', *Journal of Museum Ethnography*, no. 15, 2003, pp. 82–93.

21 William Ernest Jones to Mrs Gotto, 10 February 1915, Victorian Eugenics Society Collection, Wellcome Trust, SA/EUG/E.3.
22 Francis, 'Social Darwinism'.
23 *Argus*, 14 July 1914, p. 11.
24 KF Russell, 'Richard James Berry (1867–1962)', *Australian Dictionary of Biography*, National Centre of Biography, Australian National University, Canberra, 2006, https://adb.anu.edu.au/biography/berry-richard-james-5220/text8703 (accessed 13 October 2023).
25 RJA Berry, *Chance and Circumstance*, unpublished autobiography, University of Melbourne Medical Library, Parkville, 1954, p. 115.
26 Ross L Jones, *Humanity's Mirror: 150 Years of Anatomy in Melbourne*, Haddington Press, Melbourne, 2007, Chapter 5.
27 Michael Roe, *Nine Australian Progressives: Vitalism in Bourgeois Social Thought 1890–1960*, University of Queensland Press, St Lucia, 1984.
28 RJW Selleck, 'Frank Tate (1864–1939)', *Australian Dictionary of Biography*, National Centre of Biography, Australian National University, Canberra, 2006, https://adb.anu.edu.au/biography/tate-frank-8748/text15325 (accessed 13 October 2023); RJW Selleck, *Frank Tate: A Biography*, Melbourne University Press, Carlton, 1982.
29 Frank Tate, 'Our Neglected Opportunities', in Henry Payne (ed.), *Proceedings of the First Educational Congress*, State of Victoria, held in Melbourne, 1912, Mullet, Melbourne, n.d., p. 44; Searle argues that eugenics was an important part of this cult: GR Searle, *The Quest for National Efficiency: A Study in British Politics and Thought 1899–1914*, Blackwell, Oxford, 1971, pp. 60–1; First trip to Germany, Coblenz 9/8/07, Correspondence, Britain and Europe, 1907, Tate Papers; Irish Sea 9.30 p.m. 30/8/07, Correspondence, Britain and Europe, 1907, Tate Papers; Circular letter 12, 1933 trip, Italy, Correspondence, United States, Canada, Britain and Europe, 1932–3, Tate Papers; on illiberal progressivism, see Stephen Garton, '"Liberty of the Nation": Eugenics in Australia and New Zealand and the Limits of Illiberalism', in Diane B Paul, John Stenhouse and Hamish G Spencer (eds), *Eugenics at the Edges of Empire: New Zealand, Australia, Canada and South Africa*, Palgrave Macmillan, Cham, Switzerland, 2018.
30 Selleck, *Frank Tate*; Ross L Jones, 'Thinking Dangerous Thoughts: Post-Primary Education and Eugenics in Australia—1905–1939', in Diane B Paul, John Stenhouse and Hamish G Spencer (eds), *Eugenics at the Edges of Empire: New Zealand, Australia, Canada and South Africa*, Palgrave Macmillan, Cham, Switzerland, 2018.
31 Mark B Adams, 'Toward a Comparative History of Eugenics', in Mark B Adams (ed.), *The Wellborn Science: Eugenics in Germany, France, Brazil and Russia*, Oxford University Press, New York, 1990.
32 Mulvaney and Calaby, *So Much That Is New*; Geoffrey Serle, *John Monash: A Biography*, Melbourne University Press, Carlton, 1982; Len Weickhardt, *Masson of Melbourne: The Life and Times of David Orme Masson, Professor of Chemistry, University of Melbourne, 1886–1923*, Royal Australian Chemical Institute, Parkville, 1989; Selleck, *Frank Tate*; Geoffrey Serle, *Sir John Medley: A Memoir*, Melbourne University Press, Carlton, 1993; Desmond Zwar, *The Dame: The Life and Times of Dame Jean Macnamara, Medical Pioneer*, Macmillan, South Melbourne, 1984; Don Watson, *Brian Fitzpatrick: A Radical Life*, Hale & Iremonger, Sydney, 1979.

33 KF Russell, *The Melbourne Medical School, 1862–1962*, Melbourne University Press, Carlton, 1977; Joan Radford, *The Chemistry Department of the University of Melbourne: Its Contribution to Science, 1854–1959*, Hawthorn Press, Melbourne, 1978.

34 For Berry's statement about the importance of eugenics in his career, see Berry, *Chance and Circumstance*, pp. 189–90; Russell, *The Melbourne Medical School*; KF Russell, 'Richard James Arthur Berry, 1867–1962', in Geoffrey Kenny and Harold Attwood (eds), *Festschrift for Kenneth Fitzpatrick Russell*, Queensberry Hill Press, Melbourne, 1978, pp. 25–45; Russell, 'Richard James Berry (1867–1962)'.

35 Gabriela Soto Laveaga, 'Moving from, and beyond, Invented Categories: Afterwords', in 'Forum: Decolonizing Histories in Theory and Practice', *History and Theory*, vol. 59, no. 3, September 2020, pp. 442, 447. For a discussion, see Warwick Anderson and Gabriela Soto Laveaga (eds), 'Forum: Decolonizing Histories in Theory and Practice', *History and Theory*, vol. 59, no. 3, September 2020, pp. 369–447.

36 RJW Selleck, *The Shop*, Melbourne University Press, Carlton, 2003; RJW Selleck, 'Rocks in His Head: Importing European Science to a Nineteenth-Century Australian University', *Paedagogica Historica*, vol. 37, no. 1, 2001, pp. 153–73.

37 The publication of *The Cultivation of Whiteness* in 2002 created a major stir. See 'University Apologises to Aborigines for Past Experiments', *Adelaidean*, vol. 11, no. 2, March 2002, p. 3; Warwick Anderson, *The Cultivation of Whiteness: Science, Health and Racial Destiny in Australia*, Melbourne University Press, Carlton, 2002.

38 For Wolfe's role, see the following chapter in this text: 'The History Discipline and Aboriginal Dispossession' by David Goodman. On Anderson, see *An Onemda Decade: Ten Years of Progress in Koori Health*, Melbourne School of Population Health, The University of Melbourne, Parkville, 2010, pp. 9–12; Warwick Anderson, 'Indigenous Health in a Global Frame: From Community Development to Human Rights', *Health and History*, vol. 10, no. 2, 2008, pp. 1–15.

A Memoir

JIM BERG, GUNDITJMARA ELDER

Uncle Jim Berg.

I WAS BORN IN 1938. I was a mission kid from Framlingham Aboriginal Mission, and to me, the University of Melbourne was probably as far away as the moon. When I left school at the age of fourteen, I became a woodcutter like my grandfather and my uncles. I found it hard to even write my own name, and I could barely read, but I always worked, in lots of different jobs.

In June 1972 a meeting was organised by some young lawyers and some of the academic staff from the Law Department at the University of Melbourne, to talk about setting up a legal service for Kooris in Victoria. Elders and some others from the Koori community were invited. The meeting was held at the Moot Court at the University, and I remember feeling completely overawed and terrified.

At this time I was working at Borthwicks as a slaughterman. When the Victorian Aboriginal Legal Service (VALS) opened in January 1973, I was the only Koori staff member. My boss at Borthwicks gave me six months' leave to see if I liked the new job at VALS and he held my position for me, but I stayed at VALS as the CEO for fourteen years.

Since childhood I had always been haunted by concerns about Kooris who were not buried in their own Country. When I was appointed an inspector under the Victorian *Archaeological and Aboriginal Relics Act 1972*, I was in a position to do something about this, and take responsibility for something that was very important to me. This led to a very ugly confrontation with the University, and then to legal action, and then to a court case.

The University believed that they owned the skeletal remains of our Ancestors that were in their Anatomy Department. I believed that our Ancestors' skeletal remains should be returned to their Country and reburied in the womb of our Spiritual Mother, the Land, and the decision of the court meant this could happen. For the next twenty-five years, the relationship between myself and the University can only be described as 'cold and distant' on both sides. I was never again invited to be involved in presenting lectures to first-year medical students about the work I was doing as the chairperson of the Victorian Aboriginal Health Resources Consultative Group.

By coincidence, the last time that I lectured to the medical students, there was a young Koori in the group—the first Koori medical student at the University. His name was Ian Anderson and he went on to become the first Koori person to graduate as a medical doctor from the University of Melbourne.

Things had started to change at the University. Having Koori students at the University and having Kooris working there made a big difference. I started to feel as though the barriers surrounding the University and the academic world were beginning to crumble.

Ian Anderson was appointed to head the Koori Health Research team at the University, and later more Kooris were employed in senior positions.

I have always believed strongly in the need to work together in partnerships, and to show mutual respect. With Kooris working at the University, this is what started to happen. Koori and non-Koori academics had a chance to learn from each other, and this flows on to the students too.

Now, all these year later, I am really enjoying being able to contribute to the work of the University on committees in areas such as reconciliation, repatriation and cultural heritage, but I have noticed that it is mostly only academics who are on these committees.

As a Koori Elder, I think that it is really important to always have people from the Koori community who are not academics on these committees—to keep the academic world connected to the Koori community, and to make sure that Koori academics are always being reminded of who they are, where they come from, and their responsibilities to our Ancestors and to the future generations of our People.

I feel very proud to have been involved in some of the changes that have happened and that are happening still at the University, and I am glad that the history of Kooris and the University since the time of colonisation is being told in this book.

May the Spirits of my Ancestors be with you all.

I

Place

Place

ROSS L JONES

> 'In the act of mapping Australia the colonists began to take control of the landscape and one of the most important and powerful ways they did this was to name places.'
>
> Laura Kostanski and Ian D Clark, 2009[1]

IN 'PLACE', WE document the University of Melbourne's active erasure of the markers showing the timeless Indigenous occupation and custodianship of Country. These markers include the indigenous flora, fauna and placenames that give the land meaning. Only recently have there been attempts to reimagine the pre-settlement landscape and features.

The University's influence extends beyond the wrought-iron fences of its campuses into areas beyond. Frederick McCoy, the first professor of natural science, was one of the main founders of the Zoological and Acclimatisation Society of Victoria in 1862. This society created the first zoological gardens in Royal Park, next to the University. Here, the society introduced animals and plants from overseas, assessing their suitability to Australian conditions before releasing them. This activity forever changed the ecosystem, destroying the balance fostered by Indigenous peoples over millennia.

The willingness to refashion the environment to make it more habitable for invasive species more familiar to the settlers was expressed memorably by the Hon. Thomas Turner a'Beckett, a politician and member of the University of Melbourne Council, to the first meeting of the society. He lamented that, because 'the English song-birds which had been set free in some parts of the Colony were much persecuted by the native hawks', the 'extirpation' of the hawks would 'be an advantage'.[2] In their chapters of this book, Simon Farley explains settler attitudes to flora and landscape, and Zoë Laidlaw tells the story of how Indigenous lands were taken and worked by early settlers who then helped fund the construction of great buildings in the University.

Placenames were another aspect of the project of substituting the European for the Indigenous. For most of its history the University has made no attempt to capture Indigenous names relevant to its grounds or its other activities. Indeed, that was anathema to its vision of its role in the new colony. It was to be a new outpost of modern learning, inspired by its European compatriots, to apply Western knowledge and impose Western names on a colony it defined as uncivilised.[3] Beyond the University, Indigenous words were often adopted. For instance, the NSW surveyor-general, major Thomas Mitchell, sometimes used Indigenous names for the places through which he passed in the 1830s.[4]

The buildings erected around the grounds were accordingly named to reflect the disciplines within Western knowledge that defined the University, such as Natural Philosophy, Biology and Medicine. These names celebrated the ascendency of Western knowledge over an alien, primitive land and, while the buildings were mostly named after Western intellectual disciplines, their design was also influenced by racist science. The designer of many, Anketell Henderson, the first architecture graduate of the University, argued that his creations expressed the racial superiority of the white race, with the 'yellow races' well behind and the 'black races' last.[5] Race, according to Henderson, was the defining characteristic of architecture.[6] Henderson's firm, Reed, Henderson & Smart, designed the Natural Philosophy (housing the Murrup Barak Melbourne Institute for Indigenous Development), Pathology (Elisabeth Murdoch) and Biology (Baldwin Spencer) buildings and the professors' houses, the last surviving example being University House, now the home of the staff social club. Philip Goad writes about architecture and race in his chapter in this section, and James Waghorne discusses the naming of buildings in the penultimate chapter of this volume.

Indigenous names were first used as late as the 1970s when a new computer laboratory named its first computer servers with Indigenous words beginning with 'mu', to signify 'Melbourne University'; this is discussed in Richard Gillespie's chapter. Although a tentative step towards recognition of the First People, this way of naming with Indigenous words without identifying their provenance or significant meanings was a pattern that evolved soon after Federation. It turned away from colonial philological practice, which had been driven by the collecting mania for 'primitive' knowledge and cultural artefacts. This new approach was a product of both a new nationalism and the 'dying race' myth, which anticipated continued Aboriginal population decline and the ultimate absorption of mixed-race survivors into the general population. This new vision of Australia coopted a sanitised version of Indigenous history, stripped of 'unpleasant associations', and assigned it as decoration to give the illusion of deep history.[7]

The University's recent attempt to reconnect with pre-colonial landscapes and ecology is discussed by Shawana Andrews and Jefa Greenaway. They give examples of this new approach of acknowledging the original lands and their use by the traditional custodians, and offer inspiration for future projects to rehabilitate the place that was taken from its Indigenous inhabitants.

Notes

1 Laura Kostanski and Ian D Clark, 'Reviving Old Indigenous Names for New Purposes', in Harold Koch and Luise Hercus (eds), *Aboriginal Placenames: Naming and Renaming the Australian Landscape*, ANU Press, Canberra, 2009, p. 189.

2 Zoological and Acclimatisation Society of Victoria, *Proceedings of the Zoological and Acclimatisation Society of Victoria, First Report*, vol. 1, 1862, unnumbered pages of membership lists at the beginning and pp. 9, 19, 34–5; *Second Report*, 1863, p. 7; *Argus*, 30 August 1928, p. 12.

3 RJW Selleck, *The Shop*, Melbourne University Press, Carlton, 2003, Chapter 1.

4 Laura Kostanski, 'Toponymic Books and the Representation of Indigenous Identities', in Harold Koch and Luise Hercus (eds), *Aboriginal Placenames: Naming and Renaming the Australian Landscape*, ANU Press, Canberra, 2009, p. 175.

5 Anketell Henderson, 'Race and Architecture', *Alma Mater*, vol. 2, no. 6, September 1897, p. 13.

6 Anketell Henderson, 'University Extension Lecture', *Ballarat Star*, 28 July 1894, p. 1.

7 Kostanski, 'Toponymic Books', p. 175.

Flora and Failure

A History of Plants and People on the Parkville Campus

SIMON FARLEY[1]

In early February 1854, the *Argus* reported that a grassfire had been extinguished in 'a tract of the bush, in the north-eastern corner of the city, near the spot where it is intended the Carlton Gardens should be'.[2] By this time, there were houses, churches, pubs and a police watchhouse in the vicinity, but this was still 'the bush'. Garryowen, the iconic chronicler of early Melbourne, described the area that became North Melbourne, Parkville and Carlton as 'a vista of hill and dale, well wooded and grassed, well suited for a delightful rambling excursion'. Repeatedly he referred to the 'Carlton woods' as a 'forest' or even 'wilderness', shaded by 'luxuriant gum and she-oak trees'.[3]

'Bush' is not a word that often comes to mind when one thinks of the University of Melbourne in the early twenty-first century. The University—or more specifically, its Parkville campus—now lies very near the centre of a megalopolis that sprawls over a greater area and contains a larger population than some small nations. But when its foundation stone was set down, just a few months after that grassfire, it sat on the fringe of urbanisation. The land no longer benefited from the stewardship of its original human occupants, the Wurundjeri Woi Wurrung people, nor had it been overhauled into something useful or ornamental in the terms of the colonisers who laid claim over it. It had become a wild and unkempt place: it was, indeed, the bush.

Evidently, that changed. The University's oldest and premier campus is predicated on an immense act of ecological transformation. This chapter considers that transformation with particular regard to plants and to those who study them. The latter are as important as the former: colonisation engendered not only ecological change but epistemic change too. When *Ngamajet* (settlers) razed woodlands and drained wetlands, Wurundjeri knowledge of plant communities was left fragmented and marginalised within the settler paradigm. Throughout the institution's history, the University of Melbourne's botanists have largely ignored and overwritten the botanical knowledges of the Wurundjeri Woi Wurrung and other Indigenous peoples.[4]

When the University was founded, Melbourne had already been growing for nearly two decades. The ecological communities that the Eastern Kulin peoples had been carefully tending since time immemorial were reeling from the shock of colonisation: *Ngamajet* cut down trees, disrupted Kulin fire regimes, and ushered in a flux of animals, plants, fungi and microbes from across the world.[5] The site granted to the University in late 1853 was not exempt from this upheaval. In an annual report of the University Council written just over two decades later, its original 'unsightly state' was remembered at length.[6] The ground was rutted from cartwheels and pocked with holes where soil had been dug up and carried away; some of these pits had filled with water, others with rubbish. The largest trees had been felled, leaving cumbersome stumps. The most prominent and, from the perspective of the founding University Council, least desirable aspect of the site was 'a gully from north to south'.[7] A creek ran down this gully, roughly following the course of what is now Bouverie Street to a wetland area north of the CBD.[8] This was, in turn, the source of what was lightheartedly called the 'River Townend', the stream that, after heavy rain, flowed down Elizabeth Street and into Birrarung (which *Ngamajet* called the Yarra).[9] These waterways would not have flown continuously year-round and are perhaps better thought of as chains of ponds or linear wetlands.[10] As recently as the 1840s, Wurundjeri Woi Wurrung people had camped on the site.[11] It still is—it never ceased to be—Wurundjeri Country. But colonisation precipitated rapid and, to a large degree, irrevocable change.

Once it was granted to the University, this land—16 hectares bound by Sydney Road in the west and Grattan Street in the south—was fenced off, and a more systematic transformation began. Edward La Trobe Bateman, a visual artist and cousin to the governor, was tasked with landscaping

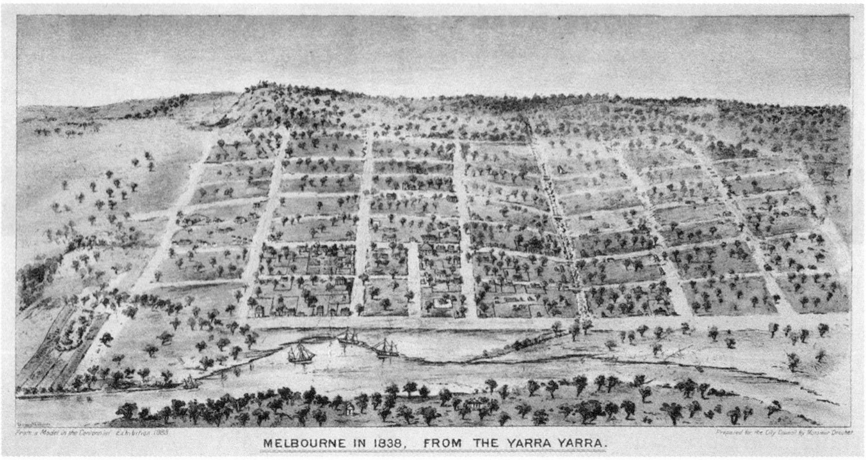

This lithograph, *Melbourne in 1838, from the Yarra Yarra*, is an act of historical imagination, based on a model created by Justin Drouhet for the 1888 Melbourne Centennial Exhibition. Note the low bridges crossing Elizabeth Street, which became the 'River Townend' in wet weather, and the hills to the north on which the University would later be built.

the site.[12] Much of the heavy manual labour involved in levelling the ground and creating roads and paths was carried out by prisoners from Pentridge.[13] Grasses, shrubs and trees from all over the world—not just Europe but Asia, the Americas, Africa and Aotearoa New Zealand—were planted.[14] These grew alongside trees such as Moreton Bay figs and Norfolk Island pines, which were 'native' to the Australian colonies but newcomers to Melbourne.[15] 'Bouverie Creek' was dammed to form an ornamental lake.[16] By the time all of this was completed in the early 1860s, the area would have been unrecognisable compared to its pre-colonial state.

This does not preclude us from speculating on what that earlier state may have entailed, however. Long before the aesthetics and the epistemes of British academics were imposed on the land, people were tending to and studying plants there as part of a holistic relationship with Country. Over countless generations, Wurundjeri Woi Wurrung people developed practical and detailed knowledge of the plant communities that existed on their Country, incorporating many species into their lifeway. Indeed, much of Wurundjeri cuisine, tools, clothing, dyes and medicine was derived from plants.[17]

Eucalypts, wattles and she-oaks are mentioned in virtually all accounts of early Melbourne, and it is clear that, at the time of colonisation, the campus site was an open woodland like much of the surrounds. The dominant trees were probably yellow box and, particularly along the gully, river red gum; a few of the latter, predating the founding of the University, still stand at the south-western corner of University Oval.[18] The chief ground cover was likely *buath* (kangaroo grass) or a similar species, the seeds of which were collected and ground into flour.[19] The flowering of *muyan* (silver wattle) signalled the advent of a bark-harvesting season, during which Wurundjeri Woi Wurrung people made canoes, *tarnuks* (bowls) and other wooden objects.[20] Red gums were a preferred source of timber.[21] Wetlands swelled in this cold, rainy period, while orchids and wattles bloomed. Bouverie Creek would have provided habitat for edible plants such as marsh cress, water ribbons and various rushes; perhaps a dense scrub of tea-tree, such as that which grew along the lower reaches of Birrarung, lined the banks.[22] The fibres of water-loving rushes and sedges—as well as various grasses and lilies—were used for weaving and to make twine. *Garawun* (spiny-headed mat rush), for example, was favoured as a source of material for 'necklaces, headbands, girdles, baskets, mats and bags', as well as traps and nets.[23] A particularly valuable plant, its seeds, core, and the base of its leaves are all edible, and the roots are used 'to treat bites and stings'.[24]

Settlers should not imagine Wurundjeri cuisine as homogeneous and utilitarian: aside from nourishment, these plant communities afforded a wide array of colours, textures and flavours, including sweet treats. The flowers of the *woorike* (silver banksia) were soaked in water to make a cordial-like beverage, while the sweet 'manna' of the eponymous gum and the fruit of the 'native cherry' (*Exocarpos cupressiformis*) were enjoyed by Wurundjeri Woi Wurrung and by the first waves of *Ngamajet* alike.[25] (It is the manna gum that gives the Wurundjeri Woi Wurrung their name: *wurun* is the name for the tree itself and *djeri* is a type of grub that lives within it.)[26] It is possible there were plots of *murnong*—also known as 'yam daisy', a chief staple of Wurundjeri cuisine—on the site, although this species is more associated with the flat grasslands to the north.[27] If not *murnong*, similar plants—orchids and lilies, for example—with appetising tubers may have been cultivated in the vicinity. Although we cannot be sure of the minutiae—of which species grew in which spots—it seems beyond doubt that the plants of this locale helped the Wurundjeri Woi Wurrung to live healthy, satisfying lives. Then, within a matter of years, they were gone; new ecosystems, maintained in new ways by new people, replaced them.

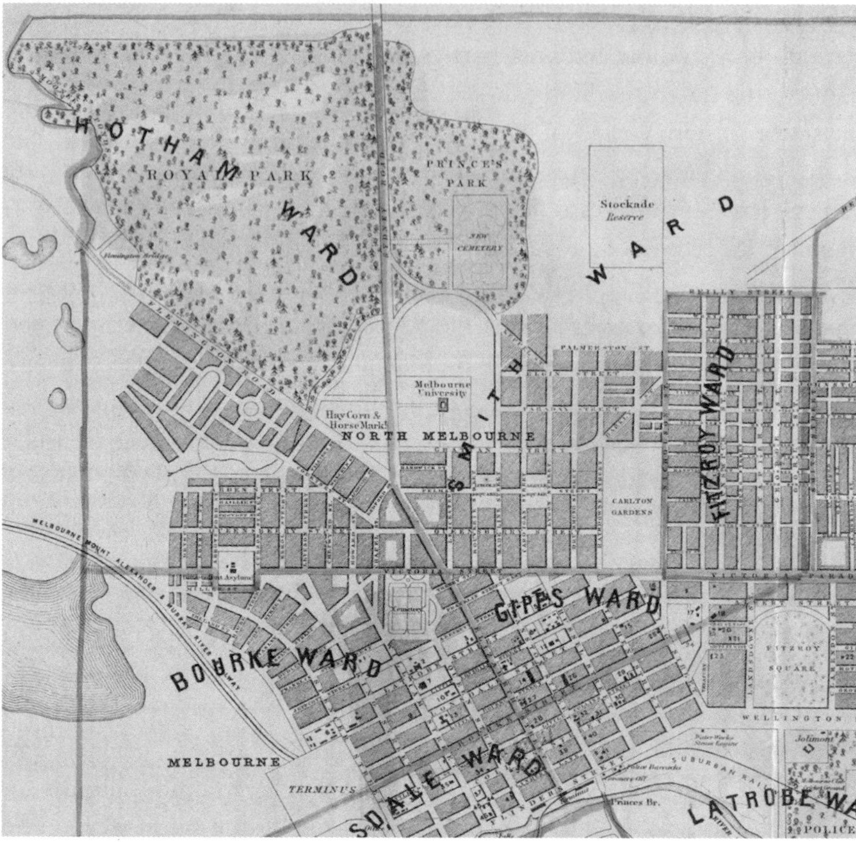

This fragment of a plan of Melbourne and its suburbs from the late 1850s shows the nascent University at the edge of Melbourne's rapidly growing sprawl. Bouverie Street and Elizabeth Street can be seen to the south.

Botany was first taught at the University by Frederick McCoy, the founding (and ultimately, the only) professor of 'Natural Science'. As Linden Gillbank has aptly put it, 'McCoy professed rather than practised botany,' or to quote one of McCoy's own students, the 'only flowers exhibited in his lectures were the flowers of rhetoric'.[28] His primary scientific interests were geology and palaeontology, but like many naturalists of his day, McCoy had his fingers in many disciplinary pies. He supervised the landscaping of the site and founded two enduring botanical institutions on campus: the Herbarium (initially as part of the National Museum, another of his projects) and what is now known as System Garden.[29] The construction of the latter began in

1856, although major additions were made as late as 1875; this entailed the cultivation of another host of species from across Australia and the world, further augmenting and altering the plant communities on campus.[30]

At the time of McCoy's arrival in the colony, Ferdinand Mueller was Victoria's government botanist.[31] Although Mueller was never directly affiliated with the University, he and McCoy often worked together, particularly through their roles in the Acclimatisation Society of Victoria through the 1860s.[32] They shared a great and mutual respect: McCoy was a pallbearer at Mueller's funeral in 1896.[33] Mueller had begun to form a rudimentary herbarium since his appointment as government botanist in 1853, but as McCoy described it, the specimens were 'tied up in bundles, and kept in the little cottage in the Botanic Garden, where the workmen took their meals and slept, and where, consequently, visitors would scarcely like to intrude'.[34] Rescued from this ignominious sanctum, a portion of these specimens were transported to the University in 1856 and exhibited in the museum.[35] Subsequently, Mueller provided additional specimens from across the Australian colonies.[36] It is almost certain that many of these were first collected by Aboriginal people, then sent to Mueller via intermediaries—usually settler landowners—before finally being identified and preserved.[37] But, typically for the time, Mueller and McCoy expressed virtually no interest in the botanical knowledge or ideas of these people.[38]

Mueller was fascinated by Australian flora, for intellectual, aesthetic and commercial reasons. 'Should we not largely surround ourselves with our own native plants, handsome and instructive as they are?' he asked during an 1871 lecture at Melbourne's Industrial and Technological Museum.[39] Wattles in particular captured his imagination. 'What delight is experienced,' he rhapsodised, 'when as the first harbingers of spring the early wattle-flowers burst into bloom, converting bushes or trees almost into one mass of gold, and diffusing fragrance widely through the air.'[40] Their 'industrial purposes' were no less exciting: 'Catechu, tanners' bark, gum, galls, scents and woods of various qualities are obtained from them; others serve for hedges.'[41] He was thrilled by the challenge of cultivating native plants and by their economic potential. Of course, wattles had been used in Aboriginal economies for millennia—had Mueller only inquired a little into Wurundjeri culture, for example, he might have learned much. The Wurundjeri Woi Wurrung had myriad uses for *muyan*: different parts of this tree were used to make everything from food to soap, medicine to adhesive, bandages to shields.[42]

It was always possible for settler botanists and their Indigenous counterparts to collaborate and cooperate, but this possibility was refused, again and again, by white settler academics whose colonialist and—increasingly as the nineteenth century wore on—racist worldview caused them to see Aboriginal people and cultures as inferior. Yet even this ethnocentric arrogance should not necessarily have prevented the likes of Mueller and McCoy from appropriating and, indeed, exploiting Indigenous botanical knowledges; indeed, they may have profited greatly from doing so. It is difficult, then, to account for their profound lack of interest. Perhaps it speaks to the fragility of the coloniser's sense of superiority—not even a trace of respect could be allowed. Or perhaps it was the result of a cultural gulf. Mueller saw great value in wattles. But where Mueller conceived of this value in relation to industrial expansion, financial windfalls, the prestige of the colony and perhaps the empire of which it was part, the Wurundjeri Woi Wurrung's goals were more modest and more humane: wattles provided sustainable ways to feed people, to heal people, to enjoy a life of abundance that was, at the same time, a life that did not demand too much of Country. Mueller saw resources; his Wurundjeri analogues saw relationships.[43] Perhaps it was this kind of distinction that made Indigenous knowledge seem worthless to settlers.

Botany scarcely existed at the University prior to 1863, and even after that, it was taught largely as a component of the medical degree.[44] Its fortunes waxed and waned. Teaching was largely taken over by the new chair of biology, Walter Baldwin Spencer, in 1887.[45] As with McCoy, botany was not Spencer's primary field of expertise, and there was little enthusiasm from students through the 1890s.[46] The university's first dedicated professor of botany—and, indeed, occupier of the first chair of botany in Australasia—was Alfred James Ewart, appointed in 1906.[47] While simultaneously working as government botanist at the Victorian National Herbarium—a successor to Mueller in both regards—Ewart rescued the discipline from its 1890s doldrums.[48] His most tangible legacy on campus today is the Botany Building, situated near McCoy's System Garden, which was constructed under his personal and close supervision.[49] The building was formally opened in 1929 by Victorian premier William McPherson and chancellor John MacFarland.[50] Ewart's first lectures in 1906 had been attended by a

Alfred Ewart.

total of six students; McPherson noted that the cohort had since grown to 220.[51] It must have felt like a triumph: Ewart himself described it as 'the culmination of 23 years' work' and 'a proud day'.[52]

Not long before—in 1924 and again in 1927—Ewart had been in very different circumstances, travelling through Australia's centre and north. In 1924 he was asked by a former student, the Northern Territory's chief veterinary surgeon, captain FAC Bishop, to investigate a rash of accidental poisonings of cattle on the overland stock route.[53] To meet him, Ewart travelled from Adelaide to Wycliffe Well—even today, a twenty-hour drive. As the *Northern Territory Times and Gazette* reported, somewhat forebodingly, 'the journey promise[d] to be an arduous one'.[54] That was early May—by late July, Ewart was 'living in a roomy tent' in Alice Springs, apparently contented from having seen several species in the wild he had previously only known from the herbarium.[55] After identifying two problem species, he instructed a local police officer in their identification; in 1925, this officer then led a group of 'aboriginal [sic] labourers' in successfully extirpating these plants from the stock route.[56] Decades before Indigenous workers were legally entitled to wages in the Territory, these labourers would likely have been compensated with only rations, if at all.[57]

Ewart's 1927 expedition was better publicised, in large part due to a series of columns he wrote for the Melbourne *Herald* and Sydney *Sun*. These unpleasant columns are worth quoting at length, not for the sake of provocation but in order to demonstrate beyond doubt that Ewart was profoundly racist. He frequently described Aboriginal people as 'blacks', Aboriginal women as 'gins' and Aboriginal children as 'piccaninnies'. These were not neutral terms, and his use of them both contributed to and reflected an overall tone of derision. In one column, titled 'Mentality of the Blacks', Ewart mused upon the 'low grade of intelligence' that he believed was common to all Aboriginal people.[58] While not utterly devoid of sympathy, he exhibited racist attitudes that were pronounced even by the standards of the day:

> Blacks have the mentality and irresponsibility of a child, with the muscular body and passions of a man. When you hear someone say that if the blacks were educated there would be as many black graduates at Perth University as white, don't believe it.[59]

Lest this be thought of as a fleeting moment of misjudgement, it should be noted that Ewart made nearly identical remarks in a letter published in the *Argus* in 1933, written in response to the Caledon Bay crisis, a series of retaliatory killings in the Northern Territory that threatened to escalate.[60] His assessment of Aboriginal women, whom he believed more intelligent than Aboriginal men, was steeped in colonial sexism of the worst order:

> If a blackfellow cannot understand what you want him to do, it is usual to call up a gin who explains to him what it is you want. Some of the black women make passably good domestics and very plain cooks, but it is best not to watch them cooking if you desire to preserve your appetite. They wash clothes quite well and with less destructive zeal than most laundries.[61]

Ewart was dismissive of the female Aboriginal assistants 'appointed' to him to help with his experimental poisoning of livestock; the labour of these women, as Ewart was not reticent to admit, was compensated with only the most modest amount of tobacco.[62] He reserved particular scorn for Indigenous botanical knowledges, as described in another column:

> Many apologists for the blacks hold very erroneous ideas as to their mental and intellectual characteristics. The average mental capacity of the adults is certainly below that of a white child of ten to twelve years of age. They are

> generally supposed to have a remarkable knowledge of plant life and of the properties of plants. As a matter of fact they do not notice or know the commonest plants which grow around them so long as these plants have no relation to their stomachs, and they regularly confuse plants which bear resemblance to one another. It is possible that in tribes certain individuals may have more specialised knowledge, but the average black knows far less about the plants and animals around him than does an ordinary white child living in the country.[63]

It is clear from such mentions of 'apologists' that he understood that many of his fellow settlers, at least in the continent's south, would not espouse such contempt, or at least not espouse the same contempt with such fervour. Elsewhere, he wrote:

> After seeing the way blacks are handled by the police, and the treatment they receive on the stations, it is difficult to credit the appalling stories ... as to the cruel handling the blacks receive ... It is greatly to be regretted that some well-meaning persons, anxious to excite sympathy for the blacks, have not always adhered to the truth ...[64]

These remarks preceded a complaint that, 'for so long as abundant supplies of cheap black labor [sic] are available, no permanent white settlement of this area is possible.'[65]

In yet another article, Ewart attempted to refute reports of the mass poisoning of Aboriginal people. He avowed, 'If any poisoning ever took place it could only have been due to either a storekeeper or a cook, usually a Chinaman.'[66] At the same time he spun lurid tales of 'wild blacks' spearing cattle and settlers alike in the north-west of the continent.[67] He advocated for these people to be contained on small reserves—which he explicitly likened to wildlife sanctuaries—or on nearby islands, further freeing up their lands for pastoral expansion. According to Ewart, some form of strict segregation, to prevent 'any inter-mixture of blood', was essential to the preservation of a white Australia.[68]

More could be quoted in evidence, but these are the passages that pertain most closely to Ewart's roles as a researcher and educator. Despite his decades in teaching, Ewart was so determined to deny Aboriginal people their humanity that he viewed them as basically ineducable; as a botanist, their knowledge of and ideas about plants were worthless to him. He had strong views, strongly expressed, which cannot be easily explained, much less excused, as a product of his time and place. One must wonder how his legacy—in this regard no less than any other—has shaped the teaching and research of botany at the University of Melbourne right up to the present day.

Although none of his successors emulated Ewart's commitment to public racism, the pervasive aversion to Indigenous botanical knowledges was entrenched in the institution. The predominant attitude is exemplified in a review of Gwen Harden's *Flora of New South Wales*, written by Malcolm Calder for the *Sydney Morning Herald* in 1993. (Calder was head of botany from 1975 to 1979 and again over 1989 and 1990.)[69] The review begins:

> Between April 29 and May 7, 1770, around the shores of Botany Bay, Joseph Banks and his small party of botanists collected some 3000 plant specimens, representing more than 200 species new to science. So started the description, documentation and depiction of the NSW flora.[70]

It would be absurd to equate this statement to those of Ewart. Certainly there is nothing overtly racist about it. Nor is it an entirely unreasonable claim: there is no doubt that Indigenous botanical knowledges were produced, organised and transmitted in very different ways to those of the Western science of botany. Yet there is an echo here of that same colonial arrogance: an underlying belief that 'genuine' botanical knowledge—the knowledge that is useful, the knowledge that *matters*—only arrived in Australia with Europeans.

Although some University of Melbourne alumni have gone on to study Indigenous botanical knowledges, this research has been conducted under the auspices of other institutions. The premier example is Beth Gott (née Noyé), who completed her undergraduate and master's degrees on the Parkville campus.[71] A plant physiologist by training, it was not until she was based at Monash University, much later in her career, that she became a revered recorder of Indigenous plant lore.[72] While settler academics from other disciplines, particularly anthropology and archaeology, have increasingly engaged with Indigenous ecological thinking since the 1970s, the University of Melbourne's botanists have largely sat on the sidelines.[73] Although 'ethnobotany' has become more prominent in Australia over a similar span of time, this discipline has proved problematic: many ethnobotanists have focused their attention on the centre and north of the continent, eclipsing the lore of Aboriginal peoples in the south-east, and often frame their inquiries as 'rescue work', trying to preserve for posterity the traditions of ostensibly dying cultures. The very separation of settler-interpreted Indigenous knowledge (ethnobotany) from the knowledge settlers produce themselves (botany) demands interrogation. Nonetheless, at least efforts like the Tropical Indigenous Ethnobotany Centre at James Cook University and Gott's Aboriginal Garden at Monash demonstrate an interest in and esteem for Indigenous knowledge, even if they are perforce translated into settler paradigms. Into the twenty-first century, botanists at the University of Melbourne have undertaken enormous amounts of research into Australian plants, but their engagement with the people and cultures who have known these plants the longest has been negligible.

In 2022, *Emu Sky*, curated by Zena Cumpston, a Barkandji researcher and writer, opened in the Old Quadrangle. It showcased the work of Aboriginal artists from the south-east of the continent, exploring 'Indigenous land management, knowledge, science, plant use, language and truth telling'.[74]

One day, while on the Parkville campus working on this chapter, I idly wandered into the exhibit—a much belated visit. One set of works made a particular impression: a wall covered in posters, depicting, in stark colours, photographs of botanical specimens, with the Woi Wurrung names of these plants boldly laid over the top. Spread across an internal wall of the Quad, I saw *buath*, *muyan*, *woorike*, *murnong* and *garawun*. The Woi Wurrung names were provided by Wurundjeri Woi Wurrung woman Brooke Wandin; the specimens were borrowed from the University's herbarium.

The exhibition guide explained:

> Aboriginal people across Australia have developed a multitude of uses for plants through scientific observation and testing over the longest time imaginable. Plant knowledge has been central to the longevity of Aboriginal communities, who use plants for medicine, nutrition and technologies, such as watercraft, tools and traps ... Each of these plants are from Wurundjeri Country and are an important part of Wurundjeri culture.[75]

A few of the posters did not show Woi Wurrung words, however. Instead, in the same bold text, were the words, 'Why don't you know me?'

It was a provocative and perspicacious question. Why did we *Ngamajet* need to rename, repurpose, reinvent these plants? Why do we not now know them as the Wurundjeri Woi Wurrung did before we invaded their Country? We can discuss racism, colonialism, genocide, ecocide, but

I suspect words like these only scratch the surface of this ecological and epistemic disjuncture.

Yet these posters also gesture towards something hopeful. They juxtapose two ways of knowing plants and, to some degree, bring those ways of knowing together. The gulf between Indigenous and Western forms of botanical knowledge is bridgeable; cooperation and collaboration have always been possible and still are. Thanks to the likes of Beth Gott and Zena Cumpston, important steps are being taken in this direction. But this is new work struggling against a century and a half of Western epistemic hubris. For most of its history, the University of Melbourne and its most prominent botanists did worse than merely fail to bridge this gulf—they never tried.

Notes

1 I must thank Zena Cumpston, Linden Gillbank, Barbara Howlett and Virginia McNally for their generous assistance in researching this chapter.

2 'Domestic Intelligence', *Argus*, 9 February 1854.

3 Garryowen, *The Chronicles of Early Melbourne*, Fergusson and Mitchell, Melbourne, 1888, pp. 29, 188, 191, 230, 352.

4 I use phrases like 'Indigenous botanical knowledges' in this chapter with some unease, though a superior catch-all shorthand term eludes me. As Palyku woman Aurora Milroy writes, such terms reduce 'our system of knowledge into something discrete, rational, linear and easy to slot into existing western frames ... But Indigenous knowledge is more than this, and also not this at all. It is non-linear, cyclical, holistic': Aurora Milroy, 'Stories in the Waterpipes', *Emu Sky*, https://emusky.culturalcommons.edu.au/blak_yarn/stories-waterpipes-aurora-milroy (accessed 13 October 2023).

5 Richard Broome, *Aboriginal Victorians*, Allen & Unwin, Crows Nest, NSW, 2005, pp. 6–9, 19–20; Gary Presland, *The Place for a Village*, Museum Victoria Publishing, Melbourne, 2008, p. 112; Gary Presland, *First People*, Museum Victoria Publishing, Melbourne, 2010, pp. 87, 90.

6 'The University of Melbourne', *Argus*, 22 July 1875.

7 Ernest Scott, *A History of the University of Melbourne*, Melbourne University Press, Melbourne, 1936, p. 14.

8 Presland, *The Place for a Village*, pp. 85, 87.

9 Ibid. This waterway has also been known as 'Elizabeth stream' and 'River Williams', among other monikers. See also Garryowen, *The Chronicles of Early Melbourne*, p. 363.

10 Cf. Robyn Annear, *Bearbrass: Imagining Early Melbourne*, Black Inc., Melbourne, 1995, p. 53.

11 RJW Selleck, *The Shop*, Melbourne University Press, Carlton, 2003, p. 6.

12 He was also involved in the design of Carlton Gardens and the Williamstown Botanic Gardens, among others of Melbourne's parks, though his lofty ambitions were seldom fully realised: Selleck, *The Shop*, p. 80. For greater detail, see Anne Neale, 'The Garden Designs of Edward La Trobe Bateman (1816–97)', *Garden History*, vol. 33, no. 2, 2005, pp. 225–55.

13 George Tibbits, *The Planning and Development of the University of Melbourne*, The History of the University Unit, University of Melbourne, Parkville, 2000, p. 16.
14 'The University of Melbourne'.
15 Selleck, *The Shop*, p. 80.
16 Scott, *A History of the University of Melbourne*, p. 14; The Clean Air and Urban Landscapes Hub, 'The Living Pavilion', https://nespurban.edu.au/platforms/living-pavilion (accessed 13 October 2023).
17 Of course, various minerals and animal products were also important in the pre-colonial Wurundjeri lifeway.
18 Presland, *The Place for a Village*, pp. 110, 122–7, 140; Murrup Barak, 'Billibellary's Walk', 2023, https://murrupbarak.unimelb.edu.au/home/about/billibellarys-walk (accessed 13 October 2023).
19 Presland, *The Place for a Village*, pp. 115, 126.
20 Jim Poulter, *The Eight Wurundjeri Seasons in Melbourne*, Red Hen Enterprises, Templestowe, 2015, p. 12.
21 Presland, *First People*, 68, 141.
22 Information on plants consumed or otherwise used by the Wurundjeri Woi Wurrung has been drawn from two main sources: Zena Cumpston, *Indigenous Plant Use*, Clean Air and Urban Landscapes Hub, The University of Melbourne, Parkville, 2020; and Tim Low, *Wild Food Plants of Australia*, HarperCollins, Sydney, 1991. See also Presland, *First People*, pp. 71–2. On the scrub surrounding Birrarung, see Garryowen, *The Chronicles of Early Melbourne*, pp. 3–4, 497. Tea-tree (also spelt 'ti-tree') can refer to various species of either the genus *Melaleuca* or the genus *Leptospermum*.
23 Cumpston, *Indigenous Plant Use*.
24 Ibid.
25 Robyn Annear half-records, half-imagines the fondness of the early *Ngamajet* for these plants in *Bearbrass*, pp. 44, 202–3.
26 Presland, *The Place for a Village*, p. 204.
27 Presland, *First People*, p. 71; Presland, *The Place for a Village*, p. 120; Poulter, *The Eight Wurundjeri Seasons*, p. 14; Bruce Pascoe, *Dark Emu*, Magabala Books, Broome, 2018, pp. 18–20, 64.
28 Linden Gillbank, 'University Botany in Colonial Victoria: Frederick McCoy's Botanical Classes and Collections at the University of Melbourne', *Historical Records of Australian Science*, vol. 19, 2008, p. 53; Selleck, *The Shop*, p. 244.
29 Tibbits, *The Planning and Development of the University of Melbourne*, pp. 16, 18; Gillbank, 'University Botany', pp. 57–66.
30 Ibid., pp. 63, 71.
31 Ibid., pp. 53, 56.
32 See, generally, Pete Minard, *All Things Harmless, Useful, and Ornamental*, The University of North Carolina Press, Chapel Hill, 2019.
33 'Baron Von Mueller', *Table Talk*, 16 October 1896.
34 Gillbank, 'University Botany', p. 59.
35 Ibid.
36 Ibid., pp. 60–1.
37 Sara Maroske, '"A Taste for Botanic Science": Ferdinand Mueller's Female Collectors and the History of Australian Botany', *Muelleria*, vol. 32, 2014, pp. 74–5.
38 It is true that several of Mueller's collectors did include information about Aboriginal uses of and words for various specimens, although Maroske

characterises such information as 'unsolicited' (albeit not necessarily unwelcome): Maroske, '"A Taste for Botanic Science"', pp. 84–5.

39 This was a different institution to McCoy's National Museum: Baron Ferdinand von Mueller, 'The Objects of a Botanic Garden in Relation to Industries', in [the committee of the] Industrial and Technological Museum (ed.), *Lectures ... Second Session of 1871*, Samuel Mullen, Melbourne, 1872, p. 169.

40 Ibid., p. 163.

41 Ibid., p. 164.

42 The Clean Air and Urban Landscapes Hub, 'The Living Pavilion'.

43 Cf. Jessyca Hutchens, 'In Abundance', *Emu Sky*, https://emusky.culturalcommons.edu.au/blak_yarn/in-abundance-jessyca-hutchens (accessed 13 October 2023).

44 Gillbank, 'University Botany', pp. 66–70.

45 Ibid., pp. 73–4.

46 Ibid.

47 TC Chambers, 'Alfred James Ewart (1872–1937)', *Australian Dictionary of Biography*, National Centre of Biography, Australian National University, Canberra, 2006, https://adb.anu.edu.au/biography/ewart-alfred-james-6124 (accessed 13 October 2023).

48 Linden Gillbank, *From System Garden to Scientific Research: The University of Melbourne's School of Botany under Its First Two Professors (1906–1973)*, School of Botany, University of Melbourne, Parkville, 2010, pp. 5–10.

49 Tibbits, *The Planning and Development of the University of Melbourne*, pp. 66–7.

50 'New Botany School', *Argus*, 30 November 1929.

51 Ibid.

52 Ibid.

53 'Town Talk', *Northern Territory Times and Gazette*, 6 May 1924; Freda Sternberg, 'Life in Central Australia', *Telegraph*, 29 July 1924.

54 'Town Talk'.

55 Sternberg, 'Life in Central Australia'.

56 'Poison Plants', *Toowoomba Chronicle and Darling Downs Gazette*, 7 September 1927.

57 See, for example, Julia Martínez, 'When Wages Were Clothes: Dressing down Aboriginal Workers in Australia's Northern Territory', *International Review of Social History*, vol. 52, no. 2, August 2007, pp. 271–86.

58 AJ Ewart, 'Mentality of the Blacks', *Herald*, 13 July 1927.

59 Ibid.

60 AJ Ewart, 'Mentality of Aborigines', *Argus*, 8 September 1933; Ben Silverstein, *Governing Natives: Indirect Rule and Settler Colonialism in Australia's North*, Manchester University Press, Manchester, 2019, Chapter 4.

61 Ibid. Ewart does not seem to have held white women in particularly high esteem either, although he counted several among his subordinates at the University. Attesting to this are his 'tempestuous [first] marriage', his bullying of Edith Derrick, and his extraordinarily acrimonious feud with Ethel McLennan (herself briefly head of botany after Ewart's death). See Selleck, *The Shop*, pp. 627–36.

62 AJ Ewart, 'Black Australia', *Sun*, 19 July 1927.

63 Ibid.

64 AJ Ewart, 'Abo. Instinct', *Sun*, 7 September 1927.

65 Ibid.

66 AJ Ewart, 'Black Spearmen', *Herald*, 23 July 1927.

67 Ibid.
68 Ibid.
69 Gillbank, *From System Garden*, p. 2.
70 Malcolm Calder, 'The Job That Banks Began', *Sydney Morning Herald*, 30 October 1993, p. 11A.
71 Gillbank, *From System Garden*, pp. 16, 21.
72 Zane Ma Rhea and Lynette Russell, 'Introduction: Understanding Koorie Plant Knowledge through the Ethnobotanic Lens. A Tribute to Beth Gott', *Artefact*, vol. 35, 2012, pp. 3–9.
73 Philip A Clarke, 'Australian Ethnobotany: An Overview', *Australian Aboriginal Studies*, no. 2, 2003, pp. 25–30. An arguable exception is Peter Attiwill (head of botany 1985–88), whose work on fire ecology evinces an interest in Aboriginal fire regimes, although this has never been a major focus of his research. See, for example, Mark Adams and Peter Attiwill, *Burning Issues*, CSIRO Publishing, Collingwood, Vic., 2011, pp. 18–19, 21–3.
74 *Emu Sky*, https://emusky.culturalcommons.edu.au (accessed 13 October 2023).
75 Brooke Wandin, with Madeline Critchley, Jax Plumley and Zena Cumpston, 'Language Posters', in exhibition *Emu Sky*, 2021, https://emusky.culturalcommons.edu.au/works/language-posters/ (accessed 13 October 2023).

Settler-Colonial Philanthropy and Indigenous Dispossession

ZOË LAIDLAW

THE FORTUNES OF the early University of Melbourne, like those of many of Victoria's most venerable institutions, were propelled by generous benefactors. The gifts of the most significant nineteenth-century donors sometimes outstripped state support and on occasion saved the University from otherwise insurmountable challenges. As well as their manifest and well-documented benefits for the University, however, these donations and bequests came at the expense of other groups—costs which have received far less attention. The donors' wealth derived overwhelmingly from Australia's pastoral industries, and especially from estates in western Victoria. And, like the University itself, the pastoral estates that contributed so much to colonial Victoria's prosperity occupied unceded Indigenous land: pastoralists' affluence was grounded in the often violent dispossession and alienation of Indigenous peoples from their Country.

This chapter considers four of the University's most significant nineteenth-century benefactors—Sir Samuel Wilson, John Dickson Wyselaskie, Francis Ormond and John Hastie—asking where, how and at whose cost they made the fortunes that underpinned their generosity. Confronting this history, long framed in ways that have diminished the historical and contemporary impact of Indigenous dispossession, is long overdue. It presses us to ask, when the University awards scholarships in the name of Wyselaskie or Hastie, or appoints a professor to the Ormond Chair of Music, or conducts examinations in the (new) Wilson Hall, what version of the institution's past is being promoted, and what obscured? Further, how can the University and its constituent communities address the long-term benefits they have derived from stolen land?

Settler Colonialism in the Port Phillip District

When British colonisers arrived in the 1830s, the Port Phillip District was occupied by multiple distinct Indigenous groups, today recognised through eleven Aboriginal corporations. Violent conflict between settler colonisers and Aboriginal peoples was particularly intense from 1836 to 1851: in under two decades, the combined effects of violence, disease and alienation reduced the Indigenous population by an estimated 80 per cent. Even when set against the brutality of settler colonialism globally, the speed and depth of the devastation wrought by colonisers made Victoria an outlier.[1] Over subsequent decades, Aboriginal survivors and their descendants would face continuing waves of dispossession, discrimination and family separation, while also becoming incorporated into Victoria's settler-colonial economy.[2] That economy, even after the 1851 discovery of gold, was heavily skewed towards pastoralism, and many of Victoria's great nineteenth-century fortunes remained connected to large pastoral estates established between 1836 and 1851.[3]

The 1853 foundation of a university in Melbourne formed one component of colonisers' early efforts to create a Victorian settler identity. Like practices of naming that evoked imperial figures and metropolitan places, the establishment of public educational institutions naturalised the presence of settler colonisers and deflected attention from their status as invaders of Indigenous land and inheritors of the benefits of Indigenous dispossession.[4] The infant University of Melbourne was acutely conscious of its role in the colony, which its early promoters conceived of particularly in relation to 'civilisation'. Thus in 1873 chancellor Sir Redmond Barry extolled the University's role as a civilising force in Victoria and its need for premises that reflected this status. When the colonial government refused to fund a hall of 'suitable dignity', in stepped the University's most significant early benefactor: Samuel Wilson of Ercildoune (later Sir Samuel) promised £30 000 towards what became known as Wilson Hall.[5]

Wilson's gift, while the University's most 'munificent to date', was not the first act of generosity from a Western District pastoralist. On his death in 1866, John Hastie of Punpundhal, near Camperdown, had left more than £19 000 to fund exhibitions in philosophy, logic and ethics. Nearly two decades later, another Western District squatter, John Dickson Wyselaskie of Narrapumelap, bequeathed £12 000 to endow six scholarships across the sciences and humanities. Wyselaskie, a Scottish Presbyterian, also left

£30 000 to the University's Ormond College for theological education. His fellow Scottish Presbyterian, Francis Ormond, donated more than £100 000 to the eponymous residential college, and made another important and direct contribution to the University itself: £20 000 to establish Melbourne's first chair of music. Ormond's wealth, too, derived from a series of Western District estates.

Other late-nineteenth-century donors and benefactors who enjoyed pastoral fortunes were William Mollison of Pyalong, who left £5000 for scholarships in modern languages, and David Aitchison of Kurucaruc (near Portland Bay), who gave £13 862. Two other long-established pastoral families of the Western District, the Blacks of Glenormiston and the Ritchies of Penshurst, made philanthropic contributions to the University in the early twentieth century: just over £2000 was bequeathed by Niel Walter Black in 1909, while RB Ritchie donated £30 000 to found a chair of economics in 1926.[6] Substantial gifts from Sir Samuel Gillott and Sidney Myer, as well as numerous smaller gifts from urban donors, had diluted the influence of pastoral fortunes on the University's coffers by the 1920s, but most of the early large donations and benefactions derived from pastoralism, and particularly pastoralism in Victoria's Western District.[7]

Wilson, Wyselaskie, Ormond and Hastie belonged to an early group of pastoralists who derived early and disproportionate benefits from the dispossession of the Western District's Traditional Owners. Three—Wyselaskie, Hastie and Ormond—migrated to the Port Phillip District between 1838 and 1843, while Wilson arrived in 1852 to join already well-established family members. Considerable evidence about each of these pastoralists and their landholdings remains; indeed, the argument put forward in this chapter—about these benefactors' indifference to and exploitation of the Indigenous peoples they displaced—relies heavily on records created or collected by settler colonisers. But such records give little insight into the Wadawurrung, Djab wurrung, Wotjobaluk and Djargurd wurrung people whose lands Wilson, Wyselaskie, Ormond and Hastie took. It is hard to assess the specific dimensions of their personal interactions with the Aboriginal peoples they dispossessed, or to quantify the harm caused by their spectacular rise.[8] However, while further research on the effects of dispossession on individuals and families is needed, this chapter draws on the evidence that is contained in settler colonial records and Aboriginal sources. Even if these accounts leave many questions open, their scrutiny allows a more open conversation about the true costs of the pastoral fortunes that shaped the University of Melbourne.

Whether or not the benefactors examined in this chapter personally inflicted violence against the Aboriginal peoples of Victoria is not a question that can be answered conclusively. However, each did benefit from the systematic, deliberate and enduring damage created by the invasion and occupation of the Port Phillip District. These prominent colonisers were conscious that they gained from Indigenous dispossession—dispossession accompanied by violence—even if they chose not to dwell on this publicly. As Niel Black, early Western District squatter and ancestor of another University benefactor, wrote privately in December 1839, it was 'universally and distinctly understood' that a new pastoral run could only be secured by the 'slaughter [of] natives left and right ... settlers agree that lead is the only antidote that effectually cures [Indigenous people of] spearing and stealing sheep'.[9] Sixty years later, the pastoralist James Dawson was prompted to write to the editor of the *Camperdown Chronicle* regarding the £122 000 estate of his peer, John Thomson:

> This amount of money was made chiefly at Keilambete by [Thomson's] occupation of country the legitimate property of the Aborigines, who were disinherited by him without the slightest compensation ... It is truly pitiable that the owners of such large sums of money chiefly derived from such a source, do not remember in their old age the condition and half-starved state of the evicted Aborigines.[10]

Very few squatters were as blunt as Dawson: as Ian D Clark has argued, while 'killings and massacres were widespread', they were accompanied by an 'attitude of silence that aimed to preserve the anonymity of those involved'. Even so, as the Traditional Owners of Victoria know, and the scholarly work of Clark, Jan Critchett, Lyndall Ryan, Richard Broome and others has documented, copious, if incomplete, evidence of this violence remains.[11] Moreover, it is undeniable now, as it was undeniable then (even if commonly denied), that regardless of the degree of violence that accompanied the seizure of Aboriginal land in Victoria, Aboriginal land was seized. Its owners were dispossessed (sometimes more than once),[12] with all the damage that entailed then and subsequently. The University needs to research, share and act on this history, and to take responsibility for its 21st-century consequences.[13]

Samuel Wilson

In December 1874, the Western District pastoralist Samuel Wilson issued a promissory note to the University of Melbourne for £30 000 to enable the construction of a hall. Wilson was an exceptionally wealthy man who had set up his fortune in partnership with three of his brothers: at that time, the colony's governor, Sir George Bowen, estimated that he owned 600 000 sheep and had an annual income of about £100 000.[14] Having promised his donation, Wilson arranged for the money's immediate transfer, allowing the University to benefit from a further £7000 in interest that accrued.[15] Laying a 'memorial' stone for the new hall some five years later, Wilson adopted a reflective mode. Predicting that the University would make Melbourne 'the Athens of Australia, and the Oxford of the Southern Hemisphere', he then mused on his own wealth. While acknowledging 'a kindly Providence' and declining to seek 'undue credit' for his philanthropy, Wilson lamented that colonial society begrudged wealthy colonists like himself—those who had deployed 'their energy and industry'—for outstripping 'their less industrious or less fortunate neighbours'.[16] Certainly, Wilson's generous gift to the University, alongside donations to charities and religious bodies, enhanced his status.[17] In 1875, on the recommendation of the grateful governor Bowen, Wilson was knighted and entered the colonial legislature's upper house as member for the Western Province.[18] In 1881 he returned to the United Kingdom, leasing Hughenden Manor, the grand former home of prime minister Benjamin Disraeli, and serving as the Conservative MP for Portsmouth from 1886 to 1892. His children married into the British aristocracy.[19] In these ways, Samuel Wilson's wealth and the way he used it brought him prestige, status and political influence, as well as benefiting the nascent University of Melbourne.

Born at Ballycloughan in Ireland's County Antrim in 1832, Samuel Wilson was the son of a farmer and landowner of the same name. His older brothers John, Charles and Alexander migrated to Australia and established squatting runs in the Wimmera before Samuel arrived in Victoria in 1852. Samuel first worked for and then entered partnership with his brothers, selling property in Ireland to raise his share of the £40 000 needed to buy Longerenong station at the junction of the Wimmera River and Yarriambiack Creek.[20] There, on the unceded lands of the Wotjobaluk people,[21] Wilson began creating the dams and watercourses that 'foreshadowed the vast Mallee-Wimmera water gravitation scheme of today'. In December 1861 he married Jean Campbell and the following year work began on a Longerenong homestead. While still in his twenties, Wilson entered the Victorian Legislative Assembly for the Wimmera, serving in the lower house between 1861 and 1864. The Wilson brothers stood firm against attempts to break up Victoria's big pastoral leaseholds through the 1860s, acquiring numerous properties across the state's north-west, including Walmer (where Charles lived) and Vectis (home to Alexander), as well as Yanko station on the lands of the Jeithi (also known as Yeidthee or Pikkolatpan) people, in the NSW Riverina. In 1869 the Wilson brothers dissolved their partnership and by 1871 Samuel had bought out his siblings.[22]

In 1873, not long before his generous donation to the University, Wilson spent £236 000 on Ercildoune, a grand homestead situated on nearly 4500 hectares of Wadawurrung land north-west of Ballarat.[23] The vendors were the Scottish Presbyterian brothers Thomas and Somerville Learmonth, and Wilson would move into the handsome house they had built on the property. In 1874 Wilson confirmed the move into south-western Victoria that his Ercildoune purchase presaged by selling several of his Wimmera properties, and buying freehold estates at Mount Bute, Marathon and Corangamite. By 1879 Wilson's freehold property extended over 100 000 hectares in Victoria and New South Wales, while he leased more than a million hectares in New South Wales and Queensland.[24] In both the Wimmera and the Riverina, Wilson not only sought to shape the land through irrigation

Ercildoune, residence of Sir Samuel Wilson.

but also favoured the introduction of non-native fauna, including salmon, trout, ostriches, camels and Angora goats. This remodelling of the colony after his own designs continued at Ercildoune.[25] Wilson invested, too, in improving his stock, commissioning the purchase of rams from Tasmania and New Zealand. By the 1890s Ercildoune would be described as the finest merino stud in the world.[26] When Wilson retired to England, management of his properties passed to two of his sons, Wilfred and Clarence.[27]

Limited evidence has been uncovered regarding Samuel Wilson's direct interactions with the Aboriginal owners of the lands he claimed as his own. In the winter of 1845, his brothers Charles and Alexander were prompted to relinquish their claim to remote Polkemmet in the Wimmera and move closer to Horsham, 'being afraid of the natives'.[28] By the time Samuel joined them seven years later, Aboriginal pastoral workers were common in the Wimmera, and a number continued to reside at or visit Longerenong with their families through the 1860s. From 1863 until 1872, rations, blankets and basic clothing provided by the colonial government were distributed from Longerenong to local Wotjobaluk people: the amount spent on these goods declined from about £120 per annum in the mid-1860s to £70 per annum by the end of the decade. Wilson was listed as one of the fifty or so 'Honorary Correspondents' (later 'Local Guardians') who reported from pastoral estates across Victoria to the Central Board for Aborigines and took responsibility for distributing the stores it provided. In one annual report, Wilson recorded twenty-three Aboriginal people at Longerenong during the shearing season, all but one of whom subsequently left.[29] In August 1866 Wilson stated that he employed Aboriginal workers to pick fleeces in the woolshed at 10 shillings per week plus rations, but noted that 'few' were 'in robust health'. The men, he wrote, also hunted for possums, kangaroos, emus, ducks and turkeys, while the women fished. Like other honorary correspondents, Wilson lamented the impact of alcohol and observed a decline in the local population, which included 'no young women and no children'. 'In a few years,' he continued, 'their race will be extinct.'

Wilson's report passively acknowledged former Aboriginal ownership of the land, but exculpated settler colonisers from responsibility for the crisis facing the Wotjobaluk:

> On the whole I cannot see any prospect of improvement in their condition. They seem to be a doomed race. In no instance, in my experience, have they been badly treated by Europeans, and still they are silently disappearing from the lands that once had no other owner. If we cannot prevent this,

> the least we should do in taking possession of their country is to make their declining years as comfortable as their habits will allow.[30]

In his final report from Longerenong, Wilson recorded that sixteen Aboriginal people received aid in 1871, noting that 'some of the more industrious' who worked during shearing were paid 'the same rate of wages as the other hands'.[31]

Ercildoune station lay north of Lake Burrumbeet on Wadawurrung land.[32] The Learmonths had brought its grand residence to a habitable state by mid-1839. Such solid bluestone foundations, however, belied the insecurity precipitated by settler colonisation in the 1830s' Western District.[33] Against a backdrop of violent, and often unreported, encounters between European colonisers and Aboriginal people across the region, a Learmonth shepherd told the Geelong police in 1838 that the Indigenous people at Buninyong had repeatedly told him 'to go or they would kill me'.[34] At least two Aboriginal men died on land claimed by the Learmonths in the winter of 1838, one reportedly drowning in a waterhole due to the weight of the chains his settler captors placed on his body.[35] By the time Wilson arrived in 1873, Aboriginal workers were less numerous on pastoral estates in the Ballarat district than in the Wimmera, but Wilson likely came into sustained, if superficial, contact with at least one Wadawurrung man: Mullawallah (c. 1821–1896), also known as 'King Billy of Ercildoune' or 'William Wilson'.

Invoking a trope common within the colonial media,[36] Mullawallah's 1896 obituary recorded that he was the 'last' Aboriginal person living in the 'district of Ballarat'; his residence at Ercildoune suggests he was possibly of the Burrumbeet balug clan of the Wadawurrung people.[37] According to settler accounts, Mullawallah was so kindly treated by Samuel Wilson that he adopted his surname at some point between 1873 and 1884. Newspapers described Mullawallah as a harmless curiosity—'the last of a once numerous tribe'—of interest to visiting aristocrats, including Lord and Lady Hopetoun.[38] In its longest form, his obituary, which was widely syndicated across the Australian press, ran to over 700 words. The *Age*, under the headline 'The King of Ballarat: Death of a Dusky Monarch. The Last of the Tribe', recounted Mullawallah's collapse (from 'senile decay' exacerbated by alcohol); his emergency transfer by rail—in the guard's van—from Ercildoune to Ballarat hospital; his subsequent death; and the touching loyalty of Mullawallah's distressed dog.[39] The earlier kindness of Samuel Wilson and his employees was widely noted, as was Mullawallah's conversion to Christianity. The *Wagga Wagga Advertiser* reported his death in the context of the ravages of colonialism, but with no suggestion that this was the fault of the colonisers, stating

> the former owners of this country are going in the direction of the Dodo and the Tasmanian blacks, of whom Truganini [Trukanini] was the last living person. It is satisfactory to find that much kindness was shown to King Billy during his later days, and that he was a welcome guest at the homesteads in the Burrumbeet district. The deceased monarch clung to his title to the last and had always claimed equal rights with all titled heads and nobles.[40]

Melbourne's *Weekly Times* published an indistinct photograph of a well-attended burial, contradicting the (more plausible and widespread) claim in other papers that Mullawallah's funeral was sparsely attended.[41]

Earlier newspaper reports about Mullawallah hint at the impact of colonisation on his life, and—both in their preoccupation with his experiences and the adoption of a tone that veered between elegiac and mocking—suggest how much had changed in Victoria since the 1830s. In 1884 the *Ballarat Star* characteristically recorded Mullawallah's arrest and incarceration for drunkenness: 'The monarch of the soil behaved himself in a matter not at all befitting his kingly dignity.'[42] In December 1895 Mullawallah was charged with using 'obscene language' and breaking into a house to the west of Lake Wendouree. Described in court as coming 'from Ercildoune, the seat of the late Sir Samuel Wilson', Mullawallah explained that his housebreaking was a response to being attacked by 'larrikins'; nonetheless he was gaoled for fourteen days. This brief and depressing account was reprinted in at least nine other Australian newspapers during the following fortnight.[43] Just a few weeks later, the *Horsham Times* noted that Mullawallah had passed through Egerton on an annual journey to collect a blanket at Yaloak Vale station. Ejected from the local pub, Mullawallah spent the night in the lock-up before continuing on his way. The article also recorded that Mullawallah had shown his appreciation to Egerton local Dr Corry by giving him 'a native song entitled "You take um up my land for me"', for which he was 'handsomely rewarded'.[44]

These accounts of Mullawallah, including fleeting and mediated references to his own words and opinions, hint at the dislocation and dispossession he endured. Where was Mullawallah's land by the time he sang of it to Dr Corry? This was not something that concerned the settler papers that patronised Mullawallah, nor the 'larrikins' who assaulted him. Certainly, by the 1870s when the University of Melbourne benefited from Samuel Wilson's largesse, stations like Ercildoune and Longerenong were no longer threatened by the sovereign owners of the lands on which they lay. Wilson largely leased and bought land after its Aboriginal owners had been dispossessed, although he continued to benefit from their labour and, as a vector for the distribution of government aid, witnessed the impact of colonisation on them. As his 1879 remarks about Wilson Hall demonstrate, however, it was not Aboriginal people but less successful settler colonisers—particularly those who sought to break up land monopolies through the 1860s—who had (if fleetingly) threatened Samuel Wilson's interests. Instead, Wilson was able to present Mullawallah as an attraction to visiting dignitaries, while focusing on the generation of a pastoral fortune that in turn enhanced his status and power in Australia and Britain as well as adorning the University of Melbourne.

John Dickson Wyselaskie

John Dickson Wyselaskie amassed his enormous fortune some 50 kilometres south-west of Ercildoune, at Narrapumelap, near Wickliffe. When he died in 1883, aged sixty-four, Wyselaskie bequeathed £8400 to the University of Melbourne for a series of scholarships. Although this was more modest than Samuel Wilson's donation, Wyselaskie also left £30 000 to train Presbyterian ministers (much of which went to the establishment of a Theological Hall at the University-affiliated Ormond College) and £5000 to Melbourne's Presbyterian Ladies College.[45] In the twenty-first century, Wyselaskie's bequest to the University continues to fund generous scholarships in history, mathematics, natural science, political economy, modern languages and logic.

Born in Scotland in 1818, Wyselaskie arrived in Van Diemen's Land in 1837 before travelling on to Port Phillip in 1838 as an agent for his Hobart-based uncle, Robert Kerr, and Kerr's business partner John Bogle.[46] Wyselaskie first took up land near Buninyong but by mid-1840 had moved to the west of Lake Bolac. Here, on Djab wurrung land along the Hopkins River, he marked out a 16 000-hectare run, Narrapumelap.[47] Wyselaskie's entry in the *Australian Dictionary of Biography*, mirroring nineteenth-century accounts, notes that while his 'first years were difficult and the Aboriginals troublesome', the '1850s brought prosperity'.[48] In fact, after Robert Kerr died in January 1846, Wyselaskie quickly used his share of his uncle's estate to consolidate his flock, and he was able to buy out John Bogle early in the 1850s.[49]

Having leased Narrapumelap since 1840, and owning a few hundred hectares outright by 1858, Wyselaskie acquired freehold ownership of nearly 10 000 hectares of the original pastoral lease in the 1860s.[50] While in that decade his merino stud flourished, Wyselaskie also deployed every available tactic to circumvent Victoria's Selection Acts, which sought to divide up large pastoral leaseholds. A fervent Presbyterian, Wyselaskie was also active in the fields of education and religion both locally—where he was instrumental in building and supporting the Wickliffe Presbyterian church—and in Melbourne.[51] Although he married Mary Jane Austin (née Farrell) in 1862,[52] it was not until 1873 that Wyselaskie began building a bluestone mansion, complete with tower, at Narrapumelap—a five-year project on which, at its height, fifty stonemasons were employed.[53] While works were underway, Wyselaskie leased out the station and sold off its stock; he and Mary Jane toured Europe, returning to Australia late in 1876.[54]

But what of the 'troublesome' Indigenous population? By the end of 1840, pastoralists like Wyselaskie occupied over 40 per cent of Djab wurrung land and, despite intense Djab wurrung resistance in 1840–42, this would rise to 96 per cent by early 1846. At least 103 Aboriginal and seven European violent deaths occurred on Djab wurrung Country between 1838 and 1844.[55] In November 1840 seven Indigenous people were massacred at Burrumbeep, about 35 kilometres north of Narrapumelap, but little direct evidence of Wyselaskie's interactions with the Djab wurrung in the 1840s and 1850s has yet been found.[56] Alexander Sutherland, in his colourful 1888 survey of Victoria, recorded of Narrapumelap that 'hundreds of sheep were taken away', 'life was constantly in jeopardy' and the 'rude homestead was stormed times out of number' by local Indigenous people, before they 'learned civilised occupations, and became useful as shearers, drovers, &c.'[57] Local historian Jennifer O'Donnell inferred that Wyselaskie's relationships with the Djab wurrung were poor; by contrast, and on the basis that his surname was adopted by some, CL Sayers placed him within a small group of pastoralists who enjoyed good relations with local people.[58]

In the early 1860s, as the colonial government sought to concentrate the Aboriginal population onto missions and reserves, colonisers recorded about seventy Indigenous people living in the Wickliffe district. Both Lake Bolac and the Hopkins River were sites of considerable cultural and economic significance to the Djab wurrung, and Wyselaskie's neighbour to the south, Charles Gray of Nareeb Nareeb, proved a relatively sympathetic local guardian for those who continued to live on Country.[59] In June 1857

James Bonwick visited Wickliffe, describing both a meeting with Wyselaskie and a violent, alcohol-fuelled fight within a large group of Aboriginal men and women near the Wickliffe hotel.[60] In response to a questionnaire distributed by the Central Board of Aborigines in 1861, Wyselaskie stated that the Djab wurrung people at Narrapumelap had 'no settled means' of livelihood and survived 'principally by begging', proceeding to describe their 'moral and social condition' as 'very much to be deplored'. He also gave his views on the rations and clothing they required, and noted that Indigenous people were 'willingly employed by settlers, who readily give them work', usually paying 8–10 shillings per week with rations.[61] Clark, however, argues that by 1867 Indigenous people who assisted with shearing at Narrapumelap received 'at most half the rations' given to their white counterparts, and no wages.[62]

By the time the Narrapumelap mansion—a powerful symbol of Wyselaskie's wealth and status—was being built in the 1870s, the local Djab wurrung population had collapsed. Some had died, while others had gone to live on either the Lake Condah or Framlingham reserves: the Aboriginal population of Wickliffe in 1877 was recorded as between five and eight people.[63] One of those who had left was also named John Wyselaskie, a Djab wurrung man born in Wickliffe around 1844. The 1869 *Act for the Protection and Management of the Aboriginal Natives of Victoria* required Aboriginal people to be granted a certificate from the Board of Protection in order to work outside designated reserves.[64] Charles Gray recommended such a certificate in September 1871 for a man he recorded as 'Johnny Wyselaskee'.[65] Wyselaskee was described in the register as a 'half-caste', about twenty-seven years old, who spoke 'English very plainly'. In 1872 another certificate was issued to 'John Wise Glascow', a 'half-caste, very muscular and powerful', but this time it was prepared by the guardians at Framlingham reserve, 75 kilometres to the south of Wickliffe.[66]

Although many details about his life remain unclear, multiple records place a Djab wurrung man named John (sometimes Jacky) Wyselaskie, born at Wickliffe in 1844, at Framlingham from the 1870s.[67] This Wyselaskie was a notable cricket player, lauded in the *Warrnambool Standard* as 'the W.G. Grace of the Framlingham team',[68] and he appears in a photo taken of the congregation at a Framlingham School House church service around 1918.[69] On 31 March 1909 he married Harriet Couzens (née Blair), an Aboriginal widow also resident at Framlingham, and became stepfather to her children.[70]

The Framlingham reserve, which was under direct government control from 1866, endured several temporary and attempted closures.[71] In 1889 the Victorian Government decided to convert Framlingham into an agricultural college but, after a struggle, 225 hectares were retained for the use of those considered 'Aboriginal' under the 1886 *Aborigines Protection Act*.[72] As Broome observes, the Act's definition of 'Aboriginal' was based 'on age and gender as well as race', and encompassed those classified as 'half-caste' who were older than thirty-four.[73] John Wyselaskie was one of four Aboriginal men who were subsequently granted 'temporary permissive occupancy' of blocks—32 hectares in size—of the original Framlingham site.[74] Although the reserve did close in 1916, the Wyselaskies remained on their block: as Critchett notes, 'as far as most people were concerned' the land belonged to them.[75]

In 1926, not long after Wyselaskie died, the Central Board for the Protection of Aborigines advertised all these blocks for lease. Widowed for a second time, Harriet Wyselaskie wrote to the Board offering to rent the land herself, having, she said,

> always thought this land was given to us older ones untill [sic] we die ... could the Board not wait untill we are dead and are all gone: as my husband had the land, I only wish that the Board would not be too hard on us.[76]

Critchett records John Wyselaskie's Aboriginal name as Woorookie Larnock but makes no comment about his parents nor how he acquired his European surname.[77] While Wyselaskie appeared (as 'Wisey' and 'Wiselasky') on lists of 'full-blooded' Indigenous people entitled to be resident at Framlingham in 1889 and 1890, this probably reflects his status under the 1886 Act rather than his parentage.[78] If Woorookie Larnock's father was indeed a settler coloniser, he was most likely one of the very few white men—including John Dickson Wyselaskie—living in or near Wickliffe in the early 1840s.[79]

The pastoralist John Dickson Wyselaskie, who built his fortune on the lands of his younger namesake, chose to lead his last years elsewhere: as building works at Narrapumelap concluded, work began immediately on a second imposing mansion, Wickliffe House, on the Esplanade at St Kilda. In early 1881 the Wyselaskies moved in, and it was there that John Dickson died in May 1883. Mary Jane continued to live in St Kilda, while Narrapumelap was sold to fund the many generous bequests laid out in Wyselaskie's will. He and Mary Jane had no children, and his will made no mention of Woorookie Larnock / John (Jacky) Wyselaskie nor any of the other Djab wurrung whose lives his pastoral activities had displaced.[80]

Francis Ormond

Like John Dickson Wyselaskie, Francis Ormond is remembered for his generosity to educational and religious causes. In 1887, having already donated tens of thousands of pounds to the University of Melbourne's residential hall Ormond College, and over £20 000 towards a Working Men's College (later RMIT), Ormond gave the University itself £20 000 to endow a chair of music. When he died in 1889 his estate was valued at nearly £2 million; in total he provided Ormond College and its theological hall with over £112 000.[81] Like Wyselaskie and Wilson, Ormond's fortune arose almost entirely from pastoralism, again mostly focused in Victoria's Western District.

Ormond, born in Aberdeen, Scotland in 1829, was a decade younger than Wyselaskie and just a few years older than Samuel Wilson. His father, also Francis Ormond, brought his family to the Port Phillip District in 1842 after a career as a sea captain. Ormond senior negotiated with the Clyde Company to lease 8 hectares of land close to its headquarters at Golfhill on the Leigh River. The family arrived in the midst of the colony's first economic downturn and were able to negotiate a favourable deal with the Clyde Company's manager, George Russell: they paid £70 per annum in rent but received a £400 remittance for the costs of building an inn at the Leigh crossing.[82] The hotel built by Ormond became known as the Settler's Arms, and the township that grew up around it was called Shelford.[83] During the Ormonds' tenure from 1843 to 1851, the Settler's Arms became an essential stop on the journey from Geelong to Hamilton.

Russell was another Scottish Presbyterian pastoralist, as were the Greeves, Robertson and Oliphant families into which Ormond's children married. Prior relationships and cultural and religious affinities helped the Ormonds become embedded in a Western District network that extended from Geelong to Skipton, Ballarat and Camperdown.[84] The flow of traffic through the Settler's Arms, and Ormond senior's reputation for hospitality and straight dealing, meant he rapidly accrued reliable information about the region's prospects.[85] Francis Ormond senior used this knowledge to manage a quickly evolving portfolio of pastoral estates, all on Wadawurrung Country. While an early interest in the Mount Gow area was informal, Ormond secured pastoral leases for Native Hut Creek No. 2 between March and October 1848; Berrybank (earlier Gherangemarajah) from 1848 to 1851; and Piggoreet West (or Mopiamnum), on the Woady Yaloak River, in 1850–51. From 1848 Francis junior had worked at Piggoreet for the previous leaseholder, Henry Gibb, a former Clyde Company employee. The twenty-year-old Ormond managed a workforce of about fifteen shepherds and hutkeepers on land carrying 7000 sheep and 400 cattle, later living in a house that Gibb built for him.[86]

In 1851 Ormond senior relinquished his lease on the Settler's Arms and sold his interest in Piggoreet and Berrybank to purchase a 12 148-hectare portion of the Borriyalloak (or Borriyalook) run on Mount Emu Creek between Elephant Bridge (Darlington) and Skipton. Ormond junior moved from Piggoreet to Borriyalloak as manager, before taking over in his own right from 1854.[87] The Ormonds enjoyed good fortune in navigating the aftermath of 1851's devastating bushfires and gold discoveries to their profit, but considerable evidence also exists of Francis Ormond junior's commitment to agricultural improvement and good standing within his milieu.[88] As a recent biographer noted, Ormond was 'a splendid flock master' and, from 1851, Borriyalloak not only 'produced the finest merino wool' but 'generated an enormous income'.[89] In the 1850s Ormond was a founder of the Western District Pastoral and Agricultural Society, which inaugurated the influential Skipton show, and was appointed as a magistrate. Later, he became a member of the Victorian Legislative Council.[90] At Borriyalloak Ormond built a large bluestone homestead, as well as a woolshed, coach-house and stables, where he lived with his first wife Mary (née Greeves) until 1876.[91]

The Ormond family—hardworking, quick to trade and to secure investments, insightful in their reading of market conditions and selection of stock—did well on the lands of the Wadawurrung.[92] Although it goes unremarked in biographical writing about Francis Ormond junior, his pastoral operations, like those of his fellow benefactors, also drew on Wadawurrung labour. Already integral to many pastoral runs before the 1850s, squatters' dependence on Aboriginal labour was intensified by the gold rush. AC Cameron, overseer of the Clyde Company's station at Terrinallum, which lay to the south-west of Ormond's Borriyalloak, wrote frequently of his difficulties in securing and keeping workers. In September 1852 he complained, 'FRANCIS ORMOND has engaged my Blackfellows. It has made me so savage ...'[93]

Late in 1858 Ormond invoked thirteen years' experience when reporting that the Wadawurrung of the Mount Emu district were 'quiet and have never committed any depredations against life or property'. They were 'employed for sheep-washing, harvesting, and cutting wood; and are paid in money for such services'.[94] This account formed part of Ormond's responses to queries circulated by a parliamentary select committee inquiring into the condition of Aboriginal people across Victoria. Ormond reported forty Aboriginal people in the Borriyalloak neighbourhood, associated with three distinct groups: 'the Mount Emu tribe, seventeen; Friendly Creek tribe, ten; Wardy Yallock [Woady Yaloak] tribe, thirteen'. He described deaths due to venereal disease and accidents due to intoxication.[95] Despite his comments about their employment, Ormond also reported that the Wadawurrung he knew lived 'mostly on the charity of the settlers', exchanging the fish and fowl they caught for alcohol. Noting that the local Wadawurrung received no assistance, in terms of supplies or reserved land, from government, Ormond indicated both that there were locations in the district 'well fitted' for an Aboriginal reserve, and that 'magistrates and settlers' (presumably such as himself) would be willing to distribute government supplies. Ormond, however, did not appear among the lists of honorary correspondents and local guardians who performed these functions from the early 1860s. He agreed with the proposition that the police should be given powers to prevent Aboriginal people entering towns.[96] No evidence has been found that either links Ormond directly to individual Wadawurrung people or documents his participation in discussions about them after 1860.

Ormond continued to acquire Victorian pastoral property near Borriyalloak through the 1860s but later expanded also into New South Wales, where he bought sections of James Balfour's Round Hill station near Culcairn in 1881.[97] His investments, however, remained limited to 'land and livestock', and he continued to manage his pastoral interests even after purchasing the Toorak mansion Ognez, where he lived from 1876. In Melbourne Ormond became more involved in philanthropic pursuits, particularly connected to secondary and tertiary education and the Presbyterian church; he also served on the colony's 1881–84 royal commission on education. After his first wife, Mary, died in 1881, Ormond married Mary Irvine (née Oliphant) in 1885: her pastoralist father had been a partner of Ormond's brother-in-law in the early 1840s. Although Ormond had no children, he adopted a boy and two girls. He died in Pau,

France in May 1889, on his fifth visit to Europe; his body was returned to Melbourne and buried in Geelong that September. Ormond's estate was valued at just under £2 million, three-quarters in Victoria and the balance in New South Wales.[98]

Like Samuel Wilson, Ormond was a generous philanthropist during his lifetime, and derived considerable status and some pleasure from contemporary recognition of his gifts. Ormond appears to have been fastidious about ensuring acknowledgement of his philanthropy—as early as 1868 he had emphasised that £80 donated towards a Presbyterian Theological Hall was an augmentation of an earlier gift; he was now 'a subscriber to the am^{t} of One Hundred pounds'.[99] Don Chambers notes that, as tax deductions for charitable donations were a thing of the future, 'there can be little question of the sincere philanthropy which activated a man who gave away such a large proportion of his fortune during his life-time'.[100] However, the motivations for philanthropy were not limited to altruism but extended to the enhancement of status and a sense of obligation to kin and religion. Ormond's largesse should not prevent us from inquiring further into the land ownership—the land seizures—that underpinned his wealth. The Ormond family benefited enormously from the dispossession of the Wadawurrung, drew on Wadawurrung labour, and stood by as the Wadawurrung became strangers on their own land.

John Hastie

John Hastie's name endures at the University of Melbourne in the form of exhibitions and scholarships in philosophy. Between his arrival in the Port Phillip District in 1840 and his death in 1866, Hastie built a fortune on the back of his pastoral estate Punpundhal, which lay on the lands of the Djargurd wurrung people and the shores of Lakes Gnarpurt and Corangamite, north-east of what would become Camperdown.[101] Hastie, unmarried and childless, was forty-eight when he died: his will provided a series of annuities to relatives, but directed that the residue of his estate be divided between the University, the Church of England and the Presbyterian Church. The complicated nature of the will's provisions meant that twenty-one years elapsed before the University received over £19 000 from the estate.

Hastie arrived in Melbourne in December 1840, having travelled, like Wyselaskie, from Scotland via Van Diemen's Land. Again, like Wyselaskie and Ormond, he was a Scottish Presbyterian, enmeshed in a trans-imperial web of religious and familial obligations that eased his passage. Prior connections, however, also brought their complications. Hastie was reputed to be an alcoholic, and his 'sin of intemperance' prompted a series of letters warning Victoria's Scottish Presbyterians, and especially those within the Clyde Company's networks, of his unreliability. Philip Russell, who had hosted Hastie in Van Diemen's Land, wrote to his younger brother George, at Golfhill, cautioning against intimacy with Hastie, while also acknowledging family obligations to fellow Scots:

> Sh^{d} he find his way to your place have nothing to do with him, as he is a sad drunk and good for nothing fellow; however, sh^{d} he be disposed to become Hut Keeper you may employ him, but by no means allow him to get under your own roof.[102]

This advice lagged behind Hastie's arrival. George Russell had already offered him hospitality and would continue to field repeated inquiries—from family and friends in Scotland as well as Van Diemen's Land—about Hastie's behaviour over the following years.[103]

In 1841 Hastie took up under licence just under 9300 hectares of land between Foxhow and Pomberneit in partnership with SP Hawkins, who records show had departed by 1844.[104] Far fewer archival traces of Hastie's life remain than for Wilson, Wyselaskie or Ormond, but, like them, he successfully navigated both the 1840s' resistance of Aboriginal people to pastoral occupation and also the early 1860s' Acts promoting closer settlement, which Hastie used to transform his pastoral leases into freehold titles.[105] The records that do remain from Hastie's lifetime reveal him as being interested in protecting squatters' rights and his own property, while also conscious of his religious and family obligations. In 1845 he contributed a pound to the 'Resistance Fund' raised by the squatters to forestall an attempt to tax them for local government, and he advertised several times through the late 1840s for the return of lost and stolen horses.[106] In 1851 Hastie subscribed £2 towards the construction of a church in Timboon, and a further £5 for the Kilnoorat church the same month.[107] He paid £30 per annum so that a Presbyterian minister, the rev. Francis Wilson, would conduct monthly Sunday services at Punpundhal.[108] In the early 1860s Hastie became the guardian of his orphaned niece, Jane Hastie, and arranged her education.[109] Like the Western District's other pastoral properties, Punpundhal welcomed travellers, such as local pastoralist Tom Anderson, who recorded spending a night there in 1853 on his way home from Geelong.[110]

Evidence of Hastie's labour force, however, is scant. In October 1851 the manager of nearby Terinallum station complained that Hastie had lured his gang of shearers away by offering them higher wages.[111] On another occasion Tom Anderson wrote of an arrangement to employ one of Hastie's housemaids, who at the last minute changed her mind.[112] In 1857 James Bonwick recorded that the Manifold brothers of nearby Purrumbete—one of whom was Hastie's executor—preferred Aboriginal stockmen, 'being far better acquainted with stock, more active on duty, more ready and willing, and not more expensive'.[113] There is, however, no explicit reference to Hastie employing Aboriginal workers, and his relations with the Djargurd wurrung people whom he displaced remain opaque. Certainly there was violence involving early pastoralists in the district, even if it is only sparsely documented in the official settler record. In 1840 the Manifold brothers and another local pastoralist, Arthur Lloyd, opened fire on a group of Djargurd wurrung people during a confrontation over sheep stealing, reporting in a deposition to the police at Geelong that they had 'no doubt some of them were wounded'. Manifold family histories record more fraught and violent encounters.[114] Notoriously, at Emu Creek—about 40 kilometres from Punpundhal—Frederick Taylor is known to have massacred thirty-five Djargurd wurrung in October 1839.[115] However, even if we set aside the violence settler pastoralism entailed for the Aboriginal Traditional Owners, by the 1850s and 1860s, dispossession in this part of Victoria:

> effectively made Aboriginals intruders on their own land. To what extent it meant total exclusion depended on the individual squatter's wishes. Some Aboriginals negotiated the right to remain and camp on what had been their own land, but all of them lost the right to care for and use the land in the old ways.[116]

Hastie died on 18 March 1866, just over twenty-five years after his arrival in the Port Phillip District. The advertising campaign promoting Punpundhal's subsequent auction conveys how he had transformed and profited from Djargurd wurrung land in that time. The estate included more than 20 000 sheep, alongside seventy horses and a small dairy herd. But it was Punpundhal's broad acres—it extended over 7300 hectares—that particularly shone in the agents' descriptions. Advertisements carried in the Melbourne papers emphasised that Hastie's 'magnificent estate' sat 'in the open plains of the western district, so well and favourably known for wool growing and producing fatstock'. Punpundhal contained 'small hills of rich black soil on the margins of numerous lakes', while 'belts of timber planted here and there' added 'much to the surrounding scenery'. Hastie's improvements were extolled as 'almost complete and substantial', including a 'fine' and 'handsome' dwelling situated on over 3 hectares of lawn, and surrounded by gardens, orchards and a vineyard. The estate's buildings were all of bluestone; 800 sheep could be shorn under cover. Punpundhal was 'securely fenced in with post-and-wire fencing' and subdivided into 'twelve sheep paddocks, besides horse and cultivation paddocks', all 'well watered by natural and artificial means'; low-lying lands were drained. Hastie, concluded the advertisement, 'devoted every care and attention to render it as nearly as possible a perfect estate, and it is not too much to say that he has been eminently successful in his endeavours'.[117] George Russell, formerly of the Clyde Company, made the winning bid in March 1867, purchasing Punpundhal for 75 shillings per acre, before renaming it Leslie Manor.[118]

Hastie's posthumous reputation was dominated by his legacies to churches and the University, and the twenty-one years it took for his estate to be finally settled. In Camperdown, stories of Hastie's intemperance persisted, including that when the dam at Punpundhal was drained after Hastie's death, it was found to be lined with bottles.[119] But no mention was made then, or subsequently, of the Djargurd wurrung people whom Hastie had so successfully displaced.

Conclusion

The point of this chapter is not to suggest that the University of Melbourne's nineteenth-century benefactors were more or less culpable for Indigenous dispossession—or more or less violent in its prosecution—than their settler-colonial contemporaries. Rather, the chapter seeks to underscore that these benefactors expropriated unceded Indigenous land and then further exploited its Aboriginal owners in other ways. There is evidence—direct in the cases of Wilson, Wyselaskie and Ormond, and circumstantial for Hastie—that these four men were conscious they had displaced the original 'possessors of the soil'. This account has demonstrated, however, that they both failed to understand the depth and dimensions of the harm they caused and were also, in important ways, indifferent to it. That harm continues to reverberate as the bicentenaries of colonial settlement in Victoria and the University of Melbourne approach, while both state and institution continue to derive benefit from it.

In sketching the lives and fortunes of four important University benefactors, this chapter has relied almost exclusively on evidence created by those men themselves or their coloniser peers. Much of this evidence lionised those benefactors both for their material success and for the generosity that flowed from it. This status is underscored by the way the names Wilson, Wyselaskie, Ormond and Hastie continue to resonate within the 21st-century University of Melbourne. By contrast, few sources directly connect these four pastoralists to the Aboriginal peoples of Victoria whom they dispossessed. Certainly the lives of Mullawallah and Johnny Wyselaskie, or of the unnamed labourers who worked for Ormond and (probably) Hastie, have not previously been considered whether on their own terms or as part of the University's history. Evidence about their lives is likely always to remain fragmentary. But, as the University of Melbourne starts to look beyond the generosity of these benefactors to the sources of their wealth, we require a history of the Traditional Owners of the lands they took, without payment and in the knowledge of the violence and injustice of those seizures.

Notes

1 Victorian Aboriginal Heritage Council, 'Victoria's Registered Aboriginal Parties', https://www.aboriginalheritagecouncil.vic.gov.au/victoria-registered-aboriginal-parties (accessed 13 October 2023); James Boyce, *1835: The Founding of Melbourne & the Conquest of Australia*, Black Inc., Melbourne, 2011, pp. 151, 167–78, 191; Richard Broome, *Aboriginal Victorians: A History since 1800*, Allen & Unwin, Sydney, 2005, pp. 54–5, 80, 91–2 and passim; Ian Clark, *Scars in the Landscape: A Register of Massacre Sites in Western Victoria, 1803–1859*, Aboriginal Studies Press, Australian Institute of Aboriginal and Torres Strait Islander Studies, Canberra, 1995; Jan Critchett, *A Distant Field of Murder: Western District Frontiers 1834–1848*, Melbourne University Press, Carlton, 1990; Lyndall Ryan, 'Settler Massacres on the Port Phillip Frontier, 1836–1851', *Journal of Australian Studies*, vol. 34, no. 4, 2010, pp. 257–73.

2 Broome, in *Aboriginal Victorians*, provides the most comprehensive overview of this experience.

3 AGL Shaw, *A History of the Port Phillip District: Victoria before Separation*, Melbourne University Press, Carlton, 1996; Margaret Kiddle, *Men of Yesterday: A Social History of the Western District of Victoria, 1834–1890*, Melbourne University Press, Carlton, 1961.

4 Cecilia Morgan, *Building Better Britains? Settler Societies in the British World, 1783–1920*, University of Toronto Press, Toronto, 2017, pp. 123–35, 144–60.

5 *Chancellor's Annual Report*, 1873, cited in Ernest Scott, *A History of the University of Melbourne*, Melbourne University Press, Carlton, 1936, pp. 57–8.

6 See Scott, *A History of the University of Melbourne*, pp. 55–67.

7 As is well documented in histories of the university: see Scott, *A History of the University of Melbourne*, pp. 69–70; Geoffrey Blainey, *A Centenary History of the University of Melbourne*, Melbourne University Press, Carlton, 1955, pp. 53, 85;

Stuart Macintyre and RJW Selleck, *A Short History of the University of Melbourne*, Melbourne University Press, Carlton, 2003.

8 See, for example, Critchett, *A Distant Field of Murder*, pp. 153–6; Broome, *Aboriginal Victorians*, p. 79.

9 Niel Black, 9 December 1839. Journal reproduced in Maggie McKellar, *Strangers in a Foreign Land: The Journal of Niel Black and Other Voices from the Western District*, Miegunyah Press, Melbourne, 2008, p. 107.

10 James Dawson, local guardian of Aborigines, Camperdown, to the editor, *Camperdown Chronicle*, 25 April 1896, p. 3. For a fuller discussion of Dawson's strident critiques of Aboriginal dispossession in the Western District, see Jan Critchett, *Untold Stories: Memories and Lives of Victorian Kooris*, Melbourne University Press, Carlton, 1998, pp. 238–48.

11 Clark, *Scars in the Landscape*, pp. 2–5; Critchett, *A Distant Field of Murder*; Ryan, 'Settler Massacres'; Broome, *Aboriginal Victorians*; The Centre for 21st Century Humanities (University of Newcastle), 'Colonial Frontier Massacres in Australia, 1788–1930', Stage 3.1, 2021, https://c21ch.newcastle.edu.au/colonialmassacres/introduction.php (accessed 16 October 2023).

12 Critchett, *Untold Stories*, pp. 122–49, argues that the multiple forced removals experienced by many of western Victoria's Aboriginal peoples—from Country to mission or reserve, and then to other missions or reserves, or, after the 1866 Act, of 'able-bodied half-castes' under thirty-five years, off reserves entirely—were 'double dispossessions'.

13 This critique extends to historians within settler-colonial institutions (and states) as well as to the institutions themselves: see Tony Birch, '"The Invisible Fire": Sovereignty, History and Responsibility', in Aileen Moreton-Robinson (ed.), *Sovereign Subjects: Indigenous Sovereignty Matters*, Allen & Unwin, Crows Nest, NSW, 2007, pp. 105–17; Chelsea Watego, *Another Day in the Colony*, University of Queensland Press, St Lucia, 2021, pp. 49–78; Vicki Hsueh, 'Reckoning with Settler Memory: Barbara Arneil's Domestic Colonies and Adam Dahl's Empire of the People', *Perspectives on Politics*, vol. 17, no. 1, March 2019, pp. 168–72.

14 Niel Black estimated that, between them, the Wilson brothers were clearing £200 000 per annum in 1873: Niel Black to Gladstone, 11 August 1873, quoted in Kiddle, *Men of Yesterday*, p. 469.

15 Scott, *A History of the University of Melbourne*, p. 58.

16 Quoted in ibid., p. 60. See also Blainey, *A Centenary History*, p. 52.

17 Kiddle, *Men of Yesterday*, p. 496.

18 Wilson represented the Western Province in the Victorian upper house between 1875 and 1881.

19 Three of his children did so: Gordon Chesney Wilson married the daughter of the seventh Duke of Marlborough and became an officer in the Horse Guards, while two daughters married noblemen: Kiddle, *Men of Yesterday*, p. 496.

20 'Sir Samuel Wilson', *Australasian Pastoralists' Review*, 15 June 1895, p. 211.

21 See Barengi Gadjin Land Council, https://www.bglc.com.au/native-title (accessed 16 October 2023). The area is in Determination Area A.

22 LJ Blake, 'Sir Samuel Wilson (1832–1895)', *Australian Dictionary of Biography*, National Centre of Biography, Australian National University, Canberra, 2006, https://adb.anu.edu.au/biography/wilson-sir-samuel-1052/text8141 (accessed 16 October 2023).

23 Ibid.

24 Wilson's freehold property extended to 47 532 hectares in Victoria and 60 704 hectares in New South Wales (including Toorale and Dunlop stations on the Darling River). His leaseholds extended over 1 011 725 hectares, including the NSW properties Coree and Goolgumbla, and in Queensland, properties on the Diamantina and Bogan rivers: Blake, 'Sir Samuel Wilson'. Kiddle estimated the value of Wilson's Victorian freehold land at £471 781 in the late 1870s: *Men of Yesterday*, p. 469. Wilson continued to own Wimmera blocks even after his move into the south-west: Drung Drung, County of Borung, Victorian Department of Lands and Survey, MAP RM 2741/67, 1887, https://nla.gov.au/nla.obj-232019882/view (accessed 16 October 2023).

25 A prominent member of the Acclimatisation Society of Victoria, he was known as Sir 'Salmon' Wilson: 'History of the Pioneers', *Horsham Times*, 24 August 1926, p. 1.

26 Obituary, Archibald McCook, *Pastoral Review*, 16 June 1925, p. 494.

27 'Death of Sir Samuel Wilson', *South Australian Register*, 13 June 1895, p. 5.

28 'History of the Pioneers', *Horsham Times*, 27 August 1926, p. 11.

29 *Sixth Report of the Central Board Appointed to Watch over the Interests of the Aborigines in the Colony of Victoria*, Government of Victoria, Melbourne, 1869, pp. 14–15.

30 *Sixth Report*, p. 30.

31 *Eighth Report of the Board for the Protection of Aborigines in the Colony of Victoria*, Government of Victoria, Melbourne, 1872, p. 23.

32 Kiddle, *Men of Yesterday*, pp. 308–10; 'Ercildoune Homestead & Garden', *Victorian Heritage Database*, 2007, https://vhd.heritagecouncil.vic.gov.au/places/67290 (accessed 16 October 2023). Wilson made further alterations to Ercildoune (including changing its name from 'Ercildoun') after his purchase.

33 See, for example, Critchett, *A Distant Field of Murder*; Broome, *Aboriginal Victorians*; Clark, *Scars in the Landscape.*

34 Joseph, shepherd of T Learmonth, deposition, 27 July 1838, VPRS 109, p. 14, quoted in Critchett, *A Distant Field of Murder*, p. 97. See also Thomas Francis Bride (ed.), *Letters from Victorian Pioneers*, Lloyd O'Neil, South Yarra, Vic., 1983, first published 1898, pp. 94–5, 98, quoted in Critchett, *A Distant Field of Murder*, p. 28.

35 Critchett, *A Distant Field of Murder*, p. 243; Michael Cannon (ed.), *The Aborigines of Port Phillip 1835–1839, Historical Records of Victoria Foundation Series, Volume 2A*, Victorian Printing Office, Melbourne, 1982, pp. 290, 309.

36 See Broome, *Aboriginal Victorians*, pp. 101–3.

37 If, as seems to have been the case, he was 'local' to Ercildoune, Mullawallah's clan was likely the Burrumbeet balug. However, an 1895 record of Mullawallah's annual trip to Yaloak Vale station near Ballan suggests it is possible 'local' should be interpreted more broadly. Ian D Clark records that he was also known as 'Frank the Black': *Aboriginal Languages and Clans: An Historical Atlas of Western and Central Victoria, 1800–1900*, Monash Publications in Geography, Melbourne, 1990, pp. 306, 311.

38 'Last of His Tribe', *Bendigo Independent*, 25 September 1896, p. 1.

39 *Age*, 24 September 1896, p. 5.

40 'The Last of the Tribe', *Wagga Wagga Advertiser*, 26 September 1896, p. 2. See also 'A Dusky Monarch', *Daily News* (Perth), 6 October 1896, p. 2; 'Last of His Tribe, A Wesleyan–Roman Catholic', *Bendigo Independent*, 25 September 1896,

p. 1; 'Death of King Billy of Ercildoune', *Leader* (Melbourne), 26 September 1896, p. 23; 'Death of King Billy. An Aboriginal Monarch. A Pathetic End', *Australian Star* (Sydney), 3 October 1896, p. 8; 'The King of Ballarat', *Western Australian Goldfields Courier*, 10 October 1896, p. 23.

41 'Burial of King Billy', *Weekly Times* (Melbourne), Saturday 3 October 1896, p. 13, photograph p. 10.

42 'News and Notes', *Ballarat Star*, 9 August 1884. Story repeated in *Tasmanian*, 16 August 1884, p. 12. On the highly disproportionate levels of Aboriginal incarceration for alcohol-related offences in this era, see Critchett, *Untold Stories*, pp. 48–9.

43 'An Aboriginal Monarch in Trouble', *Bendigo Advertiser*, 28 December 1895, p. 4. This story was also carried in the Melbourne *Leader*, 28 December 1895, p. 14; *Mercury* (Hobart), 30 December 1895, p. 4; *Evening News* (Sydney), 30 December 1895, p. 3; *Australian Town and Country Journal*, 4 January 1896, p. 13; *Barrier Miner* (Broken Hill), 6 January 1896, p. 3; *West Australian*, 11 January 1896, p. 10; *Goulburn Herald*, 17 January 1896, p. 5. The *Albury Banner and Wodonga Express* carried the same story but under the misleading headline 'Death of a Monarch' (3 January 1896, p. 28), while the *Singleton Argus* embarrassed itself with 'Le Rio [sic] s'Amuse', 1 January 1896, p. 4.

44 *Horsham Times*, 4 February 1896, p. 2. Dr Corry was likely Dr Alexander Corry (1862–1923), an Irish-educated doctor who moved to Australia, and Egerton, c. 1888: Mt Egerton Cemetery, 'Corry Family', https://www.mountegertoncemetery.com/corry-family.html (accessed 16 October 2023).

45 Scott, *A History of the University of Melbourne*, p. 63. Wyselaskie's estate was valued at just over £100 000: *Bendigo Advertiser*, 29 June 1883, p. 2.

46 Wyselaskie arrived at Port Phillip on the *Black Jack* in 1838: Alexander Sutherland, *Victoria and Its Metropolis, Past and Present*, vol. 2, McCarron, Bird and Co, Melbourne, 1888, p. 509.

47 Today, the recognised Traditional Owners of these lands are the Eastern Maar People: RV Billis and AS Kenyon, *Pastoral Pioneers of Port Phillip*, Macmillan & Co., Melbourne, 1932, p. 164. Wyselaskie was granted a pasturage licence for the year commencing 1 July 1840: *New South Wales Government Gazette*, 30 September 1840, p. 971.

48 J Ann Hone, 'John Dickson Wyselaskie (1818–1883)', *Australian Dictionary of Biography*, National Centre of Biography, Australian National University, Canberra, 2023, https://adb.anu.edu.au/biography/wyselaskie-john-dickson-4896/text8193509 (accessed 16 October 2023).

49 Melbourne agents Bell and Buchanan noted Wyselaskie bought stock with the legacy from his uncle: Bell and Buchanan to George Russell, 3 July 1846, in PL Brown (ed.), *Clyde Company Papers* (hereafter *CCP*), *vol. IV: 1846–50*, Oxford University Press, London, 1959, p. 68. See also, W. M. Bell & Co. to George Russell, 28 June 1850, in Brown, *CCP, vol. IV*, p. 500.

50 Jennifer F O'Donnell, *Narrapumelap: A Pastoral History*, Jennifer F O'Donnell, Moonee Ponds, Vic., 2018.

51 Hone, 'John Dickson Wyselaskie'. O'Donnell outlines Wyselaskie's 1860s land dealings in detail: *Narrapumelap*, pp. 6, 12–13. AC Cameron reported that 'Wiselaskie's [sic] sheep have got scab' to William Lewis, 21 February 1854. See also Cameron's letters of 29 March 1854 and 11 April 1854, in PL Brown (ed.), *CCP, vol. VI: 1854–58*, Oxford University Press, London, 1968, pp. 30, 58–60, 62.

52 Farrell was born in 1838 and died in 1895.

53 O'Donnell, *Narrapumelap*, pp. 22, 24–31.

54 Ibid., pp. 6, 10–13, 23, 44.

55 Clark, *Aboriginal Languages and Clans*, pp. 94–5.

56 On Burrumbeep, see The Centre for 21st Century Humanities, 'Colonial Frontier Massacres in Australia', https://c21ch.newcastle.edu.au/colonialmassacres/detail.php?r=525 (accessed 16 October 2023).

57 Sutherland, *Victoria and Its Metropolis*, p. 509.

58 O'Donnell, *Narrapumelap*, p. 16; CL Sayers, *Of Many Things: A History of Warrnambool Shire*, 2nd edn, Shire of Warrnambool, Warrnambool, 1987, p. 87.

59 Clark, *Scars in the Landscape*, p. 57; Clark, *Aboriginal Languages and Clans*, pp. 91–107, 114–18; Critchett, *A Distant Field*, p. 99. On policy in the 1850s and 1860s, see Broome, *Aboriginal Victorians*, pp. 119–26.

60 James Bonwick, *Western Victoria, Its Geography, Geology and Soil Conditions: The Narrative of an Educational Tour in 1857*, Thomas Brown, Geelong, 1858, pp. 146–49.

61 *First Report of the Central Board Appointed to Watch Over the Interests of the Aborigines in the Colony of Victoria*, Government of Victoria, Melbourne, 1861, Appendix 2, pp. 18, 23.

62 Clark, *Aboriginal Languages and Clans*, p. 100.

63 Ibid., pp. 101, 102, 105.

64 On the 1869 Act see Broome, *Aboriginal Victorians*, pp. 130–1, 146–7, 150; Leigh Boucher, 'The 1869 *Aborigines Protection Act*: Vernacular Ethnography and the Governance of Aboriginal Subjects', in Leigh Boucher and Lynette Russell (eds), *Settler Colonial Governance in Nineteenth-Century Victoria*, ANU E-Press, Canberra, 2015, pp. 63–94.

65 Certificate no. 35, 1 September 1871, for Johnny Wyselaskee, recommended by C Gray, Nareeb Nareeb: *Eighth Report of the Board for the Protection of Aborigines in the Colony of Victoria*, Government of Victoria, Melbourne, 1872, Appendix XIV, p. 30.

66 Certificate no. 58, 13 July 1872, recommended by W Goodhall and HB Lane: *Ninth Report of the Board for the Protection of Aborigines in the Colony of Victoria*, Government of Victoria, Melbourne, 1872, Appendix XIII, p. 24.

67 Wyselaskie was the only person at Framlingham recorded as coming from Wickliffe by the 1880s. Apart from the variations in the text, the author of this chapter has seen his name rendered as 'Wiselaski', 'Wiselasky', 'Wyselaski', 'Wiselaskie' and 'Wisey'.

68 *Warrnambool Standard*, 7 March 1876, reproduced in Critchett, *Untold Stories*, p. 108.

69 Critchett, *Untold Stories*, p. 61: this photograph includes both Wyselaskie and his wife Harriet ('Mrs Wyselaskie').

70 Harriet Blair, born before 1862, died 27 February 1928, was the daughter of Nellie Cain (Aboriginal name Whitburboin) and, probably, Barney (Aboriginal name Minimalk), who 'saw themselves as members of the Tooram "tribe" ... just to the east of Warrnambool at Allansford'. Nellie was later married to Jim Cain: Critchett, *Untold Stories*, pp. 34–8. Harriet's first husband was James Couzens, and their children included Esther Couzens and Nicholas Couzens (born c. 1903).

71 It had begun, in 1861, as an Anglican mission: Broome, *Aboriginal Victorians*, pp. 129, 132–3.

72 Jan Critchett, *Our Land Till We Die: A History of the Framlingham Aborigines*, Warrnambool Institute Press, Warrnambool, 1980, p. 95.

73 Broome, *Aboriginal Victorians*, p. 186.

74 The application of Wyselaskie was granted in 1893: Broome, *Aboriginal Victorians*, pp. 190–1, 235; Critchett, *Our Land Till We Die*, rev. edn, Deakin University Press, Warrnambool, 1992, pp. 53–4; Critchett, *Untold Stories*, pp. 111, 115–16.

75 Critchett, *Untold Stories*, p. 116.

76 Harriet Wyselaskie, Purnim, to Mr Parker, Board for the Protection of Aborigines, 21 October 1926, facsimile copy in Critchett, *Our Land Till We Die*, p. 61.

77 Critchett, *Untold Stories*, index.

78 One list, prepared contemporaneously by Colin Hood, was published in the *Warrnambool Standard* on 29 November 1889. A second was sent by the Rev. Hagenhauer to the board in September 1890: Clark, *Aboriginal Languages and Clans*, pp. 103, 116; Critchett, *Our Land Till We Die*, pp. 95, 97.

79 Online sources that suggest John Dickson Wyselaskie was John Wyselaskie's father make key errors in relation to known details of both men's lives. Michael Cannon (*Who Killed the Koories?*, William Heinemann, Melbourne, 1990, p. 25) noted of JD Wyselaskie's pastoralist neighbour at Nareeb Nareeb, Charles Gray, that he had 'several' children with a local Aboriginal woman, but provides no archival evidence for this claim.

80 O'Donnell, *Narrapumelap*, pp. 44–5, 48–51. Sutherland includes illustrations of both Wyselaskie mansions: *Victoria and Its Metropolis*, pp. 172, 448.

81 Ormond donated more than £40 000 during his lifetime, and in total about £112 000 to the college and its theological hall: Don Chambers, 'Francis Ormond (1829–1889)', *Australian Dictionary of Biography*, National Centre of Biography, Australian National University, Canberra, 2006, https://adb.anu.edu.au/biography/ormond-francis-4340 (accessed 16 October 2023).

82 George Russell to William Cross, 6 February 1843, and George Russell to William Cross, 18 March 1844, in PL Brown (ed.), *CCP, vol. III: 1841–45*, Oxford University Press, London, 1958, pp. 296, 388. In 1850 Clyde Company records indicate that the rent was renegotiated at £230 per annum, payable half-yearly: George Russell and William Lewis, 'Memorandum Regarding Clyde Co. affairs for Mr Lewis's Guidance', in Brown, *CCP, vol. IV*, p. 514.

83 Chambers, 'Francis Ormond (1829–1889)'.

84 Francis junior's sister, Elizabeth, married the Scottish Presbyterian Adam Swanston Robertson, a prominent early pastoralist who, in a partnership with Ebenezer Oliphant (dissolved in 1848), occupied the run later known as Gnarpurt near Lake Corangamite from 1841. Elizabeth had several children before her premature death in 1861. In December 1851 Francis junior married Mary Greeves, the daughter of another Scottish friend of the family, Dr George Greeves, who had a medical practice in Geelong and owned a Werribee hotel. Ormond later employed Edward Greeves, Mary's brother, as his manager and leased Borriyalloak to him in the 1860s. Ormond's second wife was Ebenezer Oliphant's daughter, Mary. See Edward (Ted) Stephens, *The Ormonds of Borriyalloak*, Waller and Chester, Ballarat, 2014, pp. 21–4, 30; PL Brown (ed.), *CCP, vol. VII: 1859–73*, Oxford University Press, London, 1971, p. 183; William Lewis to George Russell, 8 January 1868, in Brown, *CCP, vol. VII*, p. 293; RA McAlpine, *Shire of Hampden 1863–1963*, Terang Express Print, Terang, 1963, pp. 46–7.

85 Philip L Brown (ed.), *Narrative of George Russell*, Oxford University Press, London, 1935, p. 226; Mary Turner Shaw, *On Mount Emu Creek*, Robertson and Mullens, Melbourne, 1969, pp. 64–5; Stephens, *The Ormonds of Borriyalloak*, pp. 9, 55.

86 Stephens, *The Ormonds of Borriyalloak*, pp. 51–4. Native Hut Creek No. 2 was near present-day Teesdale.

87 Billis and Kenyon, *Pastoral Pioneers*, p. 122. Max Griffiths' 2015 efforts to pin down the Ormond properties suggest how difficult it is to be certain of the 1840s details: see *Francis Ormond: A Ruling Passion*, Rosenberg Publishing, Kenthurst, NSW, 2015. McAlpine documents Berrybank's history: *Shire of Hampden*, p. 46.

88 William Lewis to George Russell, 4 March 1851, in PL Brown (ed.), *CCP, vol. V: 1851–53*, Oxford University Press, London, 1963, p. 18; Stephens, *The Ormonds of Borriyalloak*, pp. 55–9; Mortlake Historical Society, *Pastures of Peace: A Tapestry of Mortlake Shire*, Shire of Mortlake, Mortlake, Vic., 1985, pp. 19–20; Shaw, *History of the Port Phillip District*, pp. 249–50.

89 Chambers, 'Francis Ormond (1829–1889)'; Don Chambers, 'Francis Ormond', *Ormond Papers*, vol. 1, no. 1, 1965, p. 32. On Ormond's interest in Bangal, see James Aitken to George Russell, 1 February 1868, in Brown, *CCP, vol. VII*, 297; Griffiths, *Francis Ormond*, p. 739.

90 McAlpine, *The Shire of Hampden*, p. 78; Shaw, *On Mount Emu Creek*, pp. 115–16; Chambers, 'Francis Ormond', p. 33.

91 Stephens, *The Ormonds of Borriyalloak*, p. 81. The homestead burned down in 1944.

92 See, for example, on Ormond's sale of stock, AC Cameron to William Lewis, 27 June 1853, in Brown, *CCP, vol. V*, p. 488; and on the quality of Ormond's flock, AC Cameron to William Lewis, 29 March 1854, in Brown, *CCP, vol. VI*, 58–60.

93 AC Cameron to William Lewis, 24 September 1852, in Brown, *CCP, vol. V*, p. 342.

94 *Report of the Select Committee of the Legislative Council on the Aborigines, 1858–9*, Government Printer, Melbourne, 1859, pp. 35, 37.

95 Ormond reported slightly more men than women, and only two children 'in the Mount Emu tribe ... a girl and a boy; the girl about thirteen years of age, the boy eleven—half-castes': *Report of the Select Committee*, pp. 26–8.

96 *Report of the Select Committee*, pp. 30–1, 33. Andrew Porteous, of variously Carngham, Mount Emu and Pretty Tower, Stockyard Hill, was probably the most proximate local guardian to Borriyalloak: Ian Clark, 'The Northern Wathawurrung and Andrew Porteous, 1860–1877', *Aboriginal History*, vol. 32, 2008, pp. 97–108.

97 Bangal (or Baangal) station, which fronted the Mount Emu Creek near Skipton, and is now known as Banongill station, exchanged hands in 2020 for $80 million: 'Historic Banongill Station Sold to Farmers for $80m', *Australian Financial Review*, 28 October 2020. Ormond named his portion of Round Hill 'Kirndeen': Chambers, 'Francis Ormond (1829–1889)'.

98 Chambers, 'Francis Ormond', pp. 32–33; Chambers, 'Francis Ormond (1829–1889)'.

99 Francis Ormond junior to George Russell, 2 December 1868, in Brown, *CCP, vol. VII*, p. 320.

100 Chambers, 'Francis Ormond', p. 34.

101 Today the Traditional Owners are recognised as the Eastern Maar people.

102 Philip Russell to George Russell, 2 February 1841, in Brown, *CCP, vol. III*, pp. 11–12. Hastie arrived in Melbourne on the *Tamar* on 27 December 1840: ibid., p. 35.

103 Apart from the question of Hastie's sobriety (or not), the Clyde Company's most significant investor, captain Patrick Wood, was left angry in 1844 over a 'vile transaction' involving £25, Hastie, corporal Jackson of the 15th Dragoons, and Wood's Melbourne agents, Bell and Buchanan: Philip Russell to George Russell, 20 February 1841, in Brown, *CCP, vol. III*, p. 17; Mrs S Russell, Edinburgh, to George Russell, 5 October 1841, in Brown, *CCP, vol. III*, pp. 128–9; William Russell, Dennistoun, VDL, to George Russell, 19 May 1841 and 5 August 1841, in Brown, *CCP, vol. III*, pp. 55, 77; captain Patrick Wood, Edinburgh, to George Russell, 28 April 1842, in Brown, *CCP, vol. III*, p. 207; captain Patrick Wood, Edinburgh, to Philip Russell, 8 August 1844, in Brown, *CCP, vol. III*, 426; Alexander Russell, Hopkins Hill, to George Russell, 22 December 1844, in Brown, *CCP, vol. III*, p. 485.

104 Billis and Kenyon, *Pastoral Pioneers*, p. 267; McAlpine, *Shire of Hampden*, p. 44.

105 Lots of Crown land at the upset price of £1 per acre were offered for sale in 1864 in Corangamite, 'west of the road from Camperdown to Geelong, and north of Mr John Hastie's purchased land, near Lake Corangamite': *The Argus*, 18 November 1864, p. 7.

106 On the resistance fund, see introductory note for 1845, in Brown, *CCP, vol. III*, pp. 542–3. On horse losses, see, for example, *Geelong Advertiser and Squatters' Advocate*, 30 December 1846, p. 3; *Geelong Advertiser*, 17 October 1848, p. 3.

107 *Geelong Advertiser*, 17 June 1851, p. 3; *Geelong Advertiser*, 20 June 1851, p. 3.

108 Rev. FMW Wilson, Camperdown, to George Russell, 20 July 1867, in Brown, *CCP, vol. VII*, pp. 866–7. Wilson migrated from Scotland to Victoria after completing a theology course in 1856, and he was based in Camperdown until 1877: *Encyclopedia of Australian Science*, 'Wilson, Francis Robert Muter (1832–1903)', 2023, https://www.eoas.info/biogs/P005525b.htm (accessed 16 October 2023).

109 Kiddle, *Men of Yesterday*, pp. 487–8.

110 Turner Shaw, *On Mount Emu Creek*, p. 80.

111 AC Cameron to William Lewis, 7 October 1851, in Brown, *CCP, vol. V*, p. 143.

112 Turner Shaw, *On Mount Emu Creek*, p. 93.

113 Bonwick, *Western Victoria*, pp. 24–5; see also Critchett, *Untold Stories*, p. 71.

114 Critchett, *Untold Stories*, p. 66; Cannon, *Who Killed the Koories?*, p. 54. The Manifold brothers' hostile encounters with the Djargurd wurrung people are recorded in a mural cycle they commissioned for Purrumbete in 1901–2: Karen Burns, 'Archive Stories/Symptomatic Histories: The Commemoration of Australian Frontier Space at Purrumbete, 1840–1902', *Architectural Theory Review*, vol. 18, no. 1, 2013, pp. 83–104.

115 Clark, *Scars in the Landscape*, pp. 105–18.

116 Critchett, *Untold Stories*, p. 98.

117 *Argus*, 21 January 1867, p. 3. The agents were King and Cuningham of Bourke Street, Melbourne. See also *Argus*, 7 January 1867, p. 3; 'News and Notes', *Ballarat Star*, 21 July 1866, p. 2.

118 Rev. Robert Russell, Evandale, to George Russell, 2 March 1867, in Brown, *CCP, vol. VII*, pp. 265–9. The entire estate realised £59 182: 'Inter-Colonial', *Bruce Herald*, 27 March 1867, p. 6.

119 Turner Shaw, *On Mount Emu Creek*, p. 80, n. 6; Blainey, *A Centenary History*, p. 52.

Stolen Stones and Bare-Faced Brick

A Material History of the Parkville Campus

PHILIP GOAD

THE DESIRE TO build and create shelter always requires taking materials from a place and then assembling those materials to provide shade or a roof overhead or walls for warmth and wind protection. Sometimes these materials are immediately at hand. At other times they are carried from places far way, sometimes across oceans. In south-western Victoria at Budj Bim, for example, more than 6000 years ago, the Gunditjmara people collected volcanic rocks and laid and stacked them in circles, then walled and roofed them with mud and branches to create permanent structures. The impetus was to collect building materials directly from the local landscape. It was expedient, pragmatic and necessary given the harsh winters and bitterly cold south-westerly winds that swept across the basalt plains.

A different impetus lay behind the creation of the buildings and landscapes that today make up the Parkville campus of the University of Melbourne. It was a desire to create an image of somewhere else—the hallowed stone walls of universities familiar to Victoria's founding citizens, like the limestone of Redmond Barry's alma mater, Trinity College, Dublin, or the fabled sandstone structures of Oxford and Cambridge. There was also a desire to transform the landscape, reshaping it in the image of an English park.

This chapter maps the contested role played by materials in the making of the Parkville campus, and in the changing of a landscape that was previously inhabited by the Wurundjeri Woi Wurrung people, and traversed by many other Indigenous peoples, such as the Yorta Yorta from north-eastern Victoria, who for centuries made their way across the site to attend ceremonies. What is revealed is a complex story of building materials travelling across Australian landscapes, having been extracted from the stolen lands of Indigenous Australians, and their reassembly as hopeful simulacra of venerable places of learning. Documenting the origins of these materials reveals a deep history of the campus, one that goes beyond the University's relatively recent history of muddled master plans. It also offers the opportunity to acknowledge and touch materials that speak of reciprocal landscapes and peoples across a much wider geography, and hence reminds us that, anywhere in the world, each time we build, we relocate—perhaps even steal—part of another's place and transfer it so it becomes our own.[1]

Ornamental Private Grounds

The University of Melbourne was founded in 1853. One of the first tasks of the University Council at its inaugural meeting on 3 May that year was to find a site for the new institution. Application was made for an 8-hectare site on the eastern side of Spring Street, at the edge of Melbourne's city grid. Architectural historian George Tibbits has surmised that the aim was to erect a landmark building that would terminate the Collins Street axis as well as the south-western axis along Gisborne Street.[2] At the time, the land that would eventually become the site of the Treasury Building and Treasury Gardens was swampy, dotted with river red gums, native grasses and the occasional scar tree, and occupied by the local Wurundjeri Woi Wurrung people. It was also land as yet undeveloped by speculators eager to capitalise on a potential eastward expansion of the city grid. Melbourne City Council objected to the proposal but the government of the day had already decided against the site.

The University's second application for a site, in September 1853, was more successful. But there were caveats. Forty hectares of undeveloped land north of the city was requested—and a University Reserve granted—but only just over 10 hectares was set aside in November 1853, and it would not be until 1908 that the entire reserve (including the land up to College Crescent) finally came under the University's control. At the time, the site on the corner of Grattan Street and Sydney Road (now Royal Parade) was considered a wasteland. On the other side of Sydney Road was the reservation for the Hay, Corn, Horse and Pig Market (functions that continued there until 1939)—the suburb of Parkville had not yet come into existence. The landscape that would become Royal Park, Parkville and the University had been continuously occupied by the Wurundjeri Woi

Wurrung people for thousands of years: they camped there and held corroborees with the neighbouring Bunurong, Wadawurrung and Taungurung peoples. It was only from the early 1850s onwards that lieutenant-governor Charles La Trobe's policy of setting aside large parcels of land close to central Melbourne for public recreation began to change this landscape where people had once lived and celebrated, and through which they'd moved.

In arguing for the Carlton reserve, Redmond Barry put the case that not only would there be the erection of university buildings, but that development of the site would

> produce other beneficial effects, in the adornment of that quarter of the town by the laying out of ornamental private grounds, as well as others to which the public may have occasional access for purposes of recreation, & in conferring an increased value on the adjacent lands of the Crown.[3]

Implicit in this argument was that the University, once it had gained the full extent of the reserve, might in due course be considered a public landscape, and that its beautification as 'ornamental private grounds' containing the University buildings was also of public benefit. At the north-eastern corner of the original 10-hectare grant was a wetland (frequently referred to as a swamp) that drained to a watercourse (outside the original grant) that sloped down to Grattan Street. Across the site and beyond to the north, given the abundant presence of water, were river red gums, natural grasses and a variety of eucalypts, including yellow box.

The Council immediately ran an architectural competition for its first building. The winner was London-born architect Francis Maloney White, who had migrated to Australia in 1848, landing in South Australia and then moving to Melbourne and commencing practice in 1851. White convinced the Council that his building should be located on the highest and most level part of the site—effectively near the centre of the entire plot of land lying between Sydney Road and Madeline Street (later Swanston Street). As Tibbits has argued, this siting decision effectively set the pattern for all future major planning, landscape and precinct decisions.[4]

White's Tudor Gothic building was planned to be a quadrangle but only the eastern and western wings were built from 1854. A picturesque turreted tower was planned for the southern wing, which faced the city, but this was never built. The construction material of both the eastern and western wings, as well as the huge flagstones in the cloister, was Tasmanian freestone (sandstone) sourced from Kangaroo Point (now Bellerive) near Hobart on Mumirimina land,[5] at a time when nearly all Indigenous peoples on

The stone for the Old Quadrangle building, including the huge flagstones underfoot, was Tasmanian freestone (sandstone) sourced from Kangaroo Point (now Bellerive) near Hobart on Mumirimina land.

lutruwita (Van Diemen's Land, then Tasmania from 1856) had been driven out and relocated to the Wybalenna Aboriginal Establishment on Flinders Island. White's northern wing of what eventually became known as the Old Quadrangle was completed in 1857.

As construction of the Old Quadrangle commenced, the works on the landscape also began. The entire reserve was cleared, stumps were grubbed out, there were levelling works, and 4 hectares were ploughed and sown with barley. Perhaps most dramatically, the grounds were enclosed on their perimeter with a timber palisade fence. The construction of fences around Melbourne's early public buildings and grounds was a common strategy to demarcate private property and keep out livestock and native wildlife, and intruders—Indigenous people among them. As the University Reserve gradually expanded with further grants in 1854, so, too, did the extent of the fencing and the delineation of a space where particular people were not necessarily welcome. Timber gates were erected on Grattan Street at what had become the main entrance to the University, aligned with White's new building. Gates and a fence in the manner of an English country estate required a gate lodge, but when a wooden cottage erected in 1855 soon burnt down, a more permanent solution was sought. In late 1858, newly appointed university architect Joseph Reed designed a Tudor Gothic brick-and-stone replacement. Gate Lodge was the earliest brick building on the campus.

Its distinctive straw-coloured bricks were sourced from clay extracted almost certainly from John Glew's brickpits in Barkly Street, East Brunswick (Iramoo), on land occupied by the Wurundjeri people who spoke the Woi Wurrung language. The gable parapets of the lodge have Stawell sandstone springers, kneelers and apex blocks transported from Dja Dja Wurrung Country more than 230 kilometres to the north-west of Melbourne, and this same stone was used for the quoin dressings and the hood mouldings for the window openings. As with all of these early buildings, the roof cladding was slate sourced from Wales, brought over as ships' ballast.

By 1873 the gates to the University were, as Tibbits has documented, 'being locked, at least on Sundays, which prevented some families in Leicester Street from walking through the University grounds on their way to St Jude's Church in Carlton'.[6] A flanking fence of iron palisades, iron gates and bluestone (basalt) entrance pillars designed by the firm of Reed & Barnes were erected in 1875, and the timber fence was replaced progressively by sections of galvanised iron.

These early buildings, whether stone or brick, had a common material connection that, unlike the sandstone shipped in from distant parts, was fundamentally local. All were built—as were almost all of Melbourne's public buildings from the 1850s until the early twentieth century—on foundations and bedding plinths of bluestone, initially from early quarries in Footscray (known as 'Stoneopolis' in the 1860s), Clifton Hill and Carlton, on Wurundjeri land, and later from quarries in West Footscray, Yarraville, Coburg and Preston. This was the stone of Victoria's basalt plains that stretch from Melbourne's inner west to the South Australian border—from the land of the Gunditjmara people, who used the same stone to construct their distinctive circular rock structures and their eel traps. Bluestone's density and hardness meant that it was an ideal material for kerbs, edgings, plinths and cobblestones. It defined not just the ground plane and the cellars of the buildings of the nineteenth-century Parkville campus but also the emerging city of Melbourne.

As the Old Quadrangle and Gate Lodge began to embody a definite 'front' address for the University, further aspects of the grounds were redefined with two imported conceptions of landscape design. The wetland was reconfigured as an artistically considered ornamental 'natural' lake in the tradition of the English picturesque landscape, and, in 1856, a scientific overlay came with the establishment of the concentric rings of the System

View across lake to Biology School, University of Melbourne, c. 1901. The building, sitting on a bluestone plinth, was designed by architects Reed, Henderson & Smart (1887, 1889) and constructed of rough-hewn Barrabool sandstone quarried near Ceres in the Barrabool Hills outside Geelong, on the land of the Barrabool and Wadawurrung people.

Garden, undertaken with the advice and expertise of Frederick McCoy, the foundation professor of natural science.

Science and the idea of encyclopaedic knowledge also informed the next major building on campus: the National Museum, built in 1863 facing the new lake. Designed by Joseph Reed, its Gothic Revival forms were constructed of the same straw-coloured clay bricks from nearby East Brunswick. The collections, mostly assembled through the zeal of McCoy, were global in scope, but of local interest were the skeletons of what was called *Biphrodoton* (now known as *Diprotodon*), an extinct Australian megafauna animal depicted in Aboriginal rock art in Quinkan Country in far north Queensland. Also, in 1865, 'the most interesting and important department of the museum' was the section devoted to colonial mining machinery, where 'models of every machine need [sic] in the various operations of boring, washing, puddling, shallow and deep sinking, quartz mining, crushing &c' and their labels 'renders [sic] every instrument and process intelligible, even to those who never handled pick and shovel, or peeped down a shaft'.[7] Museological and extractive—these were the Museum's double themes. Australia was a land to be documented and exploited regardless of continuous inhabitation.

Whale skeleton in fenced enclosure, located adjacent to the west-facing façade of the National Museum, University of Melbourne, c. 1862–99, 'proudly acclaimed at the time as the largest museum exhibit in the world'.

Outside, on the Museum's western side, for some years from 1867, exposed to the elements and at one time under a roofed canopy, there was a huge skeleton of a whale, nearly 30 metres long, that had been stranded near the Heads of Port Phillip Bay.[8] Local Indigenous people would have been shocked: for them the whale was a revered and sacred ancestor that was to be respected and laid to rest, its body not moved whole and displayed like a trophy.[9] The collection was transferred to new purpose-built museum facilities in central Melbourne in 1899 and the government gave the Parkville building to the University. Today, fragments of the straw-coloured-brick National Museum remain visible on the eastern façade of Union House and, remarkably, some of its Gothic timber trusses survive above the ceiling of the Union Theatre.

As new buildings for teaching and research were constructed, so, too, was accommodation for the University's students, all of whom were male at this time. At Trinity College, the Principal's House (1869–72, now the Leeper Wing) was, like the Old Quadrangle, styled in Tudor Gothic and constructed of Tasmanian freestone from Spring Bay on the state's east coast—part of trayapana, the Country of the Oyster Bay people. A different stone began to receive greater usage in the late 1870s at the hands of Reed & Barnes and its successor firms Reed, Henderson & Smart; Reed, Smart & Tappin; and Smart, Tappin & Peebles. It was used first at Ormond College (1879–81, 1885–87, 1888–89) on College Crescent, then on the eastern side of the main campus at the New Medical School (later Old Pathology and now the Elisabeth Murdoch Building) (1884, 1899, 1908) and the Biology School (now the Baldwin Spencer Building) (1887, 1889, 1905–06). Each of these austere Gothic Revival buildings sat on bluestone plinths and, above, were constructed of rough-hewn Barrabool sandstone with either straw-coloured brick or stone dressings. The distinctive greenish, even-textured sandstone came from quarries near Ceres in the Barrabool Hills, the land of the Barrabool and Wadawurrung people, which was also quickly surveyed from the early 1840s for squatting runs and which became the main source of wine grapes in Victoria until the industry was wiped out by phylloxera in the 1880s. These three buildings gave the late-nineteenth-century campus a form of visual unity, especially as two of them, Biology and New Medical School, both faced the ornamental lake, creating a large-scale 'outdoor room' in the north-eastern corner of the campus.

Reed & Barnes, however, had earlier completed another stone building, one that continued the University's Gothic themes and became the architectural jewel of the nineteenth-century campus. Wilson Hall (1878–82) was designed in the English Perpendicular Gothic style. Its internal walls

The south-western corner of Old Wilson Hall seen from the cloisters of the Old Quadrangle, c. 1930. Wilson Hall (1878–82) was designed by architects Reed & Barnes, its exterior clad in Hawkesbury sandstone from quarries in Sydney's Pyrmont, which were located on Cadigal and Wangal land.

The dais door of Old Wilson Hall, c. 1930. The English Perpendicular Gothic-styled building was clad in Hawkesbury sandstone from quarries in Sydney's Pyrmont, which were located on Cadigal and Wangal land.

were constructed of pale Oamaru limestone from the South Island of New Zealand, and its external walls were not Tasmanian freestone as originally intended (to match the Old Quadrangle) but Hawkesbury sandstone[10]—nicknamed 'yellow gold'—from Sydney's Pyrmont, where some fifty quarries operated on Cadigal and Wangal land.

At this point, it is important to note three figures associated with these important stone buildings of the 1870s and 1880s. The funds to build Wilson Hall came via an 1874 gift from Irish-born pastoralist Sir Samuel Wilson, whose squatting runs displaced thousands of Indigenous Australians. It was Wilson who laid the memorial stone for the University's aula magna in October 1879.

The Biology Building was later renamed the Baldwin Spencer Building, in honour of the Lancashire-born and Oxford-educated foundation chair of biology. Walter Baldwin Spencer was an evolutionary biologist whose pioneering documentary studies on Aboriginal people from the 1890s to 1920s brought him fame but also later discredit for his social Darwinist view of these people as 'dehumanized "survivals" from an early stage of social development'.[11]

Finally, Irish-born (1853) and trained in engineering at the University of Melbourne while articled to Reed & Barnes from 1869 to 1872,

Anketell Matthew Henderson was the architect who played a key role in the later reincarnations of Joseph Reed's practice and had been involved in buildings for Ormond College, New Medical School and Biology, as well as Natural Philosophy (later Old Physics) (1886–89), with its 1923 addition now the home of Murrup Barak. Henderson left the firm in 1890 and was appointed to the faculty of engineering as a co-examiner in architecture. In 1891 he was appointed lecturer in architecture, a position he held until 1916.[12] In that role he lectured on the history of architecture, which reflected his ideas on the superiority of European-based architecture, drawn largely from William Martin Conway's *Dawn of Art in the Ancient World: An Archaeological Sketch* (1891).[13] In 1897 he delivered to the University of Melbourne Historical Society in Wilson Hall a lecture entitled 'Race and Architecture', where it was reported he outlined the historical development of architectural composition 'where the white races were shown to have the greatest capacity for improvement, the yellow races the next, and the black races least'.[14] He concluded his lecture 'by showing a complete diagram of the process of the evolution of architecture during a period of 5000 years',[15] with no mention of the structures of Aboriginal Australians. It was a subject Henderson would continue to reprise as late as January 1913, when he spoke on 'Ornament and Race' to members of the Victorian Architectural Students Society.[16]

All three men were significant contributors to the University. In addition to his scholarly works, Baldwin Spencer, for example, also championed the participation of women in science. Yet all three had a complex relationship with the recognition and understanding of Indigenous Australians' existence, occupation and cultural presence.

The last two major stone buildings erected on the Parkville campus were built during and just after World War I. The first, Newman College (1915–18), was conceived by the designers of Australia's new capital city, Canberra: the charismatic American husband-and-wife partnership of Walter Burley Griffin and Marion Mahony Griffin. Constructed of Barrabool sandstone, Newman College was a direct challenge to the stylistic models of Oxford and Cambridge colleges that had previously dominated College Crescent. The design had two separate L-shaped arms of student rooms (one for men, the other for women) defining two quadrangles, at the centre of which was intended to be a chapel, also designed by the Griffins. At the corner of each L-shape was a stupa-like rotunda: one a dining room, the other a library. In the end, only one of the L-shapes was built (the one for the men, which included the domed dining room). But the Griffins also contributed a planting scheme that comprised mostly indigenous flora, a first for the University and, as Christopher Vernon has suggested, 'perhaps one of the first examples of a native flora garden designed by a landscape architect in Australia'.[17] Additionally, the lemon-scented gums (*Corymbia citriodora*) that dot the college grounds and also the Swanston Street roundabout are thought to have been planted on the instruction of the Griffins. Although the trees are not ecologically local to Victoria, Indigenous Australians in their traditional medicine use the leaves as a powerful antiseptic and natural insect repellent, and its gum to treat toothache.

With Newman College completed, construction began in 1919 on the new Tudor Gothic–styled Arts and Education Block, now known as Old Arts. Completed in 1924 and designed within the Victorian Public Works Department under government architect Samuel Brittingham (assisted by Alfred R La Gerche), the building, austere internally for economic reasons, externally suggested no lack of budgetary restraint. Clad in a golden

Clocktower of the Arts and Education Block (1919–24), now known as Old Arts. The building is clad in Kyneton freestone that was quarried at Lauriston on the land of the Taungurung people.

Kyneton freestone quarried at Lauriston[18] (also known as Keegan's Ford stone) on the land of the Taungurung people and fixed to solid brickwork behind, the building's picturesquely sited tall clocktower—its most striking feature—evokes the unbuilt FM White tower design (1854) intended for the southern front of the Quadrangle. The subject of much debate within the University and with government representatives over its suitability and cost, this was the last stone building erected on the campus.[19]

The Great Depression of the 1890s, first felt in 1892, had a serious effect on the provision of buildings on campus: there was a reduction in their number and a shift in materials choice, due not just to straitened economic times but also changes in architectural taste and fashion. There was a move to bare-faced brick, which would dramatically shift the visual character of the University. On the one hand, this strengthened the perception of the University's geographic heart as being of stone. On the other hand, its twentieth-century presentation—from the 1890s to the 1970s—was of the colours of the multiple Melbourne claypits that supplied the city's brick-making companies, all on the lands of the Wurundjeri Woi Wurrung and Bunurong peoples. The brickworks of Brunswick, Clifton Hill, Northcote and Hawthorn, and later Box Hill, Nunawading, Camberwell and Oakleigh, all sourced their clay from adjacent pits that from the 1930s became rubbish tips or swimming holes, and once filled in were converted to parks or sites for vast 1960s shopping centres.[20]

The move to brick had begun with the line of eight professors' houses designed by Anketell Henderson and built in the 1880s, and which faced inwards and framed a southern lawn with the Quadrangle and the Engineering Building (1899). All were in red brick. But it was the Public Works Department that consolidated the material's appearance across the campus, with red-brick Collegiate Gothic applied to Anatomy (1923), Old Geology (1927) and Botany (1928–29). Then, in the 1930s, they shifted to cream, deferring in colour and neighbourly propinquity to the historic sandstone campus centre with the Moderne Collegiate Gothic of Chemistry (1938), the extension to Natural Philosophy (1938–39, 1941, 1948) and Old Commerce (1938–40, demolished), all designed by then chief public works architect Percy Everett. Cream brick also defined the new Union House (1936–38), designed by Philip Hudson, which attached itself to the old National Museum, the whole complex later engulfed by later additions. Two of the key donors to this building for students were mining and related industry companies: Broken Hill Associated Smelters (owned by BHP) and the Electrolytic Zinc Company, which operated the vast Risdon Zinc Works in Tasmania, on the other side of the Derwent River from where dozens of Moomairremener people were massacred in 1804.

The use of cream brick continued after World War II with the functionalist cubic and curved forms of the three-storey (then later five-storey) New Arts and Arts Block No. 2 (1946–47, 1957), later named Babel. But Tudor Gothic and its early-twentieth-century incarnations as a stylistic choice were banished from the campus as the University surged ahead with the embrace of modernism in buildings such as the new Wilson Hall (1952–56), Baillieu Library (1957–59) and the Beaurepaire Centre (1954–57). At the same time, after the interregnum of World War II when virtually all construction ceased across campus, there was a desire—as there was across Melbourne generally—to plan for the long-term future of the campus as a whole in a coordinated way. Thus the immediate postwar decades were the years of multiple campus master plans. Up until 1945 there had been no complete vision for the campus. From its foundation, the University had grown incrementally, with the occasional master plan for various precincts rather than any overall vision for the entire University reserve. This was a circumstance driven by the gradual increase in granted land at the site and also the reality of powerful professors staking their claim on precincts that were devoted to medicine, engineering and the arts over and above any idea of coordinated planning for the entire site.

Ornamental Public Grounds

As the University expanded, its boundaries became more porous. Sections of the iron palisade fence had been removed during World War I and the iron melted down, and the corrugated-iron fencing had all but disappeared by 1940. As if to counter this, and return the University to its status as an enclosed, park-like estate, the new professor of architecture, Brian Lewis, proposed in his 1948 master plan that tall buildings be placed around the perimeter of the site, even along Tin Alley—rather like a multistorey wall—so as to keep the traditional centre of the campus open. Today, the twelve-storey Redmond Barry Building (1959–61) is one remnant of this strategy.

Of further interest is the John Stevens–designed landscape at ground level, inspired by Brazilian modernist Roberto Burle Marx but completed with Australian materials: giant pebbles taken from dry riverbeds, slate from Ngadjuri land in South Australia, and a free-form stack of natural granite boulders in a pond. The granite rocks, which came from Mount Alexander (known as Lanjanuc to the Dja Dja Wurrung people) near Harcourt in central Victoria, were draped with the Australian flag and unveiled as the memorial stones at the building's opening by Victorian premier Henry Bolte on 22 November 1961.[21]

But it was the 1970 master plan overseen by Bryce Mortlock,[22] and the accompanying hard landscaping, that transformed the campus over the next three decades and delivered a new form of visual unity to an otherwise ad-hoc collection of buildings. While the sandy tan-coloured bricks of the earlier John Medley Building (1969–71) had continued the polite deference to the University's sandstone heart, it was the completion of the South Lawn and Underground Car Park (1970–72) that signalled a new respect for the ground plane of the University campus.[23] Ron Rayment and Ellis Stones' landscape design accentuated the ceremonial axis from Grattan Street, with

The Hon. Henry Bolte, premier of Victoria (left), and Sir Arthur Dean, chancellor of the University of Melbourne (right), unveiling the stones in the courtyard of the new Redmond Barry Building, 22 November 1961. The granite boulders came from Mount Alexander, known as Lanjanuc to the Dja Dja Wurrung people, near Harcourt in central Victoria.

a reflecting pool and ordered lines of plane trees, but these gave way to picturesque zigzags of timber seats and the deliberate placing of indigenous plantings and granite rocks (now known as the Ellis Stones Garden) to the west. It was as if—finally—two traditions or understandings of the landscape might be allowed to coexist, and significantly, provide some form of echo of what might have been—even if the stones were not in themselves endemic to the place.

On the ground, tan-coloured bricks—known in the trade as 'Clifton Greys'—were used as paving. All of a sudden, the unified treatment of the ground plane and, at long last, the embrace of a completely car-free pedestrianised environment, offered a compelling precedent that might be followed for the rest of the University. The idea was adopted in what would become another critical document, the 1974 *Landscape Elements Report*.[24] A consistent palette for paving, seating and rubbish bins, and a coordinated approach to planting, were followed for the next thirty years.

The signature unmortared paving using Clifton Greys was studied and admired nationally.[25] But what was and remains important is its material nature. In many respects it brought focus not to the imported status of the University's vertical stone-faced walls, but to the very nature of the clays and the earth that had defined the grounds of the greater local landscape for

View of the 'Clifton Grey' paving bricks and bluestone steps between the South Lawn and Baillieu Library, 1980. Landscape design by Rayment & Stones.

thousands of years. It also allowed the campus, as it was progressively paved with brick over the decades, to become a place of pedestrian desire lines and myriad informal crossings over a shared public landscape, much as it might have been before the University gained its first grant of land in 1853.

Today, only remnants of the original fence that once surrounded the University remain. The original iron gates were relocated next to the Botany Building in the 1950s, and so gates no longer appear anywhere on the campus perimeter. The University's boundaries have become truly porous. The trees and the landscape have matured and the campus might now more properly be described as 'ornamental public grounds'. In some new buildings and landscapes on campus, one finds evidence of a living connection with an ancient landscape. For example, on the gently sloping ground floor of the Glyn Davis Building (2017), low, cantilevered concrete seats and polished precast concrete floor tile patterns indicate the ghosted and meandering passage of a watercourse that once flowed into the site's original wetland. It is a subtle design strategy possibly not noticed by many, but importantly it is there: an acknowledgement in today's materials of a much larger idea of Country.

While the growth of the University of Melbourne's Parkville campus has, like most Australian towns and cities, been born of stolen stones and bare-faced bricks, there is a growing recognition that even signalling a living connection to an ancient landscape might go some way to taking part in a much larger story—larger even than the University itself.

Notes

1 The concept of reciprocal landscapes is defined and explored in Jane Hutton, *Reciprocal Landscapes: Stories of Material Movements*, Routledge, Abingdon, UK, 2019.
2 George Tibbits, *The Planning and Development of the University of Melbourne*, The History of the University Unit, University of Melbourne, Parkville, 2000, p. 5.
3 Redmond Barry, file of Lands Department correspondence relating to the University, 25 October 1853, University of Melbourne Archives, cited in Tibbits, *The Planning and Development of the University of Melbourne*, p. 7.
4 Ibid., pp. 7–12.
5 George Tibbits, *The Quadrangle: The First Building at the University of Melbourne*, The History of the University Unit, University of Melbourne, Parkville, 2005, p. 27.
6 George Tibbits, 'The Lodge and the Main Gates, University of Melbourne: History and Conservation Guidelines', University of Melbourne, Parkville, October 1995, p. 12.
7 'The National Museum', *The Australian News for Home Readers*, 25 July 1865, p. 7.
8 'Melbourne', *Sydney Morning Herald*, 30 March 1867, p. 7; 'Victoria', *Telegraphic News*, 30 March 1867, p. 2.

9 Jason Cressy, 'Making a Splash in the Pacific: Dolphin and Whale Myths and Legends of Oceania', *Rapa Nui Journal*, vol. 12, p. 3, September 1998, pp. 76–7.

10 RM Crawford, *Wilson Hall: Centre and Symbol of the University*, Melbourne University Press, Carlton, 1952, p. 6. The internal and external stone choices for Wilson Hall are incorrectly cited in Emily Wubben and Jason Benjamin, 'The Art of Wilson Hall', *University of Melbourne Collections*, vol. 7, December 2010, p. 3.

11 DJ Mulvaney, 'Sir Walter Baldwin Spencer (1860–1929)', *Australian Dictionary of Biography*, National Centre of Biography, Australian National University, Canberra, 2006, https://adb.anu.edu.au/biography/spencer-sir-walter-baldwin-8606 (accessed 20 October 2023).

12 Julie Willis, 'Henderson, A & K', in Philip Goad and Julie Willis (eds), *The Encyclopedia of Australian Architecture*, Cambridge University Press, Port Melbourne, 2012, p. 322.

13 'University Extension Lectures', *Ballarat Star*, 28 July 1894, p. 1.

14 Anketell Matthew Henderson, 'Race and Architecture', *Alma Mater*, vol. 2, no. 6, September 1897, p. 13.

15 Ibid.

16 CH Strachan-Smith, 'Victorian Architectural Students Society', *Journal of Proceedings of the RVIA*, vol. 10, no. 6, January 1913, p. 275.

17 Christopher Vernon, '"A Legitimate Art Distinctive of Australia and Australia Alone": The Griffins' Contribution to the Formation of an Australian Design Ethos', *Landscape Review*, vol. 3, March 1997, p. 17.

18 David Bick with Phyllis Murphy and John Patrick, 'Shire of Kyneton Conservation (Heritage) Study', 1990, p. 267.

19 George Tibbits, 'The Old Arts Building, University of Melbourne: History and Conservation Guidelines', University of Melbourne, Parkville, October 1995, pp. 35–7.

20 Caitlin Stone, 'Quarries and Brickmaking', in eMelbourne, 2008, https://www.emelbourne.net.au/biogs/EM01213b.htm (accessed 20 October 2023). See also Laura Harper and Virginia Mannering, 'Urban Fringe Claypits: Effects of Claypit Sites on Urban Form in Melbourne', *Proceedings of the 14th Australasian Urban History Planning History Conference*, Australasian Urban History Planning History Group and Centre for Urban Research, RMIT, Melbourne, 2018, pp. 185–96.

21 'Memorial for New Building', *Age*, 23 November 1961, p. 1. The significance of the garden at the Redmond Barry Building is noted in Andrew Saniga, *Making Landscape Architecture in Australia*, NewSouth Publishing, Sydney, 2012, pp. 156–8.

22 Ancher, Mortlock, Murray & Woolley Pty Ltd, *University of Melbourne Master Plan Report 1970*, University of Melbourne, Parkville, 1971.

23 Philip Goad and George Tibbits, *Architecture on Campus: A Guide to the University of Melbourne and Its Colleges*, Melbourne University Press, Carlton, 2003, pp. 83–5, 88.

24 Ancher, Mortlock, Murray & Woolley Pty Ltd, *University of Melbourne Landscape Elements Report*, University of Melbourne, Parkville, 1974.

25 RD Marginson, MR Pawsey, Bryce Mortlock and TC Chambers, 'The Landscape of the University of Melbourne', *Landscape Australia*, vol. 80, no. 3, August 1980, pp. 180–92; RD Marginson, MR Pawsey, Bryce Mortlock and TC Chambers, 'Brick Paving at the Melbourne University', *Landscape Australia*, vol. 80, no. 4, November 1980, pp. 307–11.

A Computer Server and Indigenous Reconciliation

RICHARD GILLESPIE

COMMENCING IN THE early 1980s, staff sought unique names for the Department of Computer Science's main computers. University computer science departments were starting to build early network connections for the exchange of files and emails, within Australia and progressively with the United States and Europe, using existing telephone lines and undersea cables. The link between these networks was not straightforward. It required an intimate knowledge of which servers in which universities or agencies were acting as nodes of the network, and a clear picture of the paths that files and emails would need to take to reach the desired recipient. This in turn required finding unique and distinctive names for computer servers to reduce the chances of files being routed to the wrong destination.

Staff decided to select a series of Aboriginal names for the computer servers, starting with 'mu' to denote 'Melbourne University' (mulga, *murdu*, *mullian* and so on).[1] A visit to the University library revealed a substantial list of potential names in AW Reed's *Aboriginal Words of Australia*. At the time there was no consultation with Aboriginal communities regarding this cultural appropriation.

The word *munnari*, which means 'sleepy lizard' in the Ngarrindjeri language of South Australia, was applied to the largest computer in Computer Science, the VAX 11/780. It has become a legendary name in Australian internet history. Australia's connection to the internet was achieved on 24 June 1989 through a permanent satellite link connecting Munnari to a computer at the University of Hawaii and hence to emerging academic computer networks in the United States. This was the birth of the internet in Australia, and all internet traffic would subsequently be directed through Munnari. The network would evolve into the Australian Academic

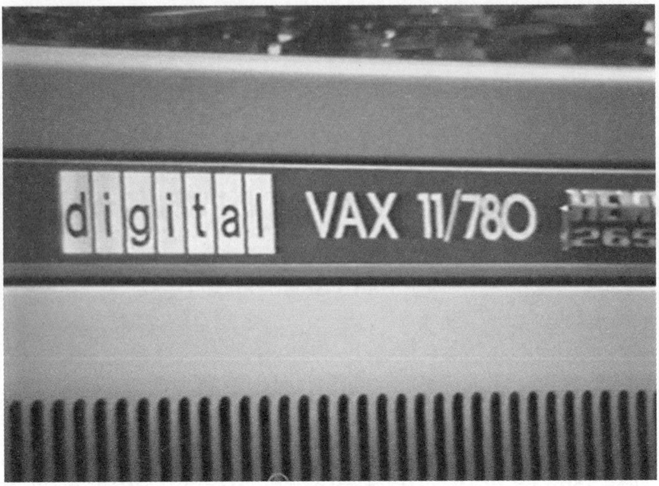

The legendary VAX 11/780 computer known as 'Munnari'.

and Research Network in 1990. Given its historical significance, Munnari continued to be used for subsequent servers.

In 2020 contact was made with the Ngarrindjeri community explaining the unauthorised past use of *munnari* and asking for permission to continue using the name, given its significance to the University and the internet in Australia. The Miwi-inyeri Pelepi-ambi Aboriginal Corporation (MIPAAC), which deals with language matters in regards to the Ngarrindjeri community, has since endorsed the use of *munnari* for a new computer server. They are pleased to have this historical association with the internet in Australia. MIPAAC has also approved use of the name for a multifunction space at Melbourne Connect, using the correct orthography *manhari* or its dialect variation *mandhari*.

Addressing past wrongs can enable the strengthening of connections now.

Notes

1 These spellings taken from AW Reed, *Aboriginal Words of Australia*, Reed, Sydney, 1965.

Billibellary's Walk

Unveiling Aboriginal Meaning of Place at a Sandstone University

SHAWANA ANDREWS

> 'Human beings—along with other entities on earth—are ineluctably place-bound. More even than earthlings, we are placelings, and our very perceptual apparatus, our sensing body, reflects the kinds of places we inhabit.'
>
> Edward S Casey, 1996[1]

ENCOUNTERS OF PLACE are complex, compellingly visceral and layered. Experience, perception and relational embodiment are the scaffolds of place that set it apart from notions of space.[2] 'Places gather things in their midst ... experiences and histories ... languages and thoughts.'[3] They also gather memories and are vessels for knowledge-keeping. Such gatherings rest on an experience of place, of being 'in place', that enables corporeal perception. Aboriginal practices of engaging place over millennia challenge many Western thinkers' assumptions about the human experience of space and time. The Western preoccupation with geographical space and Aboriginal regard for the constitution of place is the point of tension that sits at the heart of Billibellary's Walk.

The development of settler spaces relied on the removal and erasure of Aboriginal peoples in order to take land. This taking and use of land by settlers was presumed to be in perpetuity and so remains a contemporary issue. Australia's sandstone universities, of which the University of Melbourne is one, were established using lands procured in this way, facilitating the dispossession of Aboriginal peoples.[4] Bound by higher education's colonial legacies, universities are highly spatialised institutions with a carefully constructed habitus that draws heavily on settler cultural and social capital to the exclusion of Aboriginal people.

The University of Melbourne's Parkville campus is a site where notions of Aboriginal people have long been constructed in the tradition of erasure. Many academic practices and ideas, including the collection of Aboriginal remains, the study of eugenics and the promotion of social theories of natural selection, compelled the colonial narrative. Specimens for study and the production of Aboriginal people as 'objects of knowledge' purposefully sustained the pathologisation of a dying race.[5] The colonial construction of space by controlling Aboriginal 'presence' within the walls of the academy ignored the profound meaning of place held by the very lands on which the campus sits.

The Project

In 2011, a project team at the Onemda Koori Health Research Unit in the School of Population Health, at the Faculty of Medicine, Dentistry and Health Sciences, came together to consider how to engage Aboriginal place and its meaning at the Parkville campus. Drawing on Aboriginal understandings of place that consider lived experience, perception and relationality, the team wanted to challenge the colonial storying of the physical spaces that constitute the campus. The project was not intended to produce an Aboriginal history of the University, but rather a pedagogical opportunity to enable a sensory encounter with the land beyond the structural entity. As a result, Billibellary's Walk was created. In this chapter I will reflect on the process of unveiling what was discovered during the development of the walk, and the rich opportunities for learning that are revealed when Aboriginal experiences and pedagogies are brought to the fore.

Funding was secured with a Learning and Teaching Initiative Grant through the Office of the Provost to research and create an experiential, multidisciplinary teaching tool that focused on Aboriginal place. It was to be a cultural walk around the Parkville campus, with a narrative that centred Aboriginal people and voices, and drew on Aboriginal pedagogical principles.

Working on the lands of the Kulin nation, the team sought advice from the Wurundjeri Tribe Land and Compensation Cultural Heritage Council, which became a partner in the project and supported engagement with Wurundjeri Elders. A project working group was also established that included representatives of the Melbourne Medical School, Melbourne Graduate School of Education and Murrup Barak Melbourne Institute for Indigenous Development. A part-time project officer was employed and ethics approval was granted.[6] The project used four methods of data collection: historical mapping of Melbourne (the wider area known as Narrm); a literature and archival review (which included historical records, journals, paintings, photos and drawings); Elders' counsel and stories; and relational engagement with the campus. Many consultations were also undertaken throughout the project with historians, architects, horticulturists, grounds teams, campus infrastructure and construction planning teams, librarians and the Wurundjeri community. These were collectively used to generate a connection with Aboriginal place on the campus, and to understand it through one's own experience, perception and relational embodiment.

Aboriginal Land, Place and Pedagogy

The way Indigenous content is structured within curricula determines how students perceive it.[7] The use of place-based education and experiential learning in higher-education settings is not new—such pedagogy is powerful and effective. There is, however, little published literature that interrogates the nature of place as pedagogy when it is determined by the Aboriginal experience.[8] Further, land-based education offers the distinct opportunity to critically analyse and interrogate one's position in relation to colonialism and its ongoing impacts.[9] Offering a pedagogy that supports land-based education in the context of place, informed by Aboriginal knowledge, creates an opportunity for decolonised transformative learning. Understanding the nuances of the Parkville campus with respect to the layering of Wurundjeri Country, Aboriginal place and land, and colonial place and space, among others, is important.

The University has long preserved its stronghold on Parkville with land tenure, branding and spatial presence, so the project necessarily required a relational re-negotiation of the area to engage with the layers of place, distinct from space. The methods used in the project were grounded in Aboriginal methodologies and ethical practices of inquiry, and were undertaken with the guidance of the Wurundjeri Council and the wise counsel of a number of Wurundjeri Woi Wurrung Elders. The inquiry methods used in the project sought to develop a multilayered narrative of the environment and physical surroundings with the depth of Aboriginal storying of place.

Historical maps of Melbourne, the University and its surroundings were sourced through the University library and the State Library Victoria. These showed the changing landscape of Narrm with the rapid development of Melbourne town over a period of twenty years from 1835 and the establishment of the University in 1853. The maps also showed the woodland areas of river red gum and yellow box and, to the east, a forest of black she-oak. The area's significant waterways and wetlands could also be identified, including some that no longer exist or are no longer evident, such as Townend Creek, also known as Bouverie Creek. The impact of Melbourne's development could also be identified on some waterways, such as the significantly changed course of the Birrarung (the Yarra River).

The literature and archival review helped to build a basic narrative for the walk. Although many of the sources, such as the settler journal entries and early paintings, were cast through a colonial lens, the project team was able to establish a general understanding of the landscape and the nature of the impact Melbourne's development had on Aboriginal presence on and utility of the land. Importantly, the erasure of Aboriginal people was evident throughout much of the reviewed sources, and Aboriginal women in particular were patently unseen and unheard in most of the original archival material.

The Elders' counsel and stories were important methods for ensuring Wurundjeri voices were central to the stories shared through the walk. These were facilitated through the Wurundjeri Woi Wurrung Cultural Heritage Aboriginal Corporation, with both collective and individual opportunities for Elders to work with the project team to create, edit and sign off on the narrative for the walk. Building on (and critically reviewing) the scaffolding offered through the literature and archival review, the engagement with Elders provided essence and meaning to the narrative of place that was developing. This process also gave depth to the understanding of place through intergenerational lived experience and perception, and privileged Aboriginal storytelling and people in the pedagogy that would underlie the walk.

Relational engagement with the campus required the project team to regularly walk through the University across the life of the project. Connecting with the campus in person enabled the team to identify specific sites that would facilitate and anchor particular themes of the narrative. In this way, place and space were distinguished but could also be drawn together depending on the theme. The consistent mindful examination of the campus over time enabled a re-negotiation of the campus that brought new meaning for the project team, which could be captured in the walk as a resource. Themes of landscape, for example, were brought to life through the identification of sites that supported stories about water, travel, trees and land. Animals, such as eels, also featured heavily in the narrative, as they were found to be easily anchored to sites around the campus, building the meaning of place. In addition, sensory perception, including Narrm botanical seasonal cycles, time, being, voice and relationship with Country, offered a significant opportunity for linkages between the narrative and being present on Country, establishing real-time connection.[10]

The data-collection methods aimed to capture the complexities of the relationship between environment and people, and offer a rich, land-based pedagogical experience that presupposed the land as unceded Aboriginal lands. Aboriginal people have, for generations, acquired deep knowledge of and connectedness with Country, imbuing it with memory and cultural value. The creation of a cultural walk around the Parkville campus of the University sought to share a little of this with students, staff and visitors, adding value to a collective engagement with the area beyond it being a colonial higher-education site.

Unveiling Billibellary's Country

The stories and themes that were garnered through the project together revealed a continuous and living Aboriginal perception and experience of place around the University's Parkville campus. All residing in place, they referenced Kulin nation kinship; Wurundjeri diplomacy, intellect and foresight; ancient cultural practices; and a landscape and natural world that shapeshifted in defiance of the colonial overlay. The narrative that ensued was overwhelmingly grounded in Aboriginal self-determination, fortitude and resistance, and the themes identified were considered by the Elders as important to teaching and learning.

The themes supported a narrative that would necessarily slip between present and past, allowing participants to experience the place on which they stood, to imagine what was and to consider the relationship/space between the two. Such temporal linkage and fluidity within the narrative served to create important teaching moments using Aboriginal pedagogical storytelling techniques. Each theme was anchored to a specific site across the campus to form a journey, which was mapped out for participant navigation. The walk was designed as a guided tour, with a full narrative to be delivered at the prescribed stops along with questions to prompt participant responses.

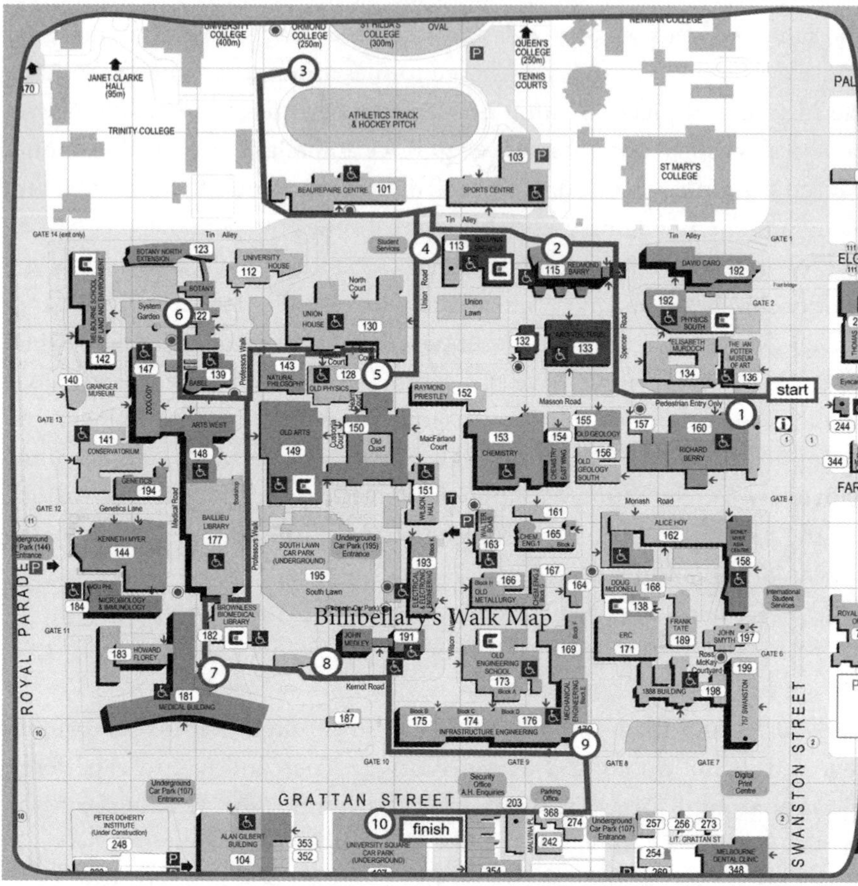

Stop	Theme	Location
1	Billibellary's Country	University entrance, corner of Masson and Swanston streets
2	Sustainable industry, farming and land management	Redmond Barry Building courtyard
3	Tools of the trade	Four river red gums around the oval
4	Aboriginal knowledge	Baldwin Spencer Building (113)
5	Self-determination and community control	Murrup Barak Melbourne Institute for Indigenous Development
6	Place	The System Garden
7	A fight for identity	Medical Building (181), rear entrance
8	Belonging to Country	Manna gum trees alongside the vice-chancellor's residence
9	A cultural landscape not lost	Corner of Grattan and Bouverie streets (University side of Grattan Street)
10	Billibellary's Country	University Square

Billibellary's Walk Map, 2011, https://murrupbarak.unimelb.edu.au/home/about/billibellarys-walk

Layers of Place

As the project developed, it was evident that the themes each contributed to an overall narrative but did not always distinctly connect with one another. To develop continuity of story and pedagogical scaffolding throughout the walk, a number of sub-themes, or layers of place, were woven through the narrative. These included Aboriginal identities and being; seasons; landscapes and places; animals; water; plants and trees; time; and sensory perception. They became the essence of the walk, unveiling a different history and sense of being, and setting participants on a path to transformative learning. The following illustrate this with excerpts from the narrative.[11]

Aboriginal Identities and Being

Centring Aboriginal identities in the narrative purposefully challenged traditions of erasure and politics of naming.[12] Naming and positioning Wurundjeri Woi Wurrung Aboriginal leaders and knowledge-holders sought to reinstate their roles as significant figures in the place of Narrm. This is often very new material to students and staff alike.

> Born in 1799, Billibellary is the Ngurungaeta, or clan head, of the Wurundjeri Willam (a distinct patrilineal group within the Wurundjeri), whose diplomacy, intellect, courtesy and skills in negotiation would, in time to come, be put to the test ...
>
> William Barak, traditionally known as Beruk Barak, was taught the ways of traditional practice by his Uncle Billibellary and, in a similar style to his Elder, provided leadership for his people with a foresight that challenged the colonial intentions.
>
> In 1863 ... William Barak and his cousin, Simon Wonga (Billibellary's son), among others, recognised the inevitabilities that lay ahead. In response they initiated and negotiated the political arena to establish Coranderrk, a self-sufficient Aboriginal farm near Healesville that soon became a thriving community and a very successful enterprise selling wheat, hops and vegetables.[13]

Seasons

The walk invites participants to move through Billibellary's land and to feel, know and imagine Melbourne's seasons, which are subtly reconstructed as the context for understanding place and belonging. In this sense the walk aims to recognise and share the idea that the land is alive.[14] It uses Gott's (undated) six botanical seasons to differentiate times of the year and to note the rhythm of the natural seasonal cycles that governed the lifestyle patterns of the people.[15]

> If it's late summer (February–March) you might smell the smoke from ancient fire burning practices, sanctioned by Elders, as it hangs in the air. The Wurundjeri people used fire to manage the land and to promote new growth, which would subsequently attract animals, and provide the right conditions for particular tuberous plants to grow, such as Myrnong or yam daisy.
>
> As the seasons change so too does Billibellary's expectation of his environment ... as late summer moves into early winter (April–May) the Wurundjeri people prepare to move to higher ground for shelter. Bunjil, the eagle ancestral creator spirit, is building his nest and the echidna prepares to go into torpor.
>
> If it's deep winter (June–July) as you stand here in 1830 the cold wind bites at you so you might pull your possum skin cloak around your shoulders ... the Wurundjeri Willam move to higher ground, near the Dandenongs, for shelter.
>
> In early spring (mid July–August) the people would have slowly returned from higher ground as the temperatures rose.
>
> Imagine it is true spring (September–October) ... you may see kangaroos whose young are graduating from the pouch or see migrating birds returning from the north.
>
> From here you could look out across the plains of the grassy woodland and if it is high summer (November–January) you might see animals congregating at dependable water sources as the land dries in the heat. Or as you walk you might hear the chatter of women digging for the roots of small tuberous plants which have died back but which are also at their best at this time of the year.[16]

Landscapes and Places

The complexities of the relationship between landscape and people are what elevate mere space to place.[17] Wurundjeri Woi Wurrung people have acquired deep knowledge of and connectedness with their extensive territory through songlines, trade routes, ceremony and seasonal cycles. Living according to the seasons, the stars and landscape, and imbuing it with memory, history and cultural value, has created a continuum that nourishes generation after generation.

The walk references a number of important yet subtle landscape features, both on campus and elsewhere, which develop a sense of continuity of connection to place throughout the narrative.

> As you walk in Billibellary's time you would find yourself in a grassy woodland dominated by river red gum and yellow box and surrounded to the east by a forest of black she-oak.
>
> You might join Billibellary, and his people, as they pass through Parkville; possibly travelling from Mt William greenstone quarry (near Lancefield) to Bolin Bolin Billabong (near Bulleen) where they will celebrate, feast, trade and share.
>
> Axes ... were quarried from Mt William, Wil-im-ee Moor-ring, a greenstone quarry near Lancefield in central Victoria (approx. 70km from Parkville) that is now heritage listed. As the last traditional custodian of the quarry, Billibellary played a central role in the management and maintenance of the quarry with many groups travelling great distances to meet with him and negotiate the exchange of items for greenstone. Mt William quarry and the greenstone axes sourced from it, however, are said to have had a far greater importance than just the economic benefits of trade. In distinct distribution patterns, Mt William greenstone axes have been found up to 1000km from the quarry and are thought to have been prized for their cosmological and ceremonial symbolism in Kulin mythology.
>
> Looking around, you may not see any evidence of a landscape that once supported the waterways, creeks, rivers and wetlands of the area. But observe the natural incline of Grattan Street as it meets Bouverie Street, down which you can see the steady slope towards Victoria Street. Take yourself back to 1830 once again—to Billibellary's time—and here you would have been standing on the bank of the creek, a tributary of the Birrarung.
>
> From this vantage point, in 1830, Batman's Hill can be seen close to the banks of the Birrarung ... covered in round-headed she-oaks.[18]

Animals

Animals were referenced throughout the narrative to give depth to the notion of place as symbols of sustainability, health, spirituality and cultural significance. Much more than a source of food, animals held important roles in the cycle of seasons and how Aboriginal people understood their existence.

> You might see many birds, such as the magpie or laughing kookaburra. Looking around through the woodland, made accessible by productive

> land management, you may come across large flocks of emus, mobs of kangaroo, echidnas and a large range of other animals.
>
> As the seasons change ... Bunjil, the eagle ancestral creator spirit, is building his nest and the echidna prepares to go into torpor.
>
> Now imagine it is true spring (September–October) and looking down the valley you would see flowers—possibly orchids, wattle and murnong. You may see kangaroos whose young are graduating from the pouch or see migrating birds returning from the north.
>
> Distracted by a splash, you peer into the clear water expecting to see Dulaiwurrung (platypus) but instead you see short-finned eel that have migrated upstream to fresh-water after their juvenile years in salt-water.
>
> As a staple part of the diet ... eel was speared or trapped using sophisticated industrial methods. Indeed, during the summer months the Kulin clans would gather at larger wetlands areas, such as Bolin Bolin Billabong on the Birrarung near Bulleen, and eels would be caught in abundance.
>
> Today, the eels continue to migrate. They travel along the Bouverie creek, beneath the roads, pavement and buildings, using the drainpipes and so maintain their ancient migratory patterns of which Billibellary and his people had intimate knowledge.[19]

Water

The eel story is also one of water. References to water throughout the narrative connect Country, people, animals and time. Waterways such as the Birrarung (the Yarra River), the seasonal creek that flowed through what is now the University's Parkville campus, and the extensive wetlands, streams and billabongs across Narrm defined the landscape and the movement of people and animals across it. They also helped to conceptualise change through time.

> The Townend creek originated from somewhere near the current Melbourne Cemetery; it flowed through the University site and down a shallow valley, along which Bouverie Street is now situated. Continuing south, the meandering creek probably flowed into the shallow creek valley that was to become Elizabeth Street and then on into the Birrarung.[20]

Plants and Trees

Plants and trees, specific to Narrm and Wurundjeri land and identity, were identified throughout the development of the narrative. Some were then mapped across the campus using grounds staff expertise as well as the *Significant Tree Study Review—Parkville Campus* to form specific stops on the walk, while others were simply integrated throughout the narrative.[21] They all served to build an understanding of place that demonstrated the integral role of landscape and the natural world to Aboriginal identity.

> [T]he Wurundjeri people would ... have used this area as a central passage—hunting on the grassy plains and in the surrounding she-oak forest and exploiting the various water sources.
>
> As a principal part of the diet, Myrnong was intensely harvested and used as both a root vegetable and herb. This plant-based diet, supplemented with meat and fish, created a low fat and fibre, nutrient and mineral-rich diet. Once European settlers arrived, the heavy stock grazing marked the rapid decline of the Myrnong, among others, which hinted at the health ramifications that were to come.
>
> Plants were not only used for food but provided important medicines, fibres for industry and utensils. The karawun (Lomandra), for example, was used to weave baskets, bags, mats and, most significantly, the funnel-shaped arrabines, or eel traps, extensively used to farm eels.
>
> Looking across you will see four river red gums ... the Wurundjeri people honour them as an essential source of shelter, bark for canoes, tools such as spears and shields, instruments such as music sticks and clapping boomerangs used in ceremony, and sap used to shrink and seal burns.
>
> The white-trunked trees you see here are wurun, manna gums, within which is found Djeri, a grub. It is from these that the Wurundjeri people take their name, symbolising the close interrelationship with the cultural landscape that Billibellary's people have.
>
> If you are unwell, you could gather the long thin leaves of the wurun and lay them over a fire; the smoke will ease your congestion and fever.
>
> Winter is ... the season of growth for many Indigenous plants ... looking down the valley you would see flowers—possibly orchids, wattle and murnong.[22]

Time

Lived time, the temporal structure of the world and our being in it, is held through its intimate connections with place, relationships and our embodied being.[23] Linear time as well as subjective 'felt' time, which is 'internally determined, socially and culturally mediated, experiential, and affected by fleeting perceptions, emotions, and cognitions',[24] is offered as a pedagogical scaffold across the narrative.

> One of seven clans of the Kulin Nation, the Wurundjeri people of the Woiwurrung language group walked the grounds, upon which the University now stands, for more than 40 000 years.
>
> Imagine the time is 1830 and the place is Wurundjeri Country, Billibellary's Country ... When Europeans arrived on the banks of the Birrarung (the Yarra River) in 1835, Billibellary, along with Derrimut, head man of one of the Bunurong clans, would employ a sophisticated method of conciliation to protect their people, their role as custodians of the land and their place. In just 20 years the rapid development of what was to become Melbourne destroyed the ancient natural landscape and decimated the Aboriginal population ...
>
> Predating the University and possibly Melbourne's settlement, these trees [river red gums] speak of the ancestors all around this land of Billibellary.
>
> Through [William Barak's] work to establish Coranderrk, and by challenging the Victorian Government for it to remain Aboriginal community-controlled in 1881, William Barak demonstrated the self-determination and fighting spirit of a true visionary.
>
> [These] are the sounds of an ancient oral tradition filled with history, memory, joy and sorrow ... By the 1850s Wurundjeri people were scarce around the University area, with references made to the occasional Koori fires burning in what we know as Royal Park ... They will travel age-old trade routes and pathways along river systems and valleys that were created by ancestral beings.
>
> And so the cycle of seasons is complete and Billibellary's people continue their lives set within a cultural landscape that holds their song and memory and which will become, in less than five years, the context within which they will fight for their lives. In 1835 Billibellary, Derrimut and others will become signatories to John Batman's ill-conceived and fraudulent treaty. William Barak will also witness this as a young boy. Upon Billibellary's death in 1846, William Barak and Simon Wonga, the last of the traditional Ngurungaetas, led their people with the dignity, confidence and distinction that only 40 000 years of history could foster.[25]

Sensory Perception

Participants are asked to be in the moment while on the walk, to 'feel' and 'know' the place that is Wurundjeri Woi Wurrung Country as they stand on the Parkville campus. A concerted effort was made by the project team not to romanticise the narrative, but rather bring place 'alive' for participants. This was done with reference to live sensory experiences such as real-time weather (rain, sunshine, wind and so on) and connecting these with the narrative at the appropriate stop (easily done by a guide), or through descriptive prose that enables participants to imagine the environment they were standing in.

> Lying within the University of Melbourne's built environment are the whispers and memories of the Wurundjeri people.
>
> ... you might smell the smoke from ancient fire burning practices.
>
> Sit on the cool grass and listen to the voices you can hear, now imagine they are speaking Woiwurrung, language of the Wurundjeri people. Hear them shout in excitement after a successful hunt, sing as they gather the yam daisy, laugh as they play and joke or whisper as child learns from Elder.
>
> ... the cold wind bites ... [i]f you are unwell you could gather the long thin leaves of the wurun and lay them over a fire; the smoke will ease your congestion and fever.
>
> Your [possum skin] cloak, and the designs on its skin, represents the reciprocal relationship and engagement with Country and imbues the wearer with Wurundjeri identity.
>
> Let the built environment around you fall away and imagine yourself there, standing by the creek, your bare feet feeling the cool ground, the smell and sounds of the bush permeating your senses.[26]

Billibellary's Walk: Unveiling Place, Revealing Story

The contexts of place and placemaking are important as they determine how communities will engage with a location and each other.[27] Multilayered meaning and different understandings of place influence the relationships held with it and within it. These are shaped by cultural, gendered and historical perception and experience.[28] Such relationships, and the associated perception and experience, are how places are 'practised'.

As a teaching tool, Billibellary's Walk aims to build on the practice of place and, through a number of important pedagogical functions, support the truth-telling of the narrative. Storytelling as a distinct Aboriginal way of knowing was used as the primary mode of teaching. This included metaphor; visual and symbolic learning; engagement of the senses; and concrete and abstract imagery as Aboriginal pedagogical practices.[29] These became powerful mechanisms with which to 'hold' participants when discussing difficult and demanding concepts, and to support safety and learning.[30]

Positioning Billibellary as the central figure in the experience and perception of place for participants of the walk challenged the colonial control of the landscape and the people within it. One of the important ways in which Australia's landscape was brought under colonial control was through placenaming.[31] Naming Billibellary and the places he belonged to drew on the symbolism of the time at which Narrm was settled. In 1835 Billibellary was thirty-four years old and a *ngurungaeta*. His leadership, preparedness for negotiation and vision for the future illustrate the important learnings bound within the walk itself. The detail of each stop offers the opportunity to build on the symbolism or metaphor of factual narrative with an emphasis on embodied learning as a process of understanding, rather than an acquisition of skills.[32]

The eel story, for example, is more than one about a staple food of the Kulin nation. It is a water story, a connecting story, and one that tells a tale of resistance and belonging. Short-finned eels, known for their extensive upstream and downstream migrations, continue to travel 'upstream' from Birrarung through the city's drainpipe and stormwater systems, where once there were streams and creeks. Finding their way along the pipes, they eventually come out into a small pond in one of the University's courtyards. The gardeners then transfer them to the Botanic Gardens, the ponds of which have established eel populations. While the significance of the summer eeling season for the Kulin nation around the Melbourne area is well known, the discovery of the eels travelling up the pipes has been an important one.[33] It has helped to story the idea of place in our teaching. The eels' defiance of the urban landscape in their attempts to find their contemporary water path offers a metaphor for survival.

In a similar way, the water story that unveils Narrm as a thriving wetland, and reveals ancient migratory patterns of eels and birds that connect lands across the Pacific Ocean, offers an opportunity for teachings about the built environment and its interface with the natural world. The possum-skin cloaking story is one of utility, but it also holds lessons of kinship, belonging and love. And the story of Coranderrk presents the existential competence of Aboriginal humanity. The stories shared in the narrative serve as critical teaching moments that have multiple lessons to offer, generating interest in and connection to place.

Broadening the Scope

The project team developed Billibellary's Walk as an interdisciplinary teaching resource available across the University. Since its development in 2012, the walk has been embedded within curricula in many disciplines across the University and is popular as a staff professional development activity. But while its success is pleasing, it proved difficult to sustain as a guided tour. In 2014, a second Learning and Teaching Initiative Grant was secured to develop a mobile phone application (or app) for the walk. This involved Wurundjeri Woi Wurrung Elders and Aboriginal academics recording the narrative and building an in-app geospatial navigation mechanism to enable Billibellary's Walk to be self-guided.

The self-guiding capacity that the app provides has enabled teaching staff to integrate the walk into their curricula and cater for large student cohorts in creative ways. The engagement of Billibellary's Walk has predominantly been as a scaffold to further teaching, such as in the Ways of Knowing in Healthcare interprofessional signature program that is delivered in the Faculty of Medicine, Dentistry and Health Sciences as an early-in-program, early-in-semester intensive. Delivered to approximately 1400 first-year graduate students across ten disciplines, this approach provides formative learning that can then be built upon in subsequent discipline-specific course material.

There are also notable examples of how the walk is used to structure other types of learning. In the School of Psychological Sciences, the walk has been used as the centrepiece for teaching students about learning and memory, identifying Aboriginal methods of storying as a powerful mnemonic structure that articulates intimately with place. Another is the use of the walk's references to traditional plants, such as the murnong daisy, to develop science-based threads across course curricula as a way of embedding Indigenous knowledge.

In 2016 the Billibellary's Walk project team worked with the University's infrastructure planning team to design and implement signage for the walk. This was erected in December that year. The walk was finally visible, with posts indicating each stop's theme and identifying the walk around the campus. These have further enhanced the utility and reach of the walk as both a teaching and learning resource and a professional development tool.

Conclusion

As a resource of the University, Billibellary's Walk supports both critical self-reflection and an active engagement with local Aboriginal history and community experience of place. It has been integral to interprofessional teaching and learning opportunities across the University and has built an important foundation for Aboriginal pedagogical practice. Through a process of unveiling, Billibellary's Walk has challenged students and staff alike to engage in Aboriginal pedagogical practices and understand the land on which the campus sits, the Aboriginal experience of it and their own relative position.

Notes

1 Edward S Casey, 'How to Get from Space to Place in a Fairly Short Stretch of Time: Phenomenological Prolegomena', in Keith H Basso and Steven Feld (eds), *Senses of Place*, School of American Research Press, Santa Fe, New Mexico, 1996, p. 19.

2 David Seamon, 'Merleau-Ponty, Lived Body, and Place: Toward a Phenomenology of Human Situatedness', in Thomas Hünefeldt and Annika Schlitte (eds), *Situatedness and Place*, Springer, Cham, Switzerland, 2018, pp. 41–66.

3 Casey, 'How to Get from Space to Place', p. 24.

4 Caitlin Harvey, 'How Commonwealth Universities Profited from Indigenous Dispossession through Land Grants', *The Conversation*, 6 July 2022, https://theconversation.com/how-commonwealth-universities-profited-from-indigenous-dispossession-through-land-grants-185010 (accessed 23 October 2023).

5 Gayatri Chakravorty Spivak, *A Critique of Postcolonial Reason: Toward a History of the Vanishing Present*, Harvard University Press, Cambridge, 1999.

6 Project ID 1137190.1.

7 Bronwyn L Fredericks, 'The Need to Extend beyond the Knowledge Gained in Cross-Cultural Awareness Training', *The Australian Journal of Indigenous Education*, vol. 37, 2008, pp. 81–9; Martin Nakata et al., 'Decolonial Goals and Pedagogies for Indigenous Studies', *Decolonization: Indigeneity, Education & Society*, vol. 1, no. 1, 2012, pp. 120–40.

8 Eve Tuck and Marcia McKenzie, *Place in Research: Theory, Methodology, and Methods*, Routledge, New York, 2015.

9 Dolores Calderon, 'Speaking Back to Manifest Destinies: A Land Education-Based Approach to Critical Curriculum Inquiry', *Environmental Education Research*, vol. 20, no. 1, 2014, pp. 24–36.

10 Beth Gott, 'Seasonal Calendars for the Melbourne Area', Herring Island, https://www.herringisland.org/seasons1.htm (accessed 23 October 2023).

11 Shawana Andrews and Ngarra Murray, 'Billibellary's Walk', Murrup Barak, https://murrupbarak.unimelb.edu.au/home/about/billibellarys-walk (accessed 23 October 2023).

12 Calderon, 'Speaking Back', pp. 24–66.

13 Andrews and Murray, 'Billibellary's Walk'.

14 Hilary Whitehouse et al., 'Sea Country: Navigating Indigenous and Colonial Ontologies in Australian Environmental Education', *Environmental Education Research*, vol. 20, no. 1, 2014, pp. 56–69.

15 Gott, 'Seasonal Calendars for the Melbourne Area'.

16 Andrews and Murray, 'Billibellary's Walk'.

17 Gary Presland, 'A Vision of Melbourne's Past', *Traffic*, no. 5, July 2004, pp. 113–28.

18 Andrews and Murray, 'Billibellary's Walk'.

19 Ibid.

20 Ibid.

21 John Patrick Pty Ltd, *Significant Tree Study Review—Parkville Campus*, University of Melbourne Heritage Documentation Part D, University of Melbourne, Parkville, 2010.

22 Andrews and Murray, 'Billibellary's Walk'.

23 Max Van Manen, *Researching Lived Experience: Human Science for an Action Sensitive Pedagogy*, 2nd edn, Routledge, New York, 2016.

24 Andrew R Hatala et al., '"I Have Strong Hopes for the Future": Time Orientations and Resilience among Canadian Indigenous Youth', *Qualitative Health Research*, vol. 27, no. 9, 2017, p. 1330.

25 Andrews and Murray, 'Billibellary's Walk'.

26 Ibid.

27 Jonathan Kingsley et al., 'Developing a Framework Identifying the Outcomes, Principles and Enablers of "Gathering Places": Perspectives from Aboriginal People in Victoria, Australia', *Social Science & Medicine*, vol. 283, 2021, p. 114217.

28 Kingsley et al., 'Developing a Framework Identifying the Outcomes'; Greg Downey, 'Seeing with a "Sideways Glance": Visuomotor "Knowing" and the Plasticity of Perception', in Mark Harris (ed.), *Ways of Knowing: New Approaches in the Anthropology of Experience and Learning*, Berghahn Books, New York, 2007, pp. 222–41.

29 Tyson Yunkaporta, Aboriginal Pedagogies at the Cultural Interface, unpublished doctoral dissertation, James Cook University, 2009; Yangarriny Bindarriy and Warlkuni Mingalpa, 'Obstacles to Aboriginal Pedagogy', in Blekbala Wei et al. (eds), *Aboriginal Pedagogy: Aboriginal Teachers Speak Out*, Deakin University Press, Geelong, 1991.

30 Cheri Logan, 'Metaphor and Pedagogy in the Design Practicum', *International Journal of Technology and Design Education*, vol. 18, no. 1, 2008, pp. 1–17.

31 Laura Kostanski and Ian D Clark, 'Reviving Old Indigenous Names for New Purposes', in Harold Koch and Luise Hercus (eds), *Naming and Re-Naming the Australian Landscape*, ANU Press, Canberra, 2009, pp. 189–206.

32 Monica Dalidowicz, 'Crafting Fidelity: Pedagogical Creativity in Kathak Dance', *Journal of the Royal Anthropological Institute*, vol. 21, no. 4, 2015, pp. 838–54.

33 Wurundjeri Tribe Land and Compensation Cultural Heritage Council, 'An Aboriginal History of Yarra', *Agora*, vol. 48, no. 4, 2013, pp. 59–65.

The Water Story

Indigenous Placemaking as Reconciliation at Scale

JEFA GREENAWAY

THE NOTION THAT Indigenous engagement and placemaking are essential to design thinking is gaining greater currency in Melbourne and, indeed, across Australia. People are coming to understand why we should consider Indigenous perspectives in shaping our places and spaces. The real challenge is less a question of *why* but rather rests on *how*. How do we implement such perspectives? How do we ensure and centre Indigenous agency? How do we foreground Indigenous knowledge and connections? Here at the University of Melbourne, we're not exempt from these questions.

In recent years, such questions have been raised—and answers ventured—in various forms on the Parkville campus. In 2018 the Melbourne School of Design held a symposium entitled 'Go Back to Where You Came from: Indigenous Design—Past/Present/Future', alongside the exhibition *Blak Design Matters*, a national survey of contemporary Indigenous design. Both demonstrated an acute appetite for meaningful dialogue around how Indigenous design practitioners can begin to inform and shape the built environment. These were followed by on-campus events and exhibitions such as *Ancestral Memory* and *The Living Pavilion* (both 2019) and 2022's *Emu Sky*, all of which celebrated Indigenous knowledge of and connections to Country.

The New Student Precinct reflects the University's leadership in this area. The Precinct project embeds reconciliation at scale. It seeks to raise the bar, demonstrating how Indigenous culture can be embedded in the DNA of a project. The project has been informed by a holistic design philosophy that centres on the core tenets of people, purpose and place, which anchor the project to the site's deep history and connectedness to Kulin nation culture. The Precinct project has moved beyond simplistic quick wins or focusing on the low-hanging fruit of surface treatment or plonk art, instead engaging with and exploring ideas co-designed by Indigenous people.

These methodologies have resulted in the cultural imprimatur to amplify the opportunity, infusing the project with an overarching cultural narrative of great richness and metaphorical resonance. The compelling narrative is the revealing of the unbroken lineage of an eel migration that traverses the Parkville campus. To this very day, eels continue to travel through the piped watercourses underneath the campus, echoing the memories, stories and histories of place.

To tell this story, we began by engaging with key Indigenous stakeholders, including representatives of the Woi Wurrung and Bunurong language groups. We needed to understand their perspectives on place and listen to their oral narratives that reside *in* place. The next step was to delve into the University archives, particularly the Map Collection, and understand that the Parkville campus is an important place that retains connections through time to a pre-colonial landscape. What transpired from this research was that the story of water has always been, and continues to be, very important to this place.

At the northern end of the campus, adjacent to the University Oval, is a group of four river red gums, a species that usually grows near watercourses. These trees are believed to predate the white settlement of Melbourne, estimated to be three or four centuries old. We can also see from early maps that, in the centre of the University, there was a swampy area, as well as a waterway that traversed the site. This ephemeral creek probably originated in what is now the Melbourne General Cemetery, flowing across campus and down the course followed by Bouverie Street today. During the initial landscaping of the Parkville campus, the so-called 'Bouverie Creek' was dammed, turning the swampy area into an ornamental lake that existed for decades on what is now Union Lawn (also known as Concrete Lawn).

Annually, young *iuk* (short-finned eels) are washed by oceanic currents into estuaries across Kulin Country.[1] For millennia they would have migrated up Birrarung (the Yarra), along the Elizabeth Street tributary and finally into what settlers would later call Bouverie Creek. Wurundjeri Woi

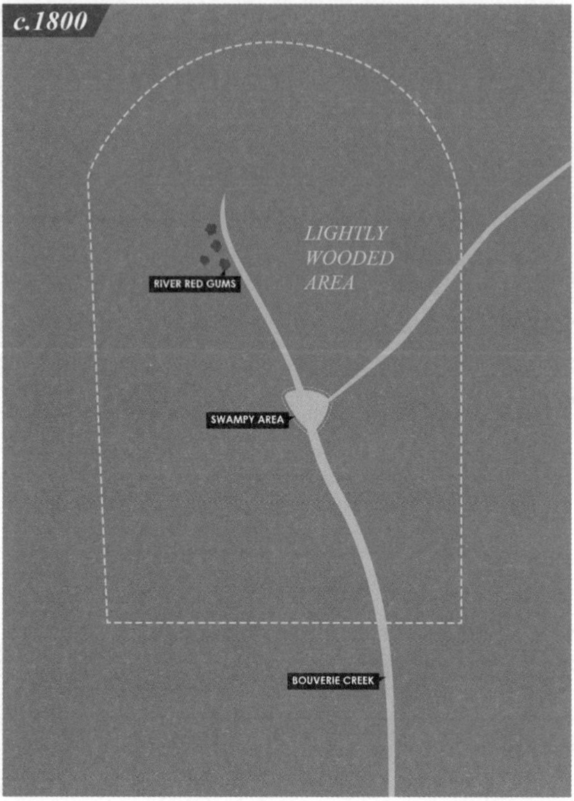

Wurrung people likely gathered up eels from the creek and wetlands on what is now the Parkville campus, using nets woven from plant fibres or spears or simply their hands. Rich in protein, fat and easy to catch, *iuk* were a cherished food source for Kulin peoples. When *iuk* reach maturity—a process which can take up to twenty years or even longer—they migrate back into Port Phillip Bay, ultimately returning to their spawning ground in the Coral Sea, thousands of kilometres away. The annual return migration, occurring in late summer, was of great significance in pre- and early colonial times: clans would meet to feast on eels and conduct business pertaining to 'justice, trade, dispute resolution, marital arrangements and firestick farming schedules'.[2] Although Bouverie Creek is long gone, we have good reason to believe that eels continue to swim through the stormwater pipes of the University—they have been spotted rearing their heads up in some of the ponds and stormwater grates that exist on campus.

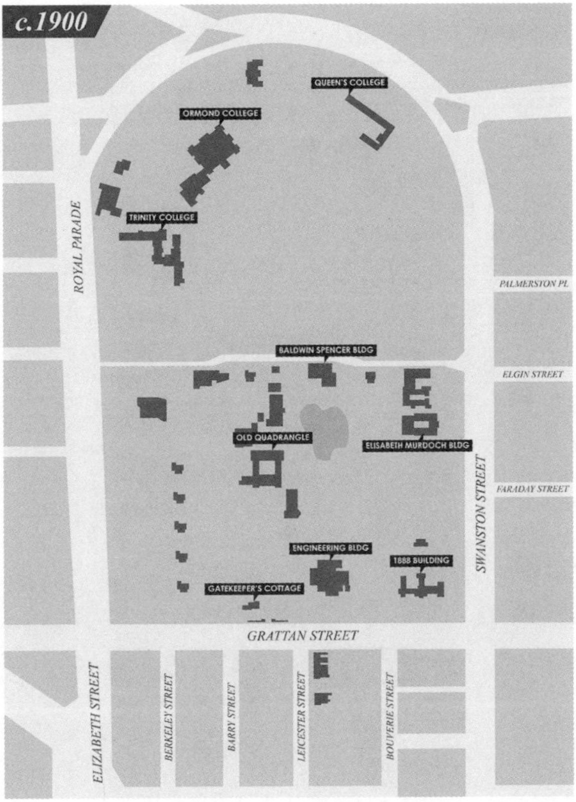

Eels are profoundly resilient animals: they are able to travel across land for short periods, climb dam walls, hibernate in cold weather and go without eating for months at a time. As their continued presence on campus shows, they are not fussy about their habitat. They have adjusted to the immense changes to Country that settler colonialism has brought about, and they continue to thrive. We can see the *iuk* as an emblem of Indigenous resilience—the ability of Indigenous cultures, despite the odds, to adapt and change, to persist and endure.

Iuk are also part of a bigger story that speaks internationally. Not only do the eels transmogrify when they move from salt water to fresh water and back again, their migration patterns also connect to global water stories. Eels were important not only to Kulin peoples but to other Aboriginal groups, particularly the Gunditjmara, who built the now-famous Budj Bim eel trap system. Water stories and water bodies connect through time and Country.

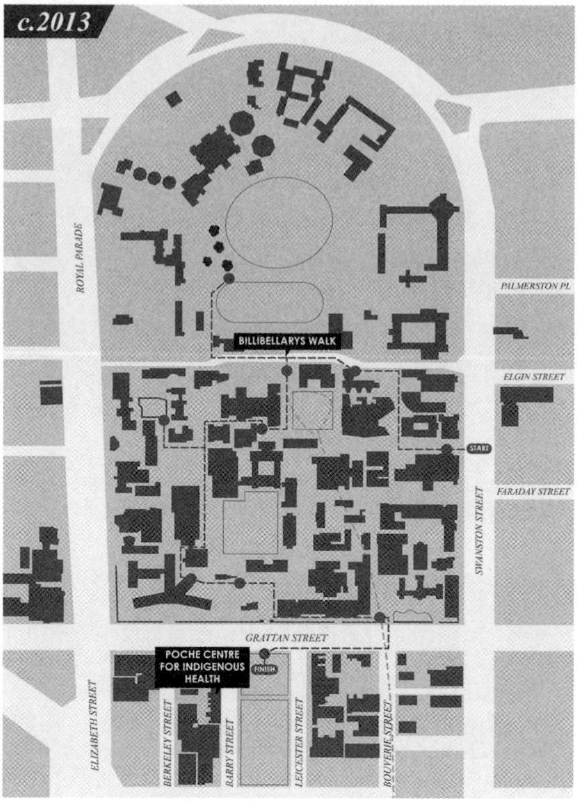

But when we look even more broadly, we start to see that the migration of the eel connects Australia to Aotearoa New Zealand and Oceania too. So when we understand that the University community is a diaspora of Indigenous and non-Indigenous people, the eel can also become an emblem of international students, of which we have a large cohort. The eel story provides an opportunity to celebrate Indigenous culture and to showcase it as part of our everyday experience; at the same time, this is a story that can resonate with anybody.

This narrative has been concealed—literally buried underground—until now. Part of the design of the New Student Precinct is to reveal a cultural narrative that speaks to watercourses in and around the Precinct and to foreground water as an important design element. This place-centred approach to reimagining Country through a water story, by actively bringing water to the surface, coupled with a distinct narrative for Murrup Barak—the Indigenous unit of the University—seeks to connect people to the deep history and antiquity of Indigenous culture, while being ever mindful of the future.

The weaving together of these stories seeks to reiterate the University's unstinting commitment to reconciliation reflected in deeds and design. This has all been supported by a carefully calibrated Indigenous engagement strategy. This strategy has been Indigenous led and supported by Greenshoot Consulting through a collective experience in culturally responsive design practice, which has privileged and foregrounded Indigenous voices, following a nuanced process of deep listening, conversation and knowledge exchange. It has also created a framework to capture the Indigenous voices of the University, including the representation of forty-five language groups from our vast island continent. Parallel to all this work has been the critical role of students in walking side by side with the design team. The outcome has been unlike most projects encountered in design practice, yet demonstrates that a community can meaningfully shape and inform the direction of even a project of vast scale.

The New Student Precinct is an exemplar project that fosters Indigenous agency, the evocative power of Indigenous design thinking, and a collaborative model that wholly normalises, embraces and celebrates a shared connection to Country. This ambitious project will create new and meaningful stories rooted in an exploration of Indigenous experience, while providing everyone with the opportunity to be enveloped by the sights, sounds and sensory echoes of place, to become a new artefact of great depth and meaning.

Notes

1 Some of the information about eels in the following paragraphs comes from the following sources: Victorian Fisheries Authority, 'Short-Finned Eel', 9 March 2021, https://vfa.vic.gov.au/education/fish-species/short-finned-eel (accessed 23 October 2023); The Clean Air and Urban Landscapes Hub, 'The Living Pavilion', https://nespurban.edu.au/platforms/living-pavilion (accessed 23 October 2023); and Zoe Kean, 'Eels Can Travel over Land, Climb Walls and Take Down Serious Prey. They May Be Australia's Most Hardcore Animal', *ABC News*, 9 January 2022, https://www.abc.net.au/news/science/2022-01-09/eels-australia-most-hardcore-animal/100572614 (accessed 23 October 2023).

2 Jim Poulter, *The Eight Wurundjeri Seasons in Melbourne*, Red Hen Enterprises, Templestowe, 2015, p. 8.

II

Human Remains

Human Remains

ROSS L JONES

'Where are you my children,
Where are you my children of this land?
As we lay exposed above the ground
At the mercy of the rain, wind and the sand,
And the heat of the baring sun bleaching our bones whiter than white.
Children of this land, can you hear the whispers of your ancestors
As you walk amongst their bones,
Asking you to bury them deep within the womb of our spiritual mother—
the land,
Where they will find peace within themselves
As you will—as I did.
Where are you my children of this land?'

Uncle Jim Berg, Gunditjmara Elder

'The subject of the dissection of the human body cannot be approached without some understanding of the prejudice which inevitably clings to it. We must admit that there is, interwoven in the whole story, the idea of the sanctity of the human body, the dislike for its mutilation and the demand that it should find sepulchre intact.'

Frederic Wood Jones, address to the Medico-Legal Society of Victoria, 1933[1]

WHY DID THE University of Melbourne start collecting human bodies and remains after its foundation in 1853, and furthermore, why did the University specifically collect Indigenous bodies and remains? What were the collecting practices and what is the significance of these practices for the University today?

The ownership of the human body in Western society (both the living and the dead) has for centuries been a three-way battle between the state, religion and the individual. For much of modern European history, the laws of the church and the state protected the sanctity of the dead body. In the case of the rights of the dead individual, the state and the church mostly worked in concert—the body was characterised by the church as the home of the immortal soul, and therefore protected from mutilation by the laws of the state. But these privileges and protections were for the mainstream. The protection offered to the majority was not extended to those defined as transgressive (such as the criminal) or 'other' (such as those of a different race, including Indigenous Australians). This was the situation at the foundation of the University of Melbourne, and the Medical School that followed in 1862.

Also, at the time of the University's foundation, the understanding and practices of medicine were undergoing a major transformation, including the introduction of asepsis, anaesthesia and germ theory, thus involving a rethinking of the traditional status of the body. The developing scientific emphasis on understanding disease and death as pathologies in tissues and cells, rather than as an imbalance in the humours, led to a greatly increased demand for corpses for teaching purposes in the growing number of medical schools across the Western world. The burning question was: how were these cadavers to be sourced?

Changes in medical research and teaching were not the only reasons behind the need for more dead bodies. Anatomical knowledge was increasingly being used by the intelligentsia of Europe and the United States to justify their self-appointed racial superiority over the other peoples of the globe.[2] The publication of Charles Darwin's *On the Origin of Species* in 1859 invigorated the search for the origins of humanity and provided yet another stimulus to racist dialogue, helping to justify the proposed inequality in the evolution of different races. The newly invigorated scientific study of races led to the creation of both local and international markets for the bodies of Indigenous Australians for the purposes of this racial research.[3] As well as sending bodies and specimens back to the centre of Empire, colonial scientists could gain international acclaim using local resources—such as the bodies of Indigenous Australians.[4]

Teaching Anatomy

The supply of bodies to medical schools and anatomy schools in the United Kingdom prior to Melbourne's foundation caused much scandal and even riots. Up until the first *Anatomy Act* in England in 1832, it was only executed criminals who filled the supply, but that avenue had proved inadequate, leading to grave robbing and even murder. The anatomy Acts solved the problem by allowing the use of the indigent population housed in poorhouses. The new government in Victoria was quick to realise that the establishment of a medical school would require legislation if it was to collect bodies legally. In 1862 a Bill to regularise dissection was brought before the upper house of the Victorian Parliament by Thomas Turner a'Beckett.[5] A'Beckett announced that Victoria's Bill 'was a transcript of the English Bill, with the necessary alterations to adapt it to the circumstances of the colony'.[6] In the second reading debate, he told the Legislative Council that:

> It was a misdemeanour at common law to be in possession of a deceased person's body. Of course it would be an outrage of common decency for a man to have anything of the kind; but they all knew what crimes were formerly perpetrated in obtaining possession of dead bodies, for the purpose of anatomical investigation; and how it was found necessary ultimately to legalise what, at first sight, appeared to be a violation of their natural feelings.[7]

The subsequent Act, however, was found to be inadequate. In an editorial on 7 August 1869, the conservative newspaper the *Argus* argued that

> it is a deficiency in the Victorian *Anatomy Act* that it does not specify from what sources bodies are to be obtained. It is not too much to say that if bodies cannot be procured from our public institutions, the practice of 'body-snatching' will be revived.[8]

The consequence of the lack of a specified source in the *Anatomy Act* was that the first bodies acquired for the new Medical School were of the homeless who had died in Melbourne Hospital and had not been claimed by family or friends. This supply proved to be inadequate, and for decades the teaching of human anatomy in the Medical School was bedevilled by a shortage of cadavers for the dissecting theatre.[9] The first professor of medicine, George Halford, repeatedly requested that the various benevolent institutions give up their dead for use by the Medical School. Naturally enough this was the cause of much angst among the inmates of the biggest charitable institution, the North Melbourne Benevolent Asylum. On numerous occasions the inmates organised petitions and demonstrated against Halford and his successor as professor of anatomy and pathology, Harry Brookes Allen. For ten years they managed to hold off the University. It was suggested by the management committee of the Asylum that Halford ask prisons and lunatic asylums for bodies, but he complained to the committee in 1873 that 'in prisons and lunatic asylums *post mortem* examinations are made, which render the bodies almost useless to us'.[10] Halford would not give up, and on 26 June 1873 yet another letter from him requesting cadavers was read at a meeting of the committee.[11] The request was again rejected. It seems that the dissection room, despite the entreaties of scientific and medical voices, was destined to be envisaged in the popular mind as 'a kind of cannibal sausage establishment, where human mince-meat is continually being produced'.[12]

The inmates of the Asylum received little sympathy from the medical profession and students. In 1889, after Allen had been in contact with every charitable institution in Victoria, with little success, the students wrote that:

> One in particular, which is supported largely by a government grant, forwarded the childish plea that were they to accede to the wish of Professor Allen it would tend to make the institution unpopular. It may be the individuals complained of have in view the time when they themselves will be eligible for a vacant allotment at the public cost.[13]

In the late nineteenth century, Allen seems to have got his way. The supply of cadavers increased and, after much futile resistance, the inmates of various benevolent institutions began to be recorded in the cadaver archives. From the foundation of the Medical School until at least the 1960s, cadavers were sourced from either the hospitals, the benevolent institutions or, increasingly through the twentieth century, the insane asylums.

The move to source bodies from government institutions was facilitated by the stripping of other rights (including the right to vote) from individuals on admission. In 1863, a year after the opening of the Medical School, the parliament passed the *Electoral Act*, which specifically disenfranchised any person who was 'receiving relief as an inmate of any eleemosynary or charitable institution'.[14] This ban on voting was further entrenched in the state constitution in the *Constitution Act Amendment Act 1890*.[15] Although narrowly failing to be amended in 1910, the ban stayed in place after the *Constitution Act Amendment Act 1958*, only being discarded in 1975 in the *Constitution Act* of that year.[16] Donations of bodies only became the main source of cadavers in the 1970s, at which time the disenfranchisement of inmates of public institutions was finally abolished.[17]

Were Indigenous Australians' bodies among those dissected in the Medical School? The surviving archives are unclear on this issue. There is, however, no doubt that some Indigenous Australians were dissected as, in 1898, one such body is mentioned in the medical students' magazine *Speculum*.[18] Were they among those from public institutions whose bodies were dissected in the University without their permission? The surviving cadaver archive in the University runs from 1898 to the present, but in the decades leading up to the middle of the twentieth century, it records individuals with just an address or place of death, not Indigenous ancestry.[19] A clue can be found, however, in the 'disappearance' of Victoria's Aboriginal population.

Disappearing Bodies

An important reason for the difficulty in identifying Indigenous people in the cadaver archives is that, from the beginning of the foundation of the state of Victoria, the Indigenous population began to 'disappear'. As Victoria was an early and closely settled area, the impact of the European incursion on the Indigenous population was severe and quick. By the 1860s the Indigenous population officially numbered only 1869, although this was only 'full-bloods'.[20] During the second half of the nineteenth century, the numerous 'half-bloods' were increasingly forcibly absorbed into Victorian mainstream society. As Ellinghaus has written:

> In the late nineteenth and early twentieth centuries, Australian policy-makers planned the disappearance of the Aboriginal people, but not though their adoption of white ways of earning a living and incorporation into the nation's economy. Rather, it was to be a two stage process: firstly the 'doomed race' theory posited that people of full descent would soon 'die out', and secondly, it was believed that Aboriginal physical characteristics, and it was hoped, Aboriginality itself, would disappear altogether through biological absorption.[21]

The consequence of this policy in Victoria was that the authorities began separating Indigenous people from each other, either through the removal of families or individuals from reserves or the removal of children from their families. As well as the early devastation caused by violent conflicts and introduced disease, the survivors of the original inhabitants of Victoria were further stripped of their heritage by then being divided into 'pure' or 'mixed race', with the latter expelled from the reserves and any government support withdrawn—they were left to fend for themselves. This was enshrined in the *Aborigines Protection Act 1886*.[22] The only fallback for those who failed to thrive when sent into the community were the benevolent institutions that, from the 1880s, were to provide the bodies for the University. Also, if you were seriously ill and unable to be looked after at home, you would end up at Melbourne Hospital and, after death, also potentially be on the dissecting table at the Medical School. It therefore seems beyond doubt that there must have been many Indigenous Australians who ended up on the dissecting table in the University. They would almost certainly have also been subjected to the further ignominy of the 'meat fights' that characterised medical student behaviour, at least up to the arrival of the new professor of anatomy, Richard Berry, in 1906.[23]

Indigenous Bodies and Racial Science

Sometime between 1907 and 1909, Richard Berry received a delivery of two preserved human heads for his research. He wrote that:

> The material employed in the present investigation consisted of the entire heads of two Australian aboriginal natives from the Lower Murray in South Australia. Of these, one was the head of a male, aged 25 years who had lived at Point McLeay near the mouth of the Murray River [a mission station], and who had died from pneumonia in 1907. The other was that of a female, aged 50 years, and who also died in 1907 ... It is almost unnecessary to add that, although both were pure-bred, both had lived under European conditions.[24]

These heads were just two of the many remains that were sent to Berry for the research project he began in racial anatomy after his arrival at the University in 1906. In the half-century prior to 1906, it seems as if Melbourne was one of the least active places for the collection of Indigenous bodies and remains for the study of racial anatomy. Frederick McCoy (the first professor of natural science, 1854–99), for example, had shown no interest in physical anthropology and was staunchly anti-Darwinist.[25] From 1863 George Halford was, however, keen to collect as many bodies and body parts (such as bones) as he could. Most particularly he collected the skulls of Indigenous Australians, but other racial groups were also obtained, measured and drawn. Some of Halford's work can be seen in Richard Shepard's drawings of the heads of the bushranger 'Mad Dog' Morgan, a Chinese individual, and a number of Indigenous people, including that of King Jimmy of the Mordialloc tribe. These were all dissected, studied and drawn for the purposes of craniological comparison and used as illustrations in Brough Smyth's *The Aborigines of Victoria* (1878).[26]

In 1906, with the arrival of Richard Berry to take up the chair in Anatomy, research in racial anatomy moved centrestage, so much so that, at the celebrations held for the first fifty years of the Melbourne Medical School at the Windsor Hotel in April 1914, the dean, Harry Brookes Allen, claimed that one of the most important achievements of the school was the *Atlas of Tasmania Crania* and the *Atlas of Australian Aboriginal Crania* by Berry.[27] By the 1930s the University had become the leader in the field in Australia. The Tasmanian surgeon and notorious collector of bodies, William Edward Lodewyk Crowther, posed the question in the Halford Oration of 1934: 'Is there any other school of medicine that can show such a tradition of anthropological work, and is it too much to say that the influence of George Britton Halford was responsible for its inception?'[28]

Berry was an enthusiastic eugenicist who believed that the mental capacity and hence the worth of an individual, or race, could be ascertained by the size of the head. He collected skulls from a wide range of races and what he called 'inferior' whites such as those in prisons and asylums, and published widely on his theories of this racial hierarchy. Berry's views were widely accepted. In the *Medical Journal of Australia* in 1919 he claimed that the heads he had measured proved that Indigenous males had the brains of thirteen-year-old white boys.[29]

The Collections

Berry did little collecting in person but rather encouraged amateur collectors and his students to send him bones for his ever-expanding collection.[30] His teaching assistant in the department, William Colin MacKenzie (later Sir), became a major collector of Indigenous remains. On the appointment of Frederic Wood Jones as Berry's replacement in 1929, much of the collection went to the Institute of Anatomy, which had been set up in Canberra under an Act of federal parliament with the encouragement and financial backing of MacKenzie.[31] The building, with busts in the foyer celebrating a number of Melbourne's anatomists, is now the home of the National Film and Sound Archive. Frederic Wood Jones also collected remains and seems to have taken many to the Hunterian Museum in London when he became its curator. This collection was destroyed by bombs in World War II. Wood Jones, however, had a different agenda as a race anatomist, as he used his studies to argue that Indigenous Australians were not inferior to whites.[32]

The most significant collector in the history of the Medical School was George Murray Black, a pastoralist and amateur anthropologist who sent a great deal of Indigenous individuals' remains, from at least the 1930s to sometime around 1950, to both the Institute in Canberra and the Anatomy Department in Melbourne. Marcia Langton, Louise Murray and Antony Sinni will discuss the collection in their chapter in this part of the book, and Jim Bowler writes about his relationship with Black and his later work at Lake Mungo. In his later years Black was accompanied on these expeditions by Wood Jones' replacement as chair of anatomy, Sydney Sunderland (later Sir), and professor Leslie Ray as well as associate professor Alex Roche (later holding various chairs in the United States).[33]

Due to personal rivalries and interests, various parts of the collection moved between Canberra and Melbourne at different times. It is not possible to completely follow these peregrinations but eventually, by the 1950s, the Anatomy Department's collection of Indigenous remains was divided into the Murray Black and Berry collections, with professor Kenneth Russell responsible for the 'Berry' and professor Les Ray for the 'Murray Black'. The story of the Berry Collection will be told in Rohan Long's chapter in this section. The Australian Indigenous remains in the Berry Collection were repatriated in 2002 and the rest is in the process of being analysed with the aim of repatriating it as well.

Racial Research

The collections have produced mediocre research outcomes. Berry published mainly on head sizes, which was criticised internationally even in his lifetime as substandard science.[34] Sunderland and Ray published very little on the collection, which was surprising in the case of Sunderland who was a prolific author in other academic areas. As the eminent anthropologist John Mulvaney wrote,

> for decades the remains were virtually unstudied. Partly due to my prompting, a summary of 'knowledge' was published in the 1959 *Proceedings of the Royal Society of Victoria*. Even with illustrations, a mere four pages sufficed![35]

More recently, even more rigorously conducted work has proved fruitless, mainly due to the virtually insurmountable problem of recovering the provenance of most of the human remains.[36] Robertson has pointed out that collection methods obscured the demographic and epidemiological patterns of the collection because Murray Black often sent specifically chosen pathological specimens and he often discarded damaged bones. She concluded that 'the Murray Black collection is not representative of biological populations'.[37]

Frederic Wood Jones published several articles on some parts of the collection of Indigenous remains in his time as professor of anatomy in Melbourne in the 1930s. All of these were part of his anti-Darwinian, pro-Lamarckian project, which aimed to demonstrate that Indigenous Australians were not inferior to white Australians but rather had perfectly adapted over a great expanse of time to be in harmony with the Australian landscape and ecology.[38]

However, James Bowler and John Mulvaney—both of whom gained their expertise at the University of Melbourne—were central to the discovery of the deep antiquity of Indigenous Australia.[39] Initially this was the product of Bowler's discovery of 'Mungo Woman' in 1968. Bowler discusses this in his chapter in this section.

Judith Ryan provides the final chapter of this section on the Benjamin Law busts of the Indigenous Tasmanians, Trukanini and Wurati. Her chapter raises the vexed question of the ownership of images of deceased Indigenous Australians. What do they represent, and how should they be approached to inform our understanding of their history as victims of settler colonialism?[40]

Conclusion

Over the University's first century, tens of thousands of bodies of the poor and mentally unwell citizens of Victoria were collected for teaching and scientific study. The numbers of Indigenous individual remains are unknown but must have been in the thousands. Also, the University actively collected the remains of Indigenous Australians for its anthropological collections. Teaching aside, very little research, and almost none of any quality, was produced on these collections.

After the Murray Black collection was repatriated in 1985, following an adverse finding in the Supreme Court of Victoria, it was almost two decades until the other significant collection of Indigenous remains, the Berry Collection, was 'discovered' in the Anatomy Department. The University had had little appetite to conduct any audit, suggesting either maladministration or passive resistance from within the department.

The discovery of the Berry Collection instigated a period of active effort by the University to establish the extent of its collections and the subsequent repatriation of remains where possible. The path taken by the University to address the ethical problems necessarily associated with the use of bodies, both as subjects for teaching and research, has been tortuous and long but seems to be reaching some sort of conclusion with the instigation of this history project.

Notes

1 F Wood Jones, 'The Legalization of the Study of Human Anatomy', in JV Barry and AE Coates (eds), *The Proceedings of the Medico-Legal Society of Victoria During the Years 1933–1934 and 1935–1936*, vol. II, Brown Prior Anderson, Melbourne, 1937, p. 135.

2 Nancy Stepan, *The Idea of Race in Science: Great Britain 1800–1960*, Macmillan, London, 1982.

3 For a discussion of this and a list of references, see Ross L Jones, *Anatomists of Empire: Race, Evolution and the Discovery of Human Biology in the British World*, Australian Scholarly Publishing, North Melbourne, 2020, pp. xi–xiv.

4 For an extensive discussion of this, see Jones, *Anatomists of Empire*, Chapter 5.

5 Victorian Legislative Council, *Victorian Parliamentary Debates*, vol. 8, 4 March 1862, p. 706.

6 Ibid.

7 Ibid., p. 837.

8 *Argus*, 7 August 1869, p. 4. While grave robbing created a sensation in other colonies, evidence of any such scandal in Melbourne is yet to surface. For detail of the Tasmanian scandals, see Helen MacDonald, *Human Remains: Dissection and Its Histories*, Yale University Press, New Haven, 2006.

9 For a lengthy discussion of this, see Ross L Jones, *Humanity's Mirror: 150 Years of Anatomy in Melbourne*, Haddington Press, Melbourne, 2007, Chapter 4.

10 *Australian Medical Journal*, June 1873, p. 170.

11 Ibid., pp. 169–70.

12 Ibid., p. 171.

13 *Speculum*, no. 16, January 1889, pp. 17–18.

14 Barbara Kerr, *The State Franchise in Victoria, 1842–2005*, Professional Intern Report, Professional Internship Program PSI3000, Monash University and the State Parliament of Victoria, Melbourne, p. 22.

15 Ibid., p. 11.

16 Victorian Legislative Council, *Victorian Parliamentary Debates*, vol. 124, 1910, pp. 416–20.

17 From 1951 until 1983, under direction from the chief secretary, the Department of Mental Hygiene supplied bodies from its institutions to the University for the purpose of dissection. See Public Record Office Victoria series VPRS 7688, 'Record of Subjects Sent to School of Anatomy, University of Melbourne'. For a complete survey of the supply of cadavers, see Ross L Jones, 'Cadavers and the Social Dimension of Dissection', in Sarah Ferber and Sally Wilde (eds), *The Body Divided: Human Beings and Human Materials in the History of Medical Science*, Ashgate, Aldershot, 2012.

18 *Speculum*, no. 40, May 1898, p. 27.

19 The cadaver archives going back to the 1860s seem to have been destroyed in the 1980s.

20 I don't have the space here to discuss this difficult calculation, so I have used Ellinghaus' figures: Katherine Ellinghaus, 'Absorbing the "Aboriginal Problem": Controlling Inter-Racial Marriage in Australia in the Late 19th and Early 20th Centuries', *Aboriginal History*, vol. 27, 2003, p. 193.

21 Ibid., p. 186.

22 Ibid., pp. 193–4.

23 Jones, *Humanity's Mirror*, Chapter 4.

24 Richard JA Berry, 'The Sectional Anatomy of the Head of the Australian Aboriginal: A Contribution to the Subject of Racial Anatomy', *Proceedings of the Royal Society of Edinburgh*, Royal Society of Edinburgh, vol. 31, 1910–11, p. 607.

25 Paul Turnbull, *Science, Museums and Collecting the Indigenous Dead in Colonial Australia*, Palgrave Studies in Pacific History, Palgrave Macmillan, Cham, Switzerland, 2017, pp. 207–8.

26 Robert Brough Smyth, *The Aborigines of Victoria: With Notes Relating to the Habits of the Natives of Other Parts of Australia and Tasmania Compiled from Various Sources for the Government of Victoria*, J. Ferres, Government Printer, Melbourne, 1878, p. 338f.

27 HB Allen, *University of Melbourne, Medical School Jubilee 1914*, Ford, Carlton, 1914, p. 53; RJA Berry and AWD Robertson, *Dioptrographic Tracings in Four Normae of Fifty-Two Tasmanian Crania*, J. Kemp, Govt. Printer, Melbourne, 1909.

28 WELH Crowther, '"1803–1876: The Passing of the Tasmanian Race", The Halford Oration', *Medical Journal of Australia*, 3 February 1934, p. 148. Crowther's collections of Tasmanian human remains were later reburied: John Mulvaney, 'Reflections on the Murray Black Collection', *Australian Natural History*, vol. 23, no. 1, 1989, p. 68.

29 See Jones, *Humanity's Mirror*, Chapter 5; Ross L Jones, 'Thinking Dangerous Thoughts: Post-Primary Education and Eugenics in Australia: 1905–1939', in Hamish Spencer, Diane Paul and John Stenhouse (eds), *Eugenics at the Edges of Empire: New Zealand, Australia, Canada and South Africa*, Palgrave Macmillan, Basingstoke, 2017; Turnbull, *Science, Museums and Collecting*, pp. 254–5.

30 Richard Berry instructed his students to collect human remains for him: see correspondence of Dr H Clive Disher in Strathfieldsaye Estate papers, file 1976.0013, University of Melbourne Archives.

31 Rob McWilliams, 'Resting Places: A History of Australian Indigenous Ancestral Remains at Museum Victoria', 2016, https://museumsvictoria.com.au/media/4273/resting_places__history_of_ancestral_remains_25_aug_2016.docx (accessed 23 October 2023).

32 For a lengthy discussion of this, see Jones, *Anatomists of Empire*; Ross L Jones and Warwick H Anderson, 'Wandering Anatomists and Itinerant Anthropologists: The Antipodean Sciences of Race in Britain between the Wars', *British Journal for the History of Science*, vol. 48, no. 1, March 2015, pp. 1–16.

33 See Shannon Faulkhead and Jim Berg with Lynette Russell, Ross L Jones and Jason Eades, *Power and Passion: Our Ancestors Return Home*, Koorie Heritage Trust, Melbourne, 2010; Sydney Sunderland to Frederic Wood Jones, 6 November (no year but must be in the late 1940s); 21 November 1951, MS0017/1/14/1-3, Frederic Wood Jones papers, General Correspondence, Royal College of Surgeons

of England, archive, London. There were Indigenous foetuses in the collections: see Lisa O'Sullivan and Ross L Jones, 'Two Australian Fetuses: Frederic Wood Jones and the Work of an Anatomical Specimen', *Bulletin of the History of Medicine*, vol. 89, no. 2, summer 2015, pp. 243–66.

34 See Jones, *Humanity's Mirror*, Chapter 5.

35 John Mulvaney, 'Reflections on the Murray Black Collection', *Australian Natural History*, vol. 23, no. 1, 1989, p. 68. The 'summary' was S Sunderland and LJ Ray, 'A Note on the Murray Black Collection of Australian Aboriginal Skeletons', *Proceedings of the Royal Society of Victoria*, vol. 71, 1959, pp. 45–52. There was one other summary: LJ Ray, 'Bilateral Coraco-Clavicular Articulations in the Australian Aboriginal', *Journal of Bone and Joint Surgery*, vol. 41B, no. 1, February 1959, pp. 180–4.

36 For the problems with the provenance of the Murray Black collection, see McWilliams, 'Resting Places'.

37 Sarah Robertson, 'Sources of Bias in the Murray Black Collection: Implications for Palaeopathological Analysis', *Australian Aboriginal Studies*, vol. 1, January 2007, p. 127.

38 See O'Sullivan and Jones, 'Two Australian Fetuses'.

39 Perhaps most tellingly their involvement in the discovery of the antiquity of Mungo woman and Mungo man. An enormous amount of literature has been written on this—see Billy Griffiths, *Deep Time Dreaming: Uncovering Ancient Australia*, Black Inc. Books, Melbourne, 2018.

40 Paul Turnbull, 'Haunting Simulacra', presentation to the Global Provenence Colloquium, University of Bern, the Museum of Ethnography in Geneva, the Museum of Ethnography in Neuchâtel and the Palais de Rumine, February 2021, https://www.paulturnbull.org/pdf/turnbull-haunting-simulacra.pdf (accessed 23 October 2023).

Unlikely Encounters

Geology and Archaeology

JIM BOWLER

TEN YEARS AFTER leaving school, I left a secure farm life growing potatoes to study geology at the University of Melbourne. Unaccustomed as I was to any contact with Indigenous people, my journey brought me to the intersection of the disciplines of geology and archaeology on the one hand, and to life-changing encounters with Australia's First People on the other. While this chapter focuses on my time in direct association with the University, it includes an account of the wider ramifications that resulted from that primary connection, after my 1965 departure to the Australian National University (ANU) in Canberra. It revisits that association on my return to Melbourne and acceptance back into this University's geological structure in 1990, a connection for which I remain grateful to the present day.

Earliest Days: Life in Leongatha

Fully engaged as they were in the demanding tasks of dairy farming and small-town marketing, to the people of the tidy town of Leongatha in South Gippsland, two items were notable in the general social agenda. The first was a general amnesia, a forgetting of the original people and the lush rainforests that once covered this entire region, memories lost in the short time since European settlement began. The second was a preoccupation with issues of daily life: fashions of the day, changing seasons and the fluctuating price of the cattle market, all contributing to a sense of local security, isolated from distant things of a university nature. The realm of lawyers, doctors and scientists was seen as a world apart, one with inevitable demands far from local agendas. These two remote concerns—the original occupants of the land and the sustained discipline of university life—were in some strange way predestined to direct me away from my own farming tradition. Potato farming did not prevent my 1963 external enrolment in University of Melbourne English and Philosophy courses; I failed English but passed Philosophy!

As someone who grew up in the cool, well-watered, fertile lands of Leongatha, I feel the circumstances were very fortunate—even if the Irish Catholic community often fell far short of understanding the Australia in which our transported culture had made a new home. It was Gippsland, the land of the Bunurong and Gunaikurnai peoples, but they lay far from the ambit of everyday life in Leongatha. The transformation of the land since European arrival was already complete. Even the towering ash, the tea-tree and the ferns, the multitude of possums, koalas and wallabies, were gone, their removal like that of the original occupants, all part of the process of converting forest to grassland. Under the joint forces of the torch and the gun, the resultant landscape, consistent with the aspirations of George Gipps, resembled the ordered fields and hedgerows of his birth country. A part of that transformation, my family was established there by my great-grand-uncle Tom Bowler.

Born in 1840, Tom Bowler alone cleared his 130 hectares of ash and blue-gum country, converting virgin rainforest into Eurocentric pastures. I recall a brief meeting with him as a small child in 1934, a short time before his death. To even have met a man born in 1840, nineteen years before Darwin's *On the Origin of Species*, puts my own life in historical perspective.

My father—like Tom Bowler, himself a migrant from the fishing country of Ireland's west coast—inherited both land and Eurocentric attitudes towards it and its traditional occupants. He arrived in Australia before the outbreak of World War I, and enlistment took him for two years of rough survival in the Somme. He came home a different man. While rejoicing in the productive years of his onion paddock and dairy farm, his deep sense of inquiry never left him. He wondered about one issue in particular: who were those who lived here before us?

That virtual absence of Aboriginal people, accepted by all in Leongatha as the mere price of progress, provided a nagging worry for my father. I remember his discovery of a stone axe in his onion paddock. It became an object of silent contemplation for us children around the dinner table. Who was the person who so carefully fashioned such an object out of stone? That axe lay on our kitchen mantelpiece for many years, a constant reminder of a mysterious past. When radio access became available, my father became a regular listener to Crosbie Morrison, who expounded upon the wonders of Australia's environments on the ABC. Simultaneously, anthropologist AP Elkin's *The Australian Aborigines* took pride of place on his bookshelf.

Slowly, he developed an awareness of the questionable nature of Anglo-Irish occupancy of these former rainforests, which produced a nagging question of identity. Although the unlawful nature of European dispossession of the First People was never actually identified or acknowledged as such in any Irish Catholic dialogue, a constant but often unspoken sense of guilt remained. Interactions with the original occupants, already confined to missions and reserves, had passed out of memory for most settler Gippslanders. In discussion of the earliest settlers, one exception was provided. It involved the development of the first pastoral station on the south-eastern Victorian coastline—the holding of Scottish immigrant George Black.

In 1851 George Black pioneered the region's first major settlement on the coastline near the Tarwin River. A highly inventive Scot, he imported best-quality Scottish cattle and established the first local dairy, complete with a self-styled butter factory. His farming methods included the introduction of strawberry clover.

As I was growing up, the comparison of George Black with my own great-grand-uncle Tom, who was of a similar age, led to my curiosity about his son, George Murray Black, one of the region's few university graduates. A degree from the University of Melbourne in 1898 led him to a career in mining engineering. Stories are told of his work in mines across remote Australia, including Kalgoorlie, but it was his somewhat idiosyncratic pastime of collecting Aboriginal skeletons that stirred much comment. 'Collecting the dead' was not a favourite tea-table discussion of the 1940s and 1950s. Many were known to ask what drove Murray Black in his virtual grave robbery. No answers emerged.

While Gippsland and the Tom Bowler legacy had been very kind to me, ten years after leaving school, an increasing awareness of the big world beyond Leongatha was stirring within me. In 1955 I departed the farm to explore the fascinating world of the University of Melbourne.

University Days: 1955–65

Like Murray Black, I, too, abandoned my legacy of land to enter the otherwise remote and challenging world of the University. It was a huge change for me, one small aspect of a pattern of wider change that had many expressions. Those years included the Melbourne Olympics, the Russian invasion of Hungary and the Suez Crisis. Fears of communism were in the air. In Vietnam, the advance of the Vietcong precipitated the return of conscription, a 'lottery of death'. The University was alive with constantly changing agendas; some critical issues awaited us.

Within the University's faculties, many major changes were also in train. In the Department of Geology, the historical priorities of mining and oil exploration were coming under increasing question. The world in general, and geology in particular, were changing in the wake of an emerging awareness of environmental issues. The focus was shifting away from the layers of oldest rocks, and new interest was awakened in the surface, the youngest rocks—the sediments and soils that defined those landscapes on which and by which we lived. In that process we were entering a world of new questions—not solely about inanimate rocks and sand but also, in geological time, the mysterious appearance of people like us!

While involvement with living Aboriginal people was minimal, within geology in this period, interest in the evolution of humanity was raising issues with particular reference to Australia. Who were the ancient Australians, and how were we to study them? Baldwin Spencer's pioneering anthropology had already stirred the field. Questions of deep time and human arrival lay in store for the next wave of scholars.

In December 1952, just three years before my entry to the University, John Mulvaney had joined the History Department. A new phase of scholarship was about to unfold. Trained in Cambridge, and with African experience under Sir Mortimer Wheeler, Mulvaney was aware of the need for closer ties between the disciplines of earth science and archaeology. Initial approaches to professor Edwin Hills in the Geology Department for joint assistance were met with caution and a lack of commitment. That reluctance was soon to change.

The Excavation at Keilor

In August 1965, evidence of human remains was uncovered in a sandpit on the western banks of the Maribyrnong River near Keilor, in a locality known as Green Gully. The earlier discovery of a cranium in a similar pit some 5 kilometres upstream had already attracted much interest, but confusion surrounding its age and the disturbed context posed more questions than answers. In contrast, the undisturbed state of the Green Gully discovery offered new prospects for a more definitive understanding. At that time, Edwin Hills, as chairman of the National Museum of Victoria board to which the discovery had been reported, directed me to undertake detailed stratigraphic work, in order to establish the age and environmental context of this new find.

Radiocarbon dating, then a new technique for accurate chronology, had recently been made available within the museum. It was now possible to establish hitherto indiscernible details of the burial's environmental context. The situation required the employment of techniques from geology, archaeology, chronology and physical anatomy, highly specialised tasks in an area of expanding public interest. The specialist team established to undertake the investigation included John Mulvaney, Thomas Darragh—a recent geology graduate in palaeontology—and Dermot Casey, brother of then governor-general Richard Casey; Dermot had previous archaeological experience with Mulvaney in Cambridge. For post-mortem analysis, the team also included the University of Sydney's professor of anatomy, NWG Macintosh.

This study provided the first radiocarbon age for any ancient burial in Australia, a finding published in the international journal *Nature*.[1] The results revealed the burial site dated to nearly 8000 years ago. Instead of a simple burial, this ancient grave enclosed a rather bizarre association of fragmented body parts, including the remains of two individuals. It provided an example of reburial after earlier disintegration of soft body parts. At the time of burial, sea levels were rising, following the end of a major glacial period. With the arrival of warmer and wetter conditions, people were beginning to experience a climate similar to today.

The site remained one of special interest. Firstly, the sheer proximity to Melbourne ensured media coverage. Secondly, the conjunction of disciplines—for me personally, that of geology and archaeology—was to remain a source of fascination. It opened a door to a much wider exploration of climatically influenced environmental change. Understanding the archaeological component required an understanding of elements of geological change and the environments that were the basis of human sustenance. Here, the Maribyrnong terrace formation proved to be contemporaneous with wetter conditions following what was earlier an arid, dune-building environment. In this context, the University of Melbourne's Geology Department played a seminal role in telling the story of Australia's climatic changes, essential in understanding the land in which we live. The Keilor study represented a foundational step towards that understanding.

Details of human remains, be they modern or ancient, evoke curiosity. Even before the Keilor study, stimulating discussions with student colleagues, especially those in the medical fraternity, often revolved around what was going on in the Anatomy Department's cadaver-dissection room. I recall one such student making reference to his vacation employment in the Department of Anatomy, in charge there of 'the Murray Black collection'. It was a topic I had explored just a year earlier.

My Interview with Murray Black

Born in 1874 at Tarwin Meadows, South Gippsland, George Murray Black had a name that had long garnered curious attention from the people of Leongatha. Intrigued by the importance attached to the collection bearing his name—and by his rather mysterious activities in my own home region—I decided it was time to satisfy my curiosity. Following a phone call to arrange a time to converse, I duly made the short trip from my parents' farm to Tarwin Lower.

On 27 February 1964, one day after Murray Black's ninetieth birthday, I sat on the sunny veranda of the Black family home, Tullaree, built in a creative style that spoke of its inventive designer. During our interview, the rather frail but friendly Murray Black seemed quite interested in someone from the University of Melbourne arriving on his doorstep. Retired but still with mind intact, he related an eloquent and detailed reflection on his work. Although my interest was the science, this man's ninety years of experience covered much more.

Murray Black recounted but a small part of his life in discussing his excavations of human remains, especially in the region of the Murray and Murrumbidgee rivers. Although to many people it was an audacious and sacrilegious invasion of the dead, it was approved by some in authority, mainly practitioners of medical science. At that time, medical research in many countries had sparked a high demand for skeletons for comparative examination. The University's Department of Anatomy welcomed Murray Black's contributions. In justification of his excavations, he provided a 1962 letter from professor Leslie Ray thanking him for service. Ray assured Murray Black that, during a planned overseas trip, he would ensure 'that the best use of your collection can be made'.

Regarding the details of field collecting, there were again more questions than answers. Murray Black's training in mining generated a familiarity with sometimes subtle landscape features, especially the small, sandy dune rises that offered possible clues to the location of buried remains. Exposures caused by the building of new roads and irrigation channels offered sub-surface evidence. Of special importance, scrapings of rabbit and wombat burrows often revealed bone fragments. After several years in the Murray–Murrumbidgee region, Murray Black became practised at recognising burial sites, some of which were virtual cemeteries offering multiple graves. Although the locations of sites were rarely precisely defined, there were several exceptions. One such, presented on a sketch map drafted on the reverse side of the letter from professor Ray, describes the location of the 'Cohuna Skull'. That site and the remains it contained later became the subject of dubious fame.

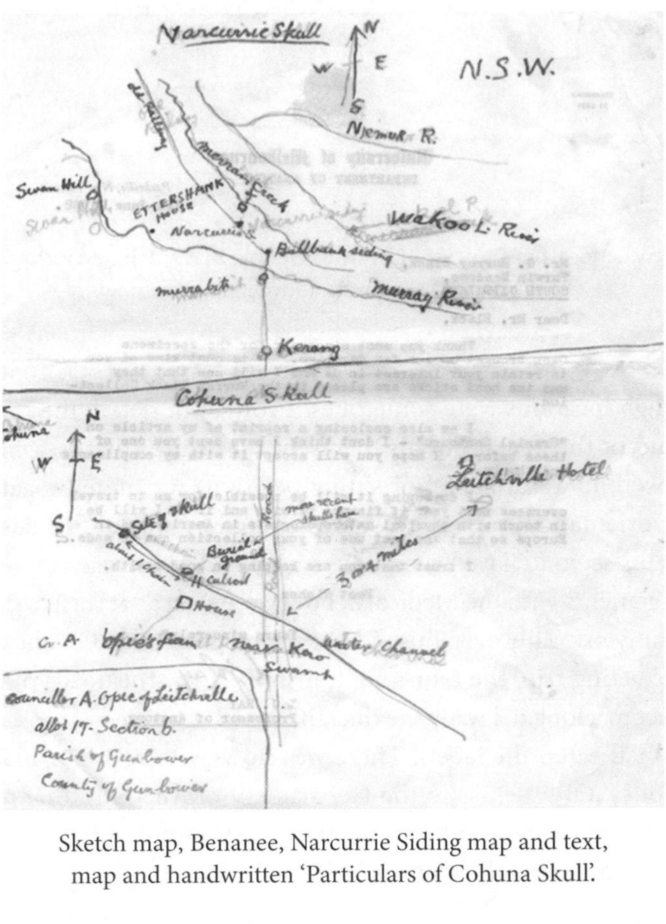

Sketch map, Benanee, Narcurrie Siding map and text, map and handwritten 'Particulars of Cohuna Skull'.

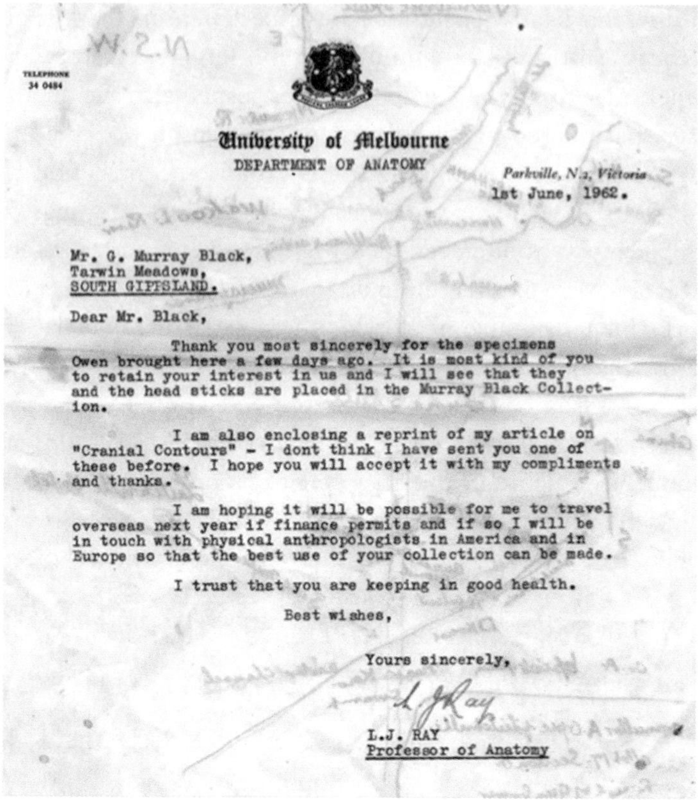

TELEPHONE
34 0484

University of Melbourne
DEPARTMENT OF ANATOMY

Parkville, N.2, Victoria
1st June, 1962.

Mr. G. Murray Black,
Tarwin Meadows,
SOUTH GIPPSLAND.

Dear Mr. Black,

Thank you most sincerely for the specimens Owen brought here a few days ago. It is most kind of you to retain your interest in us and I will see that they and the head sticks are placed in the Murray Black Collection.

I am also enclosing a reprint of my article on "Cranial Contours" - I dont think I have sent you one of these before. I hope you will accept it with my compliments and thanks.

I am hoping it will be possible for me to travel overseas next year if finance permits and if so I will be in touch with physical anthropologists in America and in Europe so that the best use of your collection can be made.

I trust that you are keeping in good health.

Best wishes,

Yours sincerely,

L.J. Ray

L.J. RAY
Professor of Anatomy

Letter from Professor LJ Ray to George Black, 1 June 1962, on the back of which the above map was drawn.

Although locations were sometimes recorded in detail, the same could not be said of the actual burials themselves. Posture (that is, whether the remains were in a horizontal or sitting position) was noted together with magnetic orientation, but little else was offered by way of fine description. The remains seem to have been treated as an end in themselves.

Arrangements with the Medical School were seen as at least one justification for this work. However, this did not always go to plan. On one occasion, after a collecting trip, the returning transport (two truckloads of remains) was subject to a long delay. By the time the remains arrived at the University, silverfish had eaten the labels. There was no way to relate crania to post-cranial bones. Of little use to the Department of Anatomy, that collection was dispatched to the Canberra Institute of Anatomy, where it remained until repatriated some thirty years later.[2]

On reflection, the 1964 interview was one of the earliest episodes of my entry into the geological discipline. I was but tapping on the door of one whose detailed record remained virtually unknown to me. Throughout, the interview remained very much matter-of-fact. We made little reference to any effects of Murray Black's work on the living, as if it was all justified by the cause of science. Lacking any first-hand experience with Indigenous cultures, I remained a neophyte in the complexities of cultural sensitivities. Now, with a somewhat belatedly enlarged understanding of the magnitude of the crimes Murray Black committed against both the dead and their living descendants, my entry into his life may be seen as abetting his invasions. Was my interest in him, in some sense, that of an accomplice? Others may judge.

Meanwhile, some items from his collection did provide substance for research. One such case involved a Sydney graduate student of our Keilor study colleague, professor Macintosh. That student, Dr Alan Thorne, undertook what was to be the final research on skeletal remains from Murray Black's Kow Swamp site, near Cohuna in northern Victoria.

After more than a century of Aboriginal graves being robbed across Australia, settlers were at last beginning to see this bizarre practice as an outrageous assault on human dignity. But two more examples were to await judgement: the Kow Swamp studies of Alan Thorne and my own identification of bones at Lake Mungo.

The Cohuna Cranium

As discussed in Rohan Long's chapter on the Berry Collection, the practice of medical anthropometry was one of long tradition. Following the influence of Darwin and the confidence in metric statistics, a longstanding theory proposed that present-day Aboriginal Australians had evolved in continuity with earlier, more archaic forms of humanity. Cranial analysis was employed to test this hypothesis. None other than TH Huxley argued that both the skulls and the lifeways of humans in Palaeolithic Europe 'clearly resembled, in several respects, those of the Australian savage tribes'.[3] In testing his ideas about extinct humanoid species, such as Neanderthals, Huxley studied the remains of Aboriginal people, in part because he believed that 'the natives of Southern and Western Australia are probably as pure and homogenous in blood, customs, and language, as any race of savages in existence', but also, crucially, because the Hunterian Museum of the College of Surgeons in

London had 'a very fine collection' of Aboriginal skulls.[4] A virtual scientific industry followed Huxley's example, using specimens exported to Britain.

This theory was given impetus by the identification within Australian samples of two morphometric types: 'robust' (heavy-boned with some archaic features) in contrast to thinner, more delicate 'gracile' forms, typical of most modern examples. This contrast between 'robust' and 'gracile' came to be part of the descriptive language of the time. One suggested explanation for the 'robust' types involved the route taken by the earliest ancestors of Indigenous Australians in their long migration to the Australian continent. It was conjectured that these people had passed through and interbred with humans in what is now the island of Java, where an archaic humanoid species, *Homo erectus*, had been present as recently as one million years ago. The 'robust' skeletons perhaps reflected relict gene traces from *H. erectus*, what Macintosh referred to as the 'mark of ancient Java'.[5]

Indigenous Australians' ancestry was vigorously explored in the University of Sydney's Department of Anatomy under Macintosh's guidance. Alan Thorne continued that tradition after joining the ANU. In 1967 Thorne discovered skeletal remains in the Museum of Victoria with cranial features typical of the 'robust' morphology. Their origin was labelled as 'Kow Swamp', the collecting site of Murray Black near Cohuna. Thorne found the site and undertook a detailed excavation. The recovery of some fifteen individual burials provided a substantial sample for analysis.

After examining a significant number of 'robust' examples, Thorne concluded that many displayed 'a complex of morphologically archaic features'.[6] His conclusions sparked widespread interest among fellow paleoanthropologists.[7] Initial radiocarbon analysis provided ages in the 9000–10 000-year range, slightly older than the Keilor remains, but a 2003 revision dated the Kow Swamp people closer to 20 000 years old.[8] This was the period of the last glacial maximum, suggesting that the observed morphologic variability may have been due to environmental stress. In the absence of any genetic evidence connecting these people to Java and *H. erectus*, later scholars have preferred what Curnoe offers as a 'more parsimonious approach', one that neither rules out but certainly does not necessarily support the *H. erectus* connection.[9]

Thorne's Cohuna samples were returned to the Museum of Victoria for curation. Meanwhile, the times were changing. Over the course of the 1960s and 1970s, settler attitudes towards Indigenous people and cultures were transformed by a wave of activism. Governments began to take interest in protecting Indigenous heritage. In 1984 the Victorian Government 'amended the Relics Act to make it an offence to be in control of or display [Indigenous] Ancestral Remains'.[10] Aboriginal Elders of the Cohuna region requested the return of the Kow Swamp remains for reburial under their supervision. Vigorous discussion followed.

John Mulvaney, at that time holding an honorary fellowship with the Museum of Victoria, protested that, as items of global importance to humanity, these remains should not be subject to the Victorian legislation. At a memorable meeting of the National Museum of Victoria board, I recall then minister for the arts Jim Kennan demanding in no uncertain terms the immediate return of the remains. In protest, Mulvaney resigned from his fellowship, untethering his long association with the Museum.

This was one of many turbulent encounters. Not before time, the pendulum was swinging to redress some of the pain meted out to an entire people for so long regarded by many as second-class. Although Thorne established contacts with Indigenous colleagues, his research, regarded now with the benefit of hindsight, would seem to be yet one more example of science's imposition on a matter of great spiritual importance. The Kow Swamp studies, although failing to produce results that Huxley and others would have preferred, remain as road signs on the journey towards a more enlightened understanding across the cultural divide—a journey that still has a long way to go.

Lake Mungo

In 1965 I moved with my family to the ANU. Although this involved a change of venue, the study of climatic change remained my central objective. Back in Melbourne, my mentor professor Hills had already planted the seeds of such inquiry. It involved major questions. This ancient landscape tells us many stories, a challenge to an inquiring mind. It provided the pathway of my choice.

Support from what was then the Department of Geography (later Biogeography and Geomorphology) permitted my exploration of salt lakes across Australia. A dry chain of basins on Willandra Creek in western New South Wales became the focal point for the study. Of especial interest was a single distinctive feature, a lunette, on early maps known as 'The Walls of China': a large north–south dune on the margin of an unnamed lake. I named that dry basin Lake Mungo, after the enclosing sheep station.

On the dune ridge, along the eastern shoreline of the basin, deep erosion revealed multicoloured complexities of internal layering, preserving evidence of ancient human presence. In September 1968 I reported a finding of burnt bones, buried at a depth that suggested they were older than 20 000 years. Despite archaeological scepticism, my account inspired genuine interest. In March of the following year, an inspection with archaeological colleagues identified those bones as traces, not simply of human activity, but of humanity itself—a moment of great excitement!

The remains, collected into John Mulvaney's suitcase, were returned to Canberra and provided to Thorne for anatomical analysis.[11] Thorne's detailed reconstruction of the fragmented cranial remains provided definitive evidence that this woman, who died more than 20 000 years ago, was fully anatomically modern. Called 'Mungo Lady', her cremated remains had two important implications. Firstly, these remains, later dated to 40 000 years ago, helped resolve the Kow Swamp controversy.[12] The remains of Mungo Lady were considerably older than the Kow Swamp remains but morphologically modern. The reality that the older remains bore no archaic features finally refuted the old contention that early Australians were anything other than fully modern *Homo sapiens*. Secondly, this cremation was recognised as the oldest known example in modern humanity—yet another cause for the celebration of our history.

In 1974 a human cranium appeared on the eroded surface of Lake Mungo, one that proved to be part of a fully articulated male skeleton.[13] Once more Thorne came to the rescue and with a specialist team removed the skeleton for return to Canberra. The grave revealed a sequence of critical environmental details. Firstly, the body had been sprinkled with ochre before the grave was filled. Secondly, beside the grave, a large concentration of blackened sands recorded the presence of a large fire, apparently created for a ritual purpose. Thirdly, sediments of the grave revealed that the burial occurred at a time of changing lake levels. Finally, despite the initial controversy, systematic dating agreed the burial took place in the time range of 40 000–42 000 years ago. Identified as 'Mungo Man', these remains told a story of a sophisticated people living in a shifting ice-age landscape of lakes and dunes. These were times of major climatic change. Mungo Lady and Mungo Man, together with the evidence of the environment of their times, had opened an entirely new chapter in Australian history.

Mulvaney, in recognition of these new contributions to the story of humanity, successfully presented a case to the United Nations Educational, Scientific and Cultural Organization (UNESCO) for World Heritage registration of Lake Mungo in 1981. In so doing, he was cautious to ensure the registration acknowledged the joint components of both natural and cultural heritage. The partnership that had begun at Keilor sixteen years earlier had enlarged to take a place on the global stage.

Premised on the foundational involvement of both scientists and Aboriginal Traditional Owners, the Lake Mungo region's future involved—and still involves—a unity of people across cultural boundaries, bridging gaps between science and traditional cultures. Initial grounds for potential conflicts in values were addressed by detailed dialogue between scientists and Traditional Owners. In June 1989, a meeting between contending groups established consensus on a working collaborative basis. Representatives of three Aboriginal groups—the Mutthi Mutthi, Nyiampaa and Barkandji—signed an agreement endorsing the value of scientific work on their lands on the basis of collaborative programs.

For forty years, successive appeals to governments—both state and Commonwealth—for the provision of an appropriate and secure location for the remains were consistently ignored. Mulvaney's last plea, in a June 2016 letter to the *Canberra Times*—just four months before his death—provides a dramatic illustration of this institutional neglect. In addition to that failing, the NSW Government's concept of site management has remained flawed. While preferential treatment for Indigenous partners is entirely justified, in this World Heritage situation, 'partnership' remains the operative word. The delegation of decisions to one partner alone inevitably raises problems for the other.

Several factors have contributed to the loss of heritage integrity. Firstly, following wide media coverage of the work carried out by settler scientists, a sense of injustice underscored a widening complaint: 'This is our history, not yours!' Secondly, placing decisions exclusively in the hands of Traditional Owners effectively silenced the views of many scientists. Important issues of natural heritage were sidelined by the prioritisation of cultural heritage. Thirdly, the widening gap between cultures was emphasised by a recurring statement from people with a sense of latent antagonism towards settler science: 'The remains were taken without permission.' This became something of a shibboleth. In 1974, the time of Mungo Man's salvage, traditional ownership of that land was completely undefined; there was no identified authority to ask. Had those remains not been recovered, there would have been no World Heritage status in the first place.

Finally, in frustration, the control group of Traditional Owners decided to undertake a secret reburial of all skeletal remains—secret in both time and place. Simultaneously, Indigenous voices arose from outside the control group offering an alternative. They pleaded with the government for a secure and publicly celebrated burial process, honourably memorialising what had become iconic treasures of Australian history. In desperation, a court injunction was enacted, effectively deferring reburial pending more public dialogue. In a final act of defiance, ignoring the injunction, the controlling owners carried out the secret burial of the remains of Mungo Lady and Mungo Man. That defiance still awaits a final legal determination.

We have experienced here something of a climactic moment, one in which Australia's international reputation has come under intense scrutiny. Following the amazing return to surface exposure of two individuals who died 40 000–42 000 years ago, and whose rites of passage reflect a highly sophisticated culture, these very foundations of World Heritage status have been secretly and unilaterally buried. To have that legacy effectively destroyed, both by government inaction and by the self-justifications of modern-day descendants, is a tragedy of Shakespearean dimensions. The collaborative agreement that emerged in 1989 was a virtual bridge between science and traditional philosophies, but it has deteriorated into a disturbing sense that the gap between cultures is widening rather than closing.

At a personal level, the failure to secure the publicly honoured status so richly deserved for those two ancient individuals remains a burden on my mind. They came to my attention unannounced. After more than 40 000 years, they returned for a reason. It is going to take time to redress the pain. What was an almost indescribable injustice inflicted on land and people by British colonisation (including by my ancestor Tom Bowler) has manifested in yet another disaster. The injustice meted out to Aboriginal dead by Murray Black has, in a bizarre way, been reproduced here, where a few inflict abuse by the secret disposal of their own ancestors.

Australians of all races and creeds have a continuing obligation, both nationally and internationally, to honour these treasures. The death and then mutual re-emergence 40 000 years later of Mungo Lady and Mungo Man on the shores of Lake Mungo stand as a rousing reminder to all Australians of the sanctity proclaimed both by this land and its ancient peoples.

Oldest Occupation: Moyjil–Point Ritchie

One particular question recurrently arises: when did people first arrive in Australia? As if the unresolved tribulations surrounding Lake Mungo were not enough, another site remains in question. Coastal cliffs near Warrnambool, in southern Victoria, contain an enigmatic occurrence of edible marine shells, suggesting human harvesting of great antiquity. Located where the Hopkins River meets the sea, and initially known as Point Ritchie but now as Moyjil, the site was reported in 1981 by a field naturalist, Jim Henry, to Edmund Gill, former deputy director of the Museum of Victoria. In much of his work in western Victoria, Gill had the assistance of a co-worker, Dr John Sherwood, a local marine biologist who initially recorded details of the site.[14]

In May 1986, Gill invited a group to inspect the site, a workshop of twenty-two participants, including John Mulvaney, myself and other specialists. The group agreed the shell deposit seemed significant in that exclusively edible species were represented, and therefore this was possibly a midden of human creation. The application of several techniques indicated that the shells were older than 40 000 years. An association with the dark-grey-to-near-black surface of accompanying stones presented a puzzle, but no sign of fire was immediately evident. That the shells were some 4 metres above the present sea level and partly cemented in calcrete suggested a date at least as far back as the last interglacial high sea level—nearly 120 000 years before the present day. As no detailed geological or archaeological analysis had been provided, a natural explanation seemed the only compromise. In its final evaluation, the group resolved that the evidence required further study, but the conviction that it demonstrated a human presence remained equivocal. The setting simply appeared too old, while, at the same time, the geological evidence for a human explanation was found wanting.

For several years I was left uneasy by the peremptory nature of this dismissal. The evidence seemed strong; dismissal was the easy way out. In 2007 I approached John Sherwood, suggesting a joint study to re-evaluate the potential of a human origin of this collection of shells. With his agreement we expanded the team to include geologist Dr Steve Carey of Federation University and archaeologist professor Ian McNiven of Monash University. Regarding it as an exercise in scientific objectivity, we aimed specifically to *disprove* any association with human agency. Our results confirmed the opposite.

The findings of our five-year study, published in 2018, warrant a brief summary.[15] The major uncertainty of age was resolved by two independent lines of evidence: new thermoluminescence dating of the sand enclosing the shells on one hand, and on the other, the identification of sea level at the time of collecting as 8-plus metres above that of the present day. Both pointed to a definitive age of the last interglacial high sea level, a global event that occurred 120 000–125 000 years ago.

The following brief account of the main data justifies this conviction:

- The appearance of only edible shells suggests a high degree of selection.
- There is evidence of multiple small fires—blackened stones—contemporaneous with the shell deposit.
- The excavation of one fire site reflects ordering in a constructed depression.
- Repeated fires on bare rock required the importing of dry wood.
- There is clear evidence of the selection of stones in fire sites, particularly the reuse of small black examples. All small black stones are a legacy of fire. Their location is essentially ordered.
- The organisation of different stones shows some older balanced over some younger, such as a large, erratic limestone boulder perched precariously on the cliff. It had been manually transported onto the shell band.

No natural explanation can be offered for any of these features. Despite the absence of stone tools, food remains or other more specific items of humanity, if we apply the principle of Occam's razor, we have firm grounds for our conviction. This is a case where one and only one explanation clarifies all.

In our attempt to disprove Edmund Gill's original human agency hypothesis, we have come full circle. From my perspective, the presence of people on the coast near Warrnambool at and therefore beyond 120 000 years ago is confirmed. Following a slight decline of maximum sea level at 8-plus metres, people occupied rock platforms at the 6-plus metres level until shoreline retreat permitted burial by later dune accretion. Multiple lines of geological evidence, thoroughly tested, especially for the validity of the 120 000-year result, offer no natural explanation. Lacking a stone tool or any other definitive trace of humanity, many will continue to contest this conclusion. However, the evidence opens a new window into Australia's ancient occupation, with unfolding significance for the global story of humanity, and raises an entirely new set of questions.

Such evidence as that offered here will be subject to scrutiny long after my departure from the scene. Still, despite signs of a long journey ahead, modest progress has been made:

1 Despite the early abuse of human remains, as in the Murray Black and Kow Swamp examples, the 40 000-year-old burials of Mungo Lady and Mungo Man received international acknowledgement by their 1981 World Heritage inscription.
2 The combination of geology and archaeology has contributed to a new story, one in which the land–people unity forms an interwoven fabric, each component helping define the others.
3 We encounter here the living story of First Australians. Embedded in their lands of origin, they invite us to walk hand-in-hand in mutual celebration of the land–people conjunction.

Following the recent failure via a referendum in October 2023 to endorse the First People's Voice to Parliament, it is clear the Australian nation has deep divisions yet to be healed. Where is the healing glue? Is it not possible that this glue resides in the reality of common ground, in communal exploration and celebration of the unified land–people context?

From ancient occupants to present descendants, for both scientists and Traditional Owners, a mutual sense of learning awaits discovery across the cultural divide. My story here is but one small example. Others will expand the sense of land–people unity, a sense that must define a new meaning for the currently divisive 26 January celebration of 'Australia Day'. The unified efforts of geology and archaeology will continue to plough that ground.

Notes

1 JM Bowler, DJ Mulvaney, DA Casey and TA Darragh, 'Green Gully Burial', *Nature*, vol. 213, no. 5072, January 1967, pp. 152–4.
2 Some of the issues with the collection, from an archaeological perspective, are detailed in Sarah Robertson, 'Sources of Bias in the Murray Black Collection: Implications for Palaeopathological Analysis', *Australian Aboriginal Studies*, vol. 1, January 2007, pp. 116–30.
3 TH Huxley, 'A Lecture on the Fossil Remains of Man', *Lancet*, vol. 79, no. 2007, February 1862, pp. 166–7.
4 Quoted in Charles Lyell, *Geological Evidences of the Antiquity of Man*, John Murray, London, 1863, p. 87.
5 NWG Macintosh, 'The Physical Aspect of Man in Australia', in RM Berndt and CH Berndt (eds), *Aboriginal Man in Australia*, Angus & Robertson, Sydney, 1965, p. 59.

6 AG Thorne, 'Mungo and Kow Swamp: Morphological Variation in Pleistocene Australians', *Mankind*, vol. 8, no. 2, December 1971, p. 87.
7 An excellent account of these complexities is available in Darren Curnoe, 'A 150-Year Conundrum: Cranial Robusticity and Its Bearing on the Origin of Aboriginal Australians', *International Journal of Evolutionary Biology*, 2011, pp. 1–18.
8 Tim Stone and Matthew L Cupper, 'Last Glacial Maximum Ages for Robust Humans at Kow Swamp, Southern Australia', *Journal of Human Evolution*, vol. 45, no. 2, August 2003, pp. 99–111.
9 Curnoe, 'A 150-Year Conundrum', p. 12.
10 Victorian Aboriginal Heritage Council, 'Timeline of Historical Events', 25 March 2020, https://www.aboriginalheritagecouncil.vic.gov.au/timeline-historical-events (accessed 23 October 2023).
11 JM Bowler, Rhys Jones, Harry Allen and AG Thorne, 'Pleistocene Human Remains from Australia: A Living Site and Human Cremation from Lake Mungo, Western New South Wales', *World Archaeology*, vol. 2, no. 1, 1970, pp. 39–60.
12 JM Bowler, Harvey Johnston, Jon M Olley, John R Prescott, Richard G Roberts, Wilfred Shawcross and Nigel A Spooner, 'New Ages for Human Occupation and Climatic Change at Lake Mungo, Australia', *Nature*, vol. 421, 2003, pp. 837–40.
13 JM Bowler and AG Thorne, 'Human Remains from Lake Mungo: Discovery and Excavation of Lake Mungo III', in RL Kirk and AG Thorne (eds), *The Origin of the Australians*, Australian Institute of Aboriginal Studies, Canberra, 1976, pp. 127–38.
14 John E Sherwood, 'The Moyjil Site, South-West Victoria, Australia: Prologue—Of People, Birds, Shell and Fire', *Proceedings of the Royal Society of Victoria*, vol. 130, no. 2, January 2018, p. 7.
15 A suite of papers was published on this topic, but see, for example, JM Bowler et al., 'The Moyjil Site, South-West Victoria, Australia: Fire and Environment in a 120 000-Year Coastal Midden—Nature or People?', *Proceedings of the Royal Society of Victoria*, vol. 130, no. 2, January 2018, pp. 71–93.

The Murray Black Collection of Aboriginal Ancestral Remains

MARCIA LANGTON, LOUISE MURRAY and ANTONY SINNI

IN 2010 Jim Berg and Shannon Faulkhead published *Power and the Passion: Our Ancestors Return Home*,[1] an account of Gunditjmara man Jim Berg's commitment to returning Aboriginal ancestral remains,[2] stolen from their graves, to their homelands. In particular, the story is both a recollection and exemplar of Aboriginal self-determination played out in a case brought against the University of Melbourne by Berg, acting in his role as inspector, Archaeological and Aboriginal Relics Preservation Regulations.[3] The University of Melbourne has rarely addressed this history. This chapter hopes to provide the transparency that many have long sought. Some may find it distressing that these events and some of the people involved are being recorded for history, but it is done with the aim of helping Aboriginal people know more about the circumstances under which their ancestors were taken, in the hope this will provide information for their own investigations and further understanding of that history.

George Murray Black

George Murray Black was one of two sons of Scottish settler George Black, a pioneer pastoralist at Tarwin Meadows, South Gippsland.[4] George Black altered large parcels of land in the area by clearing bush and draining wetlands; he introduced cattle, alien grasses and European trees.[5] The first dwelling on the Black property was made of wattle and daub, and was succeeded by a larger house built from timbers salvaged from shipwrecks along the dangerous coast.[6] The Tarwin River was either near or part of the

George Murray Black.

George Murray Black showing Don Ewart the original home at Tarwin Meadows and how it was constructed from wattle and daub, 1962.

property, forming the border for the Bunurong people to the west and the Brataualung tribe of the Gunaikurnai people to the east.

Prior to contacting academics at the University of Melbourne, Black, a graduate in Engineering from the University and a pastoralist like his father, had spent several months of each year searching for Aboriginal ancestral remains buried in graves in the southern part of New South Wales. The remains he exhumed were transferred to William Colin MacKenzie,[7] a contemporary of Black's at the University, and the first director of the Australian Institute of Anatomy, established in Canberra in 1931 to collect the 'unique and fast disappearing fauna of Australia'.[8] George Murray Black's name is an irony pointed out by some who thought 'Murray Black' 'was a description of the collection' rather than 'the name of the collector'.[9] This was because Black's collecting activities took place along the Murray River Basin, and the skeletal remains he collected were Aboriginal, those referred to historically and often unceremoniously as 'blacks'—a divisive term that pitted black against white.[10]

According to Black, MacKenzie first asked him to collect Aboriginal remains for the purpose of building up the Institute's collection so 'that visiting scientists could study the specimens for various features such as shape of skulls, malformations or malnutrition—healed fractures of bones, diseased bones, diseased (syphalyste)—teeth formations re palate formation'.[11] MacKenzie's term as director was relatively short, concluding in 1937 due to ill health. The new director, Frederick William Clements, a public health physician and researcher, continued the Institute's relationship with Black. However, Clements was critical of Black's methodology and was concerned about the unscientific way he acquired material. He wanted to engage a professional anthropologist or ethnologist to work with Black to capture comprehensive information about traditional customs, not just disassociated osteological material.

In a letter to Black dated 17 October 1940, Clements wrote: 'Undoubtedly the only scientific excuse for disturbing this ethnological and anthropological material is that it will furnish us with information on the physical characteristics [and] the tribal habits and customs of a people fast vanishing.'[12] While Clements acknowledged a debt of gratitude to Black, he emphasised 'the importance of collecting a few samples of material that could be used scientifically rather than the accumulation of a lot of material that was of doubtful scientific value'. Clements also commented: 'I feel that in some respects the characteristics of the particular tribes you have excavated have been lost for all time because of the absence of field notes made during the gathering of material.'[13]

At the time Black was excavating Aboriginal graves, the modern discipline of archaeology was a nascent area of study, with the most significant work in Australia being undertaken by 'museum curators—Norman Tindale, Frederick McCarthy and Edmund Gill—none of whom had any formal training in archaeology'.[14] In the mid-1950s John Mulvaney was still the only 'university trained prehistoric archaeologist in the country'.[15] Leaving aside the major concerns around the excavation of Aboriginal ancestral remains articulated by Rosalind Langford in her work *Our Heritage–Your Playground*[16]—Langford identified the cultural values that privileged the interests of white settler colonisers while denying the rights of Aboriginal people to control their past, culture and heritage—trained archaeologists made significant contributions to our understanding of history, as was achieved with excavations in Australia such as at Fromm's Landing and Lake Mungo. In professional archaeology, field notes, the careful mapping of areas and the detailed systematic documentation of excavations are required to give meaning and context to excavated material and therefore make a credible contribution to the study of ancient history. But none of these approaches was used by the amateur Black, and this led to a falling out between him and Clements.

This severing of ties with the Institute of Anatomy precipitated the relationship between Black and University of Melbourne academics, although there is conjecture that Black was in contact with the University before the first record of correspondence. In 1940 Black wrote to the registrar offering the University the Aboriginal ancestral remains rejected by the Institute.[17]

In their Royal Society of Victoria presentation titled 'The Murray Black Collection', Sunderland and Ray described the circumstances under which Black first began collecting for the University of Melbourne:

> One day in the early years of the last war, Professor Sunderland received a letter which stated that the writer knew where some aboriginal bones were buried and that in the view of the wartime conditions, they might be of some use for students studying Anatomy. Professor Sunderland was quick to realise that these bones would be of more use to science than as teaching instruments in normal anatomy and so contacted the writer.[18]

Thus began the relationship between Black and University academics, primarily Sir Sydney Sunderland[19] and professor Leslie Ray, which

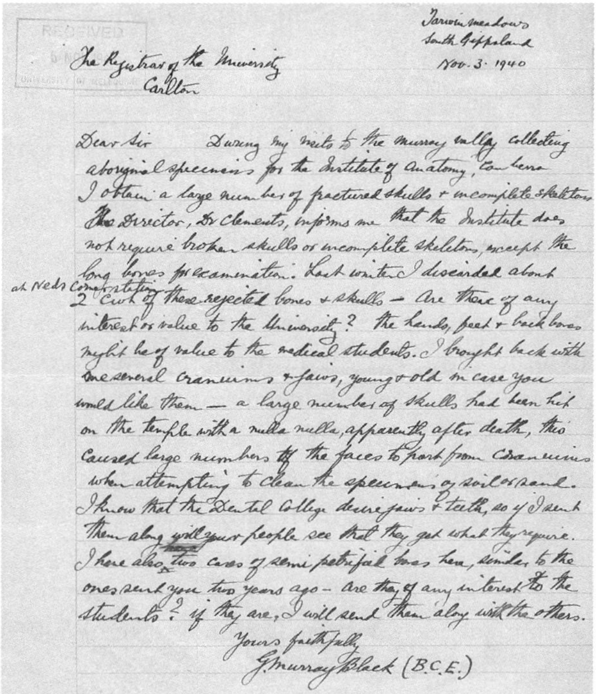

Tarwin Meadows
South Gippsland
Nov. 3. 1940

The Registrar of the University
Carlton

Dear Sir During my visits to the Murray valley collecting aboriginal specimens for the Institute of Anatomy, Canberra I obtain a large number of fractured skulls & incomplete skeletons The Director, Dr Clements, informs me that the Institute does not require broken skulls or incomplete skeletons, except the long bones for examination. Last winter I discarded about 2 cwt of these rejected bones & skulls at Neds Corner station — Are these of any interest or value to the University? The hands, feet & back bones might be of value to the medical students. I brought back with me several Craniums & jaws, young & old in case you would like them — a large number of skulls had been hit on the temple with a nulla nulla, apparently after death, this caused large numbers of the faces to part from Craniums when attempting to clean the specimens of soil or sand. I know that the Dental College desire jaws & teeth, so if I send them along will your people see that they get what they require. I have also two cases of semi petrified bones here, similar to the ones sent you two years ago — are they of any interest to the students? if they are, I will send them along with the others.

Yours faithfully
G. Murray Black (B.C.E.)

Correspondence from George Murray Black to the registrar, University of Melbourne, 3 November 1940.

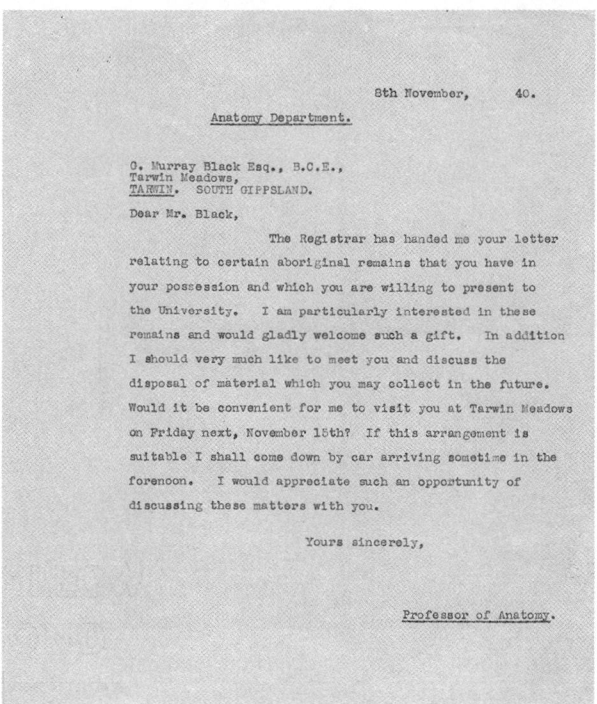

8th November, 40.

Anatomy Department.

G. Murray Black Esq., B.C.E.,
Tarwin Meadows,
TARWIN. SOUTH GIPPSLAND.

Dear Mr. Black,

The Registrar has handed me your letter relating to certain aboriginal remains that you have in your possession and which you are willing to present to the University. I am particularly interested in these remains and would gladly welcome such a gift. In addition I should very much like to meet you and discuss the disposal of material which you may collect in the future. Would it be convenient for me to visit you at Tarwin Meadows on Friday next, November 15th? If this arrangement is suitable I shall come down by car arriving sometime in the forenoon. I would appreciate such an opportunity of discussing these matters with you.

Yours sincerely,

Professor of Anatomy.

Correspondence from professor of anatomy, University of Melbourne, to George Murray Black, 8 November 1940.

continued for nearly twenty-five years. Following Black's death in 1965, other academics from the Medical School, including professor Kenneth Russell, professor Graeme Ryan and Dr Geoff Kenny, continued to curate the collection. Whereas Clements was critical of the methods used by Black, the University uncritically accepted what he offered.

Murray Black and the University of Melbourne

Insights into Black's collecting activities are detailed in documents held by the University of Melbourne. Most of the information is in the form of correspondence between Black and Sunderland and mirrors that held by the National Museum of Australia between Black and the directors. Much of the information and documents relied on in the preparation of this chapter was systematically collected and transferred from various departments to the University of Melbourne Archives. This was done in order to properly map and preserve the information as part of an audit of the University's cultural collections for Aboriginal ancestral remains undertaken in 2018 and presented to the Victorian Aboriginal Heritage Council (VAHC).

Sydney Sunderland, portrait taken during Murray Black field trip, undated (c. 1940s–1950s).

The correspondence reveals a great deal about the relationship between Black and University academics. The letters, which are informal and familiar, include information about the arrangements and locations for various trips, requests for petrol (for which the University provided vouchers), details about the individuals who accompanied Black, and commentary about the practicalities of the weather, rising floodwaters and the need to move camp, the planning for transporting cases of remains, and the suitability of vehicles. The correspondence also includes maps of areas where Black collected, including Robinvale, Euston and Lake Benanee. Some of the trips were attended by Sunderland and Ray, and photographs were taken of the excavations and camp set-ups they took part in.

The correspondence also reveals the sheer number of graves that were destroyed, burial grounds that were ransacked and material that was discarded if it was 'too damaged'. It also reveals that stone tools, axes and mourning caps were disturbed and collected at the time. In one letter, Black writes about how 'the overseer knows of some burial grounds [and] we're much impressed with the prospects and reports'.[20] Not once do Black, Sunderland or Ray speak of the graves as burial sites for the ancestors of

Murray Black's field camp (c. 1940s–1950s).

Unidentified man, one of Murray Black's party, disturbing a burial site.

the living. Their knowledge that this would never have been accepted by Aboriginal people is articulated in a letter to another collector who offered Aboriginal ancestral remains, in which Sunderland writes:

> I am particularly anxious to build up an anthropological collection of Aboriginal bones in order to determine the details, skeletal structure of the Australian Aborigine and, as you will realise, the only sources of much material are the old native burial grounds.[21]

In the same letter, Sunderland gives the following advice regarding arrangements for collecting the remains:

> (1) No publicity of any description must be given to the matter.
> (2) Excavations must be carried out in isolated areas where there are no blacks present at the time.[22]

Among the correspondence files is a small notebook titled 'Results G M Black Anthropological Expedition Lake Benanee 1946, New South Wales'. The notebook includes locations of burial sites, information about the direction in which ancestral remains were laid, and calculations of the numbers of skeletons that were exhumed at the time. It also includes hand-drawn maps of the areas where excavations took place. Apart from the details recorded in correspondence, this notebook is the only one written as a form of field journal while Black was in the process of exhuming ancestral remains. It also provides the key as to how the ancestors were catalogued.

Motivations

It is difficult today to comprehend what drove Murray Black to pursue, often at his own expense, the relentless desecration of Aboriginal burial sites, the taking of ancestors from their graves, and the endorsement of this by the University. Tom Griffiths' in-depth study *Hunters and Collectors* sheds light on the possible motivations, describing the early collectors in Australia—the amateurs and antiquarians who went out searching for Aboriginal artefacts, largely stone tools—as 'hunters'. Griffiths writes:

> Naturalists and antiquarians whether they were in pursuit of nature or culture were inspired by the thrill of the chase and the identification and possession of new specimens. They compared 'bags' and jealously guarded their hunting grounds ... they talked of 'collecting grounds', 'stamping grounds', and 'beats'. They wrote of their 'hunting' and 'flinting', they boasted of 'pickings', of 'browsing over campsites', of 'bringing back quite a useful bag', of joyfully discovering 'virgin' sites.[23]

Griffiths' description of the early collectors resonates with what we know about Black. His activities were undertaken without consulting Aboriginal people and with an obsessive zeal—a grab-and-salvage approach, taking everything before it 'disappeared'. The alignment between Griffiths' observations and Black's activities is articulated in the frequent correspondence between Black and Sunderland. Black writes, 'I have just received an invitation to prospect,'[24] 'next week we will have to pack up and so can't put in full time at the hunting,'[25] and 'we hear of a good camp site at junction of town [?] creek between here & Chowilla homestead and hope to investigate the possibility of working these new banks'. He refers to 'bags of material', 'trips', 'finds', 'a good haul', 'discarded material', 'good' and 'poor specimens' and so on. In response, Sunderland writes, 'Thanks for your letters and the news of good hunting contained in them.'[26]

The published writings of Sunderland and Ray indicate that the ancestral remains of over 800 individuals were handed over by Black. What is not recorded are the hundreds more that were unceremoniously excavated and discarded.[27] By accepting the ancestral remains of Aboriginal people, the University of Melbourne bestowed respectability on Black and sanctioned

Members of Murray Black's party at a disturbed burial site.

his activities in the name of science. Black needed an institution to donate to and the University obliged. In 1984, the same year the collection was transferred from the University to the Museum of Victoria, professor Graeme Ryan, an academic in the Anatomy Department, described Black in a seminar paper titled 'The Murray Black Collection: Preservation of a National Treasure' as 'an early conservationist'. According to Ryan:

> As well as being an engineer, he was keenly interested in archaeology and anthropology. He was particularly concerned that important skeletal material was in danger of being destroyed during civil engineering work. Through his concern, he became one of our early conservationists.[28]

Professor Ryan posits Black as a type of archaeological saviour who, by digging up the graves of Aboriginal people along the Murray River and stealing their remains, was responsible for the preservation of something of immense value for the people of Australia:

> Fifty years ago, engineers were building roads, locks and irrigation systems along the Murray River Basin. With the permission of the local authorities, George Black worked steadily and carefully ahead of the construction engineers to preserve what would otherwise have been permanently lost.[29]

The Ryan paper identifies three key reasons for justifying the preservation and continued custodianship of the University, citing the collection's importance to Aboriginal health, dental health and Australian heritage. But while University academics claimed the material for research, little of this research was produced on or about the collection,[30] and none of it had any bearing on Aboriginal health, dental health or Australian heritage. Sarah Robertson, in her article 'Sources of Bias in the Murray Black Collection', details the publications.[31] Eight papers were written prior to 1984, when the collection was seized, and nine were written in 1984 or afterwards. The most well known, and possibly the only one Ray and Sunderland wrote, was 'A Note on the Murray Black Collection of Australian Aboriginal Skeletons', published by the Royal Society of Victoria in 1959. In this short article (including images), the authors write that most 'fieldwork was carried out over the war years', 'with neither time nor opportunity to acquire any evidence regarding the antiquity of the Ancestral remains'.[32] The article lists

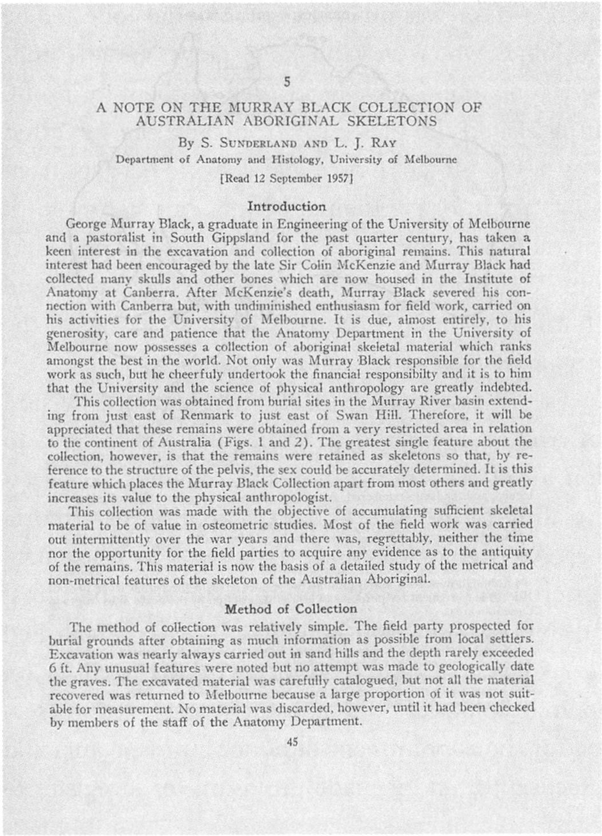

5

A NOTE ON THE MURRAY BLACK COLLECTION OF AUSTRALIAN ABORIGINAL SKELETONS

By S. Sunderland and L. J. Ray

Department of Anatomy and Histology, University of Melbourne

[Read 12 September 1957]

Introduction

George Murray Black, a graduate in Engineering of the University of Melbourne and a pastoralist in South Gippsland for the past quarter century, has taken a keen interest in the excavation and collection of aboriginal remains. This natural interest had been encouraged by the late Sir Colin McKenzie and Murray Black had collected many skulls and other bones which are now housed in the Institute of Anatomy at Canberra. After McKenzie's death, Murray Black severed his connection with Canberra but, with undiminished enthusiasm for field work, carried on his activities for the University of Melbourne. It is due, almost entirely, to his generosity, care and patience that the Anatomy Department in the University of Melbourne now possesses a collection of aboriginal skeletal material which ranks amongst the best in the world. Not only was Murray Black responsible for the field work as such, but he cheerfuly undertook the financial responsibilty and it is to him that the University and the science of physical anthropology are greatly indebted.

This collection was obtained from burial sites in the Murray River basin extending from just east of Renmark to just east of Swan Hill. Therefore, it will be appreciated that these remains were obtained from a very restricted area in relation to the continent of Australia (Figs. 1 and 2). The greatest single feature about the collection, however, is that the remains were retained as skeletons so that, by reference to the structure of the pelvis, the sex could be accurately determined. It is this feature which places the Murray Black Collection apart from most others and greatly increases its value to the physical anthropologist.

This collection was made with the objective of accumulating sufficient skeletal material to be of value in osteometric studies. Most of the field work was carried out intermittently over the war years and there was, regrettably, neither the time nor the opportunity for the field parties to acquire any evidence as to the antiquity of the remains. This material is now the basis of a detailed study of the metrical and non-metrical features of the skeleton of the Australian Aboriginal.

Method of Collection

The method of collection was relatively simple. The field party prospected for burial grounds after obtaining as much information as possible from local settlers. Excavation was nearly always carried out in sand hills and the depth rarely exceeded 6 ft. Any unusual features were noted but no attempt was made to geologically date the graves. The excavated material was carefully catalogued, but not all the material recovered was returned to Melbourne because a large proportion of it was not suitable for measurement. No material was discarded, however, until it had been checked by members of the staff of the Anatomy Department.

45

Sydney Sunderland, and Leslie J Ray, 'A Note on the Murray Black Collection of Australian Aboriginal Skeletons', in *Proceedings of the Royal Society of Victoria*, vol. 71, no. 1, p. 45.

the areas where material was collected—Chowilla, Rufus River, Euston, Lake Benanee, Poon Boon, Nacurrie, Coobool—as well as the direction, posture and position in which the ancestors were laid to rest, and the type and depth of soil the ancestors were found in, among other considerations. In addition to the publications chronicled by Robertson, Black himself appears to have written one unpublished paper titled 'Burial Methods of the Riverina Aboriginals',[33] much of which seems to have been the basis for Sunderland and Ray's article.

Legislation

The ransacking of Aboriginal graves and taking of cultural material eventually led to legislation to protect Aboriginal cultural heritage. Calls for protective legislation in Australia began in New South Wales in the 1930s when professor Joseph Shellshear of the Australian Museum in Sydney wrote an *Appeal for the Preservation of Prehistoric Remains.*[34] Much of this was in response to the vast quantities of material collected by both amateurs and professionals, who were vandalising graves and the landscape by removing prized stone tools or axe heads, selling them for profit, and destroying everything else in the process.[35] Ironically, the intention behind the legislation was not to protect Aboriginal cultural heritage from being disturbed, nor to protect it for Aboriginal people, but to prevent it from disappearing into private hands and ensure it went instead to museums and collecting institutions. Victoria was against protective legislation, and it was not until 1972 that it was finally enacted with the passing of the *Archaeological and Aboriginal Relics Preservation Act 1972.*

This Victorian Act was the first state legislation to 'make Provision for the Preservation of Archaeological and Aboriginal Relics', and to provide broad protection for all Aboriginal deposits, carvings, drawings and 'skeletal remains' relating to the Aboriginal occupation of Victoria (Section 2).[36] The Victoria Archaeological Survey, overseen by Aboriginal Affairs Victoria, administered the Act, while the minister for Aboriginal affairs had overall responsibility for decision-making.[37] The Act established the Archaeological Relics Advisory Committee to advise the minister on all matters pertaining to archaeological relics and their preservation (sections 5 and 7); it allowed for the appointment of honorary inspectors and wardens to enforce it (Section 9); and it made provision for a register to record all Aboriginal archaeological areas, all occurrences of relics, and 'all persons known to be holding private collections of artifacts or unique specimens that include relics' (Section 10). Criticisms of the Act noted that the drafting was informed and undertaken through consultation with professional archaeologists to the exclusion of Aboriginal people and local Indigenous communities.[38] The use of the term 'relic' and its connotation of a 'cultural object' associated with antiquity and embedded in a past, rather than a present culture, was also problematic.[39]

The introduction of legislation and later amendments set the course for Uncle Jim Berg's actions against the University. It coincided with the expansion of Aboriginal activism, and a pivotal historic moment when Aboriginal people found platforms from which to voice their objections to the numerous violations of their rights, especially around land rights and control of their cultural heritage. Included in their grievances was an objection to museums and institutions, both locally and internationally, holding the 'skeletal remains' of their ancestors, something Aboriginal people never approved of or consented to. Aboriginal people, including Jim Berg, wanted their stolen ancestors returned to them, and this desire gave rise to the repatriation movement.[40]

Trukanini and the Beginning of the Repatriation Movement[41]

Formative in the movement for the return of ancestors to their homelands was the repatriation of Trukanini, a Nuenonne woman and the most famous of the Palawa people of the island now known as Tasmania, who witnessed the genocide of her people; she was one of the few survivors. Aware of the terrible practices of the colonists who used Aboriginal bodies for scientific experiments—stealing them from graves and also murdering people for this purpose—she begged that her body not be used in this way. She wanted her ashes scattered in the D'Entrecasteaux Channel between Bruny Island and the Tasmanian mainland. However, when she died in 1876, her remains were exhumed and displayed in the Hobart Museum. And here, her greatest fears were realised. 'Great Men,' wrote Richard Berry, professor of anatomy at the University of Melbourne from 1906 to 1926, 'came from afar to visit Truganini [Trukanini] at the museum to make exact measurements of her skull.'[42]

After many years of demands that Trukanini's remains be returned for a proper interment, in 1976, 100 years after she had passed, the Museum finally agreed. On the fortieth anniversary of this event, Dr Stan Florek recorded the memories of that day. The late Aunty Ida West recounted:

> Truganini's [Trukanini] ashes were scattered on a lovely sunny morning ... a porpoise was swimming around us when the ashes went down. Truganini had asked for this to be done, but it took a hundred years to come about. My daughter Lennah and another lady were with the casket of Truganini before the cremation. Rosalind Langford made a speech at the cremation, and it was very good.[43]

This event was one of the first repatriations of Aboriginal ancestral remains, inspiring Aboriginal people across the country to find ancestors who had suffered the fate of Trukanini and have them returned for a dignified burial or interment according to their traditions. Over many decades, Indigenous people have demanded that museums and other collecting institutions return ancestral remains and sacred objects, but around the world, including here in Australia, some of these institutions have remained intransigent, asserting their ownership of these and their 'right' to keep them for 'scientific purposes'.[44]

Uncle Jim Berg and the University: Legal Proceedings

Eight years after the repatriation of Trukanini, the long saga of litigation and campaigning by Aboriginal people to have their Old People returned resulted in a breakthrough in Victoria when Uncle Jim Berg won a court injunction against the University of Melbourne, which was ordered to transfer the Murray Black collection to the Museums Board of Victoria. In 1984 the Victorian Government implemented important amendments to the *Archaeological and Aboriginal Relics Preservation Act 1972* (Vic.), which had significant legal implications for the custody of 'Aboriginal skeletal remains'.[45] Most notably, under Section 26B, it was now an offence to possess, display or have under control any 'Aboriginal skeletal remains' without the written consent of the secretary of the environment. The University was in possession of the Murray Black collection and other collections of 'Aboriginal skeletal remains'.[46] Despite their long-term custodianship, this possession was unlawful without the required statutory consent, and so in contravention of the Act. As the official place of lodgement, the Museum of Victoria became the lawful custodian of the collection.[47]

At the time of the amendment, Uncle Jim Berg was a member of the Archaeological Relics Advisory Committee, making him a warden and inspector under the Act.[48] Through his connections, he was aware that the University was in possession of Aboriginal ancestral remains and exercised his powers under sections 12(1) and 31 to serve the University a Notice to Impound and Detain 'all Aboriginal skeletal remains interred prior to 1834, including but not limited to the collection of skeletal remains known as the Murray Black collection'.[49]

The University's Response

University of Melbourne authorities asserted their entitlement to hold the Murray Black collection, a view that became clear in the events that followed receipt of the notice. Correspondence from the University solicitor's office reveals the interpretation of the amended provisions, with the letters stating it was 'a manifest absurdity to impound remains where possession has been enjoyed for so long'.[50] In a memorandum with the University registrar

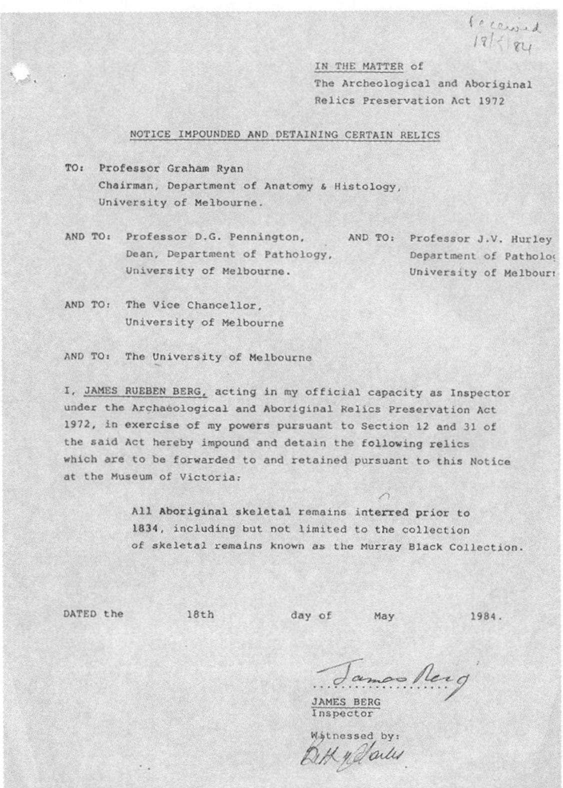

IN THE MATTER of
The Archeological and Aboriginal
Relics Preservation Act 1972

NOTICE IMPOUNDED AND DETAINING CERTAIN RELICS

TO: Professor Graham Ryan
Chairman, Department of Anatomy & Histology,
University of Melbourne.

AND TO: Professor D.G. Pennington,
Dean, Department of Pathology,
University of Melbourne.

AND TO: Professor J.V. Hurley
Department of Patholo
University of Melbour

AND TO: The Vice Chancellor,
University of Melbourne

AND TO: The University of Melbourne

I, JAMES RUEBEN BERG, acting in my official capacity as Inspector under the Archaeological and Aboriginal Relics Preservation Act 1972, in exercise of my powers pursuant to Section 12 and 31 of the said Act hereby impound and detain the following relics which are to be forwarded to and retained pursuant to this Notice at the Museum of Victoria:

All Aboriginal skeletal remains interred prior to 1834, including but not limited to the collection of skeletal remains known as the Murray Black Collection.

DATED the 18th day of May 1984.

JAMES BERG
Inspector

Witnessed by:

Notice to Impound and Detain Certain Relics, served upon The University of Melbourne by Uncle Jim Berg, 18 May 1984.

James Potter, acting University solicitor Michele Kelly concluded 'the notice itself lacks legislative authority and its description of relics is insufficient'.[51] Furthermore, 'the amendments to section 26B must act prospectively and not take away existing rights of possession that the University has under general law and 26A'.[52]

Asserting the University's right to the collection, Potter and Kelly 'dismissed the possibility of the notice itself acting as an impoundment' and recommended the University not apply to the secretary for consent to retain the relics.[53] They advised the University to 'refuse releasing the collection',[54] until the right to impound it could be established in legal proceedings.[55] Other correspondence suggests the University was deliberately unresponsive to the preliminary notice, as doing so allowed the notice (in legal terms, the doctrine) to be treated as an 'intention to impound only',[56] in order to stop any transfer of the collection.[57]

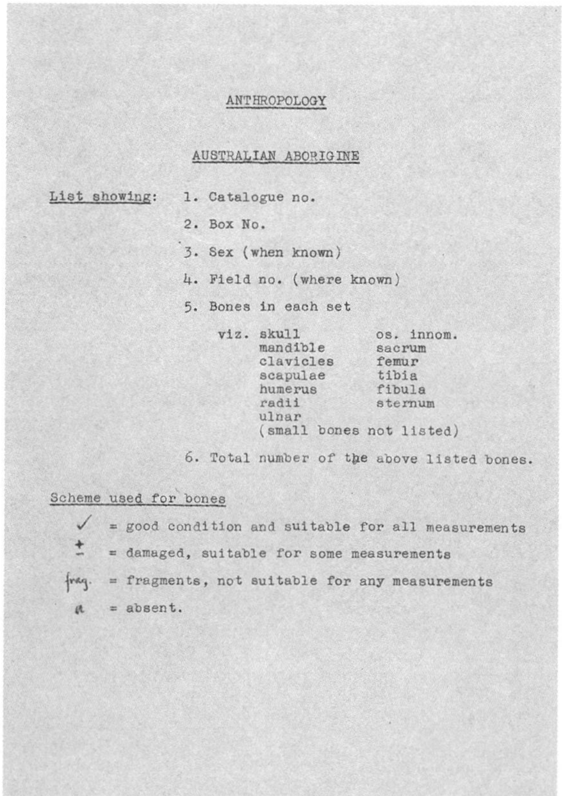

ANTHROPOLOGY

AUSTRALIAN ABORIGINE

List showing:
1. Catalogue no.
2. Box No.
3. Sex (when known)
4. Field no. (where known)
5. Bones in each set

viz. skull, mandible, clavicles, scapulae, humerus, radii, ulnar, os. innom., sacrum, femur, tibia, fibula, sternum
(small bones not listed)

6. Total number of the above listed bones.

Scheme used for bones

✓ = good condition and suitable for all measurements
± = damaged, suitable for some measurements
frag. = fragments, not suitable for any measurements
a = absent.

Catalogue of the 'Murray Black' human remains collection, title page, undated.

The University's leadership resisted meeting with Jim Berg until he hand-delivered a second notice in addition to a letter that outlined the amendments to the Act.[58] When Uncle Jim met with vice-chancellor David Caro, he insisted on a response, specifically that the University surrender the remains to the Museum of Victoria in order for the intent of the Act to become effective in allowing the repatriation of ancestral remains to their communities of origin.[59] The Victorian Aboriginal Legal Service (VALS) sent a follow-up letter on the day of the meeting requesting information on the state of the remains at the University and permission for Uncle Jim to examine them.[60] The vice-chancellor rejected the demand to surrender, prompting Uncle Jim to seek an injunction to prevent the University from keeping the remains.

Injunction Order

For Uncle Jim, obtaining an injunction order was critical, and he retained legal counsel. The challenge for lawyer Ron Merkel QC (who became a justice of the Federal Court in 1996) came down to convincing Justice Gobbo of the Supreme Court of Victoria why the injunction was required so soon after the amendments to the Act had been gazetted, and why it needed to occur without giving the University notice.[61] Correspondence between the University and Mallesons Solicitors and Notaries[62] shows that a large part of the University's defence was due to procedural grievances over the timing and nature of the notice's delivery, as the initial notice was served two days after the amendments came into effect.[63] The University's perspective was that this was the 'first official indication of the enactment of the legislation',[64] and the viability of their contravention was to be contended given the offence was newly implemented and the amendments only available in Bill form.[65] However, it should have been possible to monitor passage of the Bill through the parliament. Moreover, the implication that the University would have obtained the consent, but was obstructed by the rapid service of the notice, was not convincing, as Justice Gobbo must have noticed.

In a remarkable moment for the Aboriginal people of Victoria, Merkel convinced Justice Gobbo to grant the injunction, considering the University's clear hostility and desire to retain custody of the remains.[66] The University was still holding the remains illegally and persisted in doing so. Under Section 26B of the Act, it was drawn to the University's attention that holding the remains was illegal, and further, it had been clearly communicated that, following the amendments to the Act, retention of the remains continued to be in contravention of the legislation. The University had been reminded in three separate instances by notice and again in correspondence from VALS. Merkel made the argument to Justice Gobbo that the order was required to preserve the subject matter of the litigation—or, in other words, to ensure the case could proceed with integrity—and any notice of the injunction would defeat its purpose.[67] Justice Gobbo agreed and a Supreme Court writ and accompanying documents were then served on the University.[68]

Application for Consent under Section 26B

The University also held other collections of ancestral remains, and Uncle Jim was aware of this. Upon service of the Supreme Court writ and injunction, Mallesons Solicitors and Notaries advised the University to obtain the statutory consent under Section 26B in order to regain lawful custody over the Murray Black Collection, and thereby thwart the intention of the Act and the Supreme Court writ.[69] Vice-chancellor Caro sent an application to the secretary of planning and the environment, David Yencken, seeking written consent for the possession and control of the Murray Black and Donald Thomson collections that also held ancestral remains.[70]

The extensive application incorporated numerous national and international publications and letters in support of the University's preservation of the collection. Despite the lack of evidence of any concern for humanity or science, the University argued that the collection was '*placed*' (authors' emphasis) in their custody to 'foster the study of history and development'. It said this would benefit 'all mankind, irrespective of race', as the 'continued use of the collection gives more information about Aboriginal culture' to 'help fight racism and bigotry'. The University affirmed that there 'will be no further collections of such material in the future', which makes the collection 'even more unique' and its preservation 'more cogent', and therefore it must 'be kept in a controlled environment that can accommodate examination and study'.[71] It later emerged, in the 1990s and 2000s, that further collections of ancestral remains had been found in the University's possession, although by this time it was evident these were being held illegally.

Significantly, and upon receiving advice from the Relics Advisory Committee, the secretary rejected the University's application,[72] as it still had unlawful possession of the collection at the time of applying for consent.[73] In issuing the impounding order, the University's custody was only lawful *subject to* Jim Berg's direction as warden and inspector under the Act. As the matter was being adjudicated by the Supreme Court, the secretary directed the University to transfer the ancestral remains to the Museum of Victoria,[74] the official place of lodgement.[75]

The Judgment

In the case heard in the Supreme Court of Victoria, Justice Murphy held in favour of Jim Berg and instructed the University to transfer the collection to the Museum.[76] Justice Murphy found that, despite being the 'seat of knowledge and learning we know it is', the University was still subject to the 'strict provisions of the Act' and should have sought the statutory consent prior to the Act's promulgation.[77]

Uncle Jim's quest to see the ancestors returned to their homeland did not end with this legal case, however. Once the remains were transferred to the Museum, the distressing and onerous job of provenancing commenced. The poor collecting practices first noted by Clements meant that the ancestral remains could only be returned to regions and not specific descendant families. The cataloguing method used by the University comprised two sequences of numbers—the year of removal and an item number—but little other information. Knowledge of where Murray Black collected each year provided key information to establish where the remains came from.

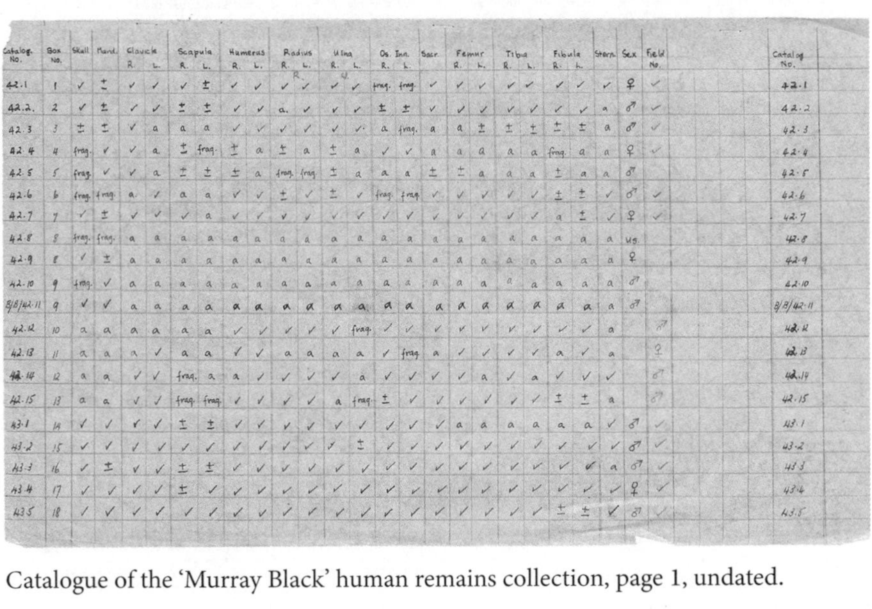

Catalog. No.	Box No.	Skull	Mand.	Clavicle R.	L.	Scapula R.	L.	Humerus R.	L.	Radius R.	L.	Ulna R.	L.	Os. Inn. R.	L.	Sacr.	Femur R.	L.	Tibia R.	L.	Fibula R.	L.	Stern.	Sex	Field No.	Catalog No.
42.1	1	✓	±	✓	✓	✓	±	✓	✓	✓	✓	✓	✓	frag.	frag.	✓	✓	✓	✓	✓	✓	✓	✓	♀	✓	42.1
42.2.	2	✓	±	✓	✓	±	±	✓	✓	a.	✓	✓	✓	±	±	✓	✓	✓	✓	✓	✓	✓	a	♂	✓	42.2
42.3	3	±	±	✓	a	a	a	✓	✓	✓	✓	✓	✓	a	frag.	a	a	±	±	±	±	±	a	♂	✓	42.3
42.4	4	frag.	✓	✓	a	±	frag.	±	a	±	a	±	a	✓	✓	a	a	a	a	a	frag.	a	a	♀	✓	42.4
42.5	5	frag.	✓	✓	a	±	±	±	a	frag.	frag.	±	a	a	a	±	±	a	a	a	±	a	a	♂		42.5
42.6	6	frag.	frag.	a.	✓	a	a	✓	✓	±	✓	±	✓	frag.	frag.	✓	✓	✓	✓	✓	±	±	✓	♂	✓	42.6
42.7	7	✓	±	✓	✓	✓	a	✓	✓	✓	✓	✓	✓	✓	✓	✓	✓	✓	✓	✓	a	±	✓	♀	✓	42.7
42.8	8	frag.	frag.	a	a	a	a	a	a	a	a	a	a	a	a	a	a	a	a	a	a	a	a	US.		42.8
42.9	8	✓	±	a	a	a	a	a	a	a	a	a	a	a	a	a	a	a	a	a	a	a	a	♀		42.9
42.10	9	frag.	✓	a	a	a	a	a	a	a	a	a	a	a	a	a	a	a	a	a	a	a	a	♂		42.10
8/8/42.11	9	✓	✓	a	a	a	a	a	a	a	a	a	a	a	a	a	a	a	a	a	a	a	a	♂		8/8/42.11
42.12	10	a	a	a	a	a	a	✓	✓	✓	✓	✓	frag.	✓	✓	✓	✓	✓	✓	✓	✓	✓	a		♂	42.12
42.13	11	a	a	a	✓	a	a	✓	✓	a	a	a	a	✓	frag.	a	✓	✓	✓	✓	a	✓	a		♀	42.13
42.14	12	a	a	✓	✓	frag.	a	a	✓	✓	✓	✓	a	✓	✓	✓	✓	a	✓	a	✓	✓	✓		♂	42.14
42.15	13	a	a	✓	✓	frag.	frag.	✓	✓	✓	✓	a	frag.	±	✓	✓	✓	✓	✓	✓	±	±	a		♂	42.15
43.1	14	✓	✓	✓	✓	±	±	✓	✓	✓	✓	✓	✓	✓	✓	✓	a	a	a	a	a	a	✓	♂	✓	43.1
43.2	15	✓	✓	✓	✓	✓	✓	✓	✓	✓	✓	✓	±	✓	✓	✓	✓	✓	✓	✓	✓	✓	✓	♂	✓	43.2
43.3	16	✓	±	✓	✓	±	±	✓	✓	✓	✓	✓	✓	✓	✓	✓	✓	✓	✓	✓	✓	✓	a	♂	✓	43.3
43.4	17	✓	✓	✓	✓	±	✓	✓	✓	✓	✓	✓	✓	✓	✓	✓	✓	✓	✓	✓	✓	✓	✓	♀	✓	43.4
43.5	18	✓	✓	✓	✓	✓	✓	✓	✓	✓	✓	✓	✓	✓	✓	✓	✓	✓	✓	✓	±	±	✓	♂	✓	43.5

Catalogue of the 'Murray Black' human remains collection, page 1, undated.

Years could be matched to locations and catalogue numbers; for example, 1942 Tocumwal, 1943 Chowilla Locks Area, 1944 Moulamein, 1945 Rufus River Area, 1946 Benanee Lakes Area, 1947 Boon Boon Area, 1949 Nacurrie, 1950 Wakool River Area and so on. In addition, the ancestral remains had been stored by bone type and not as individuals, so reuniting the ancestors also had to be undertaken. Both Aboriginal and non-Aboriginal people, physical anthropologists and museum staff, were involved and worked diligently and respectfully to establish provenance and to bring together the dispersed remains as the individuals they were before they were callously exhumed.

Relics act puts Walker off-side with academics

By BILL BIRNBAUER

The attempt by Joel Auctions to sell 92 Aboriginal artifacts late last year sparked an unlikely chain of events which today is threatening archaeological research of world importance, has given a group of Aborigines unprecedented power to determine the future of their heritage and has placed the State Government in a no-win position.

The relics were seized in October and a prosecution was launched by the Government under the Archaelogical and Aboriginal Relics Preservation Act which makes it an offence to sell relics without the approval of the secretary of the Department of Planning and Environment.

In February, Mr Maurice Gerkins, SM, said the act was so ambiguous that a prosecution under it was almost impossible. The charges against Joel Auctions and the Adelaide-based collector who supplied the artifacts were dismissed.

The next month, the Minister for Planning and Environment, Mr Walker, introduced an amendment to the act which specifically made it an offence to buy, sell or display Aboriginal relics without official approval.

The matter seemed settled at this point. But two days after the legislation received Royal assent, Mr Jim Berg, an executive officer of the Aboriginal Legal Service and a warden under the act, appeared unexpectedly at the department of anatomy at Melbourne University and impounded the entire Murray Black collection of Aboriginal skeletal remains.

The Murray Black collection, which consists of the skeletal remains of 800 people and is estimated to be between 10,000 and 14,000 years old, had been stored, preserved and studied at the university for 40 years.

The university did not have the permission of the secretary of the department, as required under the amended act, to be in possession of the remains. In the ensuing Supreme Court action, the university was ordered to hand the collection to the National Museum of Victoria by 23 August.

A professor of anatomy at Melbourne University, Professor Graeme Ryan, said yesterday that the bones were of immense scientific importance in tracing the origin of Aborigines in Australia. New techniques had recently become available overseas which could accurately date the bones without damaging them.

Mr Walker: "Legislation will stop trading in relics".

Mr Berg: seized remains from university.

"If the bones are destroyed, we will all lose the opportunity of determining the chronology of our heritage in Australia," he said. "The Aborigines of the future won't thank this current generation if this material is damaged. What has happened is that the Government has amended the legislation to outlaw an area of research at the university."

On the day the Supreme Court ruled that the collection should go to the museum — where the storage facilities are described by Professor Ryan as antiquated and overcrowded — Mr Berg said the collection and other remains would be returned to their ancient burial grounds along the Murray River.

The comment sparked a storm of protest among the international scientific community. The professor of anthropology at the University of Michigan, Professor Milford Wolpoff, said reburial of the bones would be an unparalleled tragedy which would end attempts to discover the origins of the Aboriginal population.

The Liberal Party's spokesman on the matter, Mr Chamberlain, said yesterday he had letters from the University of Kansas, the Witwatersrand School of Medicine in South Africa and other academics pleading that the bones be saved. The international journal 'Science' recently published an article headed 'Extinction threatens Australian anthropology' and it is believed Australian scientists have the support of the National Science Foundation in the US.

In an attempt to defuse the issue, Mr Walker announced recently that a committee of experts would spend the next 12 months evaluating the Murray Black collection. He said the Aboriginal community did not have a united opinion on whether the remains should be reburied.

In a letter to the 'Bulletin', Mr Walker confirmed that the intent of the legislation was to "stop commercial trading in relics and to ensure that Aborigines were consulted about the future of their heritage".

At no stage did Mr Walker refer to a committee which has been working since March this year to draft an Aboriginal Heritage Bill to replace the present act. 'The Age' revealed yesterday that the committee was considering a proposal which would give the State Government the legal ownership of all Aboriginal relics, skeletal remains and burial sites both in private and scientific collections and on private land.

Under the proposal, the Government would have the power to delegate or transfer the possession and control of Aboriginal burial and sacred sites as well as private and scientific collections or relics and remains.

Bill Birnbauer, 'Relics Act Puts Walker Off-Side with Academics,' *The Age*, 14 September 1984.

Final Comments[78]

In the twenty-first century, when the entire human genome has been mapped, revealing there is no sound scientific basis for the idea of 'race' or 'racial science', it is difficult to understand why institutions and collectors keep ancestral remains. As a result of Indigenous people relentlessly lobbying governments and museums, some ancestral remains have come home, but many international institutions hide behind legislation to prevent returns. The *United Nations Declaration on the Rights of Indigenous Peoples* (UNDRIP) makes it clear what the requirements and basic rights of Indigenous people are for their 'survival, dignity and well-being'. While the *Declaration* does not have the status of international law, it does provide a body of standards that were agreed by all the ratifying states. Underpinning UNDRIP is the articulation of the role of the state in ensuring that the rights of Indigenous people are supported through the available legal, political and administrative mechanisms. Article 12, which refers specifically to repatriation, is of particular importance:

> 1 Indigenous peoples have the right to manifest, practice, develop and teach their spiritual and religious traditions, customs and ceremonies; the right to maintain, protect, and have access in privacy to their religious and cultural sites; the right to the use and control of their ceremonial objects; and the right to the repatriation of their human remains.
>
> and
>
> 2 States shall seek to enable the access and/or repatriation of ceremonial objects and human remains in their possession through fair, transparent and effective mechanisms developed in conjunction with the indigenous peoples concerned.

The theft of ancestors and the trade in ancestral remains are not only illegal but a cause of great distress and sadness for Aboriginal people. In September 2021, Gooniyandi and Gija man Neil Carter from the Kimberley Aboriginal Law and Culture Centre came out of retirement to work on a project researching the illegal buying and selling of ancestors online.[79] According to Carter, 'it was appalling to think that people were still profiting from the sale of bones and hair samples ... It's unbelievable that this is still going on ... It's something that's been kept quiet, but it should be made public, so people know what's been happening to our people since colonisation'.[80]

Apart from the illicit trade, the other insult to Aboriginal people is the lack of a facility for unprovenanced remains, many of which are returned from overseas institutions with no accompanying records. Without any records, no-one can know who the ancestors were or where to return them. The Ngurra Cultural Precinct, approved in the 2022 Commonwealth Budget, is envisaged as the national keeping place for these Old People, providing a dignified resting place and a memorial while their histories are investigated, in the hope they can one day be returned to their communities of origin. Several important historical works recount how they were stolen from their graves and traded among institutions for the 'racial' entertainment of museum audiences, and to teach 'racial science' in universities.[81]

The University of Melbourne collected thousands of Aboriginal ancestral remains and was a major centre for the study of the now discredited field of eugenics. In Victoria, the long saga of litigation and campaigning by Aboriginal people to have their Old People returned resulted in a breakthrough when Uncle Jim Berg won his court injunction, firstly against Museum Victoria, preventing a collection of Australian Indigenous remains from Kow Swamp and Keilor being sent to America for an exhibition entitled 'Ancestors', and then the University of Melbourne. Changes in museum practices followed. In particular, the work of Uncle Jim Berg led to an important change in Victorian legislation: the amendment in 2016 to the *Victorian Aboriginal Cultural Heritage Act* that places the ownership of ancestral remains and secret or sacred objects with Aboriginal people, and the authority to manage repatriation in the hands of the VAHC.[82]

Notes

1 Shannon Faulkhead and Jim Berg with Lynette Russell, Ross L Jones and Jason Eades, *Power and the Passion: Our Ancestors Return Home*, Koorie Heritage Trust, Melbourne, 2010. In 2022, Museums Victoria published a new, updated version of *Power and the Passion*. with an expanded section on repatriation and additional contributions from those currently working in this area of important cultural responsibility.

2 This chapter uses the term 'Aboriginal ancestral remains' as defined in the *Aboriginal Heritage Act 2006* (Vic.), Part 1, Section 4, or 'ancestral remains'.

3 In 1983, Uncle Jim Berg was both CEO of the Victorian Aboriginal Legal Service, and inspector, Archaeological and Aboriginal Relics Preservation Regulations, under the *Archaeological and Aboriginal Relics Preservation Act* (Vic.) 1972: Faulkhead and Berg, *Power and the Passion*, p. 8.

4 Steven Henty, 'George Black of "Tarwin": Pioneer's Hectic Road to Riches', *Chronicle*, 5 November 1936, p. 64.

5 J Ann Hone, 'George Black (1813–1902)', *Australian Dictionary of Biography*, National Centre of Biography, Australian National University, Canberra, 2006, https://adb.anu.edu.au/biography/black-george-2999 (accessed 24 October 2023).

6 Ibid.

7 For information regarding Sir William Colin MacKenzie and the establishment of the Australian Institute of Anatomy, see Australian Government, *Official Yearbook of the Commonwealth of Australia*, no. 37, 1946 and 1947, Chapter XXVIII and p. 1186. MacKenzie, originally from Melbourne, was a colleague of Richard Berry's in the University's Anatomy Department and a friend of Murray Black's with a shared interest in collecting. MacKenzie gifted his entire private collection to the Institute, through the Commonwealth Government.

8 Ibid.

9 See Lynette Russell, 'Reflections on Murray Black's Writing', in Faulkhead and Berg, *Power and the Passion*, p. 58.

10 'Blak' was claimed by artist Destiny Deacon, who took ownership of the word for Australia's Aboriginal people. According to Deacon: 'Growing up, I always heard the words "You little black c...s" from white people. It's still common (to have) black c....s being shouted at us.' Deacon added: 'I just wanted to take the "C" out of "black". I was able to convince Hetti Perkins and Claire Williamson to alter their curated urban Indigenous exhibition to "Blakness: Blak City Culture" (ACCA, Melbourne) without the "c" in 1994.' See Kate Munro, 'Why "Blak" not Black? Artist Destiny Deacon and the Origin of This Word', *NITV*, 29 June 2020, https://www.sbs.com.au/nitv/article/2020/05/07/why-blak-not-black-artist-destiny-deacon-and-origins-word-1 (accessed 24 October 2023).

11 George Murray Black to John McEwan, minister for commerce and agriculture, Canberra, 31 May 1951, National Museum Australia, Department of Health Murray Black File 85/718, 88/563.

12 Frederick William Clements to George Murray Black, 17 October 1940, National Museum of Australia, Murray Black Collection, files 85/718, 88/563.

13 Ibid.

14 Billy Griffiths, *Deep Time Dreaming: Uncovering Ancient Australia*, Black Inc., Melbourne, 2020, p. 17.

15 Ibid., p. 23.

16 See Sandra Bowdler and Tasmanian Aboriginal Centre, 'Rosalind Langford (1946–2012)', *Australian Archaeology*, 2012, pp. 137–8 for a summary of the important work of Rosalind Langford. *Our Heritage—Your Playground* (RF Langford, Hobart, 1983) identified that 'scientific professions were underpinned by the cultural values of white supremacist imperialism and maintained by the self-serving denial of the rights over heritage, and even the continuing existence, of Indigenous people', asserting the need for 'archaeologists to take practical steps to acknowledge Aboriginal ownership and control of their past as a pre- condition for any future working relationship'.

17 George Murray Black to the registrar, the University of Melbourne, 3 November 1940, item 2018.0080.00172 in Records Relating to the 'Murray Black' Collection of Aboriginal Human Remains, University of Melbourne Archives.

18 Unknown author, 'The Murray Black Collection', unpublished paper, c. late 1950s to 1965, file USD2018115-12-001, University of Melbourne Archives.

19 Ross L Jones, 'Sir Sydney (Syd) Sunderland (1910–1993)', *Australian Dictionary of Biography*, National Centre of Biography, Australian National University, Canberra, 2017, https://adb.anu.edu.au/biography/sunderland-sir-sydney-syd-26721/text34360 (accessed 24 October 2023).
20 George Murray Black to Sydney Sunderland, 21 September 1941. Item: 2018.0080.00162 in Records relating to the 'Murray Black' collection of Aboriginal Human Remains, University of Melbourne Archives.
21 Sydney Sunderland to Mr AE Pengelly, 9 June 1944. Item: 2018.0080.00148 in Records relating to the 'Murray Black' collection of Aboriginal Human Remains, University of Melbourne Archives.
22 Ibid.
23 Tom Griffiths, *Hunters and Collectors: The Antiquarian Imagination in Australia*, Cambridge University Press, Melbourne, 1996, p. 19.
24 George Murray Black to Sydney Sunderland, 12 March c. 1950. Item: 2018.0080.00193 in Records relating to the 'Murray Black' collection of Aboriginal Human Remains, University of Melbourne Archives.
25 George Murray Black to Sydney Sunderland, Camp Coobool, c. 1942. Item: 2018.0080.00155 in Records relating to the 'Murray Black' collection of Aboriginal Human Remains, University of Melbourne Archives.
26 George Murray Black to Sydney Sunderland (not signed), 15 August 1947. Item: 2018.0080.00129 in Records relating to the 'Murray Black' collection of Aboriginal Human Remains, University of Melbourne Archives.
27 Sydney Sunderland and Leslie Ray, 'A Note on the Murray Black Collection of Australian Aboriginal Skeletons', *Proceedings of the Royal Society of Victoria*, vol. 71, 1959, p. 45.
28 Graeme B Ryan, 'The Murray Black Collection: Preservation of a National Treasure', 2 October 1984, in File 2019.0005.00002 of University Correspondence and Legal Arguments Pertaining to the 'George Murray Black' and 'Richard Berry' Collections of Human Remains, University of Melbourne Archives.
29 Ibid.
30 Other contemporaneous collections, such as the Donald Thomson Collection, were the result of sustained, locally and internationally recognised research by the academic Donald Thomson over many years, which resulted in multiple publications: see Alison Inglis, 'Retirement and Recollection: Dr Ray Marginson AM and the Donald Thomson Collection', *University of Melbourne Collections*, vol. 13, 2013, p. 35. At the same time that Black was desecrating Aboriginal graves, Thomson was starting to build his collection, a vastly different proposition that included journals, detailed field notes, maps, photographs, objects, and film and audio recordings. He would continue to do this over a period of thirty years while living and working with Aboriginal people in Cape York, Arnhem Land and the Central Desert. The collection comprehensively represents peoples, place and context.
31 For a list of publications based on the Murray Black collection, see Sarah Robertson, 'Sources of Bias in the Murray Black Collection: Implications for Palaeopathological Analysis', *Australian Aboriginal Studies*, vol. 1, 2007, p. 117.
32 Sunderland and Ray, 'A Note on the Murray Black Collection', p. 45.
33 Ryan, 'The Murray Black Collection'.
34 Griffiths, *Hunters and Collectors*, p. 76.

35 Ibid.
36 The *Archaeological and Aboriginal Relics Preservation Act 1972* (Vic.) uses the term 'skeletal remains' instead of 'Aboriginal ancestral remains', which is used in the *Aboriginal Heritage Act 2006* (Vic.).
37 See Lincoln Hayes, *Indigenous Cultural Heritage Schemes in Victoria, Queensland and the Northern Territory: An Overview—A Report Prepared for the South Australia Native Title Resolution Negotiating Parties*, Research Section, National Native Title Tribunal, May 2009, https://www.yumpu.com/en/document/view/35354709/indigenous-cultural-heritage-schemes-in-victoria-queensland-and- (accessed 24 October 2023), p. 13.
38 Ibid., p. 3.
39 Ibid., pp. 3–4.
40 The desire by Aboriginal people to challenge and change their relationship with the cultural institutions that housed and controlled large portions of their cultural heritage came in the wake of a series of historically symbolic and politically far-reaching events instigated by Indigenous people all over Australia. These included, but were not limited to, the consciousness-raising of the Day of Mourning and Protest, held on 26 January 1938, marking the sesquicentenary of the landing of captain Arthur Phillip in New South Wales in 1788; the Freedom Ride of 1965, inspired by the freedom rides in America and which drew attention to the unjust and racist treatment of Aboriginal people, particularly in regional towns; the land rights and equity for Indigenous workers expressed in the Gurindji walk-off from the Wave Hill cattle station in 1966; the referendum of 1967; and perhaps most importantly in recent times, the case launched by Eddie Koiki Mabo that led to the Mabo decision in 1992 and native title in 1993.
41 Parts of this section of the chapter are reproduced from Marcia Langton, *Marcia Langton: Welcome to Country—A Travel Guide to Indigenous Australia*, 2nd edn, Hardie Grant Explore, Melbourne, 2021, pp. 164–8.
42 Richard Glover, 'Science's Body Snatchers', *National Times*, 16–20 September 1984, p. 16.
43 Dr Stan Florek, 'Fortieth Anniversary of Returning to Truganini Land (and Water)', *National Indigenous Television*, 22 July 2016, https://www.sbs.com.au/nitv/article/2016/07/22/fortieth-anniversary-returning-truganini-land-and-water (accessed 24 October 2023); originally published at https://australian.museum/blog-archive/science/our-global-neighbours-remembering-truganini
44 Paul Turnbull, 'Managing and Mapping the History of Collecting Indigenous Human Remains', *Australian Library Journal*, vol. 65, no. 3, 2016, pp. 203–12. See also Langford, *Our Heritage—Your Playground*; and Langton, *Marcia Langton*, pp. 165–8.
45 The *Archaeological and Aboriginal Relics Preservation (Amendment) Act 1984* (Vic.) (*Amendment Act*' repealed the *Archaeological and Aboriginal Relics Preservation Act 1972* (Vic.).
46 The Richard Berry collection was still in the custody of the University.
47 Under Section 20A(1) of the *Amendment Act*, the Museums Board of Victoria became the official place of lodgement for relics that were Crown property. All other relics directed to be removed by the minister were also entrusted to be lodged at the Museum under the care of the Museum's director, unless consultation with the minister for the arts determined otherwise (Section 20A (2)).
48 *Amendment Act 1984* (Vic.), Section 5.

49 Ibid., sections 12(1) and 13. The notice was addressed to professor Graham Ryan, dean of the Medical School; professor David Penington; and vice-chancellor professor David Caro: see Notice to Impound and Detain Relics, file 2019.0005.00001, University Correspondence and Legal Arguments Pertaining to the 'George Murray Black' and 'Richard Berry' Collections of Human Remains, University of Melbourne Archives. The service of this notice marked the commencement of legal proceedings between the University and Jim Berg: see *Berg v The University of Melbourne, Caro, David & Potter, James* [1984] VicSC 290 (18 June 1984).
50 Memorandum between Michele Kelly and James Potter, 21 May 1984, file 2019.0005.00001, item 1 of University Correspondence and Legal Arguments Pertaining to the 'George Murray Black' and 'Richard Berry' Collections of Human Remains, University of Melbourne Archives.
51 Ibid.
52 Ibid., item 3.
53 Ibid., item 1.
54 Ibid.
55 This had already been established by sections 12(1) and 31.
56 Ibid.
57 Memorandum between Ian Barrah and James Potter, 21 May 1984, file 2019.0005.00001, University Correspondence and Legal Arguments Pertaining to the 'George Murray Black' and 'Richard Berry' Collections of Human Remains, University of Melbourne Archives.
58 The notice was delivered on 22 May: see *Murray Black Collection: Brief History of Proceedings*, 14 August 1984, file 2019.0005.00001, University Correspondence and Legal Arguments Pertaining to the 'George Murray Black' and 'Richard Berry' Collections of Human Remains, University of Melbourne Archives.
59 Ibid.
60 Brendan Kissane to University of Melbourne registrar, 24 May 1984, file 2019.0005.00001, University Correspondence and Legal Arguments Pertaining to the 'George Murray Black' and 'Richard Berry' Collections of Human Remains, University of Melbourne Archives.
61 Shannon Faulkhead, interview with Ron Merkel, in Faulkhead and Berg, *Power and the Passion*, p. 97.
62 The University engaged Ian Murray, senior partner at Mallesons Solicitors and Notaries, to represent the University.
63 University solicitor to Mallesons Solicitors, 24 May 1984, file 2019.0005.00001, University Correspondence and Legal Arguments Pertaining to the 'George Murray Black' and 'Richard Berry' Collections of Human Remains, University of Melbourne Archives.
64 *Murray Black Collection: Brief History of Proceedings.*
65 Ibid.
66 Faulkhead and Berg, *Power and the Passion*, p. 97.
67 Ibid.
68 *Murray Black Collection: Brief History of Proceedings.*
69 Mallesons to University solicitor, 18 June 1984, file 2019.0005.00001, University Correspondence and Legal Arguments Pertaining to the 'George Murray Black' and 'Richard Berry' Collections of Human Remains, University of Melbourne Archives.

70 Application for consent from vice-chancellor David Caro to secretary of planning and the environment David Yencken, 31 May 1984, file 2019.0005.00001, University of Melbourne Archives. The vice-chancellor sent a follow-up letter on 6 June due to the ensuing court appearance: see vice-chancellor David Caro to secretary David Yencken, 5 June 1984, file 2019.0005.00001, University Correspondence and Legal Arguments Pertaining to the 'George Murray Black' and 'Richard Berry' Collections of Human Remains, University of Melbourne Archives.

71 Ibid., items 1–3.

72 Secretary David Yencken to vice-chancellor David Caro, 14 June 1984, file 2019.0005.00001, University Correspondence and Legal Arguments Pertaining to the 'George Murray Black' and 'Richard Berry' Collections of Human Remains, University of Melbourne Archives.

73 Jim Berg to secretary David Yencken, 6 June 1984, file 2019.0005.00001, University Correspondence and Legal Arguments Pertaining to the 'George Murray Black' and 'Richard Berry' Collections of Human Remains, University of Melbourne Archives.

74 Secretary David Yencken to vice-chancellor David Caro, 14 June 1984, file 2019.0005.00001, University Correspondence and Legal Arguments Pertaining to the 'George Murray Black' and 'Richard Berry' Collections of Human Remains, University of Melbourne Archives.

75 See Rob McWilliams, 'Resting Places: A History of Australian Indigenous Ancestral Remains at Museum Victoria', 2016, https://museumsvictoria.com.au/media/4273/resting_places__history_of_ancestral_remains_25_aug_2016.docx (accessed 23 October 2023), pp. 8–13: 'In 1983 the Victorian Government passed the *Museums Act* (1983), which created Museum of Victoria from the preexisting two separate state museums. The act reaffirmed the Museum as responsible for the maintenance, storage and documentation of skeletal remains. Section 24 (3) of the Act also gave the Museum power to dispose of, to "deaccession", items in its collections.'

76 *Murray Black Collection: Brief History of Proceedings*, item 2.

77 *Berg v The University of Melbourne, Caro, David & Potter, James* [1984] VicSC 290, Murphy J judgment.

78 Parts of this section of the chapter are reproduced from Langton, *Marcia Langton*, 164–8.

79 Erin Parke, 'Online Black-Market Bone Trade under Scrutiny as Researchers Investigate', *ABC News*, 15 September 2021, https://www.abc.net.au/news/2021-09-15/black-market-bone-trade-online-under-scrutiny/100461008?utm_campaign=abc_news_web&utm_content=mail&utm_medium=content_shared&utm_source=abc_news_web (accessed 25 October 2023).

80 Ibid.

81 See Cressida Fforde, C Timothy McKeown and Honor Keeler, *The Routledge Companion to Indigenous Repatriation: Return, Reconcile, Renew*, Routledge, London & New York, 2020. See also Cressida Fforde, *Collecting the Dead: Archaeology and the Reburial Issue*, Bristol Classical Press, Bristol, 2004; and Michael Pickering, *A Repatriation Handbook: A Guide to Repatriating Australian Aboriginal and Torres Strait Islander Ancestral Remains*, National Museum of Australia, Canberra, 2020.

82 McWilliams, 'Resting Places', pp. 8–13.

‘A Precious Stone to Him That Hath It’

The Berry Collection

ROHAN LONG

> ‘I determined to go to see for myself if the anatomy department was as bad as was depicted to me. It was worse. It contained literally nothing, not even a skeleton, though later I discovered quite a lot in the cupboard.’
>
> Richard Berry, on his arrival at the University of Melbourne, 1906[1]

IT IS DIFFICULT to convey to a modern audience how commonplace and necessary collections of human remains—particularly non-European human remains—were considered to be in nineteenth- and twentieth-century museum culture. Some may be surprised to learn that the University of Melbourne's professors prioritised the collection of Indigenous remains from the institution's earliest decades, as a colonial extension of the established traditions from which the founding professors were drawn. The fact that the bodies of Indigenous Australians were considered unique and crucial to the anatomical and anthropological hierarchies being theorised by the scientists of Europe made such collections inevitable. During this era, Adelaide-based Scottish anthropologist William Ramsay Smith described Indigenous skeletons as ‘probably the most interesting anthropological specimen[s] on the face of the earth.’[2] Additionally, there was an unchallenged acceptance that Australia's Aboriginal people were on an inevitable march to extinction, and that preserving their culture in museums—‘even the skulls of their deceased men, women and children; and if possible their very bodies as mummies’—was deemed an essential institutional duty.[3]

In a paper from 1908, German anatomist Hermann Klaatsch succinctly captured the zeitgeist: ‘Man—not only his head, but every part of his skeleton, body and limbs—has now become an object of natural history to be studied like any other animal.'[4] And much like the natural history curators who discovered that Australasia's unique zoological specimens could be traded with museums in the mother country at a highly favourable exchange rate, colonial anatomists found that securing a supply of Australian skulls could open doors for them in prestigious overseas institutions and boost their academic careers. During a research tour of Southern Hemisphere museums in 1925, Aleš Hrdlička, curator of physical anthropology at the National Museum of Natural History in Washington, DC, approvingly noted the enthusiasm of Australian anatomists for this kind of collecting. While visiting anatomical collections in Melbourne, Sydney and Adelaide, Hrdlička was pleased to find 'a great deal more than was expected' in the Australian institutions and took the opportunity to analyse nearly 1000 skulls of Indigenous people, including sixty-eight from the University of Melbourne's own Anatomy Museum.[5] Well into the twentieth century, the University's Anatomy Department boasted of possessing 'a collection of aboriginal [sic] skeletal material which ranks amongst the best in the world'.[6]

The collecting of Aboriginal human remains at the University began with George Britton Halford, the foundation professor of anatomy, physiology and pathology. Hand-picked by eminent British scientists—anatomist Sir Richard Owen and pathologist Sir James Paget—Halford began his work at the University at the end of 1862 and remained there until his retirement in 1896. He worked on varied themes in his career, from snake bite cures to anatomical critiques of Darwin's theories of human evolution. Although a promising researcher in his younger years, Halford's immense teaching load left him little time for his own academic pursuits. During his lifetime, the anatomy of Indigenous skulls was often listed as one area of Halford's expertise; however, he managed only a single publication in this field. In 1878 he produced a craniological study of Victorian Aboriginal skulls as part of Robert Brough Smyth's two-volume work *The Aborigines of Victoria*.[7] Halford had collected at least eleven Victorian Aboriginal skulls for this study and sawed five of them in half to inspect the internal topography. One of the skulls was taken from Bunurong man Jimmy Dunbar. Dunbar was well known to the Mordialloc community, working for a time as a mounted trooper, and was remembered as wise, dry and amusing. He died in the Alfred Hospital in April 1877, six days after the death of his partner.[8] Halford wrote that Dunbar's skull 'was obtained through the kindness of Dr. Cooke', the Alfred's resident medical officer and honorary surgeon, and a student, future University chancellor Anthony Brownless.[9]

It is striking to a modern museum worker that little to no detail is provided for the Aboriginal skulls used in the study. Apart from Dunbar's remains, and one skull described as 'probably female', there are no descriptions or information about the individuals' geographic origin, age, pathologies or any other context whatsoever. More than one contemporary reviewer of Brough Smyth's book pointedly noted that Halford's contribution consisted merely of measurements of several skulls without providing a word of further explanation.[10] It is the earliest example of a recurring theme: a tacit presumption that holding large collections of Aboriginal bodies is justified in the name of enhancing scientific knowledge—but the science was never very good. Was it really worth exhuming almost a dozen people's skulls and carving them up, to produce an underdeveloped appendix for someone else's publication?

On 26 May 1897, German anatomist Wilhelm Krause visited the University's Anatomical and Pathological Museum (as it was known at the time) as part of a tour of Australian anatomical institutions.[11] Halford had moved from Anatomy to Physiology in 1882 and was replaced by pathologist Harry Brookes Allen, who was also made sub-conservator of the museum. Krause was received warmly by his colonial counterparts in Melbourne and given the opportunity to analyse twenty-six Indigenous skulls from the collections.[12] Eighteen were from the Anatomical and Pathological Museum, six were from the private collection of biologist and anthropologist Baldwin Spencer, and two were from other private collections.

Allen gave Krause access to the skulls in the museum and invited him to sit in on a cadaveric dissection he performed at the Melbourne Hospital.[13] During this visit, physiology lecturer Charles Martin gifted Krause with one Indigenous skull and one skeleton from his own collection. Although Krause included these remains in published research, they were never described in detail. The catalogue of the Anatomical Institute of Berlin University, where the remains were deposited in 1897, records only that they came from New South Wales. In a paper published a year after his Melbourne visit, Krause reported that Martin had personally dug up interred Indigenous remains near Sydney.[14] In 2013 the Charité (the current incarnation of the Anatomical Institute) handed over nine Indigenous remains acquired by Krause to an Aboriginal delegation in Adelaide for repatriation.[15]

One of the six skulls from Spencer's collection was taken from a tribal leader of the New England region in New South Wales, probably from the Kamilaroi, Ngarabal or Nganyaywana people.[16] Although evidently in Spencer's possession from at least 1897, this skull was entered into the register of the Tiegs Zoology Museum at the University of Melbourne sometime around 1930.[17] The skull remained in the Museum alongside zoological specimens until 2003 when it was removed for repatriation after an audit of Indigenous human remains. Another Aboriginal skull in Spencer's private collection, collected in March 1895 from New South Wales, was given to him by professor of chemistry David Orme Masson.[18]

Professor Richard Berry arrived in Melbourne in 1906 in the wake of the division of Anatomy and Pathology into separate departments. For the previous two decades, the Anatomical and Pathological Museum had been curated by Allen, producing a world-class pathological collection at the expense of anatomy specimens. Allen had added little to what Halford brought with him in 1862.[19] Appalled by the neglected state of his new workplace, Berry effectively had to establish a new museum from scratch, chiefly defined by his experience at the University of Edinburgh.[20] With great zeal, he rapidly supplemented the old anatomy specimens with frozen-tissue sections, potted dissections, and so many anthropological specimens and casts that they appeared to form the basis of a dedicated department.[21] In Berry's words, his intent for his new museum was

> to illustrate the various systems of the Human body for the benefit of students and practitioners, and further to form an anthropological collection which shall illustrate the history of the primitive inhabitants of this Continent and the Islands of the Southern Pacific—a region replete with anthropological problems ...[22]

When the Anatomy Department moved into a new building in 1923, the museum space was furnished with adjacent research rooms specifically for physical anthropology and anthropometry, the latter being a mainstay of eugenic studies. At the end of his reign, Berry considered the departmental collection he had assembled a museum of anthropology as well as anatomy.[23]

Berry's anthropological claims rested on the bioanthropological skull collection. Bioanthropological collections were assembled in numerous museums and university departments during this era as a response to scientific interest in phrenology, race science and eugenics. These collections comprised an inventory of human remains—primarily skulls—from different ethnic communities sourced from all over the world. In 2019 I visited the archetype of bioanthropological collections at the University of Edinburgh, Berry's alma mater. Established by anatomist Sir William Turner in the nineteenth century and preserved in its original state, the

Anatomy Museum from the entrance, looking east, 1906–1909.

collection is housed in a purpose-built, two-tiered, wood-panelled room containing hundreds of individuals reduced to skulls and arranged by 'race'. It is one of the most affecting and unsettling things I have ever seen. Comparable collections I have visited have been moved through multiple buildings, placed in modern containers and stripped of their original context. This was a place for elite European men to peruse a catalogue of the world's races (as they defined them) via human skulls arranged on shelves, like stamps in an album. It is a rare, unignorable material vestige of the enormously popular and influential scientific racism of the era. The Berry Collection was Berry's attempt at creating a Southern Hemisphere replica at the University of Melbourne.

Although named for Berry, the collection has existed in some form from the earliest days of the Anatomy Department, and acquisitions continued after the professor's departure; the latest documented addition was collected in 1948.[24] In a description of the early anatomy collections, Halford's Aboriginal skull collection gets special mention, and he is recorded as having deposited three Māori skulls into the Anatomical and Pathological Museum in 1894.[25] When Berry arrived at the University, he consolidated these existing remains, expanded the collection considerably, and was himself referring to the 'Berry Collection' by at least 1909.[26] For the last fifty years or so, the Berry Collection has been considered an entity distinct from the well-documented Murray Black Collection, discussed in the previous chapter in this volume.

An index card catalogue from 1909 documents various items Berry added to his collection at this time, including the preserved head of an Aboriginal person cut into six sections, produced by Berry in partnership with University of Sydney neuropathologist Dr James Froude Flashman; casts of the heads of two Indigenous people, produced by Berry in partnership with Melbourne dermatologist, wax moulage maker and fellow Edinburgh alumnus Dr Herman Lawrence; flint instruments from Aboriginal Tasmanians; and disarticulated Aboriginal limb bones.[27] The latter were kept in sets to be compared with the corresponding elements from prehistoric humans, such as Neanderthals and Cro-Magnons, and modern Europeans.[28] The existence of comparative bone sets shows that these remains were not only for museum display or research but were also used in the classroom for student instruction. These specimens would have been used to show students in the Anatomy School a simple, linear progression of development from Neanderthals to Indigenous people to white Europeans.

Anatomy Museum from the entrance, looking west, 1906–1909.

If a catalogue of the Berry Collection was produced during Berry's era, it has neither been unearthed nor referred to in any publications. According to departmental lore, the custodian of the Berry Collection in later years, professor Kenneth Russell, is said to have responded to this deficiency with the retort, 'Who needs a catalogue? Berry knew what was in the collection and so do I.'[29] A list of the remains comprising the Berry Collection compiled in 1987, before any repatriations were made, documented over 700 human skeletal remains.[30] Prior to their return, Indigenous skulls and mandibles made up three-quarters of the collection. Over sixty remains of juveniles and infants were represented, including at least four skeletons of Australian Indigenous children. Though fewer in number, in keeping with the practice of bioanthropological museums, the collection contains remains from all over the world. The second-largest group represented is skulls from Papua New Guinea and Pacific countries. Many of these skulls are ornately decorated, over-modelled with clay masks, and artificially deformed.

The provenance of the Berry Collection was never well documented. In contrast to other institutions he visited, the measurements Hrdlička recorded from the University in 1925 lacked any locality information more specific than state—and he was accompanied by Berry himself. Indigenous limb bones transferred from the Department of Anatomy to the Pathology Museum in the 1950s were described as simply 'source unknown'.[31] A number of Indigenous skulls in the collection were crowdsourced from Berry's students. William Lodewyk Crowther, a student of Berry's—and later an excavator of Tasmanian Aboriginal graves—described how his professor made an appeal to the anatomy students, particularly those from rural areas, to bring him any Indigenous skulls or bones found on their properties. 'The response was good. Much material came into the Anatomy Museum,' Crowther recalled.[32]

A handful of skulls have paper documentation associated with them, often surviving only because they have been folded up and stored, undisturbed, inside the cranial cavity. In the absence of documentation, the remains that we have the best knowledge of today are those that had information written directly onto the skull itself. Most commonly this was done by inking geographical data onto the frontal bone of the skull. Berry used a geographical code intended for categorising bioanthropological specimens and proposed by German anthropologist Rudolph Martin in 1907.[33] The code indicates a general geographic origin followed by a serial number based on how many skulls from that region were in the collection. For example:

.54(94.3) / 11	
.54	Subject code: Martin's system had numerical prefixes for details of pathology, physiology, anthropology etc. .54 indicated geographical information.
(94.3)	Country code: numerical codes were attributed to each country in the world, with supplementary numbers for that country's different states or regions. 94 coded for Australia, 94.3 for Queensland.
/11	Serial number: this is the eleventh skull in the collection from Queensland. This aspect of the code was not specified by Martin but was added by Berry for the purposes of organising his collection.

During his work on the collection in the early twentieth century, research scholar Dr Allen Robertson observed that all the skulls in the Anatomy Department were numbered with Martin's geographical codes.[34] This numbering convention was mostly abandoned after Berry's departure, so it is likely that most of the remains numbered with these codes were inscribed between the publication of Martin's system in 1907 and Robertson's observation in 1910. The cumulative nature of the serial numbers is useful, as it shows that although some numbered skulls went missing or were removed over time, the highest serial number indicates the true minimum. For example, in the 1987 catalogue there are eighty-six skulls from Victoria in a discontinuous numbered sequence. However, the highest serial number is 106, indicating that at least this many were present in the original series. Unsurprisingly, the majority of Indigenous remains in the Berry Collection that had attributed geographical data were from Victoria. Specific sites listed are Barmah, Cape Liptrap, Colac, Gunamalary, Gunbower, Kerang, Melbourne, Nathalia, Ned's Corner, Pallarang, Swan Hill, Werribee, Winchelsea and Wonthaggi—showing that the collection was assembled from locations across the state.

During their time in Australia, the Berry family regularly travelled to Tasmania, spending many 'happy summer holidays' on the island. These trips weren't just pleasant family getaways. They were an opportunity for Berry to add to the 'scanty' Tasmanian Aboriginal material held in his Anatomy Museum.[35] In January and February 1909, Berry embarked on an investigation of Tasmanian collections, searching for the most valuable specimen an anthropological museum could possess. 'Obviously a Tasmanian aboriginal [sic] skull was as a precious stone to him that hath it,' he reminisced floridly in his memoirs. In this era, Aboriginal Tasmanians were considered incontrovertibly extinct, and Berry's former teacher Sir William Turner counted only seventy-nine Tasmanian skulls recorded in the museum collections of the Western world and its colonies. After returning to the mainland, Berry published a sensational paper that revealed the existence of forty-two Tasmanian Aboriginal crania, hitherto unknown to science.[36] The anatomist could barely contain himself when reporting on his miraculous discovery:

> It does not, we feel sure, need any words of ours to emphasise, in a learned Society, the singular importance of the discovery indicated by the title of this paper; suffice it to say that in the whole annals of scientific Tasmanian literature there has never yet been recorded in a single communication such a large number of Tasmanian crania as we have the privilege to lay before the Royal Society of Victoria to-night.[37]

Berry had not undertaken any archaeological excavations but rather had discovered the skulls within existing collections of the Tasmanian Museum in Hobart and those of various private collectors. The University of Melbourne's Anatomy Department was rewarded with the gift of a plaster cast of a Tasmanian Aboriginal man's skull (originally held in the Tasmanian Museum, accession no. 4291). The resulting paper was a weighty publication dominated by over 200 full-page 'dioptrographic' diagrams of the skulls, created with an apparatus devised by Rudolph Martin to reproduce skull morphology accurately and consistently in two dimensions.[38] Much care was taken to painstakingly depict the topographic features of the crania, but details on where they came from, or the age or life history of the individual from whom they were derived, are almost totally absent—with the notable exception of Trukanini, whose skull was figured alongside Berry's discoveries. Most of the crania have no accompanying information whatsoever—one skull description records only that it came from a woman named Caroline.

Yet again, one is struck by how imprecise this all is for a purportedly scientific endeavour. When Berry et al. described the Indigenous remains they were studying, the cultural, geographical, historical and personal contexts of these people were evidently considered to be totally immaterial. A skull was simply the raw material from which valuable physiological data could be extracted and refined.

Even at that time, Berry was criticised for substandard research methodology. In 1927, English biometric anthropologist Geoffrey Morant described some of Berry's measurements of Tasmanian Aboriginal skulls as 'insufficiently defined' and others as 'obviously incorrect'.[39] Twelve years later, Melbourne Museum craniologist Dr James Wunderly backed up Morant's critique and spent a further five paragraphs pointing out inadequacies in Berry's anatomical work.[40] This weak science can often be traced to Berry's deeply entrenched biases and assumptions. He had an unquestioning adherence to physiologically based hierarchies of race and class that was almost comically unscientific.

In one comparative study grading skull size, he classed Indigenous adults as 'feeble minded', in a cluster with criminals and the 'mentally defective'. High above all of them, at the pinnacle of skull capacity and therefore intelligence, Berry—a British university teacher—had placed 'British university teachers'.[41] Another illustrative example can be found in a study from 1910 in which he ranked the skulls of apes, prehistoric hominids and various racial groups on a linear evolutionary scale derived from biometrical data. Based on the authors' own methodology, the Chaga people (Indigenous Africans from what is now known as Tanzania) topped the list as the most advanced group in the study. Without elaboration, Berry described this result as 'contradictory' and waved it away as an anomaly, while assuring the reader that it shouldn't invalidate the overarching trend—which reinforced his ideals of white supremacy—as it is 'of a very striking character'.[42]

In 1929 Berry returned to England and was succeeded as Anatomy Department head by Frederic Wood Jones. Although Berry and Wood Jones were both British anatomists brought up in traditional academic establishments, there the similarity ended. Wood Jones was a nonconformist who vigorously championed a number of unique (and wrong) theories, such as a hypothesis that humans are most closely related to tarsiers, rather than the great apes. He was one of the last great rejecters of Darwinian evolution and ascribed to a variety of Lamarckism. This radicalism never crept into Wood Jones' bioanthropological work, however, and his output in this area was largely in line with contemporary mainstream thought. He did many studies on Indigenous human remains drawn from his own departmental museum and other institutions. In the 1930s he published two papers describing Indigenous foetuses for the *Journal of Anatomy*, based on specimens to which he had first-hand access.[43] The origin of the second foetus is not provided, but the first was held in the Anatomy Museum, presented by Baldwin Spencer in 1912. Spencer took the foetus from Port Darwin and added a special label claiming it was 'probably the only one in existence'. In the first paper, Wood Jones compared measurements of the Indigenous foetus to those he took of a Portuguese foetus and a Chinese-Hawaiian foetus that he accessed during a 'routine examination of foetuses of various races at the University of Hawaii'.

Paradoxically, Wood Jones was a vocal champion of Aboriginal rights. As president of the Australasian Association for the Advancement of Science, he spoke on the moral obligation white Australians have to Aboriginal people and, although his words were interspersed with racist platitudes of the era, Wood Jones made it clear the invading colonists owe a material debt to the Traditional Owners.[44] In his November 1937 address to the Anthropological Society of Victoria, of which he was president, marking the 150th anniversary of the European invasion of Australia, Wood Jones discussed the treatment of Indigenous people. One month away from leaving the country for good, he spoke freely:

> It has been said recently and by persons of eminence, that when the white man came to Australia he found a dying and degenerate race. That is the humbug with which the white man has always gilded his extermination of native races. There is no truth in it. The aborigines [sic] were never a dying race until he started to make them die. When the white man came there were 300 000 aborigines [sic] living happily and healthily in Australia; to-day there are certainly fewer than 50 000, and twice as many half-castes existing miserably. Has there ever been any desire, on the part of Governments or of the general body of the public, to preserve the native? No Australian Government, I venture to say, has ever had any desire to preserve the native race. The Government point of view is something like this—they are going to die; it is better that they should die and get rid of the blot as quickly as possible.[45]

In his speech, the anatomist criticised not only the government of the day but also the prime minister's wife, Dame Enid Lyons, for publicly categorising Aboriginal people as a degenerate race.[46] So inflammatory and widely broadcast was Wood Jones' oratory that prime minister Joseph Lyons felt compelled to respond the following day.[47] Yet the professor apparently saw no contradiction in keeping a collection of the remains of the very people he hoped to see treated with greater dignity and respect. To the twentieth-century anatomist, even one as socially progressive as Wood Jones, it was simply taken for granted that acquiring and collecting Indigenous bodies was part of the job.

The Berry Collection should have been handed over to Museums Victoria in the early 1980s when the Murray Black remains were, but it remained at the University for a further two decades. In this era, the two collections had become separately managed and stored; control of the Berry Collection was assumed by Kenneth Russell, professor of anatomy and medical history.[48] Russell retired in 1976 but remained active in the department, being made an honorary professor in 1980. He was an avowed admirer of Berry, considering him one of the great figures of the Medical School.[49]

The return of the Berry Collection was discussed during the Murray Black repatriation but it was never handed over. In September 2002, long after the old-school anatomists had died or retired, the collection was uncovered in a locked storeroom and proved an embarrassing reminder of the University's past practices. Although described as a rediscovery, the continued presence of the Berry Collection was an open secret within the Anatomy Department. The official line was that the collection had gone 'missing'.[50] This time, all the remains of Indigenous Australians from the collection were organised and sent to the Melbourne Museum for repatriation. The University apologised for the 'hurt and understandable indignation felt by Indigenous Australians' and paid $172 000 towards the cost of repatriation and reburial of the remains. The non-Australian remains of the Berry Collection are still held by the Harry Brookes Allen Museum of Anatomy and Pathology.

Throughout the nineteenth and twentieth centuries, hundreds of human skulls were collected, measured and tabulated at the University, but the underlying assumptions of white superiority remained totally unexamined. Melbourne's Anatomy Department possessed one of the largest collections of Indigenous skeletal material ever assembled, but it never led to the University becoming a major force within anthropological thought. In many of Berry's studies, he neglected to engage with his collection at all, preferring instead to apply datasets from published scholarly works. For a time during the twentieth century, the department was well regarded nationally for anthropological research, but the shine faded as the science moved on—and yet the remains remained. Certainly, there were few direct positive medical outcomes for the people being studied, nor was there ever any real intent to pursue such avenues. As Gunditjmara Elder Jim Berg has pointed out, 'Australian Aboriginal People have been the most researched peoples in the world,' but they have 'not benefitted from any of the research carried out and published'.[51]

When Berry retired in 1928 and returned to England, the University community mourned the loss of what they saw as a brilliant academic and educational reformer. The newspaper headlines were emphatic: 'RESIGNATION DEPLORED—Great Loss to Victoria.'[52] Shortly after his departure, a gilt-framed portrait of Berry was ceremoniously unveiled in the Anatomy Museum.[53] The huge oil painting, produced by local tonalist Justus Jorgensen, shows its subject looking somewhat sinister, standing in a darkened room contemplating a human skull and a cast of an infant's head. In 2016 the University quietly removed Richard Berry's name from the old Anatomy Building on Swanston Street. It was renamed the Peter Hall Building in honour of an eminent professor from the School of Mathematics and Statistics, which had long inhabited the site. Why Berry's name was being taken off the building that he personally fought to have built in 1919 was never addressed in the University's media releases.[54] But it came in the wake of sustained campaigning from Indigenous representatives at the University and increasing global scrutiny as to who was being honoured on university campuses and other colonial institutions. This time, the headline was 'Melbourne University ... Removes Racist Professor's Name from Campus'.[55] Other academics, such as Frank Tate, Baldwin Spencer, Wilfred Agar and John Medley, are also being targeted by campaigners, as discussed in the 'Naming and Renaming' chapter.[56] Berry's portrait no longer hangs in the Anatomy Museum.

Notes

1 Richard Berry, *Chance and Circumstance*, unpublished manuscript, 1954, p. 110.

2 'The Aboriginal Skeletons', *The Advertiser*, 12 April 1911, p. 8.

3 William Henry Archer, 'Our National Museum', *Facts and Figures, or, Notes of Progress, Statistical and General*, vol. 4, no. 1, 1 September 1857, p. 28 (Queensberry Hill Press facsimile reprint, Melbourne, 1977).

4 Hermann Klaatsch, 'The Skull of the Australian Aboriginal', *Reports from the Pathological Laboratory of the Lunacy Department, New South Wales Government*, vol. 1, Part III, NSW Government, Sydney, 1908, p. 46.

5 Aleš Hrdlička, 'Catalogue of Human Crania in the United States National Museum Collections: Australians, Tasmanians, South African Bushmen, Hottentots, and Negro', *Proceedings of the United States National Museum*, vol. 71, no. 2696, 1928, p. 1. During his tour, Hrdlička was met at the University of Melbourne by Richard Berry, and at the University of Adelaide by Frederic Wood Jones.

6 Sydney Sunderland and Leslie Ray, 'A Note on the Murray Black Collection of Australian Aboriginal Skeletons', *Proceedings of the Royal Society of Victoria*, vol. 71, 1959, pp. 45–8.

7 Robert Brough Smyth, *The Aborigines of Victoria: With Notes Relating to the Habits of the Natives of Other Parts of Australia and Tasmania Compiled from Various Sources for the Government of Victoria*, J. Ferres, Government Printer, Melbourne, 1878.

8 'Last of the Mordialloc Tribe', *Illustrated Australian News*, 14 May 1877, p. 74.

9 'Doctor Fatally Injured', *Argus*, 16 December 1921, p. 7.

10 'The Aborigines of Victoria', *Leader Supplement*, 24 August 1878, p. 1.

11 Andreas Winkelman, 'Wilhelm Krause's Collections; Journeys between Australia and Germany', in C Fforde, CT McKeown and H Keeler (eds), *The Routledge Companion to Indigenous Repatriation: Return, Reconcile, Renew*, Routledge, Abingdon, 2020, p. 471.

12 José Rizal et al., 'Sitzung vom 20. November 1897', *Zeitschrift für Ethnologie*, vol. 29, 1897, p. 508.

13 Wilhelm Krause, 'Australien', *Internationale Monatsschrift für Anatomie und Physiologie*, vol. 14, 1897, p. 195.

14 Wilhelm Krause, 'Rothgefärbte Knochen von Australiern', *Zeitschrift für Ethnologie*, vol. 30, 1898, pp. 75–6.

15 'Ceremony Welcomes Ancestral Remains', *ABC News*, 6 May 2013, https://www.abc.net.au/news/2013-05-06/ceremony-welcomes-ancestral-remains/4671336?utm_campaign=abc_news_web&utm_content=link&utm_medium=content_shared&utm_source=abc_news_web (accessed 25 October 2023).

16 David R Horton, 'Map of Indigenous Australia', Australian Institute of Aboriginal and Torres Strait Islander Studies, 1996, https://aiatsis.gov.au/explore/map-indigenous-australia (accessed 25 October 2023).

17 School of Biology, Department of Zoology, 'Register of Specimens in the Museum of the Biological School', Tiegs Zoology Museum, School of BioSciences, University of Melbourne, 1893.

18 Rizal et al., 'Sitzung vom 20. November 1897', p. 531.

19 Kenneth Fitzpatrick Russell, *The Melbourne Medical School, 1862–1962*, Melbourne University Press, Carlton, 1977, p. 105.

20 'Notes and Comments', *Speculum*, May 1913, p. 9.

21 Harry Brookes Allen and the University of Melbourne Medical School, *University of Melbourne Medical School Jubilee, 1914*, Ford & Son, Melbourne, 1914, p. 36.

22 Richard Berry to Baldwin Spencer, 11 May 1909, registration XM6608, Museum Victoria Archives, http://spencerandgillen.net/objects/50ce72f6023fd7358c8a96e5 (accessed 25 October 2023).

23 Richard Berry, 'Department of Anatomy and Histology, University of Melbourne Medical School', in *Methods and Problems of Medical Education, Seventeenth Series*, Division of Medical Education, Rockefeller Foundation, New York, 1930, p. 6 (reprint pagination).

24 Peter Brown, 'Catalogue of the Berry Collection of Human Skeletal Remains', Department of Anatomy, University of Melbourne, Parkville, 1987.

25 Ibid.; Allen, *University of Melbourne Medical School Jubilee*, p. 36.

26 Richard Berry, index cards in Richard Berry lecture slides, box 6 of 6, Harry Brookes Allen Museum of Anatomy and Pathology, Melbourne, 1909.

27 Ibid.

28 Due to the scarcity of prehistoric human remains, these elements were supplied by commercially produced plaster casts of bones from European paleoanthropological sites: see Rohan Long, '"Not Man, but Man-Like': Early

20th-Century Anthropological Plaster Casts in the Harry Brookes Allen Museum of Anatomy and Pathology', *University of Melbourne Collections*, no. 25, December 2019, pp. 47–52.

29 Ross Jones, personal communication.

30 Brown, 'Catalogue of the Berry Collection', 1987.

31 Department of Pathology, 'Catalogue of the University Museum Z 7175-940/54', Harry Brookes Allen Museum of Anatomy and Pathology, Faculty of Medicine, Dentistry and Health Sciences, University of Melbourne, Parkville, 1942–54.

32 William ELH Crowther, 'The Final Phase of the Extinct Tasmanian Race 1847–1876: Being an Epilogue to the 6th Halford Oration, Canberra, A.C.T., 23.11.1933', *Records of the Queen Victoria Museum*, Launceston.

33 Rudolph Martin, 'System der (physischen) Anthropologie und anthropologische Bibliographie', *Korrespondenzblatt der Deutschen Gesellschaft für Anthropologie, Ethnologie und Urgeschichte*, vol. 38, nos 9–12, 1907.

34 AWD Robertson, *Craniological Observations on the Lengths, Breadths, and Heights of a Hundred Australian Aboriginal Crania*, Robert Grant & Son, Edinburgh, 1910. Refer to page 6: 'It will be observed that the crania in the Anatomical Department of the University of Melbourne are numbered according to the system adopted by Martin for Physical Anthropology and Anthropological Bibliography, and alongside this system number is placed the serial number of the skull.'

35 Berry, *Chance and Circumstance*, p. 127.

36 Richard Berry and AWD Robertson, 'Preliminary Communication on Fifty-Three Tasmanian Crania, Forty-Two of Which Are Now Recorded for the First Time', *Proceedings of the Royal Society of Victoria*, vol. 22, 1909, pp. 47–58.

37 Ibid.

38 Richard Berry and AWD Robertson, 'Dioptrographic Tracings in Four Normae of Fifty-Two Tasmanian Crania', *Transactions of the Royal Society of Victoria*, Part 1, J. Kemp, Government Printer, Melbourne, 1910.

39 GM Morant, 'A Study of the Australian and Tasmanian Skulls, Based on Previously Published Measurements', *Biometrika*, vol. 19, nos 3/4, 1927, pp. 417–40.

40 J Wunderly, 'The Cranial and Other Skeletal Remains of Tasmanians in Collections in the Commonwealth of Australia', *Biometrika*, vol. 30, nos 3/4, 1939, pp. 305–37.

41 Richard Berry, *Your Brain and Its Story*, Oxford University Press, London, 1939, pp. 129–31.

42 Richard Berry and AWD Robertson, 'The Place in Nature of the Tasmanian Aboriginal as Deduced from a Study of His Calvarium: Part I, His Relations to the Anthropoid Apes, Pithecanthropus, Homo Primigenius, Homo Fossils and Homo Sapiens', *Proceedings of the Royal Society of Edinburgh*, vol. 31, 1912, pp. 41–69.

43 Frederic Wood Jones, 'The External Characters of an Australian Foetus', *Journal of Anatomy*, vol. 67, 1933, pp. 549–54; Frederic Wood Jones, 'The External Characters of a Second Australian Foetus', *Journal of Anatomy*, vol. 72, 1938, pp. 301–4.

44 Frederic Wood Jones, 'The Claims of the Australian Aboriginal' (Presidential Address, Section F), *Report of the Australian Association of the Advancement of Science*, vol. 18, 1926, p. 497.

45 '"Blacks Not Degenerate": Scathing Attack by Professor', *Argus*, 18 November 1937, p. 2.

46 'Care of Aborigines, Saving a Dying Race', *Age*, 19 November 1937, p. 14.

47 'Treatment of Blacks, Prime Minister's Comment', *Argus*, 19 November 1937, p. 2.

48 Ross Jones, *Humanity's Mirror: 150 Years of Anatomy in Melbourne*, Haddington Press, Melbourne, 2007, p. 248.

49 Kenneth Fitzpatrick Russell et al., *Festschrift for Kenneth Fitzpatrick Russell: Proceedings of a Symposium Arranged By the Section of Medical History, A.M.A. (Victorian Branch), 25th February, 1977*, Queensberry Hill Press, Carlton, 1977, p. 39.

50 'Human Remains Found in Uni Storeroom', *Age*, 16 February 2003.

51 Shannon Faulkhead and Jim Berg with Lynette Russell, Ross L Jones and Jason Eades, *Power and the Passion: Our Ancestors Return Home*, Koorie Heritage Trust, Melbourne, 2010, p. 17.

52 'Professor Berry', *Argus*, 2 November 1928, p. 8.

53 'Professor Berry Honoured', *Age*, 20 July 1929, p. 23.

54 Cheryl Critchley, 'Richard Berry Building Renamed Peter Hall Building', *University of Melbourne Newsroom*, 9 December 2016.

55 Marika Dobbin-Thomas, 'Melbourne University Bows to Pressure, Removes Racist Professor's Name from Campus', *Age*, 21 March 2017.

56 Marika Dobbin, 'Heart of Darkness: Melbourne University's Racist Professors', *Age*, 30 November 2015.

Wurati and Trukanini

Benjamin Law's Portrait Busts

JUDITH RYAN

> 'The fascinating and tantalising things about Aboriginal history in Australia are often those very early colonial paintings and drawings and portraits. For many Tasmanian Aboriginal people, they're the first and only glimpse you get of your tribal ancestors.'
>
> Greg Lehman, 2020[1]

Benjamin law's portrait busts of Nuenonne leaders Wurati and Trukanini are the earliest sculptures made by a colonial artist in Australia. These portraits, modelled from life, hold a unique place in the history of Australian art, and in their confronting gaze they call us to account for the consequences of our wrongly commenced national history. Moreover, as Trawulwuy art historian Professor Greg Lehman attests:

> Violent invasion and ad hoc massacre of Indigenous people in the process of 'peaceful settlement' occurred across the Australian continent. But only in Tasmania, with its bounded, island geography did the Governor, the press and the popular colonial imagination aspire to cleanse the jurisdiction completely of its most irritating ethnic problem.[2]

In rendering these Tasmanian leaders tangible in three dimensions, the artist gives them a corporeal presence that haunts the viewer. In 1839 a bust of Wurati kept in his Melbourne office by George Augustus Robinson—the former conciliator of Aborigines in Van Diemen's Land (1829–39) and newly appointed chief protector of Aborigines in the Port Phillip District (1839–49)—was so lifelike that it struck fear in members of the local Aboriginal community, who needed Robinson to touch the sculpture to prove that it was inanimate.[3] Moreover, Law imbues Wurati and Trukanini with humanity and gravitas that impel the viewer to grapple with the atrocities of the 'Black War' of Aboriginal extirpation that occurred in Van Diemen's Land between 1824 and 1832. By engaging with the gaze of these Nuenonne leaders, the viewer confronts the enormity of the intergenerational trauma that Tasmanian Aboriginal people have suffered, through British invasion and its brutal aftermath.

These formal portrait busts, sitting on socles like early nineteenth-century bronze commemorative statues of European war heroes, prime ministers, queens or popes, do not exist in a vacuum. They cannot be divorced from the historical individuals they represent and their personal histories of colonisation, or from their more recent perception as ethnographic curios or memorials to genocide. To understand the aesthetic, cultural and political significance of Law's portrait busts of Wurati and Trukanini, we must first look at the maker in his immediate social and historical context, the Hobart Town of 1835–36, and then consider how attitudes towards the busts have altered across time.

The grandson of a Sheffield silversmith, well versed in European sculptural conventions, Benjamin Law left London in 1834 and arrived with his family in Hobart Town in February 1835. A free colonist, Law was hopeful of establishing a financially successful studio in a locale conducive to the arts. Instead, he landed in a fledging colony that, from 1820 to 1832, suffered violent guerrilla warfare between British colonists and the Traditional Owners, resulting in bloodshed, dispersal and death—largely for the First Tasmanians who stoutly defended their sovereignty against the invaders.

In 1826 colonial sentiment had been at fever pitch, as indicated by a commentary published in the *Colonial Times*:

> We make no pompous display of Philanthropy—we say unequivocally—SELF DEFENCE IS THE FIRST LAW OF NATURE. THE GOVERNMENT MUST REMOVE THE NATIVES—IF NOT, THEY WILL BE HUNTED DOWN LIKE WILD BEASTS AND DESTROYED![4]

The escalation of violence during the late 1820s prompted lieutenant-governor George Arthur to declare a state of martial law, which provided effective legal immunity for the killing of Aboriginal people. In November 1830 governor Arthur ordered a massive six-week military offensive known as the 'Black Line', in which 2200 civilians and soldiers formed a series of moving cordons stretching hundreds of kilometres across the island. The intention was to drive Aboriginal people from the colony's settled districts to the Tasman Peninsula in the south-east, where they would be permanently incarcerated.

In 1829 governor Arthur appointed George Augustus Robinson to the position of conciliator of Aborigines to negotiate an end to the warfare by affecting an amicable understanding with Tasmanian Aboriginal people, and to implement their removal to Wybalenna on Flinders Island in Bass Strait, where they would no longer threaten settlers. During Robinson's tenure as storekeeper at the mission on Bruny Island, most of the Aboriginal residents died, and those removed from mainland Van Diemen's Land to Wybalenna found their situation one of hopeless imprisonment. Many died there while waiting for the fulfilment of the promise that they would be allowed to return to their Country. In 1832, Robinson, having been party to government policies of dispossession, dispersal and genocide, wrote, 'I am at a loss to conceive by what tenure we hold this country, for it does not appear to be that we either hold it by conquest or by right of purchase.'[5]

Significantly, it was Robinson who introduced Benjamin Law to Nuenonne 'chief' Wurati and his wife Trukanini, two of his 'friendly natives'. From 1829 to 1834, they had been Robinson's most effective guides and interpreters on a series of expeditions, ironically termed the 'Friendly Mission', conducted to persuade Aboriginal guerilla fighters to cease their armed resistance to British colonisation. In August 1835, while Benjamin and Hannah Law were master and mistress of the Infant School in Hobart Town, Law began modelling a portrait bust of Wurati, believed to have been commissioned by Robinson who, after its completion in 1835, wrote to Thomas Northover, a London connection from the Aborigines Protection Society:

> Woureddy [Wurati] sat for his bust with great patience and was highly pleased with the model. The drapery is in imitation of the kangaroo skin worn by the aborigines in their primitive state. The necklace is also aboriginal and is made of the sinews of the kangaroo tail. The VDL [Van Diemen's Land] aborigines are woolly haired. The ringlets on Woureddy's head is [sic] twisted and spun out at which time in dressing they use a mixture of ochre and grease.[6]

Wurati sat for Law over several days, affording the sculptor the opportunity to engage in depth with his subject and produce far more than a superficial 'likeness'. This long sitting enabled Wurati to participate in the making of the portrait and influence its outcome. Rather than denying Wurati agency, Law's representation of the leader in customary attire, body

Wurati, an Aboriginal chief of Van Diemen's Land, reproduction cast from original, late nineteenth or early twentieth century after Benjamin Law.

ornamentation and hair-dress accorded with the proud traditional man's refusal to wear European clothes or eat European food, and his determination to retain 'an unshaken belief in his Aboriginal identity and customs through the years of dispossession'.[7] Wurati, the Nuenonne 'chief' of the Bruny Island people—a skilled hunter, boat builder and renowned storyteller who spoke five dialects—must have been startled to witness this portrait bust of himself, modelled in neoclassical Roman style according to nineteenth-century European conventions, and possessed of pride and bearing, materialise before his eyes.

Law and other colonial artists, notably Thomas Bock and Benjamin Duterrau, recognised there was a demand for likenesses of Tasmanian Aboriginal people: a demand driven in part by the colonists' growing belief that Tasmania's Aboriginal people were 'destined to disappear'.[8] Catering to this demand was a profitable enterprise. Law cast about thirty of the Wurati portrait busts in plaster, painting them in sandstone or bronze and selling them for 4 guineas each.

Buoyed by public enthusiasm for, and the sales of, the Wurati portrait bust, and encouraged by Robinson, in 1836 Law produced a companion portrait of Trukanini, then far less well known in the colony than her

Trukanini, wife of Wurati, reproduction cast from original, late nineteenth or early twentieth century after Benjamin Law.

husband. Trukanini was the daughter of Mangana, chief of the Recherche Bay people. As a young woman she had seen her mother killed by whalers, her husband-to-be shot, her two sisters abducted to Kangaroo Island and was herself raped by British invaders. Despite these experiences of violence and bloodshed, she chose to assist the conciliator in his mission to broker a cessation of the Black War in Van Diemen's Land. Hannah Law also recalled a spirited encounter with Trukanini while she was sitting for her portrait. Trukanini, a skilful negotiator, sang for a glass of wine, then demanded and secured a second glass.[9]

The portrait busts of husband and wife are likenesses of two distinct individuals of opposite genders and complementary roles in Nuenonne society. Bonyhady stated that 'the difference between the two sculptures is profound ... according to one colonial account, she is "sorrowing, mourning the slain members of her family and race"'.[10] The Trukanini bust is slightly shorter in height than that of Wurati, and her downcast pose and diffident demeanour differ considerably from the gaze of her warrior husband. Whether the sculptor observed sadness in his subject or intended to signify in her features the then untold impact of her people's history of loss is a matter of conjecture. Perhaps Law was simply conveying distinctions of gender then characteristic of 1830s British, and by extension colonial,

GA Robinson, *Pacificator*, 1838, Benjamin Law.

society. Moreover, Lehman has proposed that, by elevating both busts, Trukanini's would lose her downcast pose, enabling the husband and wife to be viewed differently.[11]

Complicating the way we view these portrait busts is a third portrait bust, commissioned by Robinson of himself, and conceived as part of a sculptural trilogy. With great self-regard and little self-awareness, Robinson intended his portrayal to sit between those of Wurati and Trukanini, commemorating what he believed to be their joint role in negotiating an uneasy armistice. This work portrayed Robinson in archetypal Roman style as a distinguished patrician: muscular and clad in toga. Since Law cast the Robinson portrait bust in white plaster to simulate marble, whereas those of Wurati and Trukanini were painted in colours of stone or bronze, these representations maintain a veneer of classical dignity yet insinuate a racial distinction.[12]

Today, Robinson, the 'pacificator', is regarded as a duplicitous figure who, in pacifying and 'civilising' the hostile original inhabitants to achieve a disquieting peace, was intent on dispersing a free people to Wybalenna, the place of their incarceration and eventual demise—a mission of deception and betrayal. Considered in this context, the unpainted plaster bust of Robinson is a politically charged object, a memorial to the cessation of the

Black War, a colonial conquest achieved at immense cost to the free people of Van Diemen's Land who had been induced to surrender.

The three portrait busts of Wurati, Robinson and Trukanini have rarely been seen together since their display in October 1836 in the office of the *Hobart Town Courier* newspaper.[13] Until the 2010 discovery of Law's portrait bust of Robinson in the State Library Victoria, this work was believed lost. Despite Robinson's belief to the contrary, the public showed almost no interest in purchasing casts of the conciliator's bust. In 1836, Gilbert Robertson, editor of the *True Colonist*, castigated

> Mr. Law [for having been] fool enough to be induced by the puffs of the courier, and the foolish vanity of the original to model a bust of Mister Commandant Robinson, the something more than Orpheus of Flinders Island. We saw a cast of it, very bad spec we guess.[14]

Law's busts of Wurati and Trukanini, meanwhile, were lauded in the same article as 'excellent likenesses' and 'works of very great merit'.[15] At that time, these portrait busts of live models heroicised as 'noble savages', as was customary in post-Enlightenment Europe, tapped into an emerging market for ethnographic curiosities. But after Trukanini's death in 1876, these busts, particularly that of Trukanini, came to be viewed very differently as memorials to genocide or portraits of the dead—equivalent to death masks, forcing the viewer to look upon the deceased. Such perceptions relive the institutionalised horror of viewers filing past Trukanini's human skeleton at the Tasmanian Museum and Art Gallery, where it was displayed and labelled as 'Lalla Rookh or Truganini [Trukanini], the last Tasmanian Aborigine'.[16] This atrocity was perpetuated against the deceased and the Traditional Owners of lutruwita, on display from 1904 to 1947. This continues to provoke outrage and sadness, and provides historical context for the presence of copies of Law's portrait busts in the collection of the University of Melbourne.

Sometime between 1905 and 1929, University of Melbourne professor of anatomy Richard Berry, a eugenicist with an interest in Indigenous human remains (see the discussion in Rohan Long's chapter on the Berry Collection in this volume), acquired copies of Law's portrait busts of Wurati and Trukanini for his department. Possessed of a fascination with Tasmanian Aboriginal people, in 1909 professor Berry published 'Dioptrographic Tracings in Four Normae of Fifty-Two Tasmanian Crania',[17] a bizarre assemblage of ghosts from the past, some of the crania with annotations from phrenologists of the time that predicted the owner's characteristics. It was originally thought these busts were the work of Law. However, comparison with other provenanced examples indicates they are copies, as they show several alterations from the originals, notably the addition of a kangaroo paw to Wurati's cloak. The casts, which are left hollow in other provenanced busts, have been filled in, obscuring the impression of Law's name and the date on the verso. A past anatomy student, Geoff Kenny, noted that Frederic Wood Jones, Berry's successor, had somewhat hastily and ineptly applied a garish 'fairground' finish to the busts, which denoted the colour of the kangaroo skin and the maireener necklace.[18]

In 1998, after extensive research, the University's Museum of Art decided to refinish the busts with a bronze patina, modelled on that of Law's busts in the National Gallery of Australia, to avoid the implication that Wood Jones' inexpertly applied paintwork represented a facile or disrespectful attitude to the memory of Wurati and Trukanini, or to the skill or intention of Benjamin Law. To ensure the reversibility of the process, the Grimwade Centre for Cultural Materials Conservation isolated the surface with a methacrylate resin and overpainted the busts to simulate, as closely as possible, the most popular painted finish applied by Law.[19]

In August 2009, controversy erupted in Melbourne when a pair of portrait busts previously on loan to the Tasmanian Museum and Art Gallery, and belonging to familial descendants of the artist, appeared in a Sotheby's auction catalogue with estimates of $500 000 to $700 000. This occasioned outrage from prominent members of the Tasmanian Aboriginal community. Michael Mansell voiced his strong opposition:

> Truganini [Trukanini] is dead and she can't defend herself against the symbolism that is portrayed by the racists of Australia who abuse her memory. The auction house should take responsibility and so should the vendor. They should be accountable for changing these racist attitudes.[20]

On 24 August 2009, five demonstrators led by two staff from the Tasmanian Aboriginal Centre (TAC) protested outside the 'Important Australian Art Auction' scheduled for that evening, chanting 'Sotheby's, Sotheby's, leave them alone, let us take our ancestors home'.[21] In response to such concerted opposition from the TAC, which had been gathering momentum in the lead-up to the auction, Sotheby's withdrew the lots from sale. Protest organiser Sara Mansell, the legal field officer of the TAC, asserted defiantly: 'These busts are not art. The image of Truganini [Trukanini] on display shows she was the last full-blooded Aboriginal, and this provides a racist image that there is no continuing Aboriginal culture in Tasmania.'[22] Fellow protester Nala Mansell-McKenna, state secretary of the TAC, likened the sale of the busts to people profiteering from images of the attempted genocide of the Jewish people, stating:

> The significance of the busts is that they depict, for racists, the myth of the extermination of Aborigines in Tasmania. They are held up as trophies, as the ultimate racist plot—if physical extermination fails, kill them off through images.[23]

Thus, as Lehman has stated, 'in this world, and never more so than at this time in Australia's history, seemingly innocent artworks are made to signify the dimensions of ideological battlegrounds that their creators could never have imagined—and certainly never intended'.[24] Following the successful campaign to veto the sale of Law's busts at auction, Nala Mansell-McKenna wrote a letter to the University of Melbourne and other public institutions requesting that any copies of busts by Law of Van Diemen's Land chief Wurati and his wife Trukanini be removed from their collections, since 'Aborigines find it offensive that images of our dead are still being used without permission. We now write seeking agreement on what items can or should not, be displayed'.[25]

On 30 September 2022, Greg Lehman and Palawa PhD researchers Neika Lehman and Tahlia Eastman viewed the University's copies of Law's portrait busts with Professor Marcia Langton, Louise Murray and Judith Ryan. The portraits of hallowed ancestors had a deeply upsetting impact, akin to a direct encounter with these ancestors and their duplicitous treatment, about which much has been written. Professor Lehman led us through a time of deeply respectful engagement with the works in their immediate historical context, Hobart Town of 1835–36, and a truth-telling dialogue about what they still signify today and how they could be respectfully displayed.

It would be disingenuous of those of us who are not Palawa to claim to sense the power of these objects for their descendants, the awe in which these ancestors are held and the pain and sorrow they invoke. Nevertheless, it is important to register that these portraits function as silent reminders of a disturbing imperial sentiment that is triumphant but also catastrophic. The tragedy of imperial conquest, an exercise of power underscored by deception and betrayal, manifests itself as art that conjures tangible, three-dimensional likenesses of Wurati and Trukanini in which their life histories remain embedded, unbearable for settlers to look upon and impossible for any of us to erase. Perhaps that is why we need to keep these works visible, so that settler descendants of the colonisers stare fixedly at the atrocity of what happened in Van Diemen's Land, ponder the enormity of what has been lost, and fight to build another Australia, one that would recognise Aboriginal and Torres Strait Islander sovereignty over their lands, waterways and cultural objects, and would enshrine an Indigenous Voice to Parliament.

Notes

1 Greg Lehman, 'Professor Greg Lehman', University of Tasmania, 10 June 2020, https://www.utas.edu.au/about/news-and-stories/articles/2020/professor-greg-lehman (accessed 26 October 2023).

2 Greg Lehman, 'Tasmania's Black War: Undermining the Foundations of Terra Nullius', *Artlink,* 1 May 2018.

3 Gareth Knapman, 'The Pacificator: Discovering the Lost Bust of George Augustus Robinson', *The La Trobe Journal*, no. 86, December 2010, p. 43.

4 *Colonial Times*, 1826, quoted in Greg Lehman, 'Benjamin Duterrau: The Art of Conciliation', *Journal of War & Culture Studies*, vol. 8, no. 2, May 2015, p. 112.

5 George Augustus Robinson, 1832, quoted by Natalie Cromb, 'Land Rights', Australian Museum, 7 October 2020, https://australian.museum/learn/first-nations/land-rights (accessed 26 October 2023).

6 George Augustus Robinson, recorded in NJB Plomley, *Weep in Silence: A History of the Flinders Island Aboriginal Settlement: With the Flinders Island Journal of George Augustus Robinson, 1835–1839*, Blubber Head Press, Hobart, 1987, p. 650.

7 Tasmanian Museum and Art Gallery, 'First Black Man', 2023, https://www.tmag.tas.gov.au/learning_and_discovery/learning_resources/online_resources/ningenneh_tunapry/first_black_man (accessed 26 October 2023).

8 In 1837 Thomas Bock produced fourteen watercolour portraits of Robinson's 'friendly people' in response to a commission from Jane Franklin, wife of the new lieutenant-governor. Benjamin Dutterau created oils of Trukanini, Wurati, Tanlebouyer and Manalargenna, which hung for many years in the chamber of the Tasmanian Legislative Council and were eventually transferred to the Tasmanian Museum and Art Gallery.

9 David Hansen, 'Seeing Truganini', *Australian Book Review,* no. 321, May 2010, p. 51.

10 Tim Bonyhady, in Daniel Thomas (ed.), *Creating Australia: 200 Years of Art 1788–1988*, International Cultural Corporation of Australia, Sydney, 1988, pp. 92–3.

11 Greg Lehman, personal communication, while viewing the bust of Trukanini, 30 September 2022.

12 For a detailed analysis of this portrait bust, see Gareth Knapman, 'The Pacificator: Discovering the Lost Bust of George Augustus Robinson', *The La Trobe Journal*, no. 86, December 2010, pp. 37–52.

13 Ibid.

14 Gilbert Robertson, 'Fine Arts', *True Colonist*, 14 October 1836, p. 2, with thanks to David Hansen.

15 Ibid.

16 Hansen, 'Seeing Truganini', p. 45.

17 RJA Berry, 'Dioptrographic Tracings in Four Normae of Fifty-Two Tasmanian Crania', *Transactions of the Royal Society of Victoria,* vol. V, Part 1.

18 Loan of Works Folder, University of Melbourne Museums and Collections Department, with thanks to Louise Murray.
19 Ibid.
20 Michelle Paine, 'Truganini Bust Sale in Ownership Battle', *Mercury*, 21 August 2009, p. 2.
21 Raymond Gill, 'Protesters Halt Sotheby's Auction of "Racist" Art', *Age*, 25 August 2009, p. 8.
22 Ibid.
23 Ibid.
24 Greg Lehman, 'Fearing Truganini', *Artlink,* June 2011, p. 52.
25 Raymond Gill, 'Museums Told to Shelve "Racist" Art', *Age*, 10 September 2010, p. 5.

III

Settler-Colonial Knowledge

Eugenics, 1853–1945

Scientific Racism at the University of Melbourne

ROSS L JONES

IN 1943, AT the height of World War II, Wilfred Agar, professor of zoology, geneticist, and dean of the Faculty of Science at the University of Melbourne, released a blueprint for a healthy, prosperous and happy future for Australia. The booklet, 'Science and Human Welfare', was part of a series called *Realities of Reconstruction*, published jointly by Melbourne University Press and Oxford University Press.[1] It argued for measures to restrict the breeding of less able ('mentally deficient') Australians.[2] In this clarion call for reform, Agar fretted about the future of the Australian 'race' and suggested a combination of sterilisation of the 'unfit' and the immigration of 'acceptable' foreigners as a solution to this problem. He cited sterilisation programs in numerous countries and remarkably singled out the German program for special favour. He then posed the rhetorical question, to which he had already provided an unambiguously positive answer in an earlier publication: 'How far are these measures likely to be effective in achieving their object?' His answer involved straightforward arithmetic:

> A total cessation of reproduction by the mentally defective would, therefore, result in the reduction of deficiency by the amount of about 15% in a single generation. A continuation of the policy would continue to reduce it generation after generation, with a gradually diminishing rate of reduction as mental deficiency got rarer and rarer in the population.[3]

A key, largely unspoken element in Agar's contention concerned race. In the final footnote of his booklet, Agar explained that his calculus relied on immigration restriction to 'only white peoples'.[4] Agar's championing of 'whiteness' represented a considerable body of contemporary opinion.

The 'eugenic imagination' in the first half of twentieth-century Melbourne had no place for the 'black' Indigenous population in the 'white Australian race'. They were the 'other' who would either be assimilated and diluted in the white population or else corralled onto reserves to slowly wither and disappear.

'Science and Human Welfare' was an especially unsubtle publication within a wider eugenic literature that rose to prominence in the first half of the twentieth century. The eugenics movement involved numerous public figures, and university personages such as Agar used eugenic thinking to influence public policy ranging from health to education. This offered relevance to academic work, but did so with a callous and brutish dismissal of people based on tenuous reasoning.

Race and the Theory of Mental Deficiency

Agar was president of the Eugenics Society of Victoria from its foundation in 1936 until the end of World War II in 1945. His predecessor as putative leader of the eugenic movement in Melbourne was another University of Melbourne professor, Richard Berry, who was professor of anatomy in the Medical School from 1906 to 1929 (and dean from 1925 to 1929). Berry claimed that most criminals, slum dwellers, 'full-blood' Aboriginal people and other 'coloured races' were mentally and racially deficient. These views received almost total consensus in all the newspapers of the day.[5]

Estimates of the prevalence of mental defectiveness in the Australian community at that time varied. In one of the first ever national social surveys, instigated in 1928 by the Stanley Bruce government, Dr William Ernest Jones concluded, after surveying every schoolchild in the nation, that 2.89 per cent of schoolchildren in Australia were mentally deficient and that the number was increasing due to the greater fecundity of mental deficients.[6] Richard Berry, meanwhile, claimed that the proportion was more like 10 per cent.[7]

In 1939, in *Eugenics and the Future of the Australian Population*, Agar argued that the problem was greater than just the prevalence of mental deficients, stating that

> there is no natural division between the low-grade normal intelligence and the defective, any more than there is between a very short man and a dwarf... [but] let us accept 15% as the proportion of all mentally defective children who have one or both parents defective.[8]

Another 15 per cent of cases, Agar argued, involved defectiveness caused by environmental factors, such as accidents, but:

> The remainder, about 70% of all mentally defective children, owe their condition to hereditary factors derived from more remote ancestors and transmitted through the parents, who, however, did not show it ... Such parents are said to be 'carriers' of mental deficiency.[9]

Professor Berry also argued that defectiveness hid behind a façade of normality. He claimed in his unpublished autobiography *Chance and Circumstance* that 'the danger to civilisation comes not from the segregated idiots and imbeciles in institutions, but from neighbours and fellow voters—so many of whom are quite definitely of the feeble-minded class'.[10]

The *Medical Journal of Australia* regularly supported Berry's work and editorialised in 1919 that 100 per cent of 'male prostitutes' and 70 per cent of 'female prostitutes' were mentally defective due to bad heredity.[11] Government intervention, it was argued, was essential and should be planned and operated by scientists: 'We have pleaded for a proper reform of this nature. We have insisted on the fact that this problem is a medical one and that it would be doomed to failure if entrusted to laymen.'[12]

The academic study of genetics had been introduced to Melbourne with the arrival of Wilfred Agar to take up a professorial chair in 1919. This meant the earlier statements of Berry and others about 'inheritance' were to be justified by a more respectable source. Indeed, as president of the Eugenics Society of Victoria, Agar used his eminence in genetics to underscore his call for sterilisation and other forms of birth control. Preceding this, eugenics and other forms of social Darwinism and racism had relied on older morphological and statistical sciences to provide justification for white supremacy, one example being head measuring.[13] By the time of Agar's arrival, as we shall see, a deep bedrock of this pre-genetic racism underpinned many facets of the University of Melbourne.

Racism in Late-Nineteenth-Century Melbourne

The work of the Melbourne eugenicists produced specious justifications for racial science, drawing on a climate of racism that long predated it. What is now called scientific racism appeared in the late eighteenth century and gained considerable intellectual ammunition after the publication of Charles Darwin's *On the Origin of Species* in 1859, along with *The Descent of Man in Relation to Sex* in 1871. Evolution came to be seen as one of the most important influences on biological, and therefore human, history and development. It became almost universally accepted that different races had different evolutionary pathways, and that the 'black' races were at an earlier stage of development than 'white' races, with the 'yellow' in-between.[14] After some initial opposition at the University, Darwin's ideas, especially those relating to eugenics (the science of improving a race by selective breeding), quickly spread, especially after the arrival of Walter Baldwin Spencer as the first chair in biology in 1887 and then Richard Berry in 1906.[15]

The two Darwinist professors arrived in a society highly receptive to their science. In 1899, the first Australian-born professor at the University, Harry Brookes Allen, appointed in 1882 as professor of descriptive anatomy and pathology (and later dean of the Medical School), paid homage to the new evolutionary creed. He wrote in 'Evolution and the Ideal':

> Thus life appears a vast ascending scale,
> Wherein the strong must constantly prevail;
> And every creature in its growth displays
> In brief the story of the earlier days ...
> Hence dull equality is deadly foe
> To upward growth, while variations show
> The play of weak and strong, with promise sure
> That evermore the fittest shall endure.[16]

Such poems show the Darwinist combination of optimistic ascent, and pessimistic scepticism of egalitarian ideas.

Evolutionary race science was widely adopted in late-nineteenth and early-twentieth-century Melbourne. In the *School Paper*, a publication of the Education Department and the Teachers College provided monthly to every state schoolchild between 1896 until 1939, children learned about the hierarchy of races and the ascendency of the white Anglo-Saxon; Indigenous peoples were frequently resiled to the bottom level. These papers also delighted in publishing mocking racist humour, encouraging schoolchildren to set themselves apart from Indigenous people. An 1899 issue joked that Indigenous people granted free admission to the Perth zoo 'spent nearly all afternoon at the monkey-houses, laughing and jabbering'.[17] They were also instructed that the natives of New Caledonia, 'although superior to the Australian aboriginal, are not so fine a race as the Fijian'.[18] These views were pervasive and helped to justify and inform the White Australia policy and legislation such as the *Immigration Restriction Act*, the first substantive Act of the Commonwealth Parliament in 1901.

Evolutionary racism also permeated the University Medical School. Racist intolerance of Indigenous people was a recurring theme in *Speculum*, the Medical Students' Society magazine. An anonymous author, 'Studentia', wrote in 1891, 'Anyone who visits our National Museum cannot fail to be struck with the resemblance between the specimens of the higher apes and our aboriginal brethren,' although they believed that 'Poor Jacky Jacky would turn away from his hairy ancestor with about the same feelings of contempt that one of our patrician ladies would show, if her aboriginal brother claimed relationship'.[19] In 1894, another author, 'W. L. F. M.', disclosed that 'I spend most Sundays at the zoo in contemplation of the vast evolutionary process which has culminated in the race of which the present writer is a member. To put it more concisely, I spend that day in visiting my poor relations'.[20] Students would have had these views reinforced when entering the University's grand buildings, as they were told by their designer, the first architectural graduate architect, Anketell Henderson, that his designs demonstrated the superiority of the white race.[21]

This constantly proclaimed 'superiority' was stimulated as much by anxiety as confidence. As Anderson has written, 'the climate was foreign, social life appeared disordered, the diseases varied, and it sometimes seemed that a new biological type might emerge from the colonial turmoil'.[22] As far as populating this new land was concerned, many academics fretted over the racial experiment, and the University was central to the successful implementation of a suitable program for change. Fear of 'degenerating' to an Aboriginal type was paramount. The widely read newspaper the *Herald* expressed this popular view of the development of the Australian 'race' in an article as late as September 1934 when discussing a prospective lecture by Dr John Cumpston (the Commonwealth director general of health and a graduate of the Medical School) at the Institute of Anatomy:

> Will climate and other influences lead to the development of a race differing greatly from the stock of the British Isles? Will the Australian be 'tall and freckled and sandy', the true Cornstalk, or retain the physique of his forefathers? ... the Federal Director General of Health ... should have something interesting to say on this subject next week ... I hope the doctor does not lean to the opinion ... that Australians would gradually assume the colour and other physical attributes of the aborigines.[23]

White superiority was the monotonous chant of the majority of Australians in the first fifty years of federation. This served to fulfil the need to reiterate white racial superiority at every turn and justify an unsophisticated act of displacement.[24]

Richard Berry and Frank Tate

The University was to be central in this intellectual justification of the racial superiority of the white races, and in the program that effectively removed from the Indigenous population any consideration of fair or reasonable treatment and acceptance. Two who were key in this were Richard Berry and Frank Tate, who formed an alliance. Unlike the anatomist Berry, who was an Edinburgh-educated Lancastrian, Tate was born in Victoria and moved up from being a student at one of the state schools set up under the *Education Act 1872* (Vic.), through the apprentice student teacher system, to become head of the Teachers' Training College adjacent to the University. He was soon appointed as the first director of education in Victoria in 1902.[25] Tate and Berry served together on the Council of Public Education, a body set up in 1910 to advise the minister of public instruction, the University of Melbourne Council and the Education Progress Association, which was formed to promote educational reform across the three sectors of education (primary, secondary and tertiary), as well as a number of other government advisory committees. Tate also advised Berry in his preparation of the 1926 Mental Deficiency Bill, a measure designed to introduce eugenic policies in Victoria.[26] They were also members of the inquiry committee appointed by the Council of the University of Melbourne in March 1913, whose recommendations formed the basis of the *University Act 1923* (Vic.) that radically reformed tertiary education in the state.[27]

Both Berry and Tate were busy proselytisers, organising congresses and public meetings and publishing regular newspaper opinion pieces. One example of this publicity was Berry's July 1917 public lecture for the Council of Public Education on 'Brain Growth and Education'. The *Herald* newspaper endorsed the lecture as one 'of more than ordinary importance, inasmuch as it furnishes, for the first time in the history of human knowledge, information as to the capacity of the brain' of the normal range for boys between the ages of six and twenty-one years.[28] The lecture, according to the *Herald*, also indicated how

> it may be possible by co-operation between the neurologist, the psychologist, and the educationist to pick out those boys who depart so much from the normal that they may not improbably be regarded

as the future inefficients [sic] or potential geniuses of adult life and be treated accordingly.[29]

Berry based his conclusions on a survey he had conducted with a psychologist, Stanley Porteus, of the head sizes of 1650 boys. He divided this survey between 1139 he classified as 'normal', measured at state and public schools and the University, '355 criminals, 53 deaf and dumb boys, 39 mentally deficient boys, and 64 living Australian Aboriginals'.[30]

In his unpublished autobiography, Berry recalled that this lecture 'aroused a good deal of interest both among the people and the Press', and even the state governor, Sir Arthur Stanley, attended.[31] The *Herald*, which promised £150 to support the research, reported that the attendance included some of the most significant figures in Victorian education. The minister of education, HSW Lawson, presided, and in the audience were George Swinburne (described as 'an Interstate Commissioner, and a leading technical educationist', and the founder of Swinburne Technical College), Theodore Fink (chairman of the Royal Commission into Education in 1901) and Frank Tate.[32] Fink moved the vote of thanks 'and remarked that the Minister for Education need not dig very deep down to find the solid substratum of people in favour of liberal education expansion'.[33]

As well as the precis of the lecture in the *Herald*, the full text was published in the *Medical Journal of Australia*, following a presentation of Berry's research findings at a meeting of the British Medical Association that preceded the public lecture, held on 2 May in Berry's Anatomy Department at the University.[34] Tate was also present at this meeting. He was singled out for a special welcome by the chairman, who announced that 'without his co-operation and assistance, the results of the work to be submitted to them by Professor Berry could not have been carried out'.[35] The chairman was referring to the financial assistance Tate had supplied to Berry in his official role, allowing him two assistants from the Education Department, one of whom was Stanley Porteus, who had been seconded part-time from his duties as headmaster of the Bell Street Special School to work in Berry's department. As well, Tate gave Berry the opportunity to measure the heads of a large number of state school students.[36]

Eugenics and head measuring were not confined to the state education system. In 1913, the legendary Wesley College headmaster LA Adamson asked Berry to address a meeting of the Parents' National Education Union on the 'correlation of size of head and intelligence',[37] the material of which was based on research Berry had conducted on Tasmanian Aboriginals and criminals' skulls, and which had been published in the *Proceedings of the Royal Society of Victoria* between 1909 and 1913. It seems that Wesley College provided boys' heads for Berry to measure.[38] It must have been this research that led Tate to provide substantial support in his efforts to measure a large number of skulls of state schoolboys.

Berry reached two main conclusions in his 1917 lecture. The first was that while head size alone could not be used as an indication of intelligence, among a large group of individuals there was 'a distinctly measurable correlation between size of head and intelligence',[39] and while he 'did not deny the possibility of brain quality entering into the problem ... he could find no proof of it. The facts seem to point to an association between size of brain and mentality'.[40] The second conclusion Berry reached was that, in any comparison of different classes in society, 'there is a distinctly measurable correlation between size of head and intelligence'.[41] The order of the groups in Berry's research (in descending order of head capacity and intelligence) were: British university teachers; London university students; Melbourne university students; average males attending the meetings of the British Association for the Advancement of Science; a number of sets of schoolboys fifteen to nineteen years of age; Melbourne criminals; schoolboys fourteen to fifteen years of age; state schoolboys thirteen to fourteen years of age; living male Indigenous people; a number of sets of state schoolboys ten to thirteen years of age; deaf and dumb boys thirteen years of age; state schoolboys nine to ten years of age; mentally deficient boys thirteen years of age; and a number of sets of younger schoolboys six to ten years of age.

Berry then sorted these groups into classes:

- Educated Class Groups—as e.g. British university teachers, university students and the average member attending the British Association for the Advancement of Science;
- Schoolboys and university students aged from 6 to 21;
- Socially Inefficient groups such as the criminal;
- Abnormal classes such as the mentally deficient and the deaf and dumb and
- One Primitive and Non-Caucasian Race—the living pure bred Australian aboriginal [sic].[42]

When this hierarchy of intelligence and head size was taken with Berry's assertion that 'it was usually accepted that no new neurons were formed after birth',[43] then education could only be for the purpose of sorting people according to their hereditary biological ability, assigning them to the appropriate classes and maximising their inherited intelligence, not for creating ability from scratch. Berry wrote of the inferior classes that they did not obey 'the laws of Man but the dictates of Nature', and the evidence of the small heads of the lower of his classes exploded 'the common error of supposing that Education could succeed where Nature had failed, and that is, put brains where they are not'.[44]

After the *Education Act 1910* (Vic.) instituted state secondary education, Tate developed a hierarchy of secondary schools based on Berry's research, with technical schools in the poorer socio-economic suburbs (with a curriculum that could not allow the students access to tertiary education) along with a much smaller number of 'high schools' that mimicked the private schools.[45] After Tate's retirement, in a book published in 1935 by the Australian Council for Educational Research, he wrote of his fear that an uncontrolled and wide-ranging extension of academic and literary secondary education leading to university could lead to social disorder:

> Because of the privileges attached to it more frequently than for the sake of the general culture that it provides, secondary education is sought by large numbers of pupils who cannot profit by it, or who, if they do meet its standards satisfactorily, are unable to find employment which they regard as suitable either for their training or their abilities. The result is the development of an educated proletariat (*Hungerkanditaten*), which becomes the centre of political and economic agitation, or, as the Japanese say, thinks dangerous thoughts. The only country where this problem has been definitely attacked is Italy, which, profiting by experience, has adopted a highly-differentiated system of post-primary education intended to deflect an excessive crowding into the higher education and liberal professions.[46]

Italy at that time was under the fascist government of Benito Mussolini.

Stanley Porteus, appointed by Tate to be headmaster of the School for Mental Deficients in Fitzroy, and seconded to Berry's lab to measure heads, followed Berry to the stage in the 1917 lecture and explained to the audience that

> it was the great fault of child education that there was but little attempt to adapt the individual's training to his special needs. They were in the habit of applying the same system of education to all children, regardless of their different intellectual endowment. The future criminal and the potential genius might be found side by side in the same class under the same teacher.[47]

Porteus' reputation was one of the first to suffer from his lifelong support of eugenics and racism, with Porteus Hall at the University of Hawaii renamed in 1998.[48]

In line with Tate and Berry's thinking, the eugenic belief in the inherent superiority of the middle classes over the poorer classes continued to be deeply entrenched in Victorian educational circles in the 1920s. In an article in the July 1926 edition of *Education Gazette and Teachers' Aid*, a magazine sent to every state schoolteacher, Dr Chris McRae (a member, along with Tate and Berry, of the committee that drew up the 1926 Mental Deficiency Bill) argued that those children attending schools in poorer socio-economic areas 'will never go to the university [and] should not follow the same curriculum'[49] as those in schools in wealthier suburbs. According to McRae, the education of the poorer classes 'should be vocational' because, 'in the main, people live in slums because they are mentally deficient, and not vice versa'.[50] This view was based on research conducted by McRae in an attempt to replicate an experiment conducted by the eugenicist Cyril Burt, McRae's teacher at the University of London.

Fitness for University

The notion that university entrance should only be available to a limited number of students from poorer suburbs was based on the eugenic view that there was a restricted number of academically gifted students, especially among the working class. After a decade of dithering by the executive and parliament, the 1913 inquiry committee's report became the basis for the Act.[51] The 1913 inquiry, which involved both Richard Berry and Frank Tate, proposed a plan for scholarships as the alternative to a free university. This eventually became government policy in the form of the 1923 *University Act* (Vic.). The committee reported to parliament that if the university were to become free,

> the inevitable tendency would be to swell the number of those who are tempted to try their fortunes in professions for which they have no aptitude, with the result of disappointment and often disaster to themselves while the State would suffer from diverting into unprofitable channels the energies of students who might have found useful and profitable careers in other occupations.[52]

The system that was put in place consisted of a limited loan facility and, as Berry had recommended in his speech at a 1912 congress convened to address perceived inadequacies in the Victorian education system, 'hundreds' of 'free' places.[53] The system of allocating free places inaugurated by the 1923 Act was also designed substantially along the lines of the system advocated by Berry in 1912. In 1925, 188 students were nominated by the Education Department, nine by University High School, one by the Railways Commissioners and thirteen by the War Bursars, making a grand total of 211 students in a student population of 2612, or 8.1 per cent.[54] In 1927, the Education Department nominated 266 students, University High School nine, the University of Western Australia one,[55] the Railways Commissioners three and the War Bursars eight, making the number of 'free' places 287 in a student population of 2985, or 9.6 per cent.[56] The proportion of free places, as well as the method of allocating them, remained substantially unchanged until 1938, when a system of half-fees was added.[57]

If the number of free places made available by the University of Melbourne in the decades after the 1923 *Education Act* substantially fulfilled Berry's aim to leave no bright working-class child without the opportunity for a university education (and neither Tate nor Berry complained about the allocation and number of such places in the 1920s and 1930s), then this allocation would seem to be a measure of those influential policymakers' regard for the natural talent pool of the working classes. Tate and his followers had no belief that Indigenous Australians should attend university. On a 1932–33 trip to the United States with Dr Kenneth Cunningham, a researcher and lecturer at the Teachers' College and then first head of the Australian Council for Education Research, when visiting a 'coloured school' he wrote that '[o]ne half caste boy inquired "What is being done for the culture of the Australian black people?" I was floored'.[58]

The first Indigenous graduate at the University of Melbourne (and in Australia) was Margaret Williams Weir, who completed her Diploma of Physical Education in 1959, more than half a century after the first Māori graduate in New Zealand, Sir Apirana Ngāta, who was born in 1874 and graduated with a Bachelor of Arts in Political Science in 1893 from Canterbury University College.[59] Before the 1950s there was virtually no hope of Indigenous Australians making it to the University.

Eugenics Societies in Victoria: 1914 and 1936–61

By the mid-1930s, a large enough group of progressive tertiary-educated people was concerned enough about the dangers of 'race suicide' and the threat of a growing class of 'mental deficients' to canvas the formation of an action group to influence public policy. 'On 29 October 1936,' wrote Victor Wallace, '[a]t a meeting in the Melbourne Town Hall ... The Eugenics Society of Victoria was born. Professor W. E. Agar, a distinguished authority on genetics, was elected President.'[60] This was the second such society, the first being the Eugenics Education Society of Melbourne, formed in July 1914 by a number of eminent citizens, including Alfred Deakin, the second prime minister of Australia. This Society only lasted a short time, due to World War I breaking out; professor Walter Baldwin Spencer had been named president.[61]

Tate had retired and Berry had returned to the United Kingdom by the time the Eugenics Society of Victoria was established in 1936, so Agar took the role of president until the end of the war in 1945. Cunningham, one of Tate's protégés, took over as president from Agar's retirement to the demise of the Society in 1961.[62]

The meeting in 1936 setting up the Victorian Society had been preceded by another earlier in the month, again chaired by Agar, that had called for a much wider scope of activities, such as environmental reform in places such as slums. An earlier group, the Victorian Council for Mental Hygiene, had a distinctively eugenic bent but also embraced many environmental reforms in the belief that the environment was an important influence on the formation of mental deficiency. It was this group that had attended the first meeting, and whose call for environmental reforms Agar and his followers clearly rejected.[63]

The manifesto released by the Society in 1936 was unequivocal:

> The Science of Eugenics has for its object the maintenance or improvement of the quality of the human race, so far as this depends upon innate inherited factors. This will be achieved if the future generations are produced mainly by persons likely to transmit good qualities of mind and body. The general aim of Eugenics Societies is therefore to bring about a state of affairs where persons of superior natural endowments shall have a higher, or at least not lower, birth rate than persons of inferior endowments; and to ensure that persons with gross defects of mind or body, known to show a tendency to be inherited, should be discouraged or prevented from producing children ... the aim of Eugenics is to ... improve, or at least save from deterioration, the innate inheritable quality of the race.[64]

From its foundation the Society grew quickly until the outbreak of World War II in 1939. Agar and Victor Wallace organised many public lectures and the Society established itself as an influential public body. As Wallace later wrote: 'We felt that we were now firmly established especially as we had, as members of our Society, prominent judges, senior University professors and other highly respected citizens.'[65]

The list of public lectures was impressive:

> The Aim and Scope of Eugenics, The Principles of Heredity, Mental Deficiency and Insanity, Birth Control and Eugenics, The Eugenic Outlook for the Future, The Relative Influence of Heredity and Environment, The Social Problem Group, Sterilization of the Unfit, The Psychological Clinic and Mental Deficiency, Eugenics and the Future of the Australian Population, The Prevention of Mental Disorder, Social Efficiency and Levels of Intelligence, The Production of Superior Races, and a great variety of other subjects.[66]

The Society used the most up-to-date methods, just as Berry had done earlier, including lantern slides. The speakers, Wallace recorded,

> were usually professors or senior lecturers from the University of Melbourne, consultant psychiatrists or people who had a special knowledge of anthropology or other subjects associated in some way with eugenics. The lectures were carefully prepared and always provoked numerous questions. I was Honorary Secretary of the society from 1936 to 1961. I regret now that I did not try to obtain from each lecturer a copy of his notes or even an article for publication. All I have which relates to the substance of the lectures is an album of newspaper cuttings. Due notice of the lectures was given to the editors of our daily newspapers and what was said at the lectures was very well reported.[67]

Another project was to set up birth-control clinics in working-class suburbs, for which a generous donation from the feminist Marie Stopes was received.[68] It seems, however, that opposition to any form of birth control in 'under-populated' Australia and the advent of war put paid to this plan.[69]

The membership of the Eugenics Society of Victoria reads like a who's who of the academic, judicial, scientific and educational elite of Melbourne society, the majority of whom had close ties with the University. The surviving subscription lists from the 1930s up until 1947 include, in addition to WE Agar, Frank Tate, James McRae and Kenneth Cunningham, the names of such eminent individuals as Sir David Rivett (CEO of the Council for Scientific and Industrial Research, the precursor to the CSIRO); Sir John Medley (vice-chancellor, University of Melbourne); Sir Sidney Sewell (president of the Royal College of Physicians); Sir Edmund Herring (chief justice of the Supreme Court of Victoria); Sir Keith Murdoch (journalist and newspaper proprietor); professor GS Browne (Education, University of Melbourne); Sir Peter MacCallum (Pathology, University of Melbourne, and vice-president of the Society); John Barry (Supreme Court justice); Alfred Foster (County Court and Arbitration Court); Dr James Booth (chairman of the North Melbourne's Children Court); Angela Booth (wife of James and prominent feminist activist); associate professor Fritz Duras (Physical Education, University of Melbourne); Dr Reg Ellery (psychiatrist); W Glanville Cook (Rationalist Society); associate professor Georgina Sweet (Zoology, University of Melbourne); and the reverend GK Tucker (founder of the Brotherhood of St Laurence).[70] In fact, the Society was effectively an offspring of the University of Melbourne, and clearly Medley provided a sympathetic environment for it.[71]

However, right up until the last decade or so of the twentieth century, material relating to the involvement of such public supporters of the eugenic movement was forgotten or ignored in biographical publications or entries.[72] Other eminent scientists, those either interested or actively involved in the eugenic movement, including professor RD 'Pansy' Wright and Sir Frank Macfarlane Burnet, did not join the Society.[73] Professor Wright, for example, supported the 1939 Mental Deficiency Bill in principle while criticising some of its provisions.[74] On the other hand, he refused an invitation to join the Eugenics Society of Victoria because, although eugenics was a subject

> in which I would be interested ... it is not one in which as far as I can see we are likely to make any significant progress unless the aim of the society is to get down to accurate investigational work. I have not heard this is the case in Victoria; if it should be the case, I will reconsider the matter and apply for membership.[75]

Other interwar academics, such as professor WA Osborne, an important public figure, gave public support to the Nazi government in Germany and its anti-Semitic policies without joining the Society, most likely due to personal animosities. Osborne reportedly had a 'low opinion of Japanese, Negroes and Aborigines'.[76] Rivett was also a Nazi apologist, as was Augustin Lodewyckx, associate professor of German, perhaps better known as the father-in-law of the historian Charles Manning Clark, while another apologist was Fritz Duras, associate professor of physical education and a member of and lecturer for the Eugenics Society.[77]

Opposition to Eugenics

Whilst eugenic thinking was widespread in the University in the twentieth century, there was some opposition. In 1938 Frederic Wood Jones wrote:

> I have many times called attention to the part that appears to have been played by the wide and unthinking acceptance of all the worst connotations of Charles Darwin's phrase 'the struggle for existence' and Herbert Spencer's 'survival of the fittest' ... [That] the Darwinian survival thesis has gone far towards producing the sinister theories that have let loose the present demons of bloodshed and destruction is not to be doubted.[78]

Richard Berry's measurements of adult Aboriginal skulls had convinced him that Indigenous Australians had the brain size and thus mentality of a thirteen-year-old Anglo-Saxon child.[79] Wood Jones disagreed violently. He wrote in *Unscientific Excursions* (a collection of essays, many of which were originally published in the Melbourne *Argus*) that 'the worshippers of the large brain claim far too much ... and many of their claims are false and that is why I range myself in opposition to them'.[80] He pointed out that Neanderthals had a much larger brain than modern individuals. In relation to the Indigenous people, he remarked that

> the Rev[erend] Mr Horton wrote of the natives of Tasmania: 'Indeed the shape of their bodies is almost the only mark by which one can recognise them as fellow-men; ... they are a race of beings altogether distinct from ourselves, and class them among the inferior species of irrational animals.' ... I should have dearly loved to tell him that many of the natives of Tasmania had brains far larger than his; and, unless his head was unusually large, the right would have been on my side ... Truly, modern civilized man is not supreme in this matter of big brains, for his forgotten ancestors and his despised, pigmented brother may both surpass him in this regard.[81]

His first argument with contemporary orthodoxy was that he disputed the notion of Aboriginal people as inferior to the white race. In three broadcasts on Melbourne radio station 3LO (on 5, 11 and 19 July 1934), he stated:

> Intelligence is an attribute that permits an individual to adjust itself correctly to the changing demands of its environment, and it is useless to attempt to establish a simple criterion, by which the intelligence of a nomadic stone-age hunter and [that] of a white politician may be measured and contrasted.[82]

Nor according to Wood Jones could the Indigenous person be seen to be physically inferior as 'it is safe to say that no more beautiful balanced human figures than those of the native in the prime of his life could be found among any race'.[83] His explanation of the evolution of Aboriginal society and culture is strikingly similar to the explanation first offered in 1997 by Jared Diamond in his popular and influential book (and subsequent television series) *Guns, Germs and Steel: The Fates of Human Societies*.[84] Preceding Diamond by some sixty years, Wood Jones argued that the development of modern civilisation is only possible with agriculture and the leisure that follows from the production of excess food. It was therefore impossible for the nomadic Indigenous people to settle and build cities, as there were no species of fauna or flora in Australia that were capable of domestication:

> Indeed the white colonist has made no more conservative use of the native animals and plants of Australia than did the aborigine [sic], for in no single instance has he adapted to his needs any animal or plant indigenous to Australia. All that can be said for the white colonist (in this regard) is that by a thoroughly vandalistic policy he has made a profit out of the destruction of native fauna and flora.[85]

It is no coincidence that Wood Jones was a friend of Sir Peter H Buck (Te Rangi Hīroa), a New Zealand physician and anthropologist who was that country's first Indigenous medical graduate and a prominent anthropologist.[86] He graduated from the University of Otago in 1904, almost a century before the first Indigenous Australian medical graduate, professor Helen Milroy.

Teaching Eugenics

As for teaching eugenics, McRae and Agar offered courses on the subject in the Vacation School at the University in the 1920s.[87] After World War II, in 1946, Agar wrote to Wallace expressing confidence in the current reputation of eugenics at the University and outlined the support that the University had given to its study. He explained he was not aware of the situation in other Australian universities, but that his university

> has shown itself quite ready to treat Eugenics as a proper subject of study. For several years I gave an official course of about 10 lectures on the subject as part of the syllabus of Political Science. With a change of syllabus in that subject the Eugenics lectures dropped off. I have since given a voluntary course of lectures—i.e. not leading to examination nor part of

> any recognised subject. The University Extension Board has always been interested & I have frequently lectured for them.[88]

It seems that Agar never lost his enthusiasm for eugenics, even after the horrors of the Holocaust had been publicised. The continuing attraction to eugenics by leading intellectuals after World War II is a separate topic, to be discussed in the last chapter in this part of the book.

Notes

1 WE Agar, 'Science and Human Welfare', *Realities of Reconstruction*, no. 4, Melbourne University Press in association with Oxford University Press, Melbourne, 1943.

2 I continue to use various forms of the phrase mental deficiency (mentally deficient and so on) without quote marks, as the reader would be aware that they represent tainted ideas from the period. For a recent discussion, see Lee-Ann Monk, David Henderson, Christine Bigby, Richard Broome and Katie Holmes, *Failed Ambitions: Kew Cottages and Changing Ideas of Intellectual Disabilities*, Monash University Press, Melbourne, 2023.

3 Agar, 'Science and Human Welfare', p. 12; WE Agar, *Eugenics and the Future of the Australian Population*, Eugenics Society of Victoria, Melbourne, 1939, p. 6. He continued: 'This rather small result has, however, another aspect. It is known that not only are a large proportion of the children of defective parents actually defective, but a further large proportion of them are in the border-line or dull class. Hence a cessation of reproduction by the mentally defective would reduce not only the number of defectives, but also the number of dulls in the next generation.'

4 Agar, 'Science and Human Welfare', p. 16.

5 Ross L Jones, 'The Master Potter and the Rejected Pots: Eugenic Legislation in Victoria 1918–1939', *Australian Historical Studies*, vol. 30, no. 113, October 1999, pp. 323–4.

6 Ross L Jones, 'Removing Some of the Dust from the Wheels of Civilization: William Ernest Jones and the 1928 Commonwealth Survey of Mental Deficiency', *Australian Historical Studies*, vol. 40, no. 1, March 2009, p. 71.

7 Jones, 'The Master Potter', pp. 333–4.

8 Agar, *Eugenics and the Future of the Australian Population*, pp. 5–6.

9 Ibid.

10 Quoted in Ross L Jones, *Humanity's Mirror: 150 Years of Anatomy in Melbourne*, Haddington Press, Melbourne, 2007, p. 107.

11 Jones, 'The Master Potter', p. 332.

12 *Medical Journal of Australia*, 26 July 1919, p. 72—one of many such articles.

13 Jones, *Humanity's Mirror*, Chapter 5.

14 Ross L Jones, *Anatomists of Empire: Race, Evolution and the Discovery of Human Biology in the British World*, Australian Scholarly Publishing, Melbourne, 2020, chapters 2 and 3 for a bibliography, including Nancy Stepan, *The Idea of Race in Science: Great Britain, 1800–1960*, Archon Books, Hamden, CT, 1982.

15 See Barry W Butcher, 'Darwinism, Social Darwinism, and the Australian Aborigines: A Reevaluation', in Roy MacLeod and Philip Rehbock (eds), *Evolutionary Theory and Natural History in the Pacific: Darwin's Laboratory*, University of Hawaii Press, Honolulu, 1994.

16 Harry Brookes Allen, 'Evolution and the Ideal', *Alma Mater*, July 1899, p. 34.
17 *The School Paper*, vol. IV, July 1899, Victorian Department of Education, Melbourne, p. 24.
18 *The School Paper*, vols V and VI, October 1899, Victorian Department of Education, Melbourne, p. 26.
19 *Speculum*, no. 23, February 1891, pp. 161, 162.
20 *Speculum*, no. 30, August 1894, p. 19.
21 For further discussion, see Philip Goad's contribution to this volume.
22 Warwick Anderson, *The Cultivation of Whiteness: Science, Health and Racial Destiny in Australia*, Melbourne University Press, Carlton, 2002, p. 11.
23 *Herald*, 5 September 1934, p. 6.
24 See Anderson, *The Cultivation of Whiteness*, pp. 27, 62f.; Aileen Moreton-Robinson, 'Duggaibah, or "Place of Whiteness": Australian Feminists and Race', in John Docker and Gerhard Fischer, *Race, Colour, and Identity in Australia and New Zealand*, UNSW Press, Sydney, 2000, pp. 240–55; Aileen Moreton-Robinson, *Whitening Race: Essays in Social and Cultural Criticism*, Aboriginal Studies Press, Canberra, 2004; Christopher Mayes, Yin Paradies and Amanuel Elias, 'Lead Essay: Institutional Racism, Whiteness, and the Role of Critical Bioethics', *Bioethical Inquiry*, vol. 18, 2021, pp. 9–12; Leigh Boucher, Jane Carey and Katherine Ellinghaus (eds), *Re-Orienting Whiteness*, Palgrave Macmillan, New York, 2009.
25 RJW Selleck, *Frank Tate: A Biography*, Melbourne University Press, Melbourne, 1982.
26 Jones, 'The Master Potter', p. 336
27 For Tate and Berry's association in committees created for the purpose of developing government policy on mental deficiency, see John Lewis, Removing the Grit: The Development of Special Education in Victoria 1887–1947, unpublished PhD thesis, La Trobe University, 1989, pp. 209–23.
28 *Herald*, 4 July 1917, p. 1; *Herald*, 6 July 1917, p. 5.
29 Ibid.
30 Ibid.
31 RJA Berry, *Chance and Circumstance*, unpublished autobiography, University of Melbourne Medical Library, Parkville, 1954, p. 143. For a list of Berry's extensive travels and lecturing, see RJA Berry, 'Publicity Campaign', *Report to the Edward Wilson (of 'The Argus') Trust on Mental Deficiency in the State of Victoria, with Suggestions for the Establishment of a Child Guidance Clinic*, Wilson and Mackinnon, Melbourne, 1929, pp. 4–5.
32 *Herald*, 4 July 1917, p. 1; *Herald*, 6 July 1917, p. 5; Don Garden, *Theodore Fink: A Talent for Ubiquity*, Melbourne University Press, Carlton, 1998, p. 121.
33 Ibid.
34 *Medical Journal of Australia*, 23 June 1917, p. 536.
35 Ibid.
36 See Berry, *Report to the Edward Wilson (of 'The Argus') Trust*, p. 3.
37 *Age*, 31 July 1913, p. 8.
38 *Medical Journal of Australia*, 14 December 1918, p. 489. For example, see Richard JA Berry and AWD Robertson, 'Preliminary Communication on Fifty-Three Tasmanian Crania, Forty-Two of Which Are Now Recorded for the First Time' [read 11 March 1909], *Proceedings of the Royal Society of Victoria*, vol. 22, Part I, 1909, pp. 47–58; Richard JA Berry and LWG Büchner, 'The Correlation of

Size of Head and Intelligence as Estimated from the Cubic Capacity of Brain of 355 Melbourne Criminals' [read 10 October 1912], *Proceedings of the Royal Society of Victoria*, vol. 25, Part II, 1913, pp. 229–53; and Richard JA Berry and LWG Büchner, 'The Correlation of Size of Head and Intelligence as Estimated from the Cubic Capacity of Brain of 33 Melbourne Criminals Hanged for Murder' [read 14 November 1912], *Proceedings of the Royal Society of Victoria*, vol. 25, Part II, 1913, pp. 229–53.

39 *Medical Journal of Australia*, 23 June 1917, p. 536.

40 Ibid., p. 537.

41 Ibid., p. 536.

42 Ibid., p. 539.

43 Ibid., p. 540.

44 Berry, *Chance and Circumstance*, p. 135.

45 Ross L Jones, 'Thinking Dangerous Thoughts: Post-Primary Education and Eugenics in Australia: 1905–1939', in Hamish Spencer, Diane Paul and John Stenhouse (eds), *Eugenics at the Edges of Empire: New Zealand, Australia, Canada and South Africa*, Palgrave Macmillan, Basingstoke, 2017.

46 Frank Tate, 'Some Problems of Administration', in PR Cole, *The Education of the Adolescent in Australia*, Australian Council for Educational Research, Educational Research Series, no. 32, Melbourne University Press, Carlton, 1935, pp. 15–16.

47 *Medical Journal of Australia*, 23 June 1917, p. 541.

48 See the James Waghorne chapter 'Naming and Renaming' in this volume.

49 Chris R McRae, 'Reports of the Psychological Laboratory, Teacher's College, no. V: "The Relation between Intelligence and Social Status"', *Education Gazette and Teachers' Aid*, 20 July 1926, p. 242. McRae lectured at the Teachers' College and eventually became deputy vice-chancellor of the University of Sydney.

50 Ibid., p. 242.

51 Ernest Scott, *A History of the University of Melbourne*, Melbourne University Press, Carlton, 1936, pp. 214–17; Geoffrey Blainey, *A Centenary History of the University of Melbourne*, Melbourne University Press, Carlton, 1957, pp. 142–5. While important, the eugenic push for fees was not the only influence on decisions made at this time: see James Waghorne and Gwilym Croucher, 'Narratives of Financial Assistance for University Students and the Emergence of HECS in Australia', *Paedagogica Historica*, 2022, pp. 1–17

52 Quoted in Scott, *A History of the University of Melbourne*, p. 216.

53 Ibid., pp. 213–14, 217; Henry Payne (ed.), *Proceedings of the First Educational Congress, State of Victoria, Held in Melbourne, 1912*, Mullet, Melbourne, n.d.

54 'The University of Melbourne: Annual Report', 1925–26, pp. 3–4, *Victorian Parliamentary Papers*, vol. II, 1926, pp. 1155–6.

55 I have not yet been able to find out why the University of Western Australia was making nominations.

56 'The University of Melbourne: Annual Report,' 1927–28, p. 1, *Victorian Parliamentary Papers*, vol. II, 1928, p. 1181.

57 See the *Melbourne University Calendar*, Melbourne University Press, Carlton, for the years from 1930 until the present. The earlier figures can be found in the *Victorian Parliamentary Papers*.

58 Frank Tate, at Lord Baltimore Hotel, Baltimore (prior to 16 December 1932), correspondence, USA, Canada, Britain & Europe 1932–33, Tate papers, University of Melbourne Archives.

59 Which is not to say that, after the initial early graduation of Māori students, all continued well in New Zealand: see Ranginui Walker, 'Reclaiming Māori Education', in Jessica Hutchings and Jenny Lee-Morgan (eds), *Decolonisation in Aotearoa: Education, Research and Practice*, NZCER Press, Wellington, 2016.

60 Victor H Wallace, 'The Eugenics Society of Victoria (1936–1961)', *Eugenics Review*, vol. 53, no. 4, January 1962, p. 215.

61 *Argus*, 14 July 1914, p. 11. On Spencer's inability to find the time to accept the position, see William E Jones to Mrs Gotto, 10 February 1915, Victorian Eugenics Society Archive, Wellcome Collection, London, https://wellcomecollection.org/works/mffnht8z (accessed 26 October 2023). Other eminent citizens were the first Commonwealth statistician GH Knibbs, Dr Felix Meyer, inspector of the insane Dr William Ernest Jones, and Dr Harvey Sutton.

62 Wallace, 'The Eugenics Society of Victoria', pp. 215–18.

63 *The Victorian Council for Mental Hygiene, By-Laws and Progress Reports*, 1930, pp. 14–15, file Mental Hygiene 1949–68, box no. 96/3/5, vicar-general's files 1911–1978, Melbourne Diocesan Historical Commission, Archives of the Catholic Archdiocese of Melbourne, Mannix Centre; Wallace, 'The Eugenics Society of Victoria', p. 215.

64 Wallace, 'The Eugenics Society of Victoria', pp. 215–16.

65 Ibid., p. 216.

66 Ibid.

67 Ibid.

68 Ibid.

69 Ibid.

70 Subscription books, The Eugenics Society of Victoria, Wallace Papers U 41/44–16; Rob Watts, 'Beyond Nature and Nurture: Eugenics in Twentieth Century Australian History', *Australian Journal of Politics and History*, vol. 40, no. 3, 1994, p. 324.

71 *Herald*, 24 April 1939, p. 10.

72 For the little that appears in biographical works, see, for Tate, Selleck, *Frank Tate*; see the *Australian Dictionary of Biography*, Melbourne University Press, Carlton, for James McRae (vol. 10, 1986), Agar (vol. 7, 1979), Rivett (vol. 11, 1988), Sewell (vol. 11, 1988), Murdoch (vol. 10, 1986), Sweet (vol. 12, 1990), Medley (vol. 15, 2000), MacCallum (vol. 15, 2000) and Duras (vol. 14, 1996); Rohan Rivett, *David Rivett: Fighter for Australian Science*, CSIRO Publishing, Canberra, 2013; WF Connell, 'The Professors: G.S. Browne and C.R. McRae', in C Turney (ed.), *Pioneers of Australian Education*, vol. 3, Sydney University Press, Sydney, 1983; Brian Williams, *Education with Its Eyes Open: A Biography of Dr K.S. Cunningham*, Australian Council for Educational Research, Melbourne, 1994; William F Connell, *The Australian Council for Educational Research, 1930–80*, Australian Council for Educational Research, Hawthorn, 1980; John Handfield, *Friends and Brothers: A Life of Gerard Kennedy Tucker, Founder of the Brotherhood of St. Laurence and Community Aid Abroad*, Hyland Press, Melbourne, 1980.

73 See Peter McPhee, *Pansy: A Life of R.D. Wright*, Melbourne University Press, Carlton, 1999; Frank Fenner, *Sir Macfarlane Burnet: Scientist and Thinker*, University of Queensland Press, St Lucia, 1988; and Christopher Sexton, *The Seeds of Time: The Life of Sir Macfarlane Burnet*, Oxford University Press, Melbourne, 1991. Sexton briefly discusses Burnet's biological determinism but makes no

mention of his relationship with, and publications for, the Eugenics Society of Great Britain: see pp. 193, 194, 235–7.

74 *Herald*, 30 October 1939, p. 10.

75 R Douglas Wright to K Cunningham, 2 June 1947, 1(e), replies to Dr Cunningham's letter 1945–47, Wallace Papers.

76 Barry O Jones, 'William Alexander Osborne (1873–1967)', *Australian Dictionary of Biography*, National Centre of Biography, Australian National University, Canberra, 2006, https://adb.anu.edu.au/biography/osborne-william-alexander-7929 (accessed 26 October 2023).

77 For Rivett, see 'Germany Today By Sir David Rivett', *Argus*, 2 January 1937, p. 14; *Argus*, 9 January 1937, p. 19. For Lodewyckx, see the chapter by Warwick Anderson in this volume. For Osborne, see letter to the editor, *Age*, 18 December 1935, p. 19; *Farrago*, vol. 9, no. 8, 18 May 1933, p. 1. For Duras, see *Age*, 8 July 1938, p. 12.

78 Frederic Wood Jones, *Habit and Heritage*, Kegan Paul, London, 1943, pp. 10–11. His indictment of Tennyson's phrase 'nature red in tooth and claw' also appears on p. 11.

79 *Medical Journal of Australia*, 23 June 1917, p. 536.

80 Frederic Wood Jones, *Unscientific Excursions*, Butler and Tanner, Frome, UK, 1934, p. 41.

81 Ibid., pp. 43–4. For a broader discussion, see Elazar Barkan, *The Retreat of Scientific Racism: Changing Concepts of Race in Britain and the United States between the World Wars*, Cambridge University Press, London, 1993.

82 Frederic Wood Jones, *Australia's Vanishing Race*, Angus & Robertson, Sydney, 1934, p. 22.

83 Ibid., p. 21.

84 Jared Diamond, *Guns, Germs and Steel: The Fates of Human Societies*, Norton, New York, 1997. The seed of this idea can be found in the writings of the co-founder of the theory of natural selection, Alfred Russel Wallace: see AR Wallace, 'On the Varieties of Man in the Malay Archipelago', *Transactions of the Ethnological Society of London*, vol. 3, 1865, p. 206.

85 Jones, *Australia's Vanishing Race*, pp. 16–17.

86 Peter H Buck to Frederic Wood Jones, 2 March 1929, MS0017/1/2/14/1-2, Wood Jones Archives, General Correspondence A–O, Royal College of Surgeons Archives, London. Of course, the debate continues: see Bruce Pascoe, *Dark Emu: Aboriginal Australia and the Birth of Agriculture*, Magabala Books, Broome, 2014; and Peter Sutton and Keryn Walshe, *Farmers or Hunter Gatherers? The Dark Emu Debate*, Melbourne University Press, Carlton, 2021.

87 See *Vacation School Handbook of General Information*, May 1924, held under the joint auspices of the University Extension Board and the Education Department at the University of Melbourne, Parkville, 26 May to 6 June 1924, pp. 16, 35.

88 Wilfred Agar to Victor Wallace, 17 December 1946, correspondence 1937–61, Wallace Papers.

Professor Ewart and 'Mr Murnane'

Botany, Veterinary Science and Mass Murder

KATE AUTY

In June 1926, a group of police officers, Aboriginal trackers and volunteers searched the land near Wyndham in north-western Western Australia looking for an Aboriginal man, later identified as Lumbia, who was accused of spearing a station owner. As the group navigated the rocky gullies and gorges, they perpetrated a series of massacres, killing at least eleven Aboriginal people and burning their bodies. The events prompted a national public outcry and the appointment of a royal commission, chaired by George Wood.[1] Two police officers would be charged with murder, although these would ultimately be thrown out for lack of evidence. One of the volunteers was Daniel Murnane, a veterinary scientist who had graduated from the University of Melbourne and was pursuing a research career at the University and the Council for Scientific and Industrial Research (CSIR, a precursor to CSIRO). The Royal Commission identified Murnane as being present at the massacre sites, although no charges against him would be laid.

Murnane had come to the Forrest River area near Wyndham in 1925 to conduct research on buffalo fly for the Commonwealth Institute of Science and Industry, and it was while undertaking this work that he volunteered to join the police patrol.[2] Murnane had served in the Second Unit of Supply during World War I.[3] He'd then obtained a Bachelor of Veterinary Science degree from the University of Melbourne in 1924, which would eventually lead to him working in research positions for much of his life at both the University and CSIR. Murnane would obtain a Doctorate in Veterinary Science in 1950, and he would be appointed an industry representative in the Faculty of Veterinary Science when it was re-established in 1962. In 2011, Ormond College created a scholarship in his honour to support a rural veterinary science student.[4]

Murnane's implication in the massacres and his comments in their aftermath, together with newspaper articles published by his research colleague Alfred Ewart, the University of Melbourne's then professor of botany, sheds an uncomfortable light on the relationship between scientific researchers and the frontier wars, where racial prejudice took on a mantle of academic authority.

The massacres followed the May 1926 spearing of Frederick William Hay, co-owner of Nulla Nulla station. Hay's body was found by his partner Leo Overheu and constable St Jack after they conducted a 'dispersal' of Aboriginal people alleged to have killed cattle. He was lying, with only his boots on, in the shade of a tree close to a billabong and a cattle carcass. The post-mortem was conducted onsite, identifying spearing as the cause of death.[5] Hay's death was declared 'murder' without any formal inquiry, generating outrage in Wyndham.[6] In response, a punitive party was put together over May, June and July 1926 to hunt down and capture those responsible for the spearing. The force comprised four white police officers; Overheu and Murnane, who had been conducting his research there; and seven Aboriginal trackers and an Aboriginal woman. It was provisioned with forty-two horses and mules. Each member was also armed, some with a pistol and a rifle, and the party was supplied with some 500–600 rounds of ammunition.[7] Their intention was clear: to deal severely with Aboriginal people in revenge for Hay's death while seeking those responsible.[8]

Such patrols had become a regular occurrence in the Wyndham region as part of the frontier conflict and the expansion of the pastoral industry.[9] Anne Scrimgeour has noted that 'Kimberley policemen were not given carte blanche to carry out the unrestrained violence that characterised mounted police activities in northern Queensland'.[10] It is apparent that police in the Kimberley also carried out unofficial and, indeed, extrajudicial actions. Few records would be kept of their deeds, and they would not publicise the names of those they had apprehended by way of reprisal.[11]

News of the patrol's actions were reported to the local Forrest River Mission, prompting a local inspector named Douglas to investigate. Detective Manning from Perth joined Douglas to support the inquiries. The investigation found evidence of a massacre and the Western Australian Government duly appointed a royal commission.

The perpetrators were called as witnesses before the Royal Commission, but three critically important trackers had been allowed to 'escape' just days before they were scheduled to give evidence. Statements taken from the trackers by Manning and Douglas would become exhibits, but their evidentiary weight was diminished by the absence of these witnesses. In his report, commissioner Wood criticised the 'very slight effort' made to locate the trackers.[12]

One of the trio, Sulieman, had given a statement to Douglas during the pre-commission investigation, as he had guided the policeman along the route the group had taken:

> While at [police patrol camp 3] the trackers went out looking for natives and found four men and four women in a gorge. We brought them into the camp. The police had a talk to them and in the afternoon Constable Regan, Barney O'Leary and another white man, I do not know his name (Murnane), together with Frank and Charlie, went away from the camp taking all the prisoners with them [this included one other person]. About dark that night Charlie and Frank came back to the camp, bringing all the horses that they had taken away with them. Regan, O'Leary and Murnane did not return to the camp that night. The following morning we packed up and started off for the next camp. Frank went ahead and picked up Regan, O'Leary and Murnane. They had no natives with them when they came up with us.[13]

Douglas corroborated Sulieman's statement by examining 'horse tracks in and out of the ravine where there had been a native camp'. He found 'the remains of a large fire and some thousands of fragments of bone in the ashes, and timber had been dragged from all around the fire [and] by the size of the fire and quantity of bone fragments' he reported having 'no doubt that the nine were cremated there'.[14]

In the final days of the Royal Commission, Murnane was called to give evidence. His testimony was evasive and his answers formed a pattern: 'I don't know', 'I have no knowledge', 'I have never heard', 'I cannot tell you', 'To my knowledge none', 'I cannot remember' in addition to simple denials. He is recorded referring to Aboriginal people as 'niggers', a not uncommon racial slur among frontier pastoralists and police in Western Australia.[15] He also rejected Sulieman's account of his involvement.[16] Murnane's evidence was similar to that of the other members of the patrol, who denied the allegations and the evidence obtained from site visits.

Shortly after the events described by Sulieman, it appears Murnane left the patrol and returned to Nulla Nulla station. He then went to Wyndham and made a number of conflicting public statements. Initially he told newspapers that 'several niggers [had been] interrogated' and to expect 'early arrests'.[17] But he later told the Royal Commission he had left the patrol because he considered the chances of catching the offenders to be 'hopeless'.[18] Sergeant Buckland, one of the officers on the patrol, testified that Murnane left the patrol 'to go to Darwin for business [and he] said he was very sorry. He would have liked to continue with the party'. However, it was also reported that Murnane told the manager of the Wyndham meatworks that the patrol was 'worse than the war'. Murnane denied this statement, calling it a 'wicked and downright lie', but it seems unlikely that the statement would have been concocted.[19]

Out of the concocted and conflicted narrative that unfolded before him, the commissioner concluded that Murnane, like all the whites in the police party, lied about the mass killings perpetrated by the patrol. Describing the actions of the police party as 'atrocities', the commissioner asked himself whether 'any reasonable man could come to any conclusion other than that the murders of the natives and the burning of the bodies were the work of members of the police party'.[20] The commissioner concluded that, during the time Murnane was a member of the patrol, four men, three women and in all probability another nine Aboriginal people had been killed and their bodies incinerated in fires that were 'restricted though intense'.[21]

These killings took place at Gotegotemerrie, Mowerie and at a ravine west of Mowerie, all west of the Forrest River Mission. At Gotegotemerrie the men were executed by gunfire in a creek bed and their bodies incinerated in a makeshift rock-slab oven that concentrated the heat for greater effect. From that place, three women—one of them old and blind—were taken to Mowerie and chained by the neck around a tree stump, then they too were shot. Their bodies were burnt where they slumped; piles of teeth were found in three places in the ashes. Murnane was a member of the patrol throughout these events. Sulieman's statement specifically implicated the veterinary scientist, along with two other whites, in the deaths of the nine people in the ravine, at the place where Douglas saw timber had been dragged in from all around the fire site.

The Royal Commission's findings led to charges of murder against two of the police, with warrants executed for their arrests and their subsequent detention in Perth in June–July 1927. The committal hearing was conducted in Perth despite the vocal objections of a north-western WA committee of pastoralists and residents, who insisted there should be no 'change of venue' and the case should proceed in Wyndham.[22] The hearing began in early July and finished the following month. St Jack and Regan were discharged on 16 August 1927 to the riotous applause of family, friends and the senior police present in the Perth magistrate's court.

By contrast, the Aboriginal man who had speared Hay was identified and convicted of murder. Lumbia claimed that, while armed with a spear and on foot, he defended himself against Hay, formerly of the 10th Light Horse and the notoriously violent and dishonest Boer War Brabant's Horse—the 'Brabinetti'. The dispute apparently concerned a dead cow that one of the women with Lumbia claimed was already deceased when the Indigenous people camped at the waterhole. Wielding his stockwhip, Hay galloped at Lumbia, discharging his pistol and inflicting a glancing head wound on the Indigenous man. The wound bled profusely—the injury was still evident months later when Lumbia was prosecuted for Hay's murder in Wyndham. Lumbia's evidence, interpreted by Angelina Noble from the Forrest River Mission, was that when he speared Hay he could barely see through his own blood.

At his trial, Lumbia was represented by a former farmer who was now a protector of Aborigines, while his jury was drawn from Wyndham's white population and his judge was a former World War I officer.[23] His claim of self-defence was rejected, and it took the jury only ten minutes to convict. Years later, bureaucrats in the Department of Native Welfare determined that Lumbia had been railroaded and the killing was not connected to the cow carcass. Rather, Hay had tried to run Lumbia down because of a dispute over an Aboriginal woman—and all the locals knew it.[24]

It was during the events surrounding the hearing of Regan and St Jack that Alfred Ewart began publishing his opinions about settler-colonial violence in Western Australia. He had come to Western Australia in 1927 to work with Murnane on a project examining Kimberley Horse Disease, building on the previous work undertaken by Murnane on buffalo fly in the Forrest River area.[25] During Ewart's stint as professor of botany at the University of Melbourne from 1906 to 1937, he enjoyed an international research reputation and gained expertise on genetics, but he was often frustrated by University protocols. He was also 'reputedly of a somewhat choleric disposition'.[26] In the wake of the Royal Commission findings, and during the course of the committal hearing, Ewart published a series of opinion pieces in newspapers supporting the actions of the patrol and defending the pastoral interests. He also, in passing, defended his 'very able colleague Mr Murnane'.[27]

The language used by Ewart in these articles reveals him as candidly racist, and it is worth quoting some sections at length. On 19 July 1927 Ewart wrote for the *Sun* in Sydney, a city where the Royal Commission and its negative findings two months earlier had been widely publicised,[28] challenging what Ewart held to be common, although ignorant, assumptions about Aboriginal Australians:

> Many apologists for blacks hold very erroneous ideas as to their mental and intellectual characteristics. The average mental capacity of the adults is certainly below that of a white child of ten or twelve years of age ... they do not know the commonest plants that grow around them so long as those plants have no relation to their stomachs ... their ideas are so few that it is very difficult to carry on even the most limited conversation with those who know English. The blacks have been stated to be sober, industrious and honest. They are sober because they are not allowed to have alcohol. They are industrious so long as their work is watched, and they are honest because they have a few temptations or opportunities to steal ... At every station one visits the blacks seem happy, contented and well fed. The children are certainly easily scared by a white man just as a white child is easily scared by a black man.[29]

In another article published on 23 July in the Melbourne *Herald*, Ewart commented directly on Murnane's role in the 1926 patrol when discussing north-western pastoralists and Aboriginal people.[30] He began with exaggerated claims about cattle killing, allegations invariably used to explain frontier conflict and justify retribution. Such claims swirled around the actions of the 1926 patrol, were used to validate the 'dispersal' after Hay's body had been found, and ultimately worked to erode the assertion of self-defence that should have been available to Lumbia.

Ewart equally confidently dismissed 'stories that have been circulated by some parties of stations poisoning blacks with arsenic or strychnine'. He claimed, again erroneously, that 'blacks' were provided with bread 'exactly the same as eaten on the stations'. This was disingenuous, as no-one was baking bread or even damper for Aboriginal people, even though Aboriginal women, unpaid, did the cooking and washing. In an act of misdirection, Ewart blamed the Chinese, stating that their 'attitude to the blacks seems to be one of amused contempt'.[31]

To justify the violence perpetrated on Aboriginal women, children and men, in his special pleading for whites on the frontier Ewart next recited uncorroborated numbers of non-Aboriginal people 'killed by blacks' and claimed many whites were 'murderously assaulted'.[32] He appears to be parroting claims made during the Royal Commission, basing his assertions on nothing more than what he had been 'told'.[33]

In this way Ewart sided with pastoralists' interests, presenting their actions as legitimised by 'wild blacks'. In his version of the events at Nulla Nulla station, Ewart wrote that

> Hay caught the blacks killing his cattle [plural] and *foolishly* attempted [my italics] to drive them [plural] off with a stockwhip. They [plural] turned on him and speared him to death. Falling from his horse he was able to fire a single shot from his pistol but without effect.[34]

None of this was true. Ewart erroneously claimed Lumbia received a sentence of a 'few years imprisonment'. In fact he was sentenced to death, a penalty that was later commuted to ten years' gaol at Rottnest and Fremantle, where all requests for a compassionate transfer to the north-west were denied.[35]

Floridly, and again channelling local views that suggested Aboriginal people were unconcerned about capital punishment, Ewart wrote that 'hanging seems to be no deterrent to other blacks'. He cited an old and exaggerated report about the hanging of three men at Mount Dockerell, describing Aboriginal people as 'disappointed that the show was soon over ... offering some of their own number as victims in order to prolong the ceremony'. Bizarre, cavalier and superficial as this claim was, Ewart was not yet finished.

Arriving at the main point of his article, Ewart wrote that the 'larger question' was not whether Murnane and the police patrol had perpetrated mass murder, but 'whether the blacks are to be allowed to render large tracts of country useless for white settlement'. Aboriginal people's actions made pastoralist retaliation inevitable, as station owners, in Ewart's view, must 'either starve to death or leave the country'. The 'solution' Ewart advocated was the removal of Aboriginal people from Country to offshore reserves. He wrote: 'We make reserves for native animals and surely we might also do the same for the black.' It was his view that such a policy would produce utilitarian benefits and support Aboriginal welfare, since their genetic inferiority meant they were 'bound to go'. He claimed that attempts at assimilation 'arouse a feeling of contempt or disgust', and he argued that the 'possibility of a future mixing of races is always present and would be a deplorable calamity'.

The Royal Commission findings, including that Murnane lied about his actions, dismissed so contemptibly by Ewart, have echoed down the years. In the 1950s workers at the Forrest River Mission, Sally Gare and Randolph Stow,[36] were both taken to the places where people were murdered.

The events of 1926 are no fiction. Neither are they insignificant. For Aboriginal people whose family members were murdered by this police patrol, there was no 'larger question'. Aboriginal people have continued to tell the story of what happened:

> To stage the mass execution of the captured men, there was a depression in the rock surface. The natives had to sit down, chained to a tree on each side, in a circle. They sat around a rock basin facing the middle, chained by the neck.
>
> When this was ready some black trackers and white men went around and shot one after another in the forehead with a revolver ...
>
> After this execution they drove the women in a chain gang about three miles upstream to Balara water hole. Here, some way from the water on sandy ground, they shot them in the same way.[37]

Truth-telling will be rooted in these narratives and we need to listen, finally.

Notes

1 GT Wood, *Royal Commission of Inquiry into Alleged Killing and Burning of Bodies of Aborigines in East Kimberley and into Police Methods when Effecting Arrests*, Government Printer, Perth, 1927, https://aiatsis.gov.au/sites/default/files/docs/digitised_collections/remove/93281.pdf (accessed 26 October 2023).

2 George Currie and John Graham, *The Origins of CSIRO: Science and the Commonwealth Government, 1901–1926*, Commonwealth Scientific and Industrial Research Organisation, Melbourne, 1966, p. 117; CB Schedvin, *Shaping Science and Industry: A History of Australia's Council for Scientific and Industrial Research, 1926–49*, Allen & Unwin, Sydney, 1987, p. 50.

3 Discovering Anzacs website, now decommissioned.

4 Ormond College, 'Ormond Announces Major Vet Science Scholarship', 14 November 2011, https://ormond.unimelb.edu.au/news/ormond-announces-major-vet-science-scholarship, accessed 26 October 2023.

5 'Killed by Natives', *Daily News*, 27 May 1926, p. 2.

6 Wood, *Royal Commission of Inquiry*, p. vi.

7 Ibid.

8 In a letter to his father in southern Western Australia, Overheu called for drastic action.

9 Lyndall Ryan, Jennifer Debenham, Bill Pascoe, Robyn Smith, Chris Owen, Jonathan Richards, Stephanie Gilbert, Robert J Anders, Kaine Usher, Daniel

Price, Jack Newley, Mark Brown, Le Hoang Le and Hedy Fairbairn, *Colonial Frontier Massacres in Australia 1788–1930*, University of Newcastle, Newcastle, 2017–22, http://hdl.handle.net/1959.13/1340762 (accessed 26 October 2023). For background on the frontier conflict in Australia's north, see Mark Finnane and Fiona Paisley, 'Police Violence and the Limits of Law on a Late Colonial Frontier: The "Borroloola Case" in 1930s Australia', *Law and History Review*, vol. 28, no. 1, 2010, pp. 144–5.

10 Anne Scrimgeour, 'This Man's Tracks: Laurie O'Neill and Postwar Changes in Aboriginal Administration in Western Australia', *Aboriginal History*, vol. 38, 2014, pp. 41, 43–4. For an overview of policing and frontier conflict in the East Kimberley during the first two decades of colonisation, see Chris Owen, '"The Police Appear to Be a Useless Lot up There": Law and Order in the East Kimberley 1884–1905', *Aboriginal History*, vol. 27, 2003, pp. 105–30.

11 On the 'conspiracy of silence' that protected settlers who killed Aboriginal people in the East Kimberley, see Owen, '"The Police Appear to Be a Useless Lot up There"', pp. 125–8.

12 Wood, *Royal Commission of Inquiry*, p. v.

13 Ibid., p. 64.

14 Ibid., p. 68.

15 Ibid., pp. 60–1.

16 Ibid., p. 59, questions 2150, 2151.

17 Ibid., p. 60, question 2222.

18 Ibid., p. 20, question 526.

19 Ibid., p. 60, question 2228.

20 Ibid., p. xi.

21 Ibid., p. xv.

22 'Murder Charges against Nor-West Constables', *Sunday Times*, 12 June 1927. The committee organised to raise funds for the defence of St Jack and Regan, and to protest the change of venue, was chaired by B George; its secretary was W Flinders. See also 'Should a Wyndham Jury Sit', *Smith's Weekly*, 25 June 1927.

23 Ernestine Hill, *The Great Australian Loneliness*, ETT Imprint, Exile Bay, NSW, 1995, p. 66.

24 Lumbia file 933 85/45, State Records Office of Western Australia. See also C McBeath, *Kimberly Oral History Program*, State Library of Western Australia, 1960.

25 Reported in the *Western Mail*, 1 December 1927; 'Walkabout: Kimberley Horse Disease—A Victory for Science', paper presented to the WA division of the CSIR. Murnane and Ewart's research was published in bulletins 36 and 50 of the CSIR. Also see TC Chambers, 'Alfred James Ewart (1872–1937)', *Australian Dictionary of Biography*, National Centre of Biography, Australian National University, Canberra, 2006, https://adb.anu.edu.au/biography/ewart-alfred-james-6124 (accessed 26 October 2023).

26 Chambers, 'Alfred James Ewart'; RJW Selleck, *The Shop: The University of Melbourne 1850–1939*, Melbourne University Press, Carlton, 2003, p. 456.

27 'Kimberley Horse Disease', *Western Mail*, 8 September 1927.

28 See, for example, 'Abo. Slaughter While in Police Custody', *Evening News*, 26 May 1927, p. 13; 'Police Blamed', *Sydney Morning Herald*, 28 May 1927, p. 15.

29 Alfred Ewart, 'Black Australia: Socialism as Natives Know It, Aborigines' Low Mentality', *Sun*, 19 July 1927, p. 16.

30 'Black Spearmen: Northern Raiders Harry Cattlemen—Aborigines' Future', *Herald*, 23 July 1927.
31 Ibid.
32 Ibid.
33 Wood, *Royal Commission of Inquiry*, p. 52, question 1891.
34 'Black Spearmen'.
35 'Aboriginal Murders', *Geraldton Guardian*, 13 January 1927, p. 3. In 1930, while imprisoned on Rottnest Island, Lumbia was photographed and interviewed for an article in the *Perth Mirror*: Geordie Bay, 'Murderers at Large at Rottnest', *Mirror*, 20 December 1930, p. 9.
36 Sally Gare and Freda Marnie, *Outback Teacher*, Allen and Unwin, Sydney, 2022; Suzanne Falkiner, *Mick: A Life of Randolph Stow*, UWA Publishing, Perth, 2016.
37 Ron Morgan of Oombulgurri (Forrest River Mission) relayed this oral history to the German anthropologist Dr H Rhoem in 1968. The comments are found in the State Records Office of Western Australia police file 430: p. 5374.

The Lost Languages of White Settler Civilisation

WARWICK ANDERSON[1]

As in other settler-colonial universities, the parameters of the 'human' in the humanities at the University of Melbourne were clearly defined and restricted in the late-nineteenth and early-twentieth centuries. Aspiring to convey 'the best that has been thought and known in the world', to use Matthew Arnold's influential formulation,[2] scholars and teachers in germinal fields of inquiry, such as classics, philosophy and history, sought to implant in the New World a canon of work by major savants of the Old World, to spread a civilisational discourse fit for conquest. Their 'humanities' were intended to nurture in strange, perhaps unfavourable, soils the best that white men in northern Europe and North America had thought and known. Indigenous peoples, Asians and Africans found no place in the antipodal humanities, not even as 'barbarians' at the classical gates. They came to signify nothing—they were not deemed to be infused with the true 'human spirit'. Therefore, in the modern university, 'antiquity' mostly meant oddly Teutonised Hellenic and Roman relics, not the ancient stories of Aboriginal culture. The humanities in Australia, even in apparently liberal and progressive forms, became a potent yet narrowly focused means of cultivating white distinction and virtue in a supposedly hostile setting.

We are familiar with contributions of biological and medical sciences to making settler colonies seem habitable and hospitable for imagined 'white' bodies and mentalities.[3] An enormous amount of work went on at the University of Melbourne in the early twentieth century in trying to invent a positive science of white settlement in Australia. While the biomedical sciences generally were predicated on implicitly white bodies and minds, they evinced at the University an especially zealous attempt to acclimatise and accommodate explicitly white physiologies to new territories, first in the temperate south of the continent and then in its challenging tropical north. The whiteness of biomedical teaching and research at other Australian institutions during this period was better concealed and perhaps more modest. Few, if any, medical schools would come to flaunt their connections with white nationalism as brazenly as the University. But the prominence of these medical votaries of white Australia has obscured a more insidious program in the humanities to naturalise white civilisation at the edge of the British Empire.[4] Extolling the accomplishments of ancient Greece and Rome or emotionally singing the Norse sagas may seem innocent, even charming, yet such devotions could covertly imply a racial agenda at least as compelling as any biomedical prescriptions.[5]

Contemplation of Greek, Latin and the Germanic languages would provide students with historical examples of how language can fashion race and nation, whereas Indigenous languages, had they been recognised at all, would have revealed instead a grammar connecting persons and places, articulating community and cosmos. But such acknowledgement of Indigenous presence and environmental embeddedness, in any expressive form, was antithetical to the function of the settler-colonial university. Since the late-eighteenth century, the comparative study of language structure, or scientific philology, or historical linguistics, had been linked to European racial projects, especially in Germany. Racial difference was fabricated linguistically as well as biologically—that is, presumed linguistic races, such as 'Aryan', were consummated along with biological races. Comparative linguistics therefore was often regarded as a natural science with a bridge to the humanities, generating prolific analogies and organic connections between philological racial categories and human physiological difference.[6] Those who engage critically with the cultivation of settler whiteness in Australia, and with white strategies of authority more generally, ignore these philological dimensions of white privilege at their peril.[7]

Here I focus on the exclusive whiteness of scholarship in the classics and Germanic languages at the University of Melbourne. Two figures take representative roles in my brief narrative: Thomas G Tucker (1859–1946), professor of classics and comparative philology,[8] and Augustin Lodewyckx (1876–1964), associate professor of German.[9] An exceptionally distinguished scholar, Tucker loomed large in the decades before World War I, while Lodewyckx took centrestage during the interwar years. Heeding the warnings of a former colleague, Charles H Pearson, that rising Asian powers threatened the European occupation of Australia, Tucker became increasingly concerned about the future of white civilisation in the country.[10] He worried that the influence of the classics, the purest and highest expression of the civilisation he cherished, was on the wane. After the war, Lodewyckx successfully elevated Germanic or Teutonic languages to the esteemed place that classics rapidly was vacating. Inspired by his reading of the racial tracts of Houston Stewart Chamberlain, Madison Grant, Lothrop Stoddard and Oswald Spengler, while admiring Nazi initiative, the Flemish Germanist became an expert on European immigration to Australia, expounding on how Teutons might bolster and uphold white civilisation in trying circumstances.[11]

I am particularly interested in the moment before World War I—with the defensive founding of the Classical Association of Victoria in 1912, the removal of any Greek language requirement at the University in 1914, and rising enthusiasm for Chamberlain's chronicling of the bonds of Hellenism and Teutonism—when a crossover or chiasmus occurred, with Germanic languages and culture soon substituting for Greek in the white pantheon. Of course, just as the classics was never associated with contemporary Greeks and Italians, Teutonic culture was not closely allied during the Great War with contemporary Germans. Teaching and scholarship in these humanistic fields strove to represent and perpetuate elite ideals of white civilisation, not give voice to ordinary white people.

Antipodal Hellenism

In 1886, Tommy Tucker, a mere twenty-seven years old, tall with the air of a dandy, strutted onto the campus of the University of Melbourne as the fourth professor of classics and comparative philology. His predecessors had come and gone quickly, leaving few marks.[12] Tucker, however, proved himself an outstanding scholar, a prolific translator and editor of Aeschylus and commentator on Aristotle, Plato and Sappho. A compelling orator, fearless in declaring his opinions, ridiculously vain, the Cambridge graduate soon became a commanding presence at the University and in the city's cultural life. He spoke frequently at the Beefsteak Club, the Melbourne Club, the Socialist Hall and the Medical Students' Society, and with Baldwin Spencer he briefly edited the aspirational journal the *Australasian Critic* (1890–91).[13] WA Osborne,[14] professor of physiology, popular essayist and fierce advocate of white Australia, was a close friend. Ernest Scott, professor of history at the University, regarded Tucker as 'the most brilliant exponent of classical literature who has taught in an Australian university'.[15] Tucker's stepdaughter, the novelist Joan Lindsay, remembered him in later years:

> Tall, slim, surprisingly upright even in old age and always something of a dandy, gloves and a light cane, a broad-brimmed fedora hat, patent leather shoes, large pearl tiepin and an unusually high white collar ... were typical accessories of his wardrobe. The lean craggy face with its gingery grey moustache and bright blue eyes was ... vivacious and ... full of charm.[16]

As Ken McKay, a subsequent classicist, put it: 'He became a cult figure; it was fashionable to invite him, to hear him, to read him and anything he recommended.'[17]

In his inaugural lecture, Tucker asserted in typical Arnoldian fashion that only the classics could sate the colony's 'craving for a higher cultivation'. Latin and Greek, he assured listeners, 'are studied as most potent aids to logical and liberal thought, literary appreciation, elevated states, humanity of sentiment—as containing in fact all the elements of culture'. Tucker believed that the study of Hellenic accomplishments 'tinges the mind with a rich and mellow intellectual colouring', presumably a rather specific shade of white.[18] The classics, he mused, 'may be expected to create a habit of logical methods, a habit of critical discrimination, a habit of taste and propriety, a many-sidedness and liberality of interest, and what De Quincey has called a strong bookmindedness'. It was a mental training or cultivation much needed in the crude colonial city. It was, above all, an apprenticeship to 'the art of citizenship' in a new settler society.[19]

In later lectures, Tucker urged his white audiences 'to go back as far into the past as we can, and to consider the mental condition of our ancestors', by whom he meant 'Indo-European' and 'Aryan' antecedents. For the classicist, 'antiquity' always referred to the ancient Mediterranean and environs, never to Aboriginal Australia.[20] Progressive and liberal, Tucker instructed his many auditors in the multiple lessons of classical scholarship. It had become clear to him and other University of Melbourne professors that Australians needed a strong federation to resist Asian incursions, just as Mediterranean civilisations once had warded off the barbarians that surrounded them. There was still more to learn from the classics. 'History,' Tucker announced, 'teaches the impossibility of realizing extreme socialistic plans. It teaches the futility of over-regulation.'[21] He was convinced that education in the classics might yet lead colonial Melbourne down the correct path to European civilisation.

In the early twentieth century, Tucker became a strident critic of degenerate vernacular patriotism. 'The prime value of literature,' he told avid listeners in 1902, 'lies precisely in that cosmopolitan, that universal, response,' not in the contemporary fashion for Australian 'colour'. 'Abandon all deliberate quest of local colour as an Australian mark,' he thundered. But Tucker did not recommend 'the humble and servile provincial'; he did not want 'exhibitions of obsequiousness to the social overlordship of Great Britain'.[22] While deploring 'the tendency to feed upon our own scanty larder of ideas and forms', Tucker still hoped for 'writing that is frankly true to its environment', derived from the best classical models. True 'moderns ... are disciples of the "Greek" school'—no matter the country in which they dwelt.[23] Only close attention to ancient Greeks and Romans could properly elevate the colonial mores of white civilisation. In Melbourne society,

> the standard of thinking, of conversation, of interest in things of the mind, is far lower than should be the case with a community which claims to be in the front rank of civilisation ... There has been no real place in it for the idealising and reverential side of humanity, for the training of the higher emotions and sensibilities.

But the classics could remedy this, providing 'an education of pure intellect, taste, and sentiment'. 'It is amazing,' Tucker concluded,

> how coldly educational proposals are received when they concern only the improvement of the culture side of humanity, and with what glib and mechanical acquiescence they are accepted when it is hinted that they may possibly have a remote bearing upon turnips or sheep-dip.[24]

Before World War I, Alexander Leeper,[25] the peevish warden of Trinity College, joined Tucker in advocating more classical education and discipline at the University. A bustling, interfering Oxford graduate, an anti-Catholic zealot devoted to the British Empire, Leeper translated Juvenal's satires and mounted Latin plays in the College, while not quite forgiving Tucker for taking the job he once had coveted. According to Scott, the warden 'never missed an occasion for striking a blow ... he was ever girt for the fray'.[26] And yet, Leeper's vision, too, could be liberal, especially before the war. In 1912 he told an assemblage of Victorian teachers:

> It is desirable to lead the young mind to realise, and perhaps especially in this White Australia of ours, how very much all human beings, whether white or black, or brown or yellow, whether ancient or modern or mediaeval, resemble each other. This would be likely to correct any tendency to a narrow national conceit, and to that spirit of jingoism which the exclusive study of British history might beget.[27]

Leeper believed the teaching of classics might help in broadening civic virtue and moral development. Addressing the new Classical Association of Victoria, the irascible warden of Trinity lamented that the University of Melbourne had been 'one of the last to hold the fort of Hellenism', but competition from applied sciences recently caused it to abandon the post. All the same, liberal education in a white settler society still required the training of character and elevation of the moral senses. 'A knowledge of classics remains the essential passport to all research in those important studies called humanistic,' he told the audience. He therefore condemned the massing of 'the armies of Philistia' at the University, those clamouring for abolition of the classics. Rather, they should learn from ancient Greece and Rome 'the dangers of unbridled mob rule, the futility of fixing prices by law ... the demoralising tendency of doles and bonuses, the results of creating a vast army of government servants, the folly of sacrificing the rural population to the city proletariat.'[28] He held such classical truths to be self-evident.

Like many other prewar classicists, Tucker and Leeper regarded Germany as the prime modern representative of ancient thought. For them, the classics passed through a Teutonic filter and came to possess a Teutonic allure—which may now seem culturally paradoxical but at the time annexed a racial logic. For Tucker, German ideals were cognate with classical thought, thus linking Englishmen hereditarily to the glories of Mediterranean antiquity. After all, he wrote in 1907, 'the basis of the English mind is chiefly Teutonic, in some measure Celtic'. Moreover, 'English literary history is the story of the Teutonic and Celtic tendencies "corrected and clarified", and the Teutonic and Celtic invention immensely assisted, by influences and ideas flowing in from other sources. There have been large ingraftings from other stocks, either partially kindred or altogether alien ...' Chief among the partially kindred stocks were ancient Greeks and Romans, the origins of 'our national genius'.[29] Before the war, Leeper was equally enthusiastic, praising Germany as the conduit for classical thought in the modern world. But this ratification soon became a matter of some embarrassment.[30]

The argument of Chamberlain's *Foundations of the Nineteenth Century* had greatly impressed both Tucker and Leeper. The British-born German philosopher, later a favourite of Adolf Hitler, extolled the Teutonic race as the bearer of European civilisation, handed down from Hellenes and Romans before it was deformed by 'senility' on Mediterranean shores or corrupted by Jews. Chamberlain even speculated on the possible influence of Teutonic blood in antiquity, ahead of its ebbing in the south through race mixing, when the remaining Greeks and Romans declined into 'half-bred souls of degenerate southern Europe'. Teutonic nations in northern Europe, the United States and Australia now possessed 'the wealth of form and the creative power of the Hellenic spirit'; they carried forward 'the immortal achievements of the Hellenes'. 'It was the Hellenes and the Romans,' Chamberlain wrote, 'who certainly gave the greatest impulse, if not to our civilisation, at least to our culture; but we have not thereby become either Hellenes or Romans.' Instead, Berlin had turned into the new and superior Athens, the bright beacon of white civilisation. Teutons now epitomised the classics. 'The German language has here,' he wrote, 'as it frequently has, infinite depth; it feeds us with good thoughts which are bountifully provided, like the mother's milk for the child.'[31] German was becoming the new Greek.

In 1916, in the dark days of World War I, Tucker lectured on German and British ideals, contrasting the German love of abstraction, system and order with British empiricism, individualism and respect for fair play, derived from cricket and the great public schools. He told his audience that the British are not only Teutonic but also boast Celtic blood. He tried out a novel term, 'Anglo-Celtic'. 'So far as Britain is concerned,' he said, 'the real facts are quite sufficient to justify patriotic love and pride, quite sufficient to induce a steady confidence in our own virility.'[32] Tucker's lecture echoed Chamberlain's essays on the same topic, published a year earlier—only emphasising British values above German qualities, which even so were not overtly disparaged.[33] Leeper showed no such equanimity; he had suddenly turned, becoming the scourge of contemporary Germany.[34] Yet he, too, could not shake off his respect for Teutonic *Kultur*, deciding in the middle of the war that the University of Melbourne needed a young Belgian, Augustin 'Kapo' Lodewyckx, to teach German. As Greek and Latin waned at Melbourne, the civilisational baton thus was passed to representatives of Teutonism and Nordicism—just so long as they were not actually German, not while the war endured.

Teutonic Attitudes

Lodewyckx became the leading standard-bearer of Teutonism in interwar Melbourne, a key figure on the front line of white nationalism. A graduate in Germanic languages and philology from the universities of Ghent and Leiden, he had taught French and German at Stellenbosch, an Afrikaans-medium, whites-only university college in the Western Cape province of South Africa.[35] From 1911 he worked in the colonial service in the Belgian Congo (now the Democratic Republic of the Congo), selecting European emigrants and caring for white settlers involved in copper mining at Elizabethville (Lubumbashi) in Katanga province. The young Belgian became obsessed with 'the future of the white race in this country', concerned with choosing those European stocks most resistant to the debilitating tropical climate. He believed Germans, who proved more hygienic and orderly, were better suited to such trying conditions than inherently dirty and irresponsible southern Europeans. 'Care of the body is indispensable in all places, but especially in hot countries,' he reported in September 1911.

Lodewyckx expected the 'white population' of Katanga would thrive so long as they kept up morale, worked hard, stayed sober, ate well and lived in proper lodgings. But it was clear to him that 'native children' were 'veritable reservoirs of malaria' parasites, a special threat to any foreigners. He therefore recommended strict segregation of the white population, who needed to maintain 'a certain distance from blacks', preferably 1000 metres.[36] He hoped to recruit and cultivate a class of white 'dominators and aristocrats', a select group superior to ordinary Europeans whom Africans would respect and admire—to whom they would submit.[37] Lodewyckx's colonial experiences thus prepared him to take the lead in advocacy for a truly white Australia; for another fifty years he would apply to Australian conditions his knowledge of white settlement in the Belgian Congo.

Worried about the effect of the tropical climate on his own young white family, Lodewyckx decided to migrate to the United States, but he got stranded in Melbourne en route when war broke out in 1914. Leeper saw Lodewyckx teaching unhappily at Melbourne Grammar School, from which he snatched the plucky Belgian, securing the émigré an appointment as lecturer in German at the University of Melbourne.[38] For the remainder of his career, Lodewyckx concentrated on expanding the teaching of Germanic languages and cultures, developing new programs in Dutch,

Old Norse, Swedish and Icelandic, thereby making available to students of the University the full Nordic suite. His contributions to scholarship, however, remained negligible. As a proud Aryan, reserved and austere, Lodewyckx soon became a leading commentator on the benefits of German migration, pleading frequently for a more 'Teutonic' Australia, a purely and securely white Australia, reiterating the lessons of Katanga. After reading Oswald Spengler's *Decline of the West* in the early 1920s, he felt the urgency of defending the local offshoot of organically European culture, or 'Western civilisation', from foreign races and white degenerates, thus preventing or retarding its retracing of the sad destiny of the Hellenic and Roman civilisations.[39] Lodewyckx interpreted Spengler as claiming that only purity of blood could forestall the *Untergang*, or civilisational downfall. He found the racial mystic immensely appealing: 'no doubt the most original thinker in Germany since the war.'[40] 'Spengler stirs our imagination as no other contemporary historian,' he wrote in 1935.[41]

In 1937 Lodewyckx warned readers of the *Australasian* that 'a decrease in vitality among British communities has set in'. The birth rate was dropping, immigration was slowing, urban degeneracy was spreading, and race mixing was on the rise. Such were 'the forerunners of national decay and disaster', putting 'White Australia in jeopardy'. The future of Western civilisation looked grim Down Under. The associate professor of German wanted 'to make Australia really white by effective occupation by white people'.[42] During the previous decade, he had illustrated the many virtues of 'Teutonic' migrants to Australia, focusing on their contributions to agriculture, especially in the wine and fruit industries. Pure Germans proved exemplary settlers, necessary 'to keep Australia permanently white'. Lodewyckx feared that 'the alternative to these European settlers is an influx of Asiatics at some further date'.[43]

After World War II Lodewyckx welcomed the arrival of greater numbers of northern European migrants to Australia, which allayed many of his prewar concerns. He continued to extol Teutonic migration into the 1950s, publishing his major book on the subject, *People for Australia*, which elicited praise from Arthur A Calwell, former immigration minister and future leader of the Australian Labor Party. According to Lodewyckx, only massive immigration from Europe—preferably from Britain, the Netherlands, Germany and Scandinavia—'can save this outpost of Western civilisation', preserving 'this continent for a pure, or at least a predominating, British-European white population'.[44] In 1957 he wrote to the editor of *Australian*

Quarterly pointing out that, in South America, those places with large German populations boasted high standards of living, distinct from 'the general backwardness of the people of mixed Latin and Indian descent'.[45]

Like many professors at the University of Melbourne before World War II, Lodewyckx was eager to express admiration for Nazi 'advances' in population management.[46] As the chief advocate for Teutonic civilisational distinction in Melbourne during the interwar years, he felt a special responsibility to explain, if not explicitly endorse, the merits of Hitler's philosophy. 'The Aryan alone, Hitler maintains, has creative genius,' Lodewyckx informed readers of the *Argus* in March 1933, adding: 'To this creative genius all civilisation and culture are due.' The professor of German rapidly morphed into a Nazi spokesman or propagandist. He went on to assert: 'The whole world's history is to be rewritten making the racial factor the dominating factor in all human events.' He observed:

> During the last century the Jews had deliberately attempted to adulterate German blood with their own, and to poison the German mind with Marxian teachings. The salvation of Germany will be found only in a purification of German blood and a revival of the German spirit and ideals.[47]

Lodewyckx therefore rejoiced in what he called 'the German national revolution of 1933', when 'powerful elemental forces were at work changing the soul of a nation by moral discipline'. As a result, Germany, 'a young nation with great reserves of energy, may yet be the educator and perhaps the saviour of the white world'—unless Herr Hitler's current successes were 'eaten away by the mass of small human vermin'.[48] Even in 1938, Lodewyckx was extravagantly praising German invasions of Austria and the Sudeten territories. He urged the *Volksdeutsche*—Germans who were subjects of other states, such as Australia—to contribute to 'spreading German culture and aiding Germany's economic expansion'.[49]

Bliss was it for the Lodewyckx family to be alive in that Teutonic dawn. Anna Hansen Lodewyckx, a casual lecturer in Scandinavian languages and Augustin's wife, along with their teenage daughter Hilma Dymphna, rushed over to Munich where they spent eight months revelling in the new Aryan regime. 'All are agreed,' Anna Lodewyckx told readers of the *Argus* in May 1933, 'that it is worthwhile, and perhaps advisable, to give Adolf Hitler a chance of proving his worth.' The new Führer's 'many excellent intentions' greatly impressed her. She had little sympathy with Jews who whined about boycotts and sackings, since they brought these problems on themselves.[50]

When Anna disembarked at Fremantle, Western Australia in February 1934, she told a local reporter: 'I came to realise the tremendous work Hitler is doing for Germany, and the brave fight he is putting up to restore the backbone and morale of the German people ... He is a great national hero.' In a talk to the International Club in Melbourne later that year, Anna also assured her audience that: 'Under Mussolini's guidance, Italy has developed self-respect outwardly and inwardly.'[51]

Dymphna, who later married a promising young historian, Manning Clark, pointed out that the Jewish girls at her school in Munich had been treated almost as normal people, causing her to doubt any allegations of discrimination.[52] Back in Melbourne, the rise of Nazism stoked Augustin's interest in Icelandic and Old Norse. After visiting Iceland in 1931 he had come to feel it was his true home, his *Urheimat*.

Afire during the interwar years with white racial enthusiasm, Lodewyckx established the University of Melbourne as a centre for teaching and research in Germanic languages. But in the 1940s he found himself on the margins of Nordicism at the University, when liberal intellectuals in the English Department poached Icelandic and Old Norse. In 1936 Keith Macartney had returned to the University of Melbourne from Cambridge, where he had studied Anglo-Saxon, Middle English and Old Norse. With his Bohemian attire, tendency to wave a silk handkerchief during lectures, and unabashed flamboyance, he definitely was not Lodewyckx's kind of Teuton. As he drifted into drama studies and theatrical directing, founding the Tin Alley Players, Macartney enlisted a substitute teacher, Hendrik Egbert 'Henk' Kylstra, a Friesian anti-Nazi activist who learned Germanic languages at Amsterdam during the war before going underground, later surfacing briefly in Iceland. He, too, was little inclined to pander to the old Fleming's racial obsessions. Kylstra initially taught Dutch, then took over Macartney's Old Norse reading circle, teaching the language and culture to AD 'Alec' Hope, Leonie Kramer and Ian Maxwell, among other future luminaries of the humanities in Australia.[53]

A spellbinding declaimer and reciter, Maxwell soon became the dominant figure in postwar studies of Icelandic and Old Norse at the University, displacing Lodewyckx's coterie of Teutonic amateurs. Having studied literature at Oxford, then taught at Copenhagen and Sydney, Maxwell returned to the University of Melbourne in 1945 as professor of English. His literary interests ranged widely, from the poetry of Milton, Yeats and Eliot to the Scottish border ballads, which he would sing to his classes with tears in his eyes. His scholarly output tended towards mere feuilletons for *Meanjin* and *Southerly*. A student, Anne Sedgley, remembered his 'noble forehead, craggy face, deep voiced, with a powerful upper body in a droopy tweed sports jacket'. It was 'the majesty of his head and the authority of his voice' that most moved her.[54] A keen axeman, Maxwell loved boxing, the bush, strong drink and horseriding—he rode his horse into the University well into the 1950s. With his wife Muriel, daughter of Richard JA Berry, the University's leading racial anatomist and eugenicist, Ian Maxwell led the local campaign against efforts to ban the Communist Party of Australia.

Setting aside studies of English literature, Maxwell's commitment to Iceland and the Norse sagas deepened over the years. He visited Scandinavia frequently and in 1966 he was appointed to the Icelandic Order of the Falcon, which also pleased him immensely. As AD Hope wrote:

> In fjords and fells his country of the heart,
> Its elder tongue his treasure. I see him there
> As his friends see him, smiling at the chart
> Of Iceland, a Viking looking from his eyes,
> The man of action in the scholar's chair,
> Like Gunnar gentle and like Ari wise.[55]

It was all very sweet, but everyone surely knew the legacy they were perpetuating. In any case, despite such heartfelt accolades, the appeal of Germanic languages slowly diminished at the University. After Maxwell's death, Old Norse occasionally was revived as Viking Studies, then abandoned altogether in 2007—a decline that partly corresponds with the rise of Indigenous studies. In any case, during the decades after World War II, during the long Cold War, the logos and ethos of white civilisation at the University of Melbourne were ever less likely to be set forth explicitly in a Germanic *Weltanshauung* or worldview, just as they had withdrawn long before from classical studies. In the postwar decades, the rationale for white settler distinction, such as it was, would much more likely be found in history or philosophy, not in esoteric European philology.

White Mythologies

These days we often see around us colleagues who like to affirm the innocence of the humanities, to proclaim their many critical virtues. Understandably, they want to believe the humanities have shed associations with racial discourses and white nationalist projects. Yet recent public debates in Australia over fate of the 'Western canon' and the establishment of the Ramsay Centre for Western Civilisation should give even the most complacent contemporary curator of the humanities pause for thought.[56] The altercation had been looming since the early 1990s, when Harvard political scientist Samuel P Huntington, inspired like Lodewyckx by Spengler's *Decline of the West*, tried to revitalise the decayed corpus of Western civilisation. 'The fault lines between civilizations,' Huntington wrote in *Foreign Affairs* in 1993, 'will be the battle lines of the future.'[57] In a follow-up book, the elderly white professor insisted that 'Western civilization is valuable not because it is universal but because it is unique'. He believed that the 'principal responsibility of Western leaders, consequently, is ... to preserve, protect, and renew the unique qualities of Western civilization'—qualities largely derived from ancient Greece and Rome, upgraded and circulated by Teutons, superior to any vernacular expressions.[58] Allegedly harried by the diversity and heterogeneity of cultural studies, the barbaric yawping of postcolonial and feminist criticism, and the insistent demands of Indigenous self-assertion, defenders of the old white citadels of Western civilisation were fighting back, preparing their backlash, arming for the counteroffensive, hoping to secure again the 'mythos' of their 'idiom'—that is, to re-establish the humanities as a space for conspicuous displays of white distinction and as a rationale and model for white imperial possession.[59] But was it not ever so?

In 1988 art historian Henri Zerner observed in passing that 'classicism means nothing more than an assertion of authority, of power under whatever form'.[60] Its continuing function as a white strategy of authority has caused dissension in North America—but less so in Australia—over the past few years. 'The discipline of "Classics" is a bustling performance site for racecraft,' writes Princeton classicist Dan-el Padilla Peralta. 'This antiquity has been and continues to be raced in scholarship and pedagogy.' He claims the classics continue to operate as a mode of white racial formation: 'the production of whiteness turns [out] ... to reside in the very marrows of classics'.[61] Although the whiteness of the discipline may generally be unmarked and obscured these days, white mythologies still infuse the study of Greco-Roman antiquity. According to Sasha-Mae Eccleston and Padilla, whiteness is actually 'baked into the habitus and hexis of classicists at every step in their professional formation'. These Afro-Caribbean Romanists, based in the United States, thus ask: 'How can we most effectively interrogate the field's Whiteness as a core property of its knowledge production? What would it mean, and what will it require of us, to historicize classical philology's co-emergence and co-dependency with race science?'[62] Such questions are rarely asked in Australia.

The study of Germanic languages has come under similar critical scrutiny along the North Atlantic littoral. Some fifty years ago, Léon Poliakov deplored the 'tyranny of linguistics', which had constructed Aryanism and Nordicism in the nineteenth century. German philological enthusiasm, culminating in Chamberlain's racial speculations, had paved the road to the Holocaust.[63] Scholars of Germanic languages were regularly scanning their texts for glimmers of the racial soul or national spirit, looking for traces of Nordic *Blut und Geist*, a golden age of *Germanentum* that might be reclaimed.[64] Since the 1990s, critics within the field of historical linguistics have examined the complicity of Anglo-Saxonism with claims of white racial superiority and justifications of imperial possession. Thus, Allan J Frantzen describes how studies of Anglo-Saxon language, literature and culture were deployed to inculcate a sense of racial prestige and to instil patriotic fervour in northern Europe, especially in England—and in its settler colonies. In the nineteenth century, during the high tide of imperialism, Anglo-Saxonism became the 'ideological partner' of Orientalism, a mode of Teutonic dynamism posed in rousing contrast to disparaging depictions of non-white others.[65] Philology thus lent lustre to a white mythos. Yet in Australia we have remained mostly immune to such concerns.

I have focused here on the collusion in the late-nineteenth and early-twentieth centuries of humanities at the University of Melbourne with imperial and national white racial projects. The philological enterprise, expressed principally through the classics and Germanic languages, served to symbolise and effect white intellectual and cultural distinction—to clear a white settler epistemic space—at the same time as it offered models of how to discipline and secure an imperial outpost. Respect for Aboriginal antiquity and acknowledgement of continuing Aboriginal cultural presence were unimaginable in this context. Aboriginal Australia was effaced, refused temporal depth, historical legitimacy, cultural significance and contemporary relevance.[66] The university humanities in this period functioned as another mode of Indigenous exclusion and denial, or 'epistemicide'—further adorning the whited sepulchre of settler colonialism.[67]

Notes

1 I am grateful to Ross Jones and Marcia Langton, who persuaded me to write this chapter. Hans Pols helped with Dutch and German translations and gave valuable comments on the Germanic languages section, while I am responsible for French translations. For their suggestions of how to improve and extend this essay, I thank Frank Bongiorno, Ann Curthoys, Cecily Hunter, Marilyn Lake, Andonis Piperoglou, Carolyn Rasmussen and Christine Winter—although I expect many of them may still be dissatisfied with its limitations. I should disclose that my father Hugh Anderson took classes with Ian Maxwell (who probably turned him onto folklore) and Manning Clark, socialised a bit with Keith Macartney, and repeatedly failed Dutch with Augustin Lodewyckx.

2 Matthew Arnold, *Culture and Anarchy: An Essay in Political and Social Criticism*, Smith, Elder and Co., London, 1889 [1869], p. 31. See also Lionel Gossman, 'Philhellenism and Antisemitism: Matthew Arnold and His German Models', *Comparative Literature*, vol. 46, 1994, pp. 1–39.

3 Warwick Anderson, *The Cultivation of Whiteness: Science, Health, and Racial Destiny in Australia*, Duke University Press, Durham, NC, 2006 [2002].

4 Perhaps the most egregious example can be found slightly later at the University of Sydney, where Enoch Powell was professor of classics (1937–40). His 1968 'rivers of blood' speech gained rhetorical force through allusion to Virgil's poetry. Although an avowed opponent of Nazism, Powell believed Germany was the white race's 'spiritual homeland'.

5 Mark Bradley (ed.), *Classics and Imperialism in the British Empire*, Oxford University Press, Oxford, 2010; Robert Dixon, *The Course of Empire: Neo-Classical Culture in New South Wales, 1788–1860*, Oxford University Press, Melbourne, 1986; Marguerite Johnson (ed.), *Antipodean Antiquities: Classical Reception Down Under*, Bloomsbury Academic, London, 2019.

6 Léon Poliakov, *The Aryan Myth: A History of Race and Nationalist Ideas in Europe*, trans. Edmund Howard, Sussex University Press, London, 1974; James Whitman, 'From Philology to Anthropology in Mid-Nineteenth Century Germany', in George W Stocking, Jr (ed.), *Functionalism Historicized: Essays on British Social Anthropology*, University of Wisconsin Press, Madison, 1984; Tsvetan Todorov, *On Human Diversity: Nationalism, Racism, and Exoticism in French Thought*, trans. Catherine Porter, Harvard University Press, Cambridge, 1993; Geoffrey Galt Harpham, 'Roots, Races and the Return to Philology', *Representations*, vol. 106, 2009, pp. 34–62. See also Christopher M Hutton, *Linguistics and the Third Reich: Mother-Tongue Fascism, Race, and the Science of Language*, Routledge, London, 1988.

7 An omission in Anderson, *The Cultivation of Whiteness*, and most, if not all, of the Australian scholarship on racial thought. But see Marilyn Lake, 'British World or New World? Anglo-Saxonism and Australian Engagement with America', *History Australia*, vol. 10, 2013, pp. 36–50.

8 KJ McKay, 'Thomas George Tucker (1859–1946)', *Australian Dictionary of Biography*, National Centre of Biography, Australian National University, Canberra, 2006, https://adb.anu.edu.au/biography/tucker-thomas-george-8869 (accessed 27 October 2023).

9 JS Martin, 'Augustin Lodewyckx (1876–1974)', *Australian Dictionary of Biography*, National Centre of Biography, Australian National University, Canberra,

2006, https://adb.anu.edu.au/biography/lodewyckx-augustin-7220 (accessed 27 October 2023).

10 Charles Henry Pearson, *National Life and Character: A Forecast*, Macmillan, London, 1893. See Marilyn Lake and Henry Reynolds, *Drawing the Global Colour Line: White Men's Countries and the International Challenge of Racial Equality*, Cambridge University Press, Cambridge, 2008.

11 Houston Stewart Chamberlain, *The Foundations of the Nineteenth Century*, trans. John Lees, 2 vols, F. Bruckmann, Munich, 1911); Madison Grant, *The Passing of the Great Race: Or, the Racial Basis of European History*, Charles Scribner's Sons, New York, 1936 [1916]; Lothrop Stoddard, *The Rising Tide of Color: The Threat against White World-Supremacy*, Charles Scribner's Sons, New York, 1920; Oswald Spengler, *The Decline of the West, Volume 1: Form and Actuality*, trans. Charles Francis Atkinson, George Allen & Unwin, London, 1918); Oswald Spengler, *The Decline of the West, Volume 2: Perspectives of World History*, trans. Charles Francis Atkinson, George Allen & Unwin, London, 1922.

12 For the very early history, see RJW Selleck, 'Classics in the Colonies: Conflict at the University of Melbourne in the 1850s', in Richard Aldrich (ed.), *In History and In Education: Essays Presented to Peter Gordon*, Routledge, London, 1996, pp. 74–97. An exception can perhaps be made for Martin Irving, the first professor, who proved a very good teacher.

13 Ken McKay, 'Thomas George Tucker', *Iris*, vol. 1, 1987, pp. 3–9.

14 Barry O Jones, 'William Alexander Osborne (1873–1967)', *Australian Dictionary of Biography*, National Centre of Biography, Australian National University, Canberra, 2006, https://adb.anu.edu.au/biography/osborne-william-alexander-7929 (accessed 26 October 2023).

15 Ernest Scott, *A History of the University of Melbourne*, Melbourne University Press, Carlton, 1936, p. 130.

16 Joan Lindsay, *Time without Clocks*, F.W. Cheshire, Melbourne, 1962. The obsession of her in-laws, the Lindsays, with the classics in their more salacious forms is well known.

17 Ken McKay, '150 Years of Classical Staff', *Iris*, vol. 25, 2012, p. 45. Tucker taught WK Hancock, and Alexander 'Sandy' Boyce Gibson.

18 Thomas George Tucker, *The Place of Classics in Education: An Inaugural Address*, Samuel Mullen, Melbourne, 1886, pp. 12, 7, 13.

19 Ibid., pp. 22–3, 30.

20 TG Tucker, 'Our Earliest Ancestors and Their Beliefs', in *Things Worth Thinking about: A Series of Lectures upon Literature and Culture*, George Robertson and Co., Melbourne, 1890, p. 9.

21 TG Tucker, 'The Teachings of History', in *Things Worth Thinking about*, p. 167. Presumably a reference to Pearson, *National Life and Character*.

22 TG Tucker, *The Cultivation of Literature in Australia*, Echo Publishing Co., Melbourne, 1902, pp. 13, 23, 29, 28.

23 Ibid., pp. 33, 29, 21.

24 Ibid., pp. 40, 41, 42. Tucker's lecture anticipates, with different emphasis, PR Stephensen, *The Foundations of Culture in Australia: An Essay Towards National Self Respect*, W.J. Miles, Gordon, NSW, 1936; and even AA Phillips, 'The Cultural Cringe', *Meanjin*, vol. 9, 1950, pp. 299–302.

25 JR Poynter, 'Alexander Leeper (1848–1934)', *Australian Dictionary of Biography*, National Centre of Biography, Australian National University, Canberra, 2006, https://adb.anu.edu.au/biography/leeper-alexander-7154 (accessed 26 October 2023).
26 Scott, *A History of the University of Melbourne*, p. 75.
27 Alexander Leeper, 'The Teaching of History in Victorian Schools', *STV: Proceedings of the Association of Secondary Teachers of Victoria*, 1912, pp. 13–14. See JR Poynter, *Doubts and Certainties: A Life of Alexander Leeper*, Melbourne University Press, Carlton, 1997.
28 Alexander Leeper, *A Plea for the Study of the Classics*, Melville and Mullen, Melbourne, 1913, pp. 4, 27, 38, 39.
29 TG Tucker, *The Foreign Debt of English Literature*, George Bell and Sons, London, 1907, p. 1. Tucker clearly knew philologist Ernest Renan's *The Poetry of the Celtic Races and Other Studies* (Kennikat Press, Port Washington, NY, 1970 [1896], http://www.bartleby.com/32/302.html (accessed 26 October 2023).
30 Leeper, *A Plea for the Study of the Classics*.
31 Chamberlain, *The Foundations of the Nineteenth Century*, p. 241. The University of Melbourne library holds the 1911 translation as well as a German version from 1912—the original German edition was published in 1899. A son-in-law of Richard Wagner, Chamberlain was convinced that Jesus Christ must have been Teutonic. He joined the Nazi Party before his death in 1927. See Michael D Biddiss, 'Houston Stewart Chamberlain, Prophet of Teutonism', *History Today*, vol. 19, 1969, pp. 10–17; Michael D Biddiss, 'History as Destiny: Gobineau, H. S. Chamberlain and Spengler', *Transactions of the Royal Historical Society*, pp. 73–100; and Geoffrey W Field, *Evangelist of Race: The Germanic Vision of Houston Stewart Chamberlain*, Columbia University Press, New York, 1981.
32 TG Tucker, 'British and German Ideals', in *University of Melbourne War Lectures*, George Robertson and Co., Melbourne, 1916, pp. 1–18.
33 Houston Stewart Chamberlain, *The Ravings of a Renegade: Being the War Essays of Houston Stewart Chamberlain*, trans. Charles H Clarke, Jarrold and Sons, London, 1915. Chamberlain praised the suppressed Teutonic (or Anglo-Saxon) elements of British culture, but he believed that decadence and incompetence had prevailed since the Norman Conquest. He extoled, in contrast, the 'mystical power' of the purer Germanic languages (p. 86).
34 RJW Selleck, '"The Trouble with My Looking Glass": A Study of the Attitude of Australians to Germans During the Great War', *Journal of Australian Studies*, vol. 4, 1980, pp. 2–25.
35 John Stanley Martin, *Augustin Lodewyckx (1876–1964): Teacher and Scholar*, working paper no. 7, History of the University Unit, University of Melbourne, Parkville, 2007. Leiden was then a centre for racialised philology.
36 Augustin Lodewyckx, Rapport à Monsieur le Ministre des colonies sur la situation des colons Belges au Katanga au mois Septembre 1911 (typescript), Box 1, Lodewyckx papers, University of Melbourne Archives. See also Augustin Lodewyckx, L'hygiène au Katanga, n.d. (typescript), 1975.0040, Box 1, Lodewyckx papers, University of Melbourne Archives; and 'Katanga, een land voor blanken', *De Vlaamische Gids*, vol. 7, no. 3, 1911, pp. 193–210.
37 Augustin Lodewyckx, Rapport à Monsieur le Ministre des colonies sur la situation des colons Belges au Katanga au mois Septembre 1912 (typescript),

Box 1, Lodewyckx papers, University of Melbourne Archives. See Bruce Fetter, *The Creation of Elizabethville, 1910–1940*, Hoover Institution Press, Stanford, 1976.

38 German (and French) had been taught at the University since 1881, but the previous lecturer, Walter von Dechend, was dismissed because he was a German national. Von Dechend's father was the first president of the Riechsbank and his daughter Adelgunde married the Welsh actor Hugh Griffiths. There is extensive correspondence with Leeper in the Lodewyckx papers.

39 Spengler, *The Decline of the West, Volume 1* and *The Decline of the West, Volume 2*. For Lodewyckx's notes on Spengler, see Box 2, Lodewyckx papers.

40 Augustin Lodewyckx, 'Spengler on World Conditions: The Spirit of Prussianism', *Argus*, 8 September 1934.

41 Augustin Lodewyckx, 'The Coloured Revolution: Oswald Spengler's Vision', *Argus*, 23 March 1935.

42 Augustin Lodewyckx, 'The World-Wide Menace to the Anglo-Saxon Race', *Australasian*, 10 July 1937, p. 5.

43 Augustin Lodewyckx, 'European Settlers for Australia: The Necessity for Population', *Australian National Review*, March 1937, pp. 12–19. See also Augustin Lodewyckx, *Das Deutschtum in Australien*, Deutscher Schutzbund Verlag, Berlin, 1926; Augustin Lodewyckx, *Die Deutschen in Australien*, Ausland und Heimat Verlagsaktiengesellschaft, Stuttgart, 1932; and Augustin Lodewyckx, 'Population Problems with Special Reference to Australia', *Australian Quarterly*, June 1936, pp. 23–35. In the 1920s, Lodewyckx had recruited Jens S Lyng as Harbison-Higginbotham scholar at the University of Melbourne, where the Danish-born leader of the Scandinavian Progress Association was able to write *Non-Britishers in Australia: Influence on Population and Progress* (Macmillan, Melbourne, 1927). See Anderson, *Cultivation of Whiteness*; and Andonis Piperoglou, 'Favoured "Nordics" and "Mediterranean Scum": Trans-Pacific Hierarchies of Desirability and Immigration Restriction', *History Australia*, vol. 17, 2020, pp. 510–24.

44 Augustin Lodewyckx, *People for Australia: A Study in Population Problems*, Cheshire, Melbourne, 1956, pp. 169, 204. He added: 'We do not want to be overwhelmed by Asiatics' (p. 214).

45 Augustin Lodewyckx, 'Letter to Editor', *Australian Quarterly*, 1 May 1957.

46 For example, Wilfred E Agar, *Eugenics and the Future of the Australian Population*, Eugenics Society of Victoria, Melbourne, 1939. For fascist intonations, see AR Chisholm, 'The Aftermath of European Romanticism', *Australian Quarterly*, vol. 8, 1936, pp. 54–62; and AR Chisholm, 'God, Man and the Reich', *Australian Quarterly*, vol. 11, 1939, pp. 45–51. An acolyte of the Sydney classicist and poet Christopher Brennan, Chisholm studied in Paris and Berlin before teaching French at the University of Melbourne from 1921, where he became a close friend and ally of Lodewyckx. Steeped in German philological scholarship, Chisholm also produced major studies of Mallarmé and Rimbaud. An admirer of the Graeco-Roman legacy, he was deeply attracted to the classicism of Charles Maurras, the leader of Action Française, and enamoured with the Nazi literary critic and anti-Semite Randolph Hughes—although the attitude of 'Chis' towards Hitler became increasingly ambivalent during the war: see David Bird, *Nazi Dreamtime: Australian Enthusiasts for Hitler's Germany*, Anthem Press, London, 2014.

47 Augustin Lodewyckx, 'Hitler's Philosophy: Importance of Pure Race', *Argus*, 4 March 1933, p. 4. See also his 'Hitler's Early Career: The Lessons of History', *Argus*, 4 February 1933, p. 4.

48 Lodewyckx, 'Spengler on World Conditions', p. 4.

49 Augustin Lodewyckx, 'The Population Policy of National Socialist Germany', *Economic Record*, December 1938, p. 237. Mark McKenna claims Lodewyckx was 'deeply committed to a European multicultural ideal in his new homeland ... For the Melbourne press, he wrote many articles on his travels in Europe, combining culture, history and politics in a personal and accessible style': from *An Eye for Eternity: The Life of Manning Clark*, Miegunyah Press, Carlton, 2011, p. 88. Lodewyckx's biographer, John Stanley Martin, states simply that his subject 'showed a deep and abiding interest in demography' (*Augustin Lodewyckx*, p. 19). Brian Matthews makes a critical appraisal in 'What Dymphna Knew: Manning Clark and Kristallnacht', *Australian Book Review*, May 2007, pp. 18–24. Of course, supporting the Third Reich in the 1930s does not necessarily imply support for Hitler in the 1940s. Nonetheless, the whole Lodewyckx family was under surveillance by the Australian security services during World War II.

50 Mrs A Lodewyckx, 'Life in Munich: A Visitor's Impressions', *Argus*, 13 May 1933. Augustin met Anna Hansen, a teacher of physical education of Scandinavian origins, in Durban, South Africa. Their son Karel Axel became chief librarian of the Baillieu Library, University of Melbourne. See KA Lodewycks, *The Funding of Wisdom: Revelations of a Library's Quarter Century*, Spectrum Publications, Melbourne, 1982; Martin, *Augustin Lodewyckx*; and McKenna, *An Eye for Eternity*. The University still offers the Anna Lodewyckx Scandinavian Scholarship annually.

51 Quoted in Anon., 'Germany and Italy Today', *Age*, 1 May 1934. Ivy Deakin Brookes introduced Anna Lodewyckx's lecture, held in the rooms of ECE Dyason's Bureau of International and Social Affairs, in Kurrajong House, Collins Street.

52 Anon., 'Life in Germany Today: Women Visitors' Impressions', *West Australian*, 28 February 1934.

53 Kylstra (originally Kijlstra) was enrolled in a PhD at Leeds when he came to Australia in 1948; after teaching at the University of Melbourne, he worked as a translator for the CSIRO before returning to the Netherlands in the early 1950s. A brief stint as a research fellow at Leeds followed, where he studied English dialects and folklore. In 1962 he followed mediaevalist Arthur C Cawley from Leeds to Brisbane to teach English at the University of Queensland, becoming an expert in Nordic drinking cultures. See Henk Kylstra, 'Via Iceland to Queensland', in Rob-Jan Mijnarends and Annelies Zeissink (eds), *Our Story: Experiences of the Dutch in Queensland*, Dutch-Australian Community Action Federation, Brisbane, 2001, p. 9. From 1951, Rein Meijhers took on responsibility for teaching Dutch at the University.

54 Anne Sedgley, 'In Fealty to a Professor', *Meanjin*, vol. 66, 2007, p. 226. Also see Hume Dow, 'Ian Ramsay Maxwell', in Gabriel Turville-Petre and John Stanley Martin (eds), *Iceland and the Mediaeval World: Studies in Honour of Ian Maxwell*, Wilke and Co., Melbourne, 1974, pp. 3–6.

55 AD Hope, 'I.R.M.: 1967', in Turville-Petre and Martin, *Iceland and the Mediaeval World*, p. 1.

56 Warwick Anderson, 'Whatever Happened to "Australian Civilisation"?' *ABC Religion and Ethics*, 24 September 2019, https://www.abc.net.au/religion/whatever-happened-to-australian-civilisation/11543430 (accessed 27 October 2023).

57 Samuel P Huntington, 'The Clash of Civilizations?', *Foreign Affairs*, vol. 72, 1993, p. 22. Also see Tony Abbott, *Battlelines*, Melbourne University Press, Carlton, 2009.

58 Samuel P Huntington, *The Clash of Civilizations and the Remaking of World Order*, Touchstone, New York, 1996, p. 311.

59 Jacques Derrida, 'White Mythology: Metaphor in the Text of Philosophy' [1971], in *Margins of Philosophy*, trans. Alan Bass, University of Chicago Press, Chicago, 1982, p. 213.

60 Henri Zerner, 'The Problem of Classicism: Ideology and Power', *Art Journal*, Spring 1988, p. 36.

61 Dan-el Padilla Peralta, 'Anti-Race: Antiracism, Whiteness and the Classical Imagination', in Denise Eileen McCoskey (ed.), *A Cultural History of Race, Volume 1: Antiquity*, Bloomsbury Academic, London, 2021, p. 158. See also Rachel Poser, 'He Wants to Save Classics from Whiteness. Can the Field Survive?', *New York Times Magazine*, 2 February 2021. Evidence for Padilla's allegations comes from classicists' earlier defensive criticisms of, and extreme discomfort with, the Afrocentric diffusionist account of Greco-Roman antiquity in Martin Bernal, *Black Athena: The Afro-Asiatic Roots of Classical Civilization*, Rutgers University Press, New Brunswick, NJ, 1987.

62 Sasha-Mae Eccleston and Dan-el Padilla Peralta, 'Racing the Classics: Ethos and Praxis', *American Journal of Philology*, vol. 143, 2022, pp. 207, 210.

63 Poliakov, *The Aryan Myth*.

64 For example, Bernard Mees, '*Germanische Sturmflut*: From Old Norse Twilight to Fascist New Dawn', *Studia Neophilologica*, vol. 78, 2006, pp. 184–98; and Jan Alexander van Nahl, 'Half-Remembering and Half-Forgetting? On Turning the Past of Old Norse Studies into a Future of Old Norse Studies', *Humanities*, vol. 9, no. 97, 2020, doi:10.3390/h9030097.

65 Allen J Frantzen, *Desire for Origins: New Language, Old English, and the Teaching of the Tradition*, Rutgers University Press, New Brunswick, NJ, 1990. See also Allen J Frantzen and John D Niles (eds), *Anglo-Saxonism and the Construction of Social Identity*, University Press of Florida, Gainesville, 1997; and Donna Beth Ellard, *Anglo-Saxon(ist) Pasts, Post-Saxon Futures*, Punctum Books, Goleta, CA, 2019. On 'Orientalism', see Edward W Said, *Orientalism*, Pantheon Books, New York, 1978.

66 Meanwhile, some equally disrespectful Aboriginal ornamentalism—what Tucker disdainfully would have called Australian 'colour'—was popular outside the University: see Tom Griffiths, *Hunters and Collectors: The Antiquarian Imagination in Australia*, Cambridge University Press, Melbourne, 1996.

67 See Dennis Masaka, 'The Prospects of Ending Epistemicide in Africa: Some Thoughts', *Journal of Black Studies*, vol. 49, 2018, pp. 284–301.

The History Discipline and Aboriginal Dispossession

DAVID GOODMAN[1]

TEACHERS AND RESEARCHERS in history at the University of Melbourne have engaged with issues of race, colonisation and dispossession since 1855. Acknowledgement of Aboriginal dispossession was stronger in the nineteenth century, then waned and almost disappeared in the middle third of the twentieth century, before reviving strongly in the 1990s and fading a little again. We should not take from this any great confidence in the stability of progress.

Students have often imbibed the terra nullius version of this history and assume earlier settler historians were either too ignorant or too self-interested to acknowledge the original ownership of country. The truth is different. The nineteenth-century historians at the University of Melbourne acknowledged and endorsed invasion and settler colonisation, propagating histories that justified colonisation and celebrated empire. They embraced theories of civilisation and its evolution that rendered an event such as the British settlement of Australia progressive, inevitable and laudable. The University history curriculum, dominated by the Roman and British empires, was full of invasions, conquests and colonisations. Until 1939 these historians did not use the phrase terra nullius, nor did they think that pre-1788 Australia was unoccupied or unowned. In fact, as Andrew Fitzmaurice pointed out in 2007, terra nullius as applied to Australia was a 1939 historiographical innovation of Melbourne's Ernest Scott (professor of history from 1913 to 1936), responding to some relatively arcane US legal scholarship about Antarctica.[2] Scott's point in saying that Australia was terra nullius in 1788 was a narrow one: that the British did not legitimately claim sovereignty over all of Australia when Cook placed some markers on the east coast; that the rest of the continent remained terra nullius until actually settled, and hence that the western part of the continent had remained claimable by other European powers until actual settler occupation, because 'effective occupation gave a valid title' but 'discovery did not'.[3]

Scott here reprised the theme of *occupation* that his predecessor WE Hearn (professor of history at the University from 1855 to 1873) had placed at the centre of *his* account of British colonisation. Conquest was the way empires grew and Hearn openly acknowledged it. He gave British colonisation a genealogy back to the Roman empire—'"*possessio*" and ... occupation thus ... became ... a form of property practically equivalent to "dominion" or ownership'.[4] Hearn was not original in saying this—Benton and Straumann write that, 'if there was a single identifiable Roman legal idea that was more prominent in empire than any other, it would seem to have been possession' rather than res or terra nullius.[5] But this is jumping ahead.

1855–1936: Aryans and Empires

It would have been astonishing had early University academics not been active participants in the nineteenth-century transnational intellectual world in which ideas about race were becoming more and more important and respectable. They carried out their teaching and research amidst a constant background hum of international debate and theoretical speculation about race and human history. Yet, while the nineteenth-century historians at the University of Melbourne never forgot that empire was based on conquest and occupation, they rarely explicitly connected their teaching and research on those issues to their own situation in a new, recently invaded British colony on unceded Aboriginal land. This is perhaps because they were also exposed to, and sometimes active in, colonial politics. Curthoys and Mitchell describe the 'settler demands that the British government recognise the right of free white men in the colonies to determine their own future and the freedom to continue the dispossession of Aboriginal people, by whatever means necessary'.[6] Those demands were all around the new professors as they read the Melbourne newspapers and followed or participated in vigorous colonial political debates about land as the key to settler freedom.

WE Hearn was the first professor of history, although he had much else on his plate. Appointed to teach modern history and literature, political economy and logic, his load reduced over time to history and political economy. Responsible for history from 1855 to 1876, he regularly taught subjects on the history of the British Empire and on ancient history (focused on Rome and its empire).[7] Like Edmund Burke, Hearn thought that English liberty rested not upon 'speculations about the rights of man or the brotherhood of nations' but on those English principles of government that were 'the maturest product of political wisdom that the world has yet seen'. From that premise flowed his enthusiasm for Britain's 'ancient empire on which literally the sun never sets': 'Our mission is to spread the British language, the British religion, the British laws, the British institutions, over this remote portion of the globe.'[8] In Hearn's time, the history of conquest was regularly placed before students and empire was presented to them as a very good thing.

Hearn was a racist in the sense that most Western social science intellectuals in the second half of the nineteenth century were—he shared ideas about stages and hierarchies of civilisation that placed white western Europeans at the top. Educated in the 1840s, he sat on the cusp of change, in some cases explicitly rejecting the more biological racial theorising developing during his lifetime and expressing scepticism about race as an explanatory category. Stocking observes that, even by the 1840s, 'ethnology had begun to provide a framework in which this linguistic identity could be expressed in explicitly "racial" terms', in the forms of 'Anglo Saxonism' and later 'Aryanism'.[9] Hearn's Aryanism was at the historical, ethnological and linguistic rather than racial end, but he subscribed to many of the tenets of social evolutionary thought that would in a later generation be taken in more explicitly racial directions. Hearn was however quite social evolutionist enough to think that traditional societies would inevitably be swept aside. Following Henry Maine, he described archaic Aryan society as governed by custom rather than contract.[10] He thought the replacement of such customary societies by more modern, individualist, competitive, nation-forming peoples was both inevitable and desirable. A free trader in politics, he knew that political economy 'requires competition' and 'free individual action' and that it was 'hopelessly embarrassed by custom'.[11]

When he became dean of law in 1873, Hearn's 1874 replacement teaching history was Charles Henry Pearson.[12] Only four years younger than Hearn, Pearson was both more liberal and more racial in his thinking. He shared Hearn's views about the all-round excellence of the Aryans but took the extra step of attributing that excellence to race and race purity, observing in 1893 that the 'most highly civilised races of the world' were 'those at present which are more or less purely Aryan'.[13] Pearson has received a great deal of notice from historians for the pessimistic predictions about the prospects for the white race in his influential 1893 book *National Life and Character: A Forecast.*[14] 'The day will come,' Pearson wrote, 'and perhaps is not far distant, when the European observer will look round to see the globe girdled with a continuous zone of the black and yellow races, no longer too weak for aggression or under tutelage.' He added: '[I]n some of us, the feeling of caste is so strong that we are not sorry to think we shall have passed away before that day arrives.'[15] Less noticed has been his brief account of the decline of Indigenous populations around the globe. In Australasia, the Americas and the Pacific, Pearson claimed, 'certain weak races ... seem to wither away at mere contact with the European.'[16] The Pearson of 1893 was a pessimistic Aryan supremacist who admitted to a 'feeling' of racial caste. It is difficult to know how much those ideas informed his history teaching in 1874, but in any case Pearson taught history at the University for only one year before moving to the better-paying job of headmaster of the Presbyterian Ladies College.

Hearn's student John Simeon Elkington followed as a lecturer and, from 1879 to 1913, professor of history. Selleck observes that Elkington 'did little to revise the curriculum he inherited from Hearn', although he 'made the history of the British Empire more extensive and more uncritical'.[17] Elkington shared Hearn and Pearson's evolutionary understanding of human society and history. He claimed in the *Melbourne Review* in 1878 that Hearn's work as a 'philosophic historian' showed 'there are processes of natural development which illustrate the universal presence of method'.[18] Elkington also had less hesitation than Hearn about turning Aryan linguistic and historical theories into imperial and racial chauvinism. The Aryan nations were, he wrote, 'by far the leading group of nations in the world at this day; its manners are purer, its laws nobler, its history is more splendid than that of any other group of mankind'.[19] He was definitely aware of contrary intellectual views—as, for example, when he chaired an 1896 meeting of the University of Melbourne Historical Society at which the professor of classics, Thomas George Tucker, argued that 'altogether too much' was made of race and that 'political, social and religious circumstances better explained the divergence of characteristics in different peoples'.[20] Elkington was against redistributive land reform and accused Pearson, who had more liberal views, of producing 'a dense tangle of error and confusion' on the issue. Citing evidence from Roman and English history, and apparently seeing no analogies with the taking of Indigenous land, Elkington contended that 'all limitations upon the right of acquisition, as well as all schemes whether of taxing or of confiscating the "unearned increment" of land, are improper'.[21]

Ernest Scott—journalist, *Hansard* reporter and author of originally researched histories—was appointed professor of history from 1913.[22] A more advanced liberal than his predecessors, as a young man he advocated women's suffrage, theosophy and Fabian socialism. Kathleen Fitzpatrick recalled: 'In university and public affairs he was always on the liberal side ... and in the 1930s he was an anti-Fascist.'[23] But like his predecessors, Scott centred his teaching on empires—including the British, Spanish, Portuguese, French, Dutch and German—and an interest in imperial rivalry underpinned his histories of Australian exploration.[24]

In *Terre Napoléon*, Scott describes French explorer Nicolas Baudin's private letter to NSW governor Philip King on 'the dispossessing of native peoples'. Baudin wrote that the Indigenous people 'were but children of nature, and just as little savages as are actually your Scotch Highlanders or our peasants of Brittany'. You have, Baudin continued, 'to reproach yourselves with an injustice in seizing their lands'. Scott, in his book, derided Baudin as a deluded noble savage theorist whose 'unsubstantiated sentiments' were 'imbibed uncritically from the rhetorical rhapsodists of Rousseau's school'. He concluded with a paean to empire and colonisation, arguing that the development of agriculture, trade and great cities in Australia 'are, in the large ledger of humanity, an abundant compensation for the disappearance of the few companies of naked savages whom, when civilisation once invaded their ancestral haunts, neither the agencies of government nor philanthropy could save from the processes of decay'.[25] Scott in 1910 was thus clear-eyed about the dispossession of Aboriginal people yet quite confident that it was necessary for the progress of civilisation.

Like Hearn, however, Scott did not go all the way with social evolutionism. He wrote critically of the way Herbert Spencer 'carried the doctrine of the Survival of the Fittest into the political and moral relations of life', describing the evolutionary process that Spencer endorsed with words such as 'hardness' and 'severity'. Here the Fabian in Scott came out, as he argued that men and women 'are not ... the helpless slaves of uncontrollable forces; and there is no sound reason for thinking that well-considered effort to mitigate the harshness of nature, to set limits to rapacity, selfishness and power ... will be mocked by inevitable failure'.[26] Did he think those mitigations should have been applied to the British colonisation of Australia? Maybe. Scott's 1916 *A Short History of Australia* went through eight editions (the last of them in 1950).[27] That book described Aboriginal people from a settler-coloniser perspective: 'Their natural inquisitiveness made them somewhat of a nuisance, perhaps, and they were thieves from the white man's point of view because, having no notion of property, to take what they wanted was natural to them.' He minimised Aboriginal resistance: 'The rapid and successful development of Australia has been facilitated by the fact that the aboriginals [sic] who occupied it before the advent of the white race were not an organized, warlike people.' None of that distinguished him from any number of other settler intellectuals of his day.

Less common by the twentieth century was Scott's frankness about frontier violence: 'The decay of the aboriginals [sic] in the settled districts proceeded very rapidly, from three main causes: from actual destruction by killing, from disease and drink introduced among them by the whites, and from the perishing due to the change of life necessitated by the limitation of their hunting-grounds.' He mentioned 'sheer brutality and treacherous murder by white settlers and their convict servants' and 'settlers who systematically gave natives arsenic in wheaten cakes, porridge, or other food'. The 'tragedy of the process' was, he wrote, 'very grim and hateful'.[28] Those unadorned words from a university professor had effects. Scott's three reasons for the decline of Aboriginal populations were quoted in Australian public life for many years.[29] Arnhem Land missionary James Watson, lecturing at the Leeton Methodist church in 1935, invoked them as authoritative, saying that Scott 'daren't tell anything that wasn't true because he was a responsible public servant'.[30] Scott used his professorial position to draw the attention of the next settler generations to the truth of what had happened in a widely read text.

For eight decades, then, the teaching of history at the University of Melbourne was in the hands of men who focused it on empire. They offered spirited justifications for colonisation, bringing the prestige of their scholarship to bear on students' and the public's view of that issue. For close to six of those decades, the teaching was conducted by men whose historical explanations for the excellence of Western civilisation centred on theories about the Aryan race. These nineteenth-century academics saw history as one of the social sciences. The fact that some of them also taught political economy and drew liberally on theories from anthropology, linguistics and sociology, increased their exposure to emerging racial theories. The trajectory is one of increasing racialisation of the history, mitigated in the case of Scott only by increasingly frank recognition of the destructive effects of past colonisation—a recognition made use of by others, but not by Scott himself, to argue for mitigation of the continuing effects of colonisation in Australia.

1937–1971: 'working out their nature from within'

RM (Max) Crawford arrived as the new professor of history in 1937, with plans for a major renovation of the teaching of this subject at the University. He explained that history was about 'societies working out their nature from within themselves and their setting'.[31] This signalled a scaling up of historical and philosophical ambition for the teaching program, not least in the way it rested upon a recentring of the curriculum on European civilisation more broadly rather than on Britain and its empire. For the honours school, Crawford chose

> certain nuclei which seem to me particularly valuable in their content—Graeco-Roman civilization; Europe + its influence in the time of the Renaissance + the Reformation (when by the way questions of present importance like liberty + authority, dogmatism and tolerance were very much in the air); the French Revolution + its importance; the Europe of the Industrial Revolution with its social problems movements, its imperialism + its international problems.[32]

Empire could thus now be named as 'imperialism', at least potentially opening up more critical perspectives. In Crawford's 1940 modern history lectures, he argued that 'there is a common quality to the civilization of Europe from the hey-day of Venice, Florence and Bruges to the early 20th century ... The unity of this course is that it is an analysis of the rise, hey-day and present transformation of European capitalist civilization'.[33] Under Crawford, the general history subjects continued to give great attention to empire—British, Spanish, Dutch, French and Portuguese.[34] But imperial expansion itself was no longer the central focus. Instead there was this dynamic and evolving history of 'European capitalist civilization'—intellectually Hegel and Marx were somewhere in the background, and RH Tawney and others would become prominent.

It is in this context that Crawford's characteristic depiction of Aboriginal society as static and dominated by tradition becomes more consequential. In a quite surprising way so many decades later, Crawford in some ways reprises Hearn's modernising criticisms of custom and tradition. In some undated (but post-1944) undergraduate Australian history lectures, Crawford characterised Aboriginal society like this: 'In their culture we saw a society which gave its members that support to personality which comes from security and attachment to the known ways, even though it was at a low material level.' He contrasted this to settler society, 'which in time offered to at least many of its members a very different support to personality, that which comes from hope and expanding opportunity'.[35] Similar contrasts were drawn in a chapter on 'The Aborigines' in Crawford's 1952 textbook *Australia*—'the authority of tradition' in Aboriginal society gave 'security', 'social cohesion' and 'support to personality', but Aboriginal people had 'no idea of self-assertion' and 'they did not set ideals of independence against their actual lot'. They had achieved 'by means of their traditions and rituals, a harmonious adjustment to a difficult natural environment, and a social cohesion and security to which civilized man in an unsettled age of the world's history may grow a little wistful in describing'.[36]

Where did these ideas come from? Crawford, like Hearn, rejected race as an explanatory schema. In a 1950 lecture he criticised 'commonly nonsensical race-theories' and said that race 'is clearly not something to be used as a ready explanation of behaviour'. Aboriginal people behaved 'with quite normal adaptability' to environment; environmental explanations were always to be preferred to racial ones.[37] Nevertheless, familiar binary oppositions ran through his work: the dynamism and individualism of Europe against the tradition and security of Aboriginal society, a contrast deeply rooted in Western historical traditions. John Mulvaney later recalled that Crawford 'appreciated that the Aborigines were factors in the Australian story and he attempted to understand their role by reading extensively of anthropological literature'. The 1952 textbook chapter was, at the time, Mulvaney added, 'a unique excursion for a general historian of Australia, and it added an important dimension to historical research'.[38] In fact the historical research came much later: under Crawford, Aboriginal society was to be studied archaeologically and anthropologically rather than historically.

Crawford may have rejected overt racial theorising, but this deeply racialised opposition between dynamic and static societies informed much of his historical thinking. The wars in Spain and China on his mind, Crawford arrived in 1937 wanting to teach the history of freedom in order to show that freedom was always under challenge—it was no longer possible, he explained, to 'regard the history of the Western world as one of steadily emergent liberty'. Freedom was

> an aspiration formulated by human consciousness. The very fact of the formulation is significant, since it shows discontent with any setting

> which condemns large numbers of people never to grow into persons; and since it shows a sense that since a man is a man, no state of society is satisfactory which imposes heavy restraints on his becoming what a man might be.[39]

Furstenberg has argued that the American revolutionaries associated freedom with autonomy and a duty to resist, and slavery with abjection and submission—an argument that resonates when we read Crawford claiming that Aboriginal people 'did not set ideals of independence against their actual lot'.[40]

These ideas about history and freedom were developed most fully in Crawford's 1939 Australian and New Zealand Association for the Advancement of Science conference address. Citing Karl Marx and José Ortega y Gasset, he advocated historical study of the 'drama of necessity and freedom', and characterised traditions and 'the heavy weight of habit' as limitations on freedom. The element of 'necessity' stemmed, he observed, from the way 'the past lives in the present' in the form of 'institutions and customary ways of doing things'. The 'imprint of the past' does not 'perfectly and rigidly control individual action' but it is to be understood as a constraint on individual freedom.[41] Aboriginal society, dominated as it was in Crawford's account by tradition, was in this way of thinking less than free and more fundamentally not a part of the history of struggles for freedom that Crawford wanted to set before students. Thus Crawford, his thought shaped and limited by these binary contrasts, failed to identify the invasion and colonisation in Australia as one of the great teachable conflicts in which human freedom was at stake. Behind his 'drama of necessity and freedom', with its evocations of the early Marx, stands Hegel and his idea that only European states had an evolving and progressive history.[42] When Crawford wrote that 'History is the study of human societies agitated from within the universe of themselves and their setting to work out their nature, a nature never defined until achieved', he was implicitly—as the new curriculum at the University confirmed—defining a European subject for history.[43] Crawford cancelled Scott's Australian history subject, observing that 'the comparative paucity of first class writing on this subject makes it, at present, of less general educational value than other branches of history'.[44] That decision, as John Poynter observed, 'made the Department's work even more Eurocentric'.[45]

Other 1930s Australians did see the colonisation of Australia in the context of a longer global history of struggles for freedom, and some of them referenced international debate about dictatorship, democracy and freedom in their discussions of the situation confronting Indigenous Australians. Anthropologist Olive Pink wrote in 1938 that

> the immediate issue is whether the aborigines [sic] are to have any rights of their own or whether their civilisation and religion are to be dictated to them ... At present, Australia in common with most other countries, is feeling deeply about the plight of the German Jews. Yet ... these aborigines [sic] of ours are ... facing religious domination and social persecution.[46]

The Australian Aborigines' League and Aborigines Progressive Association's 26 January 1938 Day of Mourning declaration asked for 'a new policy which will raise our people TO FULL CITIZEN STATUS and EQUALITY WITHIN THE COMMUNITY'.[47] Aboriginal people in 1938 were explicitly calling for 'the repeal of all existing legislation which restricts the freedom of Aborigines'.[48] That connection of living Aboriginal resistance in Australia to the longer history of struggles for freedom was not yet happening in the history program at the University of Melbourne.

Crawford decided after the war to reinstate an Australian history subject, at first teaching it himself and then appointing Manning Clark, who taught Australian history at the University from 1946 to 1949.[49] Mark McKenna, from a reading of Clark's Melbourne lecture notes, concluded that in the 1940s Clark taught Australian history from the settler point of view, depicting Aboriginal people as among the 'challenges' facing settlers.[50] Clark's 1955 *Select Documents in Australian History 1851–1900* contained only one editorial comment about Aboriginal people, noting 'the absence of a serious threat from the aborigines [sic]'.[51] That was consequential at the University in particular where, as Graeme Davison recalls, Clark's *Select Documents* was a prescribed text and 'virtually every tutorial was framed by' it, and Clark's 'sometimes enigmatic editorial comments were often the starting point for tutorial discussion'.[52] Within a few years Clark was identifying early settler Australia as an Enlightenment project, arguing that the early governors 'thought that they were advancing towards a great era in the history of human affairs', helping to 'gradually spread enlightened European civilization over the whole world'.[53] Clark's predecessors had unselfconsciously shared that optimism about the spread of British civilisation. Clark was able to identify and describe it but nevertheless opened the 1962 first volume of *A History of Australia* with the bald declaration: 'Civilization did not begin in Australia until the last quarter of the eighteenth century.'[54] Like Crawford, then, Clark did not at the time he was teaching at the University see the dispossession of Aboriginal people as worth a central place in the history curriculum.

Crawford also played a major role in fostering research in Australian history—he had indeed explained to vice-chancellor Raymond Priestley back in May 1937 that he saw Australian history as 'a matter for the schools on the one hand, for research on the other'.[55] Crawford's research plans for Australian history encompassed archaeological investigation of the distant Aboriginal past and anthropological investigation of living Aboriginal societies in the north and west of the continent. Historical research on Aboriginal people in Victoria was to be largely confined to study of the early phase of the European invasion, focused on the protectorate system and the interactions of squatters with the Aboriginal people whose land they were taking. Two of the key figures in this Crawford-era research program were ethnologist Leonhard Adam and archaeologist John Mulvaney.

On release from Tatura internment camp in 1943, Adam was awarded a research grant by the University of Melbourne to study 'The Usages of Stone among Australian Aborigines' and attached to the History Department under the supervision of Crawford.[56] Adam purchased stone tool artefacts from non-Aboriginal collectors and sent Aboriginal cultural items to museums abroad on exchange arrangements that required government permission.[57] Ethnological science as Adam understood it did not require consulting local Aboriginal people, and yet, through his wife and her family, Adam was aware of contemporaries at the University who did work closely with Aboriginal people. Crawford supported Adam in part because he hoped to establish a program in anthropology. Adam was appointed lecturer in history from 1947, tasked with giving lectures on ethnology and compiling an ethnological collection.[58] Adam retired from teaching in 1957 but remained curator of the ethnographic collection. Greg Dening recalled him as 'a lonely figure, humiliated by the university's and the community's lack of respect for his learning and his world status in scholarship'.[59]

The History Department in these years undertook field trips and archaeological expeditions. In 1946 Crawford sponsored, and Leonhard Adam and Dermot Casey co-directed, a student archaeological dig at Flinders Island, investigating evidence of Aboriginal occupation.[60] The *Age* reported that the students had collected stone implements and 'established beyond doubt that aborigines [sic] lived on the island long before' the Tasmanian Aboriginal people were removed there by George Augustus Robinson.[61] There was an expedition to Keilor and another to Phillip Island in 1947.[62] Crawford reported to the registrar at the end of 1947 that he and Jack L O'Brien, a senior lecturer in ancient history, 'wish to continue the History Department's project of examining aboriginal [sic] camping sites and of collecting aboriginal [sic] artefacts for the ethnographical museum attached to this Department'.[63] Adam managed eight field trips between 1943 and 1957.[64]

John Mulvaney studied at the University of Melbourne after serving in World War II; by 1949 he was a tutor in history. When he returned in 1953 from studying archaeology at Cambridge, Crawford offered him a lectureship, to teach ancient history and—from 1957 to 1964—an influential honours subject in Pacific prehistory.[65] Mulvaney was teaching history at the University in 1956 when he made his first major dig at Fromm's Landing (Tungawa) on the Murray River, supported by a £200 research grant from Crawford.[66] The project eventually demonstrated almost 5000 years of occupation of the site. In 1961 Crawford gave Mulvaney £125 from research funds for carbon dating.[67] Mulvaney was also receiving international funding (from the Wenner-Gren Foundation and the Nuffield Foundation). The carbon-dating work led to a dramatic pushing back of the duration of Aboriginal occupation of Australia but was conducted without consultation with living Aboriginal people.[68] Mulvaney reported he had knowingly first met an Aboriginal person only in 1960.[69] Billy Griffiths observes of that first Fromm's Landing dig: 'In 1956 there was no legislation to define the legal status and ownership of artefacts once excavated ... It never occurred to him to ask the Traditional Owners of the land, the Ngarrindjeri people'.[70]

Research work on post-contact Aboriginal history was by contrast very limited in the Crawford era. Edmund Foxcroft wrote a 1928 Master of Arts thesis under Crawford's supervision, and subsequently a 1941 book, *Australian Native Policy: Its History, Especially in Victoria*. Foxcroft called for a New Deal for Aboriginal people, but also advocated some harshly coercive assimilationist measures: 'Tribal natives must be isolated in inviolable reserves until they can all be surveyed and until agreement can be reached on the kind of policy to be followed towards them as a result of successful experiments among the half caste and detribalised'.[71] He also claimed that 'to the stories of wholesale massacres and poisoned food, little credence can be attached as far as Victoria was concerned'.[72] Foxcroft's book was assigned reading for University history students for many years.

Crawford led a field trip to research an aspect of contact history in Western Australia, a failed 1864 attempt by a Victorian group, the Camden

Harbour Pastoral Association, to settle that north-western WA area as a sheep-farming district. The 100-person expedition took 5000 sheep, all of which died, as did some of the would-be settlers. Crawford, wanting to discover why the sheep had died and if there were any 'surviving aboriginal [sic] traditions of the settlement', decided that 'the best way of finding that out was to go there and ask them'.[73] In August 1946 he set off for Camden Sound with two Worora guides from the Kunmunya Mission—an engagement with local Aboriginal people about early contact history notably different from his mode of proceeding in Victoria. The Aboriginal guides deeply impressed Crawford: 'Albert's knowledge of plant, bird or animal life is detailed + never failing'.[74] Crawford recorded lists of words, witnessed a welcome corroboree and attempted to revise local settler histories. The *West Australian* newspaper in 1947 told the 1864 Camden Harbour story, observing that 'the local blacks proved to be a nuisance at first and later developed into a menace'.[75] Crawford sought other interpretations. He told the press that his guides had described an earlier massacre of Aboriginal people as a 'reprisal' after a boat was taken.[76] What he wrote in his diary was far more specific:

> Natives had taken dinghy. Settlers set trap—long rope tied to rubbish to make noise. Chased natives round island. Took refuge in cave. Settlers' dog led them there they shot all those near our cave. One man shot thro leg climbed hill + hid in hole in rocks. Another man shot on rocks at point [blank?] while trying to escape. Natives retaliated—2 settlers swimming. Spears thrown—? one in eye.[77]

At the mission Crawford was shown JRB Love's 1932 grammar of the Worora language and described it as 'very complex' and 'v. expressive + given to variations of form to allow for rhythm and euphony'.[78] He collected Aboriginal implements as well as local plants. Mulvaney remembered that the expedition 'enthused Crawford about Aboriginal society and he came back very full of Aboriginal concerns'.[79] Margaret Kiddle, a 1938 Melbourne honours history graduate, went to Perth in 1949 to do some more research for Crawford on the—never to be completed—project.[80]

Kiddle herself made an influential contribution to contact history. Her posthumous *Men of Yesterday* depicted the Aboriginal people of Victoria as 'men from Asia' who were 'invaders' of Australia.[81] She discussed the toll of rape and violence on Aboriginal women, blaming ex-convict shepherds: 'the first squatters had intended to deal with the aboriginal [sic] people kindly but they found it impossible to control their men'.[82] Kiddle acknowledged settler killing of Aboriginal people, writing that Niel Black bought his station because 'so many of the natives had been killed he expected to have little further trouble with them'.[83] She offered this blunt judgement: 'When necessary, and when the deed was unlikely to be discovered, they murdered those who still maintained some tribal unity.'[84] Patricia Grimshaw concluded that while Kiddle 'acknowledged the appalling dispossession of indigenous peoples', she also reproduced 'a familiar colonial narrative' about Aborigines as a Stone Age people that 'indirectly, even if unconsciously, provided justification for Aboriginal oppression and white supremacy'.[85]

Crawford's History Department thus sponsored significant research on Aboriginal society and invasion history that was little reflected in its teaching program. As we have seen, there were unrealised plans for teaching in anthropology/ethnology and in archaeology. A clear statement of Crawford's teaching plans in what he called 'comparative archaeology' is in a handwritten letter to the vice-chancellor, undated but probably from 1944:

> in time we should establish a course in Comparative Archaeology specifically applying the techniques worked out in Eur. to the problems of the pre-hist + early history of the area ranging from the S.E. corner of the Asiatic mainland to Australia. (This would go hand in hand with research projects mainly into the early civilizations of Java, Sumatra + Bali, + into the history of the Australian aborigines [sic].) Out of Comparative Archaeol there might some day grow a course expounding the early history of the Western Pacific; but for the moment I think 'compar. archaeol.' is a sufficient arm in this field.

Crawford also advocated the expansion of teaching of a broadly conceived Pacific history:

> It is here that our expansion should be greatest. It begins in 1945 with the teaching of Australasian History both for the ordinary degree and for the Honour School. The next step will be the introduction of a general course in Oriental History ... The third step on the Pacific side should be a course on American History, + a fourth should be a course in Pacific History (creating of native cultures, white influence, relations, native policies + strategical situation).[86]

That was a remarkably ambitious Pacific-centric vision for a history professor anywhere in 1944. It promised attention to Indigenous history, but in an Asia-Pacific and 'comparative archaeology' frame that placed it far in the past. In 1945, fourth-year honours and second-year pass students were offered essay topics that included early colonisation in northern Australia, the Treaty of Waitangi and the Māori wars, and 'blackbirding' in the Pacific, but these topics were not at the centre of the curriculum.[87]

Some of Crawford's Pacific research vision was reflected in the intermediate-level school textbook *Ourselves and the Pacific*.[88] The book went through five editions between 1941 and 1967. By the 1960s, most Victorian Year 10 students were taking the subject for which this book was the text.[89] The book depicted Australia as part of the Pacific world, alongside Mexico, Peru, China and Japan. It thus set the British invasion of Australia alongside the Portuguese, Spanish, British and Dutch invasions of the Americas. Unsurprisingly, the 1941 first edition was written from the colonisers' point of view, emphasising the 'free' land available on the Pacific frontiers: in early nineteenth-century Australia 'there was plenty of land', we are told, but not enough labourers; later 'people pushed out into the unoccupied land with their sheep'; and a chapter on nineteenth-century North America was titled 'The Empty Lands'.[90] Crawford does not use the term, but this is beginning to sound more like a terra nullius history. The 1967 fifth edition did contain a section on 'The Aborigines' that talked frankly about settlers 'ready even to shoot or poison' Aboriginal people 'if they could get away with it, or to join them in raids intended to massacre Aboriginal people or drive them far away'.[91]

In the teaching of Australian history at the University of Melbourne, both Aboriginal history and the history of colonisation were receding from view over the later Crawford years, as a set of 'radical nationalist' questions about distinctive settler-Australia developments loomed larger. Crawford encouraged Norman Harper's interest in comparative frontier history, which tended to posit the settlement of hitherto empty lands as the core attribute of frontier societies. We can see this in Crawford's 1960 *An Australian Perspective*—lectures given in 1958 at the University of Wisconsin, where Frederick Jackson Turner had pioneered the frontier thesis in the 1890s. In the published version of the lectures, the only mention of Aboriginal people was the opening observation: 'nor were our first settlers opposed by warlike tribes of indigenous inhabitants'. Attention then turned to the nationalist themes 'Birth of a Culture' and Australia's 'Coming of Age'.[92] WEH Stanner, in his influential 1968 Boyer lectures, named a 'great silence' about Aboriginal dispossession in Australian historiography.[93] Ann Curthoys observed that nineteenth-century historians by contrast did more often acknowledge frontier conflict—the 'silence' from white historians came in the mid-twentieth century. The University of Melbourne story bears out her chronology and her observation that what ended the silence eventually was 'at least as much driven by Aboriginal people, voices, and politics' as by settler historical revision.[94]

John La Nauze, professor of economic history at the University from 1949, and appointed to a second chair of history in 1956, emerges as the most articulate Melbourne silencer. In lectures, probably from the later 1950s, he made the case for leaving Aboriginal history out of Australian history: 'European occupation ... inevitably overwhelmed the original simple cultures of the aboriginal [sic] inhabitants, and so from that time its history is necessarily that of a European society.' Australia was unique in that 'its history begins with an empty continent. By contrast, in any general account of the first two hundred and fifty years of the European settlement of North America it is impossible to ignore the American Indian.' Thus did La Nauze rule Aboriginal society out of history: 'The Australian aborigine [sic] is of great interest to the anthropologist and, as a living paleolithic man, to the pre-historian: to the history of European settlement, of economic development in Australia, he contributes nothing; except, in these latter days, a pang of conscience.' More chillingly, La Nauze wrote:

> Unlike the West or South American Indians, unlike the Africans, the Australian aborigines [sic] could not even be exploited and enslaved. They could only be exterminated or driven further into the interior, or given, in charity, rations, cotton dresses, and religion. From them the Europeans could take nothing but the land they lived in; and the only relevant earlier history is that reconstructed by the geologist, the soil-chemist and their fellows.[95]

This was an active and self-aware calling for silence about Australia's Indigenous history and violent past. When La Nauze gave the presidential address to the Australian Association for the Advancement of Science in 1959, he amplified these remarks: Australian history was 'peculiar' in that there had been 'no real experience of formidable opposition by the native inhabitants. Unlike the Maori, the American Indian or the South African Bantu, the Australian aboriginal [sic] is noticed in our history only in a melancholy anthropological footnote'. Lauding the rapid professionalisation of Australian historical research, La Nauze nominated as promising topics the history of Australian states and cities and Australia as a British province.[96] La Nauze must, however, have had some insights into anthropological research via his father-in-law JB Cleland, who conducted anthropological research in South Australia and supported the research of Olive Pink.[97]

In these postwar years, Aboriginal history was present at undergraduate level mainly in essay topics. In Pass Australian History in 1953, Geoffrey Serle set a topic on 'relations between Squatters and Aborigines in the Port Phillip district'. Pass Australian History in 1954 had one question asking students to 'compare the initial views taken by Australian settlers of the aborigines [sic] with the ways they behaved towards them', focusing on New South Wales before 1810 and the settlement of the Port Phillip area in 1835–50.[98] Students were directed to primary sources from and about the squatters, to be read in conjunction with Foxcroft's book. In Australian history annual examinations in most years from the mid-1950s to the early 1970s, there were no Indigenous-related questions. The views and behaviours of settlers towards Aboriginal people were thus cast as specialist topics fit for an essay but not figuring in the broader subject overview of the examination.

This section has shown how the surprising research engagement with Aboriginal society in the Crawford years stood in contrast to the relatively minimal teaching attention to it, but also a general trajectory in the second half of the period towards neglect and silence as Australian history professionalised, nationalised and moved away from its imperial history roots.

1971–2022: Slowly Acknowledging a Living Aboriginal History

This began to change in the early 1970s. *Farrago* evidences student discussion of racism in the period, although mostly in relation to apartheid, the war in Vietnam and the White Australia policy. The history postgraduate seminar focused on racism in 1971, hearing papers from Arthur Huck on political science and racism, Noel McLachlan and Ian Turner on history and racism, and Geoff Sharp on sociology and racism. Australian history in 1970 was mainly lectured by Noel McLachlan, but in week 9 Graeme Davison gave a lecture on 'The Aborigines'. He remembers a non-Indigenous student questioning his treatment of the nineteenth-century humanitarians—she was an activist and member of Students for a Democratic Society, and that organisation had since 1968 been active on land rights issues, including in relation to the Gurindji walk-off from the Vestey Brothers–owned Wave Hill cattle station.[99] Scripts of some ABC Radio talks for school history students that Davison also gave in 1970 show him giving significant attention to the Christian humanitarians, but he was also fundamentally critical of them for ignoring the 'material basis' of the conflict over land.[100] There was an Australian history essay topic that year on why the 1838 Aboriginal protectorates failed; Foxcroft's book had been joined on the reading list by Mulvaney's survey articles and Max's son Ian Crawford's MA thesis on William Thomas and the Port Phillip protectorate.[101]

Geoffrey Blainey moved from economic history to history in 1977, two years after the publication of his *Triumph of the Nomads: A History of Ancient Australia*, a popular account that began with the pushing back of the date of Aboriginal occupation to at least 30 000 years ago. Blainey depicted Aboriginal people as prosperous nomads who had abundant food without gardening or farming.[102] He was one of five teachers regularly listed for the second-year Australian history subject in the 1980s. In 1980 the subject promised to give attention to 'the immigrant experience and contribution, women's history, the nature of racism, urban history, class conflict and the rise of labour, Aboriginal–European conflict in the early colonial period and in modern times, Australia between the wars'. The subject description for 1982 went further: 'themes include Aboriginal society and its characteristics; the coming of the Europeans and their conflict with the Aborigines'. From 1985 to 1989 the description promised study of 'the impact of the European invasion'. By the end of the 1980s, however, the University of Melbourne still lacked a dedicated subject in Aboriginal history and appointment of someone with expertise in the field; the other history programs in metropolitan Melbourne had by then moved further.[103]

Greg Dening, a University history graduate whose study of Pacific prehistory had led him to a PhD in anthropology at Harvard, was appointed professor in history in 1971. In 1990 he convened a new subject, 'Aboriginal and Koori Histories':

> We simply indicate by the double title that we believe there are at least two sorts of history about an Aboriginal past. One belongs to the Aboriginal people themselves ... We call that Koori History. The other belongs to both Aborigines and whites, bound together by a past that has determined Aboriginal and white relationships. We call that bound-together history, Aboriginal History.[104]

The teaching team was: Andrew Anastasios, Lisa Bellear (Minjungbul, Goempil, Noonuccal and South Sea islander), Greg Dening, Pat Grimshaw,

Stuart Macintyre, Antonio Sagona and Patrick Wolfe.[105] The subject guide said: 'We believe that in a subject as sensitive and as important as this, book-learning is only one part of the experience ... We will make sure that at key moments in the subject students will hear an Aboriginal point of view directly.'[106] From 1991 to 1993 this subject was coordinated by Patricia Grimshaw and Stuart Macintyre.

Patrick Wolfe studied social anthropology at the London School of Economics and completed a PhD at the University of Melbourne in 1994. Articles published through the 1990s articulated his startlingly original perspective on settler-colonial history: the settler desire to 'replace' Indigenous society, the 'logic of elimination' underpinning it, 'repressive authenticity', the 'criminal legacy of genocidal theft' upon which the settler-colonial state was established, and invasion as a structure not an event.[107] These core ideas, developed in the 1990s at the University, became foundational to the development internationally of the highly influential settler-colonial approach to history. In 1994 Patrick coordinated Aboriginal and Koori History: Colonial and Postcolonial Contact in Australia; from 1995 to 1999 the subject was called 'Koori and Non-Koori Histories: Colonial and Postcolonial Interchanges in Australia' and covered 'relations and encounters between white settlers and Aboriginal peoples between 1788 and 1995'.

Strikingly, 1990s attention to Aboriginal history at the University was not limited to specialised subjects. In 1994 Australian history promised 'A study of Australian colonial society, and of Aboriginal/Koori–European relations, 1788–1901'; 'Australians at War 1788–1918' included 'analysis of the war experiences of Australians, beginning with their first clashes with indigenous peoples up to the end of the Great War'. In 1995 'The Oral Tradition in Australia' taught this topic 'with reference to both the Aboriginal and Western traditions', and 'A Jewel in the Crown? Issues in the History of Colonial Victoria' promised to give attention to 'Koori policies'. In 1996 and 1997 Pat Grimshaw and David Philips taught 'Colonisers and Colonised: South Africa, Canada and Australia in an Imperial Age', which examined 'the interaction of settlers and indigenous peoples in South Africa, Canada, Australia and New Zealand', and 'the expropriation of the indigenous peoples' land and livelihoods by white settlers'. From 2001 to 2003 David Philips and Patricia Grimshaw taught 'Empire, Race and Human Rights: 1900–2000' about 'the relations between white settlers and Indigenous peoples, during the 20th century', again in Australia, New Zealand, South Africa and Canada. In 1992, Chips Sowerwine and Dipesh Chakrabarty offered 'Representations of Race: Europeans, Settlers and Indigenous Peoples, 1750–2000'; Klaus Neumann taught this subject in 1994.

The 1990s was the high point so far of the attention paid to Indigenous history at the University of Melbourne.[108] In the background were the *Mabo* and *Wik* decisions and hopes for real change. A talented generation of Melbourne PhD students—including Patrick Wolfe, Lynette Russell, Tracey Banivanua Mar, Penny Edmonds, Kat Ellinghaus, Marg Stephens and Hannah Robert—was drawn to topics in the area. There was a broader vogue for 'postcolonial' studies. As Tony Birch recalled, 'from the mid-1990s ... "Aboriginal", "colonial" and Australia's "post-colonial" histories became the hot topic of history debates, public seminars and academic conferences.'[109] Activism, including demands for the teaching of Aboriginal (or Koori) history by Aboriginal people, was also a crucial factor. In 1993 the *Age* reported Gary Foley speaking to students on campus: 'What would your parents know about the truth of Australian history? What would the history department of this university know about Australian history ... Foley says he should be teaching them history.'[110] Subsequently Foley completed an honours degree in history (2002) and a 2012 PhD ('An Autobiographical Narrative of the Black Power Movement and the 1972 Aboriginal Embassy'), which argued that the history of Aboriginal activism was missing from academic and mainstream understandings of Australian history. He became professor at Victoria University, running the webpage www.gooriweb.org and creating the Australian Research Council (ARC)–funded Aboriginal History Archive that documents the 'active and engaged role played by Aboriginal people in shaping contemporary Australia.'[111]

Debate about who should be teaching Aboriginal history had surfaced earlier. Koori student Christine Stewart wrote in *Farrago* in 1984: 'Aboriginal history and culture taught by Koories should be compulsory for all Koories and non-Koories so that we can learn about the positive side of our people.'[112] In 1992 *Farrago* reported that Tony Birch was no longer prepared to tutor in 'Aboriginal and Koori History' because 'there has been no attempt made by the History Department to employ a Koori academic to develop and teach the subject.'[113] From 1995 to 1998 Sonia Smallacombe, of the Maramanindji people, taught 'Introduction to Aboriginal and Torres Strait Islander Studies', described as a 'general introductory history of indigenous/non-indigenous relations in Australia, with particular reference to Victoria, together with an overview of indigenous cultures.' From 2005, for eleven years, she worked on Indigenous issues at the United Nations in New York.

Patricia Grimshaw, who pioneered the teaching of women's and gender history at the University, was appointed professor of history in 1993. Her New Zealand upbringing gave her some comparative insights and awareness of how much had not happened in Australian history. As a researcher whose work turned increasingly to Indigenous history, as head of the History Department, teacher, PhD supervisor and contributor to public debate in these years of acrimonious 'History Wars', her contributions to the history program's engagement with Indigenous history in the 1990s were considerable.[114]

In 1998 Tony Birch was teaching a subject now called 'Koori and Non-Koori Histories'. He told *Farrago* that 'when I teach the subject it will be much more of a critique of colonial practices than it will be a course on Aboriginal history, which is not something I would teach'. He explained: 'What I want them to learn, is ... an understanding of their own history, particularly if they're people who have come from a so-called settler-society back-ground.'[115] From 2000 to 2002 Birch taught 'Aboriginal Histories' on 'relations and encounters between white settlers and Aboriginal peoples between 1788 and 2000'. Later he recalled that it was 'both a challenging and invigorating time to teach in the area'.[116] Tony Birch chose to leave the history program for a position teaching creative writing at the University and an important career as a poet, fiction writer and public intellectual who often wrote about history—out of frustration at historians' failure during the history wars to 'articulate something beyond self-preservation and a masonic attitude to legitimacy'.[117] He later became professor at the Moondani Balluk unit at Victoria University and was appointed to the Boisbouvier Chair in Australian Literature at the University of Melbourne from 2023.

Tracey Banivanua Mar was of Fijian (Lauan), Chinese and British descent. Her PhD was supervised by Patrick Wolfe and she wrote later that

> Patrick's scholarship ... grew out of implicit and explicit acknowledgements of his own racial privilege ... Most of the reading he set was written by Brown and Black authors speaking and writing their own critiques of colonialism and race, and he made students engage with the way they used their voice.[118]

In 2003 Tracey taught 'Aboriginal and Pacific Islander Histories', also emphasising that 'students will have gained access to Indigenous perspectives as well as, and in relation to, non-Indigenous writing on the major issues and themes of colonisation in Australia and the western Pacific'.[119] 'Aboriginal and Pacific Islander Histories' was not taught after 2007, when Banivanua Mar left the University of Melbourne for La Trobe University. That same year her first book, *Violence and Colonial Dialogue: The Australian–Pacific Indentured Labor Trade*, was published. Tracey sadly died in 2017 but her legacy lives on in her many former postgraduate students doing important work in this field, among them Amangu Yamatji academic Crystal Mackinnon and Ben Silverstein, currently co-editors of the journal *Aboriginal History*.

Conclusion

Ben Silverstein observed that Patrick Wolfe 'was never taken in by the celebratory mood that prevailed among non-Indigenous liberals in the 1990s'. He wanted instead 'to explain why an unending colonialism should structure the writing of Australian Aboriginal history'.[120] It was an important point. The rich offerings of the 1990s eroded as quickly as they had appeared, in the context of general reductions in staffing and subject offerings. By 2016, undergraduate offerings in Australian history were much reduced and handbooks indicated less explicit foregrounding of Aboriginal history and dispossession. The optimistic case would be that, after the Sturm und Drang of the 1990s, incorporation of some attention to Indigenous history across a range of (Australian and non-Australian) history subjects had become normalised and less in need of special flagging, but there is no doubt there was overall a decline in attention and activity in the early twenty-first century.

In 2020 Julia Hurst (Dharawal and Dharug, and a stolen generations descendant) was appointed to teach Indigenous history from an Indigenous perspective, and a new chapter began. Public events in the University now routinely begin with an acknowledgement of Country and affirmation that Aboriginal sovereignty has never been ceded. It remains to be seen how transformative this new settler consciousness will be of the teaching and research programs in history over the longer term.

Notes

1 My warm thanks to Graeme Davison, Kat Ellinghaus, Patricia Grimshaw and Sean Scalmer for generously sharing some very helpful comments, suggestions and information.
2 Andrew Fitzmaurice, 'The Genealogy of *Terra Nullius*', *Australian Historical Studies*, vol. 38, no. 129, 2007, p. 1.
3 Ernest Scott, 'Taking Possession of Australia: The Doctrine of "Terra Nullius" (No Man's Land)', *Journal of the Royal Australian Historical Society*, vol. XXVI, 1940, p. 4.
4 William Edward Hearn, *The Aryan Household: Its Structure and Its Development—An Introduction to Comparative Jurisprudence*, George Robertson, Melbourne, 1878, pp. 425–6.
5 Lauren Benton and Benjamin Straumann, 'Acquiring Empire By Law: From Roman Doctrine to Early Modern European Practice', *Law and History Review*, vol. 28, 2010, p. 30.
6 Ann Curthoys and Jessie Mitchell, *Taking Liberty: Indigenous Rights and Settler Self-Government in Colonial Australia, 1830–1890*, Cambridge University Press, Cambridge, 2018, p. 151.
7 Richard Selleck, 'Empires and Empiricism: The Teaching of History at the University of Melbourne, 1855–1936', in Fay Anderson and Stuart Macintyre (eds), *Life of the Past: The Discipline of History at the University of Melbourne 1855–2005*, History Department, University of Melbourne, Parkville, 2006, p. 8.
8 'The Colonies and the Mother Country', *Australasian*, 1 March 1879, p. 1.
9 George W Stocking, Jr, *Victorian Anthropology*, Free Press, New York, 1987, p. 62.
10 Hearn, *The Aryan Household*, p. 4.
11 Ibid., pp. 10–11.
12 John Tregenza, *Professor of Democracy: The Life of Charles Henry Pearson*, Melbourne University Press, Carlton, 1968, pp. 66–75.
13 Charles H Pearson, *National Life and Character: A Forecast*, Macmillan, London, 1893, p. 44.
14 Geoffrey Blainey, *The Great Seesaw: A New View of the Western World, 1750–2000*, Macmillan, Melbourne, 1988, pp. 80–5; Marilyn Lake and Henry Reynolds, *Drawing the Global Colour Line: White Men's Countries and the Question of Racial Equality*, Cambridge University Press, Cambridge, 2008, Chapter 3.
15 Pearson, *National Life and Character*, p. 84.
16 Ibid., pp. 31–2.
17 Selleck, 'Empires and Empiricism', pp. 12, 14.
18 JS Elkington, '"The Aryan Household" and Other Writings of Dr. Hearn', *Melbourne Review*, vol. III, 1878, p. 426.
19 Ibid., pp. 431–2.
20 *Argus*, 18 June 1896, p. 4. See also the discussion of Tucker in Warwick Anderson's chapter in this book.
21 JS Elkington, 'An Historical Glance at the Land Question', *Melbourne Review*, vol. 2, no. 7, 1877, pp. 249, 251.
22 Ernest Scott, *Terre Napoléon: A History of French Explorations and Projects in Australia*, Methuen, London, 1910; Ernest Scott, *Lapérouse*, Angus & Robertson, Sydney, 1912; Ernest Scott, *The Life of Captain Matthew Flinders, R.N.*, Angus & Robertson, Sydney, 1914.

23 Kathleen Fitzpatrick, 'Sir Ernest Scott (1867–1939)', *Australian Dictionary of Biography*, National Centre of Biography, Australian National University, Canberra, 2006, https://adb.anu.edu.au/biography/scott-sir-ernest-8367 (accessed 28 October 2023).
24 Stuart Macintyre, *A History for a Nation: Ernest Scott and the Making of Australian History*, Melbourne University Press, Carlton, 1994, Chapter 6.
25 Scott, *Terre Napoléon*, pp. 213–16.
26 Ernest Scott, *Men and Thought in Modern History*, Macmillan, Melbourne, 1920, pp. 197–9.
27 Ann Curthoys, 'WEH Stanner and the Historians', in Melinda Hinkson and Jeremy Beckett (eds), *Appreciation of Difference: W.E.H. Stanner and Aboriginal Australia*, Aboriginal Studies Press, Canberra, 2008, p. 456.
28 Ernest Scott, *A Short History of Australia*, Humphrey Milford, London, 1916, pp. 183–4.
29 See, for example, 'The Colour Bar', *Daylight*, 30 April 1927, p. 6.
30 'Rev. J. Watson Champions the Australian Abo', *Murrumbidgee Irrigator*, 21 May 1935, p. 4. See also 'Effect of Religious Missions', *Observer*, 18 June 1927, p. 27.
31 RM Crawford, 'Talk to Melbourne University Association', 1937, Box 9, Crawford papers, University of Melbourne Archives.
32 Ibid.
33 Box 10, Crawford papers, University of Melbourne Archives.
34 Anthony Disney and Inga Clendinnen tutored in this subject, which may have played some role in their subsequent career paths.
35 RM Crawford, 'Lecture II: Patterns of Settlement 1788–1850', Box 41, Crawford papers, University of Melbourne Archives.
36 RM Crawford, *Australia*, Hutchinson, London, 1952, pp. 26–7.
37 Handwritten Australian history lecture notes, Box 42, Crawford papers, University of Melbourne Archives.
38 DJ Mulvaney in 'R. M. Crawford: Some Reminiscences', *Historical Studies*, vol. 15, 1971, p. 13.
39 RM Crawford, typescript 'The Burden of Freedom', lecture to the Philosophical Association in Melbourne, June 1938, Box 9, Crawford papers, University of Melbourne Archives.
40 François Furstenberg, 'Beyond Freedom and Slavery: Autonomy, Virtue and Resistance in Early American Political Discourse', *Journal of American History*, vol. 89, 2003, pp. 1295–330.
41 RM Crawford, *The Study of History: A Synoptic View*, Melbourne University Press and Oxford University Press, Melbourne, 1939, pp. 18, 31.
42 Ibid., p. 20. See Ranajit Guha, *History at the Limit of World-History*, Columbia University Press, New York, 2002, Chapter 2.
43 Crawford, *The Study of History*, p. 33.
44 RM Crawford, 'Memorandum on Reconstruction in Department of History Honours School', Box 8, Crawford papers, University of Melbourne Archives.
45 John Poynter, '"Wot Larks to Be Aboard": The History Department, 1937–71', in Anderson and Macintyre, *Life of the Past*, p. 46.
46 Olive M Pink, 'What Is Their Future? Dictation or Freedom in Civilisation?', *Canberra Times*, 6 December 1938, p. 4.

47 Australian Institute of Aboriginal and Torres Strait Islander Studies, 'The 1938 Day of Mourning', 2023, https://aiatsis.gov.au/explore/day-of-mourning (accessed 28 October 2023).
48 'Calling All Aborigines', *Australian Abo Call*, 1 June 1938, p. 1.
49 Stuart Macintyre, 'Introduction', in Stuart Macintyre and Sheila Fitzpatrick (eds), *Against the Grain: Brian Fitzpatrick and Manning Clark in Australian History and Politics*, Melbourne University Press, Carlton, 2007, p. 5.
50 Mark McKenna, *An Eye for Eternity*, Melbourne University Press, Carlton, 2011, Chapter 8.
51 Curthoys, 'WEH Stanner and the Historians', p. 447.
52 Graeme Davison, personal communication, August 2022.
53 CMH Clark, 'Some Influences on European Civilization in Australia', *Papers and Proceedings: Tasmanian Historical Research Association*, vol. 7, 1958, p. 24.
54 CMH Clark, *A History of Australia, Volume 1: From the Earliest Times to the Age of Macquarie*, Melbourne University Press, Carlton, 1962, p. 3.
55 RM Crawford to University vice-chancellor, 5 May 1937, Box 27, Crawford papers, University of Melbourne Archives.
56 Robyn Sloggett, Dr Leonhard Adam and His Ethnographic Collection at the University of Melbourne, PhD thesis, University of Melbourne, 2009, pp. 38, 60.
57 See Tom Griffiths, *Hunters and Collectors: The Antiquarian Imagination in Australia*, Cambridge University Press, Melbourne, 1996, Chapter 3.
58 Leonhard Adam to Sydney Sunderland, 2 July 1953, Unit 14, 1995.0094, University of Melbourne Archives.
59 Greg Dening, *Readings/Writings*, Melbourne University Press, Carlton, 1998, p. 94.
60 Matthew Spriggs, '"Casey Did Very Good Work for Wheeler and You Are Lucky to Have Him": Dermot Casey's under-Appreciated Importance in Australian Archaeology', *Historical Records of Australian Science*, vol. 32, 2021, p. 8; 'Old Aborigine Relics Found on Flinders Island', *Hobart Mercury*, 30 January 1946, p. 7; RM Crawford to University vice-chancellor, 14 February 1946, Box 27, Crawford papers, University of Melbourne Archives.
61 W. R. C., 'Discovery on Flinders Island', *Age*, 20 July 1946, p. 28.
62 Leonhard Adam to RM Crawford, 30 March 1946, Unit 14, 1995.0094, University of Melbourne Archives; Crawford to registrar, 17 December 1947, Unit 14, 1995.0094, University of Melbourne Archives.
63 RM Crawford to registrar, 17 December 1947, Unit 14, 1995.0094, University of Melbourne Archives.
64 Sloggett, Dr Leonhard Adam, p. 76.
65 Ken Inglis, 'John Mulvaney's Universities', in Tim Bonyhady and Tom Griffiths (eds), *Prehistory to Politics: John Mulvaney, the Humanities and the Public Intellectual*, Melbourne University Press, Carlton, 1997, pp. 30–1.
66 Billy Griffiths, *Deep Time Dreaming*, Schwartz Books, Melbourne, 2018, Chapter 1.
67 RM Crawford to John Mulvaney, 8 March 1961, Box 27, Crawford papers, University of Melbourne Archives.
68 John Mulvaney to RM Crawford, 4 November 1961, Box 27, Crawford papers, University of Melbourne Archives; press release from Nuffield Foundation Australian Advisory Committee, 28 September 1962, Box 27, Crawford papers, University of Melbourne Archives.
69 Griffiths, *Deep Time Dreaming*, p. 27.

70 Ibid., p. 34
71 EJB Foxcroft, *Australian Native Policy: Its History, Especially in Victoria*, Melbourne University Press and Oxford University Press, Melbourne, 1941, quoted in 'People Are Reading', *Daily Telegraph*, 15 November 1941, p. 4.
72 EJB Foxcroft, 'The New South Wales Aborigines' Protectorate, Port Phillip District, 1838–50', *Historical Studies: Australia and New Zealand*, vol. 1, 1941, p. 165.
73 Typescript, 'History Open Night: Friday 16 September 1955', Box 47, Crawford papers, University of Melbourne Archives.
74 Entry for 23 August 1946, 'RMC's Camden Harbour Journal', Box 96, Crawford papers, University of Melbourne Archives.
75 Jack Rhys, 'A Settlement Gamble That Failed', *West Australian*, 25 January 1947, p. 4.
76 'Legend of Massacre', *Barrier Miner*, 19 November 1948, p. 8.
77 Entry for 19 August 1946, 'RMC's Camden Harbour Journal', Box 96, Crawford papers, University of Melbourne Archives.
78 Entry for 21 August 1946, 'RMC's Camden Harbour Journal', Box 96, Crawford papers, University of Melbourne Archives.
79 'Second Discussion Session', in Stuart Macintyre and Peter McPhee (eds), *Max Crawford's School of History: Proceedings of a Symposium Held at the University of* Melbourne, History Department, University of Melbourne, Parkville, 2000, p. 70.
80 'Authoress in Perth', *West Australian*, 9 June 1949, p. 23.
81 Margaret Kiddle, *Men of Yesterday: A Social History of the Western District of Victoria 1834–1890*, Melbourne University Press, Carlton, 1961, p. 3.
82 Kiddle, *Men of Yesterday*, p. 120.
83 Ibid., p. 122.
84 Ibid., p. 129.
85 Patricia Grimshaw and Jane Carey, 'Kathleen Fitzpatrick (1905–1990), Margaret Kiddle (1914–1958) and Australian History after the Second World War', *Gender and History*, vol. 13, 2001, p. 368.
86 RM Crawford, handwritten 'Dear V.C.' letter (1944?), Box 26, History Department records, University of Melbourne Archives.
87 Subject guides in Box 13, Department of History collection, 1975.0033, University of Melbourne Archives.
88 RM Crawford, *Ourselves and the Pacific*, Melbourne University Press in association with Oxford University Press, Melbourne, 1941. Crawford was the single name on the book (in the first edition as 'editor') but the Preface declared that it was 'the work of a number of people'.
89 Jack Gregory, 'Max Crawford and *Ourselves and the Pacific*', in Macintyre and McPhee, *Max Crawford's School of History*, p. 63.
90 Crawford, *Ourselves and the Pacific*, pp. 105, 117.
91 Ibid., p. 112.
92 RM Crawford, *An Australian Perspective*, Melbourne University Press, Carlton, 1960, p. 3.
93 WEH Stanner, *After the Dreaming: Black and White Australians—An Anthropologist's View*, Australian Broadcasting Commission, Sydney, 1969.
94 Curthoys, 'WEH Stanner and the Historians', p. 443.
95 JA La Nauze, 'Themes and Periods in Australian History', typescript, n.d., '3 lectures on Australian History', Box 26, History Department records, 1975.0033, University of Melbourne Archives.

96 JA La Nauze, 'The Study of Australian History, 1929–1959', *Historical Studies: Australia and New Zealand*, vol. 9, 1959, p. 11.
97 Julie Marcus, 'Olive Pink and the Encounter with the Academy', *Mankind*, vol. 17, 1987, pp. 185–97.
98 Subject guides in Box 13, Department of History collection, 1975.0033, University of Melbourne Archives.
99 Graeme Davison, personal communication, August 2022.
100 Graeme Davison, 'The Role of Ideas in C19 Australia', Talk IV, 5 May 1970, item 116, MON 1209, Graeme Davison papers, Monash University library.
101 Australian history essay guide Term 1, 1970, Box 13, Department of History collection, 1975.0033, University of Melbourne Archives.
102 Geoffrey Blainey, *Triumph of the Nomads: A History of Ancient Australia*, Sun Books, Melbourne, 1975.
103 *Faculty of Arts Handbook, 1980*, p. 272; *Faculty of Arts Handbook, 1982*, p. 269; *Faculty of Arts Handbook, 1985*, p. 258.
104 Handwritten notes for Aboriginal and Koorie History subject, Box 19, Dening papers, University of Melbourne Archives.
105 Tony Birch, 'Celebrating Warrior Women', *IndigenousX*, 16 March 2021, https://indigenousx.com.au/celebrating-warrior-women (accessed 28 October 2023).
106 1990 subject guide for 131-253/353 Aboriginal and Koorie History, Box 19, Dening papers, University of Melbourne Archives.
107 Patrick Wolfe, 'On Being Woken up: The Dreamtime in Anthropology and in Australian Settler Culture', *Comparative Studies in Society and History*, vol. 33, 1991, p. 210; Patrick Wolfe, 'Land, Labor, and Difference: Elementary Structures of Race', *American Historical Review*, vol. 106, 2001, pp. 868–9; Patrick Wolfe, 'Nation and MiscegeNation: Discursive Continuity in the Post-Mabo Era', *Social Analysis*, vol. 36, 1994, pp. 110–13; Patrick Wolfe, '"White Man's Flour": Doctrines of Virgin Birth in Evolutionist Ethnogenetics and Australian State-formation', *History and Anthropology*, vol. 8, 1994, pp. 189–90.
108 This chapter is focused on the history discipline, but it should be noted that elsewhere in Arts at the University of Melbourne, significant attention was also paid to Indigenous issues in the 1990s. The Australian Centre, established in 1990 under the leadership of Chris Wallace-Crabbe and Dinny O'Hearn, offered fellowships to Indigenous scholars and administered the Kate Challis RAKA awards for Indigenous creative artists. In the history and philosophy of science program, Warwick Anderson and Ross Jones taught a subject in Indigenous health in the later 1990s.
109 Tony Birch, 'The Trouble with History', in Paul Ashton and Anna Clark (eds), *Australian History Now*, NewSouth, Sydney, 2013, p. 238.
110 Martin Flanagan, 'Looking through a Black Anger: The Mellowing of Gary X', *Age*, 20 March 1993, p. 5.
111 Victoria University, 'Foley Collection', 2023, https://www.vu.edu.au/library/about-the-library/special-collections-archives/foley-collection (accessed 28 October 2023).
112 'The Koorie History Program', *Farrago*, vol. 62, 1984, p. 12.
113 'Koori Courses', *Farrago*, vol. 71, 1992, p. 4.
114 See, for example, Elizabeth Nelson, Sandra Smith and Patricia Grimshaw (eds), *Letters from Aboriginal Women in Victoria 1867–1926*, History Department,

University of Melbourne, Parkville, 2002; Patricia Grimshaw, 'The Fabrication of a Benign Colonisation?', *Australian Historical Studies*, vol. 35, 2004, p. 125.

115 'Shelley Marshall interviews Tony Birch', *Farrago*, vol. 77, 1998, p. 14.

116 Tony Birch, 'Good Patrick', *Aboriginal History*, vol. 40, 2016, p. 226.

117 Tony Birch, 'The Trouble with History', in Anna Clark and Paul Ashton (eds), *Australian History Now*, NewSouth, Sydney, 2013, p. 241. See also Tony Birch, Gary Foley and Kimberley Kruger, 'Remembering Tracey Banivanua Mar', *Overland*, 29 August 2017, https://overland.org.au/2017/08/remembering-tracey-banivanua-mar (accessed 28 October 2023).

118 Tracey Banivanua Mar, 'Talking Race: Patrick Wolfe's Scholarly Activism', *Aboriginal History*, vol. 40, 2016, p. 222.

119 '131-051 Aboriginal & Pacific Islander Histories', *Faculty of Arts Handbook, 2003.*

120 Ben Silverstein, 'Patrick Wolfe (1949–2016)', *History Workshop Journal*, vol. 82, 2016, p. 317.

Frederic Wood Jones and the Contradictions of a Race Scientist

LISA O'SULLIVAN[1]

ASSESSING HISTORICAL FIGURES for a project such as this one can create a temptation to find heroes and villains—to situate our figure of study on a continuum of progressive or retrograde opinions, whether unearthing unpalatable beliefs and practices or searching for redeeming features. Having met the facile response 'but everyone thought that way then' more times than not when teaching on the history of race science, it seems important to interrogate who the speaker's mind jumped to when considering 'everyone', which on further questioning almost universally emerges as published experts or scientists. In the anglophone imperial world, these figures were of course overwhelmingly educated white males, and it should be noted that even within this group there was always debate and division over both the contemporary practices of science and their broader social implications. Frederic Wood Jones is a particularly rich figure to explore in these terms, at once outspoken on political and social issues and dedicated to an increasingly minority view on evolution, while remaining a deeply embedded figure in the global enterprise of British imperial science.

Arguably one of the last mainstream scientists to argue for a Lamarckian vision of evolution in the early decades of the twentieth century, Frederic Wood Jones was a scientist of diverse interests, working prolifically across disciplines including comparative anatomy, anthropology and paleo-archaeology.[2] His career was likewise geographically diffuse: after completing studies in London, in 1904 he became the medical officer on the Cocos (Keeling) Islands (where he met his eventual wife, Gertrude Clunies Ross), and his subsequent work in London and Manchester as a teaching anatomist was punctuated by time spent working on the archaeological study of Nubia in Egypt between 1907 and 1909. Wood Jones arrived at the University of Adelaide as professor of anatomy in 1919. By 1929 he was at the University of Melbourne, having returned to Australia after a two-year stint as professor of physical anthropology at the University of Hawaii. He remained at the University until 1937, when he took a chair at Manchester. He ended his career as curator at the Hunterian Museum, London, from 1945, attempting to restore the collections damaged during the war.[3]

The international nature of Wood Jones' career was not untypical of scientists in the anglophone imperial world.[4] His commitment to large-scale collecting through fieldwork and expeditions meant that he was able to collect voraciously and generate vast numbers of the material specimens that acted as the currency of exchange for anatomists and anthropologists. In particular, he used his access to unique Australian fauna to establish and maintain links among the international comparative anatomy community, which relied on the global distribution of physical materials in complex networks of purchase and exchange.[5] Wood Jones' scientific theories were

Frederic Wood Jones.

deeply influenced by this time spent in the field, a practice he first came to in the coral reefs of the Cocos (Keeling) atoll and then retained throughout his career, resisting the shift towards laboratory studies. Through this on-the-ground engagement, he became convinced that the inheritance of characteristics acquired through adaptation to a specific milieu could become inheritable, a Lamarckian viewpoint that placed him increasingly at odds with the mainstream Darwinian approach in biological science.[6] By the time he came to Australia, Wood Jones' views on race science had developed in directions that in many ways took him out of the mainstream Anglosphere scientific position. Ross Jones suggests this shift seems to have occurred in the context of his time spent on the Cocos (Keeling) Islands and marriage to a woman of Malay descent.[7] Jones and Warwick Anderson also argue that his 'Australian experiences led Wood Jones to discard rigid racial typologies and fixed racial hierarchies in favour of more dynamic, adaptive models of human nature'.[8]

The position developed by Wood Jones over his many decades of expeditions, fieldwork and theorising was encapsulated in his 1942 *Habit and Heritage*, in which he argued for the need to reject the 'unthinking acceptance of all the worst connotations of Charles Darwin's phrase "the struggle for existence" and Herbert Spencer's "survival of the fittest", which had become blunt tools of propaganda and pseudo-science'.[9] Wood Jones' anti-Darwinian stance was based in part on his antipathy to social Darwinism, which he linked to the outrages of World War I, and on his encounters in the field, particularly within the Australian landscape.[10] Instead, he argued for a return to the works of earlier evolutionary thinkers such as Georges-Louis Buffon, Jean-Baptiste Lamarck and Erasmus Darwin, as well as a re-examination of the work of Charles Darwin and Alfred Russel Wallace. For Wood Jones, their work demonstrated that the ability to—over many generations—incorporate features developed in response to a specific environment into a hereditary characteristic was present across the natural world. In support of this argument, Wood Jones called attention to numerous cases of such acquired characteristics that he had encountered and documented throughout his career. The presence of bone variations in Asian populations where squatting was common, and the distinct patterns of body hair in certain animal and human populations indicating grooming habits—both were for Wood Jones small but profound markers of structural changes in the body that indicated the hereditary nature of acquired characteristics.[11]

In the Australian context, Wood Jones made key research projects of comparative studies of Australian marsupials and a concern with the status of Indigenous people. These were both scientific and social commitments; for instance, his work in Adelaide included the creation of a wildlife reserve on Kangaroo Island designed to provide an 'ark' for Australian fauna threatened by European patterns of land use, and as a commercial venture producing scientific specimens.[12] His scientific publications utilised both animal and human specimens, especially Indigenous skeletal remains, in his arguments for the adaption of species to their specific environments.

More broadly, the condition and treatment of Indigenous people preoccupied Wood Jones not only in his scientific practice but also in more public outputs, including publications, public lectures and broadcasts. In 1926 he wrote to his mentor, the British anatomist and anthropologist Arthur Keith, that 'I, for one, have learned to like, and to admire the aptitudes of, the native; and he is by no means the lowest of the low as he is depicted in almost every published account of him'.[13] He urged Keith towards action, asserting that

> anthropologists all over the world ought to take action on behalf of the Australian Aborigine. Could you get the matter taken up and have some publicity given to the thing ... You might use your influence at home. At this end I battle and get myself disliked; but the Australian politician cares not at all for the voice of science.[14]

The concern was an ongoing one. In another letter to Keith almost a decade later, in 1935, he wrote: 'I wish some outside influences could be brought to bear on Australian governments to secure better treatment for the natives. People outside Australia never know the dreadful cruelty and government apathy which is their lot.'[15]

Wood Jones' position on scientific, anthropological and social questions relating to Indigenous people should be viewed in the broader context of early-twentieth-century thinking about the colonial Australian project and the place of the country's original inhabitants within it. By the late nineteenth century, a broad consensus had been reached among scientists and colonial thinkers and administrators that Indigenous people were a 'dying' or 'doomed' race. Within the biological sciences, Darwinian thinking established a sense of hierarchy of progress and civilisation, in which so-called 'lesser' races were remnants of an earlier, more primitive stage of human evolution. Similarly, the emerging discipline of anthropology positioned itself as a science that could examine the development of progressively more civilised human societies in line with human biology. As Russell McGregor explores, the place of Indigenous people as 'the archetypal primitive man' became taken for granted in European theories of evolution.[16] As such, the data produced from Aboriginal bodies was seen as highly valuable for the light it was believed to shed on earlier forms of human biology and society (in a not dissimilar way to the scientific treatment of Australian fauna as archaic evolutionary forms, able to survive due to their isolation from competition). For most anthropologists, the Aboriginal exposure to 'higher' forms of civilisation would inevitably lead to their demise. In this context, assimilation theories that argued for the possibility of Indigenous people being able to adapt to new societal and cultural environments veered towards the liberal end of scientific orthodoxy.[17]

The first decades of the twentieth century saw the emergence of numerous humanitarian organisations concerned with the place of Aboriginal people in the newly federated nation. As Alison Holland has described, post–World War I politics also brought questions of slavery and mandates to the fore. These mandates, ostensibly designed to protect Indigenous populations in colonised lands, 'enshrined the paternalist principle that imperial powers would govern for those "not yet able to govern themselves". The decline of "Native peoples" in the face of Western intrusion was understood [to be] symptomatic of this vulnerability'.[18] Thus, while Indigenous-led organisations such as the Aborigines Progressive Association (New South Wales) and the Australian Aborigines' League (Victoria) focused on gaining civil rights for Indigenous people, including representation in parliament,[19] much mainstream white humanitarian impulse was focused on the creation of reserves to 'preserve' otherwise vulnerable groups in isolation from exposure to a 'civilisation' deemed as one to which they could not adapt.[20]

It was within the boundaries of these long-running scientific and political debates over the inevitability of Aboriginal people's demise, the possibility of their assimilation into new ways of being and their place in evolutionary chains of being, that Wood Jones, as both evolutionary scientist and physical anthropologist, made his public appeals. He was vocal in condemning, in print and in public, the treatment of Indigenous people. His arguments were widely picked up and reproduced by local media. For instance, a 1926 address to the Australian Association for the Advancement of Science, 'The Claims of the Australian Aborigine', in which Wood Jones condemned the government's approach to Indigenous affairs, was reported across the nation by metropolitan and regional media.[21] He argued that 'The aborigines [sic] racial fate was not inevitably sealed and the only hope to save him and justify ourselves in the eyes of the world was to establish properly organised and properly administrated reserves'.[22]

A decade later Wood Jones was even more explicit. His 1937 farewell address to the Anthropological Society of Victoria, of which he had been president for some years, was described in the media as 'one of the most scathing indictments that has ever been made of the Australian administration of the aborigines [sic]'.[23] He described depictions of Indigenous people as a 'dying and degenerate race' as the 'humbug with which the white man has always gilded his extermination of native races. There is no truth in it. The aborigines [sic] were never a dying race until we started to make them die'.[24] He went on to argue that no Australian governments had taken seriously their duty to protect Indigenous people, instead treating them 'first by cruelty and later by neglect', and creating 'aboriginal reservations no better than a bitter joke'.[25]

While Wood Jones had a clearly humanitarian thrust to his denunciations of the treatment of Indigenous people, his 'solution' to the question of their place in the colonial nation was one of isolation rather than assimilation. Where he differed from others making similar arguments was in the scientific basis on which he reached this conclusion. His 1934 monograph *Australia's Vanishing Race*, based on three publicly broadcast radio lectures, argued that 'something *must* be done for the aborigines [sic]',[26] because 'racially he is inevitably doomed to death once contact has been made with our alien culture'.[27] In the slim volume, Wood Jones argued that Aboriginal peoples' social organisation should not be read as that of 'savages'. Instead, he said, they had developed rules of law and custom ideally suited to maintain the welfare of their communities.[28] Physically, he said, 'it is safe to say that no more beautifully balanced human figures than those of the native in the prime of his life could be found among any race'.[29] In other words, they had adapted culturally and physiologically to a high degree to the circumstances of the Australian environment in which they found themselves. For instance, their visual and aural acuity reflected such adaptation, argued Wood Jones. Yet, with his Lamarckian approach, he felt that white individuals brought up in a similar environment would likewise eventually adapt such characteristics.[30] His admiration for this sophisticated adaptation was however focused on what he referred to as the 'uncontaminated Australian native'.[31] The preservation of a people was predicated on their isolation from other influences, while continuing to be accessible to scientists.

Whatever his knowledge of, and professed respect for, Indigenous cultures, Wood Jones remained deeply committed to extractive practices of contemporary science; throughout his career, the acquisition, description and exchange of biological specimens (including ancestral remains) remained at the core of his work. As Ross Jones and I have described elsewhere, Wood Jones was deeply embedded in global networks of material and intellectual exchange. These global networks saw individual, institutional, and national interests and agendas in play. With his access to Australian, Pacific and Asian collecting sites, Wood Jones was able to leverage the provision of coveted biological material into relationships, influence and intellectual authority. Australian biological material, both human and non-human, was in high demand and Wood Jones was well placed both to physically access material and to provide his imprimatur of the materials' origins and importance. The collection of Australian remains took place across burial and massacre sites, hospitals and mortuaries. Their perceived value straddled multiple physical, institutional and intellectual spaces, crossing the boundaries of ethnographic and scientific disciplines. This meant that they were in demand for museum collections and as sources for academic publications.[32] In addition, this value extended from the purely financial to objects of exchange to create and solidify relationships and patronage networks and academic reputations.[33]

For meaningful comparative work to be done in human anatomy, the provenance of material was of primary importance. Another aspect of the accumulation of authority and connections, as well as data generated from remains, is seen in Wood Jones' references to those who gave him material, or who first described the remains in the scientific literature. In just one 1934 article in the *Journal of Anatomy*, 'Contrasting Types of Australian Skulls', reference is made to: 'The large male skull from Wentworth (for which I am indebted to Dr Rowden White of Melbourne)'; 'The small female skull (for which I am indebted to Dr Angas Johnson of Adelaide)'; 'a loan of a cast of this incomplete skull I am indebted to Mr Gilbert Rigg'; and 'analysis ... carried out for me by the late Dr Heber Green'.[34] This pattern of attribution, acknowledgement and calls to authority can be found throughout Wood Jones' extensive publications on Indigenous remains. While his Lamarckian worldview shaped his interpretation of these remains, he used them to produce data that could be used by the broader anatomical community no matter their theoretical affiliations. Thus Wood Jones could undertake cranial measurements of Indigenous people from across Australia and argue that others were wrong to assert that skull size was a reliable indication of intelligence.[35] However, it was not the practices of race science that Wood Jones objected to, but rather the erroneous conclusions he felt that others examining the same 'specimens' came to about them.

The varied places and processes by which Indigenous remains were acquired, and became incorporated as 'specimens' into scientific networks and institutions as objects of scientific inquiry, have been well documented.[36] Curiously, however, while Wood Jones produced detailed documentation of his animal collecting, no extant records can be identified that detail how or where he acquired his personal collection of more than fifty Australian skulls.[37] His caution reflects the ongoing, and voracious, collecting of skeletal Indigenous remains that referred to their acquisition in coded language, or not at all. Colonial collectors in Australia were generally aware both that their collecting and exchanging habits were transgressive—in fact often illegal—and that their positions would allow them to bypass such restrictions.[38] Wood Jones himself complained multiple times in his correspondence to Arthur Keith about the laws controlling the export of human materials, and his temptation to work around them: 'Before I leave Australia I will break the law and send you home some material which I have hoarded. But I shall have to leave a terrible lot of stuff behind—and no one may care for it.'[39] A decade later, on a similar theme, he wrote:

> I am at a bit of a loss to know what to do with my own personal collection of marsupial and aboriginal [sic] skulls. I have a fairly good collection. Does anyone at home want them. I would give them or if possible sell them to any institution that wanted them. There is a law against the export of these things, but I could easily get a permit to send or take them out of the country.[40]

While Wood Jones was scathing in his denouncement of Australian policies relating to Indigenous people, and questioned the value of much of the science he saw being done in the country, his solution to the dismay he felt was highly reminiscent of what would later become known as 'salvage anthropology'.[41] His way of dealing with the disgust he felt over the lack of importance placed by Australian institutions on the collecting of remains was to have those remains sent overseas. Again, to Keith he complained that:

> I get very disgusted and disheartened with Australia and I often feel like risking things and sending home collections to the College—for I have a wealth of material. I shall be sending stuff to J. P. Hill for he has secured a Royal Society Grant and I am sending a man to collect in Kangaroo Island

> next month. I have also sent material to the Johns Hopkins and to Herrick in Chicago. Australia is a country of heart breaks in so many ways. No one seems to care a bit if everything is extreminated [sic] or not—but nothing must be exported—and nothing is being properly done here—all is wasted.[42]

Wood Jones' lament for the 'waste' of biological materials reflects his persistent belief that establishing the importance of Indigenous cultures was to be done by distributing knowledge—and the material remains from which this knowledge was generated—globally. This commitment to voracious collecting and publishing was passed on to students and mentees including Donald Thomson, whose anthropological collecting he supported and whose collection remains at the University of Melbourne as one of the University's most significant cultural collections.[43]

While he publicly deplored the treatment of Indigenous people and attempted to raise public awareness and concern about their wellbeing, and his Lamarckian worldview allowed him to understand Indigenous people outside the lens of hierarchical notions of civilisation to some extent, ultimately, Wood Jones remained fundamentally entrenched in the networks of extraction and exchange on which the global practices of anatomy and physical anthropology relied. At the same time, he remains an exemplar of a scientist committed to public engagement, one who refused to understand his scientific work without reference to broader social and political ideals.

Notes

1 This paper discusses the use of Indigenous ancestral remains in the creation of scientific narratives. In such narratives, these remains were reimagined and consequently referred to as 'specimens', a usage retained here. For more about the processes by which ancestral remains were 'transformed' into scientific specimens, see Lisa O'Sullivan and Ross L Jones, 'Two Australian Fetuses: Frederic Wood Jones and the Work of an Anatomical Specimen', *Bulletin of the History of Medicine*, vol. 89, 2015, p. 245.

2 Lamarckism proposed that the environment could directly influence the inherited qualities of a living organism. An eighteenth-century theory predating Charles Darwin, it has received new impetus with the recent discovery of epigenetics. See Barry Christophers, *A List of the Works of Frederic Wood Jones, 1879–1954, Including His Drawings (Published and Unpublished), His Published Letters and His Unpublished Manuscripts, with Notes*, Melbourne, 1985; and Barry Christophers, *An Addendum to a List of the Works of Frederic Wood Jones, 1879–1954, Including His Drawings (Published and Unpublished), His Published Letters and His Unpublished Manuscripts, with Notes; and Its Supplement*, Melbourne, 1988.

3 See Ross L Jones, *Anatomists of Empire: Race, Evolution and the Discovery of Human Biology in the British World*, Australian Scholarly Publishing, Melbourne, 2020, pp. 8–14.

4 Ross L Jones and Warwick Anderson, 'Wandering Anatomists and Itinerant Anthropologists: The Antipodean Sciences of Race in Britain between the Wars', *British Journal for the History of Science*, vol. 48, no. 1, 2015, pp. 1–16.

5 For Wood Jones' global reach, see Ross L Jones, 'Macaws, Elephants and Mahouts: Frederic Wood Jones, the Rockefeller Foundation and the Human Biology Project', *Australian Historical Studies*, vol. 44, 2013, pp. 189–205.

6 Jones, *Anatomists of Empire*, pp. 77–9.

7 Ibid., pp. 11–12.

8 Jones and Anderson, 'Wandering Anatomists', pp. 11–12.

9 Frederic Wood Jones, *Habit and Heritage*, Kegan Paul, London, 1943, p. 10.

10 Ibid., p. 14.

11 Ibid., chapters vi and viii.

12 O'Sullivan and Jones, 'Two Australian Fetuses', p. 256.

13 Frederic Wood Jones to Arthur Keith, 10 December 1926. MS0018/1/37, correspondence between Frederick Wood Jones and Sir Arthur Keith, 28 May 1905 – 3 May 1951, Royal College of Surgeons Archives, London (hereafter Wood Jones papers).

14 Frederic Wood Jones to Arthur Keith, 12 August 1926, Wood Jones papers.

15 Frederic Wood Jones to Arthur Keith, 20 April 1935, Wood Jones papers.

16 Russell McGregor, *Imagined Destinies: Aboriginal Australians and the Doomed Race Theory, 1880–1939*, Melbourne University Press, Carlton, 1997, p. 39.

17 Henrika Kuklick, '"Humanity in the Chrysalis Stage": Indigenous Australians in the Anthropological Imagination, 1899–1926', *The British Journal for the History of Science*, vol. 39, no. 4, 2006, pp. 535–68.

18 Alison Holland, 'The "Native Question" in Australia: Exploring the Anglo-Australian Humanitarian Response, 1904–1939', *The Journal of Imperial and Commonwealth History*, vol. 50, no. 3, 2022, p. 6.

19 Russell McGregor, 'Protest and Progress: Aboriginal Activism in the 1930s', *Australian Historical Studies*, vol. 25, no. 101, 1993, pp. 555–68; Bain Attwood and Andrew Markus, *Thinking Black: William Cooper and the Australian Aborigines' League*, Aboriginal Studies Press, Canberra, 2004.

20 Russell McGregor, 'The Aboriginal Reserves Debate of the Inter-War Years', *Journal of The Royal Historical Society of Queensland*, vol. 15, no. 11, 1995, pp. 545–52; Robert Foster, '"An Ethnographical Laboratory": Science, Religion and the Origins of the North-West Reserve', *History Australia*, vol. 16, no. 2, 2019, pp. 338–57.

21 See, for example, 'Prof. Wood Jones on the Aborigine', *Bunyip*, 27 August 1926, p. 6; 'The Aboriginal', *Townsville Daily Bulletin*, 1 September 1926, p. 4; and 'Address at Science Congress: Professor Wood Jones on The Aborigine', *Register*, 25 August 1926, p. 13. The address was subsequently published in *Report on the Eighteenth Meeting of the Australasian Association for the Advancement of Science, Perth, August 1926*, Government Printer, Perth, 1928, pp. 497–519.

22 'Address at Science Congress', *Register*, p. 13.

23 'Treatment of the Aborigines: Administration Censured', *Mercury*, 19 November 1937, p. 8.

24 Ibid.

25 Ibid.

26 Frederic Wood Jones, *Australia's Vanishing Race*, Angus & Robertson, Sydney, 1934, p. 6.

27 Ibid., p. 39.

28 Ibid., p. 17.
29 Ibid., p. 21.
30 Ibid., p. 27.
31 Ibid., pp. 17–18.
32 O'Sullivan and Jones, 'Two Australian Fetuses', p. 245.
33 The financial aspects of the trade in ancestral remains are explored in Gareth Knapman and Cressida Fforde, 'Profit and Loss: Scientific Networks and the Commodification of Indigenous Ancestral Remains', in Cressida Fforde, C Timothy McKeown and Honor Keeler (eds), *The Routledge Companion to Indigenous Repatriation: Return, Reconcile, Renew*, Routledge, Abingdon, 2020, pp. 361–80.
34 Frederic Wood Jones, 'Contrasting Types of Australian Skulls', *Journal of Anatomy*, vol. 68, 1934, pp. 323–30.
35 Frederic Wood Jones, 'The Non-Metrical Morphological Characters of the Skull as Criteria for Racial Diagnosis, Part 1: General Discussion of the Morphological Characters Employed in Racial Diagnosis', *Journal of Anatomy*, vol. 65, 1931, p. 179.
36 In the Australian context, see, for example, Cressida Fforde, 'Collecting the Dead', in *Collecting the Dead: Archaeology and the Reburial Issue*, Duckworth, London, 2004, pp. 43–59; Ross L Jones, *Humanity's Mirror: 150 Years of Anatomy in Melbourne*, Haddington Press, Melbourne, 2007, pp. 43–60; Helen MacDonald, 'The Bone Collectors', in *Human Remains: Dissection and Its Histories*, Yale University Press, New Haven, 2006, pp. 96–135; Paul Turnbull, 'Scientific Theft of Remains in Colonial Australia', *Australian Indigenous Law Review*, vol. 11, no. 1, 2007, pp. 92–104; and Paul Turnbull, *Science, Museums and the Collecting of Indigenous Bodily Remains in Colonial Australia*, Palgrave, Cham, Switzerland, 2017.
37 Frederic Wood Jones to Arthur Keith, 15 September 1939, Wood Jones papers.
38 On the tremendous volume and mobility of specimens generated from Australia in the nineteenth and early twentieth centuries, and the (il)legality of practices at the time when such remains/specimens were originally acquired, see Tom Griffiths, *Hunters and Collectors: The Antiquarian Imagination in Australia*, Cambridge University Press, Cambridge, 1996; Paul Turnbull, '"Ramsay's Regime": The Australian Museum and the Procurement of Aboriginal Bodies, c. 1874–1900', *Aboriginal History*, vol. 15, 1991, pp. 108–21; Ross L Jones, 'Medical Schools and Aboriginal Bodies', in Shannon Faulkhead and Jim Berg (eds), *Power and the Passion: Our Ancestors Return Home*, Koorie Heritage Trust, Melbourne, 2010, pp. 50–4; and Jones, 'Macaws, Elephants and Mahouts'.
39 Frederic Wood Jones to Arthur Keith, 5 October 1926, Wood Jones papers.
40 Frederic Wood Jones to Arthur Keith, 9 November 1936, Wood Jones papers.
41 Although the need to 'salvage' aspects of native cultures was expressed in the 1930s, the phrase 'salvage anthropology' came into use in the 1960s to describe efforts to collect and preserve material from cultures deemed to be threatened with extinction: see Samuel J Redman, *Prophets and Ghosts: The Story of Salvage Anthropology*, Harvard University Press, Cambridge, MA and London, 2021, p. 6.
42 Frederic Wood Jones to Arthur Keith, 12 August 1926.
43 Lindy Allen, 'Tons and Tons of Valuable Material: The Donald Thomson Collection', in Nicolas Peterson, Lindy Allen and Louise Hamby (eds), *Makers and Making of Indigenous Australian Museum Collections*, Melbourne University Press, Carlton, 2008, pp. 387–412; Jones, *Humanity's Mirror*, p. 193.

Defence Science, Expertise and Scientific Colonialism

JAMES WAGHORNE

THE BLACK CLOUD that moved noiselessly across the country surrounding Wallatinna, South Australia in October 1953 blocked out the sun and showered everything in its path with tiny particles. Its arrival had been proceeded by a loud bang, caused by the open-air firing of an atomic weapon some 170 kilometres to the south at Emu Field. There wasn't supposed to be any cloud at ground level; modelling had anticipated debris from the explosion to dissipate in the high atmosphere. Yet the wind conditions that day were still, producing the rarely observed phenomenon. Local station owners and their workers, having been warned to stay inside during the testing, watched through the windows of their houses as the cloud swept across, later washing off the sticky residue it left behind. But the message had not reached the Aṉangu community living on Country, who took no precautions, were engulfed by the cloud, and reported vomiting and other reactions. Experts at the time ignored the incident, and challenged the claims of Indigenous people that it had caused medical conditions (a claim still disputed). Oral history testimonies said otherwise, and a royal commission conducted thirty years later believed Indigenous people (supported by contemporary reports and the testimony of other, non-Indigenous people), recommending they be eligible for the same compensation as defence personnel exposed to high levels of radiation during what was a series of atomic tests.[1]

The royal commission found that the lack of precautions was a product of negligence, but the black mist had wider meaning. In part it showed hubris and wilful disregard of others' safety in the interests of personal advancement. It was a visual expression of a new phase of colonisation, as the needs of Western science claimed arid land in disregard of Indigenous people or knowledge. It also reflected how professional deference and the boundaries surrounding academic expertise left Indigenous people cruelly exposed to a technological disaster.

Postwar Weapons Development

The black mist was an unintended outcome of the second of six major atomic weapons tests conducted by the British Government, in association with Australia, between 1952 and 1963 at Monte Bello Island, Western Australia, and Emu Field and Maralinga in South Australia. These major explosions were interspersed by some 200 smaller nuclear blasts designed to test ignition detonators. These tests combined to irradiate the surrounding country, leaving it still dangerous despite repeated, inadequate clean-up efforts over subsequent years. They also sent radioactive material into the high atmosphere, where it dispersed across Australia.

The atomic tests were part of a post–World War II weapons development race, as former combatant nations sought to claim the new weapons they feared would determine the next major conflict. The Korean War had ended only recently, and few doubted that further terrible conflicts would follow. As well as the British atomic tests, the United States military sought to (but did not) conduct tests of biological weapons on the same atomic test sites, as well as others in tropical jungle in northern Queensland. Australia was an attractive site for the British atomic tests because of its vast territory separated from major population centres. US biological weapons researchers sought access to Australian sites as they offered biomes and climatic conditions unavailable in the United States. This was especially the case with tropical forests, and the US military sought to reuse airbases it had established during World War II. By offering up its territory, Australia bolstered its national defence, maintained wartime alliances and, to a lesser extent, bought itself a stake in these developments.[2]

Information about these tests was initially a closely protected secret, and some relevant files, especially those held by British archives, remain closed. Nevertheless, the documents that have been released by archives in Australia and Britain, combined with the detailed report of the 1984 royal commission about the atomic tests, and oral history work with local Indigenous communities, have informed numerous books.[3] These histories discuss the effect of Cold War geopolitics, mostly criticising Australia's deference towards British military authorities and its willingness to acquiesce with only partial information. The desecration of Indigenous lands in this testing, like that experienced at other sites such as Pacific islands, where other testing continued, has been characterised as part of wider 'nuclear colonialism' by Western powers on their former colonies.[4] The incompetence that led to the exposure of servicemen and civilians to high levels of radiation, the failure to follow up, and repeated inadequate clean-up efforts, have also rightly prompted censure.[5] The arrogance of British scientists and military leaders provides a foil for presenting the tests as secretive, cavalier and patronising, while the Australian scientists are often characterised as having been powerless to influence the tests.[6] Although the US biological weapons testing was not conducted, it still offers evidence of the effect of official secrecy in enabling discussions of extraordinary ruthlessness, with knowledge kept from public scrutiny by governments and military forces.[7]

Scientific Colonialism

Large-scale weapons testing found new uses of Country, ushering in a new phase of colonisation. The atomic testing, alongside mining enterprises, tested the postwar rendering of assimilation that had created reserves for Indigenous people living traditional ways of life, while seeking to push other Indigenous people into Western economic and social patterns.[8] Indigenous people living in the regions of the test areas were thought to be comparatively few in number, and defence imperatives were judged to outweigh their right to continue living unimpeded. These colonial processes were complicated by, and in some ways obscured by, the grossly inadequate safety measures implemented for the testing. Yet the two were connected by underlying assumptions about what was appropriate for Indigenous people, which blinded the professors who advised government and defence authorities from recognising the distinctive needs involved.

By the time the atomic testing began, policies for managing Indigenous populations had already been settled. The key figure in this management was a 'patrol officer' who would travel across the relevant areas and work with Indigenous peoples to ensure they were informed of the tests and knew to keep away from danger. This figure, one without anthropological training, would serve as the interface between Western scientists and the local population.

The patrol officer policy was a compromise reached for the earlier 1947–48 guided projectiles testing project, based at Woomera, following an acrimonious public debate about the right of defence scientists to conduct testing on Country where Indigenous people resided. The then University of Melbourne lecturer in anthropology, Donald Thomson, and a SA surgeon and Indigenous rights campaigner, Charles DuGuid, argued the rocket range presented an unacceptable risk to Indigenous people. Moreover, local groups of Indigenous people needed to be protected from disease or the moral perils that might be introduced by foreign service personnel. Australia had no right, they argued, to use lands inhabited by the Indigenous people for testing weapons, and Indigenous people should be protected on permanent reserves.[9]

These figures were consulted by military authorities, but ultimately AP Elkin, University of Sydney professor of anthropology, prevailed to become the chief adviser to the rocket range project. Elkin, a supporter of assimilation, had little time for the separatist arguments of the others and accepted the use of Aboriginal Country for weapons testing.[10] He did, however, concede the need for measures to shield remote Indigenous communities from exposure to concentrations of British military personnel, to limit both cultural disruption and exposure to Western diseases. Hence Elkin recommended the appointment of patrol officers to inform local communities about the risks of the rocket tests.[11]

In principle, patrol officers would preserve Indigenous communities' way of living around the rocket range while informing them of the potential dangers. However, the patrol officers were well versed in the paternalistic management of Indigenous people in South Australia, which offered limited scope for compromise.[12] A historian of the testing, Elizabeth Tynan, praised the first patrol officer, Walter MacDougall, for his extensive knowledge of local terrain and for the diligent application of his work (her praise was less effusive for the second officer), but acknowledged the impossibility of his task. Yet in conducting this work, patrol officers employed a range of colonial methods in common with earlier pastoral expansion, designed to move Indigenous people off Country. For example, MacDougall removed Indigenous objects from sacred sites, in order, he wrongly believed, to strip them of their sacred status and reduce Indigenous peoples' interest in returning to dangerous areas. The testing also offered a pretence for reclassifying surrounding reserves and moving Indigenous people to mission stations closer to supply links to the south, cutting them off from their lands and accelerating the assimilation project.[13] Indeed, throughout this period, patrol officers encouraged

Indigenous people to move away from the testing areas, ideally into mission stations.[14]

The patrol officers, as Tynan acknowledged, were given an impossible task. They were charged with covering vast territories, with inherent difficulties in navigating the terrain, and relied heavily on word of mouth. It was inevitable that some Indigenous people would be missed. Such safety measures reflected a general underestimation of the risks the testing might pose, especially to Indigenous groups who lived differently on Country, making different use of plants and soil from Western ways of living.[15] Indigenous people were 'managed' in the context of these tests in ways that simultaneously accorded with the practices designed by experts in this area and involved considerable neglect. As Heather Goodall has argued, the atomic issue became entangled in coincidental measles epidemics.[16]

Expertise and Technological Optimism

Three University of Melbourne professors rose to prominence in a select group of defence advisers in the period after World War II. They were chosen for their ability to offer objective advice and their pre-eminence and authority in their special areas of knowledge. With their advice, these experts helped to set the terms of government and military planning, often showing the extreme limits of what might be possible, and without necessarily endorsing the actions they described. They were part of international networks of researchers who were conducting new studies into increasingly powerful particle accelerators and nuclear reactors, or collecting biochemical and physiological knowledge in order to comprehend advanced biological weapons.

Most centrally involved in the atomic tests was Leslie Martin, a former graduate of the University who had conducted postgraduate work at Cambridge before returning in 1945 to take up the Chamber of Manufacturers chair in physics. Martin had been appointed defence science adviser in 1948 and served on several defence committees, work for which he would be knighted in 1957.[17] He resigned from the University in 1959 to become the first Commonwealth universities commissioner, and chaired the momentous inquiry that provided the basis for Commonwealth funding in a greatly enlarged tertiary-education sector. The University would later name a research centre after Martin because of his accomplishments in higher-education policy.[18] He was one of three Australian observers of the

Sir Leslie Martin.

first test at Monte Bello Island and was then appointed chair of the 'safety committee' that oversaw the test at Emu Field that produced the 'black mist'. Sir Frank Macfarlane Burnet, director of the Walter and Eliza Hall Institute, chaired the Commonwealth Radiation Advisory Committee, set up in 1957 to assess the physiological dangers posed by the testing. Martin and Burnet would be joined by professor of anatomy Sydney Sunderland, who advised government on the proposed biological weapons tests, recommending how these might be achieved most effectively.

These expert advice structures predated the weapons testing, and this form of public engagement had long been part of the expectations of university figures, who formed what Sheila Jasanoff has described as the 'fifth branch' of government.[19] University experts had helped to establish public institutions such as museums and observatories, botanical gardens and art galleries.[20] During both world wars, university academics and graduates had offered their expertise across a wide range of activities. Such work had come to be seen as intrinsic to the University's public mission.

Sir Frank Macfarlane Burnet.

In the course of World War II, scientific discoveries came to be seen as critical elements in national security, creating space for the University expert to champion and explore new ideas. The period after the war was marked by an unprecedented optimism in the potential of machines and scientific discoveries to win wars and bring social and economic change. The postwar tests extended these ideas, and the deliberations of these committees revealed a new confidence in the value of scientific discoveries.[21] Penicillin offered a new treatment for infections, while new synthetic fertilisers and pesticides improved agricultural yields. Radio waves enabled the transmission of audio across continents and beyond. Radar offered new means of sweeping the skies and directing air defences. Martin had himself worked on the creation of range-finders and a secret radar project in association with CSIR during World War II.[22] There was no more obvious example of the power of scientific knowledge than the two atomic bombs that destroyed Hiroshima and Nagasaki, offering stunning evidence of the terrible potential of the latest discoveries.

Alongside their scientific work, experts also transmitted other values and objectives, associated with development and progress that were socially determined.[23] In the case of postwar weapons development, ideas of progress, assimilation and risk permeated these discussions in a way that left Indigenous people as inconvenient intruders on testing considered essential for national security. As Tim Sherratt has astutely observed, the experts involved in postwar weapons testing combined scientific with 'public and political' roles.[24]

The role of academics in this work was not entirely disinterested. Australian researchers aimed to increase domestic research capacity, moving beyond the old Empire practices, which drew researchers of leading ability from the periphery to laboratories and libraries based in centres in Britain.[25] Researchers had come to rely on ever-more costly apparatus, pushing them to engage in fundraising beyond the academy. University professors became public champions of their work, the need for public investment, and the potential returns it would bring. One of the costliest fields was nuclear physics, with lobbying over the location of cyclotrons, treatment plants and nuclear reactors producing fierce competition between 'nuclear knights' based in Canberra, Sydney and Melbourne.[26] Another was medicine, which involved Burnet and Sunderland.[27] The pressures this created for pre-eminence and control of resources were important elements in the context in which defence scientists worked. Nuclear development also promised opportunities for developing nuclear power, an efficient source of power by contrast with fossil fuels, and one that brought ancillary scientific and medical benefits. Along the same lines, Macfarlane Burnet could argue that biological weapons offered a more efficient means of fighting than conventional warfare, or indeed nuclear weapons, in that they could reduce property destruction. They would allow an invading force to claim farmland and buildings while driving back defensive forces with comparable effectiveness.[28]

Manageable Risks

As testing implied, these new technologies involved outcomes and processes that were unknown. Testing at large scale, as in the Australian case, could affect large areas of country, increasing the potential for it to make a mess. One of the main roles for the aforementioned experts was to attempt to manage the necessary experimentation to ensure safety and contain the immediate and long-term effects. Postwar experts expressed confidence in their own ability, assisted by military manpower and facilities, to predict the likely risks associated with testing new weapons. Fear of the consequences of not pursuing the testing, of leaving Britain, and by extension Australia, beholden to other nuclear powers, spurred on the work, quietening other concerns about local safety.[29] As the costs and extent of defence projects escalated, experts rose to positions of international prominence, with influence over policy decisions and with limited public accountability.

In managing these risks, committees of experts divided the task into their specialised area of knowledge. Physicists offered technical advice on the likely scale of explosions, and the measures that would be needed to ensure safe and successful tests; psychologists assessed the mental impact on troops of witnessing the gigantic explosions, while anthropologists advised about how to work with Indigenous peoples. The insularity of these processes was heightened by the secrecy demanded by the Cold War environment, which had acted to close scientific debate rather than make discoveries public.[30]

The atomic tests were inherently unsafe, but scientists believed that the risks could be mitigated. This belief rested on an idea of the remoteness of the location, sited on an isolated claypan far from major population centres, combined with efforts to move Indigenous people out of the danger areas. The bulk of the radioactive fallout would be drawn into the atmosphere, where it would dissipate by wind shear to safe concentrations in the high atmosphere before returning to earth.[31] Such was the confidence in the capacity of scientists to manage the risks of the testing that it led them to send service personnel to fly through radioactive clouds to test radiation levels. Other personnel wore inadequate protective clothing. These methods would later be criticised by the 1984 royal commission, but they showed the readiness of safety officers, including Martin, to allow 'manageable' levels of exposure, at least according to the standards of the time.

Part of the explanation for the confidence of safety officers derived from the extensive measurement that was intrinsic to the whole idea of testing. Testing stations were established across the country. Personnel wore film badges that measured radioactivity exposure (although in fact most were not processed). Test papers were dispersed around Australia to measure the level of fallout nationwide. This measurement provided reassurance that the testing was proceeding as planned. The fallout from the explosion at Emu Field, for example, was tracked north-east as it traversed Lismore before becoming untraceable in offshore island testing stations.

Expert appraisals rested on applying the best available knowledge, but the gaps in this knowledge belied the confidence with which it was expressed. Martin, notoriously, informed the Australian Government after the first Monte Bello Island test that the risk to the population was negligible, despite Geiger counters revealing spikes of radiation in sites on the Australian mainland.[32] Yet the apparatus for the tests and the atomic explosives themselves were quite unstable, making weather delays technically difficult and costly. Martin's safety committee often found itself caught between interests. British authorities withheld technical information, providing only estimates of the potential size of an explosion, across a range of megatons, plus forecasts for wind conditions at different altitudes. The smaller atomic tests responsible for much of the local radiation were undertaken without safety committee oversight.

This confidence drew criticism from other academics, most notably the University of Adelaide biochemist Hedley Marston, who argued that the dangers of even low concentrations of radioactive fallout were not understood and would have the potential to cause illnesses.[33] Marston's arguments were disputed by Martin and other experts. Public debate about the potential effect of the atomic tests on Indigenous people was surprisingly muted, in part because of the lack of public knowledge about the dangers of nuclear testing, and also the strict secrecy that controlled the release of information.[34] However, the issue of the effect on 'tribal' Indigenous peoples was debated in Western Australia, where a reserve along the South Australian border near the Warburton Ranges became the subject of a parliamentary inquiry. This inquiry, which investigated the effects of the weapons testing and also mining, found local Indigenous people living in a parlous condition. This was at least partly caused by a short period of acute drought, which had prompted local people to seek refuge at a mission station, rather than reflecting prevailing living standards. However, a film screened widely across the major cities in 1957 showing the shocking condition of the Indigenous people who arrived at the mission station, prompted a humanitarian reaction that changed views on Indigenous welfare on reserves.[35]

In the same year, Martin recommended the formation of a Commonwealth Radiation Advisory Committee, of which he would be a member, to be chaired by Burnet, to assess the health dangers of radiation. But this committee largely dismissed public anxieties. Reflecting on these events some two decades later, in 1978, Burnet labelled public anxieties about low-level radiation exposure unscientific, since there was 'no realistic way of assessing whether the minute amounts of radiation with which we were concerned were doing any harm or not'.[36] Since the dangers could not be proved, objective advice dictated that they be dismissed.

Conclusion

A self-assured tone rings through an oral history interview recorded with Leslie Martin in 1972, reflecting his satisfaction with his role and the proper application of expert knowledge.[37] Histories of the weapons testing record Martin as a steady hand, a calm figure, but also suggestable and unlikely to push back too hard against public pressure.[38] Burnet is presented as a loner, committed to his work and a great scientist.[39] Yet this confidence also seems misplaced. While these two men assiduously analysed the data they received, they failed to appreciate what they were not measuring. Safety commission members were often not on site. Martin, for instance, insisted on continuing a full teaching load throughout the years he also supervised the safety of the testing.[40] The men also failed to see the wider horizons of their field, and they left the areas that fell between expert silos unattended. Rather than acknowledging the gaps, these professors tended to deny them. They suggested that things unmeasured by their tests were either fantasies or in any case untestable and therefore scientifically invalid, even if they were regrettable.

Such defensiveness reflects an unwillingness to adapt to rapidly changing community ideas about public work and elements of risk. Open-air atomic tests quickly came to attract public censure, leading to campaigns for international test-ban treaties that swirled around the British tests. The proposed testing of biological weapons contravened a 1925 Geneva protocol, to which Australia was a signatory. These international arrangements conceived of the atomic tests as reckless and poisoning, regardless of the technical danger as assessed by scientific measurements.[41] Similarly, recognition of the connection between Indigenous people and their Country has shifted; the country around Maralinga, for example, was returned to the Tjarutja people in 1984.[42] Both these shifts in public opinion combined to recast the weapons testing considered essential to national security, and ask whether enough was done, and whether the expertise of those involved might have overlooked crucial questions and different points of view.

That neither Martin nor Burnet published any views on Indigenous Australia shows that their actions were not malicious or motivated by an explicit racism. Others were *more* responsible for the atomic tests, including other scientists, military officials and political leaders. Yet these men chaired the committee responsible for ensuring safety and the committee appointed to assess the effect of the tests. A combination of underestimation of the risk of testing (or perhaps a commitment to its benefits, both militarily and personally) and a failure of imagination, which conceived of Australia as being unpopulated, or echoed a belief that its inhabitants ought not to live on Country, led experts to accept that military testing was safe and manageable. This had consequences for Indigenous people, who were pushed back from their Country, or exposed to risks to which Western populations were not.

Notes

1 JR McLelland, *Royal Commission into British Nuclear Tests in Australia*, 2 vols, Australian Government Publishing Service, Canberra, 1985, pp. 179–94, 613.

2 Elizabeth Tynan, *Atomic Thunder: The Maralinga Story*, NewSouth, Sydney, 2016, pp. 3–6.

3 Ibid.; Elizabeth Tynan, *The Secret of Emu Field*, UNSW Press, Sydney, 2022; Lorna Arnold and Mark Smith, *Britain, Australia and the Bomb: The Nuclear Tests and their Aftermath*, Palgrave Macmillan, Basingstoke, 2006.

4 Bengt Danielsson and Marie-Thérèse Danielsson, *Poisoned Reign: French Nuclear Colonialism in the Pacific*, Penguin, Ringwood, Vic., 1986. Eve Vincent also adopts this term: Eve Vincent, 'Nuclear Colonialism in the South Australian Desert', *Local-Global: Identity, Security, Community*, vol. 3, 2007, pp. 103–12.

5 Frank Walker, *Maralinga*, Hachette, Sydney, 2014; Roger Cross and Avon Hudson, *Beyond Belief: The British Bomb Tests—Australia's Veterans Speak Out*, Wakefield Press, Kent Town, SA, 2005.

6 Jessica Urwin, 'The British Empire's Dr Strangelove? Ernest Titterton and the Royal Commission into British Nuclear Tests in Australia', *History Australia*, vol. 18, no. 4, 2021, pp. 714–36; Tim Sherratt, 'A Political Inconvenience: Australian Scientists at the British Atomic Weapons Tests, 1952–53', *Historical Records of Australian Science*, vol. 6, no. 2, 1984, pp. 137–52.

7 Brian Toohey, *Secret: The Making of Australia's Security State*, Melbourne University Publishing, Carlton, 2019; 'US Projects: Chemical Warfare Testing in Australia', National Archives of Australia Series A1838, TS 694/7/37.

8 Eve Vincent, '"Never Mind Our Country Is the Desert"', in Tracey Banivanua Mar and Penelope Edmonds (eds), *Making Settler Colonial Space*, Palgrave Macmillan, London, 2010. On assimilation, see Anna Haebich, *Spinning the Dream: Assimilation in Australia, 1950–1970*, Fremantle Press, Fremantle, 2008.

9 Donald Thomson, *The Aborigines and the Rocket Range*, Rocket Range Protest Committee, Melbourne, 1947; Charles Duguid, *The Rocket Range, Aborigines, and War*, The Rocket Range Protest Committee, Melbourne, 1947; Sitarani Kerin, 'Doctor Do-Good'?: Charles Duguid and Aboriginal Politics, 1930s–1970s, PhD thesis, Australian National University, 2004; Geoffrey Gray, 'A Deep-Seated Aversion or a Prudish Disapproval: Relations with Elkin', in Bruce Rigsby and Nicolas Peterson (eds), *Donald Thomson, the Man and Scholar*, Academy of the Social Sciences in Australia, Canberra, with support from Museum Victoria, 2005.

10 Russell McGregor, 'Wards, Words and Citizens: A.P. Elkin and Paul Hasluck on Assimilation', *Oceania*, vol. 69, no. 4, June 1999, pp. 243–59.

11 Geoffrey Gray, 'Aborigines, Elkin and the Guided Projectiles Project', *Aboriginal History Journal*, vol. 15, 2011, pp. 153–62.

12 Heather Goodall, 'South Australia', in Ann McGrath (ed.), *Contested Ground: Australian Aborigines under the British Crown*, Routledge, London, 1995.

13 Tynan, *Atomic Thunder*, pp. 182–3.

14 Kingsley Palmer, 'Dealing with the Legacy of the Past: Aborigines and Atomic Testing in South Australia', *Aboriginal History*, vol. 14, nos 1/2, 1990, pp. 197–207; Tynan, *Atomic Thunder*, pp. 178–83.

15 Tynan, *Atomic Thunder*, p. 173; McLelland, *Royal Commission*, pp. 574–81.

16 Heather Goodall, 'Colonialism and Catastrophe: Contested Memories of Nuclear Testing and Measles Epidemics at Ernabella', in Kate Darian-Smith and Paula Hamilton (eds), *Memory & History in Twentieth Century Australia*, Oxford University Press, Melbourne, 1994.

17 RW Home, 'Sir Leslie Harold Martin (1900–1983)', *Australian Dictionary of Biography*, National Centre of Biography, Australian National University, Canberra, 2012, https://adb.anu.edu.au/biography/martin-sir-leslie-harold-14939 (accessed 28 October 2023).

18 'Media Release: New University of Melbourne Institute to Train Higher Education Leaders', *Voice*, 1 May 2007.

19 Sheila Jasanoff, *The Fifth Branch: Science Advisers as Policymakers*, Harvard University Press, Cambridge, 1998.

20 RW Home, 'Origins of the Australian Physics Community', *Historical Studies*, vol. 20, no. 80, 1983, pp. 383–400.

21 Roy MacLeod, 'The Atom Comes to Australia: Reflections on the Australian Nuclear Programme, 1953 and 1993', *History and Technology*, vol. 11, no. 2, January 1994, pp. 299–315.

22 DP Mellor, 'The Role of Science and Industry', *Australia in the War of 1939–45*, Series Four, vol. 5, Australian War Memorial, Canberra, 1958, pp. 246–81, 563; HC Bolton, 'Optical Instruments in Australia in the 1939–45 War: Successes and Lost Opportunities', *Australian Physicist*, vol. 27, no. 3, 1990.

23 Sabine Clarke, 'A Technocratic Imperial State? The Colonial Office and Scientific Research, 1940–1960', *Twentieth Century British History*, vol. 18, no. 4, 20 July 2007, pp. 453–80; Sheila Jasanoff, 'Future Imperfect: Science, Technology and the Imaginations of Modernity', in Sheila Jasanoff and Sang-Hyun Kim, *Dreamscapes of Modernity: Sociotechnical Imaginaries and the Fabrication of Power*, University of Chicago Press, Chicago, 2015.

24 Sherratt, 'A Political Inconvenience', pp. 143–4.

25 Roy MacLeod, 'From Imperial Science to National Science', in *The Commonwealth of Science: ANZAAS and the Scientific Enterprise in Australasia, 1888–1988*, Oxford University Press, Melbourne, 1988.

26 RW Home, 'The Rush to Accelerate: Early Stages of Nuclear Physics Research in Australia', *Historical Studies in the Physical and Biological Sciences*, vol. 36, no. 2, 1 March 2006, pp. 213–41; MacLeod, 'The Atom Comes to Australia'; Wayne Reynolds, 'Rethinking the Joint Project: Australia's Bid for Nuclear Weapons, 1945–1960', *The Historical Journal*, vol. 41, no. 3, September 1998, pp. 853–73.

27 Warwick Anderson, 'The Military Spur to Australian Medical Research', *Health and History*, vol. 15, no. 1, 2013, pp. 80–103.

28 Toohey, *Secret*, p. 50.
29 Ernest Titterton, *Facing the Atomic Future*, F.W. Cheshire, Melbourne, 1956; MacLeod, 'The Atom Comes to Australia', pp. 23–34; Brian Martin, *Nuclear Knights*, Rupert Public Interest Movement, Dickson, ACT, 1980, pp. 303–4; Christopher Sexton, *The Seeds of Time: The Life of Sir Macfarlane Burnet*, Oxford University Press, Melbourne, 1991, p. 197.
30 Hannah Forsyth, 'Post-War Political Economics and the Growth of Australian University Research, c. 1945–1965', *History of Education Review*, vol. 46, no. 1, 2017, pp. 18–21.
31 McLelland, *Royal Commission*, pp. 25–6.
32 Tynan, *Atomic Thunder*, p. 159.
33 RT Cross, *Fallout: Hedley Marston and the British Bomb Tests in Australia*, Wakefield Press, Kent Town, SA, 2001.
34 On secrecy about the tests, see Phillip Deery, 'Menzies, Macmillan and the "Woomera Spy Case" of 1958', *Intelligence and National Security*, vol. 16, no. 2, June 2001, pp. 23–38; and Sherratt, 'A Political Inconvenience'.
35 Pamela Faye McGrath and David Brooks, 'Their Darkest Hour: The Films and Photographs of William Grayden and the History of the "Warburton Range Controversy" of 1957', *Aboriginal History Journal*, vol. 34, January 2011; Bain Attwood, *Rights for Aborigines*, Allen & Unwin, Crows Nest, NSW, 2003, pp. 149–52.
36 Macfarlane Burnet, *Endurance of Life: The Implications of Genetics for Human Life*, Cambridge University Press , Cambridge, 1978, p. 34.
37 Leslie Martin, interviewed by Hazel de Berg, 10 August 1972, National Library of Australia, Canberra.
38 Home, 'Sir Leslie Harold Martin'; Ed Muirhead, *Leslie Martin at Melbourne*, School of Physics, University of Melbourne, Parkville, 1998, p. 10; Cross, *Fallout*, pp. 35–7.
39 Anderson, 'The Military Spur', pp. 83, 92, 94.
40 DL Caro, RL Martin and Mark Oliphant, 'Leslie Harold Martin: 21 December 1900 – 1 February 1983', *Biographical Memoirs of Fellows of the Royal Society*, vol. 33, December 1987, p. 400.
41 Arnold and Smith, *Britain, Australia and the Bomb*, pp. 236–8.
42 Odette Mazel, 'Returning Parna Wiru: Restitution of the Maralinga Lands to Traditional Owners in South Australia', in Marcia Langton, Odette Mazel, Lisa Palmer, Kathryn Shain and Maureen Tehan (eds), *Settling with Indigenous People: Modern Treaty and Agreement-Making*, Federation Press, Annandale, NSW, 2006.

Eugenics, the 1950s and Beyond

Ending or Renewing?

ROSS L JONES

ON THE EVENINGS of 14 and 15 September 1977, at the invitation of an organising committee of the Faculty of Education, professors of psychology Hans Eysenck and Arthur Jensen delivered the Fink memorial lectures in Wilson Hall in the University of Melbourne. In 1969 Jensen had published an article in the *Harvard Educational Review* that claimed intelligence was essentially heritable, accounting for 80 per cent of the effect. He also claimed that black Americans scored, on average, about 15 points (one standard deviation) lower than white Americans.[1] Eysenck had been Jensen's mentor and teacher, and soon after he published a book backing Jensen's argument.[2] The response to these publications was immediate and explosive. Their subsequent lectures were blockaded and interrupted, and both men received threats. Many in the academic mainstream attacked or dismissed their arguments.[3]

In Melbourne about 200 protestors assembled outside the first lecture by Jensen. A smaller group had infiltrated the lecture and managed to disrupt it to the extent that it was impossible to finish. The University requested more police for the second lecture, for which there were also considerable protests. Although the disturbances inside were not of the same extent as for the first lecture, most attendees were unable to hear Eysenck speak.

Such was the chaos that ensued during the lectures in Melbourne that the vice-chancellor, professor David Derham, circulated a memorandum to all deans of faculties and heads of department with instructions for it to be circulated among all staff, because what had occurred had 'disturbed many members of the University, and ... many members of the community generally who were concerned with this University and of Universities in

Australia'.[4] Derham claimed that 'a majority of those involved were not in any substantive sense members of the University, and some persons who could be expected to be responsible members of this University were either involved directly with the disruptions or were involved with their incitement'.[5]

In fact, Derham must have been aware of the identity of at least some of the protestors, as the protest leaders included the well-known Indigenous activists Gary Foley (now a professor at Victoria University) and Bruce McGuinness.[6] Even closer to home, Indigenous woman Eleanor Koumalatsos, Aboriginal liaison officer in the University (now Professor Eleanor Bourke, chair of the Yoorrook Justice Commission), also objected to the invitation.[7] Derham must also have been aware that the invitation had prompted much planning by those who objected to the views of the two eugenicists, as the student magazine *Farrago* was publicly calling for action in the period leading up to the first lecture.[8] These protests can be seen in the context of the international movement 'No Platform' that had risen in Northern Hemisphere universities in the 1960s in response to the rise of far-right ideology. Essentially it aimed to deny racist and fascist speakers and organisations any opportunity to be heard in universities.[9]

The key person behind the invitation was KB Start, recently appointed occupant of the newly created second chair in education and head of the Department of Education within the University from 1974 to 1976. He had come to Melbourne from the United Kingdom, holding a leadership role in the National Foundation for Educational Research.[10] In an article in 1967 he positioned himself as an educationist in the school of the prewar eugenicists, citing the work by the notorious US eugenicist Louis Terman (*Genetic Studies of Genius*) on the genetic inheritance of intelligence. Terman used extensive IQ testing to grade the intelligence of races, with the white race on top. Start wrote in the 1967 article, adopting the technical language of the time, that the notion that

> general intellectual level is related to physical skill over a wide range of skills and intelligence can hardly be debated. Actually, we accept this principle, as despite what we might feel, there are no mongolian idiots, cretins, or low grade defectives in the upper echelons of sport.[11]

The visit of Jensen and Eysenck coincided with a resurgence of racist eugenics in the Northern Hemisphere, starting in the 1960s. This was a counter-reaction to the immediate decline of eugenics immediately after World War II, when the full horrors of Nazi eugenics severely damaged the movement's credibility in the public arena.

In his 1977 lecture, Jensen made it clear that eugenics had not died as a subject of interest at the University of Melbourne, arguing that a biological view of intelligence had made a triumphant comeback after the decades of disgrace after 1945. He claimed that

> the de-biologizing of our conceptions of intelligence has been the greatest error of a whole generation of psychologists. But it appears that this de-biologizing of the science of human behaviour, in general, has already seen its day, with its few ardent exponents now producing only ineffectual rear-guard skirmishes in their reluctant retreat from the scientific arena.[12]

Before we return to Jensen's triumphalism, and the manifestation of these ideas in the University of Melbourne in the 1970s, we need first to revisit 1945 and the Eugenics Society of Victoria. As we will see, there was little to distinguish between the policies advocated by eugenic sympathisers connected to the University in the period from 1940 to the contemporary era, and those of their predecessors in the prewar eugenic movement in Melbourne.

Leunig, *Farrago*, 9 September 1977.

Postwar Eugenics

Immediately after World War II there was a tentative move to re-establish relations between national eugenic organisations after the hiatus during the conflict. However, many thought that, due to exposure of the Nazi eugenic policies, it was not the right time. As Kühl has shown, when 'the Nazi horrors committed in the name of eugenics and racial purity became known, the entire classical variant of eugenics fell into disrepute amongst scientists and the general population'.[13] In Australia eugenics virtually disappeared as a topic from newspapers. The popular rejection of the extreme form of eugenics was endorsed in the United Nations Educational, Scientific and Cultural Organization's (UNESCO) 1950 Statement on Race, which elevated the social over the biological in defining ethnicity and emphasised the common biological brotherhood of humanity. It announced that 'biological studies lend support to the ethic of universal brotherhood; for man is born with drives toward cooperation, and unless these drives are satisfied, men and nations alike fall ill'.[14] The statement was drafted by Ashley Montague, an admirer and correspondent of Frederic Wood Jones, one of the small group of vocal anti-racists in Melbourne in the 1930s (see Lisa O'Sullivan's chapter in this volume).[15] Montague, who later became a prominent public intellectual in the United States, wrote his doctoral thesis on the Indigenous peoples in Australia, under the supervision of the anthropologist Bronislaw Malinowski, who also had significant University of Melbourne associations.[16]

As is clear from Start's invitation to Eysenck and Jensen in 1977, even though eugenics had suffered a setback in intellectual circles immediately post 1945, there were those at the University who maintained the cause.[17] In 1947, at the annual general meeting of the Eugenics Society, it was decided to hold no more meetings under the Society's auspices but instead to work through other organisations so as to spread the eugenic message.[18] This echoed the evolution of many other eugenic societies throughout the world that had begun to refocus from promoting eugenics as a discrete discipline to influencing scientific and social research in a eugenic direction, particularly in the development of the science of genetics and, more broadly, in demographics and population policy.[19] This was the case with the Victorian society based at the University of Melbourne.[20]

Population Policy

One area where eugenic ideas continued to have influence internationally was population policy, particularly relating to migration. University of Melbourne academics and members of the Eugenics Society were vigorous participants in this debate, contributing eugenic ideas to national discussions at the highest level.

For many decades following 1945, Australian population policy was still informed by racial doctrines with their roots in eugenic theories of the racial superiority of certain groups, both in the area of migration and the forced removal of 'half-caste' Aboriginal children and their adoption by white families—although the language of justification had been somewhat modified, thereby partially disguising its eugenic provenance. From 1942 the Eugenics Society decided to concentrate its research efforts in the areas of child endowment and immigration, and it subsequently attempted to influence immigration policy directly until the 1960s at least.[21] Agar's 1943 publication 'Science and Human Welfare', quoted at the beginning of the 'Eugenics, 1853–1945' chapter in this volume, was part of this initiative, calling as it did for restrictions on the breeding rights of white Australians and the limiting of migration to white races only. In January 1948, for example, the minister for immigration (and later Labor leader) Arthur A Calwell wrote to agree with the submission of Ken Cunningham in his role as president of the Eugenics Society (replacing Agar) that:

> The quality of the migrants admitted to Australia is a very important consideration in any immigration scheme, and this matter is well to the fore in the selection of migrants. At present, however, no psychological tests are applied but each migrant has to undergo a strict physical examination ... My Department of Immigration is in close touch with the Department of Health, whose views are sought in any case concerning departures from normal.[22]

Calwell then pointed out to Cunningham that, under the *Immigration Act*, no mentally deficient migrants were allowed to enter the country.

In 1959 the Department of Immigration invited professor Sir Frank Macfarlane Burnet, director of the Walter and Eliza Hall Institute, future Nobel laureate and one of Australia's most eminent scientists, to present a paper for discussion at the Australian Citizenship Convention in Canberra. The paper, entitled 'Migration and Race Mixture from the Genetic Angle', was subsequently published in the English *Eugenics Review*, the journal of the Eugenics Society of Great Britain.[23] Burnet followed the classic British eugenic line that hybrid breeds of races (for example, white races such as Angles and Saxons) were superior to pure breeds.[24] He claimed that:

> Where healthy typical individuals of each race are concerned, the offspring can be expected to show greater physical health than either and—though the evidence is slighter—a greater likelihood of exceptional mental ability

> ... From the genetic angle, there is much to be said for allowing into the country as much non-European genetic material as the community can safely assimilate.[25]

Like many British eugenicists, however, Burnet did not believe that a random choice of individuals would necessarily uncover worthwhile genetic stock. Instead, he advised that experience

> equally points to the acceptability of upper class cross-racial marriage and, where this is accepted, clearly no general contempt for the half-breed can develop ... I should like to think [Australia should be] willing to accept into the 'gene pool' of our community a contribution from any section of the human species *that has a worthwhile inheritance to offer.*[26]

Burnet's biographers have overlooked his regular contributions to the *Eugenics Review.*[27] In 1957, for example, he wrote that:

> All educationists and psychologists know that intelligence tests show a negative correlation between the I.Q. of children and the size of the family they come from. Children from large families are on the average less intelligent than those from small ones. Why this should be so is still a matter of controversy and many geneticists hesitate to adopt the common-sense explanation that intelligence has a large genetic determinant and that under present-day conditions intelligent parents have fewer children than those of lower intelligence.[28]

Such views are virtually identical to earlier eugenic thinking, such as that expressed by the University's professor Richard Berry, concerning the dysgenic consequences of contraception among the 'better' classes in Australia and elsewhere.[29] At the 1959 Australian Citizenship Convention, Burnet argued that '[s]upreme achievement probably always demands a ... genetic contribution above all'. He also argued that the Australian nation's physical and mental vigour be maintained by genetic means 'by providing ... [a]ppropriate incentives to influence people with grossly harmful genetic defects to have few or no children'.[30]

For all this theorising about potential 'coloured' immigration, whiteness was always paramount in these debates among leading politicians. In 1957 a young Gough Whitlam, later while Labor prime minister to perform the coup de grâce on the White Australia policy, told that year's Australian Citizenship Convention that the decline in British migration was a great pity and 'we may well pull up our socks' by increasing it.[31]

Harold Holt, later Liberal prime minister of Australia and University of Melbourne law graduate, argued that another important benefit of taking immigrants from a wide range of European nations would be the support, from these nations, for the White Australia policy. This was necessary, he argued, to 'continue with our traditional policy of restricting Asian immigration. We need not delude ourselves that this policy builds goodwill for us in Asia. It is the cause of great discontent and bitter criticism'.[32] Holt later played an important role in the dismantling of the White Australia policy.[33] In the University context, however, it is difficult to ignore the racism in the postwar immigration debates and policies so well encapsulated in the annual citizenship conventions held in Canberra in the 1950s. These gatherings were not merely window dressing. They were important vehicles for influencing postwar government migration policy. At the second Convention in 1951, Holt told the delegates that 80 per cent of the recommendations of the first Convention in 1950 had been adopted by the government.[34]

Members of the Eugenics Society also published polemics to forward their views. In 1957, Wallace, as secretary of the Society, edited a collection of essays by eminent Australians devoted to the problem of world peace.[35] In his chapter 'A World Population Policy as a Factor in Maintaining Peace', Wallace argued that: 'Quality is supremely important, especially quality of intellect. As a result of research work in human genetics it is now within the power of man to improve the quality of his own species, just as he has already improved the quality of other species.'[36] Wallace advocated the application of genetic science to the population policies of developing nations because '[i]n all advanced countries there exist organizations devoted to the study of eugenics'.[37] In an attempt to keep eugenics on the agenda, he proposed that Australia's immigration policy should continue to be informed by eugenic doctrines and be dominated by white Europeans. This was, he claimed, because '[w]e may safely conclude that mass migration and miscegenation [race mixing] are not desirable in the interests of world peace'.[38] He recommended that, if there was to be 'any migration on a large scale, it should be from densely populated Great Britain'. He grudgingly accepted, however, that, owing to the developments in education and living standards in Asian countries,

> to promote friendship and good will we would be wise to admit an annual quota of people from Asia, provided adequate measures are taken to prevent the formation of colonies and provided the rate of immigration from Asia is regulated so that Australian living standards are not lowered. The Asians who come to live with us while they are students at our universities are of such a desirable type that they would do credit to any nation.[39]

Professor of zoology Wilfred Agar had expressed such views decades earlier, in 1928. He had written that '[t]he question of the restriction of alien European [non-British] immigration is not yet an important one ... and in any case ... national is far less important than individual selection.'[40] This was because Agar believed, along with British and American eugenicists of the interwar years, that while 'certain nations have a lower average intelligence than others ... a member of a low-grade nation who is above his national average may greatly exceed in intelligence a poor specimen of a nation whose average is high.'[41] After the war, these sentiments were supported by a 1949 bequest of £13 812 to the University of Melbourne from the estate of JN Peters, to endow a research lectureship on eugenics.[42] The bequest is now used to fund research in genetics.

After World War II, a group of eugenicists across Europe and the United States attempted to distance themselves from the Nazi atrocities and distinguish between 'good' eugenics and 'bad' eugenics. This has been the catchcry of many up until the present day. What we can see at the University of Melbourne is that it is not always easy to distinguish between much of what was preached by the Eugenics Society of Victoria before the war and the views of its supporters after the war.[43]

Eugenic Sympathisers

As much as eugenic influences are easily found in policy considerations after World War II, such interest was not enough to draw new members to the Society, which was wound up in 1961. But even as the Society died, stalwarts maintained their belief that it had a useful place. Dr Victor Wallace, the long-time secretary, recorded he had received 'many declarations of regret and the hope was expressed that our Society might be rejuvenated.'[44] One of the most active members, County Court judge Alfred William Foster, a socialist, pacifist and rationalist, wrote that:

> Your historical details bring memories of activities we were jointly engaged in–Peace–Racial Hygiene–Eugenics. I suppose we can note a marked change in the public's attitude to all of them; it won't be long before our 'advanced' ideas are old fashioned.[45]

In fact, some hope was expressed that the Eugenics Society of Victoria could be revivified in the near future. GS Browne (professor of education at the University of Melbourne and a long-serving member of the

Eugenics Society) wrote to Wallace about the arrangements to close down the Society, remarking that 'Professor Agar's interest in Eugenics still lingers at the University with his successors'.[46] Browne was a lifelong champion of the progressive education movement and a popular early television celebrity, hosting, after his retirement in 1956 until 1966, a television program on GTV-9, *Professor Browne's Study*.[47] He was, as well as being a central member of the Eugenics Society, also a strong supporter of the White Australia policy—a classic Australian liberal progressive.[48] Agar's successor, professor Michael White (appointed to a chair in zoology in 1957 and then genetics in 1965),[49] wrote to Wallace in December 1959 thanking him for sending the *Eugenics Review* and remarking that we 'are quite interested in problems of human heredity here'.[50] Also, in 1961, the secretary of the Eugenics Society of Great Britain stated that White would be interested in joining the British Society now that the Victorian one was folding.[51] CP Blacker said he hoped some younger people, 'perhaps pupils of Professor Macfarlane Burnet or of Professor M. J. D. White', would later feel 'it worthwhile to make a new start with an Australian Eugenics Society'.[52] Wallace thought such an arrangement was an excellent idea.[53] There is, however, no direct evidence that White supported eugenic thinking.

Perhaps the most notable student and champion of the generation that was associated with the Eugenics Society was professor Sir Gustav Nossal. Shortly after his appointment as director of the Walter and Eliza Hall Institute, he gave a number of public talks extolling the benefits of eugenic population policy. It is striking that even a figure such as Nossal, a refugee from Nazi Germany and later deputy chair of Reconciliation Australia, could find purpose in eugenics in the postwar period.[54] In a speech he gave at a meeting in the Australian Medical Association building in Adelaide on 5 December 1966, he claimed, according to the *Sydney Morning Herald*, that

> in later years great social pressure might be put on people of high intelligence and creativity to have large families, and less intelligent people to have small families. This was the reverse of the situation today ... [according to Nossal] ... The world of the future could easily contain baby farms where babies are born by artificial inseminations of semen from geniuses ... by this method people such as Einstein could have hundreds, perhaps thousands, of children.[55]

On 19 April 1967, at a Fabian Society symposium at the Kew Town Hall in Melbourne, Nossal argued that an important part of the answer to the problem of the wrong sort of people breeding was that mankind needed to practise

> some effective and acceptable form of eugenics. Strong social pressures could be brought to bear on people possessing harmful genes to adopt children rather than have their own ... it should be possible to introduce into the future world community a mild, but nonetheless definite, social pressure for the brightest individuals to have the most children.[56]

This echoes Agar's argument, first published in 1928 and, remarkably, republished in 1968.[57] Agar also expressed the eugenicists' concerns about the difference in birth rates between the working classes and the middle classes because, as he wrote,

> there is a more than average accumulation of natural talent (not merely better education) in the classes of the intellectual workers, [and] if these classes are less fertile than the rest of the population, then the average intellectual capacity of the population will decline ... generation by generation.[58]

Nossal continued to give such public lectures until at least 1970.[59] Also, in 1970 he wrote for *Meanjin* in an article titled 'Medical Research and the Future of Man' that:

> The most widely touted development, and the one which has aroused the most controversy, is eugenics. I sense a growing awareness among my colleagues that the game is not going to be as simple as mating sperm from Albert Einstein with ova from Brigitte Bardot. In fact, much recent writing on eugenics stresses instead the value of negative or remedial eugenics. By this we mean the identification of human genetic characteristics that are positively harmful, and medical counselling that points out the risks involved in the possessor's becoming a parent.[60]

While the discussion about remediating genetic diseases is new, it is remarkable that Nossal is happy to use the term 'eugenics', bearing, as it did, the weight of so much negative baggage. Is this a scientist rejecting moral usurpation of what he thought was a purely scientific concept?

A few years later the consultative body of students and staff of the University, the Assembly, tried to institute an investigation into the proposal to develop facilities for genetic engineering in the Walter and Eliza Hall Institute run by Nossal. Vice-chancellor Derham, Nossal and the University Council blocked the attempt.[61]

The Renaissance of Racist Eugenics

Much more investigation needs to be done into the influence of the Eugenics Society and its members in the period following World War II, but there is evidence that the ideas it promoted were not forgotten and rather contributed to a modern flourishing of the 'new eugenics' that was stimulated by 21st-century developments in gene technology. The demise of the Society in 1961, however, coincided with a Northern Hemisphere renaissance of racist eugenics,[62] beginning in the early 1960s.[63]

One of the key moments in the rebirth of American and European racist eugenics was the relaunch of the journal *Mankind Quarterly* in 1961, gathering funding and key individuals who had been unhappy with the triumph of environmentalism after the war.[64] Stanley Porteus became editorial adviser and Eysenck published in its pages.[65] In 1922 Porteus had been appointed professor of clinical psychology at the University of Hawaii, and his close relationship with Frank Tate and Richard Berry is outlined in the earlier chapter on eugenics in this volume. He made two research trips to northern Australia, in 1928 and 1962, to test Indigenous people and calculate their intelligence according to his models, which showed a genetic explanation for the 'inferiority' of the Indigenous population.[66] His conclusion, drawn from his return visit in 1962, was that there was little prospect for Indigenous people being able to assimilate into white society.[67] By this stage Porteus was an outlier in the psychological world, having replaced his advocacy of the small-head theory of Berry with the idea that since 'black' races lived closer to the equator, the faster spin of the earth adversely affected them intellectually. He also actively engaged with overtly racist organisations.[68]

Jensen and Eysenck's 1977 Fink lectures suggest that those sympathetic to racist eugenics remained ensconced in the University. Although the vice-chancellor claimed in his memo to staff that '[a]s distinguished Professors in their fields they were invited to speak upon matters which interest very many academic and professional people concerned with educational development in Australia', in fact they had both faced intense scrutiny and criticism from mainstream academics, academic institutions and journals. The main targets of their opponents were their intellectual simplicity and the dubious techniques of Jensen and Eysenck's research methodology. The support they received from the extreme right did nothing to allay the fears of even those maintaining moderate eugenic views. They had also long been the regular subjects of demonstrations when delivering public talks.[69] Academic publishers have since withdrawn much of their work, especially that of Eysenck, due to major problems replicating the experiments.[70]

The Endurance of Life

I have discussed Macfarlane Burnet's eugenic views as he expressed them in the *Eugenics Review* and at the citizenship conventions in the 1950s and early 1960s. It is important to point out that, after his retirement and replacement as head of the Walter and Eliza Hall Institute by Nossal in 1965, he published numerous books and gave many public lectures and interviews until his death in 1985—what Nossal described as 'an extraordinary final chapter to his career'.[71] In these summaries of his life's work and reflections, eugenics was a major feature. This was especially true of *Endurance of Life: The Implications of Genetics for Human Life*, published in 1978.[72]

Pessimism pervaded his discussion of the future of humanity because he believed that 'human nature is, for Darwin and the rest of us, the obstacle to any change in social life in the direction that modern scientists, physicists or biologists, would regard as good'.[73] He gave two reasons. First: the '80 per cent of people whose mating groups are not related to any special skills', and, secondly, because

> we have to face the question of human futures in their full bleakness. Is the 80 per cent fated to become a larger and larger fraction of the whole ... and its effectiveness, as judged either by its potential contribution to the work of the community or its level of intelligence, physical health, and mental balance, to diminish slowly but progressively?[74]

Macfarlane Burnet then claimed that, as this group had larger families, it would necessarily follow that 'the trend of intelligence *insofar as it is genetically determined* is downward'.[75] All this was based on the premise that social worth and intelligence were primarily genetically determined—even morality and therefore crime and antisocial behaviour.[76] He argued that, although environmental factors would affect such matters, '[o]f much greater practical importance are the very large numbers of people of subnormal intelligence',[77] and that overwhelmingly 'human anti-social behaviour is genetically determined'.[78] The consequences of this were potentially catastrophic:

> If healthy, vigorous, intelligent people average two surviving children per family while others of low intelligence and slovenly habits rear four

> or six to adult life, the latter is the biologically more successful group in the existent environment. Even if its existence is only made possible by payments from the state and supervision by welfare officers of all sorts, the reproductive success of the 'inferior' group marks them as biologically superior. Insofar as the relevant characters are genetic, they would be the sort of people to inherit the future, if the current pattern of the welfare state persists indefinitely.[79]

The only hope was for the 'better' 20 per cent to form mating groups that potentially could eventually evolve into a superior species, as in HG Wells' description in his novel *The Time Machine*: '[I]f society took the form of a justly and efficiently controlled meritocracy, there might soon be a diminishing movement in either direction, and if this continued for some hundreds of thousands of years a split would no doubt occur.'[80]

As a one-time Fabian, Burnet expressed disappointment that '[m]ature, well-conditioned, and socially responsible people may have most of the virtues, but may equally find themselves unattractively far to the right of the political spectrum.'[81] He concluded by expressing a glimmer of hope for the future:

> In the 1970s the idea of eugenics is completely out of fashion ... Hitler's racist policies are still anathema, and any open support of a eugenic policy would be regarded as equally objectionable by all who write for popular consumption. Just under the surface, however, I believe there is still a lot of sympathy for the Galtonian approach.[82]

Endurance of Life is peppered with discussions of the work of prewar eugenicists such as Francis Galton, Terman and RA Fisher, as well as near contemporaries such as Eysenck and Jensen. Burnet favourably quotes Jensen on the genetic inferiority of black American IQs and implies this is an unbridgeable gap:

> Most academics in [the] Americas seem to take the attitude that this may well be true but that there are good social reasons for not adopting a point of view which provides no hope of ameliorating the racial situation ... The importance of genetic factors in determining human ability, temperament, and intelligence has been recognized by intelligent people from time immemorial ... nearly all differences that could not be immediately and unequivocally ascribed to injury, infection, malnutrition, or hardship of extreme degree were to a large extent of genetic origin.[83]

While he admitted his views had prompted strong criticism within the University and wider community, it hardly diminished his influence and standing. Nossal wrote of Burnet's final publications that, although 'his views were not always popular ... the depth and originality of his mind shone through'.[84] One important difference was that, in the interwar years, the Eugenics Society and its supporters encountered little resistance. But alongside the demonstrations that greeted Eysenck and Jensen in 1977, thirty-one academics at the University publicly objected to the invitation they received in an open letter to the *Staff News*.[85] If eugenics was about to make a comeback at the University, it would face stiff opposition.

Doomed Race

In the earlier chapter on eugenics in this volume, we saw how racism characterised much eugenic thinking at the University of Melbourne before World War II. Conveniently, the most extreme race scientists, such as Berry and Agar, were able to claim partial exoneration for their views and confirmation for their science by invoking the 'doomed race' theory. A classic tautology—in fact a subset of the 'survival of the fittest' trope—this 'theory' explained the disappearance of the Indigenous people as an evolutionary certainty. Indigenous people would just fade away, with the exception of those who intermixed with the white race and thus 'bolstered' their inferior genetic make-up.[86] This view was widespread among the educated classes. University of Melbourne graduate Sir Owen Dixon, a chief justice of the High Court, told his audience in an address to the Executive Club in Memphis in 1943 that:

> We regard our country as a southern stronghold of the white race—a thing for which it is well fitted; and our population is European. The aboriginal native [sic] has retreated before the advance of civilisation, contact with which he apparently cannot survive.[87]

Although many of those attracted to eugenics in the postwar period sought to distance themselves from that racist stream—with only partial success at best—the extreme form of racism did not entirely disappear from eugenic circles in Victoria. Some scientists still believed that genetic differences between races constituted the major element in what they saw as the inferiority of the intelligence of the 'coloured' races.[88] This is evident in the attitude of some important eugenicists towards Indigenous people. In the interwar period, the widespread acceptance of the 'dying race' theory meant that the eugenic gaze rarely alighted on them. Apart from Berry's graphs purporting to show the inferior skull size of Indigenous people, there is little mention of Indigenous people in eugenic literature from the 1920s, although Dr SV Sewell (an erstwhile Stewart lecturer at the University and a member of the Eugenics Society of Victoria in the 1930s) put it to the Australian branch of the British Medical Association Congress in 1923 that: 'It is a big step from the gesture language of the lowest type of savage to the extensive word and phrase vocabulary of that finest product of evolution, the educated upper middle class English gentleman.'[89] As mentioned earlier, Frank Tate, like most eugenicists, had almost nothing to say about Indigenous people in his writings.[90]

This relative absence of the application of eugenic thinking may also be explained by the goal of assimilation policies—arguably genocidal policies—from 1938 onwards to 'breed out' the 'race'.[91] Certainly the eugenic emphasis in the period after 1945 on 'worthy' citizens, 'white' immigration and the superiority of upper-class, talented, 'worthy coloured' migrants devalued Indigenous people who had been brutally invaded, oppressed, impoverished, and denied education and advancement from the beginning of white settlement.

The Great Silence: The Legacy

Biographies of our eugenicists written after World War II have ignored their subjects' attachment to eugenics in their research and intellectual worldviews, either by deliberately removing eugenics from discussions of their published works or by discussing only those aspects of their careers unrelated to their eugenic interests.

Stephen Jay Gould has drawn attention to this critical blindness in relation to works on the eminent early British geneticist RA Fisher. For decades, major studies of Fisher were characterised by a total absence of comment on the significance of eugenics in Fisher's classic work on population genetics.[92] Thus, Gould has written of the seminal *The Genetical Theory of Natural Selection* (1930):

> The eugenical chapters are no ending frill; they represent more than one third of the book. Moreover, Fisher explicitly insists that these chapters both follow directly from his general theory and cannot be separated from his more abstract conclusions. He states that he only gathered these chapters together for convenience and might, instead, have scattered the eugenical material throughout the book. Fisher writes, 'The deductions respecting man are strictly inseparable from the more general chapters.'[93]

Likewise, the first chapter of Agar's 1943 publication 'Science and Human Welfare' doesn't mention the eugenic arguments that make up a substantial part of the book, but rather is a plea for more funding for science and the acceptance of the importance of science towards successful reconstruction. Agar's reputation as a geneticist and scientist warranted the naming of a lecture theatre after him in 1990, as Fisher was celebrated for his scientific achievements. In both instances, the material in the publications directly related to eugenics was either ignored or forgotten.

The Blindness of the Historical Gaze

In the second of Stanner's 1968 Boyer lectures *After the Dreaming*, titled 'The Great Australian Silence', he argued that, after some initial attempts at reconciliation with Indigenous tribes in the early months after the arrival of the First Fleet, what followed was a dark age in the recognition of Indigenous Australians up until a brief flickering in the 1920s.[94] However, he believed historians had effectively been complicit in the 'disappearance' of Indigenous Australia. It was in the 1960s, he argued, that there had been a stirring of the re-evaluation of Indigenous history that had led to greater respect, and that 'something very remarkable has happened: the fact that the Aborigines having been '"out of" history for a century and a half are now coming back "into" history with a vengeance'.[95]

This was not the case with the eugenic proselytisers and supporters at the University of Melbourne. Their involvement with racism and eugenics in the interwar years was forgotten. Buildings and lecture theatres were named in their honour because their history had been revised and all racist and eugenic aspects of their lives and careers had been erased or ignored. The reasons for this may vary but it is significant that there seems to be no case where any such controversial opinions were not removed.[96] This postwar revision of biographies was not unique to the University or Australia more broadly;[97] other individuals who had their biographies revised were discussed in the 'Eugenics, 1853–1945' chapter. What needs to be emphasised was that they were memorialised in buildings and lecture theatres in the decades following 1945 right up until 1990, when Wilfred Agar, along with Berry, the most notorious eugenicist produced by the University, had a lecture theatre named after him in the new Zoology building.

And while eugenics certainly did not have the same level of public exposure in the postwar period as it had in the first four decades of the twentieth century, CP Blacker, the secretary of the English Society, accurately summarised the changing fortunes of eugenics at a time when its public profile was at a low ebb, correctly foreseeing the renewal of eugenic thinking at the end of the twentieth century. This renewal has been accelerated by rapid advances in gene technology leading to the call for a 'new eugenics' among some geneticists and ethicists.[98] When discussing the winding up of the Society with Wallace in 1961, Blacker wrote that it 'is impossible to foretell how people's interests will develop in the future; and eugenics shares with other topics which occupy a sort of frontier position between science and social policies a susceptibility to tidal movements'.[99]

Conclusion

With very few exceptions, the view of the original Australian settler colonists was that the Indigenous inhabitants of the continent were an inferior race, based on early scientific theories of the history of racial development. With the meteoric growth in the popularity of evolutionism around the Western world after the publication of Charles Darwin's *On the Origin of Species* in 1859, and continuing with *The Descent of Man, and Selection in Relation to Sex* in 1871, the lowly status of Indigenous peoples, especially Aboriginal people, was confirmed in the minds of most intellectuals and the public—no more than in the newly founded state of Victoria. Later, it was universities that forgot Indigenous Australia and also the eugenic and racist policies that received intellectual justification by them—of which the University of Melbourne was a leading example.

Bain Attwood has pointed out the consensus among many leading historians that the discipline of history is essential to the formation and consolidation of settler nation-states. He writes:

> Historical narratives are critical to nations because nations are neither ancient nor eternal, but historically novel, they are invented where they once did not exist. The primary role of history has been to lend moral legitimacy to revolutionary phenomenon. This task is very difficult, if not impossible, to achieve without the telling of highly coloured stories, in which most of the time (or past) of the place the nation has occupied is forgotten.[100]

He then quotes Eric Hobsbawm, who argued that national histories comprise 'anachronism, omission, decontextualization and, in extreme cases, lies'.[101] Substitute 'nation' with 'university' and the truth holds, especially for foundational institutions in settler colonies, such as the University of Melbourne. It was, after all, as late as the 1970s, 1980s and 1990s that the University's eugenicists and racists were memorialised in buildings in a manner that erased their racist pasts.

Notes

1 Arthur R Jensen, 'How Much Can We Boost IQ and Scholastic Achievement?', *Harvard Educational Review*, vol. 39, 1969, pp. 1–123.

2 HJ Eysenck, *Race, Intelligence and Education*, Temple Smith, London, 1971 (US title: *The IQ Argument*). The following year, the two lectures were published by Melbourne University Press: Arthur R Jensen, 'The Nature of Intelligence and Its Relation to Learning', *Melbourne Studies in Education*, Melbourne University Press, Carlton, 1978, pp. 107–33; HJ Eysenck, 'The Development of Personality and Its Relation to Learning', *Melbourne Studies in Education*, Melbourne University Press, Carlton, 1978, pp. 134–81.

3 Andrew M Colman, 'Race Differences in IQ: Hans Eysenck's Contribution to the Debate in the Light of Subsequent Research', *Personality and Individual Differences*, vol. 103, 2016, pp. 183–4.

4 David Derham, vice-chancellor, the University of Melbourne, The Fink Memorial Seminar 1977, memorandum to deans of faculties and heads of departments, DPD/df 3 October 1977, file 17-135-1, n.p., vice-chancellors' correspondence, University of Melbourne, unpaginated; copy in the possession of the author.

5 Ibid.

6 *Farrago*, 5 August 1977, p. 22; *Farrago*, 16 September 1977, p. 3. For a considerable selection of the broadsheets advertising demonstrations opposing their visit, see the Genetics folder in the Fink collection of political ephemera in the State Library Victoria.

7 Aboriginal Liaison Office correspondence and subject files, 2014.0117, University of Melbourne Archives, with thanks to Margot Eden.

8 *Farrago*, 12 August 1977, p. 6; *Farrago*, 9 September 1977, p. 2; *Farrago*, 16 September 1977, pp. 2, 3. These years coincided with a significant increase in state schoolchildren coming to university and an increase in radical student politics. See Richard Teese, 'Curriculum Hierarchy, Private Schooling, and the Segmentation of Australian Secondary Education, 1947–1985', *British Journal of Sociology of Education*, vol. 19, no. 3, pp. 401–17.

9 See Evan Smith, *No Platform: A History of Anti-Facism, Universities and the Limits of Free Speech*, Routledge, Oxford, 2020, esp. pp. 4–26.

10 Private correspondence with Professor Kwong Lee Dow, 2 March 2023.

11 KB Start, 'Sporting and Intellectual Success among English Secondary School Children', *International Review of Sport Sociology*, vol. 2, no. 1, March 1967, pp. 47–8.

12 Jensen, 'The Nature of Intelligence', pp. 7–8.

13 Stefan Kühl, *For the Betterment of the Race: The Rise and Fall of the International Movement for Eugenics and Racial Hygiene*, Palgrave Macmillan, New York, 2013, p. 165.

14 UNESCO, *The Race Question*, UNESCO and Its Programme no. 3, publication no. 791, Ernest Beaglehole, Juan Comas, LA Costa Pinto, Franklin Frazier,

Morris Ginsberg, Humayun Kabir, Claude Levi-Strauss and Ashley Montagu, 18 July 1950, p. 9. See M Brattain, '"Race, Racism, and Antiracism": UNESCO and the Politics of Presenting Science to the Postwar Public', *The American Historical Review*, vol. 112, no. 5, December 2007, pp. 1386–414. Or, as the American social scientist Donald T Campbell wrote of the postwar period in 1965, 'that syndrome known as "social Darwinism", generally rejected by social scientists today ... was demonstrated in the opposition of Spencer and Sumner to social welfare legislation on the grounds that it weakened the biological race by encouraging the unfit to reproduce. The eugenics movement is an outgrowth of this': Donald T Campbell, 'Variation and Selective Retention in Socio-Cultural Evolution', in Herbert R Barringer, et al. (eds), *Social Change in Developing Areas: A Reinterpretation of Evolutionary Theory*, Schenkman, Cambridge, MA, 1965, p. 21.

15 Wood Jones denied there was such an entity as 'race': see F Wood Jones, 'There Never Has Been an Aryan Race', *Australian Jewish Herald*, 26 November 1936.

16 Ashley Montagu, *Coming into Being among the Australian Aborigines: A Study of the Procreative Beliefs of the Native Tribes of Australia; with a Foreword by Bronislaw Malinowski*, Routledge, London, 1974 [1938]. For a discussion of the drafting of the statement, see Kühl, *For the Betterment of the Race*, pp. 173–80. On Malinowski, see Ross L Jones, *Anatomists of Empire: Race, Evolution and the Discovery of Human Biology in the British World*, Australian Scholarly Publishing, North Melbourne, 2020, pp. 28–33.

17 For a discussion of the influence of eugenic thinking on youth policies in the 1950s, see Judith Bessant, 'Described, Measured and Labelled: Eugenics, Youth Policy and Moral Panic in Victoria in the 1950s', *Journal of Australian Studies*, vol. 31, 1992, pp. 8–28.

18 Victor H Wallace, 'The Eugenics Society of Victoria (1936–1961)', *Eugenics Review*, vol. 53, no. 4, January 1962, p. 217.

19 Kühl, *For the Betterment of the Race*, pp. 180–94.

20 Ibid., pp. 166–7, 171–3 for Europe.

21 Wallace's report of the Annual General Meeting, 2 July 1942, Wallace papers, University of Melbourne Archives.

22 AA Calwell, 14 January 1948, The Eugenics Society of Victoria, U 41/44–16, correspondence 1937–75, Wallace papers, University of Melbourne Archives.

23 F Macfarlane Burnet, 'Migration and Race Mixture from the Genetic Angle', *Eugenics Review*, vol. 51, no. 2, July 1959, pp. 93–7.

24 Elazar Barkan, *The Retreat of Scientific Racism: Changing Concepts of Race in Britain and the United States between the Two World Wars*, Cambridge University Press, Cambridge, 1992, p. 23. For an extensive discussion of this, see Ross L Jones and Warwick Anderson, 'Wandering Anatomists and Itinerant Anthropologists: The Antipodean Sciences of Race in Britain between the Wars', *British Journal for the History of Science*, vol. 48, no. 1, March 2015, pp. 1–16.

25 Macfarlane Burnet, 'Migration and Race Mixture from the Genetic Angle', pp. 95, 97.

26 Ibid., p. 97 (author's emphasis).

27 For example, Christopher Sexton, *The Seeds of Time: The Life of Sir Macfarlane Burnet*, Oxford University Press, Melbourne, 1991, republished as *Burnet: A Life* (Oxford University Press, Melbourne, 1999); GJV Nossal, 'Sir Frank Macfarlane Burnet (1899–1985)', *Australian Dictionary of Biography*, National Centre of

Biography, Australian National University, Canberra, 2007, https://adb.anu.edu.au/biography/burnet-sir-frank-macfarlane-mac-12267 (accessed 29 October 2023).

28 F Macfarlane Burnet, 'Biology and Medicine', *Eugenics Review*, vol. 49, no. 3, September 1957, p. 131. See also F Macfarlane Burnet, '2000 A.D.: A Biologist's Thoughts on the Next Forty Years', *Eugenics Review*, vol. 53, no. 1, April 1961, pp. 25–32.

29 See RJA Berry, 'The Menace of the Birth-Rate', *Medical Journal of Australia*, vol. 2, no. 24, 15 December 1917, pp. 491–6.

30 F Macfarlane Burnet, *Australian Citizenship Convention*, Government Printer, Canberra, 1959, p. 16.

31 Australian Government, *Report of the Proceedings of the Australian Citizenship Convention*, Government Printer, Canberra, 1951, p. 6.

32 Ibid., p. 13.

33 Gwenda Tavan, *The Long, Slow Death of White Australia*, Scribe, Melbourne, 2005.

34 Australian Government, *Report of the Proceedings of the Australian Citizenship Convention*, p. 7.

35 Victor H Wallace (ed.), *Paths to Peace: A Study of War, Its Causes and Prevention*, Melbourne University Press, Carlton, 1957.

36 Ibid., pp. 294–5.

37 Ibid., p. 295.

38 Ibid., p. 290.

39 Ibid.

40 WE Agar, 'Some Eugenic Aspects of Australian Population Problems', in PD Phillips and GL Wood (eds), *The Peopling of Australia*, Dawsons of Pall Mall, London, 1968 [1928], p. 144.

41 Ibid., p. 139.

42 *University of Melbourne Calendar*, Regulations R7, 7.41. This event stimulated Wallace to seek the advice of the secretary of the English Society, CP Blacker, on research topics: CP Blacker to VH Wallace, 24 August 1949, The Eugenics Society of Victoria, U 41/44–16, correspondence 1937–75, Wallace papers, University of Melbourne Archives; *University of Melbourne Calendar 1958*, Melbourne University Press, Carlton, 1958, p. 634.

43 Kühl, *For the Betterment of the Race*, pp. 181–94

44 Wallace, 'The Eugenics Society of Victoria', p. 218.

45 AW Foster to VH Wallace, 20 February 1961, correspondence 1937–62, Wallace papers, University of Melbourne Archives.

46 GS Browne to VH Wallace, 24 February 1961, correspondence 1937–62, Wallace papers, University of Melbourne Archives.

47 WF Connell, 'George Stevenson Browne (1890–1970)', *Australian Dictionary of Biography*, National Centre of Biography, Australian National University, Canberra, 2006, https://adb.anu.edu.au/biography/browne-george-stephenson-9604 (accessed 29 October 2023).

48 GS Browne, *Australia: A General Account*, Nelson, London, 1929, esp. Chapter 14, 'The Australian Aborigines' and pp. 250 ff.

49 JR Poynter and C Rasmussen, *A Place Apart: The University of Melbourne*, Melbourne University Press, Carlton, 1996, pp. 209, 220.

50 M White to VH Wallace, 14 December 1959, correspondence 1937–62, Wallace papers, University of Melbourne Archives.

51 GCI Bertram to VH Wallace, 29 March 1961, correspondence 1937–62, Wallace papers, University of Melbourne Archives.
52 CP Blacker to VH Wallace, 1 April 1961, correspondence 1937–62, Wallace papers, University of Melbourne Archives. On White, an important international figure in genetics research, see Jim Peacock, 'Michael James White (1910–1983)', *Australian Dictionary of Biography*, National Centre of Biography, Australian National University, Canberra, 2012, https://adb.anu.edu.au/biography/white-michael-james-15875 (accessed 29 October 2023).
53 Wallace, 'The Eugenics Society of Victoria', p. 218.
54 Nossal was deputy chairman of the Council for Aboriginal Reconciliation from 1998 to 2000.
55 *Sydney Morning Herald*, 6 December 1966, p. 10.
56 *Age*, 20 April 1967, p. 7; 'Super Race', *Farrago*, vol. 45, no. 7, 21 April 1967, p. 4.
57 Agar, 'Some Eugenic Aspects'.
58 Ibid., p. 132.
59 Professor GJV Nossal, *Medical Research and the Future of Man*, Melbourne Oration and Lecture Series 1970, *Age*, 28 February 1970, p. 9.
60 GJV Nossal, 'Medical Research and the Future of Man', *Meanjin*, vol. 2, 1970, pp. 182–3.
61 See *Farrago*, 14 October 1977, p. 6; and Pam Stavropoulos, *Short Circuit: The Melbourne University Assembly, 1974–1989*, The Assembly, Parkville, 1989, pp. 153–8.
62 See Kühl, *For the Betterment of the Race*, pp. 195ff
63 It is interesting that Holocaust denial began around this time. For Melbourne, see James Waghorne and Stuart Macintyre, *Liberty: A History of Civil Liberties in Australia*, UNSW Press, Sydney, 2011, pp. 134–6.
64 David E Stannard, 'Honoring Racism: The Professional Life and Reputation of Stanley D. Porteus', *Social Process in Hawaii*, vol. 39, 1999, p. 12; Kühl, *For the Betterment of the Race*, pp. 207–8.
65 Stannard, 'Honoring Racism', p. 12; Colman, 'Race Differences', p. 188.
66 Stanley D Porteus, *The Psychology of a Primitive People: A Study of the Australian Aborigine*, Edward Arnold, London, 1931. It also produced a scandalous film, *The Blonde Captive*: see Geoffrey Gray, 'Looking for Neanderthal Man, Finding a Captive White Woman: The Story of a Documentary Film', *Health and History*, vol. 8, no. 2, 2006, pp. 69–90.
67 Stannard, 'Honoring Racism', p. 14; Stanley Porteus, 'Problems of Aboriginal Mentality', *The Mankind Quarterly*, 1965, p. 5.
68 Stannard, 'Honoring Racism', p. 14.
69 Colman, 'Race Differences'; Kühl, *For the Betterment of the Race*, pp. 213–23.
70 For a summary, see Colman, 'Race Differences'.
71 Gustav Nossal, 'Sir McFarlane Burnet: "Wisdom of an Almost Spiritual Kind"', *University News*, May 1992, p. 9.
72 Frank Macfarlane Burnet, *Endurance of Life: The Implications of Genetics for Human Life*, Cambridge University Press, Cambridge, 1978.
73 Ibid., p. 218.
74 Ibid., p. 210.
75 Ibid. (original emphasis).
76 For the genetic basis of good and evil see ibid., p. 192.
77 Ibid., p. 150.

78 Ibid., p. 153.
79 Ibid., p. 211.
80 Ibid., pp. 186–7.
81 Ibid., p. 184.
82 Ibid., p. 209.
83 Ibid., p. 160.
84 Nossal, 'Sir McFarlane Burnet', p. 9.
85 *University of Melbourne Staff News*, vol. 5, no. 6, August 1977, p. 70. See also *University of Melbourne Staff News*, vol. 6, no. 8, August 1977, p. 105.
86 Russell McGregor, 'Representations of the "Half-Caste" in the Australian Scientific Literature of the 1930s', *Journal of Australian Studies*, no. 36, March 1993, pp. 51–64; Russell McGregor, *Imagined Destinies: Aboriginal Australians and the Doomed Race Theory 1880–1939*, Melbourne University Press, Carlton, 1997.
87 Philip Ayres, *Owen Dixon*, Miegunyah Press, Melbourne, 2003, p. 161.
88 Kühl, *For the Betterment of the Race*, p. 165; Harry M Schapiro, *Population Control Politics: Women, Sterilization, and Reproductive Choice*, Temple University Press, Philadelphia, 1985; Gavin Schaffer, *Racial Science and British Society, 1930–62*, Palgrave Macmillan, Basingstoke, 2008—Schaffer argues that, in the years since the end of World War II, 'the idea of race and the appropriateness of its usage have hardly been clarified': p. 1; Tracy Teslow, *Constructing Race: The Science of Bodies and Cultures in American Anthropology*, Cambridge University Press, New York, 2014; Alison Bashford, 'Epilogue: Where Did Eugenics Go?', in Alison Bashford and Philippa Devine (eds), *The Oxford History of Eugenics*, Oxford University Press, Oxford, 2010, pp. 539–59; Campbell, 'Variation and Selective Retention', p. 21.
89 SV Sewell, 'The Evolution of the Language Mechanism', in *Transactions of the British Medical Association Congress*, 1923, Section VII, Neurology and Psychiatry, supplement to the *Medical Journal of Australia*, 7 June 1924, p. 391.
90 Lord Baltimore Hotel, Baltimore (prior to 16 December 1932), correspondence, USA, Canada, Britain & Europe 1932–33, Tate Papers, University of Melbourne Archives.
91 McGregor, *Imagined Destinies.*
92 See also Mark B Adams, 'Toward a Comparative History of Eugenics', in Mark B Adams (ed.), *The Wellborn Science: Eugenics in Germany, France, Brazil and Russia*, Oxford University Press, New York, 1990, p. 219; Kühl, *For the Betterment of the Race*, pp. 198–206.
93 Stephen Jay Gould, 'The Smoking Gun of Eugenics', in Stephen Jay Gould, *Dinosaur in a Hay Stack*, Penguin, London, 1997 [1996], pp. 302–3. Since Gould's attack—or perhaps because of it—in 2020 Gonville and Caius College Cambridge announced that a 1989 stained-glass window commemorating Fisher's work would be removed because of his connection with eugenics. In the same year, University College London also removed his name from its Centre for Computational Biology.
94 WEH Stanner, *White Man Got No Dreaming: Essays 1938–1973*, ANU Press, Canberra, 1979. This book was published by ANU Press between 1965 and 1991. This republication is part of the digitisation project being carried out by Scholarly Information Services/Library and ANU Press; see https://openresearch-repository.anu.edu.au/handle/1885/114726 (accessed 29 October 2023). Stanner's lecture is considered to be one of the most significant in the series and this has

been well documented many times: see Ann Curthoys, 'WEH Stanner and the Historians', in M Hinkson and J Beckett (eds), *An Appreciation of Difference: W.E.H. Stanner and Aboriginal Australia*, Aboriginal Studies Press, Canberra, 2009, pp. 440–3.

95 Stanner, *White Man Got No Dreaming*, p. 207.

96 And the silence continues: see Roderick D Buchanan, *Melbourne School of Psychological Sciences: A Seventieth Anniversary History*, University of Melbourne, Parkville, 2016, https://psychologicalsciences.unimelb.edu.au/__data/assets/pdf_file/0019/2153440/Final_Digital_Version_Web_Quality.pdf (accessed 29 October 2023). For Berry's statement about the importance of eugenics in his career, see RJA Berry, *Chance and Circumstance*, unpublished autobiography, University of Melbourne Medical Library, Parkville, 1954, pp. 189–90. Also see KF Russell, 'Richard James Arthur Berry, 1867–1962', in Geoffrey Kenny and Harold Attwood (eds), *Festschrift for Kenneth Fitzpatrick Russell*, Queensberry Hill Press, Melbourne, 1978, pp. 25–45; and KF Russell, 'Richard James Berry (1867–1962)', *Australian Dictionary of Biography*, National Centre of Biography, Australian National University, Canberra, 2006, https://adb.anu.edu.au/biography/berry-richard-james-5220 (accessed 29 October 2023).

97 Stefan Kühl, *The Nazi Connection: Eugenics, American Racism, and German National Socialism*, Oxford University Press, New York, 1994, Chapter 1.

98 Robert A Wilson, *The Eugenic Mind Project*, MIT Press, Cambridge, MA, 2018; Robert A Wilson, 'Eugenics Never Went Away', *Aeon*, 2018; Ross L Jones, 'Boyer Lectures: The New Eugenics Is the Same as the Old, Just in Fancier Clothes', *The Conversation*, 15 October 2018, https://theconversation.com/boyer-lectures-the-new-eugenics-is-the-same-as-the-old-just-in-fancier-clothes-103165 (accessed 29 October 2023); Gideon Lewis-Kraus, 'Can Progressives Be Convinced That Genetics Matters?', *New Yorker*, 6 September 2021, https://www.newyorker.com/magazine/2021/09/13/can-progressives-be-convinced-that-genetics-matters (accessed 29 October 2023).

99 CP Blacker to VH Wallace, 24 August 1949, correspondence 1937–75, U 41/44—16, Wallace papers, University of Melbourne Archives. The use of the word 'eugenics' and associated words is significantly reduced in public media, such as newspapers, after 1945. See my discussion earlier concerning Kühl, *For the Betterment of the Race*, and his description of Blacker's eugenics: p. 94. At the Eugenics Society's demise in 1961, Wallace deposited its records in the University of Melbourne Archives and forwarded the small sum of money remaining in the Society's accounts to the Eugenics Society of Great Britain. GCI Bertram (then general secretary to the Society) accepted the money on the basis that it would be held in trust so that '[i]n the event of a successor society being revivified in Australia it could then feel that there is a sum of money available to be drawn upon': GCI Bertram to VH Wallace, 29 March 1961, correspondence 1937–62, Wallace papers, University of Melbourne Archives. This suggestion would not have seemed unreasonable to the Society's members considering that the main benefaction to the Eugenics Society of Great Britain was by an Australian, Henry Twitchen. In 1931 he had bequeathed £57 000 to the English Society in addition to the £1000 he had donated per annum throughout much of his life: see GA Nicholson and MT Nicholson, 'Henry Twitchen: An Australian in the Eugenics Movement', in J Covacevich et al. (eds), *History, Heritage and Health: Proceedings of the Fourth Biennial Conference of the Australian Society of the History of Medicine, Norfolk*

Island, 2–9 July 1995, Australian Society of the History of Medicine, Queensland, 1996, pp. 381–3.

100 Bain Attwood, *Telling the Truth about Aboriginal History*, Allen & Unwin, Sydney, 2005, p. 13.

101 Ibid., p. 13, quoting Eric Hobsbawm, *On History*, Abacus, London, 1998, pp. 6, 357.

IV

Indigenous Knowledge

Indigenous Knowledge

ROSS L JONES and SIMON FARLEY

On 20 August 1860, an expedition departed from Parkville, not far from the University of Melbourne. Such expeditions were at the cutting edge of colonial science, an important tool in settlers' attempts to 'tame' the Australian continent.[1] Robert O'Hara Burke had been chosen to lead a group of explorers seeking a route from the south of the continent to the north. It was the most lavishly funded and equipped expedition ever undertaken in the Australian colonies and was supposedly fully self-sufficient, being a product of the huge wealth that had flooded the colony of Victoria during the gold rushes. The establishment of the University of Melbourne in 1853 was another such product of this self-confidence. The motivation for this exercise seemed to be as much colonial rivalry as anything else, but scientific discovery was certainly one of the aims, as it had been partially financed by the Royal Society of Victoria. At the final count, it would cost well over £60 000 and seven lives, including those of Burke and his second in command, William John Wills.[2] The story of Burke and Wills—both the narrative of the journey and the subsequent plethora of histories and theories surrounding it—illustrates the wider, messy and often tragic intersection between Indigenous and settler systems of knowledge.

On or about 28 June 1861, Burke and Wills died of starvation surrounded by plenty, at what the settlers called Coopers Creek. At the end of their lives, having previously strenuously rejected Indigenous knowledge, to the point of shooting at any Aboriginal person trying to make contact, they found themselves forced to accept the help of the healthy, well-fed Yandruwandha people on whose land they were camped.[3] Along with John King, who survived the ordeal, Burke and Wills had frequent contact with the Yandruwandha in their final weeks. By the end, they were subsisting almost entirely on nardoo seeds, a nourishing staple for many Indigenous peoples in the arid centre of the continent. But while the Yandruwandha were living in perfect health, the 'explorers' grew constipated and weak. Even when accepting help, they were unable or unwilling to gain the knowledge needed to properly prepare the food to rid it of toxins. After his companions' deaths, King convinced a group of Yandruwandha to let him live with them and, despite his weakened state, he was able to do so for months before his 'rescue' and return to settler society. Settler arrogance in the face of Indigenous knowledge has often had such grave consequences.[4]

Settler Australians and Indigenous Knowledge

All across this continent—from lush rainforests to bleak deserts, from the steamy savannahs of the Top End to the sub-polar southern shores of Tasmania—Indigenous peoples have devised ways to live and thrive. And though ecosystems and landscapes have shifted time and again over the last 65 000 years, there is no doubt that much of what we settlers call 'Indigenous knowledge' has been tried and tested over centuries, even millennia. Indigenous peoples developed profound understandings of their local climates, animal behaviour and the healing properties of plants; they built sophisticated tools and infrastructure; they contemplated their place in the cosmos and created many types of society different from modern capitalist models. The importance and the ingenuity of these bodies of knowledge are difficult to overstate.[5]

Since the invasion, settler scientists have selectively drawn on this expertise. In this way, Indigenous knowledge was appropriated by settlers, but settlers rarely showed any appreciation of the worldviews or systems of thought that underpinned this knowledge. Nineteenth-century naturalists were dependent on the specimens gathered for them by Indigenous collectors—the University of Melbourne's Walter Baldwin Spencer and Ferdinand Mueller among them. Spencer told a student audience in 1895 that the famous Horn Expedition to northern Australia would not have collected any specimens other than insects without the expertise of Indigenous guides.[6] Later naturalists, such as Donald Thomson, likewise found themselves using Indigenous ecological knowledge to supplement their own research, as is discussed in the Long and Jones chapter, and the Winkel and Fijn chapter in this volume.[7]

Over the years, a few scholars have lambasted their fellow settlers for their ecological irresponsibility, comparing them unfavourably with Indigenous stewards of the land. In 1934, for example, the professor of anatomy at the University, Frederic Wood Jones, decried the 'thoroughly vandalistic policy' by which the 'white colonist ... made a profit out of the destruction of native fauna and flora'.[8] More recently, ethnobotanists such as Beth Gott—a University of Melbourne alumna—have sought to bridge the gap between Indigenous knowledge and settler science.[9] Nor is this limited to the life sciences. In 2022, the University of Melbourne's Duane Hamacher compiled a book entitled *The First Astronomers*, detailing the ways in which Aboriginal and Torres Strait Islander cultures have used their observations of the planets and stars. He shares authorship of the work with six Indigenous elders: Ghillar Michael Anderson, John Barsa, David Bosun, Ron Day, Segar Passi and Alo Tapim. (See the chapter by Duane Hamacher, Amanda Goldfarb, Bridget Kelly and Emma Barnett in this volume.)

But for the most part, Indigenous knowledge has been derided, where it hasn't been erased entirely. Settler Australians might have acknowledged Aboriginal tracking skills and other forms of 'bushcraft', perhaps even admired the ingenuity incarnated in the boomerang, but awareness of Indigenous knowledge beyond these was limited.[10] Over the last decade or so, however, popular awareness of and enthusiasm for Indigenous knowledge has greatly increased—we might call this, tongues slightly in our cheeks, the '*Dark Emu* effect', although its origins and ramifications are far broader than the trajectory of one book.[11] Tertiary students can now be awarded a Bachelor of Indigenous Knowledge from Southern Cross University or a major in Indigenous Science and Knowledges as part of a Bachelor of Science at the Australian National University; the University of Melbourne's own Indigenous Knowledge Institute was launched in 2020 (see the chapter in this volume by Aaron Corn) and in 2023 it offered a PhD in Indigenous Knowledge, the first of its kind in Australia. The new esteem for Indigenous knowledge in settler society is welcome, but it is not without its pitfalls.

Indigenous Knowledge or Indigenous Science?

The interactions—past and present—and parallels between Indigenous knowledge and Western science are increasingly studied, and the term 'Indigenous science' is becoming commonplace in Australasia and the Americas. Some commentators make tired and wrong-headed claims that Indigenous knowledge is insufficiently 'objective' or 'rigorous' to be equated to science.[12] But not all arguments in this vein are based in a racist derogation of Indigenous intellect. Science educator and Jingili man Joe Sambono has argued that

> all groups of humans around the world and throughout history have hypothesised, experimented, made empirical observations, gathered evidence, recognised patterns, verified through repetition, made inferences and predictions, and developed branches of knowledge that helped them to make sense of the world around them and their place within it.[13]

To the authors, this seems beyond doubt. But it is unclear whether all such processes of producing knowledge should be called 'science'. To begin with, there is the fundamental matter of what we even mean by the word 'science'. Some have defined the term broadly—perhaps *too* broadly—as 'the pursuit of knowledge'.[14] But 'science', as we usually mean it, refers to a particular set of values and practices that has its origin in seventeenth-century Western Europe. Some scholars call this particular way of producing knowledge 'Western Modern Science' (sometimes referred to by the shorthand 'WMS', or more commonly known as Western science) to distinguish it from other forms of knowledge production that we can describe as 'scientific'.[15] The Intergovernmental Science-Policy Platform on Biodiversity and Ecosystem Services defines 'Western science' as

> knowledge typically generated in universities, research institutions and private firms following paradigms and methods typically associated with the 'scientific method' consolidated in Post-Renaissance Europe on the basis of wider and more ancient roots. It is typically transmitted through scientific journals and scholarly books. Some of its central tenets are observer independence, replicable findings, systematic scepticism, and transparent research methodologies with standard units and categories.[16]

It is important for the reader to understand that Western science is not beyond critique. The science transported from Western Europe by settler colonisers—the science that is proposed as the objective benchmark against which Indigenous knowledge is unfavourably compared—has been subjected to decades of sustained analysis and criticism.

As just one preliminary example, widespread attention was first drawn to the so-called 'replicability crisis' within the field of psychology in the early 2010s.[17] A 2012 article by two researchers argued it was 'almost certain that fallacious results are entering the literature at worrisome rates'.[18] They went on to warn:

> Unfortunately, however, there is every reason to believe that the great majority of errors that do enter the literature will persist uncorrected

> indefinitely, given current practices. Errors will be propagated through textbooks and review articles, and people interested in a topic will be misinformed for generations.[19]

Similar issues have been found in other scientific disciplines. A 2019 meta-analysis of articles in hydrology and water resource management estimated 'that results might be reproduced for only 0.6% to 6.8% of all 1989 articles'; although this is an extreme case, troubling data has also emerged from fields such as cancer research.[20]

But this is a methodological problem within the parameters of Western science. Many have criticised those parameters themselves. As Warwick Anderson has written:

> Until the middle of the twentieth century, few could even imagine a critical history of science. Rather, science appeared to consist in a transcendent mode of inquiry or method of engaging with the world that simply unfolded, developing progressively and diffusing as Europe expanded.[21]

Over the last sixty years, however, this has changed. In his watershed book *The Structure of Scientific Revolutions*, published in 1962, the philosopher Thomas S Kuhn eloquently debunked the notion that science inevitably unfurled its knowledge at the instigation of rational experimentation.[22] A door was opened, making room for other philosophers, Paul Feyerabend and Bruno Latour prominent among them, to problematise science and its status in 'Western' societies. By the 1980s, entire fields of academic endeavour had sprung up around these topics, such as Science and Technology Studies, and the History and Philosophy of Science. No aspect of science is exempt—the 'advances' touted by medicine, physics, evolutionary biology and ecology have all come into serious question, often by scientists within these very fields.[23] For many social scientists, historians and philosophers, it has become impossible to take the findings of Western science as necessarily objective, intrinsically reliable or universally true.

The Lure of Scientism

Australia is a scientistic society. Most of us are taught from an early age to value the (modern, Western) scientific method and the knowledge it generates—science tells us what is real and what is not, and the role of scientists as arbiters of reality is often dogmatically insisted upon. If we want to say something is good or true, we say it is scientific: 'Studies have shown …', 'Experts recommend …' and so on. By describing Indigenous knowledge as science, people are trying to legitimate this knowledge; it is a way of saying, to paraphrase Tyson Yunkaporta, an artist and academic from the Apalech clan, 'See, we've been [scientists] for thousands of years, so our knowledge matters. You [settlers] wrecked all that, you bunch of bastards.'[24] Such an impulse is deeply understandable. But it is possible to assert that Indigenous knowledge and settler knowledge are equally valid without reducing the former to fit into the latter. Academic and Palyku woman Aurora Milroy writes:

> [T]he term 'Indigenous ecological knowledge' sticks in my throat … it reduces our system of knowledge into something discrete, rational, linear and easy to slot into existing western frames. The research that gains the most interest in this field—noting that even this research is often dismissed or devalued by white academics—tends to be ecological knowledge with clear cause and effect: cultural burning prevents wildfires; native plants treat illnesses. But Indigenous knowledge is more than this, and also not this at all. It is non-linear, cyclical, holistic … One of my greatest concerns about the growing interest in Indigenous knowledges is that they will only be recognised when they can be verified through western frameworks …[25]

In other words, there are important differences between Western science and Indigenous knowledge, and in this case, 'difference' does not necessarily imply deficit.[26] Western science is hard to extricate from colonialism and capitalism, systems of power that have led this continent and this planet into one catastrophe after another.[27] As Milroy suggests, the Indigenous knowledge that is celebrated by settler scientists tends to be that which, in some way or another, is also useful for the perpetuation of these systems.[28] But not all Indigenous knowledge is easily coopted. While Indigenous knowledge and Western science often make similar observations, come to similar conclusions, and complement each other in compelling ways, there are also significant points of disjuncture. Indigenous cultures have produced so much knowledge about the stars, about plants, about fire, but they have also produced much knowledge about sorcery, spirits and monsters.[29] Many settler scientists would deny that such things exist, using 'science' as the justification. This can have practical and even painful ramifications for research. Although there are generative overlaps between, say, ecological science and the Aboriginal concept of Country, there are ways of talking about and relating to Country that even the most open-minded practitioner of Western science would find difficult to write about in a journal article or speak about at a conference. It goes with knowledge as it has so often gone with Indigenous land and lives: settlers take what they like and dismiss the rest. This only becomes truer when Indigenous knowledge is challenging to how we settlers understand ourselves and our ways of life.

To be absolutely clear: none of this should be taken to imply that Indigenous knowledge is inferior to Western science. We only want to stress that the differences between them should not be papered over. Just as Western science is entangled with a 'Western' worldview, so, too, is Indigenous knowledge bound up with its own cultures, and there are myriad methodological and ethical risks in trying to separate the data from its context. Perhaps, rather than referring to Indigenous knowledge as 'science' in an attempt to make it more palatable to settlers, we should humbly reframe Western science as a form of 'settler knowledge'—a step towards a more pluralistic world, in which many truths can be allowed to stand alongside each other, even when they diverge.[30] As Brazilian scholars Charbel Niño El-Hani and Fábio Pedro Souza de Ferreira Bandeira argue, 'the solution does not lie in a broadening of the concept of science, but in putting scientism directly into question'.[31]

A Challenge to the Academy

These are difficult issues for a university to grapple with. After all, the University of Melbourne is itself embedded in a culture of scientism, colonialism and capitalism. As this very book shows, many academics at the University have failed to incorporate—or even acknowledge—Indigenous knowledge in their work. This is, perhaps, not only because the value of Indigenous knowledge has been dismissed and denigrated, but also because, as a rule, settler academics have lacked the imagination and the courage to step outside their own worldview. Once we start to question the paramountcy of science—once we start to ask whether other, non-Western worldviews might not be equally valid, equally 'real'—then the nature of academic endeavour changes.

Would this be so bad? As several chapters in this book demonstrate, many of those who did see themselves as adventurers participating in the great quest for Truth produced knowledge with vile implications—race science and eugenics prime among them. Along with Stephen Jay Gould, we wonder what 'current efforts, now commanding millions of research dollars and the full attention of many of our best scientists, will later be exposed as full failures based on false premises'?[32] In its time, this knowledge was seen as rigorous and objective, not culturally and politically influenced, because science was (and remains) widely seen as 'value-neutral'.[33] But even if Western science is all that it is often claimed to be, what good is it if it is only used to keep vulnerable and marginalised people in their powerless place?

All this said, we are settlers, and if Indigenous people want to call their own knowledge 'science', then it is not our place to object. The past of science at the University of Melbourne—as in the wider world—is mired in colonialism and racism, but that does not mean the future of science will look the same way. As more settler scientists learn to value Indigenous knowledge, and as more Indigenous scientists take leading roles in our research institutions, these debates may soon be seen as abstract and archaic. But for now, they demand our serious consideration.

Notes

1 It was an international movement: see Robert E Kohler, *All Creatures: Naturalists, Collectors, and Biodiversity, 1850–1950*, Princeton University Press, Princeton, 2006.

2 There are many accounts. See, especially, Kathleen Fitzpatrick, 'The Burke and Wills Expedition and the Royal Society of Victoria', *Historical Studies: Australia and New Zealand*, vol. 10, no. 40, May 1963, pp. 470–8.

3 Many explorers relied on Indigenous expertise. On Burke's intransigence, see Henry Reynolds, *With the White People: The Crucial Role of Aborigines in the Exploration and Development of Australia*, Penguin, Melbourne, 1990, p. 33

4 This account and the interpretation of these events are largely drawn from Philip Clarke, who writes: 'The tragedy of the Burke and Wills expedition highlights the importance of the proper transfer of landscape-based knowledge from the Indigenous occupants to the European newcomer': Philip A Clarke, 'The Use and Abuse of Aboriginal Ecological Knowledge', in Ian D Clark and Fred Cahir (eds), *The Aboriginal Story of Burke and Wills*, CSIRO Publishing, Collingwood, 2013, pp. 90–3, 100–3.

5 For just one example among many, see William J Ellwood, John B Campbell and George J Susino, 'Agricultural Hunter-Gatherers: Food-Getting, Domestication and Farming in Pre-Colonial Australia', in Jan Michal Burdukiewicz, Krzysztof Cyrek, Piotr Dyczek and Karol Szymczak (eds), *Understanding the Past: Papers Offered to Stefan K. Kozlowski*, University of Warsaw, Warsaw, 2009, pp. 115–22.

6 'Science Club Notes', *Alma Mater*, 3 September 1895, p. 14.

7 For Thomson, see Donald F Thomson, *Birds of Cape York Peninsula*, H.J. Green, Melbourne, 1935. More generally, see Penny Olsen and Lynette Russell, *Australia's First Naturalists: Indigenous Peoples' Contribution to Early Zoology*, NLA Publishing, Canberra, 2019.

8 Frederic Wood Jones, *Australia's Vanishing Race*, Angus & Robertson, Sydney, 1934, pp. 16–7.

9 Linden Gillbank, *From System Garden to Scientific Research: The University of Melbourne's School of Botany under its First Two Professors (1906–1973)*, School

of Botany, University of Melbourne, Parkville, 2010, pp. 16, 21; 'Vale Dr Beth Gott AM', Monash University, Clayton, Vic., 26 July 2022, https://www.monash.edu/vale/home/articles/vale-dr-beth-gott-am (accessed 29 October 2023); Zane Ma Rhea and Lynette Russell, 'Introduction: Understanding Koorie Plant Knowledge through the Ethnobotanic Lens—A Tribute to Beth Gott', *Artefact*, vol. 35, 2012, pp. 3–9.

10 Joe Sambono, 'Indigenous Science Goes Far beyond Boomerangs and Spears', *IndigenousX*, 11 November 2018, https://indigenousx.com.au/indigenous-science-goes-far-beyond-boomerangs-and-spears (accessed 29 October 2023).

11 The following should not be considered an exhaustive list: Bill Gammage, *The Biggest Estate on Earth: How Aborigines Made Australia*, Allen & Unwin, Crows Nest, NSW, 2011; Bruce Pascoe, *Dark Emu*, Magabala Books, Broome, 2014; Tyson Yunkaporta, *Sand Talk: How Indigenous Thinking Can Save the World*, Text, Melbourne, 2019. Thames & Hudson's 'First Knowledges' series of books (2020–23), edited by Margo Neale, provides further examples, including a collaboration between Gammage and Pascoe.

12 For a recent, controversial example of this kind of argument, see Kendall Clements et al., 'In Defence of Science', *Listener*, 31 July 2021, p. 4. The debate this letter generated was of sufficient magnitude to be recorded for posterity in *Wikipedia*: 'Listener Letter on Science Controversy', Wikimedia Foundation, October 2023, https://en.wikipedia.org/wiki/Listener_letter_on_science_controversy (accessed 29 October 2023). Further examples of this kind of critique are cited in George Nicholas, 'An Uneasy Alliance: Indigenous Traditional Knowledge Enriches Science', *The Conversation*, 19 February 2019, https://theconversation.com/an-uneasy-alliance-indigenous-traditional-knowledge-enriches-science-109212 (accessed 29 October 2023).

13 Sambono, 'Indigenous Science'.

14 For example, Jesse Pop, 'How Indigenous Knowledge Advances Modern Science and Technology', *The Conversation*, 3 January 2018, https://theconversation.com/how-indigenous-knowledge-advances-modern-science-and-technology-89351 (accessed 29 October 2023). For similar examples, see Charbel Niño El-Hani and Fábio Pedro Souza de Ferreira Bandeira, 'Valuing Indigenous Knowledge: To Call It "Science" Will Not Help', *Cultural Studies of Science Education*, vol. 3, 2008, p. 753.

15 'MWS' ('Modern Western Science') is also occasionally used.

16 Intergovernmental Science-Policy Platform on Biodiversity and Ecosystem Services, 'Western Science', IPBES, https://ipbes.net/glossary/western-science (accessed 29 October 2023).

17 Harold Pashler and Eric-Jan Wagenmakers, 'Editors' Introduction to the Special Section on Replicability in Psychological Science: A Crisis of Confidence?', *Perspectives on Psychological Science*, vol. 7, no. 6, November 2012, pp. 528–30.

18 Harold Pashler and Christine R Harris, 'Is the Replicability Crisis Overblown? Three Arguments Examined', *Perspectives on Psychological Science*, vol. 7, no. 6, November 2012, p. 535.

19 Ibid.

20 James H Stagge et al., 'Assessing Data Availability and Research Reproducibility in Hydrology and Water Resources', *Scientific Data*, vol. 6, article no. 190030, February 2019; Aaron Mobley et al., 'A Survey on Data Reproducibility in Cancer Research Provides Insights into Our Limited Ability to Translate Findings from the

Laboratory to the Clinic', *PLoS One*, vol. 8, no. 5, May 2013, e63221; 'Challenges in Irreproducible Research', *Nature*, 18 October 2018, http://www.nature.com/news/reproducibility-1.17552 (accessed 29 October 2023).

21 Warwick Anderson, 'Forum: Decolonizing Histories in Theory and Practice—An Introduction', *History and Theory*, vol. 59, no. 3, September 2020, p. 371; Jesse Pop, 'Indigenous Knowledge'.

22 Thomas S Kuhn, *The Structure of Scientific Revolutions*, Chicago University Press, Chicago, 1962.

23 To list only a few examples: James Colgrove, 'The McKeown Thesis: A Historical Controversy and Its Enduring Influence', *American Journal of Public Health*, vol. 92, no. 5, May 2002, pp. 725–9; Sabine Hossenfelder, 'No One in Physics Dares Say So, But the Race to Invent New Particles is Pointless', *Guardian*, 26 September 2022, https://www.theguardian.com/commentisfree/2022/sep/26/physics-particles-physicists (accessed 29 October 2023); Kevin Laland et al., 'Does Evolutionary Theory Need a Rethink?', *Nature*, vol. 514, 2014, pp. 161–4; Mark A Davis et al., 'Don't Judge Species on Their Origins', *Nature*, vol. 474, 2011, pp. 153–4; David Sepkoski, *Catastrophic Thinking*, University of Chicago Press, Chicago, 2020; Ken Thompson, *Where Do Camels Belong?*, Profile Books, London, 2014; Ken Thompson, *Do We Need Pandas?*, Green Books, Foxhole, UK, 2010.

24 Yunkaporta, *Sand Talk*, p. 27.

25 Aurora Milroy, 'Stories in the Waterpipes', *Emu Sky*, n.d., https://emusky.culturalcommons.edu.au/blak_yarn/stories-waterpipes-aurora-milroy (accessed 29 October 2023).

26 For an overview of these differences from a global perspective, see Douglas Nakashima and Marie Roue, 'Indigenous Knowledge, Peoples and Sustainable Practice', in Peter Timmerman (ed.), *Encyclopedia of Global Environmental Change*, vol. 5, John Wiley & Sons, Chichester, 2002, pp. 2–4. For a discussion of how these differences can be complementary, see George Nicholas, 'It's Taken Thousands of Years, But Western Science Is Finally Catching up to Traditional Knowledge', *The Conversation*, 15 February 2018, https://theconversation.com/its-taken-thousands-of-years-but-western-science-is-finally-catching-up-to-traditional-knowledge-90291 (accessed 29 October 2023).

27 The literature on these matters is abundant, but for some general overviews, see Rohan Deb Roy, 'Decolonise Science: Time to End Another Imperial Era', *The Conversation*, 5 April 2018, https://theconversation.com/decolonise-science-time-to-end-another-imperial-era-89189 (accessed 29 October 2023); and Lukas Rieppel, Eugenia Lean and William Deringer, 'Introduction: The Entangled Histories of Science and Capitalism', *Osiris*, vol. 33, no. 1, 2018, pp. 1–24. Although it is less salient to the immediate thrust of the argument here, we could easily add sexism to this list. See, for example, Carolyn Merchant, *The Death of Nature: Women, Ecology, and the Scientific Revolution*, Harper & Row, San Francisco, 1980; and Londa L Schiebinger, *Nature's Body: Gender in the Making of Modern Science*, Rutgers University Press, New Brunswick, 2004.

28 In a similar vein, researcher, storyteller and Barkandji woman Zena Cumpston writes, 'Much of the recent heightened interest in our [i.e., Indigenous] knowledge is highly extractive and damaging for Aboriginal and Torres Strait Islander peoples and our communities, as powerfully evidenced in the alarming lack of benefits we have enjoyed from the explosion of the "bush food" industry': Zena Cumpston, Michael-Shawn Fletcher and Lesley Head, *Plants: Past, Present and*

Future, Thames & Hudson, Port Melbourne, 2022, p. 14. For issues surrounding Indigenous knowledge and intellectual property from a global perspective, see Nakashima and Roue, 'Indigenous Knowledge', p. 9.

29 There have been some recent compelling calls from within the history discipline to take such 'unbelieved' (unbelieved by modern Westerners, that is) phenomena and entities more seriously. See especially Luke Clossey et al., 'The Unbelieved and Historians, Part I: A Challenge', *History Compass*, vol. 14, no. 12, December 2016, pp. 594–602; and Warwick Anderson, 'Forum', p. 3.

30 Compare the 'free society' described in Paul Feyerabend, *Against Method*, Verso, London, 1993, pp. 225–9.

31 El-Hani and Bandeira, 'Valuing Indigenous Knowledge', pp. 753, 755.

32 Stephen Jay Gould, *Eight Little Piggies*, Vintage, London, 2007, p. 187.

33 The belief in science's neutrality has been repeatedly assailed for decades. See, for example, Leslie Stevenson, 'Is Scientific Research Value-Neutral?', *Inquiry*, vol. 32, no. 2, 1989, pp. 213–22.

The Invisible Collectors

ROHAN LONG and ROSS L JONES

The development of zoological collections in the nineteenth and twentieth centuries is inexorably linked with the history and mechanisms of colonialism. The modern concept of a natural history museum has been heavily influenced by the natural history arm of the British Museum, an increasingly notorious storehouse of artefacts stolen from First Nations people. Only through the lens of colonial history do these outwardly benign collections make sense. London's Natural History Museum is full of Australian flora and fauna; the Museum für Naturkunde in Berlin has more gorilla specimens than any museum in Africa. As late as the mid-1950s it was the British Museum's official advice to would-be collectors in exotic climes that they should use 'natives' to do collecting work, thereby reducing their own workload merely to selecting localities and supervising the packing of specimens. The authors also recommended keeping preservative spirits under lock and key, lest the 'natives' attempt to drink them.[1]

It is impossible to overestimate the importance of the trade in specimens to the institutions of learning in the centres of empire—in Australia's case primarily Britain. They provided the raw material upon which theorising depended and they were the currency that allowed those in the outposts to buy honours (such as fellowships of the learned societies) or the opportunity for preferment in an ancient university.[2] Occasionally these itinerant scientists benefited in their research and reputation from their obsessive and voluminous collecting—such as Charles Darwin and Alfred Russel Wallace, the prophets of evolution. For many Australian workers, it was the only pathway for advancement within the empire science project.[3]

Even among the new and unfamiliar worlds comprising the British Empire, the striking novelty of Australia's fauna held particular thrall for museum collectors. The continent's seemingly bizarre creatures were completely at odds with a zoological paradigm that had been formulated solely on animal groups of the 'Old World'. Natural history collecting was well established by the nineteenth century. Huge numbers of specimens were used to study life's diversity, and there was demand for stocks of antipodean species to supplement the museum cabinets of Europe. Even common Australian species were valuable—'he can get Echidna material almost whenever he wants', a younger scientist remarked admiringly of Melbourne's Baldwin Spencer.[4] From the 1880s, the founders of Melbourne's Biology School sent specimens to the British Museum and when a departmental museum was established in the 1890s, donations were reciprocated from that institution, as well as from the Oxford University Museum of Natural History, Manchester Museum, and the Royal College of Science.[5]

From the earliest days of zoological collecting in Australia, however, it was Aboriginal people who worked as collectors, not the scientists who gained the rewards. Sometimes these arrangements were relatively benevolent; at other times the collectors were manipulated and abused. Regardless of the working conditions, almost without exception, Aboriginal collectors were not credited for their work.[6]

In some instances, Indigenous collectors were exploited on an industrial scale. In 1884, Cambridge University zoologist William Hay Caldwell travelled to Queensland, determined finally to solve the heretofore unknown reproductive processes of monotremes, the order of mammals that comprises the platypus and echidna. Backed by the largesse of the Royal Society, at the peak of his operations Caldwell employed 150 Indigenous collectors from the Burnett River area, who supplied him with platypus (*Ornithorhynchus anatinus*), short-beaked echidna (*Tachyglossus aculeatus*) and Queensland lungfish (*Neoceratodus forsteri*)—another unique Australian animal coveted by colonial naturalists. The collectors were unnamed and uncredited but were probably Gureng Gureng, Waka Waka or Wuli Wuli people.[7] Women and men were involved in the work, the former focusing on collecting lungfish, the latter on echidna. To accommodate the scale of the project, a camp was established as a base of operations and Caldwell became the local people's main source of supplies. Between July and August 1885, the team of collectors secured around 1400 echidnas (Caldwell didn't specify how many platypus and lungfish were collected). Caldwell had obtained this bounty by cheating the collectors out of their labour, as he stated unabashedly in his paper to the Royal Society in 1888:

> The blacks were paid half-a-crown for every female, but the price of flour, tea, and sugar, which I sold to them, rose with the supply of Echidna.

> The half-crowns were, therefore, always just sufficient to buy food enough to keep the lazy blacks hungry.[8]

In the same paper, the zoologist freely admitted that 'without the services of these people I should have had little chance of success'. Caldwell is memorialised to this day as the man who solved the mystery of monotreme reproduction. Of course, the people on whom he relied to collect the specimens already knew exactly how platypuses and echidnas reproduced—their communities had held this knowledge for thousands of years.

The zoological collections of the University of Melbourne, and Melbourne Museum, which was originally part of the University, were no exception to the colonial practice of exploiting Indigenous collectors. Most of the University's zoological specimens can be found in the Tiegs Zoology Museum, established by zoologist and anthropologist Baldwin Spencer, and later named in honour of professor Oscar Werner Tiegs who substantially reinvigorated the collection. Another major collection can be found in the Harry Brookes Allen Museum of Anatomy and Pathology, derived primarily from the activities of anatomist Frederic Wood Jones during the 1920s and 1930s. Although best known for his anthropological work, Wood Jones' protégé Donald Thomson also amassed a significant zoological collection. During his time at the University, he obtained around 2000 biological specimens from field trips to Cape York, Arnhem Land, and the Great Sandy Desert and Gibson Desert of Western Australia. All of these University museum administrators saw their collections grow due to the skills and expertise of unacknowledged Indigenous collectors.

Baldwin Spencer and the Horn Expedition

The Horn Scientific Expedition was the first expedition to central Australia with primarily scientific aims. Employed as zoologist and photographer, Spencer set out for the Country of the Arrernte and Luritja people in May 1894. The group spent about four months travelling through country largely unknown to Europeans, with the collection of natural history specimens as one of their key objectives. One hundred and sixteen animal specimens from the Horn Expedition are recorded as having been contributed to the University's Zoology Museum, and this subcollection represents one of the biggest single collection events in the Museum's history.[9] Most were catalogued and added soon after Spencer's return. Around this time, Spencer also sent consignments of central Australian zoological specimens to Frederick McCoy at the

Melbourne Museum (then situated on the University's Parkville campus) and to the Natural History Museum in London.[10]

The specimens that the Zoology Museum received from the expedition were of high scientific value. Three of them were type specimens—a biological specimen to which a scientific name is formally designated—and six were illustrated in the zoology section of the expedition's published report.[11] The three type specimens in the Zoology Museum were 'syntypes', which result when more than one specimen is designated as a species type. This is avoided today but happened regularly in the nineteenth century,

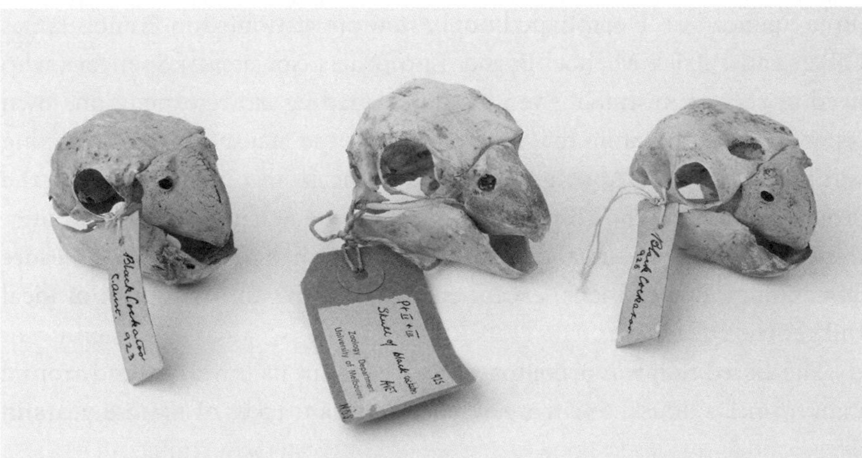

Above: Three red-tailed black cockatoo (*Calyptorhynchus banksii*) skulls collected on the Horn Scientific Expedition.

Left: Long-snouted lashtail (*Gowidon longirostris*) collected on the Horn Scientific Expedition.

when the rules of scientific nomenclature were less stringently enforced. These 'new' species were all native rodents: *Pseudomys desertor*, *Pseudomys gouldi* and *Zyzomys pedunculatus*. All three of these animals already had names—*wildjin*, *djoongari* and *antina*—given to them by the Arrernte, Luritja and Pintupi people.[12] Because of their importance, most of the Horn Expedition specimens were transferred from the Zoology Museum, a teaching collection regularly handled by students and staff, to the Melbourne Museum—one batch in 1910 and another in 1968. About sixteen specimens from the expedition remain in the Zoology Museum's collections today.

In most instances the donor of these specimens is recorded simply as 'Prof. Spencer' or 'Horn Expedition'. A few are attributed to Francis James Gillen and Patrick Michael Byrne, European associates of Spencer's who lived in central Australia. Even a cursory reading of the expedition's own report makes it apparent that much, probably the majority, of the collecting was undertaken by Aboriginal people living in the areas visited by the group. Addressing the University of Melbourne Science Club a year after the expedition, Spencer candidly reported that it had been difficult to secure 'any biological specimens, except insects' without the assistance of local Indigenous collectors.[13]

The expedition was accompanied throughout its travels by an Arrernte man from Dalhousie Springs named Harry, 'a tracker of mature years in

Harry, the Horn Expedition's tracker (detail from Members of the Horn Expedition, Alice Springs, Central Australia, 1894—Walter Baldwin Spencer, 1894).

the service of the police at Oodnadatta'.[14] Harry was a man of considerable skill; in one instance he tracked a trio of escaped emu chicks over well-trampled ground for almost a kilometre. By his third day on the expedition, he was able to identify the tracks of each member of the party, as well as each individual horse and camel. Although Harry is evidently the source of many of the animals collected, no specimen is formally credited to him. He is rarely mentioned by name in Spencer's report, usually referred to as 'our black-boy'. Harry is referenced a few times in the anthropology section of the expedition's report as a source on local customs but is not mentioned at all in the zoology section. This is in stark contrast to Gillen and Byrne, who probably didn't actually collect any specimens and just relayed requests to Aboriginal collectors, but who Spencer immortalised with the scientific names of the Centralian tree frog (*Ranoidea gilleni*) and the kowari (*Dasyuroides byrnei*).[15]

There were at least two other Aboriginal men whose contributions Spencer acknowledged in his diary but not in the published report. One was a friend of Harry's named Peter; the other, a man named Tom, joined the expedition when they reached Finke River. These are the only Indigenous collectors referred to by name in Spencer's writings, rather than the more commonplace anonymity or in the infantilising form of 'black-boy'.

Water-holding frog (*Cyclorana platycephala*) collected on the Horn Scientific Expedition.

Although the collectors are mostly not named, Spencer did record a few accounts of Indigenous collectors supplying the expedition with specimens of insects, frogs, reptiles, birds and mammals. One of the few insects from the expedition still on display in the Tiegs Museum is a striking specimen of the honeypot ant (*Camponotus inflatus*). Spencer recorded Aboriginal women collecting this species in the vicinity of Uluṟu:

> A native woman armed only with a yam stick will dig down to a depth of a few feet in a surprisingly short space of time, breaking up the earth with the stick held in the right hand while in the left a small pitchi is held and used as a shovel to clear the loosened earth away. The honey ant nest is not indicated on the surface by any mound.[16]

This is a recurring pattern: recording the expertise of Indigenous collectors without crediting them with acknowledgment.

Frederic Wood Jones

Professor Frederic Wood Jones, head of Melbourne's Anatomy Department from 1930 to 1937, was the quintessential early twentieth-century naturalist. In addition to being a world-class human anatomist, he was fascinated by the anatomy, evolution and ecology of animals. He was particularly interested in the native marsupials and birds of Australia, where he lived and worked for the majority of the 1920s and 1930s, first in Adelaide and then in Melbourne. Not content to remain in the laboratory, he regularly embarked on field trips and had a fondness for exploring islands. Natural history specimens attributed to Wood Jones, who was a prolific collector, can be found in collections across Australia, Europe and the United States, including the Harry Brookes Allen Museum of Anatomy and Pathology, Melbourne Museum, South Australian Museum, Australian Museum, Western Australian Museum, Natural History Museum London, and the Hunterian Museum of the Royal College of Surgeons London.[17] Wood Jones was a complex figure. While collecting Indigenous bones to send back to Britain, he also publicly campaigned for recognition of the Indigenous understanding of the continent as equal to, or better than, the European settlers' destructive use of the environment.[18]

There are around ninety zoological specimens that can be definitively attributed to Wood Jones in the Harry Brookes Allen Museum of Anatomy and Pathology, and hundreds of other undocumented specimens likely to be from the same source. Wood Jones' animal specimens consist

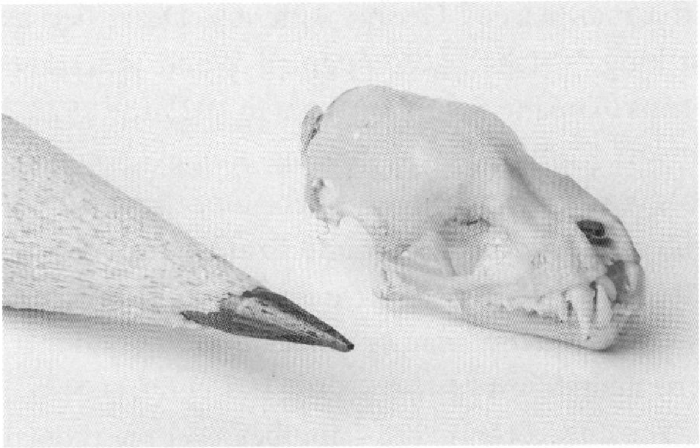

A native bat skull collected by Frederic Wood Jones from a trip to Kingoonya Well in 1921–1923.

mainly of native Australian marsupials and birds. They comprise fluid-preserved whole animals mounted in rectangular glass jars, skeletal and skull specimens, dried bird wings, and fossils. Many of the specimens in museums worldwide that are attributed to Wood Jones as a collector are from his expeditions to central South Australia in the early 1920s. At this time, Wood Jones was professor of anatomy at the University of Adelaide, and he made multiple scientific field trips to the arid inland of the state. At least one specimen in the Harry Brookes Allen Museum collections—a tiny bat skull obtained by Wood Jones at Kingoonya Well—is from one of these collecting expeditions. A number of the species that Wood Jones collected from this area, such as the lesser bilby (*Macrotis leucura*) and the golden bandicoot (*Isoodon auratus*), are now regionally or totally extinct.

Collecting in the arid interior of Australia is difficult work and, like Spencer before him, Wood Jones depended significantly on assistance and intelligence from local Aboriginal people. The anatomist gives an idea of the difficulties of collecting in this environment and his reliance on local Aboriginal collectors in a description of his 1920 trip to Cooper Creek:

> Only once did the watchful aboriginal [sic] who accompanied us come across the tracks of what was obviously a small mammal. These tracks led to a little hole among the roots of a blue-bush. The aboriginal [sic] possesses a wonderful skill and displays infinite patience in digging out the occupants of such burrows; but in this case we never came across any trace of the animal that had occupied the maze of runways that was uncovered. That was the only occasion on this, my first trip to the centre, upon which we came across any sign of the presence of a native mammal.[19]

On his collecting trips to central South Australia, Wood Jones and his colleague, dentist and anthropologist professor Thomas Draper Campbell, were assisted by a Kokatha man named George Mitchell. Described as the son of the tribe's last king, Mitchell accompanied Wood Jones and Campbell on at least two trips to inland South Australia in 1921 and 1923.[20] He showed the two professors fruitful sites for finding animal specimens and Aboriginal stone tools, and collected many such items himself. On these expeditions Mitchell collected dingo, bilby and lizard specimens for the team that, although unattributed, would have ended up in museum collections. Campbell noted that Mitchell was a proficient tracker and that, after a few collecting trips, their terms of friendship and conversational facility developed rapidly. The only recompense Campbell ever mentioned for Aboriginal expedition members was payment in cigarettes.[21]

Aboriginal collectors didn't just collect specimens for Wood Jones' museum cabinets but also obtained live animals for him. During the 1921 expedition, Mitchell emerged one morning with 'two tiny balls of cream coloured fluff'—dingo pups he had dug out from a den. In this instance at least, Mitchell was paid fairly for his efforts. From 1912, with the introduction of the *Wild Dogs Act*, the South Australian Government offered cash rewards for dingo skins with the (unsubstantiated) hope of eradicating the species. Wood Jones recognised Mitchell's right to this bounty and paid him the equivalent amount in order to save the young dingos from scalping. Wood Jones subsequently raised one of the pups to adulthood and kept it as a family pet.[22]

On another central South Australian expedition, Youngun, an Aboriginal man from the Mount Eba region, secured for Wood Jones three live boodies or burrowing bettongs (*Bettongia lesueur*). Youngun had noticed the traces made in the sand by the animals' tails, tracked them to a rabbit warren, and dug them out without harm. The trio were taken back to the University of Adelaide and thrived in captivity, and over time Youngun's boodies formed the basis of a successful breeding colony. Wood Jones attempted multiple releases of these animals onto Kangaroo Island in the early 1920s with the hope of establishing a self-sustaining population. However, these introductions were unsuccessful, and boodies became extinct on mainland Australia by the 1960s, now persisting only on a few offshore islands.

The *Itjaritjari*

The *itjaritjari* or marsupial mole (*Notoryctes typhlops*) is a unique, cryptic animal found in hostile environments that was impossible for

An itjaritjari (*Notoryctes typhlops*) potted specimen from the collections of Frederic Wood Jones.

settler naturalists to obtain without Indigenous knowledge. Although the *itjaritjari*, as it was named by the Pitjantjatjara and Yankunytjatjara people, looks exactly like a blonde version of the familiar mole of the Northern Hemisphere, it is a true marsupial more closely related to a kangaroo than any European animal.[23] *Itjaritjari* are endemic to the arid desert environments of central Australia where they are seldom seen, spending their whole lives underground, swimming through the sand with spade-like foreclaws. They are functionally eyeless and have no external ears, just a leathery shield on the front of their head. The marsupial's bizarreness and rarity made them highly sought-after specimens for natural history collections. The *itjaritjari*'s habitat and cryptic nature mean that Aboriginal people living in remote areas are the only people who reliably come into contact with them. There are hundreds of marsupial mole specimens in museums around the world and, although rarely attributed as such, you'd be hard pressed to find one that wasn't originally obtained by an Indigenous collector.[24]

At the University of Melbourne, Spencer got one for his Zoology Museum during the Horn Expedition, and then a few decades later Wood Jones acquired two for his Anatomy Museum. Any documentation relating to Wood Jones' *itjaritjari* specimens has been lost. However, in *The Mammals of South Australia*, Wood Jones thanks AG Bolam, stationmaster at Ooldea, for his contributions to science in collecting specimens of these rare marsupials—Wood Jones had personally received marsupial specimens from Bolam in the 1920s.[25] Wherever they ended up, Bolam undoubtedly had his specimens collected for him by the local Kokatha people. As for Spencer, he had been informed by Byrne that, during December 1894, 150 local Aboriginal men and women were 'enlisted in the service' of securing the professor an *itjaritjari* specimen.[26] The donor of the Tiegs Museum's *itjaritjari* is credited in the register as simply 'Prof. Spencer'. In the zoology report of the Horn Expedition, Spencer takes pains to acknowledge Byrne for providing him with a large number of marsupial mole specimens. The actual collector of the Zoology Museum's *itjaritjari* specimen was never recorded.

Conclusion

Settler-colonial societies across the world effectively stole Indigenous knowledge and expertise in order to understand the place they had taken. Without the almost completely ignored industry and knowledge of the Indigenous collector, colonial-settler scientists would have been unable to progress the Western scientific project along with the advancement of their ideas and careers.

Notes

1 John Smart and WE China (eds), *British Museum (Natural History) Instructions for Collectors No. 4A Insects*, 3rd edn, The Trustees of The British Museum, London, 1954.

2 For the success of the natural historian Frederic McCoy in receiving appropriate rewards, see Ian Wilkinson, 'Frederick McCoy and the University of Melbourne', *The Victorian Naturalist*, vol. 118, no. 5, 2001—McCoy Special Issue, part 1, p. 189; and Ian Wilkinson, 'The Battle for the Museum: Frederick McCoy and the Establishment of the National Museum of Victoria at the University of Melbourne', *Historical Records of Australian Science*, vol. 11, no. 1, 1996, pp. 1–11.

3 For early collectors and their relationships to the scientific centre, see RW Home and Sally Kohlstedt, 'Introduction', in RW Home and Sally Kohlstedt (eds), *International Science and National Identity: Australia between Britain and America*, Kluwer, Dordrecht, 1991, pp. 8–10. For a selected chronology of the discussions about global versus local production of science in the Australian context, see Roy McLeod, 'On Visiting the "Moving Metropolis": Reflections on the Architecture of Imperial Science', *Historical Records of Australian Science*, vol. 5, no. 3, 1980, pp. 1–16; Roy McLeod, 'Passages in Imperial Science: From Empire to Commonwealth', *Journal of World History*, vol. 4, no. 1, Spring 1993, pp. 117–50; and Roy McLeod, 'Introduction', *Osiris*, second series, vol. 15: *Nature*

and Empire: Science and the Colonial Enterprise, 2000, pp. 1–13. For a more general discussion of imperial connections, see David Lambert and Alan Lester, 'Imperial Spaces, Imperial Subjects', in David Lambert and Alan Lester (eds), *Colonial Lives across the British Empire: Imperial Careering in the Long Nineteenth Century*, Cambridge University Press, Cambridge, 2006, pp. 1–32; Kate Darian-Smith, Patricia Grimshaw and Stuart Macintyre (eds), *Britishness Abroad: Transnational Movements and Imperial Cultures*, Melbourne University Publishing, Carlton, 2007; and Brett M Bennett and Joseph M Hodge (eds), *Science and Empire: Knowledge and Networks of Science across the British Empire, 1800–1970*, Palgrave Macmillan, Basingstoke, 2011. For colonial membership of the Royal Society, see RW Home, 'A World-wide Scientific Network and Patronage System: Australian and Other "Colonial" Fellows of the Royal Society of London', in RW Home and Sally Kohlstedt (eds), *International Science and National Identity: Australia between Britain and America*, Kluwer, Dordrecht, 1991, pp. 151–79.

4 G Elliot Smith to JT Wilson, April 1896, MS 423/1/23.1, Andrew Arthur Abbie Collection, the Royal Anthropological Institute archive, letters and papers concerning the life and work of Professor Sir Grafton Elliot Smith (1871–1937).

5 British Museum (Natural History), Department of Zoology & Australian Joint Copying Project & National Library of Australia & State Library of New South Wales, Natural History Museum: Letters of the Keeper of Zoology Archive (as filmed by the AJCP): M2599-M2610. 1841–1973; Register of specimens in the museum of the Biological School, University of Melbourne. Tiegs Zoology Museum, School of BioSciences, University of Melbourne, 1893.

6 L Russell and PD Olsen (eds), *Australia's First Naturalists: Indigenous Peoples' Contribution to Early Zoology*, National Library of Australia Publishing, Canberra, 2019.

7 Australian Institute of Aboriginal and Torres Strait Islander Studies, *Map of Indigenous Australia*, 1996, https://aiatsis.gov.au/explore/map-indigenous-australia (accessed 29 October 2023).

8 WH Caldwell, 'The Embryology of Monotremata and Marsupialia—Part I', *Philosophical Transactions of the Royal Society of London*, vol. 178, 1887, pp. 463–86.

9 'Register of Specimens in the Museum of the Biological School, University of Melbourne', Tiegs Zoology Museum, School of BioSciences, University of Melbourne, Parkville, 1893.

10 Frederick McCoy to Baldwin Spencer, 7 January 1896, PRM1G_14, Pitt Rivers Museum, Oxford; W Baldwin Spencer forwarding list of specimens collected on Horn Expedition to central Australia, 28 October 1898, file 230/1, series DF 230, Curators of Birds Correspondence, 1896–1918 (from Natural History Museum: Letters of the Keeper of Zoology Archive (as filmed by the AJCP) [M2599-M2610] 1837–1969), https://nla.gov.au/nla.obj-838058144/findingaid#nla-obj-1552692782 (accessed 29 October 2023).

11 Walter Baldwin Spencer (ed.), *Report on the Work of the Horn Expedition to Central Australia, Part II: Zoology*, Dulau & Co., London, 1896.

12 JH Calaby, 'Baldwin Spencer's Post-Horn Expedition Collectors in Central Australia', in DJ Mulvaney and SR Morton (eds), *Exploring Central Australia: Society, the Environment and the 1894 Horn Expedition*, Surrey Beatty & Sons, Sydney, 1996, pp. 188–208.

13 'Science Club Notes', *Alma Mater*, vol. 1, no. 3, September 1895, p. 14.

14 Walter Baldwin Spencer (ed.), *Report on the Work of the Horn Expedition to Central Australia, Part IV: Anthropology*, Dulau & Co., London, 1896, p. 10.
15 See, for example, DJ Mulvaney, H Morphy and P Petch (eds), *From the Frontier: Outback Letters to Baldwin Spencer*, Allen & Unwin, Sydney, 2000.
16 Walter Baldwin Spencer (ed.), *Report on the Work of the Horn Expedition to Central Australia, Part I: Summary*, Dulau & Co., London, 1896, p. 87.
17 For Wood Jones' collecting, see Ross L Jones, *Anatomists of Empire: Race, Evolution and the Discovery of Human Biology in the British World*, Australian Scholarly Publishing, North Melbourne, 2020, chapters 4 and 5.
18 Ibid.
19 Frederic Wood Jones, unpublished autobiography, chapter titled 'South Australia I' in 'Manuscripts by Wood-Jones', c. 1953–1954. MS0017/2/1/2, Archives of the Royal College of Surgeons, London.
20 Thomas Draper Campbell, *Field Diaries, Notebooks and Other Data Relating to Fieldwork of Professor Thomas Draper Campbell, 1920–1966*, series AA 52/1/1, item 3: 'Handwritten Diary by Campbell of His Expedition to Millers Creek in August 1921 with Professor Wood Jones (AA 379) and Dr Pulleine', and item 4: 'Handwritten Diary by Campbell of His Expedition to Stuart Range in August 1923 with Frederick Wood Jones and His Wife and Gordon Jacobs', South Australian Museum Archives, Adelaide.
21 Campbell, *Field Diaries.*
22 Wood Jones, unpublished autobiography.
23 AA Burbid, KA Johnson, PJ Fuller and RI Southgate, 'Aboriginal Knowledge of the Mammals of the Central Deserts of Australia', *Wildlife Research*, vol. 15, no. 1, 1988, pp. 9–39.
24 J Benshemesh, 'Recovery Plan for Marsupial Moles *Notoryctes typhlops* and *N. caurinus*, 2005–2010', Northern Territory Department of Infrastructure, Planning and Environment, Alice Springs, 2004.
25 Frederic Wood Jones, *The Mammals of South Australia Parts I–III*, Government Printer, Adelaide, 1923–25; Frederic Wood Jones, 'The External Characters of Pouch Embryos of Marsupials, No. 6: *Dasycercus cristicauda*', *Transactions of the Royal Society of South Australia*, vol. XLVII, 1922, pp. 136–41.
26 Mulvaney, Petch and Morphy, *From the Frontier.*

Venom as a Vector of Indigenous Knowledge at Melbourne

From George Halford to Donald Thomson

KEN WINKEL and NATASHA FIJN

'Unless Australians act quickly a few museum specimens will be all that is left of the most extraordinary and interesting animals the world has ever seen.'

Donald Thomson, October 1926[1]

On 1 August 1950, Australia was transfixed by the milking of a snake at the National Museum of Victoria.[2] This particular snake had arrived by plane from Cairns where it had been collected from the wild only a few days earlier. It was the first snake of its type, collected live for the purposes of milking its venom, and it had become infamous by the time of its arrival in Melbourne. For this snake was framed as a killer. The collector, a twenty-year-old man from Sydney named Kevin Budden, was bitten on his hand while securing this snake in a bag. He then had a long journey before he could get to a hospital in Cairns, knowing that the venom was very likely to kill him. He was injected with the only snake antivenom in Australia at the time (then made in Melbourne), which counteracted the bite of the tiger snake (*Notechis scutatus*).[3] But this snake belonged to a different species and the antivenom proved ineffective. Budden, who was noted to have been initially more concerned about the welfare of the snake than of himself, had been bitten by the species colloquially known as the taipan (now scientifically known as *Oxyuranus scutellatus*). He died in Cairns Base Hospital on 28 July 1950 after making a last request that the snake be sent south for research purposes.[4]

Budden, like many Australians, was anxious for such snakes to be collected and milked for the development of a specific antivenom at the Commonwealth Serum Laboratories (CSL, now CSL Seqirus Limited). Twenty years previously, this was the institution that had first produced a commercial antivenom against the tiger snake in collaboration with the Walter and Eliza Hall Institute of Research into Pathology and Medicine (WEHI; now the Walter and Eliza Hall Institute of Medical Research). The taipan species, known as the scourge of the cane fields, had eluded capture and study for many years. Fortunately, on that fateful August day, University of Melbourne science graduate David Fleay successfully milked the snake Budden had caught, and the venom collected was instrumental in ultimately producing a commercial taipan antivenom.[5]

There was another man at the University of Melbourne, however, who had collected and milked these snakes for venom research more than twenty years earlier. He had quietly and repeatedly milked live taipans in remote Cape York during the late 1920s, before there was any antivenom in Australia. He was responsible for popularising the term 'taipan', an Indigenous common name for this snake among the people of Western Cape York, with whom he worked extensively in the field. That man, who also studied zoology at the University but graduated some years before Fleay, became renowned for his field skills in anthropology and his academic engagement with Indigenous knowledge, linguistics and an ecological form of anthropology. He will forever be known as a friend of the Yolŋu and had his ashes scattered over Caledon Bay (now Garrthalala), in north-eastern Arnhem Land. That remarkable field anthropologist and naturalist was Donald Thomson.[6]

This chapter places this pioneering work in the context of medical natural history and the practical issue of addressing the public health challenges relating to venomous snakebite. As with the larger story of the First Naturalists,[7] addressing this challenge repeatedly relied on the largely unacknowledged contributions of Indigenous people. Thence this chapter explores the history of venom as a vector of Indigenous knowledge, and its transformation, at the University of Melbourne. Although he joined the longer story of venom that has been part of the University since its first beginnings, both as a metaphor and as a practical vehicle for contact between peoples and knowledge systems,[8] Thomson developed a new way.

Since 1770, physicians and naturalists in the European tradition have botanised and dissected their way through the flora and fauna of Australia

Donald Thomson milks venom from taipan, Cape York, 1928.

and the surrounding waters of the Indo-Pacific. Like Cook, Banks and Solander with Tupaia, and Flinders and Brown with Bungaree, most had coopted Indigenous informants and resources to secure specimens that benefited Western science, as well as provided personal and professional profit. This was given full expression by the 'Fraternity of Duckmaloi', who literally hunted platypus on the Duckmaloi River, located on the Southern Tablelands of New South Wales, in pursuit of their constituent parts for anatomical analysis. These 'scientific gentlemen', based at the University of Sydney in the 1890s, including the celebrated physician and physiologist CJ Martin who subsequently was of the University of Melbourne Medical School, achieved considerable professional reward for their extractive interrogation of Australian biodiversity, including snake and platypus venom.[9]

This scientific race for 'monotreme priority' came to fullest expression in the story of William Caldwell's ruthless 1883 platypus and echidna ontogenetic enterprise, further described in Rohan Long and Ross Jones' chapter in this volume.[10] In the Medical Faculty, a similar mentality was evident in the first dean of medicine, George Britton Halford, who arrived in Melbourne from London in 1862 with a reputation as an emerging medical star. He had garnered professional respect for his experimental physiological studies of heart structure and function in mammals, birds and humans but was also an ardent anti-evolutionist.[11]

Alongside Halford, there is no clear evidence that the first lecturer in materia medica, therapeutics and medical botany, Dr Richard Eades, demonstrated an interest in Indigenous knowledge, specifically the medicinal use of plants. Further demonstrating the prevailing attitudes to Indigenous knowledge, it was Eades' colleague, Dr John Macadam,[12] who was immortalised, in 1857, by the Victorian Government botanist Ferdinand von Mueller,[13] in his naming of the Western scientific genus for the 'Queensland Nut' (*Macadamia*). Macadam, the first lecturer in chemistry to University medical students, and also famous for his role as secretary of the Exploration Committee of the ill-fated Burke and Wills expedition, was no botanist. So it is that we educate students who know the name of this Scottish-born medical doctor who spent barely ten years in Australia, but not the Indigenous names for this uniquely Australian fruit.

Among Halford's higher-profile research contributions as dean of medicine was his experimental research into Australian snake venoms. His work in this area depended on Indigenous peoples' expertise, which he failed to acknowledge. Halford's experimental studies required the venom of native snake species, often procured by unnamed Aboriginal collectors.[14] These experiments contributed to an international debate comparing secretions from various species, their mechanism of toxicity and the most appropriate method of their neutralisation. Such was the value of access to the Australian snakes and their specific venoms, particularly that of the deadly tiger snake, that Halford received requests for their export from eminent international physician experimenters. Uncharitably, Halford never shared his supplies of venom, nor did he acknowledge the Aboriginal people who helped to supply it.[15]

Through the next century, a succession of internationally significant researchers undertook studies on a variety of indigenous Australian venoms within the Medical Faculty of the University. In the late 1920s and early 1930s this included the WEHI physician and tropicalist Neil Hamilton-Fairley, as well as the pharmacologist and WEHI director Charles Kellaway,[16] working with scientists, including Donald Thomson. A multiyear venom and antivenom research program brought the University of Melbourne, Melbourne Zoo and CSL together to start Australia's first commercial antivenom production (against the venom of the tiger snake) in 1930.

After World War II, other University medical graduates working at CSL, including Saul Weiner[17] and Struan Sutherland,[18] went on to develop the full range of snake, spider, jellyfish and stonefish antivenoms. Although the sources of many such venomous species and their venoms is not always clear, many were caught and provided to researchers by Indigenous people from Australia and Papua New Guinea.[19] These products, which benefited from the knowledge and labour of Indigenous peoples, continue to save lives today.

Donald Thomson changed the narrative. He joined the longer story of venom that has been part of the University of Melbourne since its beginning, as a spokesperson and initial means of contact between the First People and their knowledge systems. Thomson's respectful approach to engaging with the Indigenous community in their own language, and to their different forms of knowledge and its keepers, began through his study of natural history, including mammals, birds and reptiles, as well as through his attention to the linguistics, kinship and rituals of the communities in Cape York. While researching broadly in the field, his particular focus was on snakes and venom for WEHI, before he began work in eastern Arnhem Land in the 1930s. As Nicolas Peterson commented, 'Thomson's writing is unique in that it names Aboriginal people, presenting them as individuals and active agents in local history in a way few other writings do.'[20]

The University collaboration with CSL, through WEHI, began with Hamilton-Fairley and Kellaway in 1928. Separately, in April of that year, Thomson took up an Australian National Research Council grant to undertake both zoological and anthropological fieldwork on Cape York Peninsula. It was during these initial eight months in the field that Thomson commenced what has become the UNESCO-listed ethno-history collection.[21] There are two separate collections. One is an ethno-history collection that includes Thomson's notebooks, manuscripts, newspaper articles, his impressive and extensive black-and-white photographic collection, Aboriginal paintings, masks and shields, tools and other rare objects. The other collection relates to natural history and contains specimens preserved in ethanol, including snakes large and small, other reptiles, mammals, marsupials, medicinal plants, eggs and even vials of venom. Thomson was a talented and highly productive field researcher. This massive two-part collection encompasses a number of different disciplines and material forms across anthropology and natural history, and is derived from Thomson's research

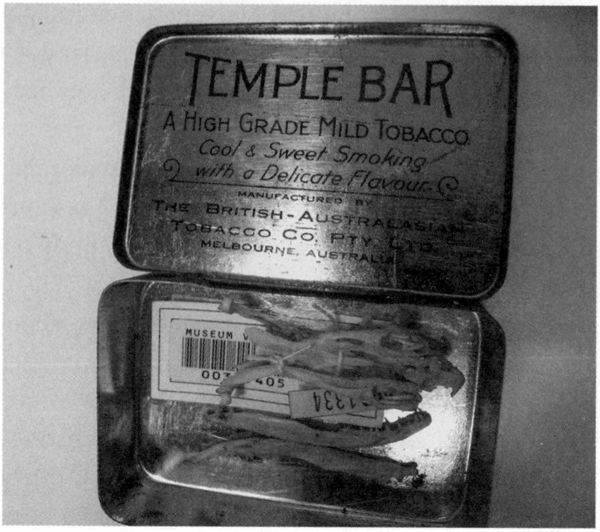

The delicate skull of a taipan (*Oxyuranus scutellatus*), collected by Donald Thomson in one of his tobacco boxes.

trips to Cape York, Arnhem Land, central Australia, the Solomon Islands and West Papua between 1928 and 1963.

During the first period of fieldwork on Cape York in 1928, Thomson learnt the local language and made an active attempt to understand Indigenous perspectives on snakes and snakebite, something no researcher had examined before. He observed the clear distinction the local tribal groups made between two snakes, now known as the taipan and the mulga snake, the largest of the black snake genus (*Pseudechis australis*). At that time, non-Indigenous understanding of these snake types was confused at best, with absolutely no studies of the relative venom toxicity. From his Aboriginal informants, Thomson learnt that these two snakes were radically different in their habits, behaviour and potential lethality to humans. The more numerous and heavier mulga snake was described thus in his field catalogue: 'They [Indigenous people] are much afraid of him, as they are of all snakes, but they all declare that he is not a "proper" venomous snake. He will kill a dog but not a man.'[22] Thomson's description of the elusive taipan had a different tone:

> The natives of the area know it as the Taipan and hold it in great dread for it is responsible for many deaths among them. I secured information about many bites—in each of which death resulted—and I have never heard of a victim recovering. A native dog that was bitten by one of the specimens that we subsequently secured alive, died shortly after, and exhibited the most intense congestion of the lung and other organs ...

> [The taipan] is nowhere very numerous but is found in greatest numbers where rats are plentiful. The natives, however, never hunt these rodents until the grass is dry enough to be burned off so real is their fear of this reptile.[23]

Thomson remarked that he collected over 200 snakes before he located a taipan in Cape York. Note that *thaypan* is the name given in the Wik languages and the Umpila-Kuuku Ya'u-Kaanju language complex of middle Cape York Peninsula.[24] It was through numerous natural history articles oriented at expanding the knowledge of the Australian public that Thomson popularised the use of the term 'taipan' for this distinctively dangerous species.

During his time in northern Queensland, Thomson noted the cultural distinction between the European conception of snakes and the way local Indigenous peoples conceived of them: 'They do not feel the necessity of killing any snake they see—as the white man does—but many are fatally bitten by this active and aggressive reptile.'[25] Until Thomson lived with and learnt from the peoples of Cape York, these facts about the differences between the mulga and taipan snakes, and the mortal impact of the taipan on the Cape York peoples,[26] were unknown by the wider community.

Aboriginal person with big specimen of *Pseudechis australis*, photographed by Gray. Stewart River, North Queensland, July 1931.

These important observations of human ecology, reflected in Thomson's natural history–based field research, were quite different from the narrow conception of anthropology as viewed by his Sydney mentor Alfred Radcliffe-Brown,[27] who tried to orient Thomson towards an analysis of the classic research of kinship and social structure, rather than attention to ecological and natural history perspectives.

A trip to Cape York in 1929 was perhaps the most productive in terms of collecting a wealth of field material as part of a diverse natural history collection. Thomson was particularly active during this time in collecting numerous snake specimens and vials of venom. He filled a field notebook with behavioural and ecological observations of the snake species his Aboriginal collaborators brought to him.

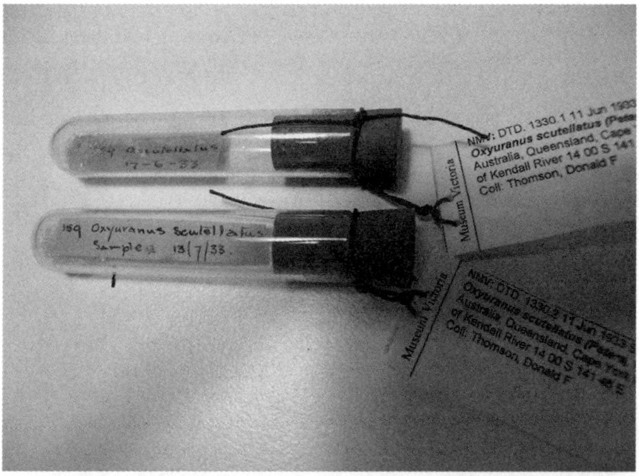

O. scutellatus (taipan) venom milked by Donald Thomson, while risking his life from potentially being bitten by this aggressive and highly venomous snake. Note the crystallised venom at the end of the two vials.

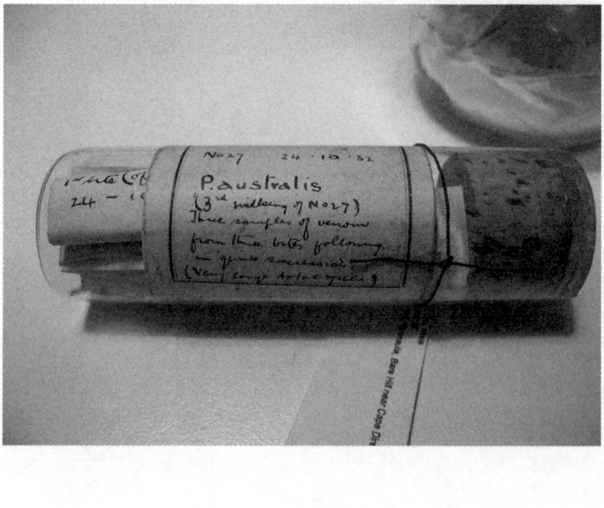

P. australis (mulga) venom, still in vials with Thomson's meticulous labelling, held in the Museum Victoria natural history collection.

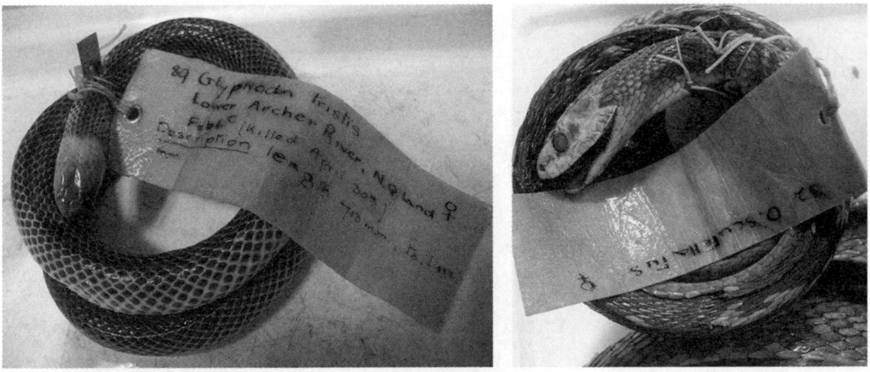

Thomson preserved snakes in jars of ethanol. The snakes and handwritten tags have retained all the detail from the late 1920s and early 1930s.

Thomson had established a friendship with mentor and research colleague Charles Kellaway, director of WEHI. The two corresponded for decades. On 29 September 1929, while Thomson was still in the field in Cape York, Kellaway writes with reference to the first taipan specimen Thomson caught: 'I do not know whether the snake you have caught alive is *Pseudechis scuttelatus* or *Oxyuranus*. For heaven's sake do not try to milk him again! ... Do not take any risks, as I would never forgive myself if anything happened to you.' (Thomson continued to repeatedly milk the taipans.) At the end of the letter, Kellaway commiserates with Thomson on an opportunity missed to head south to Antarctica on an expedition: 'I am sorry you missed the Antarctic, but I think you will make your reputation on the snakes of Australia.'[28]

Extraction of venom, 'milking' a Black Tiger snake (*Notechis scutatus*) by Tom Eades (left) and Charles Kellaway (right).

Extraction of venom at Walter and Eliza Hall Institute. February–March, 1931.

Later in 1929, Thomson was recruited by Kellaway to a position as a biologist at WEHI, where he focused on the development of snake antivenom for two years. He contributed crucial expertise on taxonomy, as well as the capacity to source wild snakes and milk their venom. He replaced Kellaway in the routine milking of the large and growing collection of venomous snakes, essential to the distribution of antivenom.[29] He researched mainly the venom and toxicity of the mulga or king brown (*Pseudechis australis*) and the common tiger snake, spurred on by his encounter with *P. australis* with local Indigenous field assistants in Cape York.

In a joint paper, Kellaway and Thomson point out that the great width of the head of *P. australis* is due to large venom glands and the powerful musculature surrounding them. They conclude that, although the king brown produces a large amount of venom, the venom is less toxic than that of the tiger snake, death adder, copperhead or brown snake, but similarly venomous to the common black snake.[30] As mentioned earlier, Thomson's research with Kellaway led to the production of Australia's first tiger snake antivenom.

Roy Kinghorn, director of the Australian Museum in Sydney, had described individual *Oxyuranus* (taipan), yet Thomson concluded that the specimens he examined from Kinghorn's collection were the same as *P. australis* (mulga). With his newly acquired specimens he decided to retain the genus *Oxyuranus*, in deference to Kinghorn. After Thomson published his findings in 1933, *Oxyuranus scutellatus* was formally recognised as a

Glasses with rubber cap for collecting venom: at laboratory, Walter and Eliza Hall Institute, 1931.

separate species and became known by its common name as the 'taipan', from the name Thomson assigned it after the Indigenous name different clans used to refer to the dreaded snake on Cape York Peninsula.[31]

Thomson joined the self-taught snake-handler-turned-curator of the reptiles at Melbourne Zoo, Tom Eades, in this work. Eades had been seconded to the WEHI snakebite project at its commencement.[32] Thomson continued working in partnership with Aboriginal peoples, repeatedly returning to Cape York for further work on taipans and mulga snakes, including milking wild-caught snakes in situ. He collaborated with Kellaway on studies of both snakes (and their venoms) as well as the tiger and black snakes. Thomson was even successful in bringing back to Melbourne a live, wild-caught mulga snake from Queensland for WEHI,[33] but never a live taipan—that unfortunate distinction awaited Kevin Budden, who appears only to have worked alone or with non-Indigenous people.

Both Thomson and Eades secured snakes from eastern and western Victoria as well as South Australia and Queensland.[34] This apparently included sourcing tiger and copperhead snakes from Lake Tyers with the help of the resident Aboriginal community.[35] 'When Thomson arrived, the men from Tyers quickly went out to find him a snake: "He wanted to know about our snakes, and we caught one for him to take to Melbourne."'[36] The extent of this fieldwork is quite remarkable, with Kellaway recording, in the 1929–30 WEHI *Annual Report*, 'This year we have collected approximately 200 death adders, 120 tiger snakes, 150 copperheads, 20 black snakes, [and] ten brown snakes.'[37]

These very large black snakes provided not just novel research material but also substantial volumes of venom for the newly commercially released tiger snake antivenom. It is quite possible these snakes were procured by the Tasmanian James Murray,[38] with the assistance of Aboriginal families resident on Chappell Island.[39] These snakes were a continual hazard to the muttonbirding community, as they shared the burrows with the birds and so were the subject of annual police 'shoots', with a bounty on their heads.

Another of the snake providers mentioned by Kellaway in the 1930–31 WEHI *Annual Report* was David Fleay. At that time, combining study in a Bachelor of Science at the University with a Diploma of Education at the Melbourne Teachers Training College, Fleay was recorded as donating three species of snake to the research program.[40] Fleay, who had a lifetime passion for collecting and caring for Australian native animals, worked with Kellaway and subsequent generations of University- and CSL-associated venom researchers, providing snakes and their venoms. This collaborative habit continued all the way up to his assistance to Struan Sutherland at CSL in the 1970s and 1980s.[41] Fleay, like Thomson, was brave enough to milk live taipans, and he was the first to successfully breed them in captivity. This feat remains largely unknown to the world when compared with his work on the platypus while director of the Healesville Sanctuary.[42]

Under the leadership of Fleay (1937–51), Healesville became known for the diligent animal-centred curation of Australian native fauna. A foundational partnership with Aboriginal people underscored the success of the Sanctuary (especially its world-leading breakthrough in breeding platypus) and Fleay explicitly acknowledged the supportive role of the Aboriginal peoples from adjacent Coranderrk Mission. In this way, like Thomson, he established new and more constructive ways for Western science to engage with the First Naturalists. Indeed, in his professional and personal life, Fleay (and his family) maintained a lifelong, mutually respectful relationship with Aboriginal communities and their culture.

Of particular importance was Frank Wandin and his mother, Jemima Donolly, known as the 'Coranderrk matriarch of the Wandin family'.[43] Fleay, who was a pallbearer at her funeral in 1944, noted in his writings:

> This fine old lady had supplied us with duckbill [platypus] food items [such as yabbies, worms, and grubs] consistently in all weathers—come what may for years—never failing to 'produce the goods' and pinpoint snake retreats for me until practically the day of her death.[44]

Indeed, such was the critical nature of such support for the platypus project that the first puggle, a female, to be bred at the Sanctuary (confirmed in January 1944, the same month as Donolly' s death) was named 'Corrie', an abbreviation of Coranderrk, the local Aboriginal name for the Sanctuary area. After her death, Frank Wandin, a son from her first marriage, not only continued the provision of platypus food but also assisted with lyrebird foods and other aspects of Fleay's work.[45] Although the Fleays moved in 1952, this time to establish an animal sanctuary at West Burleigh Heads in southern Queensland, Frank Wandin was again crucial in looking after Fleay's personal live animal collection until it could be safely airfreighted north.[46] Rosemary, one of Fleay's two daughters, described him thus:

> Frank was one of nature's gentlemen; he had the honour of being the first Aboriginal Headmaster of a Victorian school and we, the Fleay family, were very privileged to have known this quietly spoken man of enormous dignity.[47]

After completing the snakebite work with Kellaway from 1929 to 1932, Thomson moved to the Department of Anatomy as a research fellow and returned to his anthropological training and interests, including further work on Cape York funded by the University of Melbourne. He then turned his attention to Arnhem Land where, although he still observed and collected reptiles, his focus was more on anthropology. He made observations on the totemic significance of Snake Dreaming and took particular interest in pythons. He still made observations in his fieldnotes regarding encounters with highly venomous snakes, however, including the taipan and mulga. His later fieldwork was based in the Great Sandy Desert, but although he recorded plenty of reptiles, he did not come across the large, highly venomous snakes there.

When Thomson was in England at the University of Cambridge on a Rockefeller Fellowship (1938–39), he was still writing to Kellaway, indicating how he planned to travel to the museum in Germany where the type specimen for the taipan was kept. (He was invited to the zoological museum in Berlin to see it in October 1939 but, unsurprisingly, never kept that date due to the war.) It was through Thomson's ongoing connection with Kellaway that he continued venom research, even when he was drawn away to other research projects. He continued to collect snakes in alcohol and dried, crystallised venom for his own collection, which are still housed on permanent loan to Museums Victoria by the University of Melbourne.

Whilst he occasionally collected reptiles closer to home in his later years, even engaging his children in the snake-catching, it was during the early days of his fieldwork in Cape York, through the vector of venom, that Thomson pioneered a new way for Western science to engage with Indigenous knowledge. His appreciation of the breadth of natural history, behavioural and ecological knowledge embedded in the Aboriginal way of life came from months of fieldwork guided by the Traditional Owners. He integrated the extraordinary Indigenous knowledge of plants, animals, place and culture, recorded in local language, art and ceremony, by living, learning, respecting and valuing difference. He regarded his Indigenous contributors as collaborators, as they often put their own lives at risk to capture and handle highly venomous snakes as part of their work, with little monetary gain or acknowledgement in return. This includes Tjamindjinyu (Djaminjinyou) whom Thomson generally referred to by his English name Tommy. He was Thomson's main collaborator who accompanied him across Cape York Peninsula in 1928 and 1929. Thomson noted that he came from what he referred to as the Sandbeach people, eastern Cape York. In addition, Raiwalla, a Mildjingi man, became a good friend and travelled with Thomson across Arnhem Land for many years.

Indigenous people's contribution towards snake and venom research in the field has been little documented previously. This chapter is an initial glimpse of the significant contribution of Indigenous know-how and practical ecological knowledge, accompanied by on-the-ground, applied fieldwork in the identification, capture and characterisation of little-known snake species. Through these cultural gifts from the Indigenous keepers of Country, we have a message stick for a better future.

Notes

1 Donald Thomson, writing as Finlay Fergusson, *Adam and Eve*, October 1926. This quote was cited within the *Awaken* exhibition focused on the Donald Thomson Collection, situated at the Arts West Gallery, University of Melbourne during 2019–20. It was curated by Worimi nation filmmaker, curator, storyteller and Head of First Peoples at the Melbourne Museum, Genevieve Grieves, with Rosemary Wrench and Shonae Hobson (Kaantju). The same 1926 article was also cited by Ian Temby in 'Ecologist and Public Educator', in B Rigsby and N Peterson (eds), *Donald Thomson, the Man and Scholar*, The Academy of the Social Sciences in Australia, Canberra, with support from Museum Victoria, 2005, p. 66.

2 Summarised in KD Winkel, 'An Ominously Quiet Box', in J Healy and KD Winkel (eds), *Venom: Fear, Fascination and Discovery*, Medical History Museum, University of Melbourne, Parkville, 2013, p. 104. For a more expansive discussion of both Budden and Fleay's roles in these events, see P Mirtschin, 'The Pioneers of Venom Production for Australian Antivenoms', *Toxicon*, vol. 48, 2006, pp. 899–918.

3 The history of Australian antivenom production is concisely reviewed in K Winkel, P Mirtschin and J Pearn, 'Twentieth Century Toxinology and Antivenom Development in Australia', *Toxicon*, vol. 48, 2006, pp. 738–54. For more details of the tiger snake antivenom project at the Walter and Eliza Hall Institute of Medical Research, see PG Hobbins, Charles Kellaway and the Burgeoning of Australian Medical Research, 1928–37, Master of Medical Humanities thesis, University of Sydney, Sydney, 2007.

4 More details of Budden's request and the events of subsequent days, from Fleay's perspective, are available in 'Milking a Killer Taipan', in R Fleay-Thomson, *Animals First: The Story of Pioneer Conservationist & Zoologist Dr David Fleay*, Petaurus Publishing, Nerang, Qld, 2007.

5 For more details of the story of the collection of taipans for antivenom production, see K Markwell and N Cushing, 'From Snake Handlers to Wildlife Entrepreneurs', in Healy and Winkel, *Venom*, pp. 57–63.

6 For an extended examination of Thomson's work, especially that of his time spent in Arnhem Land, see D Thomson and N Peterson, *Donald Thomson in Arnhem Land*, Currey O'Neil, South Yarra, 1983.

7 The terminology 'First Naturalists' is borrowed from that of academics Olsen and Russell in L Russell and PD Olsen, *Australia's First Naturalists: Indigenous Peoples' Contribution to Early Zoology*, National Library of Australia Publishing, Sydney, 2019.

8 Formerly chair of Indigenous health at the University, Kerry Arabena explores cultural and philosophical aspects of 'venom' in the context of European and Indigenous epistemologies in her essay 'Sixty Thousand Years of Stories', in Healy and Winkel, V*enom*, pp. 23–5.

9 P Morison, *J.T. Wilson and the Fraternity of Duckmaloi*, Rodopi, Amsterdam and Atlanta, 1997. Although focused on the English-born anatomist JT Wilson, this book provided an excellent introduction to the milieu in the emergent colonial medical schools and the physician-naturalist fraternity to which the physiologist CJ Martin belonged. A concise biography of Martin is provided in P Morison, 'Sir Charles James Martin (1866–1955)', *Australian Dictionary of Biography*, National Centre of Biography, Australian National University, Canberra, 2006, https://adb.anu.edu.au/biography/martin-sir-charles-james-7501/text13077 (accessed 30 October 2023).

10 For an excellent contextualised review of the infamous events surrounding Caldwell's concise telegram, 'Monotremes oviparous, ovum meroblastic', see S Nichols, 'Étienne Geoffroy Saint-Hilaire, Richard Owen and Monotreme Oviparity', *Australian Zoologist*, vol. 40, 2019, pp. 272–89.

11 Halford's role in the emergent medical school is described in meticulous detail in KF Russell, *The Melbourne Medical School, 1862–1962*, Melbourne University Press, Carlton, 1977.

12 KF Russell, 'John Macadam (1827–1865)', *Australian Dictionary of Biography*, National Centre of Biography, Australian National University, Canberra, 2006, https://adb.anu.edu.au/biography/macadam-john-4054/text6453 (accessed 30 October 2023).

13 Deirdre Morris, 'Sir Ferdinand Jakob Heinrich von Mueller (1825–1896)', *Australian Dictionary of Biography*, National Centre of Biography, Australian National University, Canberra, 2006, https://adb.anu.edu.au/biography/mueller-sir-ferdinand-jakob-heinrich-von-4266/text6893 (accessed 30 October 2023).

14 As evidenced by extant official police receipts in the Australian Medical Association Archives held at the Brownless Medical Library: 'Expenses incurred by the snakes at Richmond Depot, 1876.' This item formed Work 16 within the exhibition *Venom: Fear, Fascination and Discovery* held at the University Medical History Museum in 2013. It is documented in the exhibition catalogue: Healy and Winkel, *Venom*, p. 118.

15 Halford himself gives an account of his work on snakebite and snake venom over the decades in GB Halford, *Thoughts, Observations and Experiments on the Action of Snake Venom on the Blood*, Stillwell, Melbourne, 1894. A more detailed review of Halford's work, and its colonial snakebite context, is presented in P Hobbins, 'Ontological Conjunctions: Dogs, Snakes, Venoms and Germs 1840–68', in P Hobbins, *Venomous Encounters: Snakes, Vivisection and Scientific Medicine in Colonial Australia*, Studies in Imperialism Book 143, Manchester University Press, Manchester, 2017, pp. 160–84.

16 In addition to Hobbins' Charles Kellaway, for details of the Hall Institute venom research program, also see PG Hobbins, 'Serpentine Science: Charles Kellaway and the Fluctuating Fortunes of Venom Research in Interwar Australia', *Historical Records of Australian Science*, vol. 21, 2010, pp. 1–34; and PG Hobbins and KD Winkel, 'The Forgotten Successes and Sacrifices of Charles Kellaway, Director of the Walter and Eliza Hall Institute, 1923–1944', *Medical Journal of Australia*, vol. 187, 2007, pp. 645–8.

17 For a snapshot of the relatively overlooked contributions of clinical allergist and immunologist Saul Wiener's contributions to CSL's antivenom development, see Healy and Winkel, *Venom*, pp. 98–9. Additional details for his work, contextualised in the story of CSL antivenom production, is given in Winkel, Mirtschin and Pearn, 'Twentieth Century Toxinology', pp. 738–54.

18 A synopsis of Sutherland's contributions to toxinology is provided in J Tibballs, 'Struan Sutherland: Doyen of Envenomation in Australia', *Toxicon*, vol. 48, 2006, pp. 860–71.

19 See the discussion of Ken Slater's procurement and milking of venomous snakes in Papua New Guinea for CSL in the 1950s, and the impact of the subsequent government bounty for public collections of Papuan black snakes and taipans, in Mirtschin, 'The Pioneers of Venom Production', pp. 899–918.

20 Thomson and Peterson, *Donald Thomson in Arnhem Land*, p. vii.

21 For a summary of the collection, see the Museum Victoria webpage page related to The Australian Register of the UNESCO Memory of the World Program: https://www.amw.org.au/sites/default/files/memory_of_the_world/indigenous-collections/donald-thomson-ethnohistory-collection.html (accessed 30 October 2023).

22 Quoted from Donald Thomson's Cape York Fieldnote, 23 August 1929, as stored in the Museum Victoria Donald Thomson Archive.

23 From a draft of an article in the Museum Victoria Donald Thomson Archive titled 'Australian Snakes: Researching on Snakes and Their Venom in Tropical North Queensland', pp. 5–6.

24 Editors' note in Temby, 'Ecologist and Public Educator', p. 70.

25 Typed version of manuscript for a newspaper article by Donald Thomson, 'The Story of the Taipan', p. 1, from Donald Thomson Collection, Museum Victoria.

26 DF Thomson, 'Snakes and Snake Lore', *Walkabout*, 2 November 1950. For a reflection on the search for a taipan antivenom and the impact of this snake, and its venom, on the life of the young George Rosendale of the Guugu Yimithirr

nation, see BJ Murray, *Venom: The Heroic Search for Australia's Deadliest Snake*, Echo Publishing, Sydney, 2017.

27 See N Fijn, 'Donald Thomson: Observations of Animal Connections in Visual Ethnography in Northern Australia', *Ethnos*, 2019.

28 C Kellaway, based at the Walter and Eliza Hall Institute, Melbourne Hospital, to D Thomson, 29 September 1929, c/f the Thomson family.

29 The Walter and Eliza Hall Institute of Research in Pathology and Medicine, *Eleventh Annual Report 1929–1930*, J. C. Stephens Pty Ltd, Melbourne, p. 7.

30 CH Kellaway and DF Thomson, 'Observations of the Venom of a Large Australian Snake, *Pseudechis australis* (Gray)', *Australian Journal of Experimental Biology and Medical Science*, vol. 7, 1930, pp. 134–50.

31 DF Thomson, 'Australian Snakes of the Genera *Pseudechis* and *Oxyuranus*', *Proceedings of the Zoological Society of London*, vol. 103, 1933, pp. 855–60.

32 For comments on Tom Eades' role in the WEHI venom research program, see Mirtschin, 'The Pioneers of Venom Production', pp. 899–918.

33 The Walter and Eliza Hall Institute of Research in Pathology and Medicine, *Eleventh Annual Report*, p. 7.

34 Ibid.

35 For more information on the Gunaikurnai people and their land, Bung Yarnda, which became the mission known as Lake Tyers in the Gippsland region of Victoria, see The Lake Tyers Aboriginal Trust website: https://laketyersaboriginaltrust.com.au (accessed 30 October 2023).

36 Lake Tyers Elder, Melbourne Museum, 1999, recorded in the *Awaken* exhibition, Arts West Gallery, University of Melbourne.

37 The Walter and Eliza Hall Institute of Research in Pathology and Medicine, *Eleventh Annual Report*, p. 7.

38 Shortly thereafter, the unfortunate nineteen-year-old James 'Jimmy' Murray died from a tiger snake bite in Tasmania. Ironically, it seems he did not receive WEHI-CSL tiger snake antivenom. He reported having recently returned from Chappell Island, where he claimed to have collected 280 snakes in four days (including catching ninety-three snakes in one day)! See this contemporary newspaper report: 'Bitten By Snake While Giving Public Demonstration: Don Man's Death', *The Advocate*, Tasmania, 9 April 1931.

39 For a detailed historical examination of the muttonbirding industry of the Flinders Island group, see I Skira, Tasmanian Aborigines and Muttonbirding: An Historical Examination, PhD thesis, University of Tasmania, Hobart, 1993, https://eprints.utas.edu.au/21596 (accessed 30 October 2023).

40 The Walter and Eliza Hall Institute of Research in Pathology and Medicine, *Twelfth Annual Report 1930–1931*, p. 8.

41 For more on Fleay's interaction with Sutherland, see Winkel, 'An Ominously Quiet Box', p. 104.

42 An insider's account of the multidecadal work towards breeding platypus in captivity is given in 'David's Greatest Achievement: The First Breeding of Platypus in Captivity', in Fleay-Thomson, *Animals First*, pp. 95–105.

43 Ibid.

44 Ibid.

45 Ibid.

46 'Paradise Found in God's Own Country, Queensland', in Fleay-Thomson, *Animals First*, p. 175.

47 Fleay-Thomson, *Animals First*, p. 103.

From Collection to Engagement

Indigenous Language Research at the University of Melbourne

RACHEL NORDLINGER and NICHOLAS THIEBERGER

THE UNIVERSITY OF MELBOURNE has long been involved in recording and describing the languages of Indigenous peoples, although the nature of this involvement has changed dramatically over time—moving from the collection of disembodied wordlists by Sir Redmond Barry through to Indigenous-centred collaboration in the present day. These changes reflect both a shift in attitudes towards Indigenous people and their languages, as well as an increased understanding of the importance of these languages to Indigenous people and the broader Australian population. This history, perhaps unsurprisingly, also coincides with the development of the discipline of linguistics at the University of Melbourne and across Australia, which saw the researchers working on Indigenous languages move from 'interested amateurs' to trained experts with a deep appreciation and respect for the languages and their speakers, and an understanding of what they can teach us about human language and human cognition. In this chapter we outline and critique this history, focusing particularly on the changing practices over time from simply collecting Indigenous language material to building long-term collaborations with Indigenous communities and researchers.

Collecting Times

The earliest interest in Aboriginal languages in Victoria by the colonists was restricted to collecting wordlists and reflected the approach to Indigenous cultures that Tom Griffiths characterises more generally as emanating from the 'antiquarian imagination in Australia'.[1] Wordlists were collected in much the same way as were artefacts, exoticised and abstracted from context and people. Donaldson, outlining the history of collecting information about western NSW languages (Ngiyampaa and Wiradjuri in particular), notes that vocabularies were collected 'first and foremost in order to make comparative study of the different Australian languages possible, rather than to help with subsequent communication with the speakers of any particular language'. She goes on to observe that word collection was an activity promoted by the 'far from scholarly monthly put out by the Royal Anthropological Society of Australasia and called, from 1898, *Science of Man*'.[2]

This is the context in which Sir Redmond Barry appears as a collector of words, the first University of Melbourne member to work with Aboriginal languages.[3] Barry was a founder of the University and its first chancellor (from 1853), a position he held until his death. He had a lifelong interest in the welfare of Aboriginal people, often acting in their defence in court cases. Barry worked to collate a set of vocabularies of Aboriginal languages for display at the Intercolonial Exhibition of Australasia of 1866 in Melbourne. He prepared a list of prompt words in the form of a questionnaire booklet,[4] which resulted in the 1867 publication of up to 683 vocabulary items for each of thirteen Australian languages.[5]

In this booklet, very little information is provided about the people these words were collected from or what the language is. Each variety is identified only with a locale, usually an English placename (for example, 'Mt Rouse tribe'), which is clearly not a traditional way of naming languages in Indigenous Australia. This makes it difficult to determine exactly which language the collected vocabularies are from, a situation exacerbated by the fact that there are only limited records for many of these languages.

The varieties identified in the booklet and the number of words for each are as follows. We have suggested a probable language name (in square brackets) in cases where this can be determined on current information:[6] Victoria Wannikin—Mt Rouse tribe [Djabwurrung?] (295 words); Victoria—Mt Talbot tribe [Nundadjali?] (482 words); Victoria. Upper Murray tribe (623 words); Victoria. Lower Murray tribe (479 words); Swan Hill tribe (509 words); Victoria. Wannon—Yarlook tribe (394 words); Victoria. Lower Goulburn tribe (672 words); Victoria. Lake Tyer tribe. North Gipps Land [Krowathunkooloong?] (152 words); Victoria. Maryborough tribe (119 words); Victoria. Dialect Bewa (Lake Hindmarsh) [Biwadjali?] (610 words);

South Australia—Dialect Maal (376 words); South Australia—Adelaide tribe [Kaurna] (289 words); Tasmania—Mt Royal and Brune Island (275 words).[7]

In the guide to the questionnaire, Barry expresses the wish that

> it may form the groundwork of future more extended inquiries of a like nature, in the progress of which the intercourse with the Aborigines may lead to improvement in their intellectual and social, as well as their physical condition; while all employed may have the satisfaction of redeeming, in some degree, the obligations they owe to the humble race—the primitive possessors of the soil.[8]

In this we see his desire that the lists not only help the 'philologist' but also lead to greater understanding between the newcomers and the original inhabitants, and result in benefits for the Indigenous people. However, Barry's language work is extremely limited, containing only individual words—mostly nouns—and no grammatical information that would allow anyone to be able to put together a simple sentence, or even a greeting. It also shows no understanding of the fact that words can carve out different meanings in different languages, so the translation of an English word may not cover the same range of meanings in an Indigenous language. The English word 'grandfather', for example, describes a male relative who is the father of one's parent (for example, a mother's father or father's father). However, many Indigenous languages do not use a single word to cover both of these male relatives but distinguish grandparents according to the mother's line or father's line. In Kaurna (one of the languages in Barry's list), the word for father's father is *madlala*, while the word for mother's father is *tamamu*.[9] Neither of these words has the same meaning as the English 'grandfather'.

This simple example illustrating the complexity of translation is replicated in many different ways throughout Barry's wordlists and reveals his lack of engagement with the speakers of the languages he was describing as well as a limited understanding of the nature of language and its differences. It also substantially limits the usefulness of such wordlists in increasing the understanding of colonisers and Indigenous peoples and forming the groundwork for future extended work in this direction. Perhaps unsurprisingly, there is no evidence of such extended research arising from Barry's work, and no comprehensive work was done with speakers of Indigenous languages at the university he led until over a century later.

There was, however, cultural inquiry and research into Indigenous peoples by researchers from other fields such as evolutionary biology and anthropology. Sir Walter Baldwin Spencer, appointed as the foundational chair of biology at the University in 1887, pioneered wax-cylinder recording and travelled through central and northern Australia with his collaborator Francis James Gillen, undertaking ethnographic work with many Aboriginal communities focusing particularly on artistic, spiritual and ceremonial

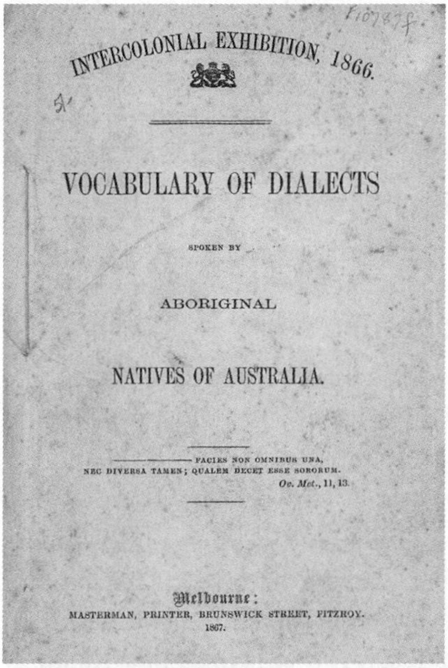

INTERCOLONIAL EXHIBITION, 1866.

VOCABULARY OF DIALECTS

SPOKEN BY

ABORIGINAL

NATIVES OF AUSTRALIA.

FACIES NON OMNIBUS UNA,
NEC DIVERSA TAMEN; QUALEM DECET ESSE SORORUM.
Ov. Met., II, 13.

Melbourne:
MASTERMAN, PRINTER, BRUNSWICK STREET, FITZROY.
1867.

Left: Front cover of Redmond Barry's vocabulary list.

Below: Sample page from Redmond Barry's vocabulary list.

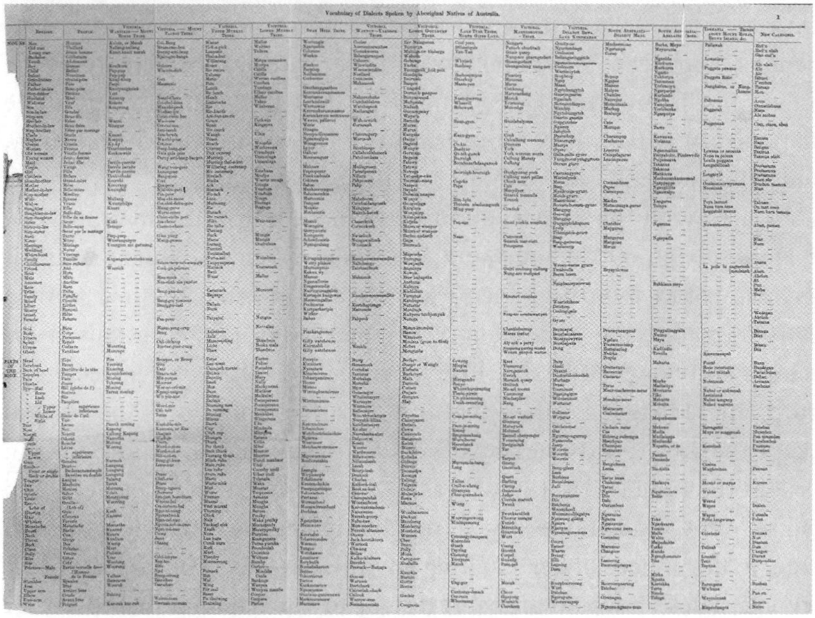

Vocabulary of Dialects Spoken by Aboriginal Natives of Australia.

aspects of their culture. In the course of their research, Spencer and Gillen recorded many words in languages of central and northern Australia, but language was not their focus and as a result their wordlists have not made any significant contributions to the documentation of the languages they interacted with. Some decades later, Donald Thomson, a zoologist at Melbourne who had studied anthropology with Alfred Radcliffe-Brown at the University of Sydney, undertook extensive research with communities in Cape York and Arnhem Land, becoming a strong advocate for the Yolŋu people and showing a deep understanding of the laws and practices of Yolŋu society. But while his important collection from this research is well known and influential, he was not a linguist and left little in the way of language records.

Early Linguistics at the University

The field of linguistics did not really separate itself from the allied field of anthropology until the 1950s, although philology and the study of language is as old as human reflection on ourselves. It can certainly be dated to Mesopotamia and China,[10] followed by Greek and Roman philosophers and a continuing tradition to luminaries such as Humboldt (early–mid 1800s), de Saussure (late 1800s) and Boas (early 1900s). Thus it was that, in the post–World War II period, there was no linguistics department at the University of Melbourne, and so there was no work being done with Indigenous languages. This is reflected in the inaugural conference of the Australian Institute of Aboriginal Studies in 1961 that included fifty-three participants, of which three were from the University (John Mulvaney, Donald Thomson and Oscar Oeser) and none was a linguist.[11]

Associated with the University of Melbourne but never an employee, Luise Hercus lived in Melbourne in the 1960s, when she taught Sanskrit to University of Melbourne students for free and in her spare time worked tirelessly to record and document Aboriginal languages, especially those of Victoria and South Australia. Hercus brought a different perspective to recording these languages than that of the earlier 'collectors'. She refused to accept the view put to her by others that the language knowledge in Victoria at the time (early 1960s) was severely limited and valueless, and instead set out to find and record all remaining language knowledge across the state. In the preface of her resulting volume *Victorian Languages: A Late Survey*, she states: 'It would probably be true to say that there are no elderly or even middle-aged persons of Aboriginal descent in Victoria and the south of New South Wales who have not at some stage been questioned by us about the language.'[12] She showed a deep respect for the people and the languages she recorded, and formed close friendships with those she worked with that lasted for the rest of her long life—and extended to younger generations as well. Hercus brought linguistic expertise to the Aboriginal languages she worked with, and thus was able to provide great insight into their grammatical systems and the interplay between language and culture. Her work is monumentally important to our understanding of the languages of Victoria and the south-east of Australia, and she is still held in deep regard by many of the Indigenous communities for whom her work is central to their language-reclamation efforts.

Yet, in a terrible missed opportunity, Hercus was never employed by the University of Melbourne. In 1967 she was appointed to a part-time research fellowship in TGH Strehlow's Department of Australian Linguistics at the University of Adelaide, and then to the ANU in 1969. Linguistics at the University of Melbourne was initially part of Russian and Slavonic Studies, and it wasn't until 1988, with the appointment of Nicholas Evans to a revamped Linguistics program, that linguistic engagement with speakers of Indigenous languages began in earnest. With his own long experience of working with a number of Aboriginal languages, and prior employment at the School of Australian Languages in Batchelor, Northern Territory (now the Batchelor Institute of Indigenous Tertiary Education), Evans developed a program that encouraged new research among a cohort of postgraduate students and established the tradition of respectful, engaged linguistic work with Indigenous communities across Australia that continues today.

Language Documentation

The 1990s saw an expansion of linguistic research at the University of Melbourne, with a particular focus on the description and documentation of Indigenous languages across Australia, bolstered by the appointment of Professor Peter Austin as the foundation chair in linguistics in 1996. By now, linguistic research was focused on developing comprehensive grammatical descriptions, texts and dictionaries based on extended fieldwork in communities and through building long-term relationships between language knowledge holders and researchers. The crisis of language endangerment across the world was becoming apparent, and the field of linguistics refocused in a global effort to record and document the world's linguistic diversity while it was still possible.[13] In his essay titled 'The World's Languages in Crisis', published in the field's leading journal *Language* in 1992, Michael Krauss made the bleak observation that: 'Obviously we must do some serious rethinking of our priorities, lest linguistics go down in history as the only science that presided obliviously over the disappearance of 90% of the very field to which it is dedicated.'[14]

In this global context of crisis, the continent of Australia was identified as 'the worst', with an estimated 90 per cent of its languages being 'very near extinction'.[15] Thus, linguists across Australia and particularly at the University of Melbourne were concentrating on working with elderly first-language speakers to document traditional languages, and to create materials that could be used by communities to maintain these languages, or revive them in the future. Evans established a successful postgraduate program that saw students and postdoctoral fellows working on languages nationwide, including Rachel Nordlinger (Wambaya),[16] Jeanie Bell (Badjala language of Gari (Fraser Island)),[17] Adam Saulwick (Rembarrnga),[18] Alice Gaby (Kuuk Thaayorre),[19] Ruth Singer (Mawng)[20] and Jennifer Green (Arandic sand stories).[21] This tradition has continued into the present day, with postgraduate projects on languages such as Gurindji Kriol,[22] Dalabon and Kayardild,[23] Tiwi,[24] Ngandi,[25] Murrinhpatha,[26] Kunbarlang,[27] Mangarla[28] and many more.

In addition to Nick Evans, staff in the linguistics program at the University of Melbourne who have worked with speakers of Indigenous languages include Peter Austin (Diyari, SA; Gascoyne/Pilbara region languages, WA; Gamilaraay, NSW); Brett Baker (Ngalakgan, NT; Wubuy, NT); Rebecca Defina (Pitjantjatjara, SA); Janet Fletcher (phonetics of Australian languages); Jennifer Green (Alyawarr and central Australian sign languages); Barbara Kelly (Murrinhpatha, NT); John Mansfield (Murrinhpatha, NT); Bill McGregor (Kimberley languages, WA); Rachel Nordlinger (Bilinarra, NT; Wambaya, NT; Murrinhpatha, NT); Lesley Stirling (Kala Lagaw Ya, Qld); Nick Thieberger (Pilbara, WA); Jill Vaughan (Burarra, NT); and Gillian Wigglesworth (Aboriginal child language).

Part of the engagement with Indigenous languages and communities during this time is reflected in the use of linguistic evidence in native title claims, a range of which is used to assert an Indigenous group's continued connection to the claimed land since what is termed 'Sovereignty', or the date at which European settlers made a formal claim to the land. Evans was the linguistic expert in the Wellesley Islands Sea claim,[29] the Lardil claim[30] and the Croker Island claim.[31] Thieberger was the linguistic expert in the Esperance Nyungar claim,[32] the Ngarluma/Yindjibarndi claim[33] and the Single Noongar claim.[34] Thieberger also co-wrote the 'State of Indigenous Languages in Australia' report (with Patrick McConvell) in 2001.[35]

Accompanying the sense of urgency to work with Indigenous speakers' languages was the field's shift to 'language documentation' from the narrower 'language description' of the previous decades. 'Language documentation' involves the creation of good records in the process of doing language description and ensuring these records are safely archived in a way that ensures their ongoing preservation and accessibility for future generations. In 2004 Thieberger developed new methods for citing primary language material in order to make it accessible in future.[36] This led to his work on the Pacific and Regional Archive for Digital Sources in Endangered Cultures (PARADISEC). PARADISEC digitises analog field recordings and makes them available online,[37] with some 1300 languages, from Australia and elsewhere, represented in the collection. The University of Melbourne is one of the founding partners in this effort, along with the University of Sydney and the ANU.

Collaboration

Although we are seeing a small increase in enrolments in very recent years, few Indigenous people have taken up postgraduate study in linguistics across Australia. At the University of Melbourne, Jeanie Bell is currently the only such graduate, having completed an MA in 2002 on Badjala, her grandfather's language. However, in the last decade or so, linguistic research has become increasingly collaborative, with teams of non-Indigenous and Indigenous researchers working together throughout all stages of a project, and academic outputs more regularly co-authored by academics and Indigenous knowledge-holders.

With the establishment of the Research Unit for Indigenous Language in 2014, there has been an increased engagement with community-led language research that serves to support communities in their own goals of language maintenance and revitalisation. These projects have focused on such topics as the repatriation of heritage language materials (the Daly Languages project[38]), developing innovative ways to make old language sources accessible to communities (the Digital Daisy Bates and Nyingarn projects[39]), and providing training and support for Indigenous community members wanting to work on their own language-revitalisation projects.

In 2018, following a generous bequest by Duncan Leary, the Research Unit launched the 50 Words Project, which aims to provide fifty words of every Indigenous language across Australia, with audio provided by language speakers.[40] The website allows a user to read and hear the words, thus avoiding the problem of reading words in a range of spelling systems, and encouraging an understanding of how Indigenous languages are written and pronounced. The principles and design behind the 50 Words Project address the inadequacies of past research practices by ensuring all contributions are community-led and only Indigenous voices are represented. Each language community also has control over the way they are represented and named on the site, with the system being flexible and adaptable enough to reflect the enormous cultural and linguistic diversity across the continent. The 50 Words Project is thus illustrative of the collaborative approach of the modern era, which stands in sharp contrast to the 'collectors' of the nineteenth century. The site has had some 100 000 users in the three years it has been online, and currently includes contributions from around ninety Australian language communities.

Despite its earlier history, the University of Melbourne is now at the forefront of engaged, collaborative research on the languages of Australia, with the Research Unit for Indigenous Language hosting the largest concentration of language-focused research with Indigenous communities across the country. In addition to work in linguistics, the Wilin Centre for Indigenous Arts and Cultural Development, and especially its Research Unit for Indigenous Arts and Cultures led by Tiriki Onus and Sally Treloyn, has a strong focus on Indigenous music and performance, of which language is often a central component.

Conclusion

There is now a recognition that academic research on Indigenous languages not only *can* be of use to the speakers of those languages, but *must* be useful to them, and that the research is improved because of its relevance to and use by those speakers. The role of academia can be to facilitate the work done by Indigenous people with their own languages and to promote understanding of those languages in the broader community.

Notes

1 Tom Griffiths, *Hunters and Collectors: The Antiquarian Imagination in Australia*, Cambridge University Press, Melbourne, 1996.

2 Tamsin Donaldson, 'Hearing the First Australians', in Ian Donaldson and Tamsin Donaldson (eds), *Seeing the First Australians*, Allen & Unwin, Sydney, 1985, pp. 81, 97.

3 The summary of Redmond Barry's language work relies on the excellent and detailed research presented in Peter Marsh, *Unravelling the Images: Redmond Barry and the Aboriginal Vocabularies*, Kitchen Table Press, 2013, p. 9. Thanks also to Barry Blake and Stephen Morey for advice.

4 Marsh, *Unravelling the Images*.

5 Redmond Barry, *A Vocabulary of Dialects Spoken by Aboriginal Natives of Australia*, compiled by the Trustees of the Public Library of Victoria, Melbourne, 1867. A scanned copy of this document is available at the National Library of Australia: https://catalogue.nla.gov.au/Record/656466 (accessed 30 October 2023).

6 The booklet also contains a vocabulary of a New Caledonian language that Professor Claire Moyse has determined to be Nyelâyu de Balade (personal communication).

7 Thieberger has created a text version of each of the vocabularies in this document, available on request: https://catalog.paradisec.org.au/collections/NT14 (accessed 30 October 2023).

8 Barry, *A Vocabulary of Dialects*, pp. vii–viii.

9 Rob Amery, Susie Greenwood and Jasmin Morley, *Kaurna Warrapiipa: Kaurna Dictionary*, Kaurna Warra Pintyanthi and Wakefield Press, Adelaide, 2022.

10 James Turner, *Philology: The Forgotten Origins of the Modern Humanities*, Princeton University Press, Princeton, 2014, p. 1.

11 WEH Stanner and Helen Shiels (eds), *Australian Aboriginal Studies: A Symposium of Papers Presented at the 1961 Research Conference*, Oxford University Press, Melbourne, 1963, p. 484.

12 Luise Hercus, *Victorian Languages: A Late Survey*, Pacific Linguistics, Canberra, 1962, p. v.

13 Ken Hale, 'Endangered Languages: On Endangered Languages and the Safeguarding of Diversity', *Language*, vol. 68, no. 1, 1992, pp. 1–42.

14 Michael Krauss, 'The World's Languages in Crisis', *Language*, vol. 68, no. 1, 1992, p. 10.

15 Ibid., p. 5.

16 Rachel Nordlinger, A Grammar of Wambaya, MA thesis, University of Melbourne, Parkville, 1993.

17 Jeanie A Bell, Sketch Grammar of the Badjala Language of Gari (Fraser Island), MA thesis, University of Melbourne, Parkville, 2003.

18 Adam Saulwick, Aspects of the Verb in Rembarrnga, a Polysynthetic Language of Northern Australia: Grammatical Description, Texts and Dictionary, PhD thesis, University of Melbourne, Parkville, 2003.

19 Alice Gaby, A Grammar of Kuuk Thaayorre, PhD thesis, University of Melbourne, Parkville, 2006.

20 Ruth Singer, Agreement in Mawng, PhD thesis, University of Melbourne.

21 Jennifer Green, Between the Earth and the Air: Multimodality in Arandic Sand Stories, PhD thesis, University of Melbourne, Parkville, 2009.

22 Felicity Meakins, Case Marking in Contact: The Development and Function of Case Morphology in Gurindji Kriol, an Australian Mixed Language, PhD thesis, University of Melbourne, Parkville, 2007.

23 Belinda Ross, Prosody and Grammar in Dalabon and Kayardild, PhD thesis, University of Melbourne, Parkville, 2011.
24 Aidan Wilson, Tiwi Revisited: A Reanalysis of Traditional Tiwi Verb Morphology, MA thesis, University of Melbourne, Parkville, 2014.
25 Brighde Collins, Aspectual Expression in Ngandi: Past and Present, MA thesis, University of Melbourne, Parkville, 2015.
26 William Forshaw, Little Kids, Big Verbs: The Acquisition of Murrinhpatha Bipartite Stem Verbs, PhD thesis, University of Melbourne, Parkville, 2016; Lucinda Davidson, Allies and Adversaries: Categories in Murrinhpatha Speaking Children's Talk, PhD thesis, University of Melbourne, Parkville, 2018.
27 Ivan Kapitanov, A Grammar of Kunbarlang, PhD thesis, University of Melbourne, Parkville, 2019.
28 Brigitte Louise Agnew, The Core of Mangarla Grammar, PhD thesis, University of Melbourne, Parkville, 2020.
29 Federal Court of Australia, *Lardil Peoples v Queensland* [2004] FCA 298, http://www.austlii.edu.au/cgi-bin/viewdoc/au/cases/cth/FCA/2004/298.html (accessed 30 October 2023).
30 Ibid.
31 Federal Court of Australia, *Mary Yarmirr & Ors v The Northern Territory of Australia & Ors* [1998] FCA 771 (6 July 1998), http://www.austlii.edu.au/cgi-bin/viewdoc/au/cases/cth/FCA/1998/771.html (accessed 30 October 2023).
32 Federal Court of Australia, *Bullen on Behalf of the Esperance Nyungar People v State of Western Australia* [2014] FCA 197 (14 March 2014), http://www.austlii.edu.au/cgi-bin/viewdoc/au/cases/cth/FCA/2014/197.html (accessed 30 October 2023).
33 Federal Court of Australia, *Daniel v Western Australia* [2003] FCA 666, http://www.austlii.edu.au/cgi-bin/viewdoc/au/cases/cth/FCA/2003/666.html (accessed 30 October 2023).
34 Federal Court of Australia, *Bennell v Western Australia* [2006] FCA 1243 (19 September 2006)http://www.austlii.edu.au/cgi-bin/viewdoc/au/cases/cth/FCA/2006/1243.html (accessed 30 October 2023).
35 Patrick McConvell and Nicholas Thieberger, 'State of Indigenous Languages in Australia—2001', Australia State of the Environment Second Technical Paper Series (Natural and Cultural Heritage), Department of the Environment and Heritage, Canberra, 2001.
36 Nicholas Thieberger, Topics in the Grammar and Documentation of South Efate, an Oceanic Language of Central Vanuatu, PhD thesis, University of Melbourne, Parkville, 2004.
37 Pacific and Regional Archive for Digital Sources in Endangered Cultures, 2023, https://paradisec.org.au (accessed 30 October 2023).
38 The Daly Languages (Australia), May 2022, https://dalylanguages.org (accessed 30 October 2023). For more on this topic, see papers in Linda Barwick, Jennifer Green and Petronella Vaarzon-Morel (eds), *Archival Returns: Central Australia and Beyond*, LD&C Special Publication no. 18, University of Hawaii Press and Sydney University Press, Honolulu and Sydney, 2019.
39 Digital Daisy Bates, n.d., https://bates.org.au (accessed 30 October 2023); Nyingarn, n.d., https://nyingarn.net (accessed 30 October 2023).
40 50 Words Project, n.d., https://50words.online (accessed 30 October 2023).

Gifts and Legacies

The Woodward Collection at the University of Melbourne

MARCIA LANGTON and LOUISE MURRAY[1]

THE ROYAL COMMISSION into Aboriginal Land Rights, or the Aboriginal Land Rights Commission (1973–74; hereafter 'the Commission'), sought to establish how land rights could be recognised in the Northern Territory. In 1973, Justice Woodward, in his role as chair of the Commission, was presented with ten objects of profound importance to Yolŋu people.[2] Each object was presented to him by a senior clan representative. The meaning expressed in the painted designs signified the ownership by the clans of traditional Yolŋu estates and emblematised the life, history and sacred narratives connected to the land and sea estates of the respective clans whose Elders created them. The designs and images on the objects and their meanings are matters of Yolŋu law and assertions of ancestral authority. Consequently, they cannot be considered as disconnected from their historical context, particularly that of dispossession and despoliation of Yolŋu estates by a major bauxite mining and processing operation and the terms of Woodward's Commission. Today, the Woodward Collection continues to attest to a rich legacy of generous engagement by Yolŋu with the University of Melbourne and the wider community. The Collection also holds the potential to challenge the University in how it conceives of its relationship with Yolŋu into the future, recognising and understanding the significance of Yolŋu communication and political assertion in relation to land rights and native title.

The Commission took place at the end of a period of cultural and political adjustment, a time of optimism for Aboriginal people, who were encouraged by the cultural recognition embodied in the results of the 1967 referendum and the establishment by the federal government of bodies such as the Aboriginal Arts Board of the Australia Council.[3] Prior to the Commission, Woodward had been a Queen's Counsel in the first native title case, *Milirrpum vs Nabalco Pty Ltd*, in the Northern Territory Supreme Court, decided in 1971. The case was heard by Justice Blackburn who, while sympathetic to the plaintiffs, found 'there could be no recognition of Aboriginal laws, despite the large amount of evidence of their existence submitted to the court'.[4] His argument rested on British common law, which, in 1788, deemed New Holland or Australia 'empty' without 'settled inhabitants or settled law'—a legal concept encapsulated in the doctrine of terra nullius overturned by Justice Brennan in *Mabo and Others v Queensland (No. 2) 1992*.[5]

Not long after the dispiriting outcome of *Milirrpum v Nabalco Pty Ltd*, Labor Opposition leader Gough Whitlam announced in an election campaign that a Labor government would 'legislate to give aborigines [sic] land rights—not just because their case is beyond argument, but because all of us as Australians are diminished while the aborigines [sic] are denied their rightful place in this nation'.[6] After winning government, Whitlam established the Royal Commission into Aboriginal Land Rights and appointed Woodward to investigate how land rights could be established.[7] Woodward's findings and recommendations had significant impact—the *Aboriginal Land Rights (Northern Territory) Act 1976* was modelled on his recommendations.[8]

After the Commission, Woodward continued his distinguished legal career as judge of the Northern Territory Supreme Court, judge of the Australian Industrial Court and judge of the Supreme Court, Australian Capital Territory. He was head of security in the Australian Security Intelligence Organisation from 1976 to 1981, and in 1977, with the establishment of the Federal Court of Australia, he was appointed Federal Court judge.[9] In 1990 he became chancellor of his alma mater, the University of Melbourne. Following his retirement as chancellor in 2001, Woodward gifted a collection of sacred bark paintings and objects to the University. In 2005 he recorded in his memoirs the circumstances under which the artefacts were given to him, describing the event and what he believed was the significance and status of these objects as 'gifts'. He wrote that, during the inquiry,

> there was one occasion when Aboriginal kindness took me completely by surprise. A big ceremony in my honour was arranged one evening

> in 1973 on Darwin's main football oval. After some dancing and other entertainment, I was asked to go down to the arena where, in front of some 1500 people, I was presented with a number of bark paintings from various communities in the Top End who had been my clients in the Gove Case. I was also given a didgeridoo and a decorated walking stick which I was given to understand, was one of the two which had been ceremonially displayed to Justice Blackburn in the course of the Gove Case—as evidence of Aboriginal title to their lands. I can only assume that it had been 'deconsecrated' and replaced, which I knew did happen from time to time[10] ... In 2003, with the consent of the Aboriginal clans involved, I gave these gifts to the Potter Museum at Melbourne University.[11]

The Gift

The original donation of the Woodward Collection to the University of Melbourne was described at the time by valuers as 'eight bark paintings and two ceremonial items by Yolŋu Northeast Arnhem Land artists'.[12] By way of provenance, it was noted that the works had been gifted to the donor in 1973 and that the historical significance of the collection lay in their collective status as 'objects and bark paintings produced by senior Yolŋu members of associated clan groups of Yirrkala Yolŋu people'.[13] At the time the works were donated, information was verbally communicated to a valuer by Rirratjiŋu clan members, other information was marked on some items, while additional information such as notes on the clan stories and the circumstances of the original gift were conveyed by the donor. It was also understood that this important collection of bark paintings and artefacts was never intended for commercial sale, nor was it simply a gift of appreciation to Justice Woodward. Each work had been created by Elders from different clans and represented ancestral designs, which might be understood as the imprimatur of traditional Yolŋu law and culture. These objects therefore occupied a very different status in the economy of Aboriginal art and exchange, within a complex framework of signification, practice and tradition.[14]

> Aboriginal transactions are not mere 'gift exchanges', as might be thought by some ... but are complicated social and economic relations like those in any human society—indeed necessary to any human society. In Aboriginal societies these transactions manifest economic as well as social, moral and religious relations, and express obligations such as rank or status, alliance, kinship and other relationships of reciprocity.[15]

The works in the Woodward Collection represent the two moieties of Yolŋu society: Dhuwa and Yirritja. Within these moieties are a number of clans, including the Rirratjiŋu, Djapu, Dhuḏi-Djapu, Gälpu, Djambarrpuyŋu, Marrakulu, Golumala, Ḏätiwuy, Marraŋu and Wägilak of the Dhuwa moiety; and the Gumatj, Maŋgalili, Dhaḻwaŋu, Maḏarrpa, Gupapuyŋu, Wangurri, Warramiri, Munyuku and Ritharrŋu of the Yirritja moiety. The estates of each clan are represented by their *dhulaŋ miny'tji* or sacred clan designs, which are coded mnemonics that refer back to the epic song cycles detailing the journeys of ancestral creation beings and the creation events.[16] The designs of these individual works belong to specific clans, and it is difficult in written descriptions to detail the many layered, deliberately nuanced and coded meanings of the works in this collection. Each *miny'tji* references hundreds of stanzas of epic poetry. The concepts and emotions in such a dense amount of text would be impossible to precis even in their original language. These designs are visual statements and may be read as a kind of text. Referring generally to Yolŋu art, Howard Morphy acknowledges that 'these designs can refer to concrete things, such as the topography of the landscape and the identity of the social group owning the design, but their most significant characteristic is that they have the capacity to encode a multiplicity of meanings'.[17]

Gifts and Legacies

Bark paintings have played an important role as conduits for the representation of religion, law and ritual of the Yolŋu and other peoples in northern Australia, whose traditions include painting on bark, on bodies and sacred paraphernalia for ceremonies, and painting on bark for anthropologists from Baldwin Spencer, Lloyd Warner and Donald Thomson onwards, and later, with the advent of the missionaries, painting on bark for the marketplace—created as a cottage industry for the missions. The production of art for economic return became a regular feature of Yolŋu creative practices following World War II.[18]

The reverend Wilbur Chaseling, founding superintendent of the Methodist Overseas Mission at Yirrkala, saw the economic viability of Aboriginal art as an opportunity to raise money for the Mission and to keep the community occupied.[19] Mungurrawuy Yunupiŋu (1907–1979), a Gumatj clan leader and famously father of the late clan leader Dr G Yunupiŋu and Mandawuy and prominent female artists, Gulumbu,

Barrama and Nyapanyapa Yunupiŋu, was one of the first artists to paint for Chaseling. He referred to the works Yolŋu produced for the missionary to sell as 'anyhow' paintings.[20] When asked by anthropologist Howard Morphy what this meant, the artist explained that reverend Chaseling had asked them 'to paint "anyhow" [paintings], and that was what they did since it was only for tobacco', during the period before the introduction of the cash economy.[21] While in some instances this was the case, it is too simplistic to draw a clear delineation between art produced for commercial purposes and *miny'tji* painted within ceremonial contexts, as Morphy has argued elsewhere.[22] Bark paintings and cultural objects were made for a range of different purposes, including, in the case of Woodward's gifts, to communicate with outsiders the deeply encoded cultural and political foundations of Yolŋu law.

The Woodward Collection holds a distinct status as an exemplar of Yolŋu intent to demonstrate, claim and assert traditional ownership by clans of defined areas of land and sea and, in other instances, to use art to protest a lack of recognition of their own religious traditions. In this sense, the Collection can be associated with other more public instances where art has been presented to non-Yolŋu people. In 1957, Yolŋu clan leaders prepared a demonstration in Galiwin'ku on Elcho Island in full view of all the residents of the mission, Yolŋu and staff alike, of *raŋga* (secret-sacred sculptures) related to burial practices.[23] Set up near the old mission church, this display was created to protest to the missionaries a lack of recognition of Yolŋu religious traditions. A small, open enclosure held a display of *raŋga* that were being made public for the first time; the central *raŋga* had a Christian cross at its apex. According to Ronald Berndt, the stimulus for the Elders was to put their relations with Europeans on a new footing.[24] It was 'an attempt to combine something of both (European and Aboriginal) to form a coherent whole which has meaning for them and is not just imposed on them from outside'.[25] The main characteristic of Yolŋu cosmology is that, through a complex system of *gurruṯu* (Yolŋu kinship relationships), it places everything in creation into an intricate unified matrix of relationality.

However, the response from both missionaries and the government was not of the kind that the Yolŋu had hoped for; their intervention was ignored. The Yolŋu did not realise that their secret-sacred knowledge held little or no value for the missionaries and their lay community, and, more than likely, was not understood.[26] Nevertheless, these treaty-seeking transactions of religious and economic import continued to be attempted by the Yolŋu clans of the region.[27]

In 1962 the clan leaders of Yirrkala in north-eastern Arnhem Land presided over the creation of two panels of sacred art, representing each of the clans of the Yirritja and Dhuwa moieties. They were displayed on either side of the altar in the mission church at Yirrkala and again represented the most sacred and secret of the clan *waŋarr* (creator ancestors), rarely revealed in public.[28] The Yirrkala church panels were painted by eight artists from each of the Dhuwa and Yirritja moieties. The paintings declare that, alongside the religion of the mission, there exists an ancient religious belief system of Yolŋu law. They are understood to be the first documented land rights statement by Yolŋu, and their context was the hallowed but public space of the church.

Howard Morphy identifies a quintessential element that unites all these works when he observed that the bark petition presented to the House of Representatives in 1963 was important because it received national attention and introduced a form of evidence—sacred paintings as title-deeds to land—that argued for new solutions'.[29]

The Woodward Collection

The works in the Woodward Collection that may be viewed by the public include paintings—all earth pigments on prepared bark sheets—and a *yiḏaki* (although its correct name may be *dhaḏalal* but this could not be confirmed; commonly referred to as a didjeridu). The paintings all date from around 1972 and were made using the methods of Yolŋu artists, which begins with the laying down of a red ochre base on a prepared sheet of the *Eucalyptus tetrodonta*.[30] The works feature single striations or cross-hatched lines in yellow, white and black, representing the artist and their clan country, and the *waŋarr* associated with that clan estate.[31] Fine dots are often carefully placed within shapes or along borders representing land and waterways, food sources, insect life and so on. Animal, plant or figurative motifs are often painted in a single hue or filled with fine cross-hatching or singular delicate lines, creating *bir'yun*, a surface intensity that is a characteristic aesthetic of Yolŋu painting and was first described by Donald Thomson.[32] These figurative representations of animals are in fact references to specific kinship identities and connections dictated by

Ganbitjun Mudinbuy
Gupapuyŋu Ḻiyaḻanmirri Marrkula clan,
Yirritja moiety
Birrkuda, c. 1972
earth pigments on Stringybark
80 × 46 cm
The University of Melbourne Art Collection
Gift of Sir Edward Woodward
Donated through the Australian Government's Cultural Gifts Program, 2003
2003.0012

Mamulinauwi (attributed)
Gupapuyŋu Ḏagurrgurr clan,
Yirritja moiety, 1934–deceased
Djaŋ'kawu story, c. 1972
earth pigments on Stringybark
70.5 × 39 cm
The University of Melbourne Art Collection
Gift of Sir Edward Woodward
Donated through the Australian Government's Cultural Gifts Program, 2003
2003.0015

Gawirriṉ Gumana
Dhaḻwaŋu clan, Yirritja moiety, c. 1935–2016
Barama and Lany'tjuŋ, c. 1972
earth pigments on Stringybark
74.5 × 36 cm
The University of Melbourne Art Collection
Gift of Sir Edward Woodward
Donated through the Australian Government's Cultural Gifts Program, 2003
2003.0016

Waḏatjaŋan Guyula
Djambarrpuyŋu Ḻiya-dhälinymirr clan, Dhuwa moiety
***Gapu Guḻarri miny'tji* (*Guḻarri waters design*)**, c. 1972
earth pigments on Stringybark
80 × 46 cm
The University of Melbourne Art Collection
Gift of Sir Edward Woodward
Donated through the Australian Government's Cultural Gifts Program, 2003
2003.0017

Larrtjanŋa Ganambarr
c. 1932–2000
Ŋaymil clan, Dhuwa moiety,
before c. 1932–2000
Djaŋ'kawu story, c. 1972
earth pigments on Stringybark
55.5 × 27.5 cm
The University of Melbourne Art Collection
Gift of Sir Edward Woodward
Donated through the Australian Government's
Cultural Gifts Program, 2003
2003.0018

Gätji
Guyamirrilil clan, Yirritja moiety
Gapu Gular̲ri – Gätji, Gapu Raŋga dhukurrurru (Gular̲ri waters – mangrove worm, freshwater and sacred rock), c. 1972
earth pigments on Stringybark
67.5 × 28 cm
The University of Melbourne Art Collection
Gift of Sir Edward Woodward
Donated through the Australian Government's
Cultural Gifts Program, 2003
2003.0019

the overarching logic of the unified system of *gurruṯu* that connects us all. Everything in the process of creation of such works is purposeful and considered. As Judith Ryan observes, 'This is not idle pattern or infill but a form of symbolic elaboration which unites the artist with his source of life, his totem spirit in the land.'[33]

The characteristic style and iconography of these works are recorded and known beyond the artists and communities that produced them, by some 'literate' anthropologists and curators with cultural knowledge of Yolŋu traditions and practices, and who can read them.[34] The importance of this is that iconography and style are recognisable and have meaning as cultural signifiers. Style in these works is not just of the individual's making but is deeply reflective of, and rooted in, complex intergenerational law, stories, beliefs, religion and, importantly, connections to land and water—knowledge of which has been passed through generations. The designs and their meanings are sacred, bestowed by *waŋarr* to different social groups, and are therefore inherited. Thus painting has a unique place in the lives of Yolŋu people because the designs provide tangible evidence of an unbroken lineage of connection to land and waterways. An appreciation of these cultural and legal dynamics is therefore essential to a deeper understanding of the significance of these gifts to Woodward.

Of equal significance is that the three restricted works presented to Woodward are attributed to highly regarded senior Yolŋu artists and ritual leaders. While these were presented at a public ceremony, they record secret Yolŋu men's law.[35] The works were created by Birrikitji Gumana (1890–1982), Wandjuk Marika (1927–1987) and Narritjin Maymurra (1916–1981). Wandjuk Marika was a member of the Rirratjiŋu clan of the Dhuwa moiety and the 'custodian of Yalaŋbara, the sacred Arnhem Land beach at which the Djaŋ'kawu sisters (creation ancestors) stepped ashore and gave birth to the first people'.[36] Wandjuk was also one of the witnesses who made and gathered sacred objects to present at the land rights case in Darwin, explaining: 'I take the sacred object to the Land Right case ... We were in that courtroom, and we show them that these things very important and we explaining to them.'[37] Birrikitji Gumana (leader of both the Dhaḻwaŋu clan and the Yirritja moiety) and Narritjin Maymurra (clan and ceremonial leader of the Maŋgalili clan and Yirritja moiety) both helped create part of the Yirritja church panel at Yirrkala. Both also gave evidence at the Gove Peninsula land rights case *Milirrpum v Nabalco Pty Ltd*, and are celebrated artists whose work is held in many national and international collections. Many of their early paintings from the 1940s were produced for and collected by Catherine and Ronald Berndt.[38]

The transcript from the Gove case reveals the importance placed on the sacred objects as evidence of ownership and connection to land:

> At 9.30 am on Wednesday, the 27th May [1970] in His Honour's Chambers, in the presence of His Honour and all counsel, sacred objects were shown and sacred songs were sung by representatives of the Rirratjunga [sic, Rirratjiŋu] and Galpu [sic, Gälpu] people. It was agreed between the parties that what took place should be treated by His Honour as a view for the purpose of understanding the evidence of the case.[39]

In the same way that the works presented at the Gove case have significance beyond their status as art, the same can be said of the open works gifted to Woodward. The six paintings on bark and the *yiḏaki* tell important waŋarr stories of both moieties and incorporate *miny'tji*, some which are customarily painted on the body for both *dhapi* (initiation) and mortuary ceremonies.[40] One work by Ŋaymil artist Larrtjanŋa references the waŋarr story of the Djaŋ'kawu, who gave birth to the first people at Yalaŋbara, connected by mala (patrilineal affiliation) to the Ŋaymil site of Yäŋunbi. A work by Dhaḻwaŋu artist Gawirriṉ Gumana represents the waŋarr story of Barama, the greatest of the Yirritja moiety creation ancestors, who is described as follows:

> He came to Gangan [sic, Gäŋgaṉ] in Dhalwngu [sic, Dhaḻwaŋu] clan territory to establish his law and teach mythical leaders of the Dhaḻwaŋu clan their songs, dances, rituals and sacred designs. To ensure the distribution of all the law, he commissioned Laitjung [sic, Lany'tjuŋ] ... to travel north along the coast from Blue Mud Bay to Yirrkala and then westwards to Miliŋgimbi and leave some *raŋga* (sacred emblems) for each of the Yirritja clans along the route. Each clan owns a part of this story and a part of the land which bears the sacred imprint or trace of these supernatural beings. They all derive from Barama and share the sacred diamond design which first formed on the body of Barama when he emerged from the sea and the foam clung to his body in diamonds. The design runs as a *leit motiv* through paintings of the Yirritja artists and encodes meanings specific to particular clans, which differ according to context like words in a sentence.[41]

The inclusion of iconography associated with the initiation ceremonies that transform male children into men is important as such designs refer to the special relationship between body painting for both initiation and mortuary ceremonies, two events that can be considered *bookends* of a Yolŋu man's life. (Women's ceremonial body painting is different and has its own distinctive logic.) One is his initiation into adulthood and with that the gaining of special knowledge and rights, and with death, the cessation of earthly existence and transition into the spirit world. According to anthropologist Jessica De Largy Healy, the body paintings for both ritual ceremonies inscribe and materialise the links between the initiate or deceased, their clan, their land and their connection to *waŋarr*. The design inscribes their place in the world on the body during initiation, which in turn survives as a palimpsest when it is reinscribed on the body in death. This process is elaborated by De Largy Healy, who explains that

> these body paintings act as relational matrixes which locate the initiands within a socio-cosmic web of connections. At the other end of the male ritual life-cycle, the bodies of the deceased undergo a similar process of transfiguration, as they are made to resemble the groups' most sacred objects, seen to instantiate the powers of specific ancestral beings. In the context of these rituals, the links between clans, places, and ancestral beings are expressed by being made visible on and around the body.[42]

As mentioned earlier, apart from the paintings on bark, there is also a *yiḏaki*, a musical instrument that is a common feature of Yolŋu '*manikay* (public ceremonial song)' in traditional and contemporary contexts, included in the Woodward Collection.[43] The *yiḏaki* is another object deeply embedded in Yolŋu cultural life through ceremony, song, dance and music, and carries important clan associations. Lloyd Hollenberg, a physicist and musician who worked with the late Gupapuyŋu leader Dr Joseph Neparrŋa Gumbula, explained, 'Yolŋu *yiḏaki* makers and players deliberately aligned instrument morphologies and playing styles with distinct clan identities.'[44] This would be determined by features such as the length and shape of the instrument, whether conical or cylindrical, as well as the decorative elements.[45]

Just as we may question the inclusion of works pertaining to initiation in the original gift, we may also wonder about the inclusion of the *yiḏaki* in the context of land rights and title deeds. Ethnomusicologist Aaron Corn explains that the *yiḏaki* is related ontologically to both traditional Yolŋu initiation and funeral ceremonies, and is 'steeped in philosophies and beliefs through which Yolŋu conceptualised life and knowledge'.[46]

More specifically, the *yiḏaki*—made from the trunk of the *Eucalyptus tetrodonta* (stringybark) that has been hollowed out by termites—is considered one form or manifestation of the *d̲upun* or *l̲arrakitj* (hollow memorial pole or ossuary), the container for the bones that many Yolŋu clans customarily used within extensive mortuary rituals. Accompanying the performance of a clan's *manikay*, the *yid̲aki* is played with the same breath or ancestral wind that rushes through the *d̲upun*, carrying the *birrimbirr* (soul) of the deceased back to their place of origin in the profound ancestral realm; the bones, having been purified of the flesh, are interred in the *d̲upun* and placed in the ground at a clan's *ŋaraka-wäŋa* (bone-country, ancestral estate).[47]

Notes in Woodward's possession that accompanied the items when the donation was made to the University include a single page describing the 'Story from the Dhal̲waŋu Clan'. The last two sentences of the note seem to indicate a clear intention for the gift to Woodward:

> This is the law for the Dhal̲waŋu clan. A hut for Barama, Lany'tjuŋ and Galparrimun. This is their traditional law. They gave this law to our great grandfathers. They gave this law to the Dhal̲waŋu through their son named Dhad̲alal the didjeridoo when Barama and Lany'tjuŋ and Galparrimun put to a place called Balambala a law for the Dhal̲waŋu and to our great great grandfathers and we are using at present the same law like this. If a man died any time young or old including children they would create the Dhad̲alal in memory of him. You see this arm, that is given by Barama when during that time he was teaching them a long time ago and to our great grandfathers, to our fathers, now to us. This paint on the mouth[-]piece which was made by a woman long time ago and we still keep it for this. On the back of the Dhad̲alal is a wild yam and the black one mean a name Baraŋgurrk. With that thing was crying a boy named Ganbulabula for this Dhad̲alal he was crying long time ago. At present we are always copying that spirit man who was crying. This time we are now giving this didgeridoo to you in memory of when you were fighting for our land so that you will talk to the government next time. [Author not named]

Conclusion

In January 2008, five years after these works were donated to the University of Melbourne and over thirty years after their presentation to Woodward, the University hosted the prestigious international art history conference titled 'Crossing Cultures: Conflict, Migration and Convergence'. Two key forums regarding the Woodward Collection were held as part of the conference, including a special closed session at the Ian Potter Museum of Art and an open session involving members of the public. Yolŋu clan leaders visited Melbourne to participate in the conference and to advise the University on the Woodward Collection's ongoing management, including any community protocols relating to restricted works.

Included in the delegation were senior women and clan leaders Dhuwarrwarr Marika, Margaret Djuwaṉdayŋu Yunupiŋu, Guḻumbu Yunupiŋu, Kathy Marawili, Djerrkŋu Marika and Dr Raymattja Marika AM, and senior men and clan leaders Mawalan II Marika, Wukuṉ Waṉambi, Waturr Gumana and Djambawa Marawili AM, along with Northern Land Council chairman Wäli Wunuŋmurra and then CEO John Christophersen. Some members of the delegation were descendants of the artists who had created the works at the time of the inquiry, over forty years prior. Information was also gathered about the gift from other session attendees, including anthropologists Professor Howard Morphy and Nancy Williams; Frank Purcell, who was also a member of the legal team who fought for the recognition of land rights for Yirrkala communities; and Sir Edward Woodward.[48] The closed and open sessions were the first time both the Yolŋu and the public had seen the works since they were presented to Woodward in Darwin in 1973.

After viewing the cultural objects, Yolŋu delegates confirmed the importance of the collection in relation to the recognition of Aboriginal land rights in the Northern Territory, and that the works held important cultural knowledge connecting current communities with their land, law and stories. They also held secret knowledge. Two of the delegates made the following comments:

> And these bark paintings are something very important to Aboriginal people, and they are still alive, even though they have been painted on bark, but the story in that painting is very much alive, and still very much a part of us ...[49]
>
> It's not just a painting. Beyond this painting it's a story, it symbolises the law and the culture.[50]

Over the past decade, both internationally and in Australia, it has become increasingly common museum practice to return certain categories of cultural material to their communities of origin. This has been done largely to redress the consequences of colonialism that saw the cultural expression and outputs of Indigenous people stolen, collected, dug up and souvenired, much of it destined for the museum diorama, international trade, or to be locked away only to be seen by the anthropologists and museum staff of the collecting institution. The current focus on 'wholesale repatriation' is sometimes understood as a type of postcolonial amelioration 'for the wrongs of colonial collecting', and this is certainly one aspect.[51] However, a much more complex project prevails that deals with the desires of communities to be reunited with their cultural heritage, and to ensure protocols of cultural practice are observed; for instance, in the burial of ancestral remains, the protection and re-engagement with secret-sacred objects, and to make sure the skills, knowledge and stories inherent in cultural material are made available to descendant communities.

Unlike works of art that are sold through art centres or held as stolen museum artefacts, the Woodward Collection at the University of Melbourne constitutes a special case of Aboriginal artistic expression that is both gift and legacy. Alongside other cultural material held in public Australian institutions, the status of this collection is unique as legal evidence, analogous to title deeds to land. The presence of this collection in the museum or institution therefore embodies a powerful gesture, a political statement, and a deliberative and formal dialogue by Yolŋu people with the non-Yolŋu world.

Notes

1 The authors would like to acknowledge the following people who have contributed their ideas, knowledge and expertise with great generosity to the development of this chapter: Yalmay Yunupiŋu, Lyndon Ormond-Parker, Samuel Curkpatrick, Bernadette Murphy, Judith Ryan, Max Moon and Will Stubbs. Some sections of this chapter are taken from Marcia Langton, 'The Art of Being Aboriginal', in J Anderson (ed.), *Crossing Cultures: Conflict, Migration and Convergence—The Proceedings of the 32nd International Congress of the History of Art*, Miegunyah Press, Melbourne, 2000, pp. 35–45.

2 Edward Woodward, *One Brief Interval: A Memoir*, Miegunyah Press, Melbourne, 2005, p. 136.

3 Langton, 'The Art of Being Aboriginal', p. 40. See also Ronald M Berndt, *An Adjustment Movement in Arnhem Land, Northern Territory of Australia*, Mouton, Paris, 1962.

4 Langton, 'The Art of Being Aboriginal', p. 40.

5 The following transcript from *Mabo and Others v Queensland* (No 2)[1992] HCA 23; 175 CLR 1, S37 (see https://derechodelacultura.org/wp-content/uploads/2015/03/Mabo-vs-Queensland.pdf) details the reassessment of the common law notion that Australia was 'without settled inhabitants or settled law' at the time of colonisation:

'37. It is one thing for our contemporary law to accept that the laws of England, so far as applicable, became the laws of New South Wales and of the other Australian colonies. It is another thing for our contemporary law to accept that, when the common law of England became the common law of the several colonies, the theory which was advanced to support the introduction of the common law of England accords with our present knowledge and appreciation of the facts.

When it was sought to apply Lord Watson's assumption in *Cooper v. Stuart* that the colony of New South Wales was "without settled inhabitants or settled law" to Aboriginal society in the Northern Territory, the assumption proved false. In *Milirrpum v. Nabalco Pty. Ltd.* Blackburn J. said (58) (1971) 17 FLR 141, at p. 267: "The evidence shows a subtle and elaborate system highly adapted to the country in which the people led their lives, which provided a stable order of society and was remarkably free from the vagaries of personal whim or influence. If ever a system could be called 'a government of laws, and not of men', it is that shown in the evidence before me."

Faced with a contradiction between the authority of the Privy Council and the evidence, his Honour held that the class to which a colony belonged was a question of law, not of fact (59) ibid., at p. 244; McNeil, Common Law Aboriginal Title, (1989), p. 292, fn. 207; Lester, The Territorial Rights of the Inuit of the Canadian Northwest Territories: A Legal Argument, (unpublished doctoral thesis (1981)), pp. 100–7, 155–7:

"Whether or not the Australian aboriginals living in any part of New South Wales had in 1788 a system of law which was beyond the powers of the settlers at that time to perceive or comprehend, it is beyond the power of this Court to decide otherwise than that New South Wales came into the category of a settled or occupied colony."

38. The facts as we know them today do not fit the "absence of law" or "barbarian" theory underpinning the colonial reception of the common law of England. That being so, there is no warrant for applying in these times rules of the English common law which were the product of that theory. It would be a curious doctrine to propound today that, when the benefit of the common law was first extended to Her Majesty's indigenous subjects in the Antipodes, its first fruits were to strip them of their right to occupy their ancestral lands. Yet the supposedly barbarian nature of indigenous people provided the common law of England with the justification for denying them their traditional rights and interests in land, as Lord Sumner speaking for the Privy Council said in In re Southern Rhodesia (60) (1919) AC 211, at pp. 233–234:

"The estimation of the rights of aboriginal tribes is always inherently difficult. Some tribes are so low in the scale of social organization that their usages and conceptions of rights and duties are not to be reconciled with the institutions or the legal ideas of civilized society. Such a gulf cannot be bridged. It would be idle to impute to such people some shadow of the rights known to our law and then to transmute it into the substance of transferable rights of property as we know them."'

6 Gough Whitlam, 'Speech, Blacktown', New South Wales, 13 November 1972.

7 Edward Woodward recalled in 'Three Wigs and Five Hats', The Fourth Eric Johnston Lecture delivered at the State Reference Library of the Northern Territory, 10 November 1989, Northern Territory Library Service, 1990, p. 8: 'I had only just completed, with my fellow members, the Report on Armed Services Pay and Conditions, when the Whitlam Government came to power and, in its first few days, I was asked by Gough Whitlam to undertake a Royal Commission into Aboriginal Land Rights. Whitlam made the decision in principle that land rights should be recognised; my task was to advise the Government how to go about it.'

8 The Aboriginal Land Rights Commission produced two reports. The first was released in July 1973. The second and final report was presented to the Australian

Government in April 1974. As explained by Colin Tatz ('From Welfare to Treaty: Reviewing Fifty Years of Aboriginal Policy and Practice', in G Ward and A Muckle (eds), *The Power of Knowledge, the Resonance of Tradition*, Electronic Publication of Papers from the AIATSIS Indigenous Studies Conference, September 2001, Australian Institute of Aboriginal and Torres Strait Islander Studies, Canberra, 2001, p. 12): 'The first forensic foray to achieve some Aboriginal autonomy over land took place a mere thirty years ago. The cases of *Mathaman and Others v Nabalco Pty Ltd* and *Milirrpum v Nabalco Pty Ltd and the Commonwealth of Australia* were decided in 1969 and 1971 respectively. The Yirrkala clans sought an end to bauxite mining on their reserve, and compensation for land that had been occupied and despoiled. In *Milirrpum*, the decision of Mr Justice Blackburn against the Yirrkala people was in some degree sympathetic because he believed he had only moral support, but no law, with which to back them. These two losses were the spur to the appointment of the Land Rights [Woodward] Commission and the subsequent Labor and then Coalition land rights legislation in the Northern Territory.'

9 See Woodward, *One Brief Interval*.

10 The sacred objects were not, however, 'deconsecrated' as Sir Edward assumed, and this was later confirmed in legal correspondence from the Northern Land Council to the University of Melbourne notifying it of the requirement to observe the condition that three items were restricted from public viewing because they were secret sacred objects.

11 Woodward, *One Brief Interval*, pp. 136–7.

12 See University Art Collection file: The 'Woodward Collection', *Sir Albert Edward Woodward*, AC, OBE, accession no. 102/26, University of Melbourne. Comments taken from valuation report by Vivien Anderson [Cultural Gifts Program approved valuer], 5 May 2003. See also valuation notes by Jan Martin [Cultural Gifts Program approved valuer], 26 May 2003.

13 Ibid.

14 See Langton, 'The Art of Being Aboriginal', p. 42: 'In 1949, Australian anthropologist Donald F Thomson refuted the idea that was long prevalent that most native title people live in a kind of idyllic "pre-economic" state. Based on his fieldwork among the Yolŋu of north-eastern Arnhem Land, Thomson's *Economic Structure and the Ceremonial Exchange Cycle in Arnhem Land* (Macmillan, Melbourne, 1949) provides an interpretation of the exchange of commodities among Aboriginal peoples of the region, describing the ceremonial or ritual exchange of "gifts" as the core of the economic system. In this work and elsewhere, the ceremonial exchange cycle has been described as a social and economic system that distributes material and non-material values rather than as merely a type of "gift exchange".'

15 Ibid., p. 42.

16 Anthropologist Howard Morphy, who lived with and learnt Yolŋu Matha, and worked with many artists, including Narritjin Maymurra (Maŋgalili clan) and Djambawa Marwili (Maŋgalili clan), defines *miny'tji* as 'a Yolŋu word for design, which can be applied to naturally occurring design as well as humanly produced ones' (*Aboriginal Art*, Phaidon Press, London, 1998, p. 423). Morphy writes further on the complex meaning of *miny'tji* in 'From Dull to Brilliant: The Aesthetics of Spiritual Power among the Yolŋu', in Jeremy Coote (ed.), *Anthropology, Art and Aesthetics*, Clarendon Press, London, p. 24. See also Lindy Allen, *Ancestral Power and the Aesthetic: Arnhem Land Paintings and Objects from the Donald*

Thomson Collection, exhibition catalogue, Ian Potter Museum of Art, University of Melbourne, Parkville, 2009, which references Donald Thomson's extensive writings on *miny'tji*: '[T]he distinctive patterns on the bark paintings and men's objects ... are sacred ceremonial designs called *miny'tji* and Donald Thomson's field writings reveal the depth of his investigation into the complexities associated with this notion and the tenets that underpin a unique artistic practice. He wrote extensively about the intrinsic importance of *miny'tji* and noted that it represented the totemic clan ancestors, *likan wangarr*. Further, he wrote that *miny'tji* was the embodiment of the ancestor—the *wangarr*—in that the patterns mirror the actual design painted on the body of the ancestor in ancestral times.'

17 Morphy, *Aboriginal Art*, p. 97.

18 Ibid., p. 27.

19 Ibid., p. 237.

20 Ibid.

21 Ibid.

22 Howard Morphy, *Becoming Art: Exploring Cross-Cultural Categories*, Routledge, London, 2020.

23 Langton, 'The Art of Being Aboriginal', p. 39.

24 Ronald Berndt and Catherine Berndt, 'Body and Soul: More Than an Episode!', in T Swain and T Bird Rose (eds), *Aboriginal Australians and Christian Missions: Ethnographic and Historical Studies*, Australian Association for the Study of Religions, Bedford Park, SA, 1988, pp. 45, 51.

25 Ronald Berndt, *An Adjustment Movement in Arnhem Land: Northern Territory of Australia*, Mouton, Paris, 1962, p. 87.

26 Ibid., p. 85.

27 Parts of the preceding section of the chapter are from Marcia Langton, 'Encountering Aboriginal Art', lecture, School of Anthropology, Geography and Environmental Studies, University of Melbourne, Parkville, 2001.

28 In 1959, Tony Tuckson, former director of the Art Gallery of New South Wales (1957–73), and Dr Stuart Scougall, an orthopaedic surgeon and researcher, commissioned an important collection of paintings on bark from Yolŋu families at Yirrkala. The paintings were by senior leaders in the community and similarly recorded important knowledge and sacred narratives. They were one of the earliest examples of such works being collected by a major Australian art gallery as opposed to an anthropological museum.

29 Morphy, *Aboriginal Art*, p. 255.

30 Judith Ryan, *Spirit in Land: Bark Paintings from Arnhem Land in the National Gallery of Victoria*, National Gallery of Victoria, Melbourne, 1990, p. 22.

31 See Judith Ryan, 'A Sacred Geometry: Yolŋu Art of North-Eastern Arnhem Land', in Ryan, *Spirit in Land*, pp. 22–7, for a discussion of the formal and sacred aspects of art of north-eastern Arnhem Land.

32 This visual effect was first noted by Donald Thomson, who translated *bir'yun* as 'brilliance': Thomson, in field notes cited by Morphy, 'From Dull to Brilliant', p. 28. Subsequent studies on the role of *bir'yun* within Yolŋu aesthetic practices have extended to consider photography and song: see Jennifer Deger, 'Shimmer', in H Callan (ed.), *The International Encyclopedia of Anthropology*, John Wiley & Sons, Hoboken, NJ, 2018; Jennifer Deger, 'Thick Photography', *Journal of Material Culture*, vol. 21, no. 1, 2016, pp. 111–32; and Samuel Curkpatrick, *Singing Bones: Ancestral Creativity and Collaboration*, Sydney University Press, Sydney, 2020.

33 Ryan, *Spirit in Land*, p. 4.

34 Morphy, *Aboriginal Art*; Ryan, *Spirit in Land.*

35 The restricted nature of these works, and their special care, was conveyed in correspondence from Wäli Wunuŋmurra, chairman of the Northern Land Council and senior member of the Dhal̲waŋu clan, to Glyn Davis, vice-chancellor, University of Melbourne, 5 February 2008. The letter reads as follows:
Dear Professor,
SACRED ART & OBJECTS HELD BY THE UNIVERSITY OF MELBOURNE
I write in my capacity as the Chairman of the Northern Land Council (NLC), and also as a senior member of the Dhalwangu clan and Yolŋu elder from north-east Arnhem Land. By way of additional background I am the only living signatory of the 1963 bark petition which is on display at Parliament House in Canberra, and I was an interpreter in the 1971 Gove Land Rights Case and the subsequent Royal Commission into Land Rights in the Northern Territory which was conducted by Justice Woodward in 1973 and 1974.
I welcomed the opportunity to attend the University of Melbourne on 16 and 17 January 2008 to view art and other objects held by the Ian Potter Museum of Art or otherwise by the University. I also welcomed the opportunity to meet University representatives, as well as the opportunity once again to meet with Sir Edward Woodward.
As discussed with university representatives, there is hidden and sacred knowledge contained within certain art held in the Woodward collection or otherwise in art or objects which may be held by the University. These items record Yolŋu law and men's business, and under Aboriginal tradition should be restricted so that they are only viewed by senior Yolŋu men or other men authorised by male Yolŋu elders.
The following items in the Woodward collection should be subject to this restriction:
2003.0014.000.00
2003.0013.000.00
2003.0021.000.00.
I would appreciate if the University would ensure that these items are restricted as explained above.
I would also appreciate if the University would ensure that it consults with Yolŋu elders regarding all future projects which concern art or objects from east and central Arnhem Land held by the University. These consultations may well provide an opportunity to more comprehensively record the mythological significance and traditional stories associated with the art and objects.
As a broader observation I look forward to the development of programs to ensure that all Aboriginal items are stored either together, or in accordance with standard guidelines to ensure that sacred information is respected.
I look forward to developing a continuing association with the University, and would be happy to discuss any matters which may arise from time to time. I may be contacted through the Northern Land Council.
Yours sincerely
Wäli Wunuŋmurra
CHAIRMAN

36 Jennifer Isaacs, *Wandjuk Marika: Life Story as Told to Jennifer Isaacs*, University of Queensland Press, St Lucia, 1995, gatefold preface; see also National Museum

of Australia, *Yalangbara: Art of the Djang'kawu—The Marika Family*, exhibition from December 2010 to September 2011, National Museum of Australia, Canberra.

37 Isaacs, *Wandjuk Marika*, p. 106.

38 Bark paintings collected by Ronald and Catherine Berndt in the 1940s are held at the Macleay Museum at the University of Sydney (see URL: https://www.atsida.edu.au/news-events/yirrkala-bark-paintings); Howard Morphy, 'Birrikitji Gumana', *100 Works of the Monash University Collection*, Monash University Museum of Art, 2022; Morphy, 'Narritjin Maymuru', *Featured Artists*, Art Gallery New South Wales, https://www.artgallery.nsw.gov.au/collection/artists/maymuru-narritjin (accessed 30 October 2023).

39 *Gove Peninsula Land Case Millirrpum v Nabalco Pty Ltd and the Commonwealth of Australia*, 'Extracts from Transcript', 27 May 1970, p. 571.

40 See Jessica De Largy Healy, '"This Painting Becomes His Body for Life": Transforming Relations in Yolŋu Initiation and Funeral Rituals', *Anthropological Forum*, vol. 27, no. 1, 2017, which details the significance of the striking body paintings given to young boys in north-eastern Arnhem Land on their initiation into adult life.

41 Patrick Hutchings and Judith Ryan, 'Religious Art: Two Cases of Iconography', *Australian Religion Studies Review*, vol. 3, no. 1, 1990, p. 7.

42 De Largy Healy, '"This Painting Becomes His Body for Life"', pp. 18–33.

43 Lloyd CL Hollenberg, 'The Yiḏaki: A Triumph of Mind over Matter in Tribute to Joe Gumbula', *Preservation, Digital Technology & Culture*, vol. 47, nos 3/4, 2019, p. 164.

44 Ibid.

45 Ibid.

46 Aaron Corn, 'Outside the Hollow Log: The Didjeridu, Globalisation and Socio-Economic Contestation in Arnhem Land', *Rural Society*, vol. 13, no. 3, 2003, p. 252.

47 Curkpatrick, *Singing Bones*, pp. 80–1.

48 Francis Xavier Purcell was a land rights lawyer and community activist. He was a member of the legal team that fought for recognition of land rights for Yirrkala communities.

49 Woodward Symposium, Closed Session, 2008, Speaker 1 (unidentified), para. 1, p. 1 of transcript.

50 Woodward Symposium, Closed Session, 2008, Speaker 3 (unidentified), para. 2, p. 2 of transcript; *Crossing Cultures*, 13–18 January 2008, University of Melbourne, Parkville.

51 Jason Gibson, '"You're My Kwertengerl": Transforming Models of Care for Central Australian Aboriginal Museum Collections', *Museum Management and Curatorship*, vol. 34, no. 3, 2019, p. 243.

The Indigenous Knowledge Institute

AARON CORN

THE INDIGENOUS KNOWLEDGE INSTITUTE (IKI) was established as a Melbourne Interdisciplinary Research Institute (MIRI) of the University of Melbourne, funded by Chancellery Research and Enterprise, in 2020. Its aim is to advance and build new interdisciplinary capabilities in Indigenous knowledge research and engagement through collaboration with internal and external partners to address global challenges. The outbreak of the COVID-19 pandemic in 2020 made such challenges starkly apparent, as it compelled us to adjust to different ways of living and working. Despite starting amid the many trials of the pandemic outbreak, IKI has grown considerably since then. Science was selected as IKI's host faculty in 2021 and, by 2022, its biennial cycle of funding schemes and events was fully operational, complete with the competitive appointment of our first cohorts of research fellows and theme leaders.

IKI supports and promotes research and collaborative engagements with Indigenous knowledge-holders that aim to strengthen capabilities in the research field of Indigenous knowledge. We aim to:

1 document, maintain, disseminate and progress Indigenous knowledge through research in partnership with Indigenous knowledge-holders
2 recognise and respect Indigenous knowledge innovations through collaborative engagements that address challenges for Australia and the world
3 create new avenues for inquiry and learning in partnership with Indigenous knowledge-holders to generate mutual benefits.

Originally conceived by the University's Associate Provost, Professor Marcia Langton, IKI's vision is to advance Indigenous knowledge research and partnerships with Indigenous communities that address imminent challenges, from the local to the global. The fact that colleagues across the University chose to pursue this important yet challenging endeavour is grounded in mature understandings of the local and global contexts in which we work.

Globally, the continent of Australia is home to the oldest continuous Indigenous cultures in the world. Ancient sites and artefacts show us that humans have lived in Australia for some 65 000 years, which long predates the human settlement of Europe and the Americas. Over this immense stretch of time, Indigenous Australians developed complex societies that enabled them to live in a wide variety of natural environments and climatic conditions. These societies changed over time but were able to continue through major climatic shifts, such as the last ice age peak around 20 000 years ago and the last major sea-level rise some 10 000 years ago.[1] The staggering antiquity and continuity of Australia's Indigenous knowledge systems are nothing but exceptional and warrant far greater and more faithful understanding and consideration in broad global discussions about the human condition, both now and into the future.

Locally, with nearly 10 000 staff and 54 000 students, including over 20 000 international students from more than 130 countries, the University of Melbourne is also one of the largest universities in the world. Though not yet at population parity, Indigenous participation in the University is similarly large. The University employs more than 100 Indigenous academics across all faculties, with more than twenty of those appointed into senior academic roles and two in chancellery leadership roles. The University also enrols one-fifth of all Aboriginal and Torres Strait Islander graduate research students in Australia. The immense breadth and depth of this research talent is what has made the interdisciplinary innovations to drive IKI's vision and approaches possible.

IKI's unique vision necessitates innovative interdisciplinary collaboration and inquiry through robust working partnerships across national borders and disciplinary boundaries. In recent decades the University has invested substantially in developing a sound cohort of world-class Indigenous researchers, as well as broader interdisciplinary and intercultural research programs that engage with Indigenous knowledge to address matters of high priority for Indigenous peoples globally.

As the only university-funded research institute in Australia with a dedicated focus on Indigenous knowledge as a cogent global research field, IKI's goals and activities span interdisciplinary research, researcher capability development, research translation, Indigenous partnerships, and national and international research collaborations at the individual and organisational levels. The University is home to a wide variety of exceptional Indigenous knowledge research across all faculties that engages beneficially with Indigenous communities and external partners. Much of this work is led by Indigenous researchers and/or co-created with external Indigenous partners. IKI works to accelerate the scale and scope of this work across the University to deliver lasting impacts and benefits nationally and internationally.

IKI has been identified as a vital Signature Project in both the present and immediate past iterations of the University's *Indigenous Strategic Plan*.[2]

Our Charter

The IKI *Charter for Research with Indigenous Knowledge Holders* has governed all research funded by the Institute since its inception, and in August 2023 it was adopted as a guiding intellectual property policy across the entire University.[3] IKI was designed to work in equitable partnerships with Indigenous communities and recognise the rights of Indigenous knowledge-holders. In keeping with the best international policies and practices, it has therefore adhered to the following research principles and guidelines since its creation.[4]

> **Principle 1. We aim to respond to the needs and interests of Indigenous people, including those who participate in research projects and others in the community.**
> Our research will seek to provide tangible benefits to Indigenous communities who are involved in our research. We commit to ensuring that Indigenous people involved in research should benefit from, and not be disadvantaged by, the research we undertake.
> Guidelines:
> - Research projects will be co-designed with recognised Indigenous knowledge-holders to ensure that they meet their community needs.
> - Research projects will aim to generate research outcomes that meet the stated needs of the Indigenous knowledge-holders and their communities.
>
> **Principle 2. We acknowledge and respect Indigenous knowledge practices and innovations.**
> We recognise Article 31.1 of the *United Nations Declaration on the Rights of Indigenous Peoples* and aim to work in accordance with the principle that
>
>> Indigenous peoples have the right to maintain, control, protect and develop their cultural heritage, traditional knowledge and traditional

cultural expressions, as well as the manifestations of their sciences, technologies and cultures, including human and genetic resources, seeds, medicines, knowledge of the properties of fauna and flora, oral traditions, literatures, designs, sports and traditional games and visual and performing arts. They also have the right to maintain, control, protect and develop their intellectual property over such cultural heritage, traditional knowledge, and traditional cultural expressions.[5]

Guidelines:

- Researchers will have a good understanding of the nature of Indigenous knowledge traditions, cultural expressions and intellectual property.
- Researchers will acknowledge the ongoing ownership, and cultural and intellectual property rights, of Indigenous knowledge-holders in ideas and materials they contribute to research and other scholarly activities.
- Researchers will acknowledge the contributions of Indigenous knowledge-holders and partners in publications arising from co-designed research, and ensure the appropriate use and publication of research results as agreed with them.

Principle 3. Free, prior and informed consent is the foundation for our research with or about Indigenous peoples.

Free, prior and informed consent means that agreement is obtained free of duress or pressure, and that Indigenous people are fully cognisant of the details and risks of the proposed research. The informed consent of people in alignment with established local Indigenous processes and responsibilities for decision-making is important.

Guidelines:

- Researchers will ensure that Indigenous knowledge-holders are equal participants in research processes.
- Researchers will engage in appropriate negotiation and consultation with Indigenous knowledge-holders about research aims and objectives to ensure their meaningful involvement in the co-design of research processes and outcomes.
- Researchers will conduct all research on the basis of free, prior and informed consent.

Principle 4. We welcome the fair and equitable sharing of benefits that arise from research.

Indigenous people who contribute traditional knowledge and practices, innovations, cultural expressions and intellectual property, skills, know-how, cultural products and expressions, and biological and genetic resources to our research collaborations will receive a fair and equitable share of benefits arising from the use and application of their knowledge, practices and innovative ideas.

Guidelines:

- Copyright in collected interviews with Indigenous knowledge-holders in any material form will be jointly owned and acknowledged by them and the University.
- Any co-owner seeking to use a collected interview will first consult with its other owners and comply with any reasonable directions given by them.
- Co-authorship with Indigenous knowledge-holders in any research output that draws upon their ideas or materials will be acknowledged by researchers.
- Prior to publishing a research output, researchers will seek the views of co-owner Indigenous knowledge-holders on ideas and materials they have contributed and comply with any reasonable directions given by them.
- Any co-owner seeking to use a research output will first consult with its other owners and comply with any reasonable directions given by them.
- Researchers will comply with reasonable directions from Indigenous knowledge-holders concerning any proposed public use of their co-owned research.

Principle 5. We respect Indigenous research confidentiality requirements, the right of Indigenous knowledge-holders to access collected data and resources, and their status as co-owners and co-authors of collaborative research content and outputs.

We seek to work as equal collaborative partners in our research with Indigenous communities and knowledge-holders, and recognise the issues of confidentiality, access to information, co-ownership of content, and co-authorship of outputs that frequently arise through this work.

Guidelines:

- Researchers will respect the confidentiality of individual and organisational research partners in any case where they deem collected information or materials to be sensitive.
- Researchers will consult with individual and organisational research partners to identify any confidential, sensitive or restricted information or materials, and determine appropriate conditions of use and access.
- All issues of confidentiality will be determined by research partners and respected by researchers.
- Researchers will make copies of any collected information and materials—including recordings, photographs and literature—requested by co-owner Indigenous knowledge-holders or their verified heirs, subject to confidentiality and privacy agreements.

- Researchers will take responsibility for arranging to appropriately store and archive any data collected during research and must not destroy or dispose of research materials.[6]

Our Team

At the beginning of 2023, three-quarters of all IKI staff were Indigenous people. Day to day, IKI was run by a directorate of academic and professional staff with a diverse array of experiences and expertise:

- Professor Aaron Corn, Inaugural Director (1.0 FTE)
- Kirsten Clark, Manager (1.0 FTE)
- Brittany Carter, Project Officer (1.0 FTE)
- Professor Michael-Shawn Fletcher, Director—Research Capability (0.2 FTE).

Michael-Shawn Fletcher was promoted from associate professor to professor, commencing in 2023. This core team was supplemented by two research fellows funded from internal University sources outside IKI:

- Dr Sangeetha Chandrashekeran, Senior Research Fellow (0.4 FTE)
- Dr Samuel Curkpatrick, Research Associate (0.2 FTE).

Since its establishment in 2020, IKI's core team of researchers has completed and released several key publications, including the following books: *Plants* by Zena Cumpston, Michael-Shawn Fletcher and Lesley Head; *Post-Capitalist Futures*, edited by Samuel Alexander, Sangeetha Chandrashekeran and Brendan Gleeson; *Ontologies and Epistemologies of Indigenous Music and Dance*, edited by Yuh-Fen Tseng and Aaron Corn; and *Law* by Marcia Langton and Aaron Corn.[7] This core research team also contributed to securing some $47.3 million for Indigenous knowledge research and research training from external public and private sources. These span four public grants from the ARC, mostly held in partnership with other universities and organisations in Australia and internationally:

1 'Has It Always Burned So Hot?' (IN210100055) led by Professor Michael-Shawn Fletcher at the University of Melbourne
2 'Fine Tuning: A Reconciliation of Indigenous and Western Musical Traditions' (IN230100005) led by Dr Dylan Crismani at the University of Adelaide in partnership with Professor Corn
3 'ARC Centre of Excellence for Indigenous and Environmental Histories and Futures' (CE230100009) led by Professor Sean Ulm at James Cook University in partnership with Professor Fletcher

4 'Improving Life Outcomes for Indigenous People Living with a Disability' (IN240100016) led by Dr Sheelagh Daniels-Mayes in partnership with Professor Corn at the University of Melbourne.[8]

IKI is also an internal partner and co-investor in the publicly funded Indigenous Data Network and the privately funded Ngarrngga national Indigenous curriculum project, which were both conceived by Professor Marcia Langton.[9]

Competitive processes initiated in 2021 to select IKI's key research themes and inaugural fellows led to the appointment of our first cohorts of theme leaders and research fellows in 2022. After a rigorous internal selection process, four theme leaders were appointed across three research themes:

1 Professor Barry Judd, Theme Leader—Culture and Heritage
2 Professor Michael-Shawn Fletcher, Theme Leader—Healthy Country
3 Associate Professor Shawana Andrews, Theme Co-Leader—Health and Justice
4 Dr Eddie Cubillo, Theme Co-Leader—Health and Justice.

After an equally rigorous external selection process specifically designed to recruit Indigenous knowledge-holders, we appointed three inaugural IKI fellows. The selection committee determined that all three successful applicants should be appointed at the University's highest academic rank, that of full professor, on the basis of their exceptional experience and standing as Indigenous knowledge-holders, and distinguished records of demonstrated commitment to Indigenous knowledge research and engagements. This decision was subsequently endorsed at a meeting of the central University Appointments and Promotions Committee (UAPC). The three IKI fellows we appointed were each the first from their respective Indigenous communities to hold the title of full professor:

1 Professor Brian Djaṉgirrawuy Gumbula-Garawirrtja, IKI Fellow (0.2 FTE)[10]
2 Professor Diane Kerr, IKI Fellow (0.2 FTE)
3 Professor Wantarri 'Wanta' Jampijinpa Pawu, IKI Fellow (0.2 FTE).

This external selection process also identified Nola Turner-Jensen as an outstanding candidate to join the University as a senior research fellow (0.2 FTE) in the Faculty of Education through IKI's co-investment in the Ngarrngga national Indigenous curriculum project. A similar co-investment was made by the University's Museums and Collections Division in professor Brian Gumbula's IKI Fellowship. IKI's first Honorary Fellow, Professor Patrick Nunn, was also appointed with UAPC endorsement in 2022, and he contributed to *A National Strategy for Just Adaptation* for publication by the Australian Academy of Science that same year.[11]

Towards the end of 2023, Brittany Carter and Kirsten Clark left IKI to take on respective promotions in the Commonwealth Scientific and Industrial Research Organisation (CSIRO) and the University of Melbourne's Indigenous Strategy unit. Among Clark's many achievements as IKI's manager were her completion of the Asialink Leaders Program and receipt of the Faculty of Science Dean's Award for Excellence in Professional Staff Support.

Professor Brian Gumbula sadly passed away in September 2023, leaving a significant legacy of continuing projects at the University of Melbourne, including his Yolŋu cultural heritage work with the Museums and Collections Division and his urgent research into Australian native bees with the School of Biosciences. His final research project, conducted with internal colleagues in the Victorian College of the Arts, Geography and Population Health, as well as external partners at the Mulka Project in Yirrkala and Universitas Hasanuddin in Makassar, took him to the Indonesian island of Sulawesi in February 2023 to investigate how his own living traditions as an expert Yolŋu ceremonial leader recounted long precolonial histories of Yolŋu trade and intermarriage with seafarers from Makassar.[12] After a lifetime of hearing and singing about this old trade network that, before 1907, linked Yolŋu society to the global economy, professor Gumbula finally met his own relatives in Makassar and was warmly received by them as family.[13] In his obituary, our Deputy Vice-Chancellor—Indigenous, Professor Barry Judd, reflected on how professor Gumbula taught the University of Melbourne to better value and engage with ardent Indigenous knowledge-holders:

> Professor Gumbula has significantly transformed the way that the University of Melbourne works with Indigenous people and their knowledges. He was an important ceremonial leader, English was not his first language, and he lived in one of the remotest parts of Australia from Melbourne. He showed us what is possible when we acknowledge and accept the inherent strength and resilience of remote communities as the primary holders and curators of Australia's ancient knowledge systems. He pointed us to a future where academics engage with Indigenous

> knowledge on terms set out by those men and women who hold it in their continuing practices of story, song, and ceremony.[14]

Following the precedent of professor Gumbula's appointment, the world's second Yolŋu full professor, the esteemed educator Yalmay Marika-Yunupiŋu, was hired by the University in April 2023.

Beyond our direct staff appointments, IKI has developed a diverse and vibrant community of practice numbering more than 100 active members from across all faculties and some professional divisions of the University. It includes University staff, graduate researchers and honorary fellows. The IKI community of practice usually meets every six weeks and encourages all members to share their research experiences and progress. Key research outcomes by community of practice members have included the book *The First Astronomers* by Duane Hamacher with Elders and knowledge-holders, and Erin O'Donnell's ARC grant 'Ending Aqua Nullius: Sustainable and Legitimate Water Law in Settler States' (DE230100622).[15] The substantial expertise of this network enabled the entire University to be selected for membership of the National Indigenous Australians Agency's Panel of Suppliers for the Provision of Indigenous Evaluation and Research Services in 2022.

Our Schemes

IKI invests heavily in administrating, advertising and supporting our biennial cycle of seven different research-funding schemes. This usually includes biennial rounds for our research themes, IKI fellows and community fellows schemes, and annual rounds for our seed funding, community engagement, PhD Research Training Program (RTP) scholarship and Indigenous PhD bursary schemes.[16]

These schemes offer a suite of funding opportunities for both internal and external applicants that are scaled from smaller to bigger grants, with the aim of enabling growth in the University's Indigenous knowledge research capabilities. Our smaller schemes for developing researchers include the Indigenous PhD bursary and community engagement grants for internal applicants, and community fellowships for external applicants. Our seed funding grants are designed to enable established internal researchers to develop new projects, while our RTP scholarships provide a living stipend to PhD students from anywhere in the University undertaking a suitable Indigenous knowledge topic. Our largest schemes are the IKI fellowships, which are advertised externally to recruit expert Indigenous knowledge-holders into mid-career and senior academic roles, and our key research themes, which are advertised internally to tender for large interdisciplinary programs of research that substantially involve external partners. All research funded through these schemes must be interdisciplinary and has been adjudicated by invited panels of internal experts against openly advertised criteria.

Details of all research projects funded through our schemes can be browsed on the IKI website.[17] Here, for example, is the official project description of the Australian native bee seed funding grant on which professor Gumbula was funded for 2023:

> **Title:** Two-Way Knowledge Sharing for Native Bee Climate Adaptation in Arnhem Land
> **Summary:** Australian native bees are important pollinators and a long-used source of medicinal products and food by First Nations peoples. However, little is known about how vulnerable Australia's 2000 native bee species are to extreme weather and climate change.
>
> The Yolŋu peoples in East Arnhem Land have a long, shared history with native bees. All Yolŋu people, clans, and traditions connect to one of two bee species: Dhuwa (*Austroplebeia spp.*) or Yirritja (*Tetragonula spp.*). Yolŋu usually harvest honey from wild nests of these bees but have been unable to in recent years, noting a lack of bees and certain flowers, possibly due to climate change.
>
> Failed harvests have serious implications for Yolŋu ceremonies and livelihoods. Elders are concerned about how to support their bees through climate change and continue their related traditions. Few Western studies of bees have drawn on Indigenous knowledge, despite First Nations peoples having a deep understanding of weather, climate, and habitats that could be used to support climate adaptation.
>
> Our project will address Western and Indigenous knowledge gaps about climate change adaptation for native bees through research with Yolŋu rangers from the Ḻaynhapuy Homelands Aboriginal Corporation. We aim to investigate:
>
> - what plants native bees use in East Arnhem Land;
> - how they are affected by climate change; and
> - how they can be managed to support climate change adaptation.

This project will advance research into Indigenous knowledge by co-developing a phenological bee forage calendar by, with and for Yolŋu peoples.

Our study may be used as a model approach for research that draws on Indigenous knowledge to enhance understanding of species and support their adaptation to climate change.

Funding:

- $20 000

Investigators:

- Professor Margie Mayfield (CI [Chief Investigator])
- Dr Rachele Wilson (RA [Research Assistant])
- Professor Brian Djaṉgirrawuy Gumbula-Garawirrtja (RA)

Organisations:

- The University of Melbourne
- The University of Queensland
- Ḻaynhapuy Homelands Aboriginal Corporation[18]

Our research theme programs, however, are typically supported by funding packages of more than $100 000 over two years, comprise components schemes of their own, and involve greater numbers of investigators and partners. Here, for example, is a short, official precis of IKI's culture and heritage theme, which culminated in an unprecedented workshop between Aṉangu Traditional Owners of Uluṟu on their nearby outstation, Patji, with visiting Indigenous leaders from Melbourne, Warrnambool and Dili in Timor-Leste in August 2023:

Title: Culture and Heritage

Summary: Led by Barry Judd (Professor and Director, Indigenous Studies, Faculty of Arts), this theme will provide mechanisms to support and grow Indigenous knowledge, so it can be applied in contemporary Australia and beyond in the critical areas of culture, land, and heritage.

The theme will investigate how this knowledge can be adapted with the guidance of Indigenous knowledge holders to meet social, environmental, and economic challenges of global significance.

Investigators:

- Professor Barry Judd (Theme Leader)
- Professor Lisa Palmer (Deputy Theme Leader)
- Professor Rachel Nordlinger (CI)
- Professor Rachel Popelka-Filcoff (CI)
- Ms Jennifer Ganske (PI [Partner Investigator])
- Ms Lynette Ross (PI)

- Joe Morrison (PI)
- Stephanie Rogers (PI)
- Dr Kirsty Sword Gusmão (PI).

Organisations:

- The University of Melbourne
- NBN Co (Indigenous Unit)
- Voyages Indigenous Tourism
- Indigenous Land and Sea Corporation
- Boon Wurrung Foundation
- Indigenous Business Australia
- Alola Australia.[19]

The outstanding calibre of our inaugural cohort of IKI fellows is evidenced by the official biography of Professor Diane Kerr:

> **Professor Diane Kerr OAM** is a respected Elder of the Wurundjeri people and identifies with the Ganun Willam Balak clan.
>
> Aunty Di works passionately on the social and emotional wellbeing of First Nations communities through her engagement with community and government in a range of fields: health, childcare, education, native title, Stolen Generation support, environment and waterway protection, and other community work.
>
> Aunty Di provides leadership and cultural advice to local councils and corporate and community organisations. She is often invited to preside at high profile Welcome to Country ceremonies, and she conducts Women's ceremonies for Aboriginal girls and women.
>
> Aunty Di is one of the most senior and well-respected Kulin nations Elders and holds uniquely rare and exceptional knowledge of the Melbourne regions on which [the] main campuses of this University are built.
>
> She holds a long and exclusive relationship with the University of Melbourne that hinges on her long-term research collaborations with colleagues in the Faculty of Medicine, Dentistry and Health Sciences and her extensive networks across the Victorian medical establishment and health sector.
>
> Aunty Di's appointment as a Fellow through this scheme will bring urgently needed understanding through her project on the impacts of Indigenous medicine and healing knowledge on infection management and antibiotic use. Indigenous peoples everywhere suffer disproportionately high rates of antimicrobial resistance, which is one of the greatest and most complex threats presently facing humanity.[20]

Bronte Gosper's IKI community fellowship directly funded her research towards the *Above and Beyond Broadcasting* report for First Nations Media Australia:[21]

> **Title:** Amplifying and Internationalising Australia's First Nations Media
> **Summary:** There is a little demonstrable evidence of the impact of Aboriginal and Torres Strait Islander journalists and reporting and positive outcomes for First Nations communities in recent years.
>
> This research will provide a case study example of impact, supporting the need for culturally relevant messaging. Then, from that case study, we will seek to learn from international examples and draw comparisons with First Nations journalism in Australia, to learn how Aboriginal and Torres Strait Islander reporters here can have greater global impact through sharing their stories.
>
> Investigators:
> - Ms Bronte Gosper (CF [Community Fellow])
> - Dr Sharon Huebner (M [Mentor])
> - Dr Lyndon Ormond-Parker (M).
>
> Organisations:
> - The University of Melbourne
> - First Nations Media Australia.[22]

The positive impacts of IKI's research funding schemes within the University and beyond are manifold. The overall standard of funding applications to IKI has risen markedly since our establishment in 2020. In 2022 our seed funding and IKI fellowship rounds received more fundable applications than anticipated, warranting the number of seed funding grants we allocated that year to rise from five to seven, and compelling us to seek alternative research fellowship opportunities in the Faculty of Science and Faculty of Education for an additional two IKI fellowship applicants. While an initial cohort of three IKI fellows was appointed as advertised, five exceptional external Indigenous researchers were identified overall and were ultimately appointed as research fellows by the University as an outcome of our recruitment process.

IKI's research-funding schemes have also begun to significantly influence how faculties are now seeking to build their own Indigenous knowledge research capabilities. The Faculty of Engineering and Information Technology, for example, sought direct IKI involvement in designing and adjudicating its own Indigenous Research Grant, which was modelled after our own seed funding scheme, while the Faculty of Science has adopted many of IKI's research-funding strategies, including the way in which it now recruits its own Indigenous research fellows.

IKI has also advised internal partners on research and related policy matters through various University committees, working groups and communities of practice, including the Indigenous Strategy Reference Group, Committee of Associate Deans and Delegates (Indigenous), Aboriginal and Torres Strait Islander Cultural Heritage Oversight Committee, Northeast Arnhem Land Advisory Academic Group, Indigenous Graduate Community of Practice, Melbourne Climate Futures Research Cluster, Ngarrngga Project Steering Committee, Indigenous Data Network Operational Stream Activity Group, Faculty of Science Executive Committee, and Contemplative Studies Centre Reference Group.

Our Students

IKI's Doctoral Academy has grown to recruit, support and enrich the research training experiences of PhD students at the University in various ways. Since its establishment, IKI has provided annual opportunities for PhD students undertaking Indigenous knowledge topics to apply for funding support through its RTP scholarship and Indigenous bursary schemes.[23]

Yet, from IKI's inception, it was also clear that the University needed to create a more streamlined and flexible interdisciplinary pathway into formal study for potential PhD students with established expertise in Indigenous knowledge and a demonstrated capability to undertake research at the PhD level. There has long been a large and influential network of established and developing Indigenous Elders in Australia and beyond, who are often widely recognised as Indigenous knowledge-holders with the authority to share and interpret their knowledge as appropriate across a wide range of contexts, including research. Many such Indigenous Elders have also worked in research and university contexts. They have frequently participated in research projects, co-authored refereed publications, led ARC and other research grants, held award degrees up to the master's level, received honorary doctorates, taught university coursework, and mentored and collaborated with graduate research students. They are already engaged in university research activities to a high degree, yet due to the paucity of high-quality intercultural educational opportunities that Indigenous people often face throughout their lives, they are rarely positioned to enter or complete award PhD programs. With his appointment as an IKI fellow, professor

Brian Gumbula, for example, became the first Yolŋu person from north-eastern Arnhem Land to hold the title of full professor in recognition of his exceptional experience and standing as an Indigenous knowledge-holder, and his distinguished record of demonstrated commitment to Indigenous knowledge research and engagement. Yet no Yolŋu person has had the opportunity to complete an award PhD, even though several have now been recognised by universities for their lifelong commitment to learning and scholarship with honorary doctorates. This indicates a structural inequity across the entire Australian education system, replicated across most of the world, that clearly needs to change.

Another matter for consideration is the challenge that Indigenous knowledge systems around the world, including in Australia, rarely fit neatly within the rigid disciplinary silos often cultivated within universities. That professor Gumbula, for example, actively collaborated so widely and readily with so many University colleagues spanning the IKI, Museums and Collections Division, Faculty of Science, Faculty of Fine Arts and Music, Faculty of Education, and Faculty of Medicine, Dentistry and Health Sciences during his tenure as an IKI fellow was no accident. His priorities, strategies, projects and collaborations within the University and beyond were driven by his research needs as he understood them in Yolŋu law and languages, where traditional songs, for example, are intentionally maintained as a source of data about biodiversity and many other fields that intersect with pressing global research concerns. Like many Indigenous intellectuals around the world, who routinely straddle such disciplinary boundaries, his research profile could not easily be surmised by any disciplinary descriptor, making the Melbourne Interdisciplinary Research Institute that is IKI his preferred and ideal home within the University.

After extensive discussion of these issues across the University in 2021, it was determined that IKI needed its own PhD course to serve this pressing need. A formal consultation process through the University's Committee of Graduate Research Associate Deans that spanned all faculties ensued at the beginning of 2022, which determined that the University should create a new interdisciplinary award course named the Doctor of Philosophy—Indigenous Knowledge (PhD-IK), to be coordinated directly by IKI with administrative support from our host faculty, Science. This would become the only PhD course in the University to be coordinated directly by a MIRI instead of a faculty. The new PhD-IK course was approved by the University's Academic Board in August 2022,[24] and it accepted its first two students, Joe Williams from Dubbo and Josh Trindale from Dili, in 2023. In keeping with his international work as a leading suicide-prevention advocate, Williams' research seeks to establish a robust evidence base for the healing effects of Indigenous ceremonies. Trindale is already established as the world's most cited ethnographic scholar of Timor-Leste, and his research will comprehensively explore the concept of *lulik* as a core set of sacred Timorese laws and values.

The PhD-IK course is the first award research doctorate in Australia to offer studies in Indigenous knowledge as an explicitly interdisciplinary field. While it conforms to all existing regulations concerning the design and delivery of PhD courses at the University, it applies these in a way that markedly enhances the visibility, appeal and accessibility of PhD study to a broader and more diverse cohort of prospective students with established expertise in Indigenous knowledge and demonstrated research capability, who seek to undertake an Indigenous knowledge topic. In keeping with IKI's global focus, expressions of interest for entry to this new course are welcome from both domestic and international applicants. Coordinated by IKI, it can be undertaken with any fitting combination of supervisors from across all faculties of the University. Our first two students, Joe Williams and Josh Trindale, are respectively supervised by IKI in partnership with Psychology and Geography. The entry requirements for this course consider all relevant forms of qualifications and professional experience, including the very real possibility that an applicant might already hold formal training and professional standing in their own Indigenous legal and ceremonial traditions. It also offers each student a flexible suite of format options for structuring a PhD thesis that aligns with their individuated strengths and research interests:

> Typically taken over 3.5 years full time (part time available), you'll be working independently on an innovative research project that makes a distinct contribution to knowledge in your field. The Doctor of Philosophy—Indigenous Knowledge gives you unparalleled flexibility with how you present your work, with four standard thesis options available:
>
> - An 80 000-word thesis
> - A 60 000-word thesis with a minor folio of work
> - A 40 000-word thesis with a medium folio of work
> - A 20 000-word thesis with a major folio of work.
>
> All thesis outputs, including folio content, will accommodate research engagements with Indigenous knowledge practices. There is no

compulsory coursework, though relevant coursework subjects may be taken with approval.[25]

IKI applies a rigorous expression of interest process, which includes prospective supervisors, to identify suitable applicants.[26] Interest in this new course from Indigenous applicants in Australia, and from others from around the world, has been overwhelming, while universities in other countries have already expressed interest in replicating our approach to its design. IKI gratefully acknowledges the Agilent Foundation in the United States for helping us to support our PhD students financially as our Doctoral Academy grows following the establishment of our new PhD-IK course.

Our Activities

Amid the challenges and travel restrictions of the COVID-19 pandemic from 2020 to 2022, IKI invested heavily in designing its research-funding programs and new PhD course, as well as strategically producing high-quality events to promote Indigenous knowledge research online. These have been attended and viewed by presenters and audiences from all over the world. IKI's events have been designed to bring together world-leading researchers, industry leaders, policymakers and Indigenous knowledge-holders. They are promoted through our website,[27] periodical newsletter, mailing list (of 676 members by 2023) and IKI's playlist on the University's YouTube channel (viewed 6242 times by 2023).[28] Nearly all of IKI's public events have been recorded and are viewable on the University's YouTube channel and IKI website. Since mid-2022, most of IKI's public events also have been delivered in a hybrid format for both live and online audiences.

Annual events that have been routinely hosted by IKI include our International Day of the World's Indigenous Peoples Symposium, Intersections Symposium, NAIDOC Week panel and Reconciliation Week panel. In 2022 IKI collaborated with the National Recording Project for Indigenous Performance in Australia to convene the first International Council for Traditions of Music and Dance (ICTMD) Indigenous Symposium, with presenters from thirty-two universities and other organisations across fourteen countries.[29] ICTMD is a non-governmental organisation in formal consultative relations with UNESCO. Other public event highlights have included the 2021 Cooking the Kangaroo Symposium on Indigenous Song, Spirituality and Connection, the 2022 Indigenous Knowledge Film Festival for Melbourne Knowledge Week, and the 2023 book launch of *Law: The*

Way of the Ancestors, by Professor Marcia Langton and Professor Aaron Corn, by Dr Eddie Cubillo, who directs the University's Indigenous Law and Justice Hub.[30]

In 2023 IKI contributed substantially to the University's Indigenous Voice to Parliament referendum public-education campaign with the 'Remote Australia and the Voice' public lecture by professor Brian Gumbula, Renelle Gandjitjiwuy Goṉḏarra and Professor Aaron Corn,[31] and the initial twenty-two episodes of the new podcast series *The Deep End* with Marcia Langton and Aaron Corn.[32] Guests we have interviewed on this podcast series are some of Australia's most prolific policy experts, serving politicians, artists, Indigenous leaders and emerging Indigenous researchers. Episodes to date include:

Episode 01 Barry Jones
Episode 02 Jack Thompson
Episode 03 Fiona Stanley
Episode 04 Shireen Morris
Episode 05 Anne Twomey
Episode 06 Paul Grabowsky
Episode 07 Peter Yu
Episode 08 Zali Steggall
Episode 09 Kate Chaney
Episode 10 Ken Wyatt
Episode 11 Eddie Cubillo
Episode 12 Joe Williams
Episode 13 Mayaṯili Marika
Episode 14 Peter Khalil
Episode 15 Glenn Loughrey
Episode 16 Allegra Spender
Episode 17 Rachel Perkins
Episode 18 Asmi Wood
Episode 19 Anne Pattel-Gray
Episode 20 Robbie Bundle
Episode 21 Sheelagh Daniels-Mayes
Episode 22 Marcia Langton

With pandemic travel restrictions easing throughout 2022, IKI's engagements with domestic and international partners began to deepen and expand greatly. We met with many of the University's Indigenous strategic partners in north-eastern Arnhem Land, the Goulburn Valley and

Melbourne, sometimes for the first time in person. We also met with visiting international researchers from the University of Taipei, Sinica Academia, Te Whare Wānanga o Awanuiārangi, University of British Columbia, Manchester University and University of Hokkaido.

In October 2022 we undertook international travel for the first time since the pandemic's onset to meet with colleagues at the University of Arizona in the United States and present at the first Association of Pacific Rim Universities (APRU) Indigenous Knowledges Workshop in Mexico, which was hosted by Tecnológico de Monterrey with delegates from eight universities around the world. IKI has contributed to hosting the second APRU Indigenous Knowledges Workshop at the University of Melbourne in November 2023, and now chairs this working group's Research and Research Training Subcommittee.[33]

In 2023 we worked hard to expand our global networks further via participation in delegations with Chancellery Indigenous, the Faculty of Arts, and Chancellery Global, Culture and Engagement to key partner universities in Taiwan, Japan and Indonesia. With support from Chancellery Research and Enterprise, IKI hosted a highly successful joint research workshop at Hokkaido University in Japan, 'Dialogues on Indigenous Knowledge: Living Cultures in a Globalised World', which centrally involved key Indigenous staff from the University of Melbourne and local leaders of the Sapporo Ainu Association.[34] Relationships built through IKI collaboration with ICTMD since 2020 and subsequent visits to Taiwan led to the esteemed Pinuyumayan Elder Akawyan Pakawyan being selected to deliver the University's annual Narrm Oration in November 2023.[35] She will be the first Indigenous speaker from Asia to deliver this distinguished oration and also the first-ever speaker to do so in her own Indigenous language. Our activities with partners in Asian nations who share a time zone with Australia exemplify one way in which IKI has successfully forged and sustained new dialogues with Indigenous peoples beyond the immediate influence of the Anglosphere, as a means of expanding and advancing vital and unprecedented discourses in global Indigenous knowledge research.

Our Commitment

IKI has been funded by the University of Melbourne though Chancellery Research and Enterprise for an initial five years over 2020–24, renewable, and is a named Signature Project in the University's new Indigenous strategy, *Murmuk Djerring*, for 2023–27.[36] From the onset of the COVID-19 pandemic in early 2020 to the 'No' vote in the Indigenous Voice to Parliament referendum in October 2023, IKI has worked constructively and pragmatically with internal stakeholders across the entire University, as well as many external partners domestically and internationally, with the singular goal of markedly strengthening the quality, recognition, resourcing and reach of Indigenous knowledge research in the academy within Australia and beyond.

All of IKI's efforts in recognising the rights of Indigenous knowledge-holders, encouraging respectful and equitable research relationships, recruiting staff and PhD students, devising our own PhD course, allocating our scheme funding, hosting and podcasting public events and content, building international partnerships, convening international conferences, securing competitive external grant funding, and publishing high-profile research outputs, have been undertaken with one purpose: building the academy's research capabilities towards achieving this singular goal for the benefit of Indigenous peoples in Australia and worldwide, and for the betterment of all humanity by fostering broader and deeper intercultural research collaborations and insights.

What IKI has asked of the University in meeting our aims is inherently challenging and difficult. We asked that the University recognise Indigenous knowledge as an interdisciplinary field requiring its own approaches, because Indigenous knowledge is not a single discipline. It is all disciplines as seen through a multitude of different Indigenous cultural lenses from all over the world. We asked that people from radically different histories and backgrounds in Australia work together in a spirit of trust and mutual respect to achieve common goals to advance Indigenous knowledge research globally, when many Indigenous people in Australia and elsewhere justifiably feel that such accommodations are unwarranted or unearned either historically or now. We asked that the University assert no rights whatsoever in any Indigenous knowledge that is used or produced by our research, and that our *Charter for Research with Indigenous Knowledge Holders* be adopted as policy across the entire University. We asked that the UAPC appoint our entire cohort of inaugural IKI fellows to the highest academic rank of full professor in recognition of their exceptional experience and standing as Indigenous knowledge-holders, and distinguished records of demonstrated commitment to Indigenous knowledge research and engagements. We asked the University and its Academic Board to allow us to develop and coordinate our new Doctor of Philosophy—Indigenous Knowledge course outside the conventional faculty structure as a means of creating a streamlined interdisciplinary pathway into formal study of unprecedented flexibility for potential PhD students with established expertise in Indigenous knowledge and a demonstrated capability to undertake research at the PhD level. We asked the University to support us in forging and sustaining new dialogues with Indigenous peoples beyond the immediate influence of the Anglosphere to expand and advance vital new discourses in Indigenous knowledge research. In doing so, we have asked the University to help us redress the greatest educational disparities and societal disadvantage imaginable across Australia and the entire world, wherever Indigenous people live.

All that IKI has asked the University in helping us meet our aims is not only challenging and difficult, but also very new and unfamiliar to many people who work in the university sector. Yet by supporting people to develop greater trust and mutual respect, by listening to each other carefully, by working through problems and concerns in good faith, by becoming increasingly open to trying new approaches and ways forward, and by appointing Indigenous leaders of outstanding judgement, academic standing and research achievement to senior roles in Chancellery, the University of Melbourne has nonetheless engaged with us constructively and delivered positively on each of these challenging requests. Despite IKI's healthy associations with bringing more than $47.3 million of external finding into Australian universities for Indigenous knowledge research and research training, the University's return on investment in supporting IKI's unique vision and approach is incalculable in terms of mere cash flow. IKI's work to expand and advance Indigenous knowledge research since 2020 has already set in motion lasting transformative change for Indigenous people who are among the most excluded from universities, and inspired faculties across the University of Melbourne and other universities around the world to build their own Indigenous knowledge research capabilities by seeking to replicate our approaches. As the University's new Indigenous strategy for 2023–27 now goes into action, IKI remains more committed than ever to working across the entire University and with our many partners worldwide to advance Indigenous knowledge research for the betterment of all humanity and, in doing so, redress immense educational disparities and societal disadvantage wherever Indigenous people live.

Notes

1 Marcia Langton and Aaron Corn, *Law*, Thames & Hudson, Melbourne, p. 33.

2 The University of Melbourne, *Indigenous Strategic Plan 2021–2022*, 2021; The University of Melbourne, *Murmuk Djerring: The University of Melbourne Indigenous Strategy 2023–2027*, 2023, https://about.unimelb.edu.au/reconciliation/murmuk-djerring (accessed 2 November 2023), pp. 35–6.

3 The University of Melbourne, 'Intellectual Property Policy (MPF1320)', Policy Library, 2023, https://policy.unimelb.edu.au/MPF1320/#section-12 (accessed 2 November 2023).

4 United Nations, 'Who Are Indigenous Peoples?', fact sheet, 2006, https://www.un.org/esa/socdev/unpfii/documents/5session_factsheet1.pdf (accessed 2 November 2023); United Nations, *United Nations Declaration on the Rights of Indigenous Peoples*, 2008, https://www.un.org/development/desa/indigenouspeoples/wp-content/uploads/sites/19/2018/11/UNDRIP_E_web.pdf (accessed 2 November 2023), p. 11; Convention on Biological Diversity, 'Article 8(j)—Traditional Knowledge, Innovations and Practices', United Nations Environment Programme, 2023, https://www.cbd.int/traditional (accessed 2 November 2023); Australian Institute of Aboriginal and Torres Strait Islander Studies, 'AIATSIS Code of Ethics for Aboriginal and Torres Strait Islander Research', 2020, https://aiatsis.gov.au/sites/default/files/docs/research-and-guides/ethics/gerais.pdf (accessed 2 November 2023); United Nations Educational, Scientific and Cultural Organization, 'Local and Indigenous Knowledge Systems (LINKS)', 2021, http://www.unesco.org/new/en/natural-sciences/priority-areas/links/related-information/what-is-local-and-indigenous-knowledge (accessed 2 November 2023); National Health and Medical Research Council, 'Ethical Guidelines for Research with Aboriginal and Torres Strait Islander Peoples', 2018, https://www.nhmrc.gov.au/research-policy/ethics/ethical-guidelines-research-aboriginal-and-torres-strait-islander-peoples (accessed 2 November 2023); United Nations Educational, Scientific and Cultural Organization, 'Traditional Knowledge', 2023, http://uis.unesco.org/en/glossary-term/traditional-knowledge (accessed 2 November 2023).

5 United Nations, *United Nations Declaration on the Rights of Indigenous Peoples*, p. 11.

6 Indigenous Knowledge Institute, 'Charter for Research with Indigenous Knowledge Holders', University of Melbourne, 2020, https://indigenousknowledge.unimelb.edu.au/resources/indigenous-research/research-ethics/charter-for-research-with-indigenous-knowledge-holders (accessed 2 November 2023); Australian Research Council, 'Grants Search', 2023, https://dataportal.arc.gov.au/NCGP/Web/Grant/Grants (accessed 2 November 2023).

7 Zena Cumpston, Michael-Shawn Fletcher and Lesley Head, *Plants*, Thames & Hudson, Melbourne, 2022; Samuel Alexander, Sangeetha Chandrashekeran and Brendan Gleeson (eds), *Post-Capitalist Futures*, Springer, Singapore, 2022; Yuh-Fen Tseng and Aaron Corn, *Ontologies and Epistemologies of Indigenous Music and Dance*, International Council for Traditional Music, Chiayi, Taiwan, 2022; Langton and Corn, *Law*.

8 Australian Research Council, 'Grants Search'.

9 The University of Melbourne, 'Indigenous Data Network', 2022, https://mspgh.unimelb.edu.au/centres-institutes/centre-for-health-equity/research-group/indigenous-data-network (accessed 2 November 2023); Melbourne Graduate

School of Education, 'Ngarrngga', University of Melbourne, 2023, https://education.unimelb.edu.au/ngarrngga (accessed 2 November 2023).

10 Professor Gumbula sadly passed away on 20 September 2023. He and his family have given permission for his full name and images to be used for professional purposes. With respect to Yolŋu law, however, his Yolŋu given name, Djaṉgirrawuy, should not be spoken for one year following his death.

11 Petra Lundgren et al., *A National Strategy for Just Adaptation*, Future Earth Australia, Australian Academy of Science, 2022, https://www.futureearth.org.au/sites/default/files/2022-09/a-national-strategy-for-just-adaptation.pdf (accessed 2 November 2023).

12 Aaron Corn, 'Friday Essay: How Indigenous Songs Recount Deep Histories of Trade between Australia and Southeast Asia', *The Conversation*, 29 November 2019, https://theconversation.com/friday-essay-how-indigenous-songs-recount-deep-histories-of-trade-between-australia-and-southeast-asia-123867 (accessed 2 November 2023).

13 Anthea Skinner et al., 'Reflections on Sustaining Trade and Kinship Traditions between Makassans and Yolŋu', *Melbourne Asia Review*, 2023, https://www.melbourneasiareview.edu.au/reflections-on-sustaining-trade-and-kinship-traditions-between-makassans-and-yolnu/ (accessed 2 November 2023).

14 Aaron Corn, 'The First, but Not the Last: Brian Djaṉgirrawuy Gumbula-Garawirrtja', *The Monthly*, 25 October 2023, https://www.themonthly.com.au/blog/aaron-corn/2023/25/2023/first-not-last-brian-djangirrawuy-gumbula-garawirrtja (accessed 2 November 2023).

15 Duane Hamacher, with Elders and knowledge-holders Ghillar Michael Anderson, John Barsa, David Bosun, Ron Day, Segar Passi and Alo Tapim, *The First Astronomers: How Indigenous Elders Read the Stars*, Allen & Unwin, Melbourne, 2022.

16 Indigenous Knowledge Institute, 'Funding', University of Melbourne, 2023, https://indigenousknowledge.unimelb.edu.au/funding (accessed 2 November 2023).

17 Indigenous Knowledge Institute, 'Research', University of Melbourne, 2023, https://indigenousknowledge.unimelb.edu.au/Research (accessed 2 November 2023).

18 Indigenous Knowledge Institute, 'Two-Way Knowledge Sharing for Native Bee Climate Adaptation in Arnhem Land', University of Melbourne, 2022, https://indigenousknowledge.unimelb.edu.au/Research/seed-funding/2023-recipients/two-way-knowledge-sharing-for-native-bee-climate-adaptation-in-arnhem-land (accessed 2 November 2023).

19 Indigenous Knowledge Institute, 'Culture and Heritage', University of Melbourne, 2022, https://indigenousknowledge.unimelb.edu.au/Research/themes/2021-2022-themes/culture-and-heritage (accessed 2 November 2023).

20 Indigenous Knowledge Institute, 'Professor Diane Kerr OAM', University of Melbourne, 2022, https://indigenousknowledge.unimelb.edu.au/Research/iki-fellows/professor-diane-kerr-oam (accessed 2 November 2023).

21 Claire Stuchbury et al., *Above and Beyond Broadcasting: A Study of First Nations Media and the COVID-19 Pandemic*, First Nations Media Australia, 2022, https://firstnationsmedia.org.au/sites/default/files/files/Submissions/Above_and_Beyond_Broadcasting%20(1).pdf (accessed 2 November 2023).

22 Indigenous Knowledge Institute, 'Bronte Gosper', University of Melbourne, 2021, https://indigenousknowledge.unimelb.edu.au/Research/community-fellows/2021-recipients/bronte-gosper (accessed 2 November 2023).

23 Indigenous Knowledge Institute, 'PhD Scholars', University of Melbourne, 2022, https://indigenousknowledge.unimelb.edu.au/Research/phd-scholars (accessed 2 November 2023).

24 The University of Melbourne, 'Doctor of Philosophy: Indigenous Knowledge—Course Overview', 2023, https://indigenousknowledge.unimelb.edu.au/Research/phd-scholars (accessed 2 November 2023).

25 The University of Melbourne, 'Doctor of Philosophy: Indigenous Knowledge—What Will I Study?', 2023, https://study.unimelb.edu.au/find/courses/graduate/doctor-of-philosophy-indigenous-knowledge/what-will-i-study (accessed 2 November 2023).

26 The University of Melbourne, 'Doctor of Philosophy: Indigenous Knowledge—How to Apply', 2023, https://study.unimelb.edu.au/find/courses/graduate/doctor-of-philosophy-indigenous-knowledge/how-to-apply (accessed 2 November 2023).

27 Indigenous Knowledge Institute, 'Event Recordings and Resources', University of Melbourne, 2022, https://indigenousknowledge.unimelb.edu.au/resources/event-recordings-and-resources (accessed 2 November 2023).

28 The University of Melbourne, 'International Day of the World's Indigenous Peoples Symposium', *YouTube*, 2021, https://www.youtube.com/watch?v=T9yhcnQLGJc&list=PLhOObpoQndRlmXwL6PeMfAv6RjlwjKheh&pp=iAQB (accessed 2 November 2023).

29 International Council for Traditions of Music and Dance, 'ICTMD Study Group on Indigenous Music and Dance', 2023, http://ictmusic.org/studygroup/indigenous (accessed 2 November 2023).

30 Indigenous Knowledge Institute, 'Cooking the Kangaroo: Conversations on Indigenous Song, Spirituality, and Connection', University of Melbourne, 2021, https://indigenousknowledge.unimelb.edu.au/resources/event-recordings-and-resources/cooking-the-kangaroo-conversations-on-indigenous-song,-spirituality,-and-connection (accessed 2 November 2023); Indigenous Knowledge Institute, 'Indigenous Knowledge Film Festival', University of Melbourne, 2022, https://indigenousknowledge.unimelb.edu.au/resources/event-recordings-and-resources/indigenous-knowledge-film-festival (accessed 2 November 2023); The University of Melbourne, 'Book Launch of *Law: The Way of the Ancestors* with Professor Marcia Langton and Professor Aaron Corn', 1 June 2023, https://events.unimelb.edu.au/ILJH/event/30209-book-launch-of-law-the-way-of-the-ancestors-with (accessed 2 November 2023).

31 Brian Djaŋgirrawuy Gumbula-Garawirrtja, Renelle Gandjitjiwuy Goṉḏarra and Aaron Corn, 'Remote Australia and the Voice', *YouTube*, 3 May 2023, https://www.youtube.com/watch?v=IKMadHZZGUM (accessed 2 November 2023).

32 Marcia Langton and Aaron Corn, *The Deep End Podcast*, University of Melbourne, 2023, https://www.unimelb.edu.au/voice/the-deep-end-podcast (accessed 2 November 2023).

33 Association of Pacific Rim Universities, 'Indigenous Knowledges Working Group', 2023, https://www.apru.org/our-work/university-leadership/indigenous-knowledges-working-group (accessed 2 November 2023).

34 Hokkaido University, 'Indigenous Research Collaboration Getting Started between Hokkaido and Melbourne Universities', 12 July 2023, https://www.global.hokudai.ac.jp/blog/indigenous-research-collaboration-getting-started-between-hokkaido-and-melbourne-u/ (accessed 2 November 2023); The University of Melbourne, 'Australian Indigenous Researchers Strengthen Ties with Collaborators in Japan',

https://science.unimelb.edu.au/about/news/australian-indigenous-researchers-strengthen-ties-with-collaborators-in-japan (accessed 2 November 2023).

35 The University of Melbourne, '2023 Narrm Oration: Cultural Reawakening—A Taiwanese Indigenous Woman's Journey through Memories and Revitalisation', 23 November 2023, https://events.unimelb.edu.au/event/34504-2023-narrm-oration-cultural-reawakening-a (accessed 2 November 2023).

36 The University of Melbourne, *Murmuk Djerring*, pp. 35–6.

Lighting the Fire, Fanning the Flame

The Wilin Centre for Indigenous Arts and Cultural Development

TIRIKI ONUS and SALLY TRELOYN

IN 2022 THE Wilin Centre for Indigenous Arts and Cultural Development celebrated its twentieth anniversary. It was established in 2002 at Southbank on Bunurong Country as part of the Victorian College of the Arts (VCA), and from 2007 it joined what is today known as the Faculty of Fine Arts and Music at the University of Melbourne, which incorporates both the VCA and the Melbourne Conservatorium of Music. The anniversary also marked twenty years of advocating for Indigenous voices in academia, arts industries and society in general; creating opportunities for First Nations artists to advance their practices and careers; and transforming University curricula and spaces to better include Indigenous knowledge and voices.

This chapter takes the form of a historical position paper from the Wilin Centre on its twentieth anniversary, written by Tiriki Onus, who was a Wilin student at the time of the Centre's inception and went on to serve as a lecturer, before becoming Head of the Wilin Centre in 2017—a role they continue to hold at the time of writing. Supplementary material has been provided by Sally Treloyn, a non-Indigenous academic in the Faculty of Fine Arts and Music who has served in an academic advisory role in various Wilin programs since 2016, and as Co-Director of the Research Unit for Indigenous Arts and Culture with Onus since 2017. The first part of this chapter relates the inception and early years of Wilin. The second looks at contributions to curricula and achieving what Andrea Hull—who, in 2007, was director of the VCA and dean of the faculty that Wilin joined—described as a 'cultural transformation' within the VCA,[1] and in the Faculty of Fine Arts and Music more broadly.

Lighting the Fire, Fanning the Flame

A student protest in 2002 gave birth to the organisation that is today known as the Wilin Centre. At that time the VCA had very few First Nations students, and there was almost no visibility of Aboriginal and Torres Strait Islander people, histories and cultures within our campus. On Wilin's tenth anniversary, playwright Andrea James reflected that, while renowned artists such as Trevor Nicholls, Gary Lang and Kylie Belling had previously been students, in James' time as a theatre-maker student at the VCA from 1993 to 1995, they were the only First Nations student in the VCA.[2] This reflected the larger problem of the absence of First Nations voices in the faculty and University, and of the inclusion of First Nations peoples in arts industries more generally.[3] This contributed negatively to a lack of safety for those First Nations students, staff and community members who were present. James, for example, describes being 'sick to the stomach' when a collaboration between drama students and a visiting drama school from Aotearoa New Zealand led to a performance of the haka on the campus without the appropriate acknowledgement of place, or consultation and permission from Traditional Owners and custodians of Wurundjeri Woi Wurrung and Bunurong land.[4]

A group of determined students—First Nations and non-Indigenous—dared to dream of a VCA that looked quite different and a future of which they all wanted to be a part. A small group of students decided they would protest the lack of representation of Aboriginal and Torres Strait Islander peoples on the Southbank campus, and they would hold physical space to make themselves heard. The students camped out on the back lawns of the VCA. James relates how senior Wurundjeri Woi Wurrung Elder Aunty Joy Wandin Murphy lit a fire with the students, who kept it going all week.[5] They made food together, and they celebrated. They invited all those passing to hear their story and their dream of a future VCA that was more diverse and had a greater dialogue with place and the history of Wurundjeri Woi Wurrung and Bunurong Country, on which the campus was built, and all the Countries and people on which Australia was founded.

Around the same time, aware of a lack of visibility of First Nations artists in mainstream public life, and of protests of students such as James, professor Andrea Hull acted with other senior staff and James to achieve change.

The goal of this, as related by Hull, was to not just focus on recruitment and supporting Indigenous students to graduation, but to work out how to 'shift the cultural consciousness of this community ... There was a real understanding that it would be a two-way thing'.[6]

In 2002 Michelle Evans founded and became head of the Wilin Centre, a role in which they served until 2010.[7] Initially the Centre was a shack, a small shed on the back lawns of the VCA, abutting the fence of the horse exercise yards behind the Victoria Police stables. There was no heating or cooling and just four rooms; however, the discussions and actions of students and allies in the rooms were impactful.

Within weeks of its establishment, the Centre received a new name, drawn from a conversation between Evans and Aunty Joy Wandin Murphy and the student fire. It centred on the Centre's inception and honoured the intrinsic centre of the student protest: the campsite, and the fire that was lit by those students to generate warmth and a movement. The Woi Wurrung and Bunurong word for fire, *wilin*, was gifted by Aunty Joy. This naming was embraced and celebrated by other Elders from within the Kulin nation who also held custodianship over that language. Through these continued acts of resistance, the Wilin Centre came to life.

In the first years of its existence, the Wilin Centre served as a mechanism to help recruit Aboriginal and Torres Strait Islander students to come and study at the VCA. As well as a recruitment agency, the Wilin Centre was also there to advocate for Aboriginal and Torres Strait Islander students. Most importantly, under the leadership of Evans, the Wilin Centre was established as a space for belonging: a refuge and safe place to which First Nations students could retreat. For Evans, as with other organisational and collective spaces by and for First Nations arts and artists, Wilin became a space 'for the development of voice, collaborative advocacy and for nourishing connection, especially for those that are otherwise disconnected and disenfranchised'.[8] Wilin's status as a safe place was marked by it being an organisational unit within the VCA and the faculty, where First Nations students were not questioned over aspects of their identity, their place or their belonging. They were not expected to speak to the complexities of life in the occupied space. It was a place where First Nations students did not have to navigate the colonised environment quite so much as in the academy at large.

In subsequent years, the Wilin Centre continued to work to recruit and advocate for First Nations students. Support began to come to the Centre from the private sector. Extraordinary financial support was offered and provided by the Dara Foundation, which kept the Wilin Centre growing and thriving, and gave it the resources to be able to support the learning journeys of emergent Aboriginal and Torres Strait Islander student-artists in transformative ways, such as by creating opportunities for those artists to connect with larger communities of practice within this continent and around the globe.

Building on an early artist-in-residence program and marking the Centre's growing presence and impact in wider public spheres, several First Nations communities of practice, each surviving and thriving in their own right, became involved in the activities of the Wilin Centre and in many cases also came to call it home. During this time, through the leadership of heads of the centre and community members, particularly Elders who empowered students and staff, Wilin continued to grow and change. A primary area of development was the creation and delivery of an innovative, community-engaged curriculum. Within a few years of its launch, the Wilin's first academic program, the Graduate Certificate in Indigenous Arts Management, had been created by Michelle Evans. This course pursued a dream of a world in which Aboriginal and Torres Strait Islander artists, makers and community members are resourced to take control of the organisations that represent their art and their communities. To give access to students from First Nations across the continent, the course was delivered via an intensive block release model that allowed arts managers to be based primarily in their home communities. This in turn allowed participants to embed knowledge in their local organisations as soon as it was gained, and served to ensure the curriculum had relevance to the organisations, communities and networks in which the student was based. The effects of this early training program can still be seen in many of our broader organisations today.

Change further accelerated and had greater effect with the merger of the VCA with the University of Melbourne, joining the Conservatorium to create a single faculty. The space that Wilin had created was held and became a significant part of the agenda of the new faculty. Likewise, the larger organisational unit lent itself to Wilin's pursuit of an expanded dream. The roles and responsibilities of the Wilin Centre changed. The Centre was not just there to advocate for and support our Aboriginal and Torres Strait Islander students in a world where the voices of First Nations people are quite often silenced. The pastoral care that Wilin had always taken as a core responsibility was now extended to include an additional remit to create spaces that were safe not only for our students but also for the community at large. A primary focus of this work has been curriculum development centred on community engagement.

Transforming the University Community and Decolonising the Curriculum

One of the first major shifts in consciousness that was effected in the VCA required a reframing of the historical positioning of contemporary arts in Australia, and with this a challenging of what was viewed as legitimate arts practice in the Western academy. Hull related that:

> One of the things I always remember Andrea James telling me [was] that her grandfather had told her that in the olden times, this whole area was really important for ritual and community celebration. And she said, 'It's so interesting how after settlement people actually think they're inventing something, but in fact, they're just reengaging with what that land had always been.' And she said, 'The fact that this whole area is now the cultural precinct is no surprise to people who understand history through a very long lens and that it was an absolute cultural gathering spot and that it is again ... the VCA is right in the heart of that.'[9]

Recognition of this, and the role of the VCA and the Conservatorium in producing many of Australia's arts professionals and practitioners, contributes to recognition of the influential role of Kulin nation place and custodians of place in the Australian and global arts scenes, and in society.

Those at Wilin dreamt of creating a space where everyone could engage with the knowledge and the stories of this place, this Wurundjeri Woi Wurrung and Bunurong Country, this Kulin nation land, to celebrate and amplify the stories that have existed in this landscape for thousands of generations, and to consider ways in which we could see these knowledges and stories as relevant to all artistic practice. In this space we would start talking about the Indigenous knowledge and stories that collectively we had missed due to these having been written out of our communal history by the colonial project, and the persistence of curricula that omitted Indigenous knowledge and silenced Indigenous voices. Building on that early dream the student group had held about representing Aboriginal and Torres Strait Islander voices, and creating safe spaces within the faculty, Wilin began addressing the question of how to change the space of the faculty itself, not just within but also outside the walls of the Centre. This was a matter of social justice and safety for First Nations students. As Andrea James related, 'It is an incredible privilege to be here and to train in your chosen art form. But with that comes an incredible responsibility and an incredible cultural responsibility.'[10] The VCA, in general, to that point lacked the knowledge and capability to fulfil this responsibility.

Wilin started offering academic programs throughout the broader University through the Breadth subject program.[11] The reasoning behind this was to contribute to the continuation of the deep, profound knowledges and technologies that have existed in this land for millennia, by creating a space in which all our students, regardless of their cultural background, are able to engage with and celebrate the stories of place. At Wilin we have believed, and continue to believe, that holding a space for everyone to be able to embrace these stories has the potential to create a far more inclusive and culturally safe environment for all our students, but particularly our First Nations students.

Critical to the academic approach to these programs has been the engagement of Elders and community members with the Wilin team concerning course design, content and delivery. Consent is a prerequisite of engagement with Indigenous knowledge, and it is accordingly typically sought by course designers prior to teaching Indigenous content. Further, when the dynamic nature of the authority to represent Indigenous knowledge and practices is recognised, consent may be sought repeatedly from delivery to delivery. Wilin has held that while this consent is vital, to deliver content, we must receive active direction and a mandate from those who are responsible for these knowledges, as well as those who are responsible for the places on which the knowledge will be taught. We do not seek permission from our Elders and community to tell the stories of this place. We seek their direction. It is not 'We are seeking permission to teach x', but rather 'We have the opportunity to teach x, so may we discuss if and how that should be done?'

This approach has been aided by long-term, community-based engagement with Elders and knowledge-holders across several domains. These engagements have created space in which Elders and knowledge-holders throughout the history of Wilin have approached us, recommending or requesting that we include certain topics, knowledges and practices in our curriculum. Over time, through these requests being met by responsive curriculum development and events, the voices of Elders and knowledge-holders have become more empowered.

A space has been nurtured in which the community is able to make meaningful, and increasingly strong and powerful, contributions at the University. Through the relationships created with community partners, knowledge-holders, and those who wish to challenge the knowledge systems that we have previously been handed, Wilin has sought to create new models of engagement, and new ways to celebrate deeply held and time-honoured knowledge systems that have existed in this land for thousands and thousands of generations. Through profound relationships and relational accountability, the Wilin Centre seeks to amplify the lesser-known stories of this continent, particularly the Kulin nation Country upon which we stand. Our mandate comes from our communities. The stories that we tell are gifts that have been given to us and which, because of the generosity, diplomacy and love of our Elders and community, we are able to share.

A common burden placed on First Nations students is the tacit and sometimes explicit expectation they will educate their otherwise non-Indigenous classrooms and teachers, challenging and changing the way in which administration and academia at universities are done.[12] It is not the job of First Nations students to fix this space. They have found their way to us to advance their artistic practices. They come to us as deeply competent artists, informed by their own identities in ways that are ever new and fascinating to us.

It is our responsibility as Wilin to support them to be the greatest artists they can be. And it is increasingly our responsibility to see that everyone around these artists is educated as well. For this reason, the curriculum that we offer is directed at all students. Each student who participates in our courses has an opportunity to engage with, celebrate and amplify the stories of place, particularly for the Country upon which they stand, live and work, and to consider the ways in which they might be able to go out into the world as practising artists to mobilise their various gifts and amplify the voice of Aboriginal and Torres Strait Islander Australia. In the creative and fine arts, this often means acquiring an understanding of the difference between appropriation and extraction, and of meaningful and productive allyship.

Conclusion

In the annual 'Lighting of the Wilin' ceremony, the Faculty of Fine Arts and Music marks the beginning of Reconciliation Week and the origins of the Wilin Centre. At the 2021 ceremony, Professor Marie Sierra, the current dean of the faculty, commemorated the actions of Wilin's founding students and community, and the need for continual reflection in the faculty to build a safe community:

> The story of the Wilin Centre is one of direct action. [It is] the result of continued effort to make this faculty safe for First Nations people ... I would like to finish by asking all of you who have gathered with us today to reflect, not just on the culture and history of First Nations, but on the ongoing responsibility each of us must play in taking an active role.[13]

In enacting each of the approaches described in this chapter, we learn as a community, and in the safety and support of our Elders. This allows Wilin to continue to grow in capacity and responsiveness, and embrace strength-based narratives of First Peoples that celebrate the incredible strength, diversity, longevity and power of knowledge systems and artistic practices that have existed in this place for thousands upon thousands of generations. When we acknowledge Country, we acknowledge that we are artists who are guests here, and that through the generosity of those around us, of those who do speak for this Country, we have been able to create our art and tell our stories, here on this place where thousands upon thousands of generations of artists have gone before us. The stories of this Country did not stop two-and-a-half centuries ago. They have been added to and added to, and we in turn now have an opportunity to keep telling the stories of this place. Each of us must decide how we are going to engage in a safe, meaningful, strength-based and productive way. In this context, while mistakes will be made, we have a framework within which to respond inclusively and to learn to do better. We hope that the history of the Wilin Centre, including its role in shaping the arts landscape of Australia, and the work we do now, stands as a model for future practice, including its status as ever evolving and changing, and always responding to the needs of our communities—both First Nations and broader.

In the same year that the Wilin Centre celebrated its twentieth anniversary, the VCA celebrated its fiftieth. Twenty years on from the foundational fire lit by students and allies, we collectively, along with the Conservatorium, dream of a future where all of us can celebrate the stories of this place together; where all of us who are guests here can talk about what it is that makes it so powerful for us to be artists and creatives here on this Kulin nation Country; and where we can each of us take up the challenge that has been issued to us by Boonwurrung Yaluk-ut Weelam Elder, N'Arwee't Professor Dr Carolyn Briggs AM to 'Come with a purpose',[14] to continually challenge ourselves to learn more, to do better, and to think about how we want to envisage the world of the future.

As artists, we have a great gift. We decide how we would like others to see the world through our eyes. At Wilin we have a great gift and opportunity, helping others to dream bigger than they have in the past. At the end of the day, we make our art because of the strength of those who have gone before us, the stories they have told, their survival and tenacity. We are here because of the strength and sacrifice of others. But we are not victims. We are contributors in every sense of the word. We reject the deficit-based discourse of the past and instead we move towards the future in a space of strength and vitality.

Notes

1 Andrea Hull, in Faculty of Fine Arts and Music, University of Melbourne, 'The Wilin Centre: 10 Year Celebration Part 1', *YouTube*, 2012, https://www.youtube.com/watch?v=jAJ-q0zJlgE (accessed 3 November 2023).

2 Ibid.

3 Michelle Evans, 'The Courage to Speak out: An Overview of Courageous Conversations', in Wilin Centre for Indigenous Arts and Cultural Development, *Courageous Conversations: National Talking Circle*, University of Melbourne, Parkville, 2010, pp. 5–10.

4 Andrea James, in Faculty of Fine Arts and Music, 'The Wilin Centre: 10 Year Celebration Part 1', 03:30–04:15.

5 Faculty of Fine Arts and Music, University of Melbourne, 'The Wilin Centre: 10 Year Celebration Part 2', *YouTube*, 2012, https://www.youtube.com/watch?v=-LyZ_PL5Cj0 (accessed 3 November 2023), 00:20–00:31.

6 Hull, in Faculty of Fine Arts and Music, 'The Wilin Centre: 10 Year Celebration Part 1', 04:26–05:04.

7 Richard Murphet, 'The Fall and Rise of the VCA: The Pulse in the Arm', *Platform Papers*, no. 28, 2011, pp. 1–62.

8 Michelle Evans and Amanda Sinclair, 'Containing, Contesting, Creating Spaces: Leadership and Cultural Identity Work among Australian Indigenous Arts Leaders', *Leadership*, vol. 12, no. 3, 2016, pp. 270–92.

9 Hull, citing James, in Faculty of Fine Arts and Music, 'The Wilin Centre: 10 Year Celebration Part 1', 07:42–08:21.

10 James, in Faculty of Fine Arts and Music, 'The Wilin Centre: 10 Year Celebration Part 1', 05:06–05:27.

11 The Breadth program requires all undergraduate students to enrol in subjects from a different area of study to the degree they are enrolled in. It is designed to embed a breadth of knowledge in their degree experience.

12 Christine Asmar and Susan Page, 'Sources of Satisfaction and Stress among Indigenous Academic Teachers: Findings from a National Australian Study', *Asia Pacific Journal of Education*, vol. 29, no. 3, 2009, pp. 387–401.

13 Marie Sierra, in Faculty of Fine Arts and Music, University of Melbourne, 'Lighting of the Wilin 2021', 2021, https://youtu.be/FI0Jf6x8570 (accessed 3 November 2023).

14 Carolyn Briggs, in Faculty of Fine Arts and Music, University of Melbourne, 'Lighting of the Wilin 2021', 2021, https://youtu.be/FI0Jf6x8570 (accessed 3 November 2023).

Indigenous Astronomy at the University of Melbourne

DUANE HAMACHER, AMANDA GOLDFARB, BRIDGET KELLY and EMMA BARNETT

THE STUDY OF Indigenous knowledge related to the night sky, and the layers of this knowledge developed through scientific processes (astronomy), have become an area of intense academic, educational and public interest over the last twenty years. Academic collaborations with Aboriginal and Torres Strait Islander communities and Elders are producing a constant stream of research outputs, revealing an increasing depth of traditional knowledge about the sun, moon, planets and stars, and the multitude of ways in which this knowledge is applied.[1] Much of this work challenges accepted narratives in public and academic discourse, and reshapes the history and philosophy of science.[2]

The University of Melbourne is currently a global leader in the study of Indigenous astronomy, as well as being one of the few leading institutions that engages in structured research, teaching and public programs in cultural astronomy. Outputs include books,[3] educational curricula,[4] astrotourism,[5] gallery and museum exhibitions,[6] musical and theatrical performances,[7] commemorative coins,[8] films and documentaries,[9] and formal names for stars[10] and asteroids[11] recognised by the International Astronomical Union.

The state of Victoria, the city of Melbourne and the University of Melbourne have all played a key role in the history of Indigenous astronomy research, with connections going back more than 160 years. This chapter examines the history of the discipline, how the University of Melbourne has been a central player in this development, and the various programs in this space.

A Brief History

The timeline for the Aboriginal discovery and settlement of Sahul (what today constitutes Australia and New Guinea) continues to reach further into the deep past, upwards of 65 000 years.[12] This Pleistocene-era settlement, along with the late-Holocene formation and habitation of the Torres Strait,[13] means that Indigenous Australians represent the longest continuing cultures in the world. Knowledge systems developed over that time describe a changing and dynamic world that has been passed down over millennia through song, story, dance, art, culture and language.

Astronomy has been described as an 'integral component of Aboriginal cultures',[14] and central to the development of calendars, celestial navigation, weather prediction and land management, in addition to informing ceremony and encoding law.[15] There are 'crucial [connections] between the Skyworld, terrestrial land and the Underworld',[16] with the sky, the sea and earth combined in a 'cosmoscape'.[17] Stories and legends helped tie this cosmoscape together, with one of the most widely spread tales relating to the Pleiades. This star cluster, also known as the Seven Sisters, is often described by different Aboriginal cultures as a group of sisters or young girls hunted by an amorous man, who is often associated with the stars of Orion.[18] In one tradition, the Pleiades women journeyed across mountains on their way to the sky, leaving behind a series of springs, which in turn fed the rivers. When a young hunter stole away with one of the girls, the remaining women sent snow and ice so that he would free their sister. However, this caused the clan hardship, and so the women ventured into the sky to find summer, so that the snow and ice would melt. Winter then served as a warning that it was 'wrong to carry off women who belong to a totem that forbade them', with the Pleiades rising in summer at the return of the warm weather.[19] Here, we can see how astronomical knowledge displays not only a rich and established understanding of the night sky, but also a reflection of the physical Country—an amalgamation of cultural practices and traditions, and an essential link to the Dreaming, that is as alive and real as the people and Country. The sky is home to rivers, ancestral spirits, flora and fauna. 'As above, then so below' is a phrase often used to describe Indigenous interpretations of the sky.[20] The narratives associated with the night sky are not only cultural or seasonal imperatives but hold within them thousands of years of history, and this knowledge provides a way to understand an ancient history encoded in story and landscape, as richly discussed in the book *The Memory Code.*[21]

Evidence for this is found in living cultures, through Elders and knowledge-holders, and also ethnohistorical accounts containing references to the planets, stars, sun, moon and Milky Way.[22] Recent investigations into transient astronomical phenomena demonstrate that Aboriginal people witnessed and recorded solar and lunar eclipses,[23] comets,[24] meteorite impacts[25] and auroral displays,[26] transmitting this knowledge over significant timescales.[27]

Applications of astronomical observations can be noted in seasonal hunting practices, plant harvesting and weather prediction. Perhaps one of the most well-known Aboriginal constellations is that of the Celestial Emu, which is located in the Milky Way. The bird's head is the dark space of the Coalsack Nebula, while its body is traced out by the dust lanes of the Milky Way down through Scorpius and Sagittarius.[28] The orientation of this dark constellation changes across the year, from its first appearance in April–May, during the emu-mating season, to June when the eggs are being incubated (the optimal time for egg collection), and August–September when the chicks begin fledging.[29] The changing position of the Emu indicates the changing seasons as well as the behavioural patterns of the bird, informing food economics and ceremony. Recent work shows how stellar scintillation (twinkling) is used by Indigenous peoples around the world to forecast weather and predict seasonal change, while observations of variable stars and possible supernovae are challenging established claims in the history and philosophy of science.[30]

Western studies of Aboriginal astronomy trace their beginnings to the work of William Edward Stanbridge, who read a paper to the Philosophical Institute of Victoria in 1857 titled 'On the Astronomy and Mythology of the Aborigines of Victoria'.[31] Stanbridge provided a summary of the astronomy of the Boorong people, a clan of the Wergaia-speaking people near Lake Tyrrell in north-western Victoria, as told to him 'as nearly as language will allow, word for word'.[32]

Originally from Astley in Warwickshire, England, Stanbridge arrived in Port Phillip in 1841.[33] In 1847 he obtained a pastoral licence at Tyrrell Downs, on the traditional lands of the Wergaia-speaking peoples.[34] Wergaia Country was divided into twenty clan regions prior to colonisation, with Lake Tyrrell associated with the Boorong clan. The name of the lake means 'night sky', as the salty waters often provide a mirror-like reflection of the stars. Over the course of a few years, two Boorong men taught Stanbridge a bit about their language, traditions and customs, and their astronomy.[35]

In his 1857 address, Stanbridge stated that 'the Booroung Tribe, who claim and inhabit the Mallee country in the neighbourhood of Lake Tyrill ... pride themselves upon knowing more of Astronomy than any other tribe'. As part of this extensive work, he learned the Boorong names and traditions about the sun and moon, Venus, Jupiter, Arcturus, Antares, Vega, Sirius, Rigel, the Pleiades, Canopus, Achernar, Delphinus, Castor, Pollux, Capella and Aldebaran, as well as stars within the constellations of Aquila, Orion, Corona Borealis, Corona Australia, Scorpius, Centaurus, Crux, Coma Berenices, the Magellanic Clouds, Milky Way and the celestial Emu.[36]

In 1857 Stanbridge was admitted to the Philosophical Institute of Victoria, and this was soon followed by admissions to the Royal Society of Victoria (1860) and the Ethnological Society of London (1861), and election as a fellow of the Anthropological Institute, London (1863).[37] He grew wealthy from gold-mining royalties from his properties and was a co-founder of the town of Daylesford. During the 1860s Stanbridge was also appointed an honorary correspondent to the Board for the Protection of Aborigines for the Upper Loddon district and a member of the first council of Daylesford.[38]

Stanbridge's work formed a key foundation for Indigenous astronomy research, leading to renewed investigations into cultural astronomy over subsequent decades. One major outcome was research by Duane Hamacher and David Frew demonstrating conclusively that Stanbridge had recorded Boorong traditions that described the 'supernova impostor' eruption of the luminous blue variable star Eta Carina in the 1840s (dubbed 'The Great Eruption'), in which the star went from an average star in a densely populated area of the Milky Way to the second-brightest star in the night sky, before fading completely from view a decade later.[39] The Boorong observed and incorporated this event into their oral traditions, which currently stands as the only Indigenous record of this transient event anywhere in the world.

Stanbridge died in his early seventies. In his will, he earmarked funds to establish the Frances Colles Stanbridge Scholarship at Trinity College at the University of Melbourne, which is still offered today. His papers formed the basis of John Morieson's seminal 1996 MA thesis in Australian studies at the University, 'The Night Sky of the Boorong'.[40] This thesis formed the foundation of the Melbourne Planetarium show *Stories in the Stars: The Night Sky of the Boorong People*, which has been shown for over fifteen years.[41] Representations of Boorong astronomy are included in the logo of the Australian Space Agency,[42] and they were the focus of the University-based play *Mirror's Edge* by Kim Ho, which won the prestigious Patrick White Playwrights' Award.[43] Boorong astronomy is taught in an undergraduate subject through the School of Physics,[44] and it is included in some of the Indigenous astronomy education modules for the Australian National Curriculum, developed at the University of Melbourne through a committee chaired by Professor Marcia Langton.[45]

Teaching and Research Programs

As a global leader in cultural astronomy scholarship (including Indigenous astronomy), the University of Melbourne offers a new cultural astronomy program developed by Hamacher, comprising four undergraduate subjects that were developed into a Breadth Track, with plans for a Minor and postgraduate programs.

Indigenous Astronomy is a first-year subject that highlights how Indigenous cultures around the world have developed complex knowledge systems focused on the sun, moon and stars. Elders teach that 'everything on the land is reflected in the sky', with the stars serving as a map, calendar, timepiece and mnemonic memory aid that inform law and social structure, and include cultural understandings of science and applications of scientific practice. As an introduction to the field of cultural astronomy, this subject examines the astronomical knowledge and traditions of contemporary Indigenous cultures around the world, with an emphasis on Australia. It is taught by Hamacher with Indigenous guest lecturers through Physics.

Archaeoastronomy is a second-year subject that focuses on ancient and Indigenous cultures from around the world. It examines theoretical frameworks, methodological approaches and historical processes that explore the role of the sun, moon and stars in culture and societies of the past, with a focus on material culture and architecture. It is jointly taught by Hamacher and Gerhard Wiesenfeldt between Physics and the History and Philosophy of Science.

Astronomy in World History is a second-year subject that examines how cultures across the globe have centred celestial phenomena in their attempts to understand the world in which they lived. Students examine the ways in which astronomical knowledge was developed throughout the world, combining simple astronomical observations with studies of historical instruments and classes discussing the development of astronomy in different cultures, ranging from East Asia, via the Middle East and Europe, to Central America and Australia. It takes a more historical approach and is taught by Wiesenfeldt through the History and Philosophy of Science.

Astronomy and Society in the Space Age is a third-year subject that focuses on the philosophical and sociological implications of astronomical research and humanity's presence in space by examining the impacts of light pollution on our view of the sky, the construction of facilities on Indigenous lands, equity and inclusion in astronomy, colonising space, and ways research can be guided by Indigenous knowledges. It is taught by Hamacher.

These subjects provide deep insights into First Nations' astronomy in Australia and around the world, and a framework for investigating scientific approaches from non-Western perspectives. Postgraduate programs are offered through the School of Physics (Master of Science), the Faculty of Arts (Master of Arts), the Faculty of Science (Master of Philosophy) and across all faculties with the Doctor of Philosophy. Current postgraduate research students have commenced PhDs and master's degrees across multiple faculties and institutions, led by a transdisciplinary team of supervisors and academics.

Hamacher is leading a range of cultural astronomy and dark sky studies research and teaching programs at the University of Melbourne. The research projects span multiple disciplines, looking into Indigenous astronomical knowledge and traditions in Australia, Central America and Thailand; studies of meteorite impacts in history and society; the role of astronomy in traditional music; and orality. A range of supervised projects is currently being undertaken by students enrolled in postgraduate research programs related to Indigenous astronomy and dark sky studies at the University of Melbourne, the ANU, the University of New South Wales, the University of Southern Queensland, and the University of Oklahoma in the United States. Research projects include constellation grouping and visual perception; star knowledge of the Torres Strait; the astronomy of the Kulin nation; mega-constellations and ethics; the night-time economy; the astronomy of the Wiradjuri people of New South Wales; the astronomy of the Kulin nation of Victoria; dark sky studies; astronomy education and pedagogy; and the Ngiyampaa astronomy of northern New South Wales.

Formal collaborations within the University of Melbourne involve the School of Physics, the School of Historical and Philosophical Studies, the School of Biosciences, the Melbourne School of Psychological Studies, the Melbourne School of Design, the Melbourne Graduate School of Education, the Department of Infrastructure Engineering, the Victorian College of the Arts, and the Indigenous Knowledge Institute.

Notes

1 DW Hamacher, with Elders and knowledge-holders Ghillar Michael Anderson, John Barsa, David Bosun, Ron Day, Segar Passi and Alo Tapim, *The First Astronomers: How Indigenous Elders Read the Stars*, Allen & Unwin, Sydney, 2022.

2 For example, DW Hamacher, 'The Stories behind Aboriginal Star Names Now Recognised by the World's Astronomical Body', *The Conversation*, 14 January 2018, https://theconversation.com/the-stories-behind-aboriginal-star-names-now-recognised-by-the-worlds-astronomical-body-87617 (accessed 3 November 2023).

3 Hamacher, *The First Astronomers*; Karlie Noon and Krystal De Napoli, *Astronomy: Sky Country*, Thames & Hudson, Melbourne, 2022.

4 Indigenous Knowledge Institute, 'Aboriginal and Torres Strait Islander Curricula', University of Melbourne, 2020, https://indigenousknowledge.unimelb.edu.au/curriculum (accessed 3 November 2023).

5 N May, 'Seeing Stars: The Astronomical Rise of Australian Dark-Sky Tourism', *The Guardian*, 11 September 2022, https://www.theguardian.com/travel/2022/sep/12/seeing-stars-the-astronomical-rise-of-australian-dark-sky-tourism (accessed 3 November 2023).

6 Scienceworks, 'Stories in the Stars', Museums Victoria, 2022. https://museumsvictoria.com.au/scienceworks/learning/school-programs-and-resources/stories-in-the-stars (accessed 3 November 2023).

7 K Ho, 'Putting Cross Cultural Stories Centre Stage', *Pursuit*, 30 May 2018, https://pursuit.unimelb.edu.au/articles/putting-cross-cultural-stories-centre-stage (accessed 3 November 2023).

8 DW Hamacher, 'New Coins Celebrate Indigenous Astronomy, the Stars, and the Dark Spaces between Them', *The Conversation*, 13 September 2020, https://theconversation.com/new-coins-celebrate-indigenous-astronomy-the-stars-and-the-dark-spaces-between-them-145923 (accessed 3 November 2023).

9 Films include National Geographic's *The Story of God with Morgan Freeman*, 2016, Season 1, Episode 4; Warwick Thornton's *We Don't Need a Map*, Ronin Films, 2017; and Werner Herzog and Clive Oppenheimer's *Fireball: Visitors from Darker Worlds*, Apple TV+, 2020.

10 Hamacher, 'The Stories behind Aboriginal Star Names'.

11 DW Hamacher, 'From 7809 Marcialangton to 7630 Yidumduma: 5 Asteroids Named after Aboriginal and Torres Strait Islander People', *The Conversation*, 25 August 2020, https://theconversation.com/from-7809-marcialangton-to-7630-yidumduma-5-asteroids-named-after-aboriginal-and-torres-strait-islander-people-144596 (accessed 3 November 2023).

12 C Clarkson et al., 'Human Occupation of Northern Australia by 65 000 Years Ago', *Nature*, no. 547, 2017, pp. 306–10.

13 M Carter, 'New Evidence for the Earliest Human Occupation in Torres Strait, Northeastern Australia', *Australian Archaeology*, vol. 52, 2001, pp. 50–2.
14 RD Haynes, 'Aboriginal Astronomy', *Australian Journal of Astronomy*, vol. 4, no. 3, 1992, pp. 127–40.
15 Hamacher, *The First Astronomers.*
16 P Clarke, 'As above, Then So below: Aboriginal Cosmology and Seasons', in C Carey (ed.), *Our Hidden State: South Australia through the Eyes of Its Scientists*, ANZAAS Handbook, Adelaide, 1997, p. 53.
17 T Leaman, 'Harmonising the Land and Sky in Aboriginal Dreamings', in N Campion (ed.), *The Harmony Debates: Exploring a Practical Philosophy for a Sustainable Future*, Sophia Centre Press, Lampeter, UK, 2020, pp. 397–406.
18 T Leaman and D Hamacher, 'Aboriginal Astronomical Traditions from Ooldea, South Australia, Part 1: Nyeeruna and the "Orion Story"', *Journal of Astronomical History and Heritage*, vol. 17, no. 2, 2014, pp. 180–94.
19 Haynes, 'Aboriginal Astronomy'.
20 Clarke, 'As above, Then So below'.
21 L Kelly, *The Memory Code*, Allen & Unwin, Sydney, 2016.
22 D Johnson, *Night Skies of Aboriginal Australia: A Noctuary*, University of Sydney Press, Sydney, 1998; RP Norris and CM Norris, *Emu Dreaming: An Introduction to Australian Aboriginal Astronomy*, Emu Dreaming Press, Sydney, 2009; Hamacher, *The First Astronomers.*
23 DW Hamacher and RP Norris, 'Eclipses in Australian Aboriginal Astronomy', *Journal of Astronomical History and Heritage*, vol. 14, no. 2, 2011, pp. 103–14.
24 DW Hamacher and RP Norris, 'Comets in Australian Aboriginal Astronomy', *Journal of Astronomical History and Heritage*, vol. 14, no. 1, 2011, pp. 31–40.
25 DW Hamacher and J Goldsmith, 'Aboriginal Oral Traditions of Australian Impact Craters', *Journal of Astronomical History and Heritage*, vol. 16, no. 3, 2013, pp. 295–311.
26 DW Hamacher, 'Aurorae in Australian Aboriginal Traditions', *Journal of Astronomical History and Heritage*, vol. 16, no. 2, 2013, pp. 207–19.
27 D Hamacher, P Nunn, M Gantevoort, R Taylor, G Lehman, K Law and M Miles, 'The Archaeology of Orality: Dating Aboriginal Tasmanian Oral Traditions to the Late-Pleistocene', Journal of Archaeological Science, https://doi.org/10.1016/j.jas.2023.105819.
28 RS Fuller, MG Anderson, RP Norris and M Trudgett, 'The Emu Sky Knowledge of the Kamilaroi and Euahlayi Peoples', *Journal of Astronomical History and Heritage*, vol. 17, no. 2, 2014, pp. 171–9.
29 Ibid.
30 DW Hamacher, John Barsa, Segar Passi and Alo Tapim, 'Indigenous Use of Stellar Scintillation to Predict Weather and Seasonal Change', *Proceedings of the Royal Society of Victoria*, vol. 131, 2019, pp. 24–33; DW Hamacher, 'Observations of Red-Giant Variable Stars By Aboriginal Australians', *The Australian Journal of Anthropology*, vol. 29, no. 1, 2018, pp. 89–107; DW Hamacher, 'Are Supernovae Recorded in Indigenous Astronomical Traditions?', *Journal of Astronomical History and Heritage*, vol. 17, no. 2, 2014, pp. 161–70.
31 WE Stanbridge, 'On the Astronomy and Mythology of the Aborigines of Victoria', *Proceedings of the Philosophical Institute of Victoria: Transactions*, vol. 2, 1857, pp. 137–40.
32 Ibid.

33 DW Hamacher, On the Astronomical Knowledge and Traditions of Aboriginal Australians, unpublished PhD thesis, Department of Indigenous Studies, Macquarie University, Sydney, 2011.
34 ID Clark, *Aboriginal Languages and Clans: An Historical Atlas of Western and Central Victoria, 1800–1900*, Monash Publications on Geography, Melbourne, 1990.
35 WE Stanbridge, 'Some Particulars of the General Characteristics, Astronomy, and Mythology of the Tribes in the Central Part of Victoria, Southern Australia', *Transactions of the Ethnological Society of London*, vol. 1, 1861.
36 Ibid.
37 C Nicholson, 'Ordinary Meeting, 26 May 1863', *Transactions of the Anthropological Society of London*, vol. 1, 1863, p. x.
38 Clark, *Aboriginal Languages and Clans.*
39 DW Hamacher and DJ Frew, 'An Aboriginal Australian Record of the Great Eruption of Eta Carinae', *Journal for Astronomical History & Heritage*, vol. 13, no. 3, 2010, pp. 220–34.
40 J Morieson, The Night Sky of the Boorong: Partial Reconstruction of a Disappeared Culture in North-West Victoria, unpublished MA thesis, Australian Centre, University of Melbourne, Melbourne, 1966.
41 Scienceworks, 'Stories in the Stars'.
42 Australian Department of Industry, Science and Resources, 'Australian Space Agency: Past, Present and Future', 12 December 2018, https://www.industry.gov.au/news/australian-space-agency-past-present-and-future (accessed 3 November 2023).
43 Ho, 'Putting Cross Cultural Stories Centre Stage'.
44 PHYC10010: Indigenous Astronomy.
45 University of Melbourne, 'Indigenous Knowledge Institute: Aboriginal and Torres Strait Islander School Curricula', https://indigenousknowledge.unimelb.edu.au/curriculum (accessed 24 November 2023).

Transforming an Engineering Worldview of the Indigenous 'Other'

JULIANA KAYA PRPIC

> 'We [Aboriginal people] have been boxed in by the Australian psyche, its fear of the other.'
>
> Alexis Wright, 2016.[1]

At its heart, this chapter is a personal reflection that explores what Alexis Wright describes as 'fear of the other'. It asks how we (non-Indigenous people) experience 'otherness' when relating to Indigenous peoples, their culture and their knowledges. This is not a story *about* the Indigenous 'other'. It is a story that invites a deeper exploration of the dark shadow of our own (non-Indigenous) truth and how it impacts engineers, engineering practice and engineering education across Australia.

How we might begin to examine the nature of the fear buried deep in our being and that impacts what we experience, and how we judge that experience, is a work not just of remembering but also of unforgetting. It is a 'work of making more conscious what was, and still is, unconscious in a past that weighs down and waits in the present'.[2]

Since the tangible, experiential and affective is easier to hold than the impersonal archetypal collective unconscious, I should say that my personal work 'began' with three significant moments. The first was in 2011 when I shared with a senior colleague that I was interested in exploring Indigenous understandings of sustainability. He rolled his eyes and responded, 'Oh, that's not science!', leaving me ashamed that I had transgressed some fundamental order, or that I was not sophisticated enough to understand this obvious 'truth'. The message was that Indigenous perspectives belonged to a world of long ago and had nothing to do with the world of science and engineering, the world of mathematical equations, chemical formulas, theoretical constructs and 'correct' answers. I have since asked myself whether this feeling resided in my own woundedness and personal complexes around being a 'displaced person', in the collective trauma of Aboriginal peoples, or in the colonial cultural complexes that operate 'in and through the group's fears and its attitudes toward other groups'.[3] This moves me to ask: what are our fears and attitudes regarding the Aboriginal 'other'?

The second moment came in 2013 when I was invited to join a project entitled Integrating Indigenous Perspectives into the Engineering Curriculum with colleagues from the University of Wollongong and the Queensland University of Technology. This led to a rich and deep quest traversing two very different worlds: the Indigenous world and that of Western engineering, where I explored how Indigenous perspectives differ from other perspectives, particularly the dominant Western perspective. It soon became evident that the deeper questions were: why is it so difficult to integrate an Indigenous perspective in the curriculum? Why is integrating an Indigenous perspective important? And what archetypal dynamics might be at play either when two worlds are kept apart or when two worlds come together?'

The third and most influential moment was when I received a message stick from Noongar Aboriginal Elder and law man Uncle Noel Nannup in 2014. I was engaged in a project aimed at bringing Noongar Elders together with mental health providers, and a colleague in Perth insisted I attend a four-week Noongar storytelling series led by Uncle Noel. Once a week I met with other *wadjelas* (non-Indigenous white people) to sit around a campfire, engrossed in ancient stories. The 'Emu in the Sky' stretched across our luminous galaxy, the Milky Way, its body constellated not by stars but by the dark nebulae seen between them, mirroring the invitation to an 'other' way of knowing.[4]

On the final evening Uncle Noel came to the group with a bundle of message sticks he had crafted, one for each person. As he walked around the group, message sticks clasped in his hands, each participant selected a stick. By the time he got to me, four sticks remained. I chose my stick. He then said, 'The sticks are all the same, except for one. I want the person with the *one* to know that the spirits have chosen you to do important work. You will play a role in bringing Indigenous and non-Indigenous people together to share knowledges and ideas.' A small shiver ran down my spine as I realised that I held the unique stick, and I wondered what the spirits had in store for me.

Uncle Noel indicated that the etchings on *my* message stick showed a group of non-Indigenous people facing a group of Indigenous people (each 'U' shape signified a person), and sharing knowledge and ideas, represented by dots.

The unique etchings on 'my' message stick from Uncle Noel Nannup.

My message stick became very significant in my work. It was a call to a quest. Not only did it symbolise the work that was being asked of me, it also became a talisman when the path ahead seemed impossible. So many times, in the course of this work, I have found myself in tears, not knowing how to proceed, feeling isolated and very small, and shouting at the spirits to choose someone else—it was all too hard. And then I would hold the stick in my hand, look at the encoded message, and remember, trusting that if the spirits had called me to do this work, then they would also support me.

My experience over the past ten years in attempting to facilitate a deep and meaningful exchange between Indigenous people and the engineering academic community, both locally and nationally, has often been fraught with difficulty. My investigations have revealed that Western engineering academics have little knowledge of, or experience with, Indigenous people and perspectives. More significantly perhaps, there is almost no awareness that Indigenous perspectives may change the Western worldview.[5] If only it were as easy as merely putting the two groups together in a room with an instruction to share knowledge and ideas!

Message from the Spirits

What is the encrypted message the spirits want me to hear? I have approached decoding the message etched on the message stick with a symbolic attitude aimed at eliciting a deeper meaning of the dynamics that are constellated when Indigenous and non-Indigenous people come together to share knowledge, ideas and learning. Who are the characters? What is the situation? What are the dynamics at play?

There are two aspects to the message stick: the unique etchings on *my* stick that I will call *the dynamics of the relationship*, and the etchings on either side that symbolise the cultural and collective aspects that we can bring to the relationship. I will explore each aspect separately, and then bring them together as a whole.

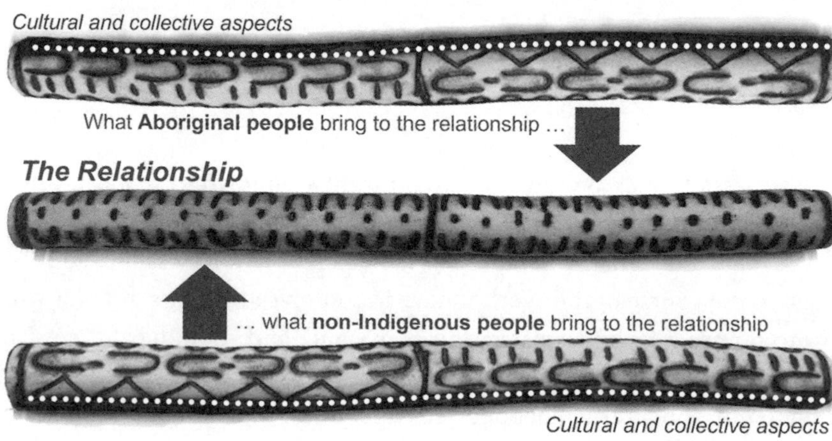

The collective and cultural aspects that are brought into The Relationship between Indigenous and non-Indigenous peoples when they come together to share knowledge and ideas. Imagine the message stick cut along the back 'seam' (shown as white dotted line) and laid out flat.

As I hope to explain, 'relationship' with the 'other' can offer powerful insights into the struggle I refer to above.

The Dynamics of the Relationship

The main characters and elements etched on the message stick that relate to the relationship between Indigenous and non-Indigenous people from the engineering community are shown diagrammatically here. Let's explore each in turn.

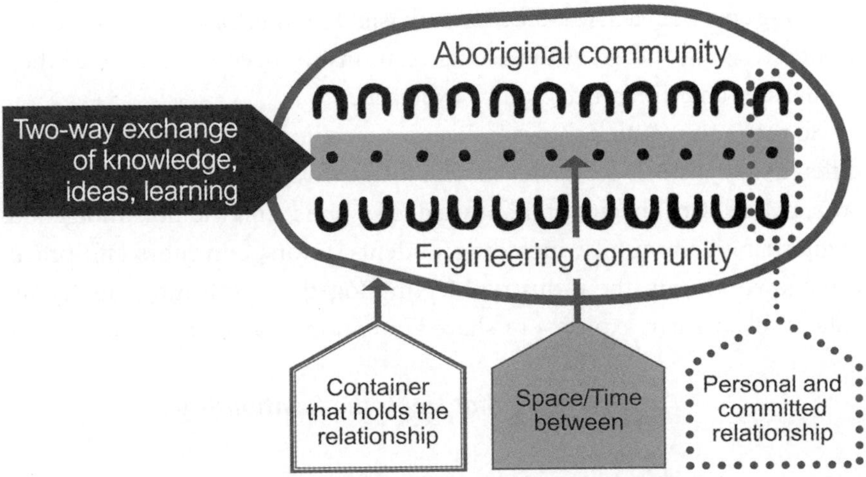

Characters and elements depicting The Relationship.

Personal Relationships

While we are a collective, relationships are forged at the individual level, and in the first instance they require personal commitment. Individuals 'stretch towards' each other, inviting authentic and honest sharing to build trust and create the reconciling or mediating 'third', a term originally coined by Homi Bhabba to describe the liminal intercultural space that occurs between people from differing cultural backgrounds.[6] Initiatives bring people together to share knowledge, ideas and learning. Ongoing commitment and awareness are essential. In Indigenous culture, a 'U'-shaped symbol is used to signify a person. There are several 'U' shapes on the message stick, arranged in two lines representing two communities—each from a different culture. Each community has its own ways of knowing, doing and being. It does not take very much imagination to see that the 'U' shape itself looks like a silhouette of a person with arms outstretched viewed from above.

To paraphrase Ronnberg et al., our arms serve the body at a fundamental level. We use our arms to forage, hunt, kill and eat, and also to embrace, comfort, push away, give, receive, reach out, take in, create, defend, destroy, craft and use tools. Symbolically, arms feed the mind by functioning as explorer and executor of consciousness.[7] The two groups of people face each other with arms outstretched. Immediately there is a dynamic between the two. They might be sitting at a banquet table sharing food, or they might be throwing rocks at each other across a chasm. In either case, there is the 'one' and there is the 'other'. A dialectical relationship becomes possible where similarities and differences can be explored.

So the message stick shows Indigenous people collectively in their many different and distinct groups, each with their own culture, customs, language, laws, beliefs, worldviews and knowledge systems, and the non-Indigenous engineering community, including students, tutors, educators and practitioners working in the industry. Meeting together, both individually and collectively, we can explore our shared intentions and shared vision.

The Container that Holds the Relationship

For the relationship to transform its members, an enclosing boundary or container must be established and maintained. Newman[8] and Ogden[9] argue that the container is itself essential to the process. The two other important aspects of containment are framing and holding.[10]

This was beautifully illustrated in the metaphor of the coolamon offered by Jimmy Cocking, the CEO of Desert Knowledge Australia, during a recent on-Country learning experience in central Australia. The coolamon is a solid and enduring traditional Indigenous vessel used for everything from protection from the weather, to holding gathered resources or carrying a baby. Cocking invited engineers to develop solid and enduring frames and flexible protocols that support the diverse relationships between Indigenous and non-Indigenous communities, such that resources can be gathered, safety can be assured, trust can develop, space for deep listening is guaranteed, and newly emerging creations (knowledge, ideas, learnings) can be nurtured and supported to maturity, so that we can all benefit.

Space/Time-between

Between the two lines of people in the message stick there is the 'space-between'. Like the proverbial fish unaware of the water in which they swim, we do not often perceive the space-between that is created when we engage with an 'other'. It could be an intimate space that invites authentic and honest sharing, or a psychological chasm that seems impossible to bridge. This liminal 'betwixt and between' space holds unlimited possibilities as the interface between people from differing cultural backgrounds.[11] Indeed, Martin Nakata's cultural interface theory argues that

> what is needed is consideration of a different conceptualisation of the cross-cultural space, not as a clash of opposites and differences [but as] a multi-layered and multi-dimensional space of dynamic relations constituted by the intersections of time, place, distance, different systems of thought, competing and contesting discourses within and between different knowledge traditions, and different systems of social, economic and political organisation.
>
> Australian Indigenous peoples have often experienced the space-between as both a social and an ontological divide. In attempting to bridge this divide we need to be mindful that it embraces so much more than trading one engineering know-how with another.[12]

To build a successful relationship takes time, particularly in the initial emergent stage. As we sit at the frontier of our unknowing, we need time to explore common ground, time to connect and learn about each other, time to make mistakes and learn from them, time to imagine what is possible. Time is a particularly challenging concept since, in a Western worldview, time is perceived as linear and chronological, something you can seize, parcel, package and measure. Life becomes structured by milestones and deadlines, and failure to meet them is interpreted as having a poor work ethic or being incompetent. Concepts such as efficiency, a short timeframe and rapid turnover are valued in Western culture, particularly in engineering. In a profit-driven world, time is a precious, even a scarce commodity.

As Walker has observed, 'forcing the western view of time on Aboriginal people continues the colonial sins of the past'.[13] For Indigenous peoples, time is eternal. McGrath has argued that 'the Indigenous concept of "deep time" ... asks us to rethink our narrow conceptions of time by looking back far into Earth's history and looking forward far into the future'.[14]

Awareness of the Western Worldview

Uncle Noel's message stick also had etchings that symbolised the cultural and collective aspects we bring to the relationship. These include 'Relationship', 'Place', 'Worldview' and 'Belonging'. The most significant of these is *worldview* since it impacts the other aspects.

The cultural and collective aspects we bring to The Relationship.

Again, turning to the message stick, we see the people sitting facing each other with arms outstretched, indicating a movement towards the 'other'. The response can be either an action or a reaction, which suggests volition. But before our arms can act, before our emotions respond, we need to 'see', taking the world in through our eyes, forming an image, or a worldview. As Carl Jung observed, 'the eye, like the sun, is a symbol as well as an allegory of consciousness'.[15]

Although philosophers, poets, religious spokespeople and others from different philosophical backgrounds have been questioning the assumptions of the dominant worldview for over 500 years,[16] 'worldview analysis' is a relatively recent field of scholarly inquiry. The term 'worldview' is the English rendering of the German term *Weltanschauung*, coined by the philosopher Immanuel Kant in 1790.[17] *Weltanschauung* is derived from the German *Welt* meaning 'world' and *Anschauung* meaning 'to look at with meaning, contemplate, experience'. Our worldview not only gives meaning to our lives but also requires active reflection.

We use our worldview as a map to help navigate our way through the social landscape. These maps are rich constructs and evolve throughout our lifetime as we try to integrate our experience, knowledge, values, beliefs and assumptions. They shape the ideologies that provide meaning, simplifying existence and creating certainty; involve mind, heart and action; and represent our most fundamental beliefs and assumptions about the world we inhabit. They are the cognitive, perceptual and affective 'maps of reality' through which we interpret the world and interact with it. But perhaps more fundamentally, worldviews lie deep in the inner recesses of the human self (unconscious). Our worldviews develop through socialisation and social interaction and are encompassing and pervasive in both adherence and influence. Yet they are usually taken for granted unconsciously and uncritically as the way things are.[18] To begin to address Alexis Wright's 'fear of the other', we can ask: how can we become conscious of our 'Western' worldview and how does our worldview determine how we perceive the 'other'?

Hess and Strobel point out that engineering has adopted and shaped aspects of the 'dominant' Western worldview, including an ever

> greater reliance on science and technology, the refusal to set limits on production and consumption, the fragmentation of human labour, the reductionist approach to understanding life and the interrelationships between phenomena, and the concept of progress as a process of continually transforming the natural world into more valuable [through

> exploitation] and more human-made environment ... [T]he engineering worldview, is quintessentially reductive and deterministic.[19]

Worldviews include 'strategies of defensiveness, suppression and subterfuge, and they are concentrated around false certainties or spuriously objectivised modes of rationality, into which the human mind withdraws in order to obtain security amongst the frighteningly limitless possibilities of human existence'.[20] They can thus harden into 'objectivised boxes' (*Gehäuse*), set against 'content and experiences which threaten to transcend or unbalance'.

How do we respond when our worldview is threatened? The image within the message stick offers a further insight into the spectrum of psychological responses that are constellated in the relationship between Indigenous and non-Indigenous people. When we face an Indigenous 'other', what do we 'see'? What emotions, values and attitudes are triggered? How do we interpret what we 'see', and how does that interpretation influence our initial, and ongoing, response?

In the figure here, I have used the image from the message stick to illustrate the possible perceptions and attitudes Westerners have had towards Indigenous peoples, and the responses that have ensued. Perceiving Indigenous peoples and their ways of being, knowing and doing as 'alien', 'savage', 'enemy', 'indigent' and 'ally' is not only an illustration of the historical flow of perceptions, but also forms a mosaic of contemporary responses held by different factions within non-Indigenous peoples in general, and the engineering community in Australia in particular.

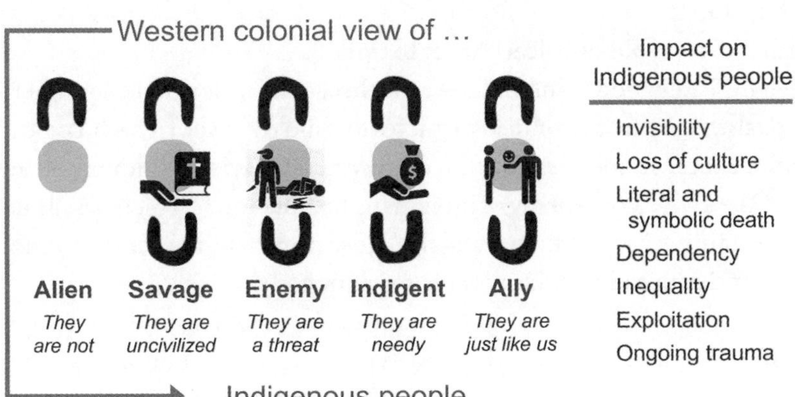

A spectrum of Western 'colonial' views of Indigenous peoples.

Seeing the 'other' as 'alien' makes them invisible, and the 'alien other' becomes abject. Kristeva describes the abject as that which cannot be named or imagined, the jettisoned object that is radically excluded and the place where meaning collapses.[21] This cloak of invisibility covers every aspect: people, their culture, their knowledge systems and their engineering practices. Indeed, evidence suggests that, among engineers in both industry and academia, even seeing, let alone understanding, the needs, values and priorities of Indigenous peoples remains a serious challenge.[22]

There is an inseparable relationship between 'civilisation' and 'engineering', as we understand it, bringing a structure to culture and peoples' relationship to the environment that is easily recognisable. Did the lack of easily seen Indigenous structures, such as buildings (homes, markets and temples), roads and transportation vehicles, or the absence of metalwork with gold, silver and precious stones, contribute to the conclusion that Indigenous Australians were uncivilised? Did the absence of recognisable hierarchical social structures, kings and emperors do likewise? Did Indigenous peoples lack advanced knowledge structures?

Sadly, the notion that Indigenous peoples are uncivilised continues to resound within the engineering community. Some of the comments I have heard include:

- We can no longer provide sponsorship because your organisation is now clearly engaged with 'those stone-age people'.
- Indigenous knowledge is primitive!
- You don't expect us to go back to hunting with spears!
- What has Indigenous knowledge got to do with modern engineering? They don't have any engineering!
- What can we possibly learn from them?

Seeing Indigenous Australians as a threat has informed a number of historical actions, from frontier massacres to child removal.[23] Psychologically, our arch enemy resides deep within our own unconscious. Anthony Stevens defines the archetypal enemy of humans as the Shadow,[24] which has, as Jung says, 'certain features which offer the most obstinate resistance to moral control and prove almost impossible to influence'.[25]

What is this evil we want to turn our backs on? Who is this enemy we want to obliterate? I suggest that the evil is our own modern-day hunger for 'progress'.[26] This is central to our Western thinking, and it drives the philosophy and values underpinning engineering, ruthlessly prioritising 'efficiency' and 'growth', and coloured by the development dogma 'bigger is better and biggest is best'. The enemy becomes anyone who stands in the way of progress.

Engineering is littered with examples of what Shephard refers to as 'pioneering triumphalism'. In an article describing how the overland telegraph brought colonial triumph and Aboriginal devastation, he writes:

> That meant the liberal use of euphemisms by the overseers and pastoralists as massacres continued. 'Dispersals' meant not the scattering of Aboriginal people, but their deaths. 'Stern reprisals' was the same. Then there was 'teach a lesson', and 'justice was done'. All mean 'killed'.[27]

Engineering, together with agriculture and private land ownership, has played a significant role in the dispossession of Indigenous lands. Until very recently, consideration of Indigenous priorities and interests in Country and cultural sacred sites has been of minimal concern within engineering industries such as mining, urban development, construction, transport, water supply and energy infrastructure.

Consider the destruction of the Juukan Gorge Caves by the mining giant Rio Tinto in May 2020. The Australasian Centre for Corporate Responsibility noted how a recent parliamentary inquiry found 'serial and cumulative failures' that continue to demonstrate 'the atrocious treatment of First Nations Australians by governments and mining companies'.[28] Or consider the case of *Ankerre Ankerre* (Coolibah Swamp in Alice Springs). *Ankerre Ankerre* is a sacred site, a place of antiquity and deep cultural significance; a place where the great caterpillars (Yeperenye) of the *Altyerre* (Dreaming) entered and continue to dance, in the form of the twisted coolibah.[29] The landscape is a vital water-catchment area. Today, however, through urban development, altered water flow and the construction of a major road through the site, when the rains do come, all the water is diverted. As a result of this diversion of the stormwater and the drying out of the swampland, the coolibah trees, some of which are at least 400 years old, are dying along with the rest of the wetland ecosystem, leaving a scrubby wasteland.[30]

These are only two examples of where engineering has failed to address the needs and perspectives of Indigenous peoples. While engineering purports to adopt triple bottom line (TBL) approaches that supposedly consider the social, environmental and economic aspects of development projects, research indicates that the 'conceptual roots of TBL are embedded in a quantitative, economic paradigm ... and that the TBL reporting system depicts a negative outlook of what corporate sustainability should aim to be, in spite of raising awareness of multiple objectives for corporations to report against'.[31] In the figure below, Josh Lloyd, a Wajarri Yamatji man and civil engineer, summarises a major difference between the dominant (Western/engineering) philosophy and an Indigenous philosophy as being a difference of focus, where the Western view is human-focused while the Indigenous view is Country-focused.

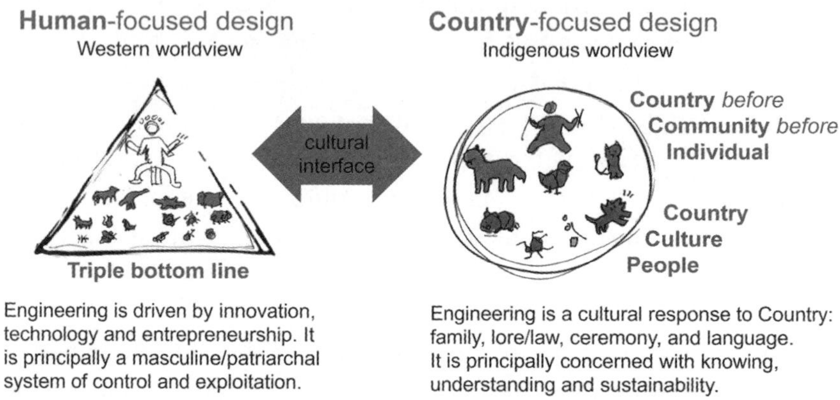

Western and Indigenous worldviews: a different focus.

Author and artist: Josh Lloyd

Perceiving Aboriginal peoples as indigent, another way of reading the 'other', sets up a psychological dynamic where we maintain both our vision of being the benevolent and anti-racist 'do-gooders' and being superior, while responding to the 'deserving neediness' of the Aboriginal subaltern. This is particularly evident within the academic sphere of engineering where most of the funding in education supports student scholarships and bursaries, aimed at addressing parity and equity of access for Indigenous students. However, this has been criticised because these initiatives 'largely continue the status quo by engaging potential students in exploration of how they could partake in western engineering education and the profession as it exists now, with students often facing conflicting family or community values, and study pressures'.[32] In general, across Australian engineering schools, little attention (and funding) is given to co-creating educational programs with Indigenous communities, where Indigenous values, knowledges and practices are placed on an equal footing with Western engineering approaches.

The danger of seeing the 'other' as 'just like me', by contrast, is that we eclipse their unique individuality with our own projections. The question here becomes, as medical anthropologist Emma Kowal puts it:

> How can we make Indigenous people have the health statistics of white people without making them white, and thus continuing the assimilationist project?' And the answer is, 'Because in the imagined future time when Indigenous people have the same health statistics as white people, they will not be white because they will still have their culture that is Aboriginal'.[33]

It is important to distinguish between acknowledgement and assimilation. Acknowledgement (to have knowledge of) is concerned with respect for Aboriginal peoples and their ways of knowing, being and doing, while assimilation (to make similar) is bound up with making 'them' like 'us'.

Transformation

Transformation is not easy. In fact, it is extremely difficult. Since our individual and collective worldviews are an intricate part of our very being, they are tenaciously held on to. Indeed, as Ray and Anderson suggest, 'changing a worldview literally means changing what you think is real'. They go on to say: 'Most of us change our worldview only once in a lifetime, if we do it at all, because it changes virtually everything in our consciousness.'[34]

So how might we think about transformation such that it doesn't instantly trigger a defensive response, or plunge us into an existential and ontological crisis? Transformation is not a 'problem that can be fixed'. Nor is it a 'problem' that can be addressed through an engineering philosophy usually founded in technical rationality and employing systematic, logical, analytical systems that are applied in reductive frameworks to prove outcomes or maximise efficiencies.[35] One of the dangers of a Western worldview and its reductionist approach to understanding life, with a strong push to generalise phenomena and universalise narratives, is that we become blind to other ways of knowing, doing and being. Effort is required to engage not only with the Indigenous 'other' but with a plurality of knowledge, perspectives and ways of being. Australia comprises many different and distinct groups of Aboriginal and Torres Strait Islander peoples, each with its own culture, customs, language, laws, beliefs and knowledge systems. Every engagement with an Indigenous community is unique. Further, working with difference requires commitment, patience and the capacity to listen. Consider what Verran says about working with difference:

> Becoming sensitive to this level of difference can be crucial in successful working together of disparate knowledge traditions. These structural differences are embedded in language use and in the ordinary generalising we do when we use numbers. Here people are working at the level of assumption; things are usually just taken for granted as people go on together. In working disparate knowledge traditions together people must bring these assumptions and what they take for granted out into the open. Often, especially in the beginning, that is not comfortable.[36]

As a way of deepening my reflections on transformation, I want to elaborate on three aspects I have already touched on: the space-between, the interaction between a pair of individuals, and the importance of relationship.

The Space/Time-between

Being in this space/time-between where the Western and Indigenous worlds come together has opened my eyes to just how powerfully our *Weltanschauungen* are embedded in who we are as humans—two worlds with vastly different landscapes, histories and cultures, where our view of the 'other' is distorted through the lens of our conscious and unconscious cultural complexes.

In my own personal journey and experience of being in this space-between, I have been very aware of the struggle involved in stepping outside the safety of my own worldview, particularly when it contributes to my sense of identity and belonging. It is my relationship with the space-between that has seen the greatest personal transformation. Just before I began my journey of working with Indigenous people, my experience of being in this space can be seen in an entry I made in my reflective journal:

> What is liminality? Displaced, misplaced, in between, on the fringe, on the run, forgotten, ignored, pilgrim, nomad, refugee, eternal wanderer, no-man's land, neither/nor ... What gives us a sense of identity, of belonging? Is it our location that makes us easy to categorise, classify, pigeonhole?

My relationships with Indigenous people have offered new images of this space-between that move beyond the Western 'either/or' polarisation to a more inclusive 'both/and' perspective. I have been struck by the power of image, and how a small change in the way we imagine something can bring a big change in attitude.

Hannah Rachel Bell, who spent forty years of her life working with the Ngarinyin people in the Kimberley, introduced me to a different image of the space-between: the littoral. Bell had learned this from Ngarinyin Elder David Mowaljarlai. The littoral is 'the intertidal of both land and sea—sometimes land, sometimes sea—both not actually, fully belonging to either'. This littoral zone has its own distinct character:

> Having happened quite recently upon this littoral revelation kindly offered up by Nature, I began to understand why Ngarinyin people call many, if not most animals, birds and reptiles of littoral zones, 'Chosen Animals'. Take the frog. Ngarinyin call it 'Banman Frog' which means that it intercedes between environments and dimensions. Mowaljarlai explained, 'See that frog? 'E spits up in the air ... makes a pipehole in the air ... when those heavy clouds come over, those Wanjina clouds, 'e spits up at them. Lightning come shooting down through that pipehole, hit the ground, go under, travel everywhere then joining everything up.'
>
> I asked if the frog makes the lightning come down. 'Lightning go up before 'e come down!' he exclaimed. 'Banman Frog spits up, then lightning come down.' Here is an example of a littoral-living animal interceding, not just between water and land, not just between the heavens and the earth, but also relationally between man and environment. Similar stories are associated with all the Chosen Animals.[37]

Another image of the space-between, *ganma*, from the Yolŋu, is a place where salt water and fresh water meet to form a lagoon. The water looks quiet on the surface but is turbulent underneath, symbolising the emotional challenge of engagement and transformation.

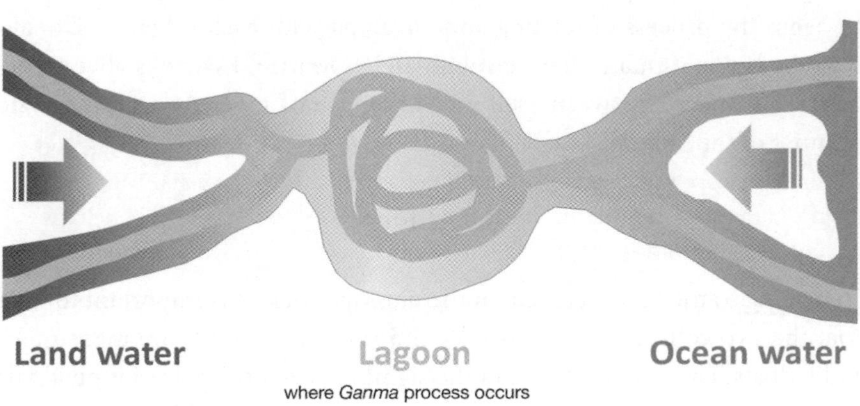

Ganma: A Yolŋu image for relationship and transformation.

In the English language we often use the metaphor of a 'bridge' as a way of understanding our relationship to the space-between. 'Bridging the chasm' is a more empowering image than 'jumping into the void'! In his essay 'Building Dwelling Thinking', Heidegger offers a beautiful reflection on the nature of bridges:

> The bridge ... does not just connect banks that are already there. The banks emerge as banks only as the bridge crosses the stream. The bridge designedly causes them to lie across from each other. One side is set off against the other by the bridge. Nor do the banks stretch along the stream as indifferent border strips of the dry land. With the banks, the bridge brings to the stream the one and the other expanse of the landscape lying behind them. It brings stream and bank and land into each other's neighbourhood ... The bridge gathers the earth as landscape around the stream. Thus it guides and attends the stream through the meadows ... Even where the bridge covers the stream, it holds its flow up to the sky by taking it for a moment under the vaulted gateway and then setting it free once more ... The bridge gathers, as a passage that crosses, before the divinities—whether we explicitly think of, and visibly give thanks for, their presence, as in the figure of the saint of the bridge, or whether that divine presence is obstructed or even pushed wholly aside.[38]

Heidegger's prose suggests that it is through the very act of bridge-building that we bring to consciousness the many points of difference ('banks') within the landscape of our worldviews. In other words, identifying and arguing about points of difference does not lead to a resolution nor new learning. Rather, it is through conscious intention, and the act of bridge-building itself, that we invite each other into the 'space-between' to begin the process of relating and engaging with each other. As Donald Kalsched puts it in an interview with Helen Marlo: 'Psyche is alive in the relational space "between" self and other [that] gives us a mythopoeic glimpse of the human soul.'[39]

Relatedness

Returning to the image etched on the message stick, it is important to note that the two collectives (Indigenous and non-Indigenous) are made up of individuals. Until we understand the significance of the pair of individuals highlighted earlier, our unconscious fears, prejudices and projections will continue to dominate our experience. This brings me to the realisation of how critical it is for each and every individual to bring to consciousness their relationship with unconscious material, how it shapes their worldview, and how their responses in turn contribute to the shaping of the collective worldview.

My colleague Craig San Roque has worked as an analyst and community therapist in central Australia. In a 2017 article, Fleming suggested that

> San Roque's intercultural work might help *kardiya* [whitefella] understand how an inherited cultural framework can obscure our capacity to fully understand the Aboriginal lifeworld. Reflexive in philosophy, exploratory in intention, and privileging the imagination above all, San Roque's work is unique among those working in, and with, Central Desert communities.[40]

In his reflection of what emerges in the interpersonal, ethnographic, dialogical space, San Roque writes:

> And the question might be, 'What is in our minds as we sit together, you and I?' with the fire simmering, tea stewing, ants busy on the sand, and maybe the heat of coals drifting through the shade of a mulga tree. These settings are fitting for reflective conversations between men of two worlds—Indigenous Warlpiri, perhaps, and the travelling Caucasian. Such conversations take place on the edges of campsites, on the edges of settlements, on the edges of and between dreams, between times, between languages, a shimmering, dusty place where nothing much is really what it seems. And nothing spoken is exactly what it might mean and nothing heard is quite what is intended, perhaps. Ambiguous answers and ambiguous tracks of thought are exchanged between persons in exactly the settings where transference phenomena might readily be found, if Freud or Jung had time enough and the chance to sit there long enough—learning, letting go of anticipation, observing the flow of desire and projection. Seated between the eyes of two worlds. That sort of thing.[41]

In a recent series of seminars entitled Black Knot, White Knot, San Roque presented a painting created in conversation with Spencer Japaljarri about being 'seated between the eyes of two worlds'. This painting was influenced by Jung's work exploring all the possible interactions of the conscious and unconscious when two people come together in an analytic, or indeed in any, relationship.[42] When we sit together 'between the eyes of the world' with open minds, and hearts, humility and a willingness to confront our own ignorance, we give birth to something new.

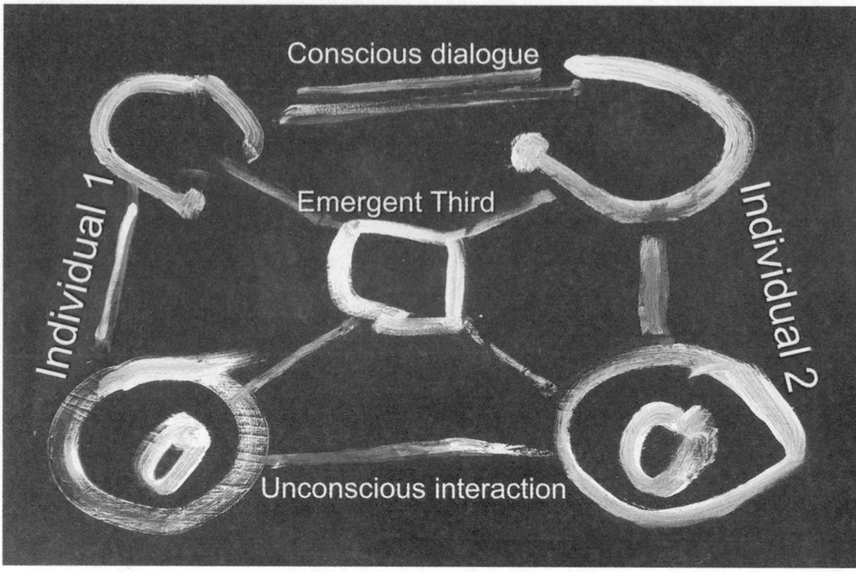

Seated between the Eyes of Two Worlds. A painting by Craig San Roque in conversation with Spencer Japaljarri.

It is through relatedness that we can be in *conscious dialogue* with our own unconscious *and* with peoples from other cultures and other parts of the world. It is through relatedness that consciousness expands, and our horizons broaden. It is through relatedness that we discover that the many and various expressions of an archetype as it takes form in archetypal images—appearing as motifs in myths, legends, stories and the creative arts—arise from a shared collective unconscious, putting a great array of symbolic representation at our disposal. We develop a deeper capacity to amplify archetypal images as they emerge in our dreams and active imagination. Personal stories gather to become a collective story and collective stories are retold and relived in personal stories. Or, as Joseph Campbell put it, dreams are private myths, and myths are public dreams. They beat with the same heart.[43]

It is only through relatedness that we can stand with one foot on a bridge, the other firmly planted in 'my world', and reach across the chasm of the great cultural divide that separates one from the 'other', reaching with hand outstretched, leaning forward, straining to breaking point until our fingers meet, human flesh touching human flesh, 'my world' meeting 'your world', becoming 'our world', enlivened with a broader range of archetypal images painted with palettes of new and vivid colours.

If, however, our experience of other worldviews is limited, either through lack of experience or because our worldview dominates all others, we become one-eyed. We start to believe that 'everyone' sees the world as we do. Our world becomes 'black and white', and our worldview become narrower in range, sometimes ossified, always exclusive. This is particularly significant for the Western worldview.

Notes

1 Alexis Wright. 'What Happens When You Tell Somebody Else's Story?', *International Journal of Applied Psychoanalytic Studies*, vol. 15, no. 2, 2018, p. 136.

2 Robert D Romanyshyn, *The Wounded Researcher: Research with Soul in Mind*, Spring Journal Books, New Orleans, 2007, p. 114.

3 Samuel Kimbles, 'The Cultural Complex and the Myth of Invisibility', in Thomas Singer (ed.), *The Vision Thing: Myth, Politics and Psyche in the World*, Routledge, London and New York, 2000, p. 159.

4 Robert S Fuller, Michael G Anderson, Ray P Norris and Michelle Trudgett, 'The Emu Sky Knowledge of the Kamilaroi and Euahlayi Peoples', *Journal of Astronomical History and Heritage*, vol. 17, no. 2, 2014, pp. 171–9.

5 Thomas Goldfinch, Juliana K Prpic, Lesley Jolly, Elyssebeth Leigh and Jade Kennedy, 'Australian Engineering Educators' Attitudes Towards Aboriginal Cultures and Perspectives', *European Journal of Engineering Education*, vol. 42, no. 4, 2017, pp. 429–44.

6 Homi K Bhabba, *The Location of Culture*, Routledge, London and New York, 1994, p. 53.

7 Ami Ronnberg, Kathleen Martin and Archive for Research in Archetypal Symbolism, *The Book of Symbols: Reflections on Archetypal Images*, Taschen, Cologne, 2010, p. 378.

8 Kenneth D Newman, 'The Riddle of the Vas Bene Clausum', *Journal of Analytical Psychology*, vol. 26, no. 3, 1981, pp. 229–41.

9 Thomas H Ogden, 'On Holding and Containing, Being and Dreaming', in Thomas H Ogden, *This Art of Psychoanalysis: Dreaming Undreamt Dreams and Interrupted Cries*, Routledge, London, 2005, p. 101.

10 August J Cwik, 'From Frame through Holding to Container', in Murray Stein (ed.), *Jungian Psychoanalysis: Working in the Spirit of C.G. Jung*, Chicago, Open Court Publishing, 2010, pp. 169–78.

11 Arnold van Gennep, *The Rites of Passage*, Routledge, London, 2013; Victor W Turner, *The Ritual Process: Structure and Anti-Structure*, Routledge & Kegan Paul, London, 1969; Victor W Turner, *Dramas, Fields, and Metaphors: Symbolic Action in Human Society*, Cornell University Press, Ithaca, NY, 1974; Victor W Turner, *From Ritual to Theatre: The Human Seriousness of Play*, Performing Arts Journal Publications, New York, 1982.

12 Martin Nakata, *Disciplining the Savages, Savaging the Disciplines*, Aboriginal Studies Press, Canberra, 2007, p. 272.

13 Rebecca Walker, 'Eternity Now: Aboriginal Concepts of Time', *Others*, 3 July 2016, https://others.org.au/features/eternity-and-aboriginal-concepts-of-time (accessed 5 November 2023).

14 Ann McGrath, '"All Things Will Outlast Us": How the Indigenous Concept of Deep Time Helps Us Understand Environmental Destruction', *The Conversation*, 19 August 2020, https://theconversation.com/all-things-will-outlast-us-how-the-indigenous-concept-of-deep-time-helps-us-understand-environmental-destruction-132201 (accessed 5 November 2023).

15 Carl Gustav Jung, 'Mysterium Coniunctionis', trans. RFC Hull, in H Read et al. (eds), *The Collected Works of C. G. Jung*, vol. 14, 2nd edn, Princeton University Press, Princeton, 1970 [1955–56], p. 14, para. 47.

16 Bill Devall and George Sessions, *Deep Ecology*, Gibbs Smith Publishers, Salt Lake City, 1985.

17 Immanuel Kant and Werner Pluhar, *Critique of Judgment*, Hackett, Indianapolis, 2010.

18 Devall and Sessions, *Deep Ecology*; Mark E Koltko-Rivera, 'The Psychology of Worldviews', *Review of General Psychology*, vol. 8, no. 1, 2004, pp. 3–58; David K Naugle, *Worldview: The History of a Concept*, W.B. Eerdmans Publishing, Grand Rapids, MI, 2002; Karl Mannheim, *Ideology and Utopia: Collected Works*, Routledge, London, 1997; Laura Nader, 'Up the Anthropologist: Perspectives Gained from Studying up', in Dell Hymes (ed.), *Reinventing Anthropology*, Pantheon Books, New York, 1972; James W Sire, *Naming the Elephant: Worldview as a Concept*, InterVarsity Press, Downers Grove, IL, 2014.

19 Justin Hess and Johannes Strobel, 'Sustainability and the Engineering Worldview', *Proceedings: Frontiers in Education Conference*, Oklahoma City, 2013, p. 646.

20 *Stanford Encyclopedia of Philosophy*, 'Karl Jaspers', 7 March 2022, https://plato.stanford.edu/entries/jaspers (accessed 5 November 2023).

21 Julia Kristeva, *Powers of Horror: An Essay on Abjection*, Columbia University Press, New York, 2009, pp. 1–2.

22 Xavier Hollis and Thomas Goldfinch, 'Experience, Education and Training on Aboriginal Cultural Heritage in Engineering', *Australasian Journal of Engineering Education*, vol. 22, no. 1, 2017, pp. 54–62; Goldfinch et al., 'Australian Engineering Educators' Attitudes'.

23 Paul Daley, 'Australia's Frontier War Killings Still Conveniently Escape Official Memory', *The Guardian*, 8 June 2018, https://www.theguardian.com/australia-news/postcolonial-blog/2018/jun/08/australias-frontier-war-killings-still-conveniently-escape-official-memory (accessed 5 November 2023); Bridget Brennon, 'New Map Records Massacres of Aboriginal People', *ABC News*, 5 July 2017, https://www.abc.net.au/news/2017-07-05/new-map-plots-massacres-of-aboriginal-people-in-frontier-wars/8678466 (accessed 5 November 2023).

24 Anthony Stevens, *Archetypes: A Natural History of the Self*, Routledge & Kegan, London, 1982, pp. 210–43.

25 Carl Gustav Jung, *Aion: Researches into the Phenomenology of the Self: Collected Works of C G Jung*, vol. 9 (part 2), ed. and trans. Gerhard Adler and RFC Hull, Princeton University Press, Princeton, 1979, p. 9.

26 Eric Cohen, *In the Shadow of Progress: Being Human in the Age of Technology*, Encounter Books, London, 2008.

27 Tory Shephard, 'Two Sides of the Wire: How the Overland Telegraph Brought Colonial Triumph and Aboriginal Devastation', *The Guardian*, 21 August 2022, https://www.theguardian.com/australia-news/2022/aug/21/two-sides-of-the-wire-how-the-overland-telegraph-brought-colonial-triumph-and-aboriginal-devastation (accessed 5 November 2023).

28 Australasian Centre for Corporate Responsibility, 'Juukan Gorge Caves Inquiry: Serial and Cumulative Failings', 9 December 2022, https://www.accr.org.au/news/juukan-gorge-caves-inquiry—serial-and-cumulative-failings/ (accessed 5 November 2023).

29 RG Kimber, *Cultural Values Associated with Alice Springs Water*, Northern Territory Department of Natural Resources, Environment, the Arts & Sport, Darwin, 2011, https://denr.nt.gov.au/__data/assets/pdf_file/0005/254606/Cultural-Values-of-Alice-Water-Kimber-2011.pdf (accessed 5 November 2023).

30 Linda Wells, 'Alice's Enchanted, Endangered Forest', *Alice Online*, 17 September 2012, https://aliceonline.com.au/time-to (accessed 5 November 2023).

31 Kaushik Sridhar and Gant Jones, 'The Three Fundamental Criticisms of the Triple Bottom Line Approach: An Empirical Study to Link Sustainability Reports in Companies Based in the Asia-Pacific Region and TBL Shortcomings', *Asian Journal of Business Ethics*, vol. 2, no. 1, 2012, pp. 91–111.

32 Jillian Seniuk Cicek, Stephanie Masta, Thomas Goldfinch and Bruce Kloot, 'Decolonisation in Engineering Education from Four Global Perspectives', in Aditya Johri (ed.), *International Handbook of Engineering Education Research*, Routledge, London, 2023.

33 Emma Kowal, 'Moving Towards the Mean: Dilemmas of Assimilation and Improvement', in Tessa Lea, Emma Kowal and Gillian Cowlishaw (eds), *Moving Anthropology: Critical Indigenous Studies*, Charles Darwin University Press, Darwin, 2006.

34 Paul H Ray and Sherry R Anderson, *The Cultural Creatives: How 50 Million People Are Changing the World*, Harmony Books, New York, 2001, pp. 4, 17.

35 Heather Stonyer, 'Making Engineering Students: Making Women—The Discursive Context of Engineering Education', *International Journal of Engineering Education*, vol. 18, no. 4, 2022, p. 394.

36 Helen Verran, 'Knowledge Systems of Aboriginal Australians: Questions and Answers Arising in a Databasing Project', in H Selin (ed.), *Encyclopaedia of the History of Science, Technology, and Medicine in Non-Western Cultures*, Springer, Dordrecht, 2008, p. 2445.

37 Hannah Rachel Bell, 'Considering Ultimate Questions from an Indigenous Perspective', *Dialogue Australasia*, vol. 25, 2011, p. 19.

38 Martin Heidegger, *Poetry, Language, Thought*, trans. A Hofstadter, Harper and Row, New York, 1971, p. 150.

39 Helen Marlo, 'Between the Worlds: Healing Trauma, Body, and Soul—A Conversation with Donald Kalsched', *Jung Journal: Culture and Psyche*, vol. 7, no. 3, 2013, p. 118.

40 Joan Fleming, 'Seated between the Eyes of Two Worlds: The Intercultural Work of Craig San Roque', *PAN: Philosophy, Activism, Nature*, vol. 13, 2017, p. 36.

41 Craig San Roque, 'On Tjukurrpa, Painting up, and Building Thought', *PAN: Philosophy, Activism, Nature*, vol. 6, 2009, p. 41

42 Carl Gustav Jung, 'The Practice of Psychotherapy', trans. RFC Hull, in H Read et al. (eds), *The Collected Works of C. G. Jung*, vol. 16, 2nd edn, Princeton University Press, Princeton, 1970 [1935], p. 16.

43 Joseph Campbell, *Myths to Live By*, Penguin Books, London, 1993.

The West Arnhem Land Dog Health Program

ELIZABETH TUDOR and CAMERON RAW

THIS IS A STORY about people and their dogs, a story that spans the millennia of human existence and crosses language and cultural barriers.

In the Beginning ...

For the Bininj Kunwok people of western Arnhem Land, this is a story that began as the land as we know it was forming. Two *duruk* (dogs), Adjumarlarl, the brother one, and Omwarl, the sister one, moved across the land from the west. They travelled to the Country near Gunbalanya, and there they stopped and dug a waterhole at a place called Ngindjarnh—a soak with a spring, surrounded by pandanus palm, paperbark trees and tea-tree, where people now come to drink the water. In Kunwinjku, this place is called Duruk Benegadbom, which means 'Two dogs have dug this hole and they created water'.[1]

After resting in this spot, the dogs continued on to Gunbalanya, creating two more small waterholes, before they ran towards the Arnhem Land escarpment. In the area called Mandjaworlbidji, Adjumarlarl scrambled up the escarpment beside a waterfall, but when Omwarl tried to follow him up the rocky slope, she fell and broke her leg. Then Omwarl became a *djang* (spirit) at Ngindjarnh. To this day her image endures in the rock.[2] When Adjumarlarl saw what had befallen his sister, he returned to the bottom of the waterfall and put himself there as a rock. Together, as *duruk djang*, they remain in this place.

Dogs created the waterholes that sustain the landscape and all who dwell within it. Could there be any more powerful expression of the relationship between humans and their dogs?

Omwarl, who, after breaking her leg, was turned into stone as a dreaming Ngindjarnh.

Observations of the First Invaders

Prior to colonisation, dingoes and humans formed close bonds across much of continental Australia. Indeed, Aboriginal people often adopted young wild animals—of all kinds, from possums to skinks to cockatoos—as companions.[3] As with other species, dingoes generally left camp once they reached maturity.[4] Rather than the domestication seen in sedentary agricultural societies, these relationships between Aboriginal people and non-human animals reflected 'an ecocentric tradition of cohabitation', in which the agency and autonomy of the non-human was respected.[5] Once settlers introduced the domestic dog, these older traditions were augmented and altered; elsewhere—particularly Tasmania, where the dingo did not occur—new traditions emerged as domestic dogs were enthusiastically embraced and incorporated into Aboriginal cultures.[6]

Among the settlers who first invaded this continent were some who used pen or paintbrush to record their observations of the everyday lives of the first custodians of the land. And as they created their images in words or pigments, inevitably they told the story of the people and their dogs.

George French Angas, *South Australia Illustrated*, 1846–47.

Augustus Earle, *A Native Family of New South Wales Sitting Down on an English Settler's Farm*, c. 1826.

George French Angas was a naturalist and painter who arrived in Adelaide in January 1844, only eight years after Kaurna Country was first invaded.[7] During 1844–45, he spent two periods of six months each travelling to the Coorong district and to Kangaroo Island and Port Lincoln, recording in watercolour sketches the way of life of the first inhabitants of the land. We see men, women and children in their dwellings, and in many of these images, the dogs with whom they shared their lives are depicted as well. The relationship between these people and their dogs is apparent—one of mutual affection and trust.

Robert Brough Smyth arrived in the colony of Victoria seventeen years after the founding of Melbourne and was motivated to gather information about, and artefacts of, Victorian Aboriginal cultures at a time of enormous disruption and displacement for Aboriginal people.[8] In his two-volume compilation *The Aborigines of Victoria* (1878), the sentiments evident in Angas' paintings are corroborated:

> Native dogs are found in every encampment. They are in all conditions, some mature and strong, and some in the stage of puppyhood. Not less than twenty, perhaps forty, may be seen at any time when a number of

> natives camp for the night. Before European dogs were introduced, the blacks took the puppies of the wild dog, and brought them up, and trained them to hunt. They are very kind to their dogs, and indeed nothing more offends a black than to speak harshly to his dogs, or to depreciate them; and if any one gave a black man's dog a blow, he would incur bitter enmity.[9]

Smyth reported that these dogs were 'of the greatest use to the natives', not only as 'affectionate and faithful companions' but as hunters, helping to track and catch 'opossums, snakes, rats, and lizards'.[10] This was reciprocated with 'gentle treatment and kind words'; so tender were the ties between human and dog that Aboriginal women 'not infrequently' nursed puppies themselves.[11]

Similarly, in the colony of New South Wales, Augustus Earle travelled widely to sketch landscapes and Aboriginal people, which he published in *Views in Australia* (1826). His work *A Native Family of New South Wales Sitting Down on an English Settler's Farm* paints a tragic picture of dispossession and loss, but in the midst of this, dogs appear as loyal companions and perhaps even a source of solace. Across the records of early settlers, a consistent story emerges of dogs as esteemed intimates and essential partners in Aboriginal life.

Dog Ownership in Modern Indigenous Australia

In present-day Australia, Indigenous dog ownership reflects these past themes, although these relationships remain complex and multilayered. In many communities, just like Gunbalanya, dogs have spiritual associations. Senior et al. reviewed observations gleaned from multiple communities and language groups, and while stories and beliefs about dogs may vary, a spiritual dimension to dog ownership is widely evident.[12] Dogs play multiple functional roles for their owners. They provide protection from malevolent wildlife, spirits and humans alike; some dogs are also valued hunting assistants.[13] Many dog owners take great pride in the specific roles that their dogs play in the hunt; for example, some identify prey and alert their owners, while others run the prey to ground. In some communities dogs are included in kinship systems. They are given skin names as the brothers or sisters, sons or daughters of specific family members, and this can have significant implications when decisions are to be made about the care or medical treatment of the animal. Most of all, however, the universal role of the dog as companion prevails—the adage of 'man's best friend' endures.

Despite all the benefits of dog ownership, dogs present many challenges in Indigenous communities. Firstly, the sheer size of dog populations can create issues. Without access to veterinary care in many remote communities, uncontrolled breeding results in a dog population beyond the capacity of people to feed and care for them. Scavenging dogs create litter, spilling rubbish from bins and depositing faeces. Dog noise, particularly barking and fighting, disturbs people's sleep. Aggression from uncontrolled 'cheeky dogs' leads to a high incidence of dog bites.

Of course, dog health matters intrinsically, as we have a responsibility to attend to the welfare of animals in our care. But it matters also because the health of dogs is important to the wellbeing of their owners. People take pride in having a healthy dog and feel shame when a dog in their care is diseased or otherwise in poor condition.

The 'One Health' approach to veterinary medicine recognises the interplay of animal, environmental and human factors in the health and wellbeing of all.[14] This is starkly evident in the context of life in remote Indigenous communities. A variety of factors contributes to the poor health outcomes experienced by too many people in these settings: substandard, overcrowded housing; limited access to health hardware such as running water; poor sanitation; and the cohabitation of humans and pets in a hot and often humid environment.

Zoonotic diseases transmitted from dogs to people are of significant concern. Dogs harbour a range of internal parasites—roundworms, hookworms and threadworms—that can infect and cause disease in humans, particularly children. Some are known collectively as soil-transmitted helminths: heavy faecal contamination of soil by dogs, combined with wet soil and a lack of footwear, markedly increases the risk of infection.[15] Dogs also harbour external parasites. The common dog flea, along with mosquitoes and sandflies, inflicts bites that can result in infected skin sores. Of greater zoonotic significance is the mite *Sarcoptes scabiei*, which is endemic in the dog population of many communities and may cross species boundaries to infect humans.[16] The resulting infestation, just like the human variant of *S. scabiei*, causes intense itching in people, frequently resulting in weeping, infected skin sores. These sores, when infected with the bacterium *Streptococcus GpA*, are the cause of acute rheumatic fever and rheumatic heart disease (RHD)—over 5000 Aboriginal and Torres Strait Islander people live with RHD, at a rate sixty times higher than that for non-Indigenous Australians.[17] In their 2017 systematic review, Smout et al. provided evidence that dogs are acting as a reservoir for human scabies in Indigenous communities. They identified a need for large-scale, high-quality, comparative studies of dogs and humans from the same household to assess the occurrence and importance of transmission of *S. scabiei* and other diseases.[18]

Despite the obvious need for veterinary care of dogs in Indigenous communities, dog health program delivery to remote communities is at best patchy and often non-existent. People may reside many hundreds of

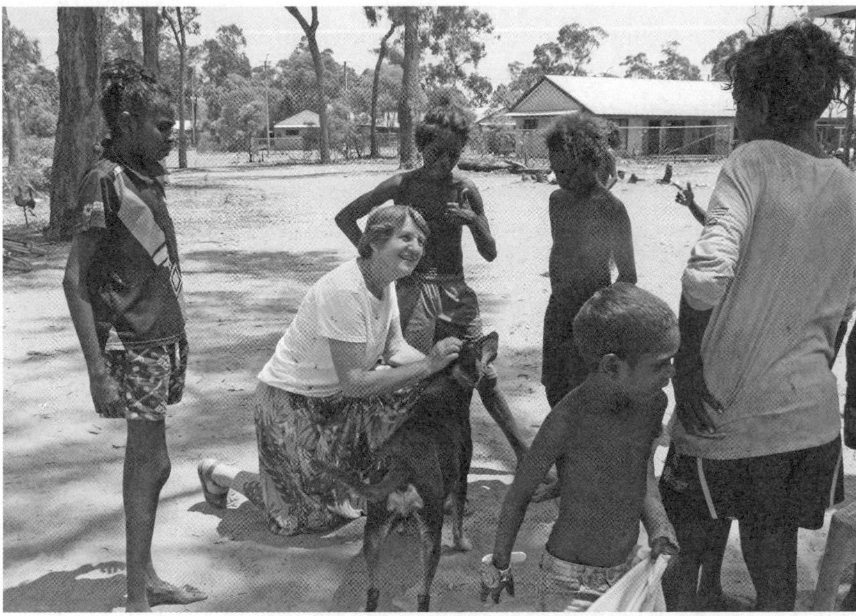

Above: Elizabeth Tudor speaking with children in Galiwin'ku about health care for their dog. Right: Cameron Raw (front left), as a student, assisting the veterinary team. Manmoyi homeland community, Arnhem Land, 2013.

kilometres from veterinary clinics, and most do not have the means to transport their animals the required distances for treatment. Efforts to address this need have been made by veterinarians at the request of individual communities and local government authorities, as well as collectively through the advocacy, education and veterinary program delivery of Animal Management in Rural and Remote Indigenous Communities (AMRRIC).[19] However, many challenges remain in ensuring that, across Australia, all dogs are part of a healthy and happy community ecosystem.

West Arnhem Land Dog Health Program (WALDHeP)

The origins of WALDHeP can be traced to Elizabeth Tudor's experience of a veterinary student placement at Gunbalanya, at that time known as the Oenpelli CMS mission station; some sixty years earlier, Gunbalanya had won the heart of another University of Melbourne academic, Walter Baldwin Spencer, who, on his first visit to see his friend Paddy Cahill, described Oenpelli as 'the most beautiful spot that I have seen in the Territory'.[20] Elizabeth Tudor's return to Gunbalanya in 2002 resulted in the development of deep personal and family ties. During this visit, she received multiple requests for veterinary assistance. In 2005, following an initial veterinary program in the homeland communities of Malkawa and Kabulwarnamyo, WALDHeP was established with the support of the Faculty of Veterinary Science at the University of Melbourne. Every year since then, WALDHeP has sustained an annual program, interrupted only in 2021 by pandemic-induced biosecurity restrictions.

The goal of WALDHeP is to make a measurable difference to the health and wellbeing of the dogs (and other companion animals) of West Arnhem, and thereby contribute to the wellbeing of their owners and communities. Annual visits provide house-to-house consultation, offering parasite control medications, surgical desexing of dogs and cats, general veterinary care, and euthanasia (on request) of debilitated animals. At each visit, an audit of dog population size and health is also recorded. The WALDHeP surgical team generally includes up to four veterinarians working as volunteers (of whom two are Melbourne Veterinary School staff) and a similar number of final-year veterinary students. In smaller communities and homeland settings, the group is very much smaller.

A secondary goal of WALDHeP is to foster engagement with veterinary students and recent alumni. In doing so, the aim is to introduce them to the richness of Indigenous knowledge and cultures, to increase awareness of the issues facing First Nations people living in remote Australia, and to demonstrate the role that veterinarians can play in improving animal and human wellbeing. Student interest in WALDHeP is very high. The selection process includes submission of an expression of interest, followed by an interview, providing all students with the opportunity to explain the basis of their interest in participating, their commitment to the principles of reconciliation, and past evidence of commitment to community projects. Following selection, students participate in pre-trip planning and fundraising activities, as well as cross-cultural orientation sessions. Over eighteen years, more than 150 students have participated in WALDHeP programs, and thirty young alumni have returned to contribute. Several have gone on to establish their veterinary careers in the Top End and have led their own programs in remote communities.

In the years since 2005, the reach of WALDHeP has extended beyond Gunbalanya and its associated homelands, with services offered to a number of West Daly communities (2009), the West Arnhem island communities of Minjilang and Warruwi (2015), and through a memorandum of understanding with the East Arnhem Regional Council to Galiwin'ku, Ramingining and Milingimbi in 2016. Colleagues in the Melbourne Veterinary School established a similar program servicing Lake Tyers in eastern Victoria and the Goulburn Valley, so that in 2019 almost 20 per cent of final-year veterinary students participated in a placement in an Indigenous community. This expansion of service has been achieved partly because, as companion animal population numbers stabilise in a community, less work is required on subsequent annual visits to maintain the health of this population; additional days can then be devoted to neighbouring centres.

Program Outcomes

Achieving change in any health-related metrics requires sustained effort over time—progress is not necessarily evident in the early years. The short funding cycles and tendering contracts of most government authorities typically do not allow for sustained effort over the timeframe required to effect change, particularly in remote communities. Additionally, policy and funding changes lead to 'visitor fatigue' and disengagement on the ground, where stakeholders must adjust to new approaches and establish new relationships with every change of contract.

The progress that WALDHeP has made speaks to what is most important in any community engagement: sustainability over time. To be sincere, engagement must be consistent, but it must also reflect the core values of respect, relationship and reliability. When the WALDHeP team say, 'Same time, every year, we'll be back,' there is trust among stakeholders that actions will match words.

Notes

1 Words of the late J Nayinggul, Traditional Owner of nearby Red Lily area, as told to Theo Read and published in *Omwarl dja Adjumalarl*, Theo Read Kormilda Science Project Gunbalanya, Northern Territory, 2004.

2 Words of the late Aunty P Balmana, Traditional Owner of Gunbalanya area, as told to Theo Read and published in *Omwarl dja Adjumalarl*.

3 Justine Philip and Don Garden, 'Walking the Thylacine', *Society and Animals*, vol. 24, 2016, pp. 37–47, 51–2.

4 Ibid., pp. 52–3.

5 Ibid., p. 57.

6 Ibid., pp. 57–8. On the introduction of the domestic dog in Tasmania, see James Boyce, 'Canine Revolution: The Social and Environmental Impact of the Introduction of the Dog to Tasmania', *Environmental History*, vol. 11, no. 1, 2006, pp. 102–29.

7 EJR Morgan, 'George French Angas (1822–1886)', *Australian Dictionary of Biography*, National Centre of Biography, Australian National University, Canberra, 2006, https://adb.anu.edu.au/biography/angas-george-french-1708 (accessed 7 November 2023).

8 Michael Hoare, 'Robert Brough Smyth (1830–1889)', *Australian Dictionary of Biography*, National Centre of Biography, Australian National University, Canberra, 2006, https://adb.anu.edu.au/biography/smyth-robert-brough-4621 (accessed 7 November 2023).

9 R Brough Smyth, *The Aborigines of Victoria*, vol. 1, John Ferres, Melbourne, 1878, p. 147.

10 Ibid.

11 Ibid., pp. 147–8. Cf. Philip and Garden, 'Thylacine', pp. 53, 57.

12 Kate Senior et al., 'Dogs and People in Aboriginal Communities: Exploring the Relationship within the Context of the Social Determinants of Health', *Environmental Health*, vol. 6, no. 4, 2006, pp. 40–4.

13 Ibid. See also Philip and Garden, 'Thylacine', p. 53.

14 See, for example, John S Mackenzie and Martyn Jeggo, 'The One Health Approach: Why Is It So Important?', *Tropical Medicine and Infectious Disease*, vol. 4, no. 2, June 2019, p. 88.

15 See, for example, Meruyert Beknazarova et al., 'Opportunistic Mapping of *Strongyloides stercoralis* and Hookworm in Dogs in Remote Australian Communities', *Pathogens*, vol. 9, no. 5, May 2020, p. 398.

16 Felicity Smout et al., 'More Bark than Bite: Comparative Studies Are Needed to Determine the Importance of Canine Zoonoses in Aboriginal Communities—A Critical Review of Published Research', *Zoonoses and Public Health*, vol. 64, no. 7, 2017, pp. 499–500.

17 Rosemary Wyber at al., *The RHD Endgame Strategy: A Snapshot—The Blueprint to Eliminate Rheumatic Heart Disease in Australia By 2031*, Telethon Kids Institute, Perth, 2020, p. 5.
18 Smout et al., 'More Bark', pp. 501–2.
19 Animal Management in Rural and Remote Indigenous Communities, 'Our Approach', 2023, https://www.amrric.org/our-approach (accessed 7 November 2023).
20 John Mulvaney, *Paddy Cahill of Oenpelli*, Aboriginal Studies Press, Canberra, 2004, p. 44.

The Art of Healing

Australian Indigenous Bush Medicine—Collections Creating Connections

JACQUELINE HEALY

'We look for these plants in rocky country, we can find a little purple plum that we use to clean the kidneys and sometimes for flu. The yellow flowers are used for scabies; we boil them and add water and wash our skin with it. The pink flowers we use for when we have sore eyes; we mix the flowers with water and the colour changes to a light green.'

Rosie Ngwarraye Ross, 2015[1]

THIS CHAPTER FOCUSES on a new era of collecting at the University of Melbourne. It traces the development and tour of an exhibition, *The Art of Healing: Australian Indigenous Bush Medicine*, from the Medical History Museum. The exhibition demonstrated how museums and their collections play an important role in the life of the Faculty of Medicine, Dentistry and Health Sciences in pursuing the values and strategic goals of the University.

As part of its fiftieth anniversary celebrations in 2017, the Medical History Museum expanded its collections policy to encompass contemporary Aboriginal and Torres Strait Islander art. Established in 1967 through a grant from the Wellcome Trust, the diverse collection to that point consisted of over 8000 items covering the history of the Melbourne Medical School and the broader history of medicine in Australia and internationally, including medical equipment, photographs, archives and artworks. Yet it had not encompassed the traditions and knowledge of 65 000 years of Australian Indigenous healing practice. The revision of the collections policy allowed for art and material that related to Australian Indigenous health care. The focus was to collect contemporary art that illustrated the prevalence and potency of these healing traditions.

Sharing bush medicine stories through art has become one of the ways in which Elders maintain a strong knowledge and culture for their communities. So the emphasis on contemporary Indigenous art in the Medical History Museum collection was to underline the continuing practice of bush medicine by revealing it through a current lens. It also visually demonstrated the distinct and varied cultures that make up Aboriginal and Torres Strait Islander Australia. This initiative was supported by Professor Marcia Langton, Associate Provost and Foundation Chair of Indigenous Studies; Professor Shaun Ewen, pro vice chancellor (Indigenous) and director of the Melbourne Poche Centre for Indigenous Health; and Romlie Mokak, CEO of the Lowitja Institute. There were two stages in implementing the new collection policy: firstly, to purchase a significant collection of Aboriginal and Torres Strait Islander art that represented the theme of bush medicine and healing practices; secondly, to show these works as part of an exhibition to be displayed at the Medical History Museum from 15 May 2018 to 2 March 2019 and then toured to London and Berlin.

For 65 000 years, Aboriginal and Torres Strait Islander peoples have occupied this land, with distinct cultural boundaries defined by intimate relationships with Country. A fundamental aim of the exhibition was to acknowledge those connections. *The Art of Healing* followed the premise of *Tjukurpa*, which has many meanings—including the creation period or Dreaming, as well as the foundation of Aṉangu life and society—and has various equivalents in other Aboriginal languages. It examined traditional Indigenous healing practice as simultaneously past, present and future. Through contemporary art and objects, the exhibition presented examples of healing practice and bush medicine from many distinct and varied Indigenous communities across Australia.

The Art of Healing had a national perspective and works were sought from throughout Australia. Some of the artworks were directly commissioned for the exhibition, while others came from existing projects. Engagement with the artists and communities was a crucial part of the process. Each artist was asked for a work that represented healing practice and bush medicine in their Country. Some items were sourced from artists represented by the extensive network of Aboriginal-owned and controlled art centres, while others were sourced directly from individual artists.

The first art centre to be approached was Hermannsburg Potters, which responded immediately. Judith Inkamala, an Elder and leading ceramic artist, was keen to participate. The work matched the narrative of the exhibition because it explained the whole process of making medicine and caring for the community. As Inkamala stated:

> Bush medicine has always been with Aboriginal people. It was before, and we will always be making bush medicine. There are all kinds of bush medicine and they grow all over. You'll find they're different in each place, and we have these ones that I've painted.[2]

The distinctive Hermannsburg pots are renowned for their rendition of Country, people, animals and plants. All these elements appear in Inkamala's pot titled *Bush Medicine* (2017). The body of the pot is painted with a scene depicting the collecting, making and administering of bush medicine. The *knunkura* (medicine woman) is part of this scene. Underlining her importance, the *knunkura* is also moulded in clay on top of the pot, with a coolamon full of medicinal plants that she is preparing using a grinding stone.

Other art centres that were approached included Warmun Art Centre, Waringarri Aboriginal Arts, and Warlayirti Artists (all in the Kimberley); Warlukurlangu Artists of Yuendumu, Iltja Ntjarra/Many Hands Art Centre and Tjanpi Desert Weavers (central Australia); Merrepen, Injalak, and Buku-Larrnggay Mulka (North East Arnhem Land); and Jilamara and Munupi (Tiwi Islands). Commissions were also sought directly from individual artists. Kathrine Clarke, Treahna Hamm and Marilyne Nicholls in Victoria and Judith-Rose Thomas in Tasmania contributed works specifically created for the exhibition.

Fifty-six artworks were selected for *The Art of Healing* that represented a variety of techniques and media, including painting in ochre and acrylic, printmaking, weaving and ceramics. Each work was accompanied by information provided by the artist. As well as statements about the bush medicine or healing practice represented in each artwork, this information included the skin name, language group, Country (traditional lands) and artist's location. This readily shared with the visitors the rich cultural diversity in language and cultural practice of First Nations Australians.

The artworks told stories of bush medicine from many parts of Australia, not in a comprehensive manner but rather as an introduction to a vast bank of knowledge that precedes and parallels other great healing traditions. Some of the artworks were the result of major projects that have been undertaken over many years. For instance, senior Gija Elder and artist Shirley Purdie has been working for several years with linguist Frances Koford to document medicinal and other plants of the eastern Kimberley, identifying individual species and recording their Gija, Latin and English names. This project preserves vital information and cultural memory for future generations, through written records and individual artworks. Nine paintings by Shirley Purdie were commissioned for the exhibition.

In a similar project, Yolŋu Elder Mulkuṉ Wirrpanda was motivated by her concern that young people were forgetting the uses of local plants. Mulkuṉ, working with landscape artist John Wolseley, produced a series of works recording the uses of plants in north-eastern Arnhem Land. This project culminated in a major exhibition titled *Miḏawarr/Harvest: The Art of Mulkuṉ Wirrpanda and John Wolseley*, and held at the National Museum of Australia in Canberra from 17 November 2017 to 19 February 2018. Wirrpanda's woodblock print *Buṉdjuŋu* (2014) from this project was included in *The Art of Healing*.

Many of the works in the exhibition illustrated specific bush medicines and their uses. The descriptions of the plants and, in some instances, their preparation for medicinal use were generously provided by the artists. For instance, the artists at the art centre of Ampilatwatja in the central desert express their knowledge of bush medicine through their art, the intention being to share this knowledge with their children and grandchildren. Artist Beverly Pula Luck commented: 'There are lots of different medicines, we know what their stories are, we learnt them from our parents and we teach these stories to our children.'[3] The medicinal plants found in this part of the central desert were depicted in intricate detail in the acrylic painting *Bush Flowers and Bush Medicine Plants* (2015) by Rosie Ngwarraye Ross, and Beverly Pula Luck's *Bush Medicine Plants* (2017). Pula Luck vividly shows the flowering *Alperrantyey* and *Therrpeyt* plants, whose flowers are boiled and used for drinking and washing, whereas Ngwarraye Ross paints the plant that produces the purple fruit used 'to clean our kidneys and sometimes for flu'.[4]

A series of works illustrating certain treatments was also commissioned from renowned artists at Waringarri Aboriginal Arts. For example, Peggy Griffiths' painting *Larrgen—Spinifex and Water* (2016) revealed Country in the Keep River area, where *Gajarrang* (spinifex) and grass grow on the plains. The *Gajarrang*, when picked and boiled like tea, is used as a contraceptive. Other remedies include the remarkable properties of *Goongoolong* (bloodwood gum tree). Kittey Malarvie comments: '*Goongoolong* is blood tonic. I collect it out bush then boil it up and drink it. Some people use it for cancer too.'[5] Her work *Goongoolong* (2016) shows in ochre the dripping sap of the bloodwood tree.

Senior women Miriam Baadjo, Tossie Baadjo, Jane Gimme, Gracie Mosquito, Helen Nagomara, Ann Frances Nowee and Imelda Yukenbarri from Wirrimanu (Balgo) produced a painting titled *Bush Medicine: A Collaborative Work By the Women from Wirrimanu (Balgo)* (2018). Two trees dominate the centre of the painting: the *Wirrimangulu* (bloodwood tree) and *Tinjirl* (mulan tree or river red gum), which grow beside rivers. These represent two important aspects of healing: the medicinal and the spiritual. Acknowledging the medicinal power of the bloodwood tree, like Kittey Malarvie, these artists mention the use of the sap as a powerful medicine for serious ailments including cancer tumours. *Tinjirl* has powerful cultural significance, forming part of the seven sisters *Tjukurpa* for the region. 'It is used for law and for smoking ceremony to cleanse bad spirits. It can also be inhaled for respiratory problems.'[6]

Treahna Hamm, from Victoria, commemorated the ancestral knowledge of healing of the Yorta Yorta people in *Dhungala Cool Burn* (2017), a major triptych depicting ancestral figures gathering bush medicine on the banks of Dhungala (the Murray River). On their shoulders are dillybags and in the foreground lie coolamons for the preparation of the medicines. These coolamons are outlined in local river-bark ink, an ingredient in bush medicine.

In another work titled *Yorta Yorta Bush Medicine First Aid Kit* (2017), Hamm created a box including instruments and remedies from materials used in bush medicine. As Hamm explains:

> During the European settlement of Australia, the bushland, wetlands and waterways were seen as barren, and empty of medicinal knowledge and practices ... This bush medicine first aid kit contains bush and river remedies that have been in use for many thousands of years. Paperbark, from which the kit is constructed, was also used as bandages, having antiseptic qualities ...[7]

The iconography used to represent bush medicine differs between communities and language groups across Australia. In the Daly River area of the Northern Territory, the fruits of the *Miwulngini*—red lotus lily (*Nelumbo nucifera*)—are collected from the bottom of billabongs. Senior women locate the fruit with their feet as they slowly and carefully wade through the water, and a medicine to treat constipation is made from this plant. In the coloured etching *Miwulngini—Red Lotus Lily* (2016) by Margaret Gilbert, the shape of the lotus leaf (outlined in blue) appears to float over the images of three lotus pods. On Melville Island, the centre of the *Purnarrika* (waterlily) flower is eaten to cure sore throats and colds. Michelle Woody's painting *Purnarrika (Water Lily)* (2017) in ochre shows an abstract pattern of lines and circles, reminiscent of body painting.

The use of bush medicine should not be viewed in isolation but as part of a rich healing practice with cultural and spiritual aspects. An important theme in the exhibition was the role of healers. In a project of the Lowitja Institute led by Brian McCoy, old and young people from Wirrimanu (Balgo), including senior *maparn* (healers) such as Helicopter Tjungurrayi, produced a series of paintings in which they share their perspectives on healing and men's health and wellbeing. In *Maparn* (2003), for instance, Flakie Stevens Tjampitjin used the image of the *maparn*'s hand as the physical source and symbol of healing, and told of a *maparn* travelling between communities. These works were borrowed for *The Art of Healing* exhibition from the South Australian Health and Medical Research Institute (Sahmri).

In Alice Springs, the Ngaanyatjarra Pitjantjatjara Yankunytjatjara Women's Council (NPYWC) offers *ngangkaṟi* (healers) a mental health program that examines factors contributing to wellbeing. This is also an example of two-way learning: Western and traditional practice working hand in hand. In the exhibition was the work *Tjulpu Wiltja: Bird Nest Basket* (2017) by Elder and *ngangkaṟi* Ilawanti Ungkutjuru Ken. She created a basket based on observing birds' nests, to show the power of family and community for a person's wellbeing. She says: 'My basket is like a nest. In our community, that's how it should be ... Altogether the community stays strong, healthy and happily looking after their family.'[8]

The voices of the *ngangkaṟi* were heard at the Faculty of Medicine, Dentistry and Health Sciences dean's lecture on 9 July 2018 as part of NAIDOC week. *Ngangkaṟi* Maringka Burton, Betty Muffler and Ting Pullier Mervyn from the NPYWC outlined their roles in their communities and their relationships with Western medicine practitioners. Burton described the nature of the working partnerships with Western-trained doctors and how these relationships were valued:

> I ... give you one example of my work, which is to work alongside the male *ngangkaṟi* healer. The two of us work in the Alice Springs hospital

> and we work really closely with the doctors there. We're on call ... but primarily we're looking after their spiritual wellbeing, and their spirit, and that can be helping someone, you know, to get a sense of their self, and they might [be] really anxious or worried about being in hospital and dealing with their sickness, and we can really help them in that way.[9]

Angela Lynch, manager of the Ngangkaṟi Project, and interpreter Patrick Hookey enabled the *ngangkaṟi* to share their stories of healing while speaking in Pitjantjatjara, as well as share their knowledge through songs about the *Tjukurpa* (law) of healing.

The exhibition was accompanied by a 170-page full-colour catalogue representing the perspectives of Indigenous communities, with fourteen authors and the fifty-six artists bringing together Indigenous and Western medical knowledge. Professor Marcia Langton stressed in the introduction that

> the most pressing social problem in Australia today is the health disparity between our Indigenous and non-Indigenous people ... if we were more knowledgeable of the history of Australia, of the diversity and depth of our Indigenous cultures, and more accommodating of the continuing traditions, allowing them their rightful place in our nation, [I] believe that we would overcome the life-threatening disadvantages faced by Indigenous Australians more quickly.[10]

A series of essays then provided examples of this knowledge and practice from throughout Australia. Contributions include Kathrine 'Kat' Clarke sharing the medicinal practices of the Koori nation based on the knowledge of the Koori Elders. Similarly, Professor Kerry Arabena expressed the power of the knowledge passed down by Elders in the Torres Strait Islander communities and the importance of continuing these practices. Importantly, Sharon Dennis, a member of the Aboriginal Land Council of Tasmania, wrote about the reclamation of Tasmanian Aboriginal knowledge. Healing and the power of culture and education were covered from various perspectives, ranging from central Australia Elder and artist Mervyn Rubuntja explaining what was involved in running a health service based on traditional practice provided by Akeyulerre—a central Indigenous healing centre in Alice Springs—to Professor Shaun Ewen and Odette Mazel covering the medical training of Aboriginal and Torres Strait Islander students in universities. Elder Bruce Pascoe, author of *Dark Emu*, visited the exhibition and commented that he felt its significance was that it was not exhibited in an art gallery but in the Medical History Museum, located in the heartland of the University of Melbourne medical precinct. It brought First Nations' bush medicine and healing into the mainstream of medical knowledge and research. The artworks were not just art but time capsules of cultural knowledge.[11]

The Art of Healing was attended by over 8000 visitors. Professor Shaun Ewen was instrumental in ensuring that the exhibition had an international reach. It was part of the International Academic Engagement Program 'to support the development of academic networks and relationships that facilitate an understanding of Indigenous cultures and knowledges'.[12] This view set the framework for taking *The Art of Healing* to Europe. An exhibition tour presented a strategic opportunity to develop academic networks and relationships that facilitated an understanding of Indigenous cultures and knowledges through major international universities. And so a highlights exhibition consisting of twenty artworks was curated to be shown at Bush House, King's College London from 15 May to 28 June 2019, and then move to the Berlin Museum of Medical History of the Charité—Universitätsmedizin from 24 October 2019 to 2 February 2020.

At each venue, the exhibition was part of a broader cultural program. In London, *The Art of Healing* was to be part of a series that the Menzies Australia Institute was undertaking in relation to Australian Indigenous culture and health, partnered with the University of Melbourne, including the Poche Leadership Fellows program. This celebrated the long-term partnership between King's College London and the University of Melbourne, as well as establishing new connections.

Issues of mental health and wellbeing were addressed with London audiences in Pitjantjatjara and English. *Ngangkaṟi* Rene Kulitja and Pantjiti Lewis from NPYWC, along with Professor Sandra Eades, associate dean (Indigenous) at the Faculty of Medicine, Dentistry and Health Sciences, talked about the healing role of *ngangkaṟi* (16 May) followed by a workshop (18 May). The exhibition was then included in the program of the Border Crossings Origins Tenth Anniversary Festival of First Nations, which was held from 11 to 23 June 2019.[13] Professor Helen Milroy, who was the first known Australian Indigenous person to graduate in medicine in 1983, gave a lecture on mental health. In Berlin, as part of the public programs at the Berlin Museum of Medical History of the Charité—Universitätsmedizin, Professor Marcia Langton gave a lecture on 'Traditional Healing Practice' (24 October).

Two publications were developed for the tour. One was a room brochure for visitors to Bush House, to enhance their understanding of the exhibition.[14] At the Berlin Museum of Medical History, the director, Thomas Schnalke, supported the production of a bilingual publication to accompany the exhibition. In 'The Message from Australia', vice-chancellor Professor Duncan Maskell and pro vice chancellor (Indigenous) Professor Shaun Ewen shared the importance of the public acknowledgement of First Nations peoples' knowledge systems:

> *The art of healing* provides an example of Indigenous knowledge and how it sits comfortably side by side with other healing and artistic traditions. To reach our aspiration of being a great *Australian* university, examples such as those presented in this catalogue should become visible across all intellectual disciplines, and in our teaching and learning, and research ... The University of Melbourne recognises the great knowledge gift expressed in *The art of healing* exhibition. We will continue to reform our institution to ensure that Indigenous knowledge is a visible, vibrant and integral part of our present and future work. [Emphasis in original][15]

The exhibition tour to Berlin coincided with the University of Melbourne's plan to form major partnerships with the Berlin-based universities. The exhibition was an opportunity to extend knowledge of Indigenous healing practices in Europe.

In London and Berlin, *The Art of Healing* was supported by the Australian embassies in those cities. The exhibition in London was opened by Australian High Commissioner George Brandis on 14 May, and in Berlin by Australian ambassador Lynette Wood on 23 October. It was received with immense interest by the visitors, and student guides were present at both venues to answer questions. In London, *The Art of Healing* received over 1300 visitors—all of those surveyed rated the exhibition either 'excellent' or 'good', which was an impressive result.[16] In Berlin, the major newspaper *Berliner Zeitung* gave very detailed and positive coverage of the exhibition. An article connected the exhibition to the fires in Australia and climate change, and acknowledged the importance of Indigenous knowledge.[17] Schnalke commented at the end of the exhibition: 'Everything went really well. The last 4 days we had over 10 000 visitors. Many were asking about the "Australian" exhibition.'[18]

Acknowledging the importance of recognition of First Nations knowledge systems, the University of Melbourne gifted artworks to both universities. *Tjulpu Wiltja: Bird Nest Basket* by *ngangkaṟi* Illawanti

Ungkutjuru Ken was given to King's College London, and a work on paper by Sidney Moody, *Birriwa Tree Leaves* (2015), was given to the Berlin Museum of Medical History.

The response by viewers of these artworks, individually or collectively, has been the same wherever they have been displayed: disbelief that this rich and expansive knowledge system is not more widely known and acknowledged. The University of Melbourne is committed to incorporating Australian Indigenous knowledge throughout its curriculum and research projects, so this situation will be rectified. The resulting partnerships between Western medicine and traditional Indigenous healing practices will offer greater benefits for all in the provision of health services.

In 2022, Professor Jane Gunn, Dean of the Faculty of Medicine, Dentistry and Health Sciences, launched the strategic plan for the faculty, *Advancing Health 2030*. Artworks from *The Art of Healing* were chosen to enhance the strategic plan's themes of collaborate, innovate and nurture, not for decoration but for inspiration. An explanation of their use was included in the plan itself. *Thalngarrji/Snappy Gum/Eucalyptus brevifolia* (2016) by Gija Elder Shirley Purdie was selected by Aboriginal and Torres Strait Islander students in the faculty to represent nurture. Second-year medical student Joel Bones commented:

> This work symbolises the flourishing body of knowledge that First Nations Peoples in Australia have so successfully nurtured through the passing of knowledge from elders to young people. As First Nations students, we should aspire to continue to learn, nourish and contribute knowledge as done by our ancestors.[19]

The Art of Healing exhibition has transformed the Medical History Museum collection. All of the artworks collected on the theme of bush medicine and healing are linked by the strong connection of Aboriginal and Torres Strait Islander peoples to Country, and the passing down of cultural knowledge to the next generation. We are privileged that these individuals and communities have chosen to share this rich repository of healing and knowledge with us through their art. The works are a significant addition to the Medical History Museum's permanent collection. They have been installed in public areas, meeting rooms and student study spaces across the Faculty of Medicine, Dentistry and Health Sciences, and will continue to inform and engage students, staff and the broader community through their aesthetic value and cultural significance. They also remind us of the importance of cultural and social frameworks for the wellbeing of all communities.

Rosie Ngwarraye Ross (b. 1951)
skin: Ngwarraye
language: Alyawarre
Country: Ampilatwatja, Northern Territory
Bush flowers and bush medicine plants, 2015
acrylic on linen
91.0 × 91.0 cm
MHM2017.3, Medical History Museum

Judith Pungkarta Inkamala (b. 1948)
skin: Pungkarta
language: Western Arrarnta
Country: Ntaria, Northern Territory
Bush medicine, 2017
terracotta and underglaze
43.0 × 31.0 × 31.0 cm
MHM2017.17, Medical History Museum

Treahna Hamm (b. 1965)
language: Yorta Yorta
Country: Yorta Yorta (Central Murray Region, Victoria)
Dhungala cool burn, 2017
acrylic paint, river sand, bark ink, paper on canvas
100.9 × 114.0 cm (each of three panels)
MHM2017.2, Medical History Museum

Treahna Hamm (b. 1965)
language: Yorta Yorta
Country: Yorta Yorta
Yorta Yorta bush medicine first aid kit, 2017
Paperbark, Kurrajong pods, bark ink, riverbed clay, charcoal, raffia, ash, possum bone, mussel shell, river sand and other materials
4.0 × 12.0 × 27.0 cm
MHM2017.1, Medical History Museum

Balgo artists: Miriam Baadjo (b.1957), **Tossie Baadjo** (b.1958), **Jane Gimme** (b.1958), **Gracie Mosquito** (b.1955), **Helen Nagomara** (b.1953), **Ann Frances Nowee** (b.1964) and **Imelda Yukenbarri** (b.1954)
language: Kukatja
artist location: Wirrimanu (Balgo), Western Australia
Bush medicine: a collaborative work by women from Wirrimanu (Balgo), 2018
acrylic on linen, 120.0 × 180.0 cm
MHM2017.20, Medical History Museum

Shirley Purdie (b. 1947)
skin: Nangari
language: Gija / Kimberley Kriol
Country: Gilburn (Mabel Downs Station)
artist location: Warmun, Western Australia
Thalngarrji / Snappy Gum / Eucalyptus brevifolia, 2016
natural ochre and pigments on canvas
45.0 × 45.0 cm
MHM2017.20, Medical History Museum

Notes

1 Jacqueline Healy, 'Sharing Medical Knowledge through Art', in Jacqueline Healy (ed.), *The Art of Healing: Australian Indigenous Bush Medicine*, Medical History Museum, University of Melbourne, Parkville, 2018, p. 96.
2 Ibid., p. 85.
3 Ibid., p. 98.
4 Ibid., p. 96.
5 Ibid., p. 126.
6 Ibid., p. 108.
7 Ibid., p. 70.
8 Ibid., p. 81.
9 Maringka Burton, through interpreter Patrick Hookey, July 2018. Transcribed by Outscribe Transcription Services.
10 Healy, *The Art of Healing*, p. 1.
11 Visit to Medical History Museum on 29 June 2018 by Bruce Pascoe, author of *Dark Emu*; Penelope Joy Smith, research assistant, Indigenous Studies Unit; and Vicky Shukuroglou—and meeting with Jacqueline Healy.
12 The University of Melbourne, *The University of Melbourne Reconciliation Action Plan: April 2018 – December 2022* (RAP 3), 2018, https://about.unimelb.edu.au/__data/assets/pdf_file/0020/75350/Elevate-RAP-2018-2022.pdf (accessed 7 November 2023).
13 Border Crossings, *Border Crossings Origins Tenth Anniversary Festival of First Nations, London, 11–23 June 2019*, *Issuu*, 29 May 2019, https://issuu.com/originsfestival/docs/brochure_origins_2019_sent-singlepa (accessed 7 November 2023).
14 King's College London, *The Art of Healing: Australian Indigenous Bush Medicine*, Menzies Australia Institute, Bush House, King's College London, London, 2019.
15 University of Melbourne and Berliner Medizinhistorisches, *The Art of Healing: Australian Indigenous Bush Medicine / Die Kunst Des Heilens: Australische Indigene Buschmedizin*, Medical History Museum, University of Melbourne, and Berliner Medizinhistorisches Museum der Charité, Germany, 2019, p. viii.
16 Ian Henderson, 'Visitors to "The Art of Healing" Gain New Perspectives', News Centre, King's College London, London, 10 July 2019, https://www.kcl.ac.uk/news/visitors-to-the-art-of-healing-gain-new-perspectives (accessed 7 November 2023).
17 Suzanne Lentz, 'Aborigine-Kunst in Berlin: Als das Feuer noch heilen konnte', *Berliner Zeitung*, 13 January 2020, https://www.berliner-zeitung.de/kultur-vergnuegen/als-das-feuer-noch-heilen-konnte-li.4831 (accessed 7 November 2023).
18 Thomas Schnalke, email message to Jacqueline Healy, 'Farewell Exhibition', 3 February 2020.
19 Faculty of Medicine, Dentistry and Health Sciences, *Collaborate + Innovate + Nurture + Impact: Advancing Health 2030*, University of Melbourne, Parkville, 2022, p. 3.

V

Conclusion

Naming and Renaming

JAMES WAGHORNE[1]

DURING THE CELEBRATIONS for the University of Melbourne's 150th anniversary in 2003, which included a series of public events as well as the release of new histories and the staging of exhibitions, students raised questions about the University's colonial legacy and its complicity in historical racism.[2] Aboriginal human remains that had been collected almost 100 years earlier by then professor of anatomy Richard Berry had been discovered stored in the Medical School, prompting an outcry (as discussed in Rohan Long's chapter in this volume).[3] The critics observed that Berry, who had a building named after him, had also recently been publicly identified as an active eugenicist, and they expanded their critique to include other so-honoured individuals, including Berry's contemporaries, namely professor of biology Sir Walter Baldwin Spencer, education reformer Frank Tate and professor of zoology Wilfred Agar. Recent scholarship had revealed that Berry, Tate and Agar had advocated eugenic measures to limit the reproduction of people of 'inferior' genetic stock, as they viewed it; and a major Indigenous history survey had uncovered comments Spencer made to the *Herald* newspaper at the end of his career disparaging Aboriginal people's capacity to benefit from education.[4] At the same time, new scholarship had criticised the role of anthropologists such as Spencer in managing policies that brought harm to Indigenous people. While Northern Territory Protector of Aborigines, Spencer promoted child-removal policies, among others.[5]

Where, in the sesquicentennial moment, were these 'unsavoury' aspects of the University's past, these students asked? How could the University have named buildings and lecture theatres after men associated with such ideas, and why did it tolerate this now? At this moment, when the University's history had come into prominence, wasn't it time for a 'fuller recognition and acknowledgement of the university's past'?[6]

Acknowledging or Erasing?

The article in *Farrago* was followed by letters to vice-chancellor Alan Gilbert pointing out the contradiction between the actions of Berry and Spencer and the University's 1998 'Reconciliation Policy', which recorded the University's 'deep regrets for the injustices suffered by the Indigenous people of Australia as a result of European settlement', including 'the hurt and harm caused by the forced removal of children and families and its effect on the human dignity and spirit of Indigenous Australians'.[7] Renaming the Berry and Spencer buildings would be a 'meaningful gesture which admits all the historical practices and deeds of the University' and a 'good start', the petitioners argued.

Gilbert's response was sympathetic, short and revealing. He conveyed that the request had prompted 'a lot of careful consideration'. He and his colleagues agreed with many of the criticisms raised against Berry and Spencer, which he saw as a 'warning about the dangers of universities voicing and endorsing indefensible conventional wisdom'. However, he felt that 'rewriting history is far from the best way to deal with past injustices', implying that renaming a building could be interpreted as the University erasing past connections rather than acknowledging them.[8]

Gilbert's letter reflected the quandary naming presented. Naming a building or lecture theatre conveys honour on the recipient, binding them and their legacy to their university. For past professors, it recognises their achievements and standing among the university community. For philanthropists it reflects the university's gratitude for major donations without which the university would be diminished. Naming spaces connects the university to its past and urges students to revere and be inspired by the names they look up at as they cross building and lecture theatre thresholds. Names give personality to a campus.

Renaming or even denaming a space is not easily done. It appears to go back on decisions made by previous generations, and risks damaging that individual's reputation even more than if they had not received the honour in the first place. However, like many other universities across the world, the University of Melbourne was facing new critiques, often championed by students and Indigenous scholars, compelling it to reassess the careers of its past academics and the continuing use of their names.

Naming Policy

Before World War II, the University of Melbourne's buildings were mostly named for the disciplines they housed, such as Natural Philosophy, Biology and Medicine. These names were impermanent and could follow the changing uses of buildings. The Biology Building, for example, became the Zoology Building on the retirement of Spencer and the appointment of Agar in 1919.

Only a small number of buildings were named after individuals, mostly in recognition of those who had donated funds towards their construction. The ceremonial hall was called Wilson Hall after Samuel Wilson, who had given £30 000 to pay for its construction, as discussed by Zoë Laidlaw in this volume.[9] Melba Hall was named after Dame Nellie, who sang at a fundraising benefit concert in 1909. The composer Percy Grainger donated funds to establish the Grainger Museum in 1938, while the Beaurepaire sports centre and swimming pool, constructed as a training facility for the Melbourne Olympic Games, was named in 1956 after its funder, Sir Frank, the industrialist and former Olympic cyclist. Some affiliated organisations also had names, including the Walter and Eliza Hall Institute, named after the Cobb & Co. magnates who gave funds in 1912, and Ormond College, named after the pastoralist Francis Ormond, who also funded the Ormond Chair in Music in 1887.

The names of donors also permeated the University in the form of named scholarships, such as for the pastoralist John Wyselaskie and the newspaper proprietor David Syme, among many others. Along similar lines were memorials for the fallen in wars. Both the Ritchie Research Chair in Economics and the clock in the Old Arts tower, named for ET Stevens, were different forms of war memorial for the fallen on the Western Front.[10] This naming was reckoned an important measure to give proper acknowledgement of munificent gifts, and to offer an incentive to other would-be philanthropists to follow. Critical to the University, dependent as it was on public funding, such gifts were practical demonstrations of public support.[11]

A new movement to recognise the names of longstanding and notable former members of staff who had made major contributions to their disciplines arose during the middle decades of the twentieth century. The lecture theatre in the Chemistry Building that opened in 1940 was named after the celebrated professor of chemistry Sir David Orme Masson, who had died in 1937 just before work had begun on the building.[12] Colleagues of Jessie Webb, associate professor in history, raised funds for a history library after her death in 1944.[13] Then, in 1956, the University Council named the roads constructed through the grounds after Masson, Spencer and Sir John Monash—respectively, a four-time graduate, former vice-chancellor and decorated World War I general.[14] These men all combined significant and longstanding service to the University with major contributions to public life recognised by their respective knighthoods. Their contributions would be highlighted in Geoffrey Blainey's centenary history, published the following year, which showed them to be part of a great generation that shaped the University.[15] And, when it opened 1961, a high-rise, cream-brick edifice that had been known on plans as the North Building, because of its location on the University's northern boundary, was renamed after the founding chancellor, Redmond Barry. Its four theatres honoured two former science professors, Sir Thomas Lyle (natural philosophy) and Sir David Rivett (chemistry); a former deputy chancellor, Sir John Latham; and the most recent chancellor, Sir David Lowe. Lyle and Rivett had been leading public scientists, the latter the CEO of CSIR, while Latham had been chief justice of the High Court and Lowe was a longstanding justice of the Supreme Court of Victoria. Naming theatres after Latham and Lowe broke new ground by bestowing this honour on living former members of staff.

The appeal of naming buildings and theatres after the University's greatest figures accelerated in the following decade, with the new administration building, opened in 1970, called after the first salaried vice-chancellor, Raymond Priestley. In the same year the Anatomy Building was renamed for Berry in recognition of his fundraising work almost half a century earlier, which had produced a building of such size it came known as 'Berry's folly'.[16] Meanwhile, the University pressed the Arts Faculty to decide on names for its three buildings, then simply Old Arts, Arts North and Arts South. Old Arts was held to have currency and would be kept, as was the informal naming of Arts North as the Babel Building, which name had been adopted into general usage despite vice-chancellor David Derham's personal disapproval.[17] At length, in 1972, after repeatedly failing to reach agreement on a figure acceptable to all of its internal departments, the faculty voted unanimously for the late former vice-chancellor John Medley as the compromise candidate for Arts South. Although having no formal association with Arts, the faculty commendation upheld Medley as a 'man of the humanities'.[18]

Such moves for major buildings were seen as worthwhile. However, the interest in naming extended beyond large central buildings and into rooms for smaller departments. Extraordinary post–World War II expansion helped to create this pressure as the range of University departments swelled with increases in staff and students. By 1970 student numbers had grown from 3511 in 1944 to 14 727, while the number of academics had increased more than five and a half times from just 359 to 2020.[19] To house the expansion, and supported by funding from the Commonwealth Universities Commission, numerous new buildings were erected and others extended, creating new opportunities for naming, while also producing greater churn as departments were shuffled around the University. These rooms provided bastions for older departments feeling themselves overrun, while newer departments often sought to identify their deeper roots by identifying their earlier originators.

Naming was the responsibility of the University Council, but the Council delegated the nomination of candidates to faculties with little formal process. It had been odd to name the mathematics building for Richard Berry, for example, since the medical faculty had since vacated the building in its move to the south-western corner of the campus. Furthermore, the similar-sounding Redmond Barry, Richard Berry and Raymond Priestley buildings caused confusion, especially among first-year students, prompting calls to improve planning.[20]

Derham drafted guidelines for nominations in 1970 to introduce some order into the process. The first, that 'not all permanent buildings need to be named for individuals', reflected anxiety about the increasing number of nominations and the possibility that the University could be stuck with a campus adorned with the names of individuals important in their time but with less enduring significance. Derham's other guidelines endorsed the custom of naming buildings after the academic disciplines they housed, since this left space for future changes. A clear distinction was drawn between buildings, which were now only to be named for individuals of 'university-wide significance', and rooms within departments, which could be named for individuals of local meaning—these named rooms could be transported with departments if they relocated to new premises.[21] The Council would name buildings only after consulting with their tenant departments, thus recognising the interest of their primary users—a policy that would become relevant as names were later challenged.[22]

While these general principles were helpful in controlling the process, the difficulty in assessing the merits of nominations led the Council in December 1974 to appoint an advisory Committee on Naming, a subcommittee of the University Buildings Committee. The committee comprised a lecturer in English, Hume Dow; the professor of botany, Tom Chambers; Dr Neil Lewis of the University Council; and the executive officer (buildings), MR Pawsey. Professor of history Geoffrey Blainey declined to join the committee because of other commitments, but he offered informal advice to the members when asked.[23]

This committee met annually, adjusting policies in response to changing needs. At its December 1975 meeting it recommended that only surnames should be applied to buildings, with titles and given names left off for simplicity. At the same meeting it decided that the names of living persons would no longer be eligible, a policy it later retracted for internal rooms, provided the individual was 'no longer in the service of the university'. Such policies, however, lasted only as long as the committee.

The greatest difficulty remained how to assess the merits of nominations. The Naming Committee was unwilling, or insufficiently resourced, to conduct independent assessments of all the nominations. Instead, it delegated this responsibility to the nominating department, which it asked to provide a formal citation listing the career achievements, positions held, memberships of academies and societies, and public honours. In 1978 it stipulated the form and structure required of these and, although it reserved the right to 'interview a representative of the proposing faculty', its capacity to assess their merit was limited. It conceded that 'responsibility to provide adequate details for assessment lies with initiators of proposals for naming. In a broad sense, this has always been the case'.[24] These citations were effective in recording the justification for nominations, but they hardly offered a searching appraisal. The process trusted that behind the paperwork lay an informal endorsement, derived from personal and historical connections between present academics and those of the past.

In the decades after 1970, the University acquired a patina of named spaces. These added a singular quality to the campus, creating landmarks that made it comprehensible. The naming of the Hearn and Deakin courts surrounding the Law Quadrangle, for instance, helped to convey which door people should enter. The Naming Committee fell into abeyance in the 1980s amid restructures within the Property and Buildings Department, but the broad principles it established remained: responsibility for researching and understanding the life of the nomination lay with the nominating department, and the Council would approve based on formal citations.

Many of these rooms and buildings honoured longstanding, retired colleagues, and these were happy occasions when the individuals and their families could be toasted at unveiling ceremonies. Professor of psychology Oscar Oeser, for example, attended the opening of the room in his honour; Lady Medley joined the gathering for the naming of the building named after her late husband. The opportunity to host such an event itself seemed to be motivation for proposing a name.[25]

Another impulse was to recover great names from the University's history, to counter the tendency to recognise the University's recent achievers over their sometimes more notable forebears. It also parried the inclination to offer naming rights as inducements for public donations. Baldwin Spencer, venerated in a recent biography, was extracted from the University's past to name the Old Zoology building after renovations in 1989, in partial recognition of Spencer's role in securing government funding for the original building in 1888.[26] Wilfred Agar became the candidate for naming the new Zoology lecture theatre in 1990, so as to connect with the first professor of zoology. However, while Spencer's citation stressed his leadership roles, it omitted reference to his arguments about Indigenous peoples' heritable qualities and intellectual capacity. While Agar's citation is not recorded, the proposing letter recorded only that he was the first professor of zoology.

In recognising figures from the past, citations highlighted how past activities reflected current priorities. Early professors' research initiatives or their administrative roles, for instance, were expanded upon, while their teaching skill mostly went unacknowledged.[27] These historical names highlighted some of the University's most significant figures, their greatness magnified by their singular position in colonial Australia and the comparatively tiny institution they inhabited. The format allowed for little ambiguity about an individual's suitability, and relied on historical scholarship that sometimes overlooked race.

Challenging the Names on Buildings

Little in the processes for naming rooms and buildings anticipated opposition. There had been few such examples internationally. An early example, notable mostly as an outlier, was the opposition of students at the University of Hawaii to its 1974 naming of the political science building after Stanley Porteus, an Australian-born psychologist whose studies into intelligence rendered non-white people into lower categories. As related in the earlier 'Eugenics, 1853–1945' chapter, before transferring to Honolulu, Porteus had conducted eugenic research with Richard Berry at the University of Melbourne, and Frank Tate had appointed him the first headmaster of the School for Mental Deficients in Fitzroy.[28] The protests were led by Indigenous students who were disparaged by Porteus' research. Similar protests were raised during the 1980s by Native American students from the University of Colorado Boulder against the naming of its student hall after a former donor, David Nichols, over his participation in the 1864 Sand Creek massacre.

Victories were slow in coming for these activists, whose claims took time to be appreciated. Nichols Hall was renamed Cheyenne-Arapaho Hall in 1987, after a formal inquiry and public debate.[29] The University of Oklahoma renamed its DeBarr Hall the following year, since its namesake, as well as chair of chemistry, was a Ku Klux Klan leader.[30] Porteus Hall endured longer, the governing body relenting only in 1998.[31]

Criticisms of some of the building names emerged at the University of Melbourne during the 1990s, spurred by increasing numbers of Indigenous students and a new politics of reconciliation. In 1992 Paul Keating delivered his 'Redfern address' acknowledging past harm to Indigenous peoples. In the same year the landmark *Mabo* judgment acknowledged native title, prompting a heated backlash from conservative groups. The 1997 *Bringing Them Home Report* detailed the deplorable, longstanding policy of child removal, while new histories such as Ann McGrath's collection offered a more comprehensive national overview of Indigenous politics than had previously been available.[32] The naming of buildings was a comparatively minor yet symbolically significant issue in what came to be described by Anna Clark and Stuart Macintyre as the 'History Wars'.[33] In 1992, Indigenous activists, including Gary Foley and others, staged a mock public trial of the statue of John Batman, the 'founder' of Melbourne, for his participation in frontier violence.[34] In a 1998 article in *Farrago*, lecturer Tony Birch called on students to 'reflect on' the naming of the Baldwin Spencer Building.[35] Associate professor of history Ann Trindade, writing a letter of support in the next issue, stated her view that 'if I were Koori I would feel shamed and insulted every time I walked past'.[36] Other critics suggested the naming question was not peripheral but fundamental. Student leader Mark Cunningham argued that Spencer's name, alongside those of other luminaries after whom buildings had been named, was 'synonymous with Melbourne University; as an institution, as a landscape and as a place'. These names were ways of 'writing a history into and onto a landscape'.[37] Stickers appeared around the campus declaring 'Baldwin Spencer was a racist'.

Cunningham, with others, formed a 'rename the buildings' pressure group, which petitioned the vice-chancellor. The citation for Spencer revealed that the University had not considered Spencer's role in the stolen generations when the building was named. His biography, published in 1985, had tried to contextualise his racism, arguing that it 'should be compared with the naked and aggressive racism of tropical Australian contemporaries, rather than with the United Nations Charter'.[38] This form of extenuation had since been rejected by 1990s writers, including Patrick Wolfe, Tony Birch and Mark Francis.[39] Gary Foley, who had enrolled in an arts degree as a mature-aged student in the late 1990s, recalled how disturbed he was by the presence of the names of individuals who had expressed racist views and whose work had served to disparage Indigenous peoples.[40] Yet, while these new perspectives were increasingly expressed, the names appeared permanent.

Behind the scenes, however, the University made tentative arrangements to release it from the permanent decisions of previous councils. A 2007 revision of the University naming policy included provision for twenty-year reviews of all building and room names. It also created new categories of 'fixed-term' names, which could recognise philanthropic project support.[41]

The ongoing pressure over building names was finally released in the 2010s, led by a new generation of Indigenous scholars, including Tyson Holloway-Clarke. The *Age* newspaper and the *Conversation* website published articles that framed the issue in stark terms, the names representing a failure to confront a 'racist past'.[42] In September 2015, the Faculty of Arts Equal Opportunity and Diversity Committee and University Indigenous Employment Framework Working Group held a seminar titled 'Naming "Whiteness" in the University: Constructing Erasure, Creating Visibility', which addressed the University's links to the eugenic movement, generating further media coverage.[43] The Richard Berry Building sign was defaced in June 2016, and several months later the pro vice-chancellor (engagement), Professor Ian Anderson, sought endorsement from the University Executive for a strategic review to address the naming of buildings and places to acknowledge the University's colonial and eugenic history, and to foster a critical and scholarly engagement with this history. The review would also aim to promote respect for diversity, including Indigenous peoples. The proposed review was then incorporated into the University's third *Reconciliation Action Plan* as a Signature Project with associated targets, timelines and accountabilities to ensure the work was prioritised.[44] This book is one outcome of that initiative.

In December 2016, anticipating this work, the Council voted to rename the Richard Berry Building. It did so with little consultation or public fanfare. The sign was changed for one in identical font, now bearing the name of the late professor of mathematics and statistics, Peter Hall, and a short press statement was released that explained the longstanding residency of mathematics in the building, but offered no comment on Berry.[45] There is to date no plaque or other form of communication explaining the name change and the reasons behind it.

Other names have followed. The Frank Tate Building has become Building 189, following its renovation as part of the New Student Precinct redevelopment, which opened in 2022; the building was smoked in 2023 to cleanse it of this history. In 2023 one of the University of Melbourne's residential colleges, Medley Hall, moved to find a new name after long campaigns against the association with former vice-chancellor John Medley. Medley had been a member of the Eugenics Society of Victoria (see the chapter 'Eugenics, 1853–1945' in this volume), and residents of that college, including Indigenous people, who make up almost a third of those residents, objected to their address bearing his name. With the approval of the University's Traditional Owners Advisory Group in 2023, a new name for the College in the Woi Wurrung language was requested from the Wurundjeri Woi Wurrung Cultural Heritage Aboriginal Corporation. This followed the University naming its newest student accommodation facility Lisa Bellear House in 2020 in honour of the Minjungbul, Goernpil and Noonuccul woman from Minjerribah (North Stradbroke Island). Bellear was an alumna and lecturer who was a prolific and widely admired Indigenous activist, photographer, broadcaster, poet, feminist, academic and performer.

Renaming Buildings Worldwide

The renaming of the Berry Building was part of a major change in the approach of universities around the world to historical racism. Trailblazing works such as Craig Stephen Wilder's 2013 history *Ebony and Ivy* had uncovered deep historical connections between US universities and slavery, both in terms of the use of slaves by former staff, and even the trading of slaves on university grounds, to the acceptance of donations from individuals whose wealth derived from the slave trade. This work was followed by numerous others, including student efforts to air these difficult histories, with initiatives such as the College of William and Mary's Lemon Project.[46] Concerns with the legacies of slavery have led to calls to rename Yale University's Calhoun Building, while Brown University renamed one of its residential colleges.[47] In 2022 Harvard University published a website detailing its history of slaveholding, including offering reparations to current descendants of former slaves.[48]

Outside the United States there was the South African 'Rhodes Must Fall' campaign, launched in 2015 at the University of Cape Town to call for the removal of a statue of Cecil Rhodes. Rhodes made major donations to universities, including establishing the Rhodes Scholarship that supports students from around the world to attend Oxford University. While the statue of Rhodes has been removed at Cape Town, his name remains on international scholarships supporting students to study at Oxford and elsewhere, in recognition of his donations.[49]

The campaign was taken up across the former British Empire, and many names of university buildings have been challenged across Australia. At the University of Sydney, activists challenged the naming of the Wentworth Building.[50] The Monash student union has removed John Medley's name from its recreational library, which had been named in recognition of his donation of non-academic books.[51] Deakin University has had petitions calling for a new name, owing to Deakin's role in creating the White Australia policy, and James Cook University faces similar pressure, renaming its Townsville campus Bebegu Yumba, or 'place of learning' in the Birri-Gubba language.[52] In 2022, following the revelations in Henry Reynolds' *Truth Telling* of Sir Samuel Griffith's judicial role acquitting participants in reprisal raids against Indigenous peoples, Fiona Foley called for Griffith University to be renamed.[53]

External cultural moments have also shaped these policies over recent years. The killing of George Floyd by a police officer in Minneapolis in 2020 strengthened moves to change names in the United States, as it revealed a structural racism in the community, and the need for universities to show leadership in countering this scourge. One of the more striking examples was Princeton University, which removed the name of former president Woodrow Wilson from its School of Public and International Affairs in 2020, following student protests against his segregationist policies.[54] Another was Stanford University, which renamed its Jordan Hall because of its founding president David Starr Jordan's eugenic advocacy.[55]

In the United Kingdom, renaming debates have become embroiled in culture wars about the legacies of the British Empire, producing contrasting approaches. University College London removed the name of Francis Galton, the man who coined the phrase 'eugenics', from its lecture theatre. It also renamed its Pearson Building, Pearson Lecture Theatre and R.A. Fisher Centre for Computational Biology, because of the two men's leading roles in the eugenics movement.[56] Imperial College London has taken a different approach, rejecting the recommendation of its History Group to rename the building named after the noted nineteenth-century zoologist Thomas Henry Huxley.[57] The recommendation provoked a concerted counter-campaign that framed the recommendation as an attempt to 'cancel' Huxley and repudiate his standing as a great scientist.[58] A member of the committee that wrote the report countered that the issue should be seen in two ways: the continued presence of Huxley's name belittled black staff members and also reflected 'structural racism' that was 'intertwined into the building itself'.[59]

History and the Present

These challenges to buildings show how different stories can be told about the lives of people from the past. Yet these conversations are complicated, for people after whom rooms or buildings are named live two lives: their own and their life as an inscription above the doorway of a building or room. The act of naming has its own history, giving names contemporary as well as historical meaning. The individuals represent not only their own lives and times but also those of current and future generations. By naming places, universities write them into the contemporary lives of staff and students, asking the current university to identify with figures from the past and draw inspiration from them. The question about whether a person's name is valid covers multiple historical stages: the individual's life and legacy, the later decisions of universities to honour that individual, and how the ideas the person represents align with changing university values.

It is to untangle these complications and resolve these tensions that universities have appointed history committees, drawing on historical research and interpretation, and heritage policies, and consulting members of the university and the wider public as well. The recommendations of these committees are thus tested in informed public debates and decided on by university governing bodies. The countervailing arguments raised can make these wrenching choices. Figures of undoubted public importance and standing, whose work produced new knowledge and influenced public discourse, who were great teachers, or whose activities helped to fund the construction of new buildings or enhance the university in some other way, can also be ineligible to have buildings named after them.

History committees have parallels in earlier decisions to name buildings. Like their predecessors, these committees must separate broader questions about a person's historical legacy from more-specific questions about whether their name is appropriate for a contemporary university. This is a forensic process, judging an individual by their actions as expressed in their published record, their public works and their commercial activities.

Such debates involve ideas and ways of thinking that have since been repudiated. They also reflect universities' changing make-up and the diversity of the people who study and work in them. Universities are no longer composed of select groups of people, mostly from similar class and cultural backgrounds. Different groups bring different perspectives on the past, and it is striking that students from minority groups have argued loudest and longest, and most persuasively, against certain names. They see obvious parallels between the racism they continue to experience on university campuses and racist intellectual work from the past that has been the subject of this book.[60] The incongruity between universities' continuing efforts to encourage diversity and their heralding of historical intolerance through room and building names appears stark and hypocritical.

Recent changes to the University of Melbourne's naming policy have sought to address these issues and encourage greater diversity in the range of people honoured. Individuals who have made a 'distinguished contribution … to community, or to society' are now eligible alongside philanthropic donors or University leaders, as are Indigenous Elders in recognition of the 'land upon which the University property is built'. The measures also create new, considered ways of reviewing existing names.[61]

What, then, of the other named places around the University? Names can inspire, but will new critiques challenge those who manufactured weapons, or contributed to environmental degradation, or opposed other minority groups? The answer is almost inevitably in the affirmative. Oxford academic, and participant in the Rhodes Must Fall movement, Simukai Chigudu, reflecting on the multitude of portraits adorning the walls of the colleges in which he worked, observed that each had difficult connections with the past. Chigudu argued that each should be viewed as 'quiescent': 'they patiently await excavation' and critique.[62]

Universities can change names without distancing themselves from troubling histories; removing a person's name from a building need not mean the university severs its relationship with its past. On the contrary, if changes are fully discussed and properly acknowledged, they become a focus for thinking about universities and their current directions. They can inform teaching and open discussion about the social, political and cultural aspects of universities' histories.[63] If the University of Melbourne's naming citations were published, they would give an overwhelming impression of the substantial contributions that past members have made within the University and across public life. They would also inform discussion not only about building names but also how academic roles and disciplinary knowledge have changed. By assessing universities' current values, and associating them with those of the past, we have a chance to redefine their future.

Notes

1 Ross Jones contributed to an earlier version of this chapter, and I am grateful to Peter McPhee and Margot Eden for detailed comments on the draft.

2 'Why Do We Honour These Men?', *Farrago*, vol. 82, no. 2, 2003, p. 30; RJW Selleck, *The Shop: The University of Melbourne, 1850–1939*, Melbourne University Press, Carlton, 2003; Stuart Macintyre and RJW Selleck, *A Short History of the University of Melbourne*, Melbourne University Press, Carlton, 2003; Philip Goad and George Tibbits, *Architecture on Campus: A Guide to the University of Melbourne and Its Colleges*, Melbourne University Press, Carlton, 2003.

3 William Horton, 'Shameful Remains', *Farrago*, vol. 88, no. 4, 2009, pp. 38–41.

4 'University Apologises to Aborigines for Past Experiments', *Adelaidean*, vol. 11, no. 2, March 2002, p. 3; Warwick Anderson, *The Cultivation of Whiteness: Science, Health and Racial Destiny in Australia*, Melbourne University Press, Carlton, 2002; Ross L Jones, 'The Master Potter and the Rejected Pots: Eugenic Legislation in Victoria, 1918–1939', *Australian Historical Studies*, vol. 30, no. 113, 1999, pp. 319–42; Ross L Jones, Skeletons in Toorak and Collingwood Cupboards: Eugenics in Educational and Health Policy in Victoria, 1910 to 1939, PhD thesis, Monash University, Clayton, 2000. The earliest article on Berry was Mary Cawte, 'Craniometry and Eugenics in Australia: R.J.A. Berry and the Quest for Social Efficiency', *Historical Studies*, vol. 22, no. 86, 1986, pp. 35–53. Also see Richard

Broome, 'Victoria', in Ann McGrath (ed.), *Contested Ground: Australian Aborigines under the British Crown*, Routledge, London, 1995, p. 144.

5 Patrick Wolfe, *Settler Colonialism: The Politics and Poetics of an Ethnographic Event*, Bloomsbury Publishing, London, 1998.

6 'Why Do We Honour These Men?', p. 30.

7 'University of Melbourne Reconciliation Policy', University of Melbourne, Parkville, 1998.

8 Alan Gilbert to Daniel Fleming and Laura Smelter, 23 June 2003, Buildings & Properties: Naming Buildings, Lecture Theatres and Seminar Rooms, 93/00472.

9 Council minutes, 18 June 1877.

10 Kate Darian-Smith and James Waghorne, 'Australian Universities and the Commemoration of the First World War', *History of Education Review*, vol. 45, no. 2, 2016, pp. 241–3.

11 RJA Berry, 'The Modern University and Its Upkeep', in Henry Payne Mullet (ed.), *Proceedings of the First Educational Congress, State of Victoria, Held in Melbourne, 1912*, n.d., pp. 118–41.

12 RJW Selleck, *Finding Home: The Masson Family*, Australian Scholarly Publishing, North Melbourne, 2013; Len Weickhardt, *Masson of Melbourne: The Life and Times of David Orme Masson, Professor of Chemistry, University of Melbourne, 1886–1923*, Royal Australian Chemical Institute, Parkville, 1989.

13 'J.S.W. Webb Memorial' (pamphlet), University of Melbourne Special Collections.

14 *Farrago*, vol. 32, no. 12, 1956, p. 3—along with Main Drive, Conservatorium Road, Vice-Chancellors Road, Professors' Road and Tin Alley.

15 Geoffrey Blainey, *A Centenary History of the University of Melbourne*, Melbourne University Press, Carlton, 1957.

16 RKF Russell, *The Melbourne Medical School, 1862–1962*, Melbourne University Press, Carlton, 1977, p. 130.

17 Buildings & Properties: Naming Buildings, Lecture Theatres and Seminar Rooms, 93/00472

18 JR Poynter to RD Marginson, 22 June 1972; 'Annual Report 1972', *University of Melbourne Calendar 1973*, p. 7.

19 Commonwealth Year Books, various years.

20 EJ Williams, professor of statistics, to RD Marginson, 3 March 1971.

21 Naming of Buildings: Executive of Council Discussions, 1 October 1970, file 22-31-1.

22 Minutes, University Council Executive, 31 March 1971.

23 University of Melbourne Buildings Committee, Committee on Naming, Notice Paper, inaugural meeting, 10 December 1974.

24 University of Melbourne Buildings Committee, Committee on Naming, Policy Guidelines and Terms of Reference, 20 December 1978; Policy and Guidelines, 1979.

25 Buildings & Properties: Naming Buildings, Lecture Theatres and Seminar Rooms, 93/00472.

26 DJ Mulvaney and JH Calaby, *So Much That Is New: Baldwin Spencer, 1860–1929, a Biography*, Melbourne University Press, Carlton, 1985.

27 See, for example, 'Walter Baldwin Spencer (1860–1929)', Nomination Citation, University of Melbourne Special Collections.

28 Stanley D Porteus, *A Psychologist of Sorts: The Autobiography and Publications of the Porteus Maze Tests*, Pacific Books, Palo Alto, CA, 1969; David E Stannard,

'Honoring Racism: The Professional Life and Reputation of Stanley D. Porteus', *Social Process in Hawaii*, vol. 39, 1999, pp. 85–125.

29 Ari Kelman, *A Misplaced Massacre: Struggling over the Memory of Sand Creek*, Harvard University Press, Cambridge, 2013, pp. 90–3; Patricia Limerick, *What's in a Name? Nichols Hall: A Report*, University of Colorado, Boulder, 1987.

30 James W Loewen, 'The Shrouded History of College Campuses', *Chronicle of Higher Education*, 28 January 2000.

31 Kaylee Miki, 'What a Name Stands for: Stanley Porteus', *Horizons*, vol. 5, no. 1, 2020, pp. 20–5; Stannard, 'Honoring Racism', pp. 85–125.

32 Ann McGrath (ed.), *Contested Ground: Australian Aborigines under the British Crown*, Routledge, London, 1995.

33 Stuart Macintyre and Anna Clark, *The History Wars*, Melbourne University Publishing, Carlton, 2004.

34 Penelope Edmonds, 'Monuments on Trial: #BlackLivesMatter, "Travelling Memory" and the Transcultural Afterlives of Empire', *History Australia*, vol. 18, no. 4, 2 October 2021, pp. 16–21.

35 Tony Birch, 'Forget History', *Farrago*, vol. 77, no. 7, 1998, pp. 26–7.

36 Ann Trindade, letter to editor, *Farrago*, vol. 80, no. 2, 2001, p. 4.

37 Mark Cunningham, 'Navigating Baldwin Spencer', *Farrago*, vol. 80, no. 1, 2001, p. 9.

38 Mulvaney and Calaby, *So Much That Is New*, p. 289.

39 Wolfe, *Settler Colonialism*, p. 11; Tony Birch, 'A Mabo Blood Test?', *The Australian Journal of Anthropology*, vol. 6, nos 1–2, 1995; Mark Francis, 'Social Darwinism and the Construction of Institutionalised Racism in Australia', *Journal of Australian Studies*, vol. 20, nos 50–1, 1996, pp. 90–105.

40 Gary Foley, 'Eugenics, Melbourne University and Me', *Tracker Magazine*, February 2012.

41 Policy and Guidelines for Naming Proposals, 2007.

42 Ross Jones, 'Eugenics in Australia: The Secret of Melbourne's Elite', *The Conversation*, 21 September 2011; Marika Dobbin, 'Heart of Darkness: Melbourne University's Racist Professors', *Age*, 30 November 2015.

43 E Cervini, 'Human Remains Found in Uni Storeroom', *Age*, 16 February 2003; E Cervini, 'A Theory out of the Darkness', *Sydney Morning Herald*, 13 September 2011; E Cervini, 'It's Time Melbourne Uni Stopped Honouring Eugenicist Richard Berry', *Sydney Morning Herald*, 6 March 2016; Jeff Sparrow, 'Naming and Renaming Uni's Racist Monuments', *Eureka Street*, 2015, http://www.eurekastreet.com.au/article.aspx?aeid=45760#.VylRl_l95hE (accessed 7 November 2023); J Pearlman, 'Melbourne University Pressured over Buildings Named after Racist Founders', *Telegraph*, 1 December 2015; Natasha Mitchell, 'The Hidden History of Eugenics: The Eugenic Turn in Schooling', *Earshot, ABC Radio National*, 2016.

44 The University of Melbourne, *The University of Melbourne Reconciliation Action Plan: April 2018 – December 2022* (RAP 3), 2018, https://about.unimelb.edu.au/__data/assets/pdf_file/0020/75350/Elevate-RAP-2018-2022.pdf (accessed 7 November 2023).

45 The University of Melbourne, 'Richard Berry Building Renamed Peter Hall Building', media release, 9 December 2016, https://about.unimelb.edu.au/newsroom/news/2016/december/richard-berry-building-renamed-peter-hall-building (accessed 7 November 2023).

46 Craig Steven Wilder, *Ebony and Ivy: Race, Slavery, and the Troubled History of America's Universities*, New York, Bloomsbury, 2013; Leslie M Harris, James T Campbell and Alfred L Brophy (eds), *Slavery and the University: Histories and Legacies*, University of Georgia Press, Athens, 2019; The Lemon Project, 2023, https://www.wm.edu/sites/lemonproject (accessed 7 November 2023).

47 Brown University Steering Committee on Slavery and Justice, *Slavery and Justice: Report of the Brown University Steering Committee on Slavery and Justice*, Brown University, Providence, RI, 2006; Yale University, 'Report of the Committee to Establish Principles on Renaming', Yale University, New Haven, CT, 2016, https://president.yale.edu/sites/default/files/files/CEPR_FINAL_12-2-16.pdf (accessed 7 November 2023); Susan Hudson, 'The Men behind the Names', *The Well*, University of North Carolina, Chapel Hill, 17 July 2020, https://www.unc.edu/posts/2020/07/17/names-of-dishonor (accessed 7 November 2023).

48 President and Fellows of Harvard College, *Harvard & the Legacy of Slavery*, Harvard University, Cambridge, MA, 2022, https://legacyofslavery.harvard.edu (accessed 7 November 2023).

49 Rekgotsofetse Chikane, *Breaking a Rainbow, Building a Nation: The Politics behind #Must Fall Movements,* Picador Africa, Pan Macmillan, Johannesburg, 2018; Antje Daniel, 'Rhodes Must Fall: Different Layers of Intersectionality in Students' Protests in South Africa', *Interface: A Journal for and about Social Movements*, vol. 13, no. 1, 2021, pp. 12–37.

50 Evelyn Araluen, 'Resisting the Institution', *Overland*, no. 227, 2017, pp. 3–10.

51 Editors, 'A Medley of Evil: A Dark History of Our Student Union Library', *Lot's Wife*, 25 February 2017, https://lotswife.com.au/a-medley-of-evil-a-dark-history-of-our-student-union-library (accessed 7 November 2023).

52 Peter Neil, 'Rename Deakin University', Change.org, 23 January 2022, https://www.change.org/p/deakin-university-executive-board-rename-deakin-university (accessed 7 November 2023); James Cook University, 'JCU's Townsville Campus Indigenous Name Unveiled', media release, 4 December 2020.

53 Joe Hinchcliffe, '"Enabler" of Massacres: The Push to Reexamine the Legacy of Founding Father Samuel Griffith', *Guardian*, 5 June 2022. See discussion of Griffith in Henry Reynolds, *Truth Telling: History, Sovereignty and the Uluru Statement*, NewSouth Publishing, Sydney.

54 Kenneth O'Reilly, 'The Jim Crow Policies of Woodrow Wilson', *The Journal of Blacks in Higher Education*, no. 17, 1997, p. 117; Office of Communications, 'President Eisgruber's Message to Community on Removal of Woodrow Wilson Name from Public Policy School and Wilson College', Princeton University, Princeton, 27 June 2020, https://www.princeton.edu/news/2020/06/27/president-eisgrubers-message-community-removal-woodrow-wilson-name-public-policy (accessed 7 November 2023).

55 Jessica Riskin, 'A Poisonous Legacy', *New York Review of Books*, 22 June 2023.

56 University College London, 'UCL Denames Buildings Named after Eugenicists', *UCL News*, 19 June 2020, https://www.ucl.ac.uk/news/2020/jun/ucl-denames-buildings-named-after-eugenicists (accessed 7 November 2023). Karl Pearson was founding professor of eugenics at University College London.

57 Imperial College London, 'Community Report of the History Group, Imperial College London', November 2021.

58 Why Evolution Is True, 'Huxley at Imperial', reproduced in 'Our Letter to Nature', 21 January 2022, https://whyevolutionistrue.com/2022/01/21/our-letter-to-nature-also-rejected-but-published-in-shortened-form-by-the-telegraph (accessed 7 November 2023).

59 Philip Ball, 'Imperialism's Long Shadow: The UK Universities Grappling with a Colonial Past', *Nature*, vol. 610, no. 7932, 19 October 2022, pp. 593–6.

60 Rhonda Povey, Michelle Trudgett, Susan Page and Michelle Lea Locke. 'Hidden in Plain View: Indigenous Early Career Researchers' Experiences and Perceptions of Racism in Australian Universities', *Critical Studies in Education*, vol. 64, no. 4, 2023, pp. 355–73.

61 The University of Melbourne, 'University Naming and Memorial Policy (MPF1201)', 31 March 2023, https://policy.unimelb.edu.au/MPF1201 (accessed 7 November 2023).

62 Simukai Chigudu, 'Rhodes Must Fall in Oxford: A Critical Testimony,' *Critical African Studies*, vol. 12, no. 3, 2020, p. 303.

63 Derek H Alderman and Rose-Redwood Reuben, 'The Classroom as "Toponymic Workspace": Towards a Critical Pedagogy of Campus Place Renaming', *Journal of Geography in Higher Education*, vol. 44, no. 1, 2020, pp. 124–41.

Conclusion

MARCIA LANGTON

Dhoombak Goobgoowana takes up the challenge of truth-telling about the history of the University of Melbourne in its engagement with Indigenous people. It shows the willingness of the contributing authors to confront the past with candour and place their lines of investigation and research on the public record. This has so rarely occurred in the University's history, as so many chapters reveal.

The history of interactions with Indigenous people from 1853 to the twenty-first century has required a reckoning for some time. Several Aboriginal leaders and intellectuals—including Jim Berg; Professor Eleanor Bourke AM, now the Chair of the Yoorrook Justice Commission overseeing a truth-telling inquiry in Victoria; Professor Ian Anderson AO; and many others—have played a role in steering the University towards an approach that honours the Traditional Owners and their dispossession and suffering from earliest colonial times. Importantly, Indigenous leaders involved as staff, Traditional Owners, Elders, students or advisers have been aware of the need for truth-telling about the history of the University and the need for transparency.

Now, at a modern and leading university not only in Australia but the world, Indigenous leaders have developed programs with an auspicious track record in enrolling and recruiting Indigenous students and staff. They have instigated groundbreaking research in Indigenous matters by both Indigenous and non-Indigenous researchers. They have established fruitful partnerships with a range of Aboriginal communities, foundations and corporations. Yet progress towards parity in education outcomes and reconciliation activities, by themselves, cannot remove the stain of the University's role in furthering the usurpation of the land from its owners, in eugenic experiments and the creation of collections of

Aboriginal corpses and body parts. This book has shown that teaching and promoting discredited eugenic theories and racial scientism to generations of impressionable students and publics, and lending the authority of the academy and the sciences to theories and tropes that in the twenty-first century have been shown to lack rigorous evidence, were wrong.

Similarly, the University's continued commemoration of individuals discussed in this book prolongs trauma. For many, there is palpable shame in working in a place where frontier settlers and their works are celebrated because they donated some of the wealth they extracted from stolen land and resources to the University. Correcting the history by merely adding the long-suppressed details of the fatal impact of the colonial mission on tens of thousands of Aboriginal people is rightly regarded as an insufficient response to naming and renaming practices. Yet, finding an honourable solution—and informing the decisions to rename or not—must involve factual historical accounts, such as appear in the chapters in this volume. The perpetrators of injustice should be named, and their roles in historical events fully recounted. However, merely deleting their names from buildings, rooms, courtyards and roads, and not explaining why, compounds the injustices with further acts of denial. This kind of truth-telling is necessary to make just, transparent and worthwhile University practices and policies, if our community is to prevent the repetition of commemorative rituals that honour racists, thieves and body snatchers.

Truth-telling is one form of restorative justice. Writing factual histories that fully acknowledge the Aboriginal peoples impacted and their fates can make some recompense for this history. In 2021 the University acknowledged and apologised 'for the historic and current injustices which have been and are to the detriment of the health and well-being and educational and living standards of the Aboriginal and Torres Strait Islander peoples of this country'.[1] A further form of restorative justice would be a full and specific apology for the eugenic and racial scientism supported at the University, along with the industrial-scale use of Aboriginal bodies obtained by grave robbers—and clearly by other means, as some records suggest—for the teaching of dissection and anatomy. It is the hope of the editors of and contributors to this volume that a permanent place for truth-telling and correcting the record will be embedded in our campus environments.

What other conclusion could be drawn from reading these chapters? What image, what history, what legacy should the University of Melbourne present to the world? All of the chapters raise the urgency of continually delving into the records and informing the narrative of the University's past. We must not stop at acknowledging failures and triumphs but address injustices and violations with corrective actions that engage our community. Not only must we talk, we must also help to overcome the often-traumatic historical legacies and contribute to initiatives that redress the wrongs with respect and with regard to the rights of Indigenous peoples, as they are now elaborated in the *United Nations Declaration on the Rights of Indigenous Peoples*.

What other reparations are available to the University community to make amends for the murders, grave-robbing and humiliation inflicted on Aboriginal people in pursuit of false scientism? In the second volume, *Voice*, some of the efforts of University staff, students and alumni to make amends for this history are discussed. That volume will be important in a rigorous assessment of the burden of this history on the University of Melbourne, and the adequacy of the responses to it.

Notes

1 University of Melbourne Council, 'University's Apology to Aboriginal and Torres Strait Islander Peoples', 4 August 2021.

Acknowledgements

A project of this scale has been possible only with support from many people from the University of Melbourne community, and expert readers beyond. It has involved careful, challenging work across disciplines, and we are grateful for the hard work of our multiple contributors.

We'd first like to thank Margot Eden, without whose major contribution this project would not have happened. We were also ably supported by members of her team, including Ben Pearce, David Semmens and Cate Roy, as well as Karen Davis, who organised public events to profile the project. The original impetus for the project was provided by Professor Richard James, deputy vice-chancellor (academic and undergraduate).

The project has been overseen by an Indigenous-led Steering Committee, and we acknowledge its invaluable leadership and support. This committee was first chaired by Professor Shaun Ewen, and after he left the University at the end of 2021, by Professor Barry Judd. Other members, with the editors, were Uncle Jim Berg, Professor Michael-Shawn Fletcher, Associate Professor Sana Nakata, Margot Eden, Dr Julia Hurst, Tyson Holloway-Clarke and Raelene Nixon. The University's Traditional Owners' Advisory Group and Committee of Associate Deans Indigenous also provided important guidance and support.

The text has been read by experts in the fields of Indigenous history and the history of education, including Professor Richard Broome, Professor Richard James, Professor Peter McPhee and Professor Lynette Russell. Another of our readers, Dr Carolyn Rasmussen, took on an additional role, compiling and formatting the manuscript, particularly the illustrations. Her ongoing help has been indispensable.

Several research assistants also contributed to the project, including Simon Farley, Will Gorton, Antony Sinni and Katie Wood.

Elsewhere across the University, we have received assistance from Gioconda Di Lorenzo, who provided access to recent archival material;

Dimity Flanagan, who offered guidance on open-access publishing; Keryn Fortsmanis, who provided legal assistance; Stella Marr and other members of the University of Melbourne Archives; and Georgie Meagher, who provided information about the University's estate planning.

This project has been funded by the University of Melbourne Chancellery and hosted by the Centre for the Study of Higher Education, and we thank successive directors, Professor William Locke and Professor Sophie Arkoudis, for their ongoing support.

Contributor Biographies

Warwick Anderson, MD, PhD, based on the land of the Wangal of the Eora nation, is an historian and anthropologist of science and medicine, and a pioneer in postcolonial studies of science. He is Janet Dora Hine Professor of Politics, Governance and Ethics in Health at the University of Sydney and an Honorary Professor in the Centre for Health Equity at the School of Population and Global Health, University of Melbourne. His books include *The Cultivation of Whiteness: Science, Health and Racial Destiny in Australia* (2002).

Shawana Andrews, BA, BSW, MPH, PhD, is a Trawlwoolway Palawa woman. She is Director of the Poche Centre for Indigenous Health, and Associate Professor in the Department of Social Work at the University of Melbourne. Shawana has had a clinical and academic career in Aboriginal health that has spanned over twenty years. At the Poche Centre she leads signature programs that focus on Aboriginal doctoral advancement and health leadership.

Kate Auty is a member of the Victorian Bar and holds qualifications in history, law and environmental science. Roles to which she has been appointed include magistrate in Victoria and Western Australia, commissioner for environmental sustainability in both Victoria and the Australian Capital Territory, and Vice Chancellor's and Professorial Fellow at the University of Melbourne.

Emma Barnett is a Graduate Diploma in Science (Advanced) graduate who focused on cultural astronomy education, working alongside the Victorian Space Science Education Centre and the Melbourne Graduate School of Education to create programs for secondary-school students.

Jim Berg is a Gunditjmara Elder.

Jim Bowler is a University of Melbourne graduate in Geology (MSc, 1960). His 1970 PhD at the Australian National University, involving the study of climatic change in dry lake basins of south-eastern Australia, led to archaeological discoveries on the shores of 'Lake Mungo' in western New South

Wales. Lakeshore erosion had revealed human remains we know today as those of 'Mungo Man' and 'Mungo Lady'. Dated to 40 000 years ago in ice-age climates, these highly sophisticated burials challenged the way we saw ancestral Australians on one hand, and the legacy of ice-age landscapes and the urgency of our response to anthropogenic change on the other.

Aaron Corn, PhD, is Professor and Inaugural Director of the Indigenous Knowledge Institute at the University of Melbourne. Collaborating closely with Indigenous colleagues over the past three decades, his work strives for broader recognition of Indigenous knowledge through multiple research and education initiatives, including major grants and fellowships led by Indigenous colleagues. He serves as Director of the National Recording Project for Indigenous Performance in Australia, and as a Board Director of the International Council for Traditional Music and Dance Indigenous Study Group. He is founding Coordinator of the University of Melbourne's PhD–Indigenous Knowledge course.

Simon Farley is a PhD candidate in History at the University of Melbourne. He is researching settler-Australian attitudes towards non-native wildlife from the 1820s to the present.

Natasha Fijn is Director of the Australian National University's Mongolia Institute. She has been awarded a mid-career Australian Research Council Future Fellowship to conduct research on 'A Multispecies Anthropological Approach to Influenza' (2022–26). Natasha wrote a seminal multispecies ethnography based in Mongolia called *Living with Herds* (2011), and has co-edited several books and journal volumes, including three special issues oriented towards visual anthropology and ethnographic filmmaking, and three engaging with sensory and multispecies anthropology in the journals *Inner Asia* (2020), *The Australian Journal of Anthropology* (2020) and *Anthropology Today* (2023).

Richard Gillespie is curator of collections in the Faculty of Engineering and Information Technology, and an Honorary Principal Fellow in the School of Historical and Philosophical Studies at the University of Melbourne. He was previously head of the Humanities Department at Museums Victoria, where he led the curatorial development of over thirty exhibitions and associated public programs. Dr Gillespie trained as a historian and sociologist of science at the University of Melbourne and the University of Pennsylvania. He has published widely on the history of science and technology and the history of museum collections.

Philip Goad is Chair of Architecture and Redmond Barry Distinguished Professor at the University of Melbourne, where he is also Co-Director of the Australian Centre for Architectural History, Urban and Cultural Heritage. He is the co-author of *Architecture on Campus: A Guide to The University of Melbourne and Its Colleges* (2004) and co-editor of *The Encyclopedia of Australian Architecture* (2012) and *Australia Modern: Architecture, Design and Landscape Architecture 1925–1975* (2019). In 2019–20 he was Gough Whitlam and Malcolm Fraser Chair of Australian Studies at Harvard University. He is a Fellow of the Australian Academy of Humanities.

Amanda Goldfarb is a qualified archaeologist with a BA/BSc, BA (Hons) and MA from the University of Melbourne. She has worked for over eleven years in the heritage consulting industry and has a strong background in research and writing. Amanda's MA focused heavily on archaeoastronomy. She is a member of the Australian Archaeological Association, an Associate Member of the Australian Association of Consulting Archaeologists Inc, and a Full International Member of the International Council on Monuments and Sites. Amanda is also listed as a Heritage Adviser with First Peoples—State Relations in accordance with the *Aboriginal Heritage Act 2006*.

David Goodman is Professor in History in the School of Historical and Philosophical Studies at the University of Melbourne. He has a BA (Hons), MA and Dip. Ed. from the University of Melbourne and a PhD in History from the University of Chicago. He has taught at the University of Melbourne since 1990, in areas including US history, Australian studies and the history of history/historiography.

Jefa Greenaway is a University of Melbourne senior academic whose work spans two decades, an Australian Institute of Landscape Architects National Cultural Ambassador, and a founding Director of Greenaway Architects. He has championed Indigenous-led design thinking for three decades as a registered architect in New South Wales, Victoria and the Australian Capital Territory; as founding Director of *Indigenous Architecture + Design Australia*; and as co-author of the *International Indigenous Design Charter*, with a particular interest in design equity and Country-centred design. He was a 2020 Design Institute of Australia Hall of Fame inductee, signifying an outstanding contribution to Australian design, and was recently named among Qantas' '100 Inspiring Australians', celebrating the airline's centenary.

Duane Hamacher is Associate Professor of Cultural Astronomy in the School of Physics at the University of Melbourne. His work examines humanity's connection to the stars with a focus on Aboriginal and Torres Strait Islander communities. He is President of the Australian Association for Astronomy in Culture, Vice-President of the International Society of Archeoastronomy and Astronomy in Culture, and Associate Editor of the *Journal of Astronomical History and Heritage*. He has worked on films with Warwick Thornton, Werner Herzog and Morgan Freeman, and has published dozens of works on cultural astronomy, including the book *The First Astronomers: How Indigenous Elders Read the Stars*.

Jacqueline Healy is Director, Museums, Faculty of Medicine, Dentistry and Health Sciences (MDHS) at the University of Melbourne, including the Medical History Museum, Henry Forman Atkinson Dental Museum and Harry Brookes Allen Museum of Anatomy and Pathology. In 2018 she was awarded a University of Melbourne Excellence Award for the transformation of the museums in the Faculty of MDHS. Previously, she was the director of, respectively, Bundoora Homestead Art Centre, the Museum and Art Gallery of the Northern Territory, and public programs at the National Gallery of Victoria. Jacqueline was awarded her PhD in 2006 on marketing art from remote area communities, focusing on Balgo and Warmun.

Ross L Jones is Senior Research Fellow in the Indigenous History of the University of Melbourne Project in the Centre for the Study of Higher Education. After teaching for some years, he completed a Master of Educational Studies and a PhD at Monash University on the eugenic movement in Victoria. He then taught in the Department of History and Philosophy of Science at the University of Melbourne, after which he took up an Australian Research Council postdoctoral position at the University of Sydney. In 2016–17 he was awarded the Redmond Barry Fellowship at the State Library Victoria.

Bridget Kelly is a PhD candidate at the University of Melbourne. She is examining the power of visual patterning, narrative cognition, socially created experiences and memory methods in order to explain similarities between constellations and the associated traditions of different cultures separated by space and time.

Zoë Laidlaw is Professor of History at the University of Melbourne. She grew up in western Victoria and completed honours degrees in Arts and Science at the University of Melbourne, and a doctorate at the University of Oxford. Having worked at the University of Sheffield, and Royal Holloway, University of London, Zoë returned to Melbourne in 2018. A historian of nineteenth-century imperialism and colonialism, she has published widely on British imperial networks and governance, settler colonialism, Indigenous dispossession and humanitarian activism. Her current research focuses on imperial inquiries and the legacies of British slavery in Australia.

Marcia Langton, AO, is a granddaughter of Yiman and Bidjara people in Queensland, where she was born and raised. She is qualified as an anthropologist and geographer. Since 2000 she has held the Foundation Chair of Australian Indigenous Studies at the University of Melbourne, and since 2017 she has held the role of Associate Provost. She is Chair of the Aboriginal and Torres Strait Islander Cultural Heritage Oversight Committee at the University of Melbourne and advises on collections of art and cultural heritage. Her current research concerns alcohol management and domestic and family violence in Aboriginal settings, and Indigenous data governance and community data projects. She has published in the areas of political and legal anthropology, Aboriginal arts and cultural heritage, Indigenous agreements and engagement with the minerals industry, Aboriginal land tenure, native title, and Indigenous resource management.

Rohan Long is the curator of the Harry Brookes Allen Museum of Anatomy and Pathology in the Faculty of Medicine, Dentistry and Health Sciences at the University of Melbourne. He has been managing and curating biological museum collections at the University for over a decade, previously working as the collection manager of the Tiegs Zoology Museum from 2013 to 2018.

Louise Murray has over twenty-five years' experience working in the cultural sector in curatorial and research roles, most recently in the role of research manager, First Peoples Collections, Museums and Collections Department at the University of Melbourne. She previously worked in the Indigenous Studies Unit on projects including the reporting of Aboriginal ancestral remains to the Victorian Aboriginal Heritage Council, and establishing protocols and procedures for the management of Indigenous cultural material in the University's collections; she was also part of the team working on the Donald Thomson Collection review. Louise worked closely with collections incorporating Aboriginal cultural heritage material at the University of Melbourne, including the Donald Thomson Collection.

Rachel Nordlinger is Professor of Linguistics and Director of the Research Unit for Indigenous Language at the University of Melbourne. Her research focuses on the description and documentation of Australian Indigenous languages and their implications for our understanding of the complexities of human language more broadly. She has worked for many years with communities across the Northern Territory, especially the Wambaya, Bilinarra and Murrinhpatha communities, to record and document their languages and support their educational and language-maintenance efforts.

Tiriki Onus is a Yorta Yorta and Dja Dja Wurrung artist, academic and filmmaker. Tiriki's research specialism is in the histories and practices of Indigenous arts in south-eastern Australia. As Head of the Wilin Centre for Indigenous Arts in Cultural Development, Co-Director of the Research Unit for Indigenous Arts and Cultures, Associate Dean (Indigenous Development), and Deputy Dean (Place), in the Faculty of Fine Arts and Music at the University of Melbourne, Tiriki fosters innovation in research, development, advocacy, representation and inclusion of Indigenous arts and cultural practices and practitioners, in the academy.

Lisa O'Sullivan trained in the history of medicine, completing her PhD at Queen Mary, University of London. She was senior curator of the London Science Museum's medical collections, including the Wellcome Collection, leading the Museum's repatriation program and advising on the care of human remains and culturally sensitive objects in the collections. She then became founding director of the New York Academy of Medicine Library and Center for History. She has taught on the history of the European race science in Australia and the United Kingdom. Until 2023, she managed engagement and outreach activities for the University of Melbourne's Archives and Special Collections.

Juliana Kaya Prpic is Associate Professor in the Faculty of Engineering and Information Technology at the University of Melbourne. She works exclusively in close collaboration with Indigenous communities around Australia using an iterative process that embraces the five key principles of people, place, philosophy, practices and projects. Her projects include inspiring Indigenous students to undertake engineering as a career option, developing two-way learning exchanges for engineering students, and promoting cultural exchange and understanding for engineering staff based on immersive on-County experiences. She has served as co-editor for the recent publication *Indigenous Engineering for an Enduring Culture* (2022).

Cameron Raw is a Palawa man from the far south of lutruwita (Tasmania) and a veterinarian, lecturer, researcher and Assistant Dean (Indigenous) within the Melbourne Veterinary School in the Faculty of Science at the University of Melbourne. His work has involved veterinary programs in several Arnhem Land communities for more than ten years, as well as One Health research in zoonotic parasite spread and control in Aboriginal and Torres Strait Islander communities. His teaching interests lie in traditional knowledge, professional veterinary skills, One Health, and diversity and inclusion.

Judith Ryan received a BA (Hons) in Fine Arts and English Literature at the University of Melbourne, and a Certificate in Education at Oxford University. In 1977 she began her art museum career at the National Gallery of Victoria (NGV), where she was senior curator of Indigenous art on her retirement in 2021. Judith greatly contributed to planning, initiating and advancing the NGV's Indigenous art collection from 1987 onwards. She has curated over fifty exhibitions, focusing on increasing the visibility and accessibility of Indigenous art, and revealing its importance. In 2017 Judith was awarded a Member of the Order of Australia 'For significant service to the visual arts ... as a curator of Indigenous exhibitions and as an author'.

Antony Sinni is a research assistant for the University of Melbourne Indigenous Studies Unit. He holds a BA/LLB (Hons) from Monash University and a GDLP (Graduate Diploma in Legal Practice) from the College of Law. He is currently based in Darwin and practising as a civil law solicitor for the North Australian Aboriginal Justice Agency.

Nicholas Thieberger set up the Pilbara Aboriginal Language Centre in the late 1980s, then worked at the Australian Institute of Aboriginal and Torres Strait Islander Studies. His PhD research was conducted in Vanuatu, and his main focus has become finding, digitising and providing access to language records, primarily through the Pacific and Regional Archive for Digital Sources in Endangered Cultures, of which he is Director. He currently leads the development of Nyingarn, a platform for manuscript sources on Australian languages. He is Associate Professor in the School of Languages and Linguistics, University of Melbourne.

Sally Treloyn is an applied ethnomusicologist with a primary-area specialism in Indigenous song and dance practices and historical collections relating to the Kimberley and Pilbara regions of north-western Australia. They have published widely on the compositional practices and processes of Indigenous song, and over the last decade on issues of archives and access, repatriation, sustainability, revitalisation and resurgence, in collaboration with Indigenous scholars and knowledge-holders. As Associate Professor in Ethnomusicology and Intercultural Research and Co-Director of the Research Unit for Indigenous Arts and Cultures at the University of Melbourne, Treloyn has convened the graduate program in Indigenous Arts and Cultures, delivers undergraduate courses in Indigenous music, and supports the inclusion of Indigenous knowledge, research and researchers in the academy.

Elizabeth Tudor, AM, is a veterinary graduate and Professor who has worked for twenty years in the Faculty of Veterinary and Agricultural Sciences at the University of Melbourne, where for ten years she was the associate dean, curriculum. Since 2005 Liz has led the West Arnhem Land Dog Health Program, delivering, along with veterinary students and alumni, veterinary care to companion animals in remote Northern Territory Indigenous communities. In 2016 Liz, Rick and their children founded the Melbourne Indigenous Transition School (MITS). MITS exists to provide educational opportunities to First Nations students from regional Victorian and remote Top End communities who aspire to pursue their secondary-education journey in Melbourne schools.

James Waghorne is official historian of the University of Melbourne, based in the Centre for the Study of Higher Education. His history of the Melbourne University Student Union, *By Students, For Students*, was published in 2022, and his history (written with Gwilym Croucher) of the Australian Vice-Chancellors' Committee, *Australian Universities*, was published in 2020. He is Chief Investigator on the 'Expert Nation' and 'Universities and Post-War Recovery' Australian Research Council projects, tracing the careers of university graduates who served in both world wars.

Ken Winkel is Associate Professor within the School of Population and Global Health at the University of Melbourne, and Honorary Fellow of the University's Medical History Museum (MHM). Long interested in the nexus between natural history and medicine, he trained in medicine and medical science at the University of Queensland (BMedSci MBBS) and the University of Melbourne (PhD WEHI). A leading Australian toxinologist, he was formerly director of the Australian Venom Research Unit (1999–2015) and is a past president of the Australasian College of Tropical Medicine. In 2013 he co-curated the *Venom: Fear, Fascination and Discovery* exhibition with MHM curator Dr Jacqueline Healy.

List of Illustrations

'A Precious Stone to Him That Hath It'
Rohan Long

Wurati and Trukanini
Judith Ryan

Benjamin Law,
English, 1807–1882, lived in Australia from 1834
Trukanini, wife of Wurati
reproduction, cast from original, late nineteenth or early twentieth century
plaster, paint
68.5 × 39 × 27.2 cm
Harry Brookes Allen Museum of Anatomy and Pathology
Faculty of Medicine, Dentistry and Health Sciences
The University of Melbourne
LL 0000.0284

Benjamin Law
English, 1807–1882, lived in Australia from 1834
G. A. Robinson, Pacificator, 1838
plaster, paint
60 × 54 × 26 cm
State Library Victoria, Melbourne
Presented by Henry Downie, Esq., c. 1870–71
LTS 58

III SETTLER-COLONIAL KNOWLEDGE
Frederic Wood Jones and the Contradictions of a Race Scientist
Lisa O'Sullivan

Frederic Wood Jones, c. 1937, UMA/I/2141, University of Melbourne Archives.

Defence Science, Expertise and Scientific Colonialism
James Waghorne

Sir Leslie Martin, 1970, 1994.0025.00111, University of Melbourne Archives.

Sir Frank Macfarlane Burnet, [no date], 1994.0025.00111, University of Melbourne Archives.

Eugenics, the 1950s and Beyond
Ross L Jones

Leunig cartoon, *Farrago*, 9 September 1977, p. 11, courtesy Michael Leunig.

IV INDIGENOUS KNOWLEDGE
The Invisible Collectors
Rohan Long and Ross L Jones

Three red-tailed black cockatoo (*Calyptorhynchus banksii*) skulls collected on the Horn Scientific Expedition, photograph by Gavan Mitchell, MUZD923, MUZD925, MUZD926, Tiegs Zoology Museum.

Long-snouted lashtail (*Gowidon longirostris*) collected on the Horn Scientific Expedition, photograph by Gavan Mitchell, MUZD957, Tiegs Zoology Museum.

Harry, the Horn Expedition's tracker (detail from *Members of the Horn Expedition, Alice Springs, Central Australia*, 1894 – Walter Baldwin Spencer, 1894).

Redmond Barry, 'Vocabulary of Dialects Spoken by Aboriginal Natives of Australia', Melbourne, 1866–1867.

Gifts and Legacies
Marcia Langton and Louise Murray

Colour plates are fully captioned.

Transforming an Engineering Worldview of the Indigenous 'Other'
Juliana Kaya Prpic

Images 1–5 courtesy of the author.

Raymattja Marika, 'Milthun latju wana romgu yolŋu: Valuing yolŋu knowledge in the education system, *Ngoonjook*, no. 16, Dec 1999, p. 113.

Seated between the eyes of two worlds. A painting by Craig San Roque in conversation with Spencer Japaljarri.

The West Arnhem Land Dog Health Program
Elizabeth Tudor and Cameron Raw

Photograph: Elizabeth Tudor.

George French Angas, 'South Australia Illustrated', 1846–47, 1966.7.1–10, National Gallery of Australia, Canberra.

Augustus Earle, 'A native family of New South Wales sitting down on an English settler's farm', c. 1826, NK12/45, NLA.

Elizabeth Tudor speaking with children in Galiwin'ku about health care for their dog. Photograph courtesy Elizabeth Tudor.

Photograph: Meg Hewett (permission provided). Photograph courtesy Meg Hewett.

Cameron Raw as a student, assisting the veterinary team. Manmoyi homeland community Arnhem Land, 2013. Photograph courtesy Meg Hewett.

The Art of Healing
Jacqueline Healy

Colour plates are fully captioned, photography by Matthew Stanton.

Index

Note: University of Melbourne is referred to as 'the University' in subheadings